T0368323

THAT POWERLESS FEELING

BY
AARON HANDY JR

Order this book online at www.trafford.com
or email orders@trafford.com

Most Trafford titles are also available at major online book retailers.

Printed in Victoria, BC, Canada.

ISBN: 978-1-4251-3155-5 (sc)
ISBN: 978-1-4251-3156-2 (eBook)

*Our mission is to efficiently provide the world's finest, most comprehensive book publishing
service, enabling every author to experience success. To find out how to publish your book,
your way, and have it available worldwide, visit us online at www.trafford.com*

Trafford rev. 3/02/2010

 **www.trafford.com**

North America & international
toll-free: 1 888 232 4444 (USA & Canada)
phone: 250 383 6864 ♦ fax: 812 355 4082

INTRODUCTION

Any exposure to the arena of armed conflict teaches that there is no glory in combat and nothing scarier than its purported thrill. It minimizes the life of a citizen soldier and is arguably the most thankless task facing modern man. For in spite of and in contradiction to our democracy, war can be prosecuted at the sacrifice of many, under the authority of one, for reasons that occurs to few others. When our constitution fails to protect us from the eagerness of our leaders to invade, we become cannon fodder for wars with no end in pursuit of victories that can't be achieved. To that purpose, any given reason for fighting a ground war should be held under a scrutiny that our government of people could never easily explain away.

The enactment of compulsory service to wage war in response to anything less than an attack on our sovereignty and an absolute victory in its defense is an injustice that penalizes youth and alienates an entire generation. Given the choice, we would all rather live inside of Fortress America than to represent its citizenry on a foreign battlefield fighting an undeclared war. With no real or imagined threat to our security at home, fighting on distant soil for any loosely defined reason is a wasteful imposition on those facing the carnage and, regrettably, impossible to accomplish without a draft.

Historically, being involved in a conflict fought by draftees has always exposed our country's disdain for conscription. This resentment, over the course of an extended engagement, measures the limit of our patriotism and produces an understandable reluctance to maintain the vigil of continuing to send our sons off to fight.

Once America grew accustomed to victorious defenses of its borders and triumphant returns from all excursions abroad, it became invincible in the eyes of its constituents as well as its adversaries. Surely, many thought, war with the US was the ultimate deterrent. Our advanced technologies, enormous wealth and resources coupled with our industrial capabilities always gave us an advantage that couldn't be matched. Yet in spite of our perceived might, there was never a sufficient pool of volunteers to exercise this superiority in time of war. Our edge in the military applications of these technologies always relied heavily on able bodies willing to fill in the ranks making the draft necessary.

The Vietnam War was the ultimate test of a generation's willingness to submit to military obligation while internally struggling with the conflict's many debatable aspects. On the whole, we passed the test but failed to accomplish the mission as we fought an enemy abroad to a standstill and lost the internal struggle at home. In the face of the debate, the war continued on as most of our draft-eligible men answered the call to engage in mortal combat that, in retrospect, pursued nothing more than a distant light at the end of a very long tunnel.

Throughout the history of warfare, there was always the gratification of the easily definable victory for the survivors to enjoy before moving on to the next campaign, operation or battle. Victory was always sought but, in the eyes of the participants, surviving each battle was the only worthy achievement. To stand on a battlefield over a vanquished foe counting the dead and collecting the spoils of war is normally a combatant's definition of victory. In Vietnam, however, all of our victories were illusory as we became mired in an endless war. Our supposedly weaker opponent's philosophy of surviving to fight again was a battle plan that frustrated our conventional forces. This method of fighting redefined our victories as we mounted meaningless body counts against an outgunned army that stood ready to lose as many men as necessary. Their willingness to accept these losses negated our superior firepower as they always knew that we could neither stay forever nor kill them all. The war of attrition that followed was a losing struggle as time and public opinion continually mounted against us. To even define a victory against this patient, resilient and resolute army while lacking support from home was impossible. On a more personal level, any attempt at moving on after shedding blood or suffering losses meant to leave behind more than unfinished business. For the survivors it meant literally to leave behind a part of our psyche and wonder how or if it could ever be retrieved. This process of moving on after battle, unfortunately, guaranteed that these traces of ourselves would be sowed in Asian soil as we continued to cross paths with our destinies. Coming home to live without these pieces, no matter how big or small, has proven to be an uneasy truce for all who fought there. For too many of us, coming home to the cold reception that awaited us was more like reaching the end of that long tunnel finding the proverbial distant light had been turned off leaving us in the dark unable to find a way out or a way back.

As a group, we are doomed to suffer from being the actual participants of our government's foreign policy blunders in Vietnam. For us, the war never ends. Losing as much of what is so essential to our continuing development has proven to be more damaging than any analytical or clinical study has yet to discover. The experience of living without as much of our former selves has been and continues to be a source of pain and helplessness. We will always be left to ponder the "what ifs" of life past, present and future while convincing ourselves that our actions were just and worthy of the sacrifices made. The memories of close friends lost in combat and the accompanying effect of guilt for having survived, however, has become an unexpected burden that still affects members of our ranks well into our middle age and beyond. Our attempt at living as whole individuals, who had not been separated from that part of our souls we left in Vietnam, has been a complex endeavor. It has shaped the ensuing years since the war's end into yet another story that is still unfolding. A story of nightmares, alienation, addiction, failed relationships and endless psychiatric treatment that has defined us as less than our more celebrated war veteran counterparts. This story is a microcosm of the day to day life on the action end of the foreign policy mistakes, the deterioration of a mission that lasted too long and the beginning of the suffering that never ended. It is also a story about some of the dynamics involved in losing that part of us that we may never reconnect with.

In a saner world, lessons are learned from previous mistakes and measures are taken to prevent any recurrences. Nothing could be worse for America than to repeat these tragic errors of its past. As a reminder of what has been learned, the memories of those who died in Vietnam, the stories told by its survivors and the internal damage we suffered as a nation should stand out and offer a concrete testimony to the fallacy of using our military to shape the affairs of other countries. Our experiences should have put an end to America's involvement with all wars fought for questionable reasons. Ours should have redefined war as an instrument of last resort because, in the end, memorializing the dead and commemorating the conflict is not enough. It only justifies the insanity that is war and keeps the door open for the next needless incursion into the pain and suffering that only the survivors will know. In that same world, the ultimate sacrifices made in Vietnam and the visible scars of the survivors would have also served as a legacy for a part of our history that should have taught us a lot more than we have obviously already forgotten.

A. H. 2007

PART ONE

1

Crossing the international dateline caused a little confusion onboard about what the new date had become. We couldn't understand if the event meant moving one day ahead or backwards but I figured it must have been the 29th of November. As we were still flying somewhere over the South Pacific Ocean, I also realized my relationships with family and friends would soon be reduced to written correspondence and the exact date had become less significant. The Vietnam War had claimed me as a soon-to-be participant and our arrival there, as well as coping with life apart from family, had become the most important issue. Two hundred other GIs who had left Oakland behind were on board with me that day. Our moods had changed dramatically. All of the horseplay and the spirited bravado were, by then, replaced by a silence that reflected our somber mood. We had all been consumed by thoughts of our destination which had become the number one preoccupation of every young man in America. This endless war had lasted long enough to become our war. A conflict we barely understood and never imagined would grow into the unmanageable monster it had become. Our youth and innocence had shielded us from its slow development, while making us prime candidates for warring. Vietnam, to my dismay, was no exception to the design of using the young and politically naïve to do the fighting. The average age of a soldier in Vietnam was said to be 19 and the plane was packed with so many teenagers that I almost felt like an elder at 21.

Seated beside me was a close friend from back home in New Orleans. William Howard (I'd called him Gathar) and I had known each other since our early teens. We lived on the same street in the same housing project and of course attended the same high school. At one time or another we even dated the same girls. We were real fortunate to have been drafted together and did all of our training as members of the same company. It was unusual but we had a nice thing going for the previous six months as we enjoyed the kind of buddy system the Army couldn't guarantee the average two enlistees. Being grouped in alphabetical order, we were also always bunkmates, and as we went from one phase of our training to another, we ceremoniously flipped a coin to see who would get the upper berth. We had a lot of fun but it was obvious that sooner or later our military career as a duo would end and we could possibly be serving in separate units. Gathar assumed that volunteering for jump school sealed our fate on the Vietnam issue. He believed we never would have been sent over had we just ignored the recruitment pitch made during the summer while in basic training. It was hopeless trying to convince him otherwise but Uncle Sam would have probably sent us to Vietnam with or without jump wings. Gathar was only second guessing himself for following my lead when I showed interest and signed up for the extra training.

Incredibly, the Army only gave us 18 days at home before reporting. Considering the duty that awaited us, another two weeks of leave would have been more appropriate. We were facing the job of doing the actual fighting and felt we deserved more time at home before being deployed. To add insult to injury, we were ordered to report on Thanksgiving Day and had to be at the Oakland processing center at 7:00 a.m. that morning. After fighting the war for almost five years without us, I was sure they could have easily held out for another 24 hours. My family ate Thanksgiving turkey a day early just to accommodate me. Mom made a huge effort to put on a good day on my behalf in spite of her anger over the untimely holiday departure. It was a little too cruel for her to comprehend.

Our flight itinerary took us to Alaska first and then to Yokota AFB in Japan. Unlike the so-called trendy state of California where it was impossible for anyone as young as Gathar at 20 to buy a beer before going off to fight a war, we had no problems buying a drink during our quick stop in Alaska. While in Yokota we ran into a group of GIs wearing faded fatigues and grim expressions who were returning from Vietnam. A group of them were paratroopers like so many of us heading in the other direction. We talked with them for a few minutes to see if we could get any idea of what to expect over there. Although we were all about the same ages, they seemed to have a seasoned look on them that spoke volumes of their past experiences. They were members of the 101st Airborne Division, a unit that gained a lot of fame and notoriety during WWII. Three of then said they were survivors of a battle earlier in the year in the Ashau Valley; a battle that cost them a lot of their best friends. Most of their losses were incurred, they said, on one particular hill they nicknamed "Hamburger Hill". As one survivor struggled to recount details of the battle and broke under the trauma of the re-visitation, another picked up the story and continued until he needed help from the third to finish. Their dramatic method of storytelling offered us a study in mutual cooperation; a byproduct of the close bond they had formed while serving together. Those guys were closer than Gathar and I were, yet they'd only known each other for a matter of months. Their intense exteriors suggested they really hadn't survived the battle and will probably be haunted by all of their memories. We thanked them for their graphic accounts then boarded our planes and headed in opposite directions. It was a dose of reality that was not overlooked. Our little talk gave the two of us a lot to digest for the rest of our flight.

Obviously Gathar and I weren't the only ones to talk to those paratroopers. The plane was probably so quiet for the last leg of the flight because everyone got a chance to listen to their stories. About the only noise to be heard, aside from jet engines, was the snickering of the old-timers who were returning for their second and third tours. They all seemed to relish their status of having already been there before and were amused at our deflated spirits. All of the chatter and horseplay we exhibited before arriving in Yokota had seemingly boarded the plane going in the other direction. The seniors were undoubtedly just as concerned as anybody else on their first trip over. Half of those old farts were probably cooks, mechanics and clerks anyway. With cushy jobs like that waiting for them, Vietnam was nothing more than another tour of duty comparable to going to Germany or Korea. "What do you think that cab driver is doing now?" Gathar mused in reference to a cab driver we met in San Francisco's Airport. We were somewhat stranded because our promised helicopter ride across the bay was nowhere in sight upon our arrival. We had flown a thousand miles to get there on Thanksgiving Day and didn't think more could be expected of us. All we could do was ask ourselves, "What's the worst they could do to us for showing up late? Send us to Vietnam?" Being sent over to fight this war was about the worst thing we could imagine happening to us. Asking "What's the worst?" had become a question sarcastically asked by all facing our predicament. Answering the question was a realization that our worst fears were about to become our own little nightmare come true. In a twisted sort of way, we all felt privileged to be able to both ask and answer the question aloud at every opportunity. "He's probably driving some poor bastard crazy right about now," I answered remembering how the cab driver camped himself next to us when he realized we were stranded. He started a conversation about his Army days that just went on and on.

He was a middle aged black guy who we assumed was looking for a fare. Since we had spent every dime we had in New Orleans, all we could do was listen to the cab driver bore us with his never-ending story about his days in the military. As annoying as he was, we both tolerated his presence hoping he would give us a free lift across the bay to Oakland.

I should have gotten a few dollars from my girlfriend while we were standing at the airport two nights before. She was so depressed about my leaving that I couldn't even mention my lack of funds to her. Barbara and I had been through a lot together and she feared the worst. We were already committed to marriage after the war and life without her for a year was expected to be tough. The prospect of her losing me as a war casualty was unimaginable. Coming back alive and in one piece was the only ending we ever considered

In the darkness, flying seemed scary for someone who, like me, had only flown a half dozen times. With total darkness outside the windows, there was nothing but my imagination running wild thinking about what could go wrong while in the air over the ocean. Earlier during our flight, when there was sunlight, our plane reached a part of the Pacific that was so vast we actually flew for hours without seeing land. It gave me my first true perspective of the expanse between our West Coast and SE Asia. It also rekindled my confusion about our involvement there and about how such an insignificant country could require so much commitment and sacrifice from a people from so far away.

"Well at least he did give us the ride." Gathar said under the muffled drone of the engines that had already signaled the start of descent.

"Yes he did." The cab driver finally offered to drive us across the bay. We were reunited with all of the guys we jumped with at Ft. Benning. Gathar and I trained with two of them earlier at Ft. Polk. They were both Louisiana natives, Lonnie Ray Jackson from Homer and C. L. Larks from Opelousas. We had a lot in common being black, underprivileged, and drafted to be trained in our home state. We didn't enjoy the best Thanksgiving in Oakland but it was special to have so many of the guys I trained with accompany me on the flight over.

As the plane touched down and started to taxi down the runway, I remembered an incredible story we heard from one of our training cadre who was being mortared while stepping off of the plane that brought him over. "Gathar, do you remember the story that Drill Instructor told us about when…."

"Man, I was just thinking about the same thing." he interrupted.

After the plane came to a stop, we quietly waited for the flight attendants to give us the order to disembark as we were reluctant to make the next move. When the door finally opened, an odor swept through the plane that fouled the entire cabin. It was as if a hundred people were just outside the door spitting on a very hot tin roof. In spite of the late November date, the humidity was almost similar to a typical spring night in New Orleans. I easily overcame the odor and Gathar grabbed his nose in reaction to the muggy pungent air. It was a surprising introduction to the war and I could only imagine what else awaited me outside of the door. All we knew for certain was that we were in Ben Hoa, S. Vietnam, it was November 29, 1969, 10:30 p.m. and day one 365 to go.

2

After leaving the plane and while walking across the tarmac, we filed past a crowd of about 200 wildly cheering guys who, we assumed, were about to board the same 727 we had just arrived on for their return trip. They were ecstatic. Their enthusiasm bordered on being sarcastic and it seemed impossible for as much noise to be created by so few. Of course, they had earned the right to act as they pleased. To their delight, the same plane that brought over a mostly unwilling and unknowing group of passengers would take back a group of newly crowned Vietnam veterans.

We then assembled in a nearby area for an outdoor briefing given by an Air Force NCO. The old timers had been through the routine and the rest of us were busy taking in the initial experience of having finally arrived. The NCO soon realized that nobody was listening to him at all. He tried raising his voice again but all new guys like Gathar and I remained in the same state of distracted wonderment mostly impressed by the faint sounds of gunfire and explosions going of in the distance. They sounded harmless but of course it represented more. We tried to imagine the struggle somebody somewhere out there was living through. We also privately wondered how long it would be before we were put into the line of fire. To my right front was a makeshift newsstand with the latest copy of The Stars & Stripes. The biggest story for the day, oddly enough, was the lottery. Our government had decided to pull straws or draw lots to decide who gets drafted in the future. "A lot of good this is going to do for me," I said to Gathar while pointing to the headline. I didn't know how the lottery worked but it was probably instituted to appease the protestors. They had already brought down LBJ and were by then probably gloating over how Nixon was playing to their protests with the lottery.

The NCO started passing out some toothbrushes and some toothpaste that he promised would be gritty. It was designed to help protect our teeth from the anticipated neglect we were about to subject them to. We assumed it was safe to try and complied with the NCO and brushed them without water. We were then assigned to temporary barracks for a few hours of sleep. Gathar and I ceremoniously flipped that coin for what we feared would be the last time for a while and used the few hours to confront the possibility of our finally being separated. The sleeping arrangement mattered little as our six-month run was seemingly coming to an end. After the coin flip, we sat around and waited for our first sunrise in Vietnam.

Breakfast was expected to be an adventure. The crude accommodations at Ben Hoa suggested an experience unlike anything we had ever encountered. After we got in line and grabbed a platter, we became concerned about the green stuff they spooned out to each of us.

"Powerderd eggs" said the guy with the spoon.

"Powdered eggs! Don't tell me there's no chickens in Vietnam" Said Gathar as he stabbed it with his fork perhaps expecting it to move or change colors.

"Man don't eat this shit, it can't be eggs. Eggs aint green," I said as we walked further down the chow line where we were each handed a slice of bread that was equally suspect. We disposed of our platters and made for the exit. It seemed cruel, inhuman and shouldn't have been too much to expect some real food since we had to be there.

After skipping breakfast, we were assigned to work details, the never ending shit details. Our duty for the day was to clean out a swimming pool. As unusual as it should have been to find such amenities, I was assured that for bases as large as Ben Hoa, it was common. The guy in charge of our detail claimed he had been stationed there for a couple of years. "I have no idea what his MOS is but I bet it sure in hell aint swimming pool attendant". Gathar joked. Talk about lucky; he was sporting a Fu Manchu mustache, wearing fatigue pants that had been cut into shorts with no shirt and all sorts of wild trinkets and hand made necklaces that defied the Army's sacred dress code. He also had a tan that would have made many white Americans green with envy. I thought we must have done something real bad in a previous life to be in such a different predicament than he was. Tan notwithstanding, we would have traded places with him in a heartbeat.

After the pool detail we assembled to watch a film put together by one of the fighting units, the 173rd Airborne Brigade. The film was about the effort to win some of those proverbial hearts and minds of the S. Vietnamese people throughout the countryside. During our training we learned that this PR effort was reported to be as important as the actual fighting going on in the mountains and jungles. It made sense but was still a little disturbing to me. The U.S. had been involved in combat for almost five years yet we were still selling the war effort to the troops with films and, at the same time, still trying to win over the people we were supposed to be helping. Suddenly all of the failures of the war started to shape up before me. On one front we had the American people demonstrating and voicing displeasure about our being in Vietnam and on the other, we still hadn't impressed the Vietnamese with the sacrifices we had already made. After the film they really rubbed it in with some literature explaining our mission there as if our not understanding the war was to be expected. The Army really knows how to run a show.

Later that evening we were assembled for assignment to our respective units. All paratroopers, we were told, were to be assigned to the 173rd Airborne Bde. The same unit that prepared the film we watched earlier. There was of course an assumed correlation between the film and our assignment but we really didn't care. After all, it meant that all of the guys I jumped with would be going to the same unit. Of course it also meant that Gathar and I would be together at least for a while longer. The buddy system continued. After dark, a truck pulled up and we all loaded our gear onto it and left the huge complex at Ben Hoa. Our destination was in Bin Dinh Province. A place called Charang Valley where the 173rd's Jungle School was located. The valley would be our home for a one-week period of more training. Along the way, during the truck ride, we were exposed to our first glimpse of the Vietnamese countryside, the people and more significantly, the abject poverty commonly associated with all third world underdeveloped countries. In spite of all we had been trained for, nothing could have prepared us for the culture shock of riding through that stretch of Vietnam. Ben Hoa's close proximity to Saigon exposed us to a swelling refugee problem that reportedly got out of hand after the Tet Offensive of 1968. The refugees sought the so-called safety of living close to large American troop concentrations such as the one at Ben Hoa, one of many bases in the area. Their living condition was appalling by any definition. It was unbelievable the way people were literally living on top of each other in squalor. It did go a long way to explain the odor that permeated the area though. In spite of it all, the people seemed content to live under those extreme conditions. Evidently, in some way, our presence in Vietnam had caused almost as much hardship on the people as any other factor. If we had struck some kind of balance with whatever we had achieved up to that point, it was not readily apparent to us during that truck ride.

The fear and paranoia of riding on the back of that truck through unfamiliar territory was nerve wracking. According to the news, there was no real safe area in Vietnam and we could have been killed at any time along the route. The truck ride sort of only increased our chances for calamity. But we were in no position to turn down the ride.

The ride took us to an airstrip for a flight to our next stop along the way. We then boarded a C-130 for a short flight to Phu Cat A.F.B. and then awaited a truck for a ride to Charang Valley. While waiting around for our truck, an N.C.O. came up to us and asked for a volunteer. To everyone's surprise one of my jump school buddies, Danny Dangerfield, volunteered to go with him. We all thought he was a little crazy for doing so but that was his choice. The rest of us waited on the truck for a ride up the highway to Jungle School. I assumed Dangerfield would have to catch up later.

3

After a long truck ride, we arrived at Charang Valley which was mostly a tent city. We then lined up for some individual B&W Polaroids to be sent to our next of kin informing them of our new status as members of the 173rd. This was no ordinary outfit. According to the pamphlets handed to us at Ben Hoa that briefly detailed the history of all of the units in Vietnam, it just happened to be one of the most distinguished units to ever unfurl its colors. The Brigade was formed in 1963 and was originally stationed in Okinawa where it was trained to fight in the jungles of S.E. Asia. Since there was no war going on there, it demonstrated just how early the U.S. was leaning towards getting involved in the fighting in Vietnam. When the time came for the Army to start sending combat units to Vietnam, the 173rd got the call. They were already acclimated with both the climate and terrain making them a natural choice. It was in the spring of 1965 when they or we rather, were given the distinction of being the "First In" (in country). On Feb.22, 1967 the "Sky Soldiers" or the "Herd", as the unit had come to be known as, made the first and only combat jump of the war. That was nice because the jump pay never stopped after that putting us in line for the $55 that was so tempting to me when they first made their recruitment pitch. On the other hand, if another jump had to be made or even planned, we would have been the only logical choice. With a little luck and Nixon slowly getting us out of the war, I hoped that maybe it would be possible to collect the jump pay for a whole year without ever having to strap on a parachute.

Later that same year the Herd had the misfortune to be sent into battle against a formidable contingent of North Vietnamese Army regulars in two of the bloodiest engagements of the war. The battles were fought in the Central Highlands at a place called Dak To. The first battle happened that summer and the cost in lost American lives was heavy. The second was the more difficult and newsworthy of the two, as they had to assault the enemy surrendering both the tactical as well as the numerical advantage. The NVA savagely fought off repeated assaults from fortified bunkers and made several attacks of their own. I could still remember when the second battle was going on. It was the month of November and the battle lasted more than a week. Every day Walter Cronkite was giving the latest on the battle of Dak To and a deadly, senseless battle for one particular hill that was named simply for the amount of meters it reached skyward. From where I sat in my mother's kitchen watching the news reports of the battle, it seemed like a waste of young men dying needlessly while fighting their way up a hill that reportedly had no strategic value at all. The battle had obviously become the Herd's most significant moment in Vietnam. In the end they ate Thanksgiving turkey at the summit of Hill 875 and then vacated the area. The guys we met in Japan never saw the likes of Dak To and Hamburger Hill was definitely no Hill 875. I'm sure they realized it too.

Before we were sent to our tents, I was taken out of the pack to receive a recruitment pitch from the Rangers. Since I never really wanted to go to Vietnam in the first place, it was easy to decline their commando training offer. Becoming a Ranger would have been beyond explaining. So we all, Gathar,

Larks, Jackson and the rest of the guys from jump school, took up residence in the same big tent to await the beginning of the next training class which would be the following morning. That night we were awakened by the sound of a large number of boots stomping rhythmically in cadence and chanting in "that" foreign language. We feared the worst. I peeped out and found about two platoons of shirtless Vietnamese soldiers running in formation. In spite of my fear I had to laugh at myself. I remembered a funny line from a movie Barbara and I saw a couple of weeks earlier called Butch Cassidy and the Sundance Kid. In the movie, while being chased doggedly by an unusually aggressive posse, Butch comically asked Sundance..."Who are those guys?" I looked at Gathar and laughed as I momentarily likened our predicament to Butch and Sundance's. Although the men outside the tent were Vietnamese, they couldn't have possibly been the enemy. So just who were these guys? Before long, one of the training NCO's walked into the tent to put our fears to rest.

"They are ARVN soldiers in training. ARVN, in case none of you cherries have heard, is an acronym that stands for Army of the Republic of Vietnam." In his own reassuring way, he was explaining that they were S. Vietnamese soldiers. I was astounded by the news of their (ARVN) existence. "You mean they have an army!"

"Of course they do".

"Then what in the hell are we doing here?"

"We are assisting the S. Vietnamese in their struggle against communism." he said. The war against communism or the cold war was an answer that we could all relate to. After all, we were the baby boomers who as children "ducked and covered" under our school desks and wondered who would bomb a schoolhouse with little kids in it. We rooted for our astronauts against the cosmonauts in the space race and our Olympic athletes against those from the communist bloc nations. We were on this side of the Iron Curtain and witnessed the building of a wall dividing the city and people of Berlin. Vietnam was of course the newest flashpoint. The answer to my question, however, did little to educate me on our involvement in the former French colony. I was tempted to resort to sarcasm but then remembered my own Vietnam War education; or how little I really knew. I remembered sitting at my jump school graduation, when one of the not so politically naive graduates rudely interrupted the guest speaker's address and asked, "Why are we over there?" Before the General could answer, I realized I had never even bothered to find out. Before recovering from my embarrassing lack of knowledge, the General replied, "To prevent communist aggression from the north". I temporarily got over my embarrassment, reverted to my ever-present wit, turned and asked Gathar, "Does he mean Milwaukee, Chicago or Canada?" The good General's explanation seemed as meaningless as the Sergeant's reason for our being there. It was a startling revelation to find out about our ally yet inexcusable for someone about to go to war to not understand why the war was being fought.

My ignorance on the subject of the war had me scrambling for knowledge about it and how we found ourselves knee deep in what seemed to any casual observer as an Asian conflict. I had to find a way to increase my understanding of the war I found myself headed for. I didn't know how hard being in Vietnam would make the pursuit of this knowledge and only hoped I wouldn't get killed before fully understanding the reason for the hostilities. I did a little reading on the subject while home on leave and read in a 1954 year book about the French losing the decisive battle at Dienbienphu but somehow I never came upon a defining reason for our involvement. I felt uncomfortable being in a war I didn't understand and frustrated over not being able to find out more before being deployed.

Although we had been training for six months for our assignment, the Army figured we needed another one-week refresher course I guess. Of course there had to be some shit details to keep everything familiar. For the first night, we were trucked to a nearby compound that might have been just another part of the same complex that we were training in. Our job for that night was guard duty, and it was quite an experience. It was, in essence, our first exposure to the actual danger we were expected to face on a regular basis. We were each assigned to guard towers that were at least four stories tall. The best description of the tower's construction was a gun nest situated atop an oil derrick. Gathar was on the tower next to me shining a searchlight on my position for laughs. It was a good sign because he still hadn't shown any signs of accepting his being in Vietnam and absolving me of all of his imaginary blame for dragging us into the war. After the guard detail he was in good spirits and couldn't stop laughing at his prank.

The training went on for a week covering a lot of what we were about to experience. We had classes on language barriers, trip flares, medivac evacuations, slang, and in between we had to perform more shit details. It was fun but only because we were doing it as the same group that trained together. It was disappointing to know that we were going to be sent to different battalions and companies throughout the brigade. The adjustment was going to be tough.

Occaisionally we acquired some pot from the ARVN's and we all got stoned. The potency of the weed was noticed but the availability of it should have made an even bigger impression on us. When I started to come down off of the stuff, I felt depressed and started feeling as if doing a year in Vietnam was nearly impossible. We had formed some close ties with each other and I started having regrets about our impending separations. Not having Gathar as a sidekick was expected to be even more difficult.

The training cadre spoke using a lot of fascinating slang. Firefights were known as being "in the shit" and the enemy was named according to the two alphabets in our military code; Victor Charlie or Charlie for short. Sometimes it was Chuck or Sir Charles but Charlie was the most commonly used name. No matter how large the contingent of enemy soldiers, the singular Charlie was always used. The name was already ingrained in our minds during training. One word in particular, "boo coo", was a very familiar term used extensively throughout our military. It was a mispronunciation of the French word beaucoup. The Vietnamese had literally incorporated the word into its own language and it just stuck with the Americans after we replaced the French as the foreign influence in Vietnam. The Vietnamese, as we were told, also had a very comical numerical rating system for all facets of life. If someone or something were good, then he she or it would automatically be regarded as Number One. A bad performance would always be rated or branded Number Ten. There was never any other number used in the rating. A fair to moderate effort or impression would always garner a number one rating without any mention of two or three. Conversely, there was never any slow climb up from the dreaded number ten. Number nine or eight just didn't exist. It was feast or famine; one extreme or the other. When it came to the locals and their rating system there could never be any middle ground.

We were taken to the finance center to have all of our allotments taken care of. During that process, I was served by a clerk that knew how to spell Tchoupitoulas St. It was a great revelation because only New Orleanians can even pronounce the name. We enjoyed the brief encounter and he wished me the best of luck. The jungle training continued afterward as the Brigade Surgeon, a colonel, gave us the most interesting orientation talk of all. He was a very entertaining middle aged guy who had a weakness for comedy. He talked about dysentery, malaria and of course VD. While on the subject of sexually transmitted diseases, he dispelled the rumor and thoroughly debunked the myth about the untreatable strain of V.D. known as the "Black Syph." We had heard volumes about the disease and never could tell if the storytellers were pulling our legs or not. The story was that if you caught it you would be exiled on some island and quarantined for the rest of your life for fear of spreading the disease in America. A letter would then be sent to your parents or your wife misinforming them that you were M.I.A. and assumed dead or captured by the enemy. According to the Colonel, the story was elaborate, well detailed, and impressive in its construction. He jokingly added that it would make good fiction if anyone wanted to take credit for starting the story. "Just don't believe it". His response triggered a huge laugh and of course we all felt relieved at the same time. The guy had a wonderful sense of humor. I would have paid admission to one of his orientation talks. He also spoke about drugs. Surprisingly, he never mentioned anything along the line of abstinence. What he did was give us a detailed list of all that was going to be made available to us by the local hustlers. He warned us about getting caught and for an added effect; he called for one of the guys from the back of the class; gave him a big fat joint; told him to light it and walk around the room so that everybody could learn to distinguish the smell of burning marijuana. The smoker was not a member of our class and seemed to be part of the entourage that arrived with the Colonel. As the guy circled us puffing and blowing the smoke around filling the room with a white cloud, I turned to Gathar and tried to understand the whole scene. "Do you believe this shit?" I mumbled to him.

"I believe it. Do you think we'll all get a turn?" He said as he kept his eyes focused on the smoker.

"Probably not, I'll bet that guy was busted sometime ago and is being used by these lifers for demonstrations like this."

Being in Vietnam, I figured, wouldn't be a picnic but being in the Herd started to look interesting to all of us then. Just what kind of unit was it anyway? There was definitely a kind of swagger about the Brigade that stood out and made a first impression that we weren't about to forget. One that, I might add, we were eager to duplicate. Class definitely ended on a high note that day.

Later that evening, while going over all of the paraphernalia handed to us upon our arrival, I came across a pamphlet that seemed more appropriate for tourists. It reminded us we were guests or visitors in Vietnam and that we should respect the Vietnamese people and their customs. It also gave a brief history of the country and the many invasions they had endured and repulsed over their long recorded history that spanned millenniums. With a bit of politicking injected, the booklet went on to say that the current struggle the country was engaged in was but another invasion they would eventually overcome. But the current invaders mentioned in the booklet were Vietnamese suggesting maybe we were in the middle of a civil war. As an added strange twist of irony, huddled to my right was a bunch of GIs listening to a radio rebroadcast of a football game with huge implications. The game was played the previous day on the other side of the planet in the southwest part of the States. It was a rare match of the two top ranked college teams at the time. Texas and Arkansas had already battled it out for supremacy of the football polls and as expected, interest was high among the troops. Significantly, it also marked a sad ending to the decade of radical change. In spite of all that had transpired in the '60's, these two teams played to a packed stadium and the only black people that probably witnessed it first hand was selling peanuts or sodas. It seemed odd that America hadn't reached the point in its history where people of all color could play interscholastic athletics together but could send troops overseas to defend the Vietnamese from the Vietnamese. Sadly, in the process of this questionable defense, we had managed to kill hundreds of thousands of Vietnamese right, left, front and center and obviously planned to continue until our Vietnamese were able to kill the communist Vietnamese with the same dispatch. We were, in a sense, encouraging the Vietnamese to live apart from each other, meet only on the battlefield or negotiating table and never to consider coming together for anything certainly as mundane, I supposed, as education or athletics.

We were each issued a ration card which was to be used whenever we purchased items from any of the large P.X.'s (Purchasing Exchanges) in country. The card was introduced to somehow counter Back Market dealings. The Black Market, we were told, was more than just the pervasive illegal buying and selling of goods that the name usually implied. The illicit dealings in Vietnam had grown to monstrous proportions. In some corners, it was bigger than the war itself. We were warned our rations card was one of the most coveted pieces of paper we would come across during our tour. Some of our own fellow GI's would, reportedly, do anything to separate it from us for the quoted $200.00 it could fetch on the streets. We were also told some guys come back for second and third tours to deal on the market and some guys do so well on the market they never go home at all. Our cards were to be protected with our lives because they could sometimes cost a life or two. Even worse, on the Black Market, there was a prevailing attitude that just about anything goes. There was a price on anything and everything including, of course, the ration card countermeasure. Some of our unscrupulous comrades, we were warned, would stoop to stealing our weapons and selling them also. The enemy almost always bought these stolen weapons and used them against us. While at Ft. Benning, I was once told that Vietnam was like one large corporation with an entire workforce that had all gone mad. The guy who told me that was probably referring to the Black Market. It sounded like an exercise in madness.

That night, while enjoying a marijuana-induced altered state of mind, I stretched out on my cot and started listening to some music someone was playing on his cassette player. It was both a lot different from what I had been listening to, and very intriguing. I felt as if the dope had a lot to do with enhancing the music's appeal. I had to ask the guy who was playing the tape....

"Just who are those guys?"

"Led Zeppelin man." he answered as the group belted out continuous choruses of "Whole lot of Love" spaced by some eerie guitar chords that, coupled with the background voices, seemed otherworldly. It had to be the drugs doing a number on my faculties.

"Led Zeppelin? I never heard of that group."

His name was Karl Kyler. He was a short white kid from California who wore thick glasses and a personality as odd as the music he was playing. There was something weird about the little guy and he seemed to enjoy being visibly different than the rest of the guys. He was not in our jump school class but was definitely on our flight over from Oakland. I remembered seeing him sitting in the back of the plane.

"I volunteered for a tour of duty in Vietnam to get away from those fucking lifers at Ft. Bragg. You got any dope?" he asked suddenly.

"No but check out the ARVN's. They've got boo coo weed." I couldn't imagine volunteering for a tour in Vietnam under any circumstance. I thought that maybe he wasn't the spit and polish type they were looking for at Bragg, or maybe he thought the lifers in Vietnam were different. Maybe somebody lied to him and told him he was going to Japan. It just didn't add up. Volunteering for a tour in Vietnam went against my conventional wisdom. If I didn't have to be in Viet Nam, I wouldn't have made the trip. Of course he did seem to be unconventional. I accepted him as being a little different and we listened to some more of his personal favorite tapes he made to take with him. I liked Zeppelin and Blind Faith the most. The music and the high were a perfect match that created a special moment.

11

We were also introduced to the Chieu Hoi program. Chieu Hoi or Open Arms was a plan designed to induce the enemy into surrendering to us through the use of pamphlets dropped by aircraft. Unbelievably, any enemy soldier carrying a Chieu Hoi pamphlet, according to story, was to be granted safe passage and was not to be killed. After realizing that we couldn't kill all of them, we had apparently changed our strategy by trying to get the rest of them to surrender to us. The cadre even gave the talk with the most obvious tongue-in-cheek delivery by telling us of how nice each Hoi Chan would be treated after we turned him in. It was a weird part of our training session and in the end we decided to shoot anybody carrying a pamphlet if the opportunity ever presented itself. Giving the enemy an easy way out of what we all still had to face was just unimaginable.

The end of our training came too quick and we accepted the anticipated breakup of our close knit jump school class. It was tough but we took our assignments in stride. We then wished each other the best of luck and acted as if we all expected to be around a year later for a big reunion in the valley to pick up our orders for our trip back to the states.

4

As expected, we were all scattered throughout the brigade. Gathar & Larks were assigned to one battalion. Jackson and I became a part of another. It was good enough to see that they didn't send the four of us to all four different battalions. We loaded up on our truck with our records, files and fatigues and left Charang Valley for LZ English (Landing Zone English). After arriving at English we had to spend the night there and were treated to our first mortar attack. It was no real threat to our exact location but it was still a little scary wondering if the falling rounds would start walking in our direction. Apparently mortar attacks were common and easily tolerated by the troops stationed at English. For as the mortar rounds were landing in another area of the very large base, the guys in our area continued their activity as if nothing was happening. Having just arrived and being very cautious and afraid, we took cover behind a wall of sandbags stacked around a small building. "What are you cherries doing? Those rounds are landing at least 100 yards away from here." said a very cocky passer-by who laughed at our position cowering behind the sandbag protection. "Of course it is." I said as we all got up in unison laughing at ourselves but still jerking at the sound of each distant explosion. We were trained to take mortar attacks serious. Standing, we were told, was a no-no during one and that lying in the prone position lessens the possibility of being wounded by any of the flying shrapnel. We were not told anything about judging the distance of the impacting rounds and were taking no chances. Naturally we must have looked like a bunch of scared sissies to that guy. The nickname "Cherry", a moniker which I already knew to be commonly associated with being new in country, didn't sit well with me. I knew I was going to have problems with it. After being a lowly trainee for almost seven months, another unappealing name like cherry or F.N.G. (Fucking New Guy) was like a cruel joke.

The next morning, all of the guys assigned to L.Z. Uplift were trucked down the highway to our new home. Some of the guys were assigned to the two battalions at English so the breakup began right there. Kyler and "Red" were both assigned to C co. with Jackson and me. Talley, Tarrer and Byrd were going over to B. co. Sgt. Tita was a cook so he was to be assigned to Headquarters co. Dangerfield volunteered for that detail while we were sitting around waiting for a ride. The detail had something to do with typing but volunteering for anything in Vietnam was taboo. I didn't know what he was thinking about and exactly where he would be stationed was still up in the air because he never came back from his detail before we left. When we arrived at Uplift, we reported to the 1st Sgt. and asked where our quarters were. He laughed and informed us that..." Line companies ain't got no quarters. Give me those new fatigues" he said. He then started going through our duffle bags as if he owned them. He took our fatigues and started passing them out to a bunch of guys who obviously hadn't seen the bush in a while.

"What will we wear?" I asked.

"You'll be resupplied with some clean fatigues periodically." He said. I felt robbed as I stood by watching ungrateful strangers admire the new fatigues that we brought to them all the way from Oakland, Ca.

The company was out in the field at the time and we were told that they would be coming in shortly for a stand down delaying our deployment a while longer. We were relieved of our records and files and sent to a hooch. A hooch was as close to what we knew as barracks as could be found at that base. From the outside, it bore a strong resemblance to a chicken coop for people. A wall of sandbags such as the ones we hid behind at English surrounded it. Along side each of these buildings was a rugged sandbagged fortified shelter that was mostly below ground level. We entered the hooch, sat on some available cots, and waited for nothing to happen.

Christmas was less than two weeks away and there was no holiday spirit to be found. Pretty soon I heard some guys outside doing their version of caroling. Or should I say, anti Christmas caroling. "Jingle bells, mortar shells, V.C. in the grass. Take your Merry Christmas and shove it up your ass." they sang as they passed outside our hooch. Christmas, it seemed, was a million miles away or just some lost practice of an ancient civilization. Maybe it was just something the guys missed so much that they tried to pretend it didn't matter. To a new arrival though, it represented a total abandonment of all that once mattered so much more. Missing Christmas at home for the first time was depressing and somehow the guys around me forced me to act as if it was no big deal.

There was an artillery battery located about 150 yards from the hooch and every time they fired a round the walls shook. Each loud explosion prompted Jackson and I to get up and make a mad dash for the door, only to be stopped by the two strangers who were lounging around in the hooch. "OUTGOING!!!" they yelled each time we ran. Jackson and I couldn't tell the difference because the explosions were extremely loud and we were spooked every time another round was fired. The strangers in the hooch with us had been in country for a while. We sort of depended on them to tell us we weren't about to die. They were black guys who referred to us as cherries or F.N.G.'s (Fucking New Guys) and they both learned quickly how much I resented it. Being new in country was about as unforgiving as any experience ever was. It was understood that all new arrivals would be called one or the other. Fitting in would be difficult for sure and having two assholes like them around didn't figure to make it any easier. They said they were ghosting and that ghosters were troops whom for an alibi, ailment or injury, real or imagined, get to spend some time in the rear. Most of these injuries, we assumed, were contrived and could never be confirmed by any real physician. These guys had probably elevated ghosting to an art form.

The N.C.O.I.C. (Non Commissioned Officer in Charge) suddenly walked into the hooch and announced that he wanted all cherries to fall out. I defiantly remained but with the rest of the guys falling out for formation, it made my stance just that much more difficult. "You'd better fall your cherry-ass out there with the rest of those fucking new guys." one of the ghosters laughed. The N.C.O.I.C. came storming back into the hooch five minutes later. "I said all cherries fall out."

"I'm not a damned cherry, I'm a man!" I shouted.

"Yes sir," he laughed. "Would you please fall out with the rest of those men? "I'm giving you the shit burning detail." he said.

"You're giving me what?"

"The shit burning detail! You're going to burn some shit!" I thought he was joking, but he wasn't. He went back into the hooch and returned with one of the ghosters.

"Teach this cherry how to burn shit." he told him. Without hesitation, the ghoster led me to a primitive looking outdoor latrine with four seats in it. We went around the back of it; dragged a collector out which was a sawed off 55 gallon drum; poured some diesel fuel on it and lit it. He told me to stir it up every few minutes and assured me that shit burning was one of the best jobs in the rear. For the next few hours, I stirred and stirred. I also steamed and dreamed of revenge for the humiliation. Surprisingly, burning feces wasn't the final step in waste disposal I thought it was. It was a measure thrown in to fight against the outbreak of disease. It was crude but obviously effective. Without the sewerage treatment, that I had come to take for granted living in America, we were at the mercy of diseases such as cholera, dysentery and a host of other nightmarish maladies. It was still humiliating, just the same, to be standing with stick in hand burning the stuff. Such was the life in the rear it seemed. Everything performed there, I was told, was done in support of the troops in the field. I just couldn't see what burning feces in the rear had to do with supporting the company in the field.

L.Z. Uplift was a rolling landscape carved out of the middle of Bon Song which was another part of Binh Dinh Province situated near the coast adjacent to the Central Highlands. The Central Highlands was the site of many of the major battles of the war. Our base camp was part of a complex of bases straddled alongside Highway 1. Uplift was a crudely constructed home away from home of about 300 sq. yards ringed with fortified bunkers that formed the defensive perimeter. The ground was littered with marijuana cigarette butts that signified a drug situation that was either out of hand or well under way, depending on which side of the divide one stood. There was also a disturbing situation I couldn't help but notice. There were a few young Vietnamese boys who were maybe 10 years old located on the base camp dressed in fatigues with 173rd patches on each shoulder, jump wings and C.I.B. patches on their chests. They definitely weren't American soldiers and their presence eating in the mess halls, lounging around in the hooches or in the showers bathing with the GIs stationed there seemed out of place or at least inappropriate. Their status seemed to be residential.

The next day the N.C.O.I.C. gave me the garbage detail. Before I could utter a word in objection, the two ghosters came running out of the hooch complaining that First Sargent Crowe had promised them the job. They were furious and unruly about being slighted. "Let them have it. I'll find something else to do." I said.

"You'll do as you're told, cherry!"

"O'kay, but they are so willing".

"Look Sarge, could we show him how to do the detail?" one of the ghosters asked.

"I don't care. Just get that shit off of this compound!"

The two ghosters then whisked me away and told me that the garbage detail was the best job available. We agreed to disagree and headed for the mess hall. Parked outside was a truck full of garbage with a driver waiting nearby. "Are we going to have to unload all of that?" I asked."

"Just get on the truck." he said as they grabbed three shovels and jumped atop the smelly cargo. We then drove down the highway to a designated dump area. They smoked pot all the way to the dumpsite.

When we arrived, the place was swarming with civilians. They started chasing after the truck as soon as we turned off the highway. Old men, women and children were jumping onto the truck while it was still moving. The two ghosters were punching, kicking and clubbing them with their shovels. When the truck came to a stop, we were inundated. The two ghosters were like a couple of slave drivers. They ordered them to take every morsel and paper plate off of the truck in 5 minutes or they would not come back again. The truck was clean in about 60 seconds. They were actually eating some of it on the spot and putting some away for later. The brutal beating they suffered at the hands of the two slave drivers paled in comparison to what they inflicted upon each other while fighting over the scraps. We might have been winning some hearts and minds according to the six o'clock news, but as long as the people had to fight over garbage brought to them by the black Hitler Youth, we were losing face.

We finished up and made it back in time to catch Charlie Co. coming in for a stand down. It was raining and they were standing in it as if it were sunny and dry. They were dirty as hell but full of spirit. They unloaded their gear as the N.C.O.I.C. stood before them giving a briefing that was being ignored. After dropping off all of their excess gear they started taking off to all points unknown. Some talked about going to the steakhouse, some to the N. C. O. club, and some to the highway to hitch a ride. There was an air of wild lawlessness about them. They talked back to the lifers and actually defied them to the point of insubordination, which I always thought was supposed to be taboo in the military. I couldn't wait to get to know them. I was fed up with the ghosters and wanted to get away from Uplift in the worst way. Unfortunately, I was informed that I wouldn't be able to join them when it was time to return to the field. It seemed as if they couldn't find my dental records. I probably lost them in transit between Uplift and the valley. Dental records are essential in identifying bodies in one of those unfortunate scenarios. They couldn't get the Battalion dentist to make some new records because he was on R&R. The ghosters thought I was lucky, but at that time I was ready to get the hell away from both of them.

The stand down only lasted one night. The following morning they were gearing up in the rain for a return to the field. They had all made an amazing adjustment to the elements. In sharp contrast to Jackson and me, getting wet meant nothing to them. They packed and left seemingly as sudden as they arrived the day before.

Christmas came and I was still in the rear waiting for the dentist. The mess hall was serving turkey dinner and eggnog, a whole quart! It didn't matter because I was really homesick and not adjusting too well. They were right about making us miss being home by bringing so much of home over too us. The turkey and eggnog only reminded me of the early Thanksgiving dinner my mom put on for me. I missed Barbara a lot and I started to lose confidence in myself about our doing a whole year separated. Christmas is normally that time of year set aside for holiday cheer. In Vietnam, I was told, it's best to be in the rear during Christmas. The idea was that at least there was the chance to celebrate in any way one chose to. In the field, it was duty and nothing else. As they always taught us in training, one day is just like all the rest. There were no holidays when you're in the bush and weekends existed on calendars only. There were only long hard workdays in the field awaiting my arrival.

That night the ghosters took Jackson and me to a roof top party that had lots of grass to smoke, alcohol to drink up and plenty of beer to cry in. I helped myself to as much as I could to try to forget where I was. After the party we returned to the hooch and listened to the radio. A new group called the Jackson 5 debuted with a song titled "I Want You Back". Sly & the Family Stone followed it up with a real nice one called "Everybody is a Star." The mixture of drugs and alcohol made a sad and also memorable music moment. "I'll always remember where I was when I first heard those two songs." I told Jackson who was drunk and lying on the floor unconscious. He had helped himself to a lot more liquor at the party than he could hold. I had a feeling I was in for a lot of similar moments that would etch its way into my memory both musically and emotionally. Hopefully nothing would happen that would render me as stricken as those paratroopers we met in Japan or as comatose as Jackson was on the floor next to me.

The following morning the two ghosters invited Jackson and me to accompany them to the village. We were sort of reluctant to go on unofficial business and without any weapon.

"Don't worry about it. Nothing will happen to you. I hear that the Dentist will be returning from R&R soon. Ya'll better come with us and get ya'self a shot of ass before going out to the field. You never know when you might get a chance to get laid again. It might be the last time too." He said. His suggestion started to make sense to us in a twisted sort of way.

"Okay, we'll go with you." I said.

"First tell me, do ya'll got any money. The hoes in Bong Son don't work for free you know."

One of them asked. I laughed as Jackson and I both went into our pockets to show the two ghosters our money. Their eyes bulged out of their sockets when they saw that we had in excess of $100.00 between us. Their reaction to the sight of our cash made us remember our black market orientation speech. After adding a little caution to our plans we went along with the two characters anyway. We smoked some pot along the way to the highway and for some reason the high was more than any I had experienced before we hitched that ride. By the time we finally got one of the passing trucks to stop, I felt as if I was on another planet. The ground beneath me was almost in motion or so it seemed. I jumped aboard and took the short ride to the whorehouse but could not get over the paranoia that accompanied the high. I was rendered helpless and could not overcome the ominous feeling that something was about to happen to me and that the hookers were somehow linked to the impending disaster. The two ghosters had a big laugh as they were obviously aware of my predicament. As their laughter seemed to echo inside of my head I fought to maintain my cool and just waited patiently for the end of our excursion. The effects of smoking the pot for some reason proved to be a little more than I could handle. The trip was miserable. Hopefully, I thought, the marijuana wasn't always as potent as that particular joint or that maybe the two ghosters had added some secret ingredient to amuse themselves with me. It was good to see the ugly confines of Uplift that evening and after that I stayed away from the ghosters.

The dentist finally arrived and made a set of dental records on me as was procedure. I was immediately issued a weapon, some gear and sent out to the company's location in the field. My first helicopter ride was surprisingly nauseating and the weather was equally unappealing. It was the rainy season and the monsoon was in full swing. As we hovered before starting our descent, I noticed that every one below was not only soaking wet but also covered with quite a bit of mud. Our landing site was atop a hill or mountain that had all of its trees removed seemingly to create the L. Z.

With me were Jackson and a new arrival named Anderson, a black guy who hailed from somewhere in rural Georgia. I had spent an eternity at Uplift waiting for my turn to come for deployment. I was beginning to feel forgotten and overlooked. As much as I didn't want to go through any of the war, Uplift was not an appealing alternative. In fact it was almost like a deterrent.

While flying overhead, I found Vietnam to be a beautiful country. The view from above was breathtaking. The landscape was full of low-range mountains spaced by rice paddies that formed a pattern of squares occupying all of the low-lying areas. The villages dotting the countryside offered a beauty that should bring shame to anyone who would disfigure its landscape with all of the bomb craters that served as a constant reminder of the war going on. As we continued our descent, all of the beauty slowly disappeared. Soon, there was nothing but a muddy mountain top covered with tree stumps. The trees were obviously removed to form the LZ as I had suspected.

When we landed we were taken to the C.O. (Commanding Officer) He greeted us warmly and welcomed us to the war as if it were a picnic. He assigned us to the 2nd platoon whose platoon leader, Lt. Garson, was sitting with his RTO, (Radio Telephone Operator) a short black guy. "My RTO Edwards will take you to your new squad leader. Before you go, tell me, where are from back in the world?"

"I'm from New Orleans sir." I replied as his eyes lit up when he learned that I was from way down yonder. It had taken me my entire life to realize just what a storybook city New Orleans was to the rest of the world. I knew it was unique but I was surprised at all of the attention that came with being from there.

"One of these days I'm going to the Mardi Gras. When is it, anyway?"

"The day before Ash Wednesday sir." I said.

"Okay, Edwards will take you over to the 2nd squad. Sgt. Griffey will be your squad leader. When he introduced me to Sgt. Griffey, I was offered some hot chow. On resupply day, I imagined it was common to have hot food or maybe it was because it was New Year's Eve and the special treat of having turkey, yams, and eggnog was the least they could do for us. "No thanks. I just ate back in the rear." I said while watching the guys eat as raindrops watered down an already unappealing meal. I tried to imagine myself doing the same thing in three months and wondered how I could ever have my turkey, mashed potatoes, peas, yams and peaches served on a platter without separating each dish and eating it all together as if it didn't matter. All of the guys I came over with, and some that arrived since and sent out ahead of me, had made the adjustment. Red had already taken on the appearance of someone who had been in country for months. Almost all of them seemed to be at home in their new surroundings. Kyler, however, had a despondent look about him and didn't want to talk much as he passed by.

Griffey introduced me to the rest of the squad. There was Raymond Floyd, a large hairy white guy. There was a short mustachioed curly haired white guy called Boogie Man whose real name seemed unimportant, Purvis, another buck sergeant like Griffey and Jones, the only black guy in the squad. Boogie man was the RTO and was more than ready to dump the job on one of us new guys. He had decided that his days humping the PRC 25 had lasted long enough.

"I've paid my dues, let one of those cherries carry it now." He said as Griffey simply ignored him and continued conducting C-Rations distribution. Everyone sat in a circle while taking turns choosing one meal at a time. The old timers knew what to expect in each box and we were just picking blindly. Right in the middle of the ritual, Boogie Man was summoned by a guy who was from another squad. Boogie Man dropped what he was doing and left with him. I thought it was odd to leave at that time, but continued to make my selections. We then started to pack all the food while sitting and talking. "Where you from back in the world Handy?" Griffey asked.

"New Orleans."

"Really, Do you know Reb?"

"No. Should I?"

"Well he's from Baton Rouge."

"C'mon, man. Baton Rouge is about 80 miles away from New Orleans."

"I just thought you might have known him." After we finished distributing the C rations, Griffey handed me a stick of plastic explosive called C-4. The stuff was more powerful than dynamite but as pliable as a piece of clay. Everybody humped a stick to be used when moving the huge trees for our next landing zone. When Boogie Man returned to the squad and started packing up all of his food, his eyes were red as fire and his breath smelled like a burning forest. He turned to me and stared for a moment.

"Where you from back in the world, cherry?"

"The name's Handy I'm from New Orleans and while you're at it, back up with that cherry shit."

"Really."

"That's right. I don't like it." I said angrily.

"My buddy's from Baton Rouge." He said practically ignoring the name-dropping.

"No shit."

"Yeah man, do you know Reb?"

"I already asked him. He never heard of him." Griffey interjected. Obviously Boogie Man meant no harm, but he came close to forcing my hand with the cherry issue. To keep everything from getting out of hand, I tried my best to ignore him and continued packing. As I started to throw away my candy Jones almost went berserk when he realized I was unloading the stuff. He informed me that we were in the Crow's Foot where humping the boonies will totally exhaust me. They call it the Crow's Foot because the terrain's features on the map, resembles a birds claw. We have been humping the area for weeks looking for Charlie. Every two maybe three days we will clear the top of another hill for resupply."

"Like the area I landed in?"

"Yeah, that's an LZ. That mother fucker takes a lot of work to complete. I don't know what's worse, the humping or clearing an LZ." Personally I found the rain to be the real monster. If the rain stopped for five minutes, it felt like an eternity. The sound of raindrops pelting my steel pot literally drove me insane during my first few hours in the elements. Standing in the rain was something different for me to get accustomed to. The instinct to seek cover was tough to overcome. Everything about being soaking wet and not expecting any dry moments was totally unnatural.

My first day humping drained me just like Jones said it would. He reached in his pocket and handed me a piece of that candy I'd given him a couple of hours earlier. When I ate it I experienced a boost in energy that I never imagined I could get from the stuff. Jones gave me a look as if to say…"Well, what'd I tell you?" After acknowledging his tip about the energy he gave me my candy back and told me about another new guy in one of the other squads who wasn't quite hacking it. He was said to be unable to go uphill without everybody else carrying his load.

"All of it?"

"Weapon and ammo included." He said creating a picture in my mind about how humiliating it would've been to not be able to cut it. It was strange to feel that way. Vietnam was not a cherished destination for me but while in training, the Army had somehow instilled this performance thing in me that kept me driven. As long as someone else could, it would automatically become necessary for me to at least be as able.

While humping up a very muddy mountain, Purvis and some of his buddies in the platoon would take advantage of every dry break along the way to resume a never ending poker game played with a mixture of both MPC and Vietnamese money. The money could get wet but of course not the cards. One of his friends, Cantrell, seemed to be doing most of the wining.

As it started to get dark, our squad was dropped off along the trail to pull ambush. The practice was intended to catch Charlie creeping up on our rear end. This was real scary stuff for someone spending his first night in the bush. As the rest of the company moved up the hill, we silently went about deploying our anti-personnel mines (Claymores) and setting trip flares in their paths. I placed my trust in the system and went along with the practice. All during the night we took turns alternating between pulling guard shifts and sleeping. The biggest mistake that could be made was falling asleep on guard. Such mistakes had cost the lives of many young men. There were also stories of GI's being executed by their own for committing such an unpardonable sin. Every hour on the hour C.P. (Command Post) called every position for sit-reps (Situation Reports). Answering these sit-reps while on ambush, was mandatory because no answer could usually represent the worst. Depending on the situation, a sit-rep could be whispered or negotiated by breaking squelch twice on the radio handset. No answer usually meant that someone was asleep at their post or everyone was dead. We managed to make it through the night without incident and rejoined the rest of the platoon. The following night, I was told, would be another squad's turn. I liked that. We made it to the top of the hill and found that everybody was working their tails off. Our job for the following 2-3 days would be to clear the top of the mountain for resupply which meant axes, saws and mule teams of guys pulling trees away. Upon reaching the summit, our squad took up position in the perimeter and alternated between clearing the L.Z. and perimeter guard. I took advantage of my first break and wrote a letter to Barbara. Floyd insisted that I was wasting my time writing her because she would eventually write me a Dear John letter. He said that everybody gets one sooner or later.

The rain was incredibly constant and at the same time B.J. Thomas was singing the ironically appropriate "Raindrops Keep Falling on my Head." It was a song from the "Butch Cassidy and the Sundance Kid" movie. One day when the war ended for me and the letter writing became unnecessary, that song would always be special to Barbara and me. Too bad Floyd and all of the guys he talked about didn't share the same with someone back in the world.

5

A loud explosion went off sending everyone scrambling for their weapons. Fortunately, it was only platoon Sergeant Calvin reminding everybody that it was the beginning of a new year with a grenade. "It's 1970 you poor bastards. Happy New Year." He said giving me some bad feelings about him. Getting past his unlikable personality and performing my duties would be easy as he would naturally try to come across as a hard-ass. He was very deep into his second tour status and he wore it like some proven mantle that defined his fortitude or his courage. He wore a Screaming Eagle patch on his right shoulder signifying that he served in Vietnam with the 101st on a previous tour. He was obviously disliked by most of the guys and his second tour meant nothing to them. Actually being a lifer was about all it took to become a second or third tour guy. It was questionable to keep returning to fight a war that was coming to an end but who said that lifers had any brains.

The next day while humping around in the rain and mud, I heard over the horn that Army Intelligence had come up with information about a regiment of NVA regulars operating in our area. Calvin paused, took his rucksack off and searched through it until he came up with his baseball cap with his master jump wings pinned on the front of it. "I'm gonna need all the help I can get." He boasted in true airborne fashion. His gesture only produced an exasperated response from those who were standing around him at that moment. There was no doubt about it, the guys definitely didn't like him and didn't care for any of his airborne bullshit. His presence in our platoon was more like being tolerated by the rest of the guys. He did seem to relish his role of the second platoon's head non commissioned hard ass-and talked endlessly about his chances of becoming the platoon's "Field First Sgt." Whatever that meant.

We continued on and eventually our day ended going uphill. After we reached the summit of a moderately tall hill, Cantrell passed by carrying an extra rucksack. He was followed shortly by a machine gunner who was carrying an M-16 along with his weapon. They carried it over to a designated area, dropped them on the ground and retired to their respective areas along the platoon's perimeter. I gave it no further thought and concentrated on our duties at our location in the perimeter. The ground was extremely muddy inside of the perimeter. Our boots were all caked with what seemed like an extra five pounds of mud that had to be removed with a bayonet only to be reaccumulated when we moved about again. The monsoon was proving to be a little bit worse than those drill sergeants said it would be. The only respite we had to look forward to was the little field hooch constructed by stretching our ponchos out and tying its corners to the bushes, trees or whatever was available. The makeshift canopy was never more than a few feet off the ground. It was a crude implementation but a welcome one that afforded us the only dry moments of the rainy season. They could only be deployed within the platoon's perimeter. The unfortunate ambush squad had to lie in the rain. The sound of raindrops falling onto the stretched poncho was a violation of the sound discipline rule employed in the bush during the monsoon. Charlie had been trained to listen for the distinctive sound of raindrops pelting the taught surface of one of those field shelters easily giving away our position. The position was always a highly guarded commodity.

Compromising the position by sight sound or odor, especially during ambush, was the ultimate and sometimes fatal betrayal.

Resupply day came around again and our C.O. was about to end his tour. The old man's time ended and I never got a chance to get to know him. Everyone spoke highly of the man. They say that he was always approachable, and in general, the kind of Captain everybody needed to have in Vietnam. One that I think I just missed out on enjoying being around. His replacement, it was hoped, would be equally as squared away as he was but my instincts told me different. I was being cheated by the early departure of a very popular Captain and his replacement, more than likely, would not be as well thought of at the end of his tour. It always seemed to work out that way for me.

Boogie Man was obviously the only pot smoker in Griffey's squad. Expecting an invitation from him was, quite expectedly, out of the question. To him I was just a cherry he was trying to unload his radio off to. Not someone he wanted tagging along when he and one of his friends from the other squads came wandered off to get high. Resupply day seemed to be the ideal moment to sneak off for a quick smoke with or without me. I never really felt snubbed though, after all, in Vietnam the new guy had to earn his respect and nothing would ever change that. Jones, however, had a different opinion in the subject. "Boogie Man can have that shit. I tried it before but at night the stuff can give you the whores real bad man."

"The whores?"

"Yeah, it's like an attack of the worst case of paranoia that you can imagine. At night, a lot of things can go on in the dark and there are a lot of little sounds that the jungle is famous for that can drive you mad. Marijuana just makes it worse for me. Nothing is worse than the Short Timers Whores that comes when you get short like Griffey and everything scares you." Griffey showed no signs of the malady and I suppose it was to his credit. I did, however want him to make up his mind about whatever he was going to do with that radio issue. It was getting a little angry listening to Boogie Man bitch and moan about how long he had been humping the thing. The longer the issue was allowed to just sit, the more uncomfortable my stay became. Being in the second squad had become as undesirable as being at Uplift with those two ghosters. My stay in the bush was off to an unimpressive start.

After resupply, we geared up and started beating the bushes conducting the search for the very elusive "Charlie" who was apparently very familiar with the Crow's Foot. Our method of attempting to engage him made us look like a bunch of assholes. Hiding was the only way to fight a war against our superior firepower. In training we were taught that Charlie only strikes when he has the numerical advantage. His method would always be to hit and run. The guerilla tactics of the enemy had confounded our conventional army. He intended to outlast us and wear down our resolve to continue to carry on the war. Obviously Nixon's election had given him (Charlie) a sense of accomplishment. He felt as if the war had already been won and I couldn't blame him. With whole units being redeployed, who would want to really try to fight under such circumstances? I knew that the majority of draft age Americans wouldn't want to.

During a lull in our progress, Cliff Wheelhouse, one of the machine gunners and I were standing around when I heard over the horn that there was a Bengal tiger alert. "Bengal tiger alert. What are they talking about now?" I asked him.

"That means a tiger has been spotted in the area; A Bengal tiger." He noted.

"Yeah right!"

"No seriously, a Bengal tiger. You are aware that we're in tiger country aren't you?" He said as I finally realized the reason for the name of Ft. Polk's infantry training school; Tigerland.

"Of course. I just thought that they wouldn't be caught dead in this weather." I said as we both laughed. Actually I had never made the connection before he mentioned it.

"Don't worry about them eating you alive though. I hear that they are surprisingly skittish."

"Tell me something. Why were you and Cantrell carrying that extra gear earlier?" I asked.

"One of the new guys can't cut it out here. He can't carry his load when we have to go uphill. Someone always has to carry his stuff for him. He's pathetic."

"I think I heard about him."

When our platoon had to take over point, Garson put the third squad up front and the pace picked up considerably; those guys must have been running. Garson went berserk trying to slow them down. He started screaming at them over the horn but their squad leader was acting as if he couldn't hear him. The third squad did seem to have a certain air about them. To say that they marched to a distant drumbeat was an understatement. Calvin tried to get Garson to lower his voice, which only angered him, more. "We're the only damned fools out here!" he screamed at the top of his voice. This was good news to me. It cleared up a lot of apprehension about the possible presence of Charlie. If Garson could make such a statement, I believed it because I wanted to believe that we were truly the only damned fools out there. I couldn't wait to mention in my next letter home that we were in a very safe area.

We continued to hump the rain soaked hills and valleys and I couldn't tell if it was harder to hump uphill because going downhill presented the same problems with footing. Our boots were caked with mud and there never was enough time to remove the muck from its bottom. There was always someone sliding down the muddy trails knocking aside whoever was standing in the way. Twice sliding bodies knocked me down like a bowling pin as I was frozen in my tracks both times waiting for the collision. Any sudden move in either direction would have sent me sliding down the trail in advance of them. The well beaten trail was always like a greased skid that made the footing treacherous. We tried to negotiate the path by walking along the edge to avoid being knocked down by the human bowling balls. I tried to imagine myself negotiating a path uphill during the monsoon with the added disadvantage of being shot at while struggling to maintain any footing. It seemed foolish to think that we were actually looking for someone to fight against at that moment.

We humped for a few more clicks and came up on a swollen stream that figured to be deep enough to be up to our necks. I assumed there was no way we would cross it. We would be too vulnerable to attack. However, since we were the only damned fools around, why not? We started fording the stream and, though it wasn't as deep as I thought, it was still chest high with a swift current. When I made it to the other side, I found a group of guys standing with their pants down bent over allowing each other to sort of examine each other. "What the hell is going on?" "Leeches!" said Floyd as he dropped his pants, bent over and asked me to check him. I reluctantly looked up his sphincter as he spread his cheeks for me to get a good look.

"Well, what do you see?" he asked.

"I can see your asshole and a lot of hair. Boo coo hair!" I said without really knowing what else to look for.

"O.K. now it's your turn." he said.

"Not on our first date you won't thank you." I joked.

"If a leech gets up your ass and starts sucking blood, you'll catch hell the next time you take a shit." He warned me. Floyd had no sense of humor. He actually thought I wouldn't let him check me. I dropped my pants and bent over with my cheeks spread to let him examine me. I passed with flying colors. "Floyd, listen man I knew that nothing was up my ass. Why didn't you just believe me? And what kind of country is this where leeches crawl up your ass and start sucking blood? That sounds disgusting." I joked.

"Check your dick. They like to get into the urethra too." He said while giving himself a close examination. Without a bit of hesitation, I checked my urethra and breathed a sigh of relief.

"Alright break up that cluster-fuck up there. One frag could kill every one of you bastards!" Calvin shouted as he waded ashore

"What's a cluster-fuck anyway? Is it some kind of weapon?" I asked Jones.

"A cluster-fuck is when you have a bunch of guys standing around with their heads up their asses. Of course today we really do have our heads up each other's ass but it's still a cluster-fuck. Out here it's a no no because if Charlie does throw a frag at the group, he could do a lot of damage. Of course Calvin will declare a gathering of two a cluster-fuck because he is a prick."

When we reached the area designated for our platoon to cover, Garson had a meeting with all of the N.C.O.'s. Most of them were buck sergeants with the exception of Calvin and Don Sayut. Don was such an exceptional trainee at the NCO School that he was said to be awarded the rank of E-6 upon graduation. One of the buck sergeants had a very famous nickname. It was Westy and I couldn't help but wonder if he was related to the famous General Westmoreland who was once running the war. Griffey confirmed that the General was his uncle and that he had spent nearly 18 months in the bush. He was nearing the end of his extended tour and was about to accept a job as a writer for our unit newspaper, The Firebase 173. "Jones, how much have the lifers been kissing his ass?"

"Boo coo man. Boo coo. But nothing goes to his head though. He is one squared away dude."

At the meeting Garson passed out grid coordinates for each squad to patrol. So we set out to check out our designated area. The constant rain wreaked havoc as we attempted to negotiate the area which unfortunately took us up a few small but muddy hills. Humping uphill during the rain, of course, made for a memorable trip. It was always one step forward and then slide ten feet down hill. All progress made uphill was done at the expense of having your face scraped and your neck hung by some of the most persistent wait-a-minute-vines in all of Vietnam. The wait-a-minute-vine was the most comical description I had heard up until then. Every time one of those vines would grab my equipment or me and yank me in the opposite direction, I had to laugh at my predicament. Most of the time, I tried my best to not show just how much the uphill struggle and the mud was getting to me. When we returned to C.P., all I could do was silently hope we didn't have to go back out on ambush. We had been patrolling all day.

The 3rd squad was picked to go out on ambush and it seemed as if those guys were always being chosen to take risks and put themselves in danger. I thought they were being punished for being so rebellious. I also noticed that when they were chosen to go out, nobody complained. "Doc" Bueno volunteered to go out with them and one of the two machine gunners volunteered to bring along an M-60; which was thought to be your best friend in a fire fight. Everybody else stayed back with C.P. and formed a protective perimeter around them. I almost felt guilty for being with the numbers and not out there with the potential of being outnumbered and cut off. Of course I figured our turn would come around often enough to erase all of the guilt.

The following morning Boogie Man brought up the radio issue again. This time I volunteered to take the radio and to put the issue to rest. He continued to grumble even after turning the thing over. Griffey thanked me for making the move. I figured that once I'd carried the radio long enough, the next squad leader would take it away and turn the job over to a new guy with a minimal amount of pouting. Or maybe the war would end first.

The rain was unbelievably constant. There was hardly a pause between showers making me feel fortunate that I had already missed most of the rainy season. My hands were like prunes and so were my feet. My feet took most of the abuse because taking off my boots at night was an unwise practice. During a pause on a trail a guy loosened his bootlaces and peeled his socks down to scratch the leg area along the top of his boots. The skin was full of scabs and his scratching of course removed the scabs and created a bloody mess as he just sighed in ecstasy.

"What happened to your legs man?" I asked.

"They started itching one day along the tops and I started scratching it. After a couple of days, it became a mess." The rain had softened his skin and caused a very delicate area at that spot. Overall, our feet suffered tremendously. Changing socks and using powder did little good because we were always sloshing around in water and mud. I had already gone through a complete 72 hours without even untying my boots. The kind of war we were engaged in made it unwise to take the chance of being caught by Charlie with your boots off. The ugliest problem that came with the monsoon was the "Jungle Rot he was suffering from. The continually wet skin made the slightest scratch turn into the nastiest puss infected sores I had ever seen. Doc Bueno was forever changing dressings on someone's rot. The rot would often form on the buttocks, which made for a funny sight as Doc changed the dressing with someone's ass in his face. The guys seemed to have a name for everything. There was a whole new vocabulary for me to learn and in spite of the physical torture; I began to enjoy the experience of being in the wilderness. Being a city boy that never even went out camping, it was like some kind of seduction of the mind. Once I accepted the fact that I had to be there, it became easier to deal with mentally. When I heard B.J. Thomas singing about the raindrops again, I realized the radio had played the song again for at least the third time that morning. The routine of being in the bush and suffering through the elements sometimes only played as a backdrop to the music that was always playing around us on someone's radio. The lyrics were practically carrying me through the day.

Kyler walked up to me with his head hanging low. He was in the dumps about his performance in the bush. He was, as it turned out, the other new guy Jones told me about on my first day. The one who he claimed couldn't hump worth a shit and the one who had to surrender his equipment to make it uphill. He was sent to the field almost two weeks ahead of me and, unfortunately, he never got any better at humping. I could only imagine what the guys in his squad thought of him. Humping the bush was truly the ultimate physical test Jones said it would be and Kyler was rumored to be facing being banished from the field. Banishment! A lot of guys would love to have been in his shoes right then. Instead, Kyler was demoralized. He wanted to be in Vietnam and he wanted to be out in the bush as a fighting man. Not being able to hack it was really killing him. It was easy for me to relate to something like that. Being dismissed for any reason other than being wounded seemed unreal. Kyler's size had little to do with his inability to hump his load. There were other guys in the platoon who were about the same size as Kyler. They showed no problems at all handling their rucksacks. He had the misfortune of being physically unfit to perform his duties. The Army needed to do something about screening out the guys who possessed little more than desire. Kyler, it seemed, should have been weeded out long before he finished basic training. At least the oversight wouldn't have to go on much longer. A lot of guys back home would've welcomed being told that their services weren't needed in Vietnam. Kyler had made the trip over only to fail the physical challenge and be told he would have to be excused from having to fight.

The following day found us moving uphill again and our squad was in the lead for a change. Jones was our point man and I always wondered if he and others were assigned that duty. I hoped not because it wasn't like being told you're the new R.T.O. or being assigned to carry the "thumper"(M-79 grenade launcher). This was point man, which meant that you'd get to step on all of the booby traps or shot at first. There were stories about how a lot of guys got hurt walking point on the previous mission. Jones was a good guy and I would've hated to see him get maimed doing that point man thing. He seemed confident in his abilities as he led the company uphill in the rain and mud. When we paused for a break, he walked back down the line to talk with me. "Handy, how long have you been with your girlfriend?"

"Almost five years. Why?"

"I was just wondering if you think she knew any girl who would be interested in writing me. I don't have a girlfriend back in Brooklyn and I want to write one of those sisters from New Orleans." I thought little of his request and gave him the address of a sister of one of my correspondents. Her name was Cynthia. I had been writing her sister Beverly since I was in Basic. Cynthia had already asked me to give her name to one of the guys and Jones gave me the chance to accommodate. Cynthia would be a perfect pen pal and nothing more of course. The two of them were about the same age and, I thought, could've possibly provided each other with a very entertaining correspondence.

We continued humping the Crow's Foot and of course it continued to rain on us. The fact we were constantly exposed to the elements was the hardest thing to adjust to. After a while I realized how the rain forest managed to create such a never ending rainfall. It was like the perfect water wheel my sixth grade teacher taught us about. The climate was continually raining and evaporating. The end result was a condensation/precipitation effect that transformed the mountainous area into a treacherous, rain soaked bog replete with heavy runoff, tall grasses, mosquitoes, leeches and all of the associated diseases like malaria and dysentery that came with being exposed to the area. It was fascinating to learn about but a nightmare to experience and I was slowly adjusting to it. Cliff Wheelhouse had made his adjustment and was quite amused at my predicament.

"Don't worry man, I hear the season is about to change and this rain will soon be ending. You came along at the right time. Of course next season's monsoon will be in full swing when your turn comes to DEROS." He said as the lull in our caravan continued to be stalled along that trail leading uphill. "What's the problem up there anyway?" I asked.

"They're arguing about our location."

"Our location?"

"Yeah, every now and then, all of the map holders get together to disagree about exactly where we are. Today's argument happened when we started up this hill they can't seem to find on the map. Some of these guys take the navigation issue a little too serious. They get into some really heated arguments about our exact grid co ordinates. We always manage to find our way around this place and today will be no exception. I'm putting my money on Don though. He really knows those maps. You want some cookies. My Mom sent them." He said as he handed me a couple of wet chocolate chips.

"There's a snail on your elbow." I said pointing to the slimy creature that had somehow crawled onto the underside of his forearm.

"That's no snail Handy. It's a leech. Here's one on you." He said as he removed a smaller one from my shoulder and plucked the other away leaving a spot of his blood on his arm. I didn't realize how much blood one could extract. The leech that had attached himself to Wheelhouse must have been there for an extended period of time. It was scary to think that they could do as much damage without being noticed by its host. Then I remembered when Floyd had me checking my urethra and tried to imagine having one anchored to such a sensitive area.

After the argument ended, we continued and obviously Wheelhouse was right. Those guys could have waited until we were at least at the top of whatever mountain it was or wasn't. When we did make it to the top, there was a peculiar scene awaiting us. The mountain's summit was above the white carpet of low hanging clouds that was providing us with all of the rain just a short distance below. The surreal scene of being above the clouds was one that sent all of the guys scrambling for their cameras. They all wanted to be photographed standing along the incline with the white mist behind them. "Handy, take my picture!" Said Wheelhouse calmly as he handed me the Instamatic and retreated to a spot along the mountain slope that would give the illusion that he had just ascended to the heavens. I should have bought one of those little Kodaks while I was ghosting away waiting for my dental records. Wheelhouse shot all of the remaining pictures and prepared to have the roll of film sent home to his folks. "I'm planning to have them there waiting for me when I get back. I've got a huge collection of all of the places I've been and everything I've seen since I came over.

"When did you arrive anyway?"

"September. I don't count the days like some of the short timers. At this point, there are too many days ahead and these guys would tease me about having over two hundred plus days left."

"I guess they'd really laugh their heads of if I announced I had more than three hundred days left."

"I would laugh with them too. Do you realize how funny that would sound if someone would yell short, three hundred and ten days?" I had to admit he was right. Being short is a privilege that should be guarded by the fortunate few.

6

After humping with the second squad for a brief period, it was decided to spread the three of us new arrivals around. Anderson remained with Griffey's squad while Jackson was moved to one of the machine gun crews and I, along with Purvis, was sent over to the third squad. It meant that I had to get used to answering to another call sign or referring to that new sign every time I talked on the radio or "horn" as we called it. Anyway, I welcomed the move because the guys in the third squad were always having fun just being together. When I arrived at the third squad's area in the perimeter, I immediately detected a problem within and fortunately it wasn't centered on me. There was a mild controversy brewing about whom was the squad leader. I could have been wrong about "Bear" being the squad leader because Purvis seemed to be in charge. The rest of the squad, Black, Speedie, and Shave, quietly disagreed. I thought maybe the lifers appointed him as the squad leader to rein them, or rather us, in. I didn't think the ploy would work. Purvis was a good guy but if he was truly appointed leader of the group, he could never command the respect of the rest of the guys that comprised the squad. Bear, on the other hand, had already earned the respect of his men and nothing could ever replace that. Purvis could only hope for respect due to his appointment. In Vietnam, as I was told countless times before, you earned your respect. With an appointment, such as that which Purvis appeared to be saddled with, about all he could offer was an extension of the lifers' brand of leadership. The Bear lead by example and everyone seemed to prefer it that way. Purvis had one thing going for him though. Bear was not offended nor threatened by Purvis' presence. His reaction to Purvis's arrival to the squad added a huge element of irrelevance to the issue. Bear seemed too happy just being in Vietnam to be caught up with something like who was in charge. He was the consummate team player and his style was the kind of example that stood out and made a favorable first impression. Everyone in the squad rallied around his style of leadership and I couldn't blame them.

When the time came for us to move out again, it was our squad's turn to walk point. Bear seemed to prefer walking point because he was either in a hurry or maybe he thought there might be some action around. Comparatively speaking, his intensity level was a bit higher than Jones and he seemed to live for such moments. He moved very fast, which explained the accelerated pace we used when the third squad was up front. It didn't take Garson five minutes to call us on the horn to try to get us to slow down. There was no way to talk on the horn and keep up with Bear at the same time so I didn't try. I didn't get the impression that he was about to stop running and start prowling anyway. He seemed to be looking for Garson buttons as he led a relay uphill at breakneck speed. We ran for a few minutes, sat for a few and when everybody caught up, we would take off again. He seemed to know his pace would get a certain reaction from our tempestuous leader and continued to press on at his ridiculous pace.

The conventional order to line up was point man, squad leader, R.T.O. and then the rest. Bear just liked the action. He couldn't care less about order. Being a grunt, or "Boonie Rat" was his passion. It was hard to imagine the guy doing anything else. Hell, it was hard to imagine him being anywhere else as long as he could be in Vietnam. Vietnam seemed to fit some of the guys just right. Bear was one of those guys. He was on a high that he didn't want to end.

"Speedie" was a Chicano from California. He carried this one tape, "Santana" and played it just loud enough for the rest of the squad to hear. Carlos Santana, he noted, was an acquaintance of his back in the world. I, on the other hand, had never heard of Santana and it seemed to disturb him in a way that didn't really threaten our relationship. He played the tape continually and fortunately it had a very infectious beat. I was rapidly becoming a big fan of this new Latin sound. "He's my homie man." He reminded me twice in the first half hour I had known him. Speedie and Bear were real close. They occasionally called each other by their real names for fun. Bear's name was Roger Hill and Speedie was Carlos Diaz. I was amazed at how close some of the guys were. They seemed to feed off of each other's presence and made the most out of the situation in spite of the constant rain and the threat of war. As miserable as the situation was, nothing could change their pursuit of having a good time with each other. There was a family quality about them that really stood out. I was constantly entertained by the closeness of the group and by the way they enjoyed tweaking authority. Going uphill was probably just one of many games they played.

Speedie openly expressed his objection to Purvis' appointment. If Bear were half as objectionable, we would have had a real serious problem. My only problem was getting to feel as if I had become a part of the group. I couldn't expect to achieve any measure of acceptance that soon and I was being patient waiting for it to happen. It was just too early to expect to make any kind of impression on them. I could only hope that being the one that came over to their squad with Purvis wouldn't hurt my chances of becoming a part of their close knit group. Just being in the squad wasn't enough. Becoming a member of their family mattered more and had become my goal.

Black, a nondescript oddity, was just glad to be with the squad. He was a white guy with dark hair, a pointed chin and a noticeable overbite. It was pretty obvious he had less time in-country than the rest of the squad members. He was happy to have someone in the squad newer than he was. He offered assistance to me at every opportunity and although some of his tips were a bit redundant, I still appreciated the help. He was not as sharp as the rest of the squad but it didn't seem to matter as they just continued along having fun and treating the war as some kind of big camp out.

Shave was a thin, sandy haired white guy that spoke with a high pitched voice and was at times somewhat animated. Shave, who was also short, seemed to be an intellectual of sorts and I liked that. The notion that all grunts were dumb had become a source of irritation and seeing Shave in the bush was just the kind of rebuttal to that theory I needed to witness.

"Tell me, are you as short as Griffey?" I asked as we came to a pause in our pace to allow the rest of the procession to catch up.

"Not quite. He's got a few wake ups on me." He said. Besides counting days, he also counted his money. How much he had and how much he expected to have upon DEROS (Date Expected to Rotate Overseas), and what he planned to do with it when he got home.

"I'm a Jew, you know how we like to save our money." He said jokingly.

"There's another member of our squad we call Burt. Whenever he's not assigned to the mortar squad, he humps with the third squad. Burt is the coolest guy who ever lived." He said.

"There it is." Speedie said as everybody nodded in agreement with him.

"Burt was sent to a Fire Support Base. He'll join us later." Black added. I had become the only black member in the squad and had no idea if there were any before my arrival and wasn't aware of who the RTO was prior to the shift in personnel. To our squad's credit, race never seemed to matter. I could sense that in time we would all be one. It was reassuring to know there would only be the anticipated problems associated with being the new guy and not the only black guy or the new black guy. I felt extremely comfortable with my new squad.

When our trek resumed, Bear continued to move along at a rapid pace in spite of the rain, mud and Garson's objections. Being first in the long line of marching boots had its advantages in spite of the obvious dangers. The ground was not as well beaten meaning less muddy and a lot less slippery. Our sure footing seemed to inspire Bear to move faster. He was driven to extreme performances by some kind of demon that would not let him slow down. All one could do was maintain eye contact with the guy in front. Losing this visual means getting lost which also means that everyone behind he who loses contact would have also been lost. This further underscored the point man's importance. He was the only one paying any attention to where we were going. The rest of us just concentrated on the guy directly ahead or would occasionally scan our flanks for whoever was hiding in the bushes as we continued along. It was creepy the way the guy in front of you would just disappear right before your very eyes. He could be standing in front about ten meters ahead and then suddenly he would become difficult to distinguish from all of the jungle around him. The phenomenon made it important to occasionally look back to see if the rest of the procession was still following you. To occasionally make eye contact with that person behind you was very crucial. Doing it with Bear at point only added a degree of difficulty to the effort.

When we finally reached the top of the hill, everybody was gasping for breath as we laughed at the fuss we created with the pace we set. We picked out a nice spot on the hill, dropped our rucks and waited for the rest to arrive. When they reached the top, Garson did a beeline for Bear and chewed him out for not answering his call. I was just glad that he didn't jump in my shit for not answering the horn. Bear put on a pretty good poker face and faked ignorance about being called on the way up the hill. The show was very entertaining. Like all lieutenants were, Garson would lose his cool in grand fashion. The way he went after Bear only demonstrated to any casual observer just who was regarded as the real leader of the third squad.

After getting chewed out by Garson, we were ordered back down the hill to pull ambush as a form of punishment I suppose. Again, nobody complained and we were ready to move out almost immediately. Before we left Doc Bueno volunteered to come along and Al Milles followed along with the M-60. Neither one of those guys had to do it but they did it anyway. My squad, without a doubt, preferred to be away from the main body and the practice went against my philosophy about being out in the bush. I'd always believed in strength in numbers but would have to get used to being with 6 or 8 guys because they preferred it that way.

When we reached the bottom of the hill, we deployed our Claymores and set up the post. Then I decided to take advantage of the remaining daylight hours to write a letter to Barbara and was immediately joined by Speedie. "How do you like our little war so far?" he asked."

"I don't."

"Do you always speak in fragments?" he asked pouncing on that little flaw in my English. Humping the boonies with him around could be like humping with a schoolteacher but I expected it to be fun. I may have been the only black guy in the squad but it was obvious that race had nothing to do with the teasing. Charlie Co. was just one big happy family where racial problems did not exist. We were all brothers. "Whom are you writing?" he asked in his best grammatical form.

"My girlfriend."

"Where are you from back in the world."

"New Orleans."

"New Orleans! Do you know Reb?"

"Every time I mention that I'm from New Orleans, someone asks if I know this Reb. Tell me, just who is this guy?"

"Reb used to be our squad leader. He went home a couple of months ago. He was at Dak To."

"Dak To. I've heard about that place, Hill 875, 300 men lost and then turkey dinner. I guess it was special to have him with you."

"Damn Right, he was a real squared away dude. Say, how did you know about the turkey dinner?"

"It was on the news. I hear that he was from Baton Rouge and although New Orleans isn't exactly next door to the place, everybody somehow expects me to know him. Forgive me but I do find that sort of weird."

"Well, I was just wondering."

Doc Bueno was another Mexican-American who, according to Speedie, was also from California. I had overheard him boasting about how short he was on my first day in the field. Which was too bad because, I liked being in the medic's favorite squad. In the bush, who wouldn't? I figured that by volunteering for ambush, he was also avoiding all of the guys who were trying to get out of the field with fake ailments. I remembered the two ghosters in the rear and asked Bueno if he thought they would ever be coming back out to the field. He said they were junkies who would never be expected to return.

"Like that character "Heavy". He would shoot peanut butter into his veins if he thought it would give him a buzz." said the machine gunner.

"Where are you from back in the world?" I asked him.

"I'm from upstate N.Y. A place called Rochester." Milles seemed to be a real true spirit. He kept a permanent smile on his face as he obviously enjoyed being in Vietnam.

"Ever heard of lacrosse?" he asked.

"I've heard of the game but I've never been to Wisconsin."

"I was a near club level player back home. The game is real popular in the upstate region and across the border in Canada. There's a Canadian in the first platoon who plays the game. We call him "Baby San" because he looks like a little kid. He joined our Army so that he could come here." Up until that moment I had always thought of Canada as a place where draft evaders ran to. I never thought of it as a place where their youth came from to volunteer. I started to wonder how many north-of-the-border enlistees were there in Vietnam and then I remembered a story I read about Al's hometown. "Rochester, you know I've heard of that place before. It used to be a stop for runaway slaves on the Underground Railroad heading north to Canada." I said

"That's right and I hear you're from New Orleans. What's the Mardi Gras like man?"

"You gotta see it to believe it."

"Last guard." Speedie said suddenly.

"Next to last guard." Bear announced while laughing. After hearing Bear chime in, Doc Bueno ran over to our little gathering and said,

"First guard"

"Second guard" said Shave

"Third guard." said Black while laughing his head off.

31

"I'll go ahead of Bear." said Al with an air of confidence. There was something going on around me but I couldn't understand exactly what it was.

Jackson, who was on the same gun team with Al, looked at me as if to ask, "What are these guys talking about?" He was about as confused as I was.

Then almost as if the entire little play never happened, Al continued talking about New Orleans.

"One of these days I'm coming down there to look you up, okay?"

"Please do." I said still wondering what the guard thing was about. My curiosity wouldn't rest either. Black, of course, explained that they were sort of jockeying for position in the guard rotation for the night. As darkness neared, Purvis gave the order of guard duty. Doc was first and then Shave, Black, Purvis, Me, Jackson, Bear, followed by Speedie. Everyone was to pull 90 minute shifts before waking up the next guy. The reason for all the frantic positioning was that either Charlie was a hopeless insomniac or maybe the guys in the squad all believed in ghosts. Midnight was thought to be our adversary's preferred hour to attack. It was comical the way everyone felt relieved to not be up at that time. I personally preferred to be wide-awake prior to attack as opposed to being wakened by gunfire or explosions. As long as they preferred to be asleep at the Witching Hour, I'd just pretend to always be stuck with whatever position they left me with. There was a tradition regarding the way they handled guard duty. In Griffey's squad the squad leader assigned the order of guard, in the third squad, it was up for grabs. They took something as serious as guard duty and made it into something they could laugh at.

That night, when Purvis woke me up to pull my shift at the post, it was so dark I couldn't see anything. I needed more time to allow my eyes to adjust to it and Purvis, to my embarrassment, took me by the hand and walked me over to the post. He then sat with me and waited until my eyes made the adjustment. While sitting there, I quickly got over the embarrassment of my temporary blindness and started to wonder how often it happened. As my eyes became adjusted to the dark, I noticed Speedie was sleeping in a hammock which seemed a lot more appealing than sleeping on the ground. Of course, it also meant there would have to be two trees around to make use of the above ground sleeper.

The following morning there was no movement up the hill. I was anticipating more lumberjack duty but instead we remained at our ambush site that morning. Suddenly someone lit up a joint and I realized why they liked to be alone; or why Doc always volunteers to tag along; and, of course, why we could expect to have a machine gun with us more often than not. The third squad was a crew with a partying spirit and everybody knew it. Being a member of the third squad was going to be a lot of fun. It was all I could hope for. The party was short lived though. We had to move to an extraction site and wait for a ride. The ride, surprisingly, was going to be provided by a giant Chinook helicopter. The Chinook is a craft large enough to transport the entire platoon and often used for lifting heavy loads. The biggest surprise was that we were to be lifted to an R&R site set up for us on the beach at Qui Nhon the province capital of Binh Dinh. While inside the "Shit Hook" as we affectionately called the big bird, Cliff Wheelhouse sat next to me making conversation about our respective home towns.

"Are you kidding me, Virginia Beach is a very popular East Coast resort area and one of America's first settlements." he boasted. I never doubted his claim about his hometown. He was just a little upstaged by the fact that I was from New Orleans. A place that everyone had heard about, including him. Wheelhouse was a tall good-natured guy who really enjoyed being in the bush and relished the role of machine gunner. He offered to show me how to surf when we got off the chopper but I declined because I wasn't a very good swimmer at all.

Our flight was surprisingly long. We arrived and were looking forward to the rest of the day in Qui Nhon. We shopped at a PX and then headed to the beach. Wheelhouse and some of the other guys took off for the waves with boards in tow. The waves were too rough but just being out there trying to catch one was enough to keep them happy for a while.

The R&R site was less than impressive but anything beats the bush. We had a basketball court, ping pong, pool tables, and of course there was the beach. While sitting around killing time, Calvin invited himself to our little gathering and tried to make conversation. "I remember back in '65 when the N.V.A. came down from the mountains and kidnapped all of the women in this city." he said. The war was full of legend about how the enemy was always terrorizing the local populace. There was also a story I had heard about Binh Dinh Province being a former communist stronghold during their war against the French. The story was that Ho Chi Minh wanted the D.M.Z. to be situated below the province because of all of the work he had accomplished in the region. Relinquishing the area was said to be a bitter pill for the old beard to swallow. It made me wonder how they lost the so called South Vietnam territory through negotiation after winning the war of liberation against the French. The French's ouster should have given them total rule over the entire country and not have the south occupied by American troops. Everything about our presence in Vietnam seemed to redefine Ho Chi Minh's victory. Winning only meant they had to face us next. Of course we were expected to do a lot better than the so called inferior French Army. Their poor performance against Hitler during WWII seemed to fuel a low opinion about their fighting prowess or lack there of. Getting their asses kicked by the Viet Minh was the ultimate insult. The prevailing attitude was that we had to bail them out during WWll and were just doing it all over again in Vietnam. Calvin's demeanor, as he spoke, possessed the same air of arrogance that defined the French as being militarily incapable. Surely the NVA could never chase us out of Vietnam and definitely not out of the province. Too many of our decisions were born of that same attitude and had already cost us dearly. But at that moment, the beach was just a place we were going to use for a brief respite from life in the bush.

We played a little basketball and then spent the rest of the evening sitting around the court. Somebody reached me a small bottle of black liquid. Before I drank any of it, I wanted to know more about its contents. I assumed it of course was a drug. "What is it?" I asked Wheelhouse.

"Obesitol. Be careful, two swallows of that stuff and you'll be wired for the next 24 hours."

"Wired?"

"Yeah man, its pure speed." he said. Obesitol was one of the drugs the Brigade surgeon talked about during his orientation. It was a weight reducing liquid the French manufactured and sold over the counter back in the colonial days. After they were kicked out, the Vietnamese continued production of the drug. Using speed to combat obesity is common but Obesitol, according to the good doctor, is a highly concentrated form that would be outlawed in any other industrialized nation including modern day France.

In spite of Wheelhouse's warnings, I took a swallow and passed it on to the next willing drug abuser. Vietnam had a smorgasbord of drugs available. It was a totally corrupt country with a segment of people willing to cater to our every whim and desire in exchange for our currency, the vaunted M.P.C. (Military Payment Certificate). The hustlers, seemingly, didn't care about the threat of a communist takeover and was certainly unconcerned about which form of government was in power. The manufacture of a packaged, marketed illegal drug like Obesitol only underscored the degree of corruption that existed around us. The American G.I. wanted the dope and the dealers were willing to accommodate. The market only existed because of our presence and our considerable drug habits. "These people will do anything for a buck." I asserted as Wheelhouse and I sat and talked.

"Actually the people that we mostly come in contact with are Black Market operators; the hookers, drug dealers and money hoarders who are always somewhere nearby. The rest of the civilians are just hard working people who would be glad to see us go home." he said which would make our presence in Vietnam questionable at best. If our efforts weren't being appreciated then we didn't need to be prolonging our stay. If I thought I didn't know about the war before that guy at Benning interrupted the General's speech, being involved was proving to be a continuing lesson. The stories told by people like Wheelhouse, were all I had to rely on for my learning experience. Unfortunately, anything that came from the lips and minds of a GI was of course subject to conjecture. The newspaper accounts were too current and told me nothing about the history of the war. My memory of the slow development could only be traced to the years leading up to our introduction of combat troops. Even then it seemed as if we were already in Vietnam. I still couldn't understand the reason for our presence and how much earlier did it begin. Learning about our involvement in Vietnam seemed to be almost impossible from where I was at that time. I just had to know more about why I was sitting on that beach staring out at the South China Sea wishing it was our own polluted Lake Ponchartrain.

That evening, our stay ended and we returned to the treacherous rain forest nicknamed "Crow's Foot". The sudden change in background was disturbing. That night the effects of the Obesitol lingered as I was transformed to a wind-up toy. I couldn't even bring myself to lie down for the night and just stood up with my rucksack on my back. It was all right with the rest of the guys because it meant someone would be wide-awake for the night; someone that just happened to be carrying the radio too. While standing under a tree, my imagination started conjuring up what could only exist in my mind. I thought I heard noises that couldn't be heard and sensed movement that no one else could detect. The Obesitol was too much for me to handle.

The following morning, rumors started spreading around about our new C.O. who was expected to join us soon. One story had him down as an ex-Marine, another had him as an ex-Green Beret; and I even heard one about him being both. I imagined the worst character would replace our CO and expected Attila the Hun in jungle fatigues would show up.

Wheelhouse tried to keep me perked by telling me stories about his nephew. The guy would start talking and eventually would laugh his head off. The nephew must've been his first and only one. He was obviously very attached to the little fellow. He then went into his rucksack and pulled out a photo of himself taken when he was stationed in Germany. He was all starch, spit and shine. He was posed on one knee next to all of his gear. Judging from the way all of his stuff was situated neatly stacked, folded and positioned; I had to ask the obvious questions. "Inspection day right?"

"You guessed it"

"No gigs, right?"

"Right again."

"So tell me, why aren't you still in Germany?"

"I just wanted to be here."

"You left Germany to come here?"

"Germany's not a great place to be. Besides the women had too much hair on their legs." he joked.

"What's wrong with a little hair on the legs?"

"You like hairy women? Hey guys! Handy likes women with hairy legs, good lord!" he said as he went into hysterics. Wheelhouse was a true free spirit who was really going out of his way to be nice to me.

"You got any photos?" he asked sending me into my rucksack for a photo album that I prepared before I left home.

"The pictures in here cover a span of about four years." I said as I handed it to him. "Who's the pretty girl with the baby on her lap?

"Her name is Barbara."

"You have a lot of pictures of her. She must be your girlfriend." he said as he flipped through the album.

"Yes she is. What about you? What's your girl's name?"

"I don't have a girlfriend at home." he said which I found hard to believe because he was so likeable and he looked reasonably attractive. Then I realized that at his age, and having already been to Germany, he had to enlist at 17. While most guys were trying to invent ways to delay turning 18, he was in a hurry. Vietnam was full of guys like him though. Guys who wanted to go to war. It was either tradition (Gramps fought in WWI, Dad in WWII, etc.), the pursuit of adventure, or just out of boredom they went to Vietnam to say that they went. One of my best friends, Carter McKnight, joined the Marines at 18, wound up at Khe Sahn and then went through TET '68. He was wild and out of control for sure but loved the attention he received while there. Wheelhouse, aside from Carter's reckless abandon and race, differed very little from him. They both came from good homes with two loving parents. Wheelhouse must have kept close tabs on his folks because in the little time we had known each other, he'd asked me to take quite a few pictures of him to send home. Although he should've been home chasing teenage girls like the average teenage boy and not posing for pictures in some foreign country while at war, I had to admit it was fun having him around.

We picked up and started to move out again. The first platoon had point, third platoon followed and our platoon had drag. Our squad was last in line so with a slight breeze blowing in our face, we lit up a joint and tried our best to keep it dry. It was fun being with those guys but somehow I just didn't feel accepted. It wasn't rejection or ostracism. It was just a matter of making the grade with the rest of the squad. Being the only black guy in the squad had nothing to do with it either. All I could do was be patient and keep performing. Time was on my side because I had so much of it left to do.

When we reached our designated area for resupply, I decided to change fatigues because the brand new set that was issued to me in Oakland had become part of my new guy persona. I thought that maybe a set of old fatigues would do the trick. So when the fatigues arrived I started searching through them for a pair that might fit but couldn't find anything close to my size at all. "Forget about fit and just make the change. Nothing will ever fit the way you want them to. Those fatigues will never fit like Irtenkauf's over there." Wheelhouse said pointing to a buck sergeant wearing fatigues that had obviously been tailored to fit him. "Top took my fatigues when I first arrived at Uplift and gave them to some of those guys in the rear." I said.

"I know. He does that to all of the new guys." Then Purvis walked over to me and handed me my first letter. It was from Barbara. He said it was sent to the first platoon by mistake.

"They sent it to the first platoon and had been trying to find you." he said. I read the letter and realized that in spite of being told to wait until I was assigned to my unit, she wrote me as soon as she got my letter from the valley. That was classic Barbara. When I last saw her, I told her that she was holding our relationship in her hands and not to drop it. Actually, she never knew how to let go. I was fortunate to have her on the other end at that time. The Dear John letter Floyd was predicting was out of the question.

Resupply day should have been the day that the new C.O. would come out but he didn't show. This would give us at least until the next resupply day to do without him. Undaunted, we loaded up on our new supplies and moved on without his presence. The rain continued to make life miserable for us but at least we were in the low lands and not going uphill. It did seem like a relief to not have to tackle mountain climbing with a full ruck. Unfortunately our course was taking us to a mountain range straight ahead. The distance, I assumed, wouldn't take us more than an hour to reach but it was almost impossible for me to judge. It always looked a lot easier to negotiate than it actually was.

As we continued on our way to the mountains, the terrain again proved to be as misleading as ever. This trip was no exception as what appeared to be a one-hour hump turned into an incredible six hours. As we reached the base of the mountain, we decided to set up for the night. Before we could settle down we got word that our new CO was arriving and was in fact on his way. There was nothing like the disruption of a loud chopper to drop off one passenger. If his entrance wasn't staged, then it must have at least been designed to avoid making the trip to our spot on foot. When he finally arrived and stepped off of the chopper, the ground did not shake and when he approached our area, the mountains did not part. My guess was that whenever we reached our next swollen stream, he wouldn't be able to walk on water either.

All rumors about the new CO were to be expected. Vietnam, according to the guys, was famous for rumors and wild speculation. His arrival managed to expose him as just another lifer and that would place him in the ranks of the rest of us mere mortals. I just hoped he could stand it. He was a rather unimposing figure with wavy dark black hair on his head and a lot more of it everywhere else on his body. He was gruff, aloof and I suppose he preferred to create that kind of aura around him. His name was Mercein and his exterior was as exaggerated as the pistol he wore on his side. According to the patch on his right shoulder, he was also an ex-Green Beret. He conferred only with his platoon leaders and talked a lot on his radio. He spent the next few hours doing nothing else. He seemed to be observing our execution of duty. His ploy was unnerving to others but as far as I was concerned, the less heard from him the better it would be. Our squad spent the night inside of the perimeter situated close enough to his majesty's area to make me wish I were on ambush. In the moonlight I could seem him as he surveyed our manner of performance. It was possible that we were being graded as the night went along.

The following morning we started uphill with our new CO in tow. He continued his method of not addressing anyone in general except for an occasional radio transmission. When on the horn he talked in strong, forceful exaggerated tones. He was asserting himself while trying not to interfere with our climb up the mountain. Again, his mannerisms were more tolerable than his presence but he continuously gave off a lot of bad vibes.

When our path took us through another mountain pass, the rain stopped for an entire ten minutes. It was the first extended period without precipitation I had experienced since first stepping off of the helicopter. There was something weird about walking along a muddy trail without the rainfall. It didn't make maters any better but it was different. The sun came out and started to assert itself in a manner that I had yet to witness in Vietnam. It became hot enough to almost dry the fatigues we were wearing and then cause us to sweat. After the unusual phenomenon was over the rain resumed and restored the area to normalcy.

When resupply day came around again my anticipation level was high because I expected to start receiving mail. While standing around waiting for the next helicopter or slick as they called it; a guy walked up to me carrying a little vial with a label on it. "You got any piss?" he asked.

"Some what?"

"Piss man, you got any piss?" he asked again.

"No man. I'm fresh out." I answered. He walked away and went about asking some others. Then a short black guy that bore a strong resemblance to a friend of mine from back home stood up.

"I've got some." He said as he unzipped his pants and started urinating in a small bottle he already had in his hands. When he filled the bottle he reached it to another guy and started filling up another. He then handed the bottle of urine to another guy and then continued to empty his bladder on the ground. "Run Away Child". Don't waste it man. Smitty needs some." someone else said.

"Well Smitty had better get his ass over here now because I'm not waiting all day for him." he said as the guy who first asked me for some urine returned to have his bottle filled. Smitty was an olive complexioned white guy with little or no chin features and a very extroverted personality. It was easy to see that he was well liked in the company. The urine samples were being collected for early malaria detection. Everyone had to submit a sample to the aid station to find out who wasn't taking his malaria pills or who had contracted the disease. The Brigade surgeon gave us a talk about it when we were in the valley. He said that the samples were to be collected periodically but it only provided the guys with an amusing distraction. Everyone was supposed to take one small pill daily and one large pill once a week to protect us from it. There were a couple of problems with the testing procedure though. First of all, the human body can only produce urine when there is some in the bladder. The process does not work on command. The other problem was that none of the guys in the field seemed to take malaria serious enough to commit to the regimen of taking the pills. The attitude was that the worst that could happen to us if we caught it would land us in a nice dry hospital bed. Personally I figured that if the two pills couldn't guarantee that I wouldn't catch it (and it didn't), there was no use in taking them at all (and I didn't). The biggest joke was that out of about 30 bottles of urine collected from our platoon, there might've been three guys filling them all up. Everybody had fun with Piss Day. I collected urine from a guy who had a waiting line in front of him. He was one of the guys with a full bladder. The black guy who everybody called "Run Away Child" was the one of the few filling up the piss bottles that day. Obviously it was hoped the guys with the full bladders would never have malaria. It would have caused quite a problem for the guys in the rear doing the testing. The brigade surgeon warned us that contracting malaria was misery and that a relapse was possible up to a year or two after we returned home.

A Vietnamese civilian barber came out on one of the slicks and started cutting hair. I needed one but was hesitant to get in line with the rest of the guys. "Jones, can the Vietnamese barbers cut a black man's hair?"

"Hell no. Those guys can't cut hair at all. Whatever you do, don't ever let one of those people cut your hair. They will fuck your shit up real bad man. Calvin will bug you about it so just ignore him." he said confirming my suspicions.

My mother wrote me a letter. She never finished school and her lack of education was always evident in her letters but her handwriting never looked better. The last three letters were from Barbara and I read them all before I rejoined the rest of the Company. "Handy, we're going to take over a fire support base (F.S.B.) called Beaver from a company of legs." Bear said as I returned from my moment of privacy.

"Sounds like the best news I've heard since the rain started. It doesn't matter to me that a bunch of legs constructed the place. I don't care who was there first. Just get me out of this rain." I said. A leg is any soldier who never experienced the thrill of jumping out of an airplane. In the eyes of the paratrooper, these people represented the lowest life forms on the planet. The lifers always talked of the non-paratroopers in the worst way. "They were scum sucking, no good, dirty low down legs and can't do anything as good as paratroopers." As they always said at Ft Benning. Sometimes they would get real personal with lines like… "The poor lousy bastards were probably inbred." There was an endless line of derogatory descriptions used whenever the conversation turned to the dreaded legs. Personally, after stumbling around in the muddy jungle, a firebase sounded like a winner to me. It couldn't have happened at a better time either. The jungle rot had infected half of my knuckles and rendered my hands useless. I couldn't write a letter and I doubted if I could even pull a trigger properly. I also had developed a nasty sore on my knee that made it hard to bend. I was pretty close to asking Doc Bueno to send me to the rear to spend a few drier moments for the remainder of the monsoon season.

7

They sent us a fleet of helicopters for the flight over to Firebase Beaver. I was told to sit in the door which, as in all slicks, had been removed exposing the occupant to a very open view of all below. Although everybody seemed to enjoy sitting there, I didn't. I found it kind of nauseating as I sat next to Speedie and tried to pretend I was enjoying the ride. Helicopters fly as if they were intended to crash. With more time I expected to get used to sitting in the door like all the others. Enjoying it was a little too much to expect that soon because helicopters tilt, sway, and bounce occasionally. When tilting to the side, or when banking, it feels as if you're about to fall forward out of the door. Considering I never flew before I first jumped, flying was still relatively new and very sickening to me. Maybe if I had a parachute I could have felt a lot more at ease. When we arrived at Beaver, we were assembled for a talk to be given by the C.O. "You mean to tell me that guy actually talks." Wheelhouse mumbled as he stood to my rear.

"Fire Base Beaver is a decent compound. It's in a strategically situated area with an ample amount of firepower on it. The only problem is that it was constructed by a bunch of legs." Mercein said as he began his little briefing with true airborne bullshit bravado. I could see where he was taking us with his pep talk.

"We are going to have to go to work on this place and bring it up to airborne standards." he concluded.

The new CO was not going to be fun. If the last commander was half as good as the guys said he was, Mercein just had to be bad which was standard for the Army. Expect the worst and still get the big let down. After the formation and we were put to work digging, filling sandbags and constructing a huge shelter that when completed would probably withstand an artillery strike. We also started construction on a kitchen that no one wanted because it meant that someone would have to pull K.P. We even worked on improving the road to the bottom of the hill to the valley that no one wanted to visit. This would surely mean patrols and ambush too. There was absolutely nothing wrong with Beaver before we arrived. The airborne mentality could drive the average guy nuts. Being airborne meant we always had to go the extra mile, do the extra deed or meet the extra challenge. All I wanted to do was jump from an airplane and feel the sensation of it. The airborne standard thing was an unexpected byproduct. Sometimes, being airborne seemed similar to being a Marine and that really scared me.

Mercein did bring in the mortar crew, which reunited the squad with "Burt." He was a likeable guy with a very warm personality. That night after a hard day of digging, we assembled over at his bunker. Burt had a flair for decorating that incorporated all of trappings of the insufferable life we lived. The shipping crates that once packaged the armaments were used as tables and chairs. The parachutes from flares were used as ceiling cover and poncho liners were on the wall. "Everything this guy touches turns into a work of art." Black said. Burt was a lean lanky blonde guy of about 20 who was happy about being reunited with the third squad again. It was a special event for him to be playing host to the guys he was so attached to. He tried real hard to get acquainted with me since I was the new guy in the squad. Burt was every bit as cool as the guys said he was. Shave told him the radio he bought in Qui Nhon was to be kept in the squad and that he would leave it with one of the guys who had been with the squad during the old days. It meant that Burt and not Speedie would get it in April and probably hump it until his turn came to DEROS. Speedie was almost as short as Shave was. Shave had demonstrated the kinship within the squad that made us all feel we were special; a feeling that went far beyond the radio gesture.

The following morning as we rolled out of Burt's bunker still feeling the effects of our all night party, we started another morning of hard work. Our new CO relished the role of upholding the airborne standard with his demand for a complete makeover of the base. He strutted around the place with a swagger, a gruff attitude and an equally abrasive manner of address that he used whenever he communicated with any of us. He acted as if he had something against us or maybe he didn't want to give the impression there was a human side of him beneath his hard-ass exterior.

As we worked toward the CO's goal of transforming the place into something fitting his vision, things really started rolling. The huge shelter we were constructing was going to be used as a combination T.O.C. (Tactical Operations Center) and a hospital. A recon platoon was brought in along with some vehicles from our mechanized unit E Troop. The little hill, although not much larger than a football field, seemed to be gearing up for something big. The hospital really had me worried though. I didn't think they were building it just to treat jungle rot. Suddenly the monsoon and the Crow's Foot didn't seem all that bad after all.

Firebase Beaver was situated in the An Lo Mountains atop a hill no higher than 100 ft. There must have been some recent activity nearby or we wouldn't have been sent in. The lifers were getting edgy. Garson chewed me out when he made a spot check on my weapon and declared it dirty because of some corrosion he spotted. The corrosion was the product of exposure to the morning dew. I had mistakenly left the protective flap open and that one inch area of the bolt accumulated some harmless corrosion that was only superficial. It was bad enough to be wrongly accused but my fellow squad members believed him. There was nothing left to say because there was no one to listen to my side of it. So I re-cleaned my weapon and let the issue pass. All of the progress I made fitting in went down the drain. It mattered little to the lifers though. They seemed to be expecting trouble, and naturally they needed to know that everyone was carrying a well-oiled weapon. I accepted the treatment and considered myself back at square one. While sulking around the firebase later that day, I found a large bag of loose marijuana and stuck it in my leg pocket and started searching for a pipe to smoke it with. Instead I found Wheelhouse who was always nearby. "Handy, I overheard Garson chewing you out about that weapon. Don't get the wrong impression about the guy. He's better than you think. If he wasn't, someone would have probably fragged him by now." he said with a laugh. He was only monitoring the damage to my feelings but what he didn't know was the only thing that mattered to me was the way my fellow squad members reacted after Garson spoke up. I did appreciate Wheelhouse's gesture though. He was an extremely confident guy and his confidence sometimes bordered on being outright cocky. Confidence was a big factor in the bush. Surprisingly, courage was never used as a measuring stick. It was always the confidence level that mattered. Nothing ever disturbed Wheelhouse as he always seemed to maintain the same demeanor no matter what. Of course I had yet to see him or any of those guys operate under duress. Wheelhouse was good for a laugh and obviously good for some confidence building talk whenever he thought it should be applied. I would've rather sulked until I was able to exact some measure of revenge or whatever I could gain from my position but he would not let the issue bother me long at all. We were quickly becoming good friends.

The next day our squad was sent down to the bottom of the hill for a patrol. After covering a considerable amount of ground we were told to set up shop for a while. The decision to stay a while longer was, at first, well received because there were so many shit details going on that we were glad to get away from the extra duty. There was KP, shit burning, and anything else the lifers could think of. There was a continuous water relay going on that exhausted the unfortunate few assigned to the detail. Going up and down that hill carrying those water cans was a killer. Setting up that Mess Hall was a bad idea. It would have been good enough to eat C-Rations. Just having that kitchen atop the hill was causing more headaches than anything else. Under any other circumstance, being at the bottom of the hill would have been an unacceptable alternative to life at the top of it. There was no real lesser of the two evils.

We were expected to be at the bottom of the hill for days. We took up the same position the previous squad used earlier. While there, they attracted the company of a VD infected hooker and her 10-yr. old pimp. She looked like death. After the previous squad passed the word around about her working the bottom of the hill, everyone was sneaking down to get a dose of the clap. Wheelhouse came down looking for her too. "Where's the whore Handy." he asked.

"She's got the clap man."

"That's what penicillin's for."

"She's over there in the bushes." I said. Wheelhouse must have been carrying a condom. I didn't think that he would go in the bushes unprotected. Later that day, Doc Bueno came down looking for her too.

"Where's your whore?" he asked jokingly.

"She's his whore." I said pointing to the kid expecting shock but obviously Doc had seen his share of child pimps.

"Five dollars. That's all." he told the kid before being led into the bushes.

"She's got the clap, Doc." I warned him as he started to crawl out of sight.

"Don't worry, I'm the medic.

When he came out, he said that he only came down to give her a shot of penicillin. She had caused a mini-epidemic atop the hill and Doc figured he could do a lot of good by going right to the source. He sat and smoked a few joints with us, as he would have done had we been out in the bush instead of at the bottom of that hill. "I would stay but it's getting dark now and I gotta go." he said before returning to the comfort of the newly constructed hospital. Bueno was really putting in some legwork. Only he would have come up with the idea of giving shots to the hooker to stop the outbreak. When the kid asked me if I was interested in sleeping with his hooker, I told him that I was only interested in smoking my next joint. He took off in a hurry and returned with two packs. It seemed that any service we wanted was available to us. There was nothing we could not expect the hustlers of Vietnam to produce. Anything short of an armistice was possible and I doubted if any of the black market operators wanted to see the end of the war.

After all of our visitors had returned to the top of the hill, we spent the night in place in the middle of a cemetery. Our defenseless position at the bottom of that hill was scary enough. Spending the night in a graveyard added a macabre element to our predicament. For some odd reason my attention had turned to the condition of the graves. I imagined that the cemetery was no longer being used or even visited probably due to our military's decision to relocate the village of the surviving families.

The individual plots were all showing an advanced state of neglect. It was a far cry from what I was accustomed to seeing. The cemeteries in New Orleans often resemble miniature cities that received a lot of care. Ambush that night again, exposed us as the root cause of a lot of inconvenience to the people we were supposed to be helping. After I did my turn at guard, I retired for the night atop a plot and tried to forget about where we were.

I never quite fell asleep in that compromising site at the bottom of that hill. The hooker and her ten year old pimp returned early and sat to wait for some more action. Wheelhouse came down but only to kill a little time with us. He had grown tired of the pace atop the hill and was hiding out from his next shit detail. "You guys are lucky to be down here you know."

"You wouldn't say that if you had to spend a scary night down here with us."

"Did your girlfriend spend the night over there in the bushes?"

"Are you serious? She is way too smart to try that shit. In fact, she just arrived. She had been over there squatting in that deep knee bend waiting for you for at least an hour now." I joked.

"Have you noticed how the Vietnamese can squat in that position for hours on end?"

"Yes I have noticed and by the way, what is that shit she's chewing on?" I asked.

"It's a small mixture of twigs, leaves and something called beetle nut. I don't know why they use the stuff but it will eventually turn their teeth into one continuous black ring. You might have also noticed a lot of the older people already have the condition."

"Yes I've noticed."

"I'm telling you the stuff must be as addictive as heroin. I mean why else would they do that to themselves?" The beetle nut was not covered in our orientation and I was as curious as Wheelhouse was about the natives' attraction or addiction to the chaw.

Wheelhouse returned to the top of the hill as we continued to sit around waiting for nothing to happen. The ten year old pimp continuously tried to feel us out but could never sell us on the proposition of exchanging five of our dollars for ten minutes with his hooker. "You do realize that she just might be his mother don't you." said Black.

"No way man. Are you serious?"

"I've seen it before. When we were on pacification last year, a kid once offered his momma to me and never tried to conceal their relation."

"Incredible. I didn't realize that things over here were so desperate."

"At least she did look a lot better than that one over there." he said pointing at the hooker and at the same time unintentionally beckoning her to his position.

"Go back! I wasn't calling you. Didi mau! Didi mau!" he said sending her back to her deep knee bend before she could make more than a few steps in our direction. She looked less like a hooker and more like a desperate poor woman who sat patiently waiting for the next willing horny GI to come down the mountain. But of course desperate situations always did call for equally desperate solutions. "Last Guard." said Speedie as the rest of the guys started laughing their way through another session of jockeying for position on the guard detail. It was barely 11:00 a.m. and the issue was already settled. Of course I was again left with the unenviable task of facing the boogie man at midnight.

We spent the entire day doing little or nothing and after another scary night in the cemetery, we finally received notice to return to the top of the hill. I was real glad because the nights were getting too scary. I was curious about why we weren't replaced by another squad though. When we made it to the top we were told that it was Tet. Of course what it really meant was that it was the second anniversary of Tet '68 when Charlie staged his infamous and disastrous offensive that signaled a change in our war policy. The firebase was full of activity. Everyone was circling the wagons and getting their bunker mentality fixed. Nobody would be sleeping and there would definitely be no partying. Everybody would be too scared to have any fun. It was weird the way Charlie ruled the night and how we naturally spoke in whispers when it got dark. Beaver was a relatively secure area. It was well armed, staffed and fortified. We all felt confident until somebody said Tet. Then everybody was laying in wait for an all out assault on the firebase. That night Wheelhouse came to me with a wild idea. "I'm going to toss a couple of frags just to be sure that there's nobody out there." he said with a serious look on his face. His confidence in what he was about to do exposed that pseudo cocky side of him.

"The lifers will have a shit fit if you do that." I warned him.

"Probably, so don't let the noise freak you out O.K." Having said that, he calmly tossed the frags and whispered, "Frag Out" in barely audible tones. The two explosions attracted Calvin in a hurry.

"Who did that? Who threw those grenades?

"I did." Wheelhouse answered.

"What in the fuck are you doing?"

"I thought I saw something out there." he said with a good poker face. The two of them were like a stand up comedy team. Wheelhouse played the straight man and Calvin provided the hysterics. The noise did loosen up quite a few of the guys in our sector of the perimeter though.

The following morning, we were ordered to go on a patrol in the valley. In defense of the patrols, we almost had to constantly check out our surrounding area. The patrols were designed to search for the enemy, confirm his presence, and destroy him head on so that he wouldn't be able to concentrate his forces and resources to mount an attack on his terms. The French, according to history, lost the decisive battle against the Vietminh by sitting in one spot and allowing the enemy to gear up for an artillery barrage followed up by ground assault. The performance of the French was always used as a measuring stick of sorts. They had made every mistake in the military book and, of course, we were supposed to be showing them how it should have been done. The problem was that the correct way to handle our Vietnamese adversaries was taking too long and costing too many lives.

While patrolling, Wheelhouse came up with the idea of taking more pictures of the squad as we forded another swollen stream. Sometimes he made it seem as if he was only in Vietnam to take pictures or rather pose for them. I was definitely going to get me one of those Instamatics and was kicking myself for not already having one.

After our patrol, we came back to Beaver and found a group of Red Cross girls waiting for us. Someone had already decided that their presence in Vietnam would be some kind of morale booster. Actually, they needed to come up with more than their mere presence. When we went back down the hill to bathe in the stream, the slick came to pick up the girls and the pilot made a second pass over our wading spot. The girls got a bigger boost in their morale than that which they provided for us. One of them almost fell out of the door as she tried to get a closer look at us. "Those are the ugliest Red Cross Girls that I have seen since I arrived last year." Wheelhouse said as we stood along side of the swollen stream in our birthday suits. "How many have you seen?"

"They were the third group of girls so far."

"Give them a chance. They're supposed to be here to lift our spirits and make us feel better?" I said as we both laughed.

That night a mad minute firepower display was planned. It sounded like we were going to have some fun. I was sure it would have been different if the enemy was firing back at us, but who cared. It would give us a chance to unleash our firepower and the show was expected to be awesome. I'd been carrying my weapon for weeks and, up until that moment, never had a chance to pull the trigger. It would have been nice to never have to shoot at anybody but it would also be nice to know if the thing worked.

When zero hour arrived, the signal was given and the mad minute began. The M60 and 50 caliber machine guns were sending tracer rounds out in a frenzy that exaggerated the ferocity of what went on in a fire fight. The dusters were unloading on the mountains across the valley with their 40mm exploding rounds and causing so much noise that the little pops caused by the M16's were being drowned out. After the shooting ended, Wheelhouse brought over his M-60 to show off his barrel, which was glowing, white-hot. "How 'bout that mad minute Handy?"

"I liked it man. It was insane."

"Milles and I must have shot up two cans between the two of us. What about you?"

"Well, now I know the thing works. It was the first time I had a chance to shoot it."

"I think we ought to do that every night. It would keep Charlie on his toes." he said.

The mad minute, according to legend, was first used by the 1st Cav in '65 at Ia Drang in America's first major battle of the war. They used the ploy to root out NVA forces hidden in the tall grasses. The mad minute had arrived and, from that moment on, was to become a part of our way to fight the war.

The next night a MARS station was set up on the firebase that actually made it possible for us to call home. I passed because I knew the lifers probably would've limited the amount of time and amount of calls made anyway. The waiting line would have been discouraging too. We decided to spend the time over at Burt's hooch getting stoned instead. The MARS hook-up provided us with just the right distraction that night. The novelty of having another of the comforts of being back in the world was just too much to ignore for the rest of the guys and all of the lifers. It was another one of those nights when nothing else mattered to us but us.

8

The following morning, while sitting around shooting the breeze, we were interrupted by a disturbing call over the radio. Someone was in the shit. It was a recon patrol somewhere out in the valley. They had already suffered one casualty and were still engaged with the enemy. Shortly thereafter we got the call to scramble over to the helicopter pad for extraction. That long dreaded moment, it seemed, had finally arrived. It appeared as if we were about to be thrown into the fray with little knowledge about the firefight, or more significantly, its severity. I instantly looked to my squad members to get a sense of what we were about to get into. They were all frantically packing their gear with no wasted energy. I followed their lead and moved with equal dispatch. We were ready in less than a minute and started moving towards the helicopter pad. Garson stopped us along the way and said that our platoon would stay behind to provide security for the base. We then all split up and occupied all of the bunkers along the perimeter. My bunker was near the emergency L.Z. where the wounded came in by helicopter. As I stood there watching them being carried in by litter and on foot, the sight of the blood and bandages sent shivers through me. Their voices screaming in pain was equally traumatic. One of the wounded, who was on foot with no shirt, had shrapnel all over his back. He was undoubtedly a victim of one of those-hand made Chicom (Chinese communist) grenades. The shrapnel consisted of small pieces of metal, rocks; shards of glass and what seemed like small screws. My heart started pounding so hard I could almost hear it and my legs started to wobble like one of those frightened cartoon characters. I struggled to get a grip on myself.

In the distance an Air Force F-4 Phantom fighter jet was seen dive-bombing and strafing the area with loud 20mm cannon fire. The sound of the roaring jets and their cannon fire could be heard for miles. It turned out that an NCO named Washington had been killed and all of the wounded men were hit trying to recover his body as it lay out in the open. It was impossible for me to imagine exactly how they were going to succeed in retrieving him while taking casualties at the same time. Our platoon had to spend the night on the base and was expected to be sent out to the fight the next day. That night, I suffered through the agony of not knowing exactly what to expect. We made a lot of mental preparation for all of the worst case scenarios that our imagination could conjure up. It was a little more trying for me because I was still untested in battle and the difference in our outward emotions was more than evident.

The following morning, we boarded slicks for insertion onto the battle ground that had become silent overnight. When we arrived the LZ erupted around us with gunfire. It was from the fleet of gunships laying down a base of covering fire and possibly the return fire from an identified target. We were said to be taking fire from the mountains as we landed and had to exit the choppers in a hurry. There was a lot of confusion for sure but I could not hear any rounds cracking overhead as I stepped off of the slick and scrambled for cover. Nothing else happened for the rest of the day and we spent the entire evening in the same spot we took up upon our arrival. That night someone in the third platoon scored a kill on his first night in the field. He caught the intruder sneaking up on their position and took him out with a Claymore. He was immediately extracted from the field for a one day R&R at a beach somewhere called Vung Tau.

Sgt Washington's body was finally recovered, Charlie disappeared and we combed the area for any more signs of his presence. As we swept the valley on the way back, we came upon the dead body killed by the new guy during his first night. I expected to find it in pieces but he obviously wasn't as close to the Claymore as I thought. He was, nonetheless, as dead as any severed corpse. He had actually swum across another section of the same stream we were bathing in earlier. Clad in only a pair of short pants with the underside still damp from his trip across the stream, he made his date with a flying ball bearing that took his life. We continued our sweep but when we did come to a pause, Wheelhouse came and asked me to watch his weapon and the rest of his gear while he went back for a picture of the dead N.V.A. soldier. He seemed to chronicle everything he came across with his ever-present Instamatic. Again, he was not going to have the role of film developed. My mom would have had a fit if I had sent her a roll of film to develop with pictures of dead bodies in it. Wheelhouse obviously had two very understanding parents. After the morbid photo session, we sat talking about home and family while eating more of his goodies from home. He mostly talked about his little nephew and some of those memorable things that little kids often say and do. He could never hold back his laughter whenever he told another episode. "Do you have any nieces or nephews back home?" he asked as he regained composure.

"Boo Coo man. More than I can count on both hands. I even have about a half dozen of them who are older than I am."

"Really?"

"Dig it."

"Any of them been here?"

"No. My nephew Johnny did a tour in Germany but I am the first of the entire family to come here." I said before he went on telling more stories of his nephew. Some of the stories were repeated but it didn't seem to matter. He laughed as hard that day as he did when he first told them back in the Crow's Foot.

The company then completed the sweep all the way back to the firebase. Although there were no significant findings along the way, the first platoon did have more to report than any of the rest of the platoons. Their platoon leader, Lt. Mack, displayed a knack for his role. During the sweep, his voice was all that could be heard as he continued to find tracks, old enemy equipment, small holes dug into the ground and all of the kind of things that would seemingly go unnoticed by everyone else. Fortunately none of his findings were enough to warrant any further concerns.

The next day we were told that a B-52 strike was planned for an area in the mountains and that we were to be inserted behind it to search for any damage. The area was suspected to be the home of an N.V.A. regiment. Just when I thought it was safe enough to breathe a sigh of relief, something else came up. The war had started to look every bit like the war I had come to fear so much. Privately I was hoping for something to happen that would hasten the end of the conflict and send me home. I was inspired by news of the end of the civil war in Nigeria. There was a picture of a Biafran soldier and a Nigerian soldier embracing each other that gave me an illusion of just such an ending for the war in Vietnam. Unfortunately the war in Vietnam was not a civil war. It had become to look like the intrusion that both sides always claimed it was. There would never be any embracing between the U.S. and the NVA. To them, we were the intruders and they wanted us out. To us they were aggressors that needed to be placed in check and sent back across the DMZ. Time was on the side of the other guys because it had seemingly run out on us. We were redeploying and they would of course be staying behind because the battle ground was their turf. They were going to have the opportunity to say that they ran us out of Vietnam and evidently we could do little to change the outcome. We could not be defeated but we couldn't stay on an indefinite basis either. Our open ended commitment to Vietnam ended somewhere between Johnson's resignation and Nixon's inauguration.

That night, as we assumed the air strike was taking place, we were wide awake in anticipation of the following day's assault. "Speedie, has anybody else in the company been sent to Vung Tau for that one day R&R deal? How long has it been in practice?" I asked.

"Ask Shave. He went in my place once." Speedie said with a bit of sarcasm in his voice.

"They just sent me, I didn't ask to go." said Shave defensively. According to Black (whom else), Speedie went into a tunnel and came up with a prisoner.

"Shave was with him, but, it was Speedie who went in and got him." he said

"But why not send Speedie?"

"Because Speedie had recently got busted with some pot and the lifers were still holding it against him." In spite of it all, there was no real animosity between the two of them. In fact if I had to call it like I saw it, I'd say that the lifers were actually trying to drive a wedge between them but had only succeeded in bringing them closer. I was impressed with the solidarity exhibited within the squad as they continued to amaze me with their unity.

Their story distracted me from my preoccupation with the B-52 strike which must have been far away from where we were. There was no ground quaking and no distant rumbling to be heard that night; only Santana playing Soul Sacrifice.

The following morning we boarded the slicks and took off for the area of the B-52 strike. Our squad was designated to be on the first craft to land. I couldn't complain because the one who chose us (Garson) was on our chopper with us. There is something about leading by example that really inspires. If he had chosen us to lead and delayed his arrival by about 3or4 sorties (flights), I would have felt differently about his leadership qualities. In spite of his tantrums, Garson was an effective platoon leader. He would have no trouble with the men under his command. He seemed to make all of the right moves that would solidify his control without being too heavy-handed. He knew when to have his moments and when not to. Riding on the first slick with us was just the kind of move that would be noticed by all.

The flight over was more stressful than usual. The usual queasiness that came with sitting in the door coupled with the added fear of the unknown was rough. My wild imagination started working against me as I remembered the news accounts of that battle at Dak To about how the NVA withstood constant bombardment and still repulsed repeated ground assaults.

When we arrived there were no fresh craters and no dead bodies lying below our slick as we came in for a landing. We had some Cobra gunships riding shotgun for us and they carpeted the area with machine gun and rocket fire before we landed. The closer we came to the ground, the more the anxiety ate at me. The threat of being surprised by a well-concealed ambush team lying in wait was huge. One of my old drill instructors at Ft. Polk once told us about one chopper assault he made back in '65 when Charlie allowed the first craft to land to lull the rest of them into a sense of false security. Then after the rest of their helicopters came in, all hell broke loose as Charlie opened up on them when they neared the ground.

We landed without any problem and immediately took up a defensive position until the next slick landed. After the following squad landed and took up our position, we started our movement up the nearest mountain. Each succeeding landing initiated the preceding group's movement uphill. The process continued until everybody was on the ground and moving uphill. Bear, was naturally at point and moving at his usual pace. He lived for such moments. I only hoped he wasn't disappointed at not having someone shooting at us as we moved up the hill. The slope of the mountain was a heavily forested region with the largest and tallest trees I had ever seen. The ground had no trails at all. Unlike like the Crow's Foot where there were well-beaten paths everywhere. There was litter strewn about the place from GIs on previous missions. The area was about as pristine as any place I could imagine existed on earth.

Garson rose to the challenge of keeping up with our fast moving squad and maybe that is why he chose us. He never once said anything about our pace and was glad to reach the summit as quickly as we did. After we reached the top we set up a perimeter and waited to be sent out on patrol. I was as eager to explore the mountain pass as the rest of the squad. We were also eager to see some of the huge bomb craters that I had heard so much about in training. The craters, we were told, made some pretty large swimming pools during the monsoon season and probably hatched a lot of mosquitoes too. Fortunately the monsoon season was over and we didn't have to deal with that problem. Humping without the added burden of the rain, I thought, should be easier. Too bad Kyler was no longer around to prove he could do better during the dry season. His days in the bush ended before we left the Crow's Foot.

We received our coordinates and set out on our own. The scenery was absolutely breathtaking. The beauty of the country was evident at every turn in the mountains. The size of the trees was mind-boggling making it easy to understand why those little "ghosts" were so hard to locate from overhead reconnaissance. The foliage on those skyscraper like trees completely blocked out the sun. After living in such a flat terrain like New Orleans all of my life, it was an experience in itself being in the mountains or just seeing them. The only thing I ever climbed in New Orleans was the levee. "Last guard." Bear announced which sent the rest of the guys scrambling for a spot on the guard list to avoid being the one awake at midnight. The guard list for the night was settled before noon. There was absolutely no way to determine when one of them would blurt out those two words. Their little ritual was the most comical event of our day.

After patrolling around for hours, we returned to C.P. and reported our findings to Garson. We felt good about our patrol but figured that we would fare better the next day. That night we were sent down to the bottom of the mountain to pull ambush. Al Milles volunteered to go along with us. Once we arrived and set up for the night, Al squeezed off about fifty rounds at nothing in particular. When the lifers called to ask what all of the noise was about, we could hardly hold back the laughter long enough to tell them he thought he saw something. Afterwards Al decided to volunteer to go with us on our next patrol.

The following day we patrolled along the bomb strike. The craters were every bit as huge as I was told they would be. The awesome power of the bombs actually uprooted some of the largest trees and left them sprawled in their wake. One of the huge trees was splintered by direct impact and left so much debris that it rendered the ground impassable. So we gave up on the designated path and ventured out on our own. It was obvious that the free-lance style of patrolling was more to the liking of the squad. They hardly ever followed orders or directions anyway. Our route took us through an extended mountain pass. It was the kind of area that I wished that we could have been in during the monsoon.

None of the trails were too traveled and never could have created the quagmire that the trails in the Crow's Foot became. We walked for what seemed like hours and I figured that we were overdue for a sit-rep and became concerned about not hearing from C.P. So I decided to call one in but couldn't make contact. The radio could only operate for so many kilometers and we had obviously wandered outside of its range. "Bear I can't make contact with C.P." I said.

"We're probably out of range." he said redundantly as he continued to study his map and check his compass. He couldn't have cared less about being out of C.P.'s range of radio intrusiveness. Purvis, on the other hand, cared very much. He tried to place an emphasis on the situation without coming across as being any more concerned than the rest. He obviously wasn't the risk taker that Bear was. He only wanted to be in charge and in that situation no one was about to listen to him. "Man, I wish I had some dope." said Speedie.

"Yeah man, me too." said Black.

"You mean nobody's go any?" said Speedie. Then I remembered the bag of pot I found at Beaver back when Garson chewed me out for that so-called dirty weapon.

"I got some weed but I don't have anything to smoke it in." I said alerting them in a most pleasant way. As they all looked at me I felt I had finally made it with the squad. When I pulled the bag out of my leg pocket and they saw how big it was, I knew I had really scored big time. Black pulled out an ivory pipe, Speedie pulled out an ivory pipe and Bear pulled out still another one. "You mean you don't have a pipe." Bear laughed as he reached for the bag and started to pack his pipe before passing it on.

We temporarily forgot about our predicament and got stoned. In spite of Purvis's concern, he smoked with us anyway. Shave was not a head and didn't want to smoke the stuff. He claimed that a drug habit would cost him some of his precious money and he was having none of that. In spite of all the smoking habits around him he said he never considered indulging or moving to another squad. We were like family; dysfunctional, but family just the same. After the smoking session, we continued our patrolling moving further out of radio range. Purvis continued to worry and the whole scene started to look like some comedy. "Say, I can't find my knife." Black alerted us as he searched himself continuously for his trusty Bowie knife prompting a further departure from sanity. The patrol then turned into a search party. The war had to wait until we found Black's knife. The decision to look for the knife didn't sit too well with Purvis.

Our search soon led us to a weathered, well-concealed enemy bunker dug into the side of the mountain. It was camouflaged with some shrubs that was picked elsewhere and stuck in the ground in front of the bunker. The temporary shrubs had withered with passing time leaving the bunker exposed to view. Bear jumped into the bunker and found a small bomb shelter, or spider hole, dug inside of the bunker. It was just big enough for one of those little bastards to squeeze into when the moment of impact came. We also found some wire running from the bunker. We followed it and came upon another bunker. Then we looked up the mountainside and found that the entire face of the mountain was honey-combed with bunkers all connected by wire for communication. We had discovered the regimental compound and it wasn't in the path of that bomb strike. Fortunately it was unoccupied and had been so for some time. We could have walked into a world of trouble had Charlie been home when we came along looking for the knife.

We returned to C.P. and naturally Garson was a little irritated about our not calling in. Of course all it took was for Bear and Purvis to tell him of our finding the bunker complex. The following morning we were to bring him to the complex to make his own assessment and report it to his superiors. While we were out discovering the bunker complex, a new medic arrived from the world. He was a slightly round blonde guy with twelve o'clock shadow sitting alone looking out of place and every bit as new in country as he actually was. I sat next to him as I cleaned my weapon and he tried to take notes on the dismantling procedure. He was excited when I told him I was from New Orleans. He was from KC and the Chiefs had just won the recent Super Bowl played there. Those Vikings didn't stand a chance." he said with pride. "Would you show me how to take apart my rifle? I haven't even held one of these things since basic."

"Gimme that thing." I said as I took his M-16 and started to strip it for him. The new medic seemed like a real cool guy and no one ever had to tell me that it's good to be close to the medic. It wasn't that I didn't feel that close to Bueno or that I thought he wouldn't try hard enough to save me either. It was just that Bueno was short. He was down to his last 65 days and the new medic was just starting. So when he asked me to show him how to clean his rifle, I just decided to clean it for him. As I serviced his weapon he asked me a lot of crazy questions about New Orleans, Bourbon Street, the Mardi Gras and anything else he had heard about the place. Confusingly he said he was drafted out of college and accepted his fate.

The next morning we took Garson to the complex. He was excited about the size of the complex. It was the same old story; when something goes wrong, he gets all the blame. When things go right, he gets all the credit. When we returned to C.P. he filed his report and was told that we had to destroy the entire complex. It sounded a lot better than shooting at a complex full of inhabitants, but the Army's method was questionable from my point of view. Destroying the complex sounded like a lot of hard work. We started to regret reporting it but it was, however, the only thing we could offer as an excuse for staying so long and not calling in any sit-reps.

The following morning we received some 40lb cratering charges to hump all the way to the complex to clear an L.Z. The rest of the guys in the platoon were a little pissed at us because we had to carry all of those charges for such a long distance. Unfortunately we had to carry them up a watery trail that winded its way from the area of the bunker complex. The route was supposed to be shorter than the one we took following the B-52 strike but we had yet to determine if it were so. We emptied our rucks and replaced the contents with one cratering charge each. We started out that morning and although the hot sun was blocked out and the scenery was beautiful, the task of humping such a cumbersome load was frustrating. A full ruck was usually heavier but the cratering charge was awkward due to its tubular shape and length. In the middle of all of the hard work and the unanticipated backlash from the rest of the platoon, we realized how foolish it was to report our findings.

The view along the way up the water trail was breathtaking. I was really kicking myself for not having a camera that day. I could have run out of film in less than 100 yds. It was unbelievable that any part of the planet Earth could look as interesting and as beautiful as the watery path formed by mountain runoff. The water level was never higher than the knee and we only had to climb when we came across another part of the stream that was cascading from cliffs of various heights. After our first trip to the bunker complex it became highly unlikely that we would ever report any such finding again. The guys in the other two platoons were complaining too much. We were beginning to feel as if we were being blamed for the long trip. There was a popular saying the guys were always repeating...."What goes on in the bush, stays in the bush." It would never happen to us again.

After blowing up our explosives on some trees we returned to the wet trail for the trip back. Going downhill was easier but we couldn't tell by the amount of complaining we had to listen to. We made it back that evening and settled down knowing that we had to do it all over again the following morning. "Last Guard." said Speedie.

The following morning we loaded up our cumbersome cargo and returned along the almost idyllic route. Garson amused himself by constructing little firecrackers with blasting caps crimped to fuses and throwing them at us. Of course they were all carrying long fuses and exploded harmlessly underwater as we walked past them. It was always good to see the guy in a playful mood. He always seemed one moment away from his next tantrum. But of course, it was one of the things that made him such an interesting character. He did manage to hold onto enough blasting caps, detonation cord and fuse to finish the job when we made it to the bunker complex. After finally clearing an L.Z. we started receiving the rest of the charges at the complex site by helicopter and started the process of destroying each bunker.

The work continued as the air around the bunker complex became full of smoke, fumes and cries of "Fire in the hole" followed by the sound of explosions. By blasting the bunkers with the charges, we were creating larger bunkers for Charlie to occupy whenever he returned. There was no doubt that he would someday return either. The ebb and flow of the war had created a strange practice of cat and mouse movement throughout the countryside. Even after some of the major battles of the war, we had always left the area after the battle and Charlie always returned. Charlie had the upper hand and was continually dictating our strategy. As large as the complex seemed to us, it could have been no more than a temporary station along the way for any large unit passing through the area. For all we knew, Charlie could have been across the valley watching us from the adjacent mountain range.

Our work was interrupted by the visit of some old codgers wearing starched fatigues and spit shined jump boots. It was the brass who, no doubt, thought it was a good idea to come out. We immediately started to escape to a nice secluded area to light up a few joints. We figured that with all of the backslapping and ass kissing about to take place on top of that hill, it would be the perfect time to steal away. We expected to be able to stoke up quite a few bowls while the lifers engaged in stuffing themselves with each other.

As soon as the party started to get warmed up, we looked up the trail and found a party headed our way. We assumed that the Colonel or whoever wanted to talk to us. We hoped not because we all smelled like a burning forest. "It's Westy." said someone.

"Westy, I thought he was back in the world." I said as we looked up the trail to see our former platoon member being led to our location by one of the straight guys (non smokers). They all greeted him warmly as I kind of stood in the background. Having arrived in the bush near the end of his tour, I never really got to know the guy. He'd taken the job as a reporter for the Firebase 173 and was back to do his first story which happened to be on his former company. He was as thrilled to be at the complex for his story as the guys were to see him again. As I stood back taking in the whole scene, I realized just how much camaraderie existed in the bush and felt proud to be among them even if our potential was being wasted fighting a war of loosely defined reasons.

After getting all the details for his story, Westy boarded the helicopter and, along with the rest of the brass, returned to HQ. We then finished our work on the complex and started gearing up for our departure. "Alright let's break up that cluster fuck. One frag and every one of you bastards will be dead." said Calvin again.

9

Our next stop was not going to be Beaver. We were, instead, going to another place in the bush to take over a position from another company. The new area, we hoped, would stop the grumbling about our finding that bunker complex. We didn't enjoy that mission anymore than they did. They alternated on those trips up that waterfall. We had to go every day. They were making too big a fuss over the entire matter. We needed to be more focused on the war with the real enemy and not each other. All of the bickering was just the kind of mess they warned us about back in jungle school. We were sort of self-destructing in the face of adversity. I thought they were exaggerating over there at Charang Valley but it could and would happen. It might have been impossible for Charlie to defeat us but we definitely could defeat ourselves. There were too many guys fighting the war that, like me, didn't know much as about our presence in Vietnam. One guy stated that we were really after the oil in the delta. Calvin, who was on his second tour, said that we wanted to keep air bases close to communist China. I even heard one ridiculous claim that we were interested in the rubber tree production. I didn't know that Vietnam had rubber trees. The only two crops that seemed to be in abundance were rice and marijuana.

After the quick helicopter ride, we got off and started toward the mountain with the first platoon at point. Lt. Mack was at it again, just like when we made that sweep to Beaver after Sgt. Washington was killed. There was constant chatter on the horn between the C.O. and the Lieutenant. His point man spotted someone and blew him away. It was the point man's dream to find the enemy before he spotted you and getting the kill with one shot. Lt. Mack's uncanny knack for finding action seemed to rub off on his men as he continued to get the maximum out of them. Rumor was that Mack had some kind of death wish to fulfill. The rumors were turning out to be a bigger monster than anyone ever said they would. Jones told me that if the world would come to an end, it would be preceded by a rumor started in Vietnam. Someone else said that the reason Jesus hadn't returned yet was because no one in country was smart enough to start the rumor first. Mack would be around for the rest of his tour because Charlie wouldn't be able to get near him without getting his ass shot off first. He had a promising career ahead of him in the Army, but his zeal was too extreme for the average draftee just fulfilling his military obligation.

After chalking up the kill, we moved quickly up the mountain. The trail was a well traveled path. Everywhere we looked there were signs of U.S. troops having been there before. Old C-rations cans, boxes and wrappers littered the trail. Unlike the area on our previous mission where the ground always seemed unmolested by anything other than fallen leaves, pine needles and pine cones, this was a well traveled piece of turf. Our squad was last in the procession so we were dropped off along the trail to be the first line of defense along the trail leading to the rest of the company. I didn't like the way the lifers got to decide where our ambush site was to be situated. It left no room to deviate at all. Without delay, we started hacking our way into the bushes straddling the trail on the down slope side. The space we occupied was small and risky; just the way the lifers would've wanted it. Our best scenario would have the intruders coming up the trail as opposed to down the face of the mountain.

The rest of the company moved up the mountain trail and took up positions further up the trail from our location. According to Bear, the company we replaced got a kill about five days earlier and had been sitting in place waiting for more action. When our first platoon got that kill it was all the lifers needed to see. We settled in that one area for an extended stay waiting for something to happen. About all that happened though, was a lot of bonding and a lot of smoking. Bear even once went on patrol alone out of boredom. Purvis developed a fear or deep concern about his girlfriend Debbie dating one of his friends and started to melt down. I thought I was hearing voices and a motor running every night I pulled guard. It was some of the scariest nights I ever had to spend since arriving in country. I thought I was losing it until Shave mentioned that he was hearing the voices and then everybody said they were hearing voices too. The motor or engine was, I thought, a lingering buzz or ringing in my ears.

Mercein delayed resupply to extend the window of opportunity to let Charlie get a chance to die for his cause. He figured that three more days wouldn't hurt that much. What he didn't know or probably didn't care about was that some of us didn't have enough rations to last more than a day. At our location, we had more pot than food or water. A couple of days into our extended occupation of the mountainside, Shave gave us a treat from home. His mom sent him a canned, tubular loaf of what he called brown bread. It tasted more like brown cake but we were fortunate that he saved it until after the unanticipated resupply delay. After those extra days, I wished that someone had saved something. In spite of the hardship imposed upon us by Mercein, we maintained our same behavior. Everyday someone would start the "Last Guard" routine. We loved it. Of course I was up at midnight every night. I thought it was comical the way they avoided that time slot reminding me of little kids who would always hide under the sheets during scary moments. Hiding under their poncho liners was literally what they did every night. Midnight was the scariest part of their lives in Vietnam. They just couldn't take being awake during that mystically haunting one hour. The Last Guard routine was an inventive way to trivialize their own personal fears about being in the field. During the daylight hours we still maintained a vigil because we couldn't afford to feel safe just because it wasn't dark. Although the "Charlie only strikes at midnight" theory still existed, we still had one hour shifts during the day stationed along the trail. A lax attitude had sent too many young GI's home in a body bag.

Purvis's crisis with his girlfriend started shaping up like one of those scenarios that Floyd always talked about. Vietnam was the worst place for a young man to be while dealing with matters of the heart. To gain an understanding of the dynamics of the average failed relationship for grunts, one must take youth in consideration. Since the average age of the soldier in Vietnam was 19, it meant that the age of their girlfriends back home was 18 or 17. It must have been hard for a girl that young to cope with having a boyfriend on the other side of the planet fighting for his life. I could see where they might've wanted to reconsider the whole thing and be relieved of the pressure of writing, waiting and hoping nothing bad happens. The Dear John letter probably became the easy way out of a stressful situation. I sat down to write another letter and went through a tablet of stationery and a pack of envelopes in one sitting. Mercein had gone a little too far extending our stay. Delaying resupply because of the noisy helicopters was absurd. He was less concerned about the noise of our growling stomachs. In that unreal world of elimination by fragging, the CO had become an imaginary candidate for removal. I could only picture him sitting atop the mountain like a reigning monarch waiting for one of the ambush positions below his perch to come up with a precious kill to present before him.

After spending an extra few days waiting for nothing to happen, Mercein gave up and called for resupply. When we finally got word to come up the mountain and join the rest of the company, we were angry and not about to run at our usual speed. While taking a slow and more casual stroll up the mountain, the buzzing sound of that motor or engine kept getting louder and louder. I started to believe that someone up the hill was actually running a motor in the middle of the jungle. Just before I became convinced that there was one, however, I started to smell a very foul odor and it made the buzzing sound more appropriate. It was the noise of about ten million flies buzzing around the burial site of the kill scored by the previous company. Flies were everywhere in Vietnam and were probably on him before he fell. By the time we came up on the mound of dirt covering the hole dug for him, it was oozing maggots from the ground. The odor was suffocating. "How can you guys handle being around this odor as long as you have?" I asked the squad assigned to camp out near the body.

"You kind of get used to it after the first 24 hours." one of them said over the sound of the flies that was by then almost deafening. Their location was the level just below the mountain's summit or the first one on the way down. Resupply had already started up top, so we just went up to grab some much needed supplies and a breath of fresh air. The unfortunate squad that had spent the last week around the dead body had to spend resupply day there too. It was better them than us.

Baby San, the Canadian guy Al told me about, almost hacked his leg off swinging a machete as he walked point up the hill and was extracted for the self-inflicted wound. I wondered if he would receive a Purple Heart for his accident. I never got to know the guy and I feared that he wouldn't be coming back because of his time left in-country. Al said that he would miss him because the two of them shared the same love of the game of lacrosse. Hopefully the guy would still be able to play after he was discharged from the Army.

After the resupply was resumed, a burst of automatic gunfire was discharged from somewhere down the mountain. It was from the area of the dead body. We rushed back to the area only to find the squad still in place. "One of those mother fuckers was right over there!" one of them said pointing in the direction of the trail leading up to their location. Charlie had waited until he thought we were leaving the area. Missing their target and allowing the intruder to escape only infuriated Mercein. With all of the experience he had, I figured that it wouldn't be as troubling to him. After all, Charlie Co. wasn't exactly the Green Berets and he should have expected as much from our daring enemy.

We wrapped up our operation at that location and returned to Beaver. Awaiting us were a few new arrivals. They were Darryl Ellis, Bill MacMahon a Native American named Leonard Big Goose and another guy named Robert Bargas. Big Goose became an immediate interest with me because I had never met an Indian before. He was a Ponca City Indian. I never heard of that tribe and of course never met an Indian before either." It took no time at all to realize that living on a reservation had both preserved his culture and denied him of the melting pot experience. His English was almost like that of someone who was foreign to America, yet his people are the only ethnic group native to what we all called home. Once he became one of us, nothing else mattered though.

I was sent over to TOC to learn a new encryption to be used. The new code was called KAK (cack). All future grids given over the radio were subject to be cacked on command. Charlie had ears all over the country. He was resourceful enough to force us to adapt to his capabilities.

Bear was getting ready to go to Bangkok for R&R. The Thailand destination was a very popular site if not the most popular on the list available to us. I was leaning towards Tokyo because I wanted to see the World's Fair in Osaka when it was completed. I'd always wanted to see one and I figured that it might be my only chance. In spite of the added attraction of the Fair, Bangkok remained the No. 1 favorite among the troops in Vietnam. Bear had either heard a lot about the place or had been there before. He talked a lot about what he was going to do and where he planned to go while there.

In the distance a helicopter was approaching with a carcass in a sling dangling beneath. It was a huge wild boar. "Now what?" I asked.

"A door gunner shot it. The cooks are gonna prepare it for us." said Black.

"I think I'll pass on it. I can wait until I get back to Uplift." I said. It was obvious we would not pass on any opportunity to amuse and entertain ourselves. There was nothing we wouldn't at least hunt. Nothing was sacred to us and everything was open game. We were playing the role of the ugly Americans on a mission conceived by the devil. It was like a saying I heard from one of the returning veterans who trained us at a Fort Polk rifle range. "Kill everything that moves and let God sort the mess out later."

A list of recent Combat Infantry Badge recipients was being circulated around. The C.I.B. is a very coveted medal. Forget about the Congressional Medal of Honor. Too many of those were awarded posthumously. The C.I.B is awarded to all infantrymen seeing action in a combat zone. It's also awarded for spending 30 days on the front lines and was the little badge of honor we all connected with. Unfortunately my name wasn't on the list. I had been in the field for at least six weeks and was alleged to have been fired upon when Sgt. Washington was killed. It wasn't easy looking at all of those names and not finding my name on it. Although I was content being a civilian and felt shanghaied to be picked for the forced induction ceremony, I wanted a CIB. The Army scene had turned me off completely and there was nothing about the life that impressed me. Still, every loudmouth that pushed me around at Ft. Polk and Ft. Benning wore that little badge. It had a Kentucky long rifle with a wreath on a blue enamel background. Each recipient even wore an embroidered replica on their fatigue shirt which made it more intriguing. Not knowing the significance of the badge mattered little. The little rifle somehow completed one's uniform and made us trainees feel somewhat naked without one.

Our time at Beaver came to an end as we were told to gear up for our return trip to Uplift. I couldn't say that I would miss Beaver or the valley either. I did, however, expect to take a lot of memories with me. As we stood on the chopper pad, spirits were high. Everybody was talking about where they we're going, what they we're going to do and consume when we got back. As we took off, the usual anxiety that came with sitting in the door had dissipated. It was good to finally get used to flying with the open view. My next project would have to be for me to ignore all of the craters we we're passing over on our way back to Uplift. There was an amazing don't give a damn attitude about the guys that wouldn't lend itself to caring about the landscape. To us, there were more important matters like how many days we had left in the cratered country. Maybe it was the paratrooper thing.

When we landed at Uplift, the lifers immediately went into their control mindset. They were telling us where to line up, where to drop our gear and everything else they could think of. The scene was reminiscent of that rainy day in December when I first saw the guys come in for that brief stay. We were ignoring the lifers as much as they were then. When the N.C.O. I. C. finished talking everybody took off for wherever they had been talking about going since we were at Beaver. It was either the steakhouse, the whorehouse, the N.C.O. club and of course, the opium den. Everybody else did a beeline for the bunker line. Our platoon was assigned bunkers 9-11. L.Z. Uplift, like any other base camp, is ringed by sandbagged, fortified bunkers. The bunkers at Uplift were tiered fortresses. Some of them were like sandbag castles, two and three levels high and a sharp contrast to those towers at Charang Valley. Whenever a line company was in the rear on a stand down, they were usually assigned to the bunker line to provide security. When there was no company in the rear, the duty fell on the guys who worked in the rear. Most of the cooks, clerks and drivers or as the grunts affectionately call them, R.E.M.F.'s (Rear Echelon Mother Fuckers), were once "Boonie Rats" like us. As I noticed in December, most guys in the Company on stand down preferred to spend their nights pulling guard when they come in the rear. There was expected to be a party going on at every bunker and the gatherings were highly anticipated.

Setting up for bunker guard was a lot different than being in the bush. In the bush, it was Claymores, trip flares, and "last guard." With bunker guard, it was getting all of the party favors or treats in time. Having enough marijuana and beer on hand was all that mattered. Of course there was always music playing in the background wherever we were. We all expected to have a great time.

The party went on all night and nobody actually pulled guard. The lifers were mostly too scared or too drunk to check up on us. All we needed to look out for was the Officer of the day, which was a bullshit protocol the Army had used for about the last 200 years. He always arrived by jeep and we could usually spot him a mile away. I finally left the party and made it to my assigned bunker where the new guy, MacMahon, and I were pulling bunker guard together with a couple of others. When he turned the watch over to me I fell asleep on guard. The Officer of the day woke me up saying that I didn't look like I was pulling guard. I was so stoned and out of it that I forgot MacMahon had already pulled his shift. I instinctively told the officer it wasn't my turn yet. When Mac started to dispute my incorrect story I realized the officer didn't care who was supposed to be asleep or awake. He just hopped into his jeep and had his driver pull off. They hated that duty. There was no doubt about it.

The morning after the sleeping incident, a truckload of us took a ride to L.Z. English where Brigade headquarters was. This was like a field trip for school kids. Along the way, all of our baseball caps blew off. Losing the caps was no big deal to us. It wasn't, that was, until we arrived and ran into General Cunningham who just happened to be standing around talking to the Command Sargent Major. They both blew a gasket at the sight of a truckload of GIs parading around on the back of a deuce-and-a-half violating the Army's sacred uniform code. Purvis had to run over to the two highest ranking hard-asses in the Brigade, stand at attention and get his ass chewed out for being in charge. It was funny the way Purvis stood there while they had their way with him. It wasn't funny when we had to all buy some baseball caps for the sake of uniformity. I also bought some film and a camera to take some pictures of rice paddies for Barbara on our way back to Uplift. It was like stealing a page from Wheelhouse and trying to take as many pictures as possible while in country. I had already missed capturing some real beautiful shots in the An Lo's and it seemed unlikely that another chance at seeing anything as picturesque could possibly come along.

After we returned to Uplift, Wheelhouse was eager to return back to the highway. He suggested that after the last formation, we take off for Phu Cat to spend a night in one of the whorehouses. Jones, Jackson and Anderson decided to come along with us. So we left the compound right after the last formation. We all stood outside of the base camp under a sign that read....

WELCOME TO LZ UPLIFT
HOME OF THE ROCK
3rd BATTALION (AIRBORNE) 503rd INFANTRY
"BEST DAMNED FIGHTING UNIT IN NAM"

Surely every American unit in Vietnam made similar claims about their own personal prowess. The Herd was no exception. The sign was, however, only a source of shade for an old Vietnamese woman selling trinkets, bandanas and a lot of assorted junk that was so popular with GI's. I wanted to price a bracelet but Wheelhouse said it would probably cost too much. "So what do you do in such a situation?" I asked as he continued to browse the goods.

"Just take what you want Handy."

"What do you mean take what I want?"

"If you want the bracelet just take it and forget about the cost. After all you are armed aren't you?" he said as he took the bracelet and handed it to me. The woman selling the goods began to look confused. She obviously couldn't understand any English but realized she was being ripped off.

"How much for this?" he asked holding up a bandana with Vietnam embroidered on it.

"Two dollah" she said. To my surprise, she spoke enough English to consummate the deal.

Two dollars! You're crazy!" he said as he dropped it and walked away. I picked it up and gave it to him and with the reminder that he too was also armed. We laughed and then the four of us hopped a ride on a passing truck. When we made it to Phu Cat corner and went into a nearby whorehouse. We grabbed four girls and went into a large room where blankets were used to partition off each cubicle. We were interrupted that night though by a lot of shooting outside in the street. Since the walls were made of mud and bamboo we became concerned about our safety. The shooting went on with the sound of running footsteps passing outside the door then suddenly the shooting stopped. We were all waiting for the worst to happen but everything returned to normal. After things quieted down, I smelled a strange odor coming from the back room. One of the girls got up and went in the back. She came back and said that everything was all right. I had a suspicion that Charlie came sneaking around to get some "nooky" and found the place occupied. The shooting outside, I imagined, was probably from some ARVN soldiers who spotted them.

We were constantly warned about going to places like whorehouses and opium dens. They said that it was a dangerous trip and that we could be killed or captured. They were all full of it because Charlie collected taxes from all businesses. The guys knew it wouldn't be smart for Charlie to make our stay inhospitable, it was bad for business. Charlie operated like the Mafia. Paying taxes to him was like paying for protection from him. In the villages or the more rural areas, Charlie also took a portion of the rice crop. At Tigerland we learned that the enemy took full advantage of all the resources available to him. He used the money to purchase brand new American-made weapons and ammo. Doing business with the locals had its way of working against our efforts in Vietnam. Of course, somewhere down the supply line, someone was selling us out big time.

I kept my suspicions to myself and spent the rest of the night smoking Bong Son Bombers, a local brand of ready rolled joints dipped in opium that made me feel extremely paranoid. I felt that it would do me good to stay alert if we were truly visited by Charlie after all of that shooting. I wrestled with my suspicions for the rest of the night and before I knew it, it was time to leave the place. We left early to get back to Uplift before the morning formation. "The first formation is when most guys get charged with being AWOL." Jones said as we tried to walk along the side of the highway hoping to get a lift on a passing truck before the MP's caught us. We were too early to get a ride on one of our trucks as the only traffic out at that hour was civilian. Our only hope was to take a ride on a Vietnamese Lambretta which was only slightly larger than a Volkswagen van and usually crowded with passengers and surprisingly a few small livestock. Wheelhouse jumped out in front of one to make sure it came to a stop. When we got on, all of the civilians got off quick. The civilians were naturally afraid of armed GI's s and although the driver was terrified, he gave us the ride to Uplift anyway.

We got there in time and in formation that day was a new face or one that I hadn't seen before. They called him Dickey. Dickey was a very street-wise black guy just released from the L.B.J. ranch (Long Binh Jail). He wore a black beret and talked constantly about how the war was the white man's war. "We don't belong over here brother. This is not our war." he said after he introduced himself to me. The Vietnam War had produced a lot of black guys who always talked about how the war was about oppressing the yellow man and eliminating the black man. I had already heard the theory repeatedly before my draft notice was given to me. Although the story was mostly preached by the anti war crowd, it was more than just another cop out. Since I still hadn't found a credible reason for our being in Vietnam, I couldn't dare challenge Dickey's stand. After all, I was the one who never gave the war's necessity any second thought. Without a doubt the more militant guys like Dickey had a better understanding of the situation than most. Just the same, I had already decided to avoid the discussion about the war's intention, invention, moral conviction, direction and any other of its many debatable aspects. I figured that since I allowed myself to be drafted I might as well do the duty. There was little else I could do about our involvement in the conflict; only learn about it. "Where you from back in the world, blood?" he asked me.

"New Orleans."

"Really. I know a brother who is still on the ranch from there."

"What's he in for?"

"The white man's fucking with him but when the revolution comes, we'll change all of that."

In spite of his militancy and slanted views, everybody seemed to be glad to see him back. The white guys showed no resentment toward him and in fact seemed to respect his opinions. The company was truly an unbelievable group of individuals. The guys just would not let anything stop them from getting along with each other. Racial polarization of the troops could never exist in Charlie Co. If someone like Dickey could show up popping off with inflammatory statements like he did without rubbing anyone the wrong way, the sky was the limit. It had to be the best place in Vietnam. I couldn't have asked for a better situation.

Although the race relations were incredibly good, the company was still segregated. I detected a noticeable imaginary line in the sand had already been drawn along of all things, substance abuse. Although there were no real hostilities between the two groups, the line seemed impassable. The two factions were sarcastically called the juicers and the heads. The juicers thought that smoking pot was dumb and risky because of its illegal status. Alcohol was legal and therefore they always felt comfortable about getting shitfaced. The heads would occasionally drink beer but were known to avoid the juicers when the hard liquor flowed because they always got rowdy when drunk. They were said to be notorious for always starting fights among themselves. Some of the fights, I had been told, were brutal. The heads claimed they always made sure that there were no weapons around during any of the fights, because the juicers would surely kill each other. The overwhelming majority of the heads were enlisted men with no rank of significance (E-4 & below) and most of the juicers were lifers. Alcohol use was widely practiced and probably encouraged among the lifers. The heads didn't trust anyone who wouldn't light up and even referred to coffee as lifer juice, because they needed so much of it after one of their parties. The lifers listened to mostly C&W, and the heads preferred Rock and R&B. The comparisons and contrasts went on and on. The difference in one's race however had nothing to do with the separation of the two groups of substance abusers. There were black juicers as well as white. Similarly, drugs also crossed all racial lines. I was surprised that we were able to keep up the war effort.

After breakfast Wheelhouse introduced me to what he claimed to be the most popular opium den in the province, Linda and Monique's. It was a residence located a few miles down the highway deep in the village and was very crowded. Linda and Monique were two young girls of about 21 who sold dope and entertained anybody who showed up. Wheelhouse was no head and claimed he only occasionally dropped by for fun. True to form, not everyone in attendance was a head. I assumed they just came to escape the boring life at Uplift. It was the same at the whorehouses also. There were always some guys hanging around smoking and playing cards or just listening to music. Linda and Monique had a policy that was very endearing to their clientele. They allowed the customers to consume as much as they wanted for free and only charged for the take-out. The free heroin was a bit too much for me to understand. It was weird the way some of the guys would shoot pure free heroin in their veins fully aware of the addiction that came with it. They were getting their systems adjusted or conditioned to a grade of heroin that could never be found back in the world. In a way I could almost understand some naive farm boy from Iowa sampling the stuff and getting hooked. The inner-city guys, however, saw junkies every day and had witnessed the life of the heroin addict.

Linda and Monique also claimed to be sisters but no one believed them. They were probably as related to each other as Wheelhouse and I. "Is this place wild or what?" Wheelhouse asked me.

"It could be if it weren't for all of that skag being cooked up over there." I said pointing to one of the junkies burning a spoonful of heroin and water over a small flame provided by his lighter.

We had a ball while we were there, but we left after about an hour. We took a nickel bag with us for bunker guard and returned to Uplift. Later that day I found out we were going out on ambush. "Ambush? But this is a stand down. Why are we going on ambush tonight?" I asked Purvis.

"The same reason we go when we're in the bush." he said. It felt disturbing and unnatural to pull ambush on a stand down. We just wanted to have fun at the time and it didn't seem fair to be the squad that had to go. We did have strength in numbers though. Wheelhouse, Doc John, Anderson, Edwards, Moose, Jones, Sgt. Watson, Big Goose, and Dickey joined us for the trip. Since Bear was still on R&R Speedie was less objectionable about Purvis taking us out on ambush. After all, he could just pretend that Watson was in charge of the patrol if he wanted to. Speedie seemed alone in the world without Bear around. As he prepared to lie down on the ground, I remembered the hammock he normally uses in the mountains.

"Say man, where can I get myself one of those hammocks?"

"The black market man. It's the only place they can be found. For some reason, the things are never distributed to line companies but sold openly by the hustlers. I got mine for five bucks MPC." Again the black market figured in the equation. I could only wait for an opportunity to acquire one. I hated the way that the goods meant to be issued to us weren't making it down the supply line. As we left the perimeter, Purvis informed me that back in December a guy stepped on a booby trap in the area we were patrolling giving me too much to think about as we continued on. When we reached our site, we deployed our Claymores and trip flares. Then Purvis handed me a grid coordinate and told me to "Cack" it. Fortunately I still remembered how to use the scheme I learned at Beaver. "No problem" I said confidently as I handed the "Cacked" code to him before lying down for the night. Purvis took the radio and gave the code to whoever was listening on the other end. He ended his transmission with a look of concern. "Are you sure about this code, Handy?"

"Of course I'm sure. Why do you ask?"

"Because they're about to send some live mortar rounds to encircle the grid," he said placing a seed of doubt in my mind. The sound of the rounds exploding out of the tube at its point of origin started the seed to grow. The low whistles of the rounds closing in on our location really made me think twice. Then the reassuring sound of the impacting rounds landing safely around us restored my confidence. "Piece of cake." I said as I silently breathed a sigh of relief. Somehow I managed to keep my same face on throughout. A calm exterior always did seem to ease the troubled minds of those around you.

We had a quiet night and started to recover our Claymores and the rest of our gear for our return. A grenade exploded beyond our perimeter as we left our ambush site. Dickey threw it for no apparent reason angering Purvis. After returning we posed for some pictures, for Wheelhouse of course, and then went to breakfast. The C.O. had a BBQ planned for that evening which meant that we would get a chance at some free cokes and beers. Of course we had to act quickly before the lifer's reputed behavior started to materialize. I expected them to act like a group of idiots once under the influence and I didn't want to get shot by any of them.

10

The bunker line party went on as scheduled. Everybody who was somebody joined us on bunker #8 and the fun started early. The generator was out of order and left us in total darkness. It didn't matter though and in fact it only added to the fun. We couldn't see each other but all of the voices were familiar. Smitty had a camera and a fist full of flashcubes. It turned out to be quite an event. The party had all of the main ingredients, lots of good music, good pot and good company. Every time one of those flashcubes went off, it left a picture burned onto our retinas. It was like an unsynchronized strobe light going off from different spots in the crowd. And every picture was memorable too. Other than the occasional flash about all we could see was the glow of a well-lit ivory pipe being passed around the circle.

To our left was Duster Hill, the highest elevation on the base camp where the dusters fire their rounds in support of units operating in the area of operation. Jones said that every night a party, complete with whores, took place up there. The hookers walked up the hill every night from beyond the perimeter wire in what had to be considered a risk to our security. They were let in every night to perform favors for the crew manning the hill. Everybody knew what went on up there too. The lifers just couldn't seem to break it up. I hoped to get a chance to get an up front and personal look at what went on up on that hill one night before my tour ended.

After the party, many of us left with the impression that it was the best ever. I had always assumed that there could never be a party without any women around but it had to be the most fun I ever had in my young life. Of course we were all so young that we really hadn't started to live yet. Hopefully there were many parties ahead for all of us back home. When I thought of all of the young men that had already lost their lives in Vietnam, I imagined all of the things they never got a chance to do. It was probably the reason we had so much fun at the bunker line parties. Life was short and war made life shorter. Privately we all realized that the next party could've been our last and we wanted to have as much fun with each other as we could. Our loved ones back home would miss us if the worst happened but being in Vietnam made us want to be remembered by each other long after the war ended. The parties seemed to be an expression of that feeling.

While someone fumbled around in the dark changing tapes Wheelhouse said he agreed with my impression of my new squad. "Those guys will always be fun to be with. They love to drive Calvin crazy. You are going to have a ball being with them."

"I'm already having a ball with those guys." I said.

"How about that Last Guard routine? Are they insane or what?" He laughed.

"It's a riot man. It's always a surprise when the first one claims a position on the guard rotation and then the rest of them follows through. You never know when it will kick off."

"Bear is one great guy. He earned his stripes in the bush and is by far the most popular squad leader in the platoon." He said and again I couldn't argue against it. Being in the third squad was turning into the most enjoyable part of my tour. Wheelhouse was content to be carrying his beloved M-60 though. He didn't belong to any one squad and enjoyed being attached to all of them at one time or another.

A nice little controversy started when we realized that a new heavyweight boxing champ had been crowned. Joe Frazier had moved up to the throne and of course the issue in Vietnam was always focused on Muhammad Ali. I supposed it was appropriate since we were in the war and Ali wasn't. The prevailing attitude that day was anti-Ali. I had nothing against him personally but we all felt that if we had to be in Vietnam, so should everyone else. That included Frazier too. The war seemed to be fought by the poor and the underprivileged guys with no real connections to people of influence or affluence. If you were somebody, you didn't have to worry about getting drafted. The whole situation caused discontent amongst the guys who were in the war. It probably worsened after Nixon took office with a promise to get us out but continued to draft and send guys over. In spite of it all, America could still produce enough thrill seekers, patriots and guys that just wanted to be there to help fill the ranks with the ordinary guys who, due to the draft, had to be there. It was a shining testament to our resources. And a sharp contrast to the college types who seemingly protested the war for their own personal reasons. We even had the good fortune to have the company of a Canadian and the nephew of a famous high ranking general serve with us. Someone should have been doing a story about those two instead of the draft dodgers/students and prima donna athletes. We only made the headlines when civilians died at our hands.

My sister-in-law Pearl sent me a week-long edition of all of the Mardi Gras season copies of our local newspaper, The Times Picayune. It was late February and I suppose that Mardi Gras was at least a couple of weeks earlier. I really didn't like missing it but at least I got a chance to let Wheelhouse see what it was like for the first time in his life even if it was just a newspaper account. Then he read about Al Hirt getting hit by a bottle at a parade and said he didn't know that Hirt was from New Orleans. "Man I've got to see the Mardi Gras when the war ends for us. I'll be looking you up when that time comes, OK."

"I'll be waiting for you." The list of future visitors was growing and I was doing nothing to discourage their planning. The Mardi Gras was proving to be too much of an attraction to the average guy who never witnessed it.

That night we were assigned to pull guard at a bunker behind the company headquarters. Wheelhouse was assigned to the bunker next to ours. "Listen I've got a good idea. I'm going to fire a few rounds out into the area immediately in front of us from my position over there." He said. "Look man, the lifers will probably come running over here if you shoot that thing." I said.

"Handy listen, I didn't live to see nineteen by taking unnecessary chances."

"Of course you didn't. You're the surfer that had to come to Viet Nam because you wanted to be here." I said before he fired off the rounds to put his mind at ease about the safety of his position. There was nothing as reassuring as the sound of an M-60 mowing the area in front of you. Wheelhouse had become addicted to both the sound and the feeling that accompanied it. After his burst, we all settled down for another uneventful night.

Back in New Orleans, everyone was coming back from another big pre-Lenten celebration. On the other side of the planet I was gearing up for our next mission. I paused and sat watching Wheelhouse pack his ruck with the supermarket goodies his mother kept him well stocked with. "Say man, who are those Vietnamese kids on the base camp? I mean, what is the story behind their being here?" I asked him.

"I'm not sure but I think they're war orphans. I think that they were orphaned during some battle our battalion was involved with back in the earlier part of the war."

"How long have they been living with the Herd?"

"Probably longer than they can remember. I've heard that they can't even speak Vietnamese. They never leave the perimeter and, in a way, are virtual prisoners in their own country. They are well cared for but are not being allowed to engage with their own culture." he said showing a surprising concern for the plight of the kids.

"That's ridiculous. What's going to happen when the Herd gets called home?"

"I guess we'll just release them into the wild like animals."

In the distance I could see Kyler sitting in a jeep looking at us and probably wishing he could be with us. I hadn't seen much of him during our stand down. He was taking his reassignment hard. The little guy had all the heart in the world but not enough stamina to hump the boonies. Too bad things happened the way they did. He wanted to do better.

While sitting on the helicopter pad taking pictures of each other, I knew that I didn't want to go back out to the field. Being in the rear had spoiled me. The recent stand down was quite an enjoyable one. About the only thing that I had to look forward to was that I would be with the same guys I had just finished enjoying my stand down with. Our next mission was about to begin and we didn't even know where we were heading. At least nobody bothered to tell me anyway. I only wanted to write home and tell everyone where the hell we were. I guess it was expecting too much to be informed about as much. I got over not knowing when I saw our slicks approaching. "Handy, take my picture." Wheelhouse asked as he handed me his Instamatic again. We all took pictures of each other until our helicopters came to whisk us away to our next destination.

We flew high above the thatched roofs nestled beneath the rows of leaning coconut palm trees. The dark green bamboo bordered the wet rice paddies with the sun reflecting a glare on its surface that made us squint. The height made the picture below smaller but the beauty was still there. When the helicopters started its descent, it was easy to see our intended landing zone. It had to be beyond the last complex of villages across a neglected rice fields that must be some kind of no man's land. It was once used for rice production but it seemed to be a barrier between the mountains and the nearest village.

After disembarking we lined up and started moving across the dried up field and then paused near the foot of the mountain. As we sat and waited for Garson to give the command to move on, I looked around the area and found a nice spot in the bushes and opened a can of applesauce. It was expected to be a tough readjustment to life in the field after that stand down. Eating out of a can again was expected to be especially hard. Maybe, I thought, it's not a bad idea to stay out in the bush and never go back. "Look at those coconuts Handy." said Wheelhouse as he got up from his spot on the ground pointing to a nearby tree situated at the base of the mountain. It was a healthy cluster of them all right but the trouble was that climbing one of those trees was no minor task. Creatively, he grabbed his M-60 and started to shoot the coconuts hoping to knock them down. Other than perforating the coconuts and draining them of all of the juice, nothing fell. "Well, can't say that I didn't try." he said before Garson gave the word to start moving up the mountain. After at least ten long days in the rear, climbing had turned into an arduous task. The objective was there but not the will. We had been spoiled by the stand down and had lost our feel for climbing. Guys were actually sweating for the first time in quite a while. Suddenly we got the word to turn around. After only about 100 ft. uphill, we were ordered to make it to an extraction site for a return to Uplift. This was my kind of mission, climb until we get tired and then go back to the steakhouse for some more char-broils and beer. We didn't have to wait too long for our ride either. As soon as we passed the bullet riddled coconut tree, we could see our slicks coming in over the village. And just like that we were on our way back to resume what we had started earlier, the greatest stand down of all time.

When we got back to Uplift, the C.O. was waiting for us with a quick briefing. It was one of those rare moments when he addressed us as a unit. "When I first arrived here I wanted to know what kind of company I inherited. I wanted to know how good you were." he said.

"Charlie Co. is a good company in the field but we haven't got that body count yet." he said. His observation really had me worried. Until he made the statement, I thought that it was good to say that we hadn't made any real contact with the enemy.

"We must have that body count to gauge our effectiveness. So I've been talking to higher-ups and I managed to get us a mission in Tuy Hoa. The N.V.A. is on a campaign of terror and aggression in the area. Some of the village chiefs have been assassinated and the populace is under the enemy's control. Our job will be to restore control of the area to the Saigon government. I know we will get that body count in Tuy Hoa."

"Oh no! Not pacification again." said Black from the rear of the formation.

"Pacification? I keep hearing about this pacification thing. Just what is pacification anyway? "

"That's when we work alongside those fucking ARVN soldiers."

"What's so bad about that?" I asked.

"What's so bad? Those mother fuckers won't fight. All they do is run every time we get into a firefight. Just wait. You'll see what I mean. They're just a bunch of cowards. Fucking gooks!" he said angrily.

"Man you can't be serious. Those guys can't be that bad." I offered. Black then laughed at my reply.

"Handy listen at this. On the black market they use a sales pitch whenever they sell ARVN rifles. They always claim that the rifles are brand new, never been fired and only dropped once." he said as a lot of other guys started to laugh with him. The joke wasn't as funny as they all made it sound but their laughter only made me worry about how serious they were. Black had been consistently honest and informative about everything he had told me since I became a part of the third squad. His joke about the brand new ARVN rifles scared me. Mercein had either placed us in a challenging situation or, according to Black, we we're about to go on what amounted to a suicide mission. We would also be going without Bear because he had come down with malaria and there was no way of determining if he would be coming back soon or at all. None of the guys were happy about going on pacification again. They were on a pacification mission before the Crow's Foot and most of the memories of that job were bad ones.

Wheelhouse explained that pacification, in theory and application, meant going into villages on a sort of good will mission to win some hearts and minds of the Vietnamese people that was so essential to our goals. This explained the film we watched at Bien Hoa in November. We were expected to accomplish this by giving more than just the armed presence fighting alongside the ARVN soldier. He said we would also have the added responsibility of assisting the civilians in their day to day life and providing health care and education. It all sounded like what we went to Vietnam for, to help the people. I was personally in favor of this pacification thing.

"Handy, I'm telling you this mission will give us a chance to work with the little kids in this country." He said. He was happy to be going on pacification again and didn't share Black's pessimism. On the surface, I couldn't find anything wrong with the concept. I thought Black was exaggerating about the issue of cowardice. After all, there were almost 50,000 dead American soldiers who had given their lives fighting the war. I doubted if we would still be involved in the war if the ARVN wasn't fighting against the enemy. Vietnam was their country, their war, for their freedom. It had already been established that the war was theirs to win, not ours.

As I stood in formation waiting for someone to tell me that Black was just kidding about the ARVN, I looked to my right and noticed Griffey accepting congratulations and farewells. His tour was coming to an end or at least he wouldn't be going to Tuy Hoa with us. I thought he would be happier than he seemed. Floyd was talking to him and from where I was standing. It seemed as if Floyd was happier than Griffey was. I imagined that it would be rough on Floyd, losing his good friend "Grif". He seemed to be taking it alright though. Soon our squad would be decimated with the losses of both Speedie and Shave. With Bear already down with malaria, and Bueno leaving shortly it figured to be a lot different real soon. We would be assuming a new identity in the not too distant future. I didn't even know who would be included when the word "we" was used later on. It was the biggest handcuff of the war; the dreaded one-year tour of duty. Every guy in "Nam" had to return back to the states one year after his arrival. It was nice to know that you didn't have to spend but a year in the war, but there were some drawbacks; like being short. Jones said that nothing could hurt the effectiveness of a grunt more than being short because he would literally become obsessed with counting his days. After that, he'd lose all of his effectiveness and would easily become a burden to all whom depended on him. All of the fears, apprehensions and anxieties that were common to us would become exaggerated. The enemy, on the other hand, had to fight to the end. He had nothing to look forward to but victory. Being short was sheer torture for the GI. I hoped that I would be able to handle being short in the same manner that Speedy, Shave and Doc Bueno.

Our company received a few new men while away on our aborted mission. Wheelhouse was assigned one of them as an ammo bearer/asst. gunner. He was complaining about having to work with him almost immediately. "This guy is driving me crazy with his know-it-all attitude." He said. His name was Young and he rubbed everybody the wrong way. Surely with time, everyone would grow accustomed to his cocky confident approach to his job. Maybe he was just trying to make rank or show his ability to Wheelhouse. It could've been worse though. He could have been one of those totally incompetent assholes that always find themselves positioned where they would do the most damage to everyone around them. Young had yet to separate his training experience from his in-country baptism. In the bush you had to be willing to accept all advice as well as criticism. We were all judged constantly by our willingness to absorb as much as we could.

We had another new guy; a native Hawaiian that everybody called "Punch". He hated being in Charlie Co. He had asked around and found out that we hadn't been in any firefights lately. We weren't seeing enough action for his consumption. After we returned to Uplift, he finally got to meet us and thought that we were a great group of guys but he wanted to get him some kills. The new mission to Tuy Hoa had not warmed his interest at all as he had already put in for a transfer to another unit. He would probably go to a Ranger or Recon group. He had already gotten his wish and although we had just met the guy, he was already considered a former member of Charlie Co. Wheelhouse really got a kick out of the way he said that we weren't "getting any kills." Although I hadn't been in country very long, I knew that our enemy deserved every bit of the respect he had earned. Punch thought he was on some kind of adventure. I was glad to see him get his wish for reassignment. His brand of enthusiasm could have gotten some of us killed

Another new arrival, Phelam, was a second tour guy. He was someone who I wished would have transferred to another company, any other company. Phelam was a misfit if there ever was one. His first tour was with the 101st back in '65. I didn't know what to make of the guy. On his first day with us, he demonstrated a bad habit of walking that thin line between them and us, the juicers and the heads, the lifers and the guys. He tried not to fall off of that line but sooner or later it had to happen, it was impossible to live both lives in the bush. He'd been over before and should've known better. He spent practically that whole day with "Moose". Moose was from California and an admitted misfit. He'd been in the army for at lest 5 or 6 years and had never achieved any rank of significance. He stayed in just enough trouble to keep from being promoted to E-5. Moose was also on his second tour and was also a former member of the 101st. Other than both being white, the comparisons ended there. Moose was one of the guys and enjoyed it. Phelam only paid token visits to keep the lifers from thinking that he had gone over to the other side. Phelam had already attained the rank of E-5 and used it to maintain his close ties with the lifers.

On the bright side, our platoon had gained still another new guy. His name was Dowd. He wanted very much to be thought of as one of the guys in spite of his Sgt. E-5 rank.

"Call me LSD it's my initials, Louis S. Dowd." he said repeatedly. His name was actually Carter Wayne Dowd but his attitude was encouraging. So we chalked up another head in our camp. Dowd was a graduate from the N.C.O. School at Ft. Benning. We called it Shake and Bake school. I never knew if the Army always had the N. C. O. School or if it was a product of the Vietnam War. I was just glad it was there to produce the number of E-5's needed to provide us with an adequate amount of squad leaders. They took a lot of abuse from the guys in the field but I think that we all realized how important it was to have them around.

The C.O.'s guaranteed body count in Tuy Hoa gave me a lot to think about. I doubted if the enemy was willing to just lie down and die to be counted for him though. They were expected to put up a fight and possibly get a count of their own. The boldness of their actions (assassinations) was almost like an invitation to do battle. Our arrival was to be anticipated and we were definitely on our way.

One more night at Uplift and then it would be on to Tuy Hoa. Bunker #11 attracted a crowd of heads for a big party before the trip in the morning. I headed over and found Wheelhouse and a crowd of guys from the third platoon. We sat and talked for a while. Jones joined us and was in the best of spirits. "I got another letter from Cynthia." he said. I'd forgotten about the address I had given him when I was in Griffey's squad.

"What's she talking about?" I asked.

"Love man, love."

"Be serious. You've only been writing each other for what, less than two months now?"

"I'm telling you man the woman is in love with me."

"C'mon man, she lives in New Orleans and you're in Vietnam. You've never even met the girl."

"We're in love." he jokingly insisted.

"You're both crazy." I said feeling sort of outdone by the amount of progress made by Jones. Her sister never would've been as accommodating for me.

The party was a lot of fun. The crowd was made up with a lot of strange faces too. Wheelhouse retired up to the top level and fell asleep before waking up suddenly with a loud frightened outburst.

Assuming that sappers were attacking us, everyone took up defensive positions expecting the worst. Wheelhouse jumped down from the upper level breathing heavily.

"There was a giant rat sitting on my chest when I woke up. He was eating the joint right out of my mouth!" he said as the rest of us got in a good laugh. The party turned out to be one of the best laughs I ever had thanks to Wheelhouse and his little friend. If Tuy Hoa was going to be the kind of place that Mercein said that it would be, I felt fortunate to be going in with the kind of people that I was surrounded with that night. I could only hope to be coming out with them too; all of them. Black had always been honest with everything that he had to offer me in the way of advice and assistance. This was going to be one time I was hoping he wasn't. Somewhere along the way, someone should have mentioned that ARVN soldiers wouldn't fight.

PART TWO

1

After the second end to the stand down of all stand downs, we packed our gear for a truck ride to English for a flight on some C-130's destined for Tuy Hoa AFB (Air Force Base). When we arrived at English, I laughed as I remembered the last time I was there. Old General Cunningham was standing in the right place at the right time when we arrived at his location on that truck. He must have gotten his rocks off chewing Purvis's ass out for that uniform infraction. At first I wondered where he was but then I assumed he was somewhere getting his ass kissed by our C.O. for letting him have the trip to Tuy Hoa. What mattered most was the confident mood that everyone was displaying. The spirited bravado tactic seemed like the only thing we had in our arsenal at that moment. The promise of a body count was still ringing in my ears as we jumped off of the trucks and surveyed the crowded airstrip.

There must have been at least 200 men standing around lined up waiting to board. The huge planes were poised on the tarmac with their cargo doors open. The planes resembled giant whales with their mouths wide open as men and material disappeared into their vast cargo bays. The loud noises caused by the engines shut off all but the thought process. During that pensive moment, I started to wrestle with the possibility that some of us were not going to come back from Tuy Hoa. The thought of any of us shedding blood or losing our lives had me shaken. My tour had been somewhat of an extended camp out and the war was just something that went on elsewhere. Our new CO's aggressiveness gave me a lot to think about and I could do a lot of thinking when the situation called for use of my wild imagination.

As we rolled down the runway for take off, I was reminded of my first flight on a C-130 at Ft. Benning. The thrill of jumping, however, had been replaced with the ominous fear of the unknown. We landed at Tuy Hoa AFB and started to deplane amidst the busiest strip I had ever seen. There were F-4 Phantom fighter planes landing and taking off every two minutes. Their decibel level was deafening. The Phantom ruled the sky over Vietnam. The valued existence of air superiority allowed us to roam the jungles and mountains with near impunity. That goes for every war we had been in since the advent of flight. While it was good to have them on our side, the enemy was not that impressed with all of the supposed advantages of having the edge in air support. Whenever Charlie was confronted with having to deal with the superior firepower from above, he went underground and caused an entirely new problem for us with an amazing complex of tunnels. From there he would practically dare us to come in and at the same time, wage war from an improbable staging area. Nothing was going to deter him from his goal of winning the war. He was willing to do whatever it took to achieve his victory. From what I had witnessed, his biggest weapon was his patience. The war was no more than a big waiting game and we were the only ones getting impatient.

The airbase was every bit as accommodating as any facility back in the world. Off duty personnel were even allowed to wear civilian attire. A couple of friends of mine from back home joined the Air Force after high school. In fact, a lot of guys joined the Air Force to beat the draft. My two friends,

Walter and Bobby just wanted to be in that particular branch of the service. I was sure they were enjoying the lifestyle. If the living conditions were that good for the Air Force guys in Vietnam, it was probably great everywhere else. Walt, who was also my classmate, was stationed at Clark AFB in Okinawa after having already done a tour in Taipei. I really never second-guessed myself for letting the draft catch up with me. I could have joined the Air Force and been done with my military obligation before I turned 20. The draft evaders overwhelmed the recruiters seeking a quick way out of the draft. The Air Force eventually changed the rules and made it an initial four-year hitch. Four years was like an eternity to me. I couldn't surrender an extra two years to Uncle Sam just to get out of going to Vietnam.

We loaded up for a truck ride to our rendezvous with our ally the ARVN. While riding through downtown Tuy Hoa, I saw a lot of the French influence in the architecture. It reminded me of the French Quarter in New Orleans. I imagined it also had a lot to do with Ho Chi Minh's success against the colonialists. He probably used the French's dominance of the region as a rallying point and easily won his war against them. I was certain that most aspects of our presence were also equally as irritating to the same belligerents that kicked the French out.

When we reached the outskirts of the town, we got off the trucks expecting to meet up with a company of ARVN soldiers. There were no ARVN's in sight though. "It must be their day off." Said Black as he laughed at the absentee soldiers.

"Tone it down will you." said Young showing the part of his personality that was so irritating to Wheelhouse and others. When he spoke up Wheelhouse turned around to say something to him but I was able to change his mind about whatever he was about to say. It wasn't very hard as Wheelhouse was not in any real hurry to say anything at all to his new sidekick.

"I guess we'll just have to go find them." Garson suggested before we started to search for the missing ARVN Company. Unfortunately Black was right about the ARVN. If one of our units failed to make such an objective there would be cause for concern or alarm. The thinking would be that the missing unit was being kept from making the appointment due to its inability to separate itself from the throes of combat. Anything less might cost the head of an officer or two for gross dereliction of duty. Garson's reaction to the absence of the ARVN's and his decision to search for them should've been considered unusual and not the only solution.

After an hour long search we finally came upon a couple of them sleeping in their hammocks. We had them take us to their main body. When we reached the destination we found the so-called main body to be widely dispersed, and to a large extent well hidden. The ARVN, it seemed, was every bit the shrinking violet Black said they were. I still held on to my belief that if they were bolstered by our presence they would stand and fight. "Black, I have to believe these guys will give a good fight since we're gonna be here to assist them". I said.

"Don't count on it, Handy. These are not your average soldiers." He warned me as we waited around for the rest of the ARVN's to show up. According to the interpreter, the ARVN soldiers had not been conducting any operations in the area since the NVA converged on the village which created numerous worst case scenarios. I had to stop thinking about the worst and concentrate on what it would take for us to survive our predicament. I couldn't let the ARVN's lack of motivation affect me so adversely.

Our contingent of ARVN's were more like a reserve force that worked the villages. We were aligned with a bunch of weekend warriors and had to go up against a unit of real soldiers. The NVA were the tough guys and the "Ruff Puffs," as Black called them, were less than impressive. As the late arriving soldiers started to finally show up, I was sickened by what I saw. They were all wearing starched fatigues and shiny boots. They carried their rifles by the gun sights like suitcases or purses, I should say and half of them were arriving by motorcycle. The scene made me wonder if Nixon's so-called Vietnamization program had any real chance of being implemented. His plan to turn the war over to the ARVN was a disaster in the making. Hopefully the regular ARVN soldier was more formidable than his RF PF counterpart. They looked like a bunch of pretty boys and there was nothing pretty about combat or combat readiness.

As Garson conferred with the ARVN C.O., I sat back and started to observe the simple lifestyle of the villagers. Everywhere I looked I saw another aspect of the rural Vietnamese. Slowly, a little boy of about 10 came walking alongside a canal that flowed in front of us. He was leading a huge gaggle of geese that was swimming in the water below the bank. The geese could barely see the kid from the vantage afforded by the low water level. He was, just the same, still able to keep them following him by carrying a long bamboo stick hovering over the water path. When he stopped, the birds stopped in unison. When he spotted us and reversed his direction, they all did an immediate about face. The choreography, along with the pure white color of the geese superimposed against the dark murky water in the canal, was another spectacle all by itself.

To my left, was an old man carrying two piglets by their hind legs. He squatted near a small pen in front of me and placed one of the animals inside. He then took the other and cut a tiny slit along the underside of his thigh. After placing his finger inside of the freshly cut hole, he pulled out some string like tissue. "What's he doing to the poor little fellah." I asked.

"He's fixin him or her." said Anderson who was from some rural part of Georgia. Being a county boy, I assumed he knew more about it than I who had never seen a live pig before.

"Papa San don't want this one reproducin'; he's just gonna fatten him up and take him to market or eat him later." Anderson continued as the old man repeated the procedure on the other piglet and left both of them lying in the pen squealing their little lungs out.

Over the horn, I heard someone spelling Jones name out. I wondered what it was all about until a helicopter came out to pick him up shortly after the message came over the radio. Jones was placed on the slick and was taken away immediately. I had never seen anyone snatched away so suddenly. After the commotion was over, I looked in on my two little newly sterilized patients and noticed that one of them was not going to make it. Poor little dude; Papa San decided that he would never get laid and he had to die because of it. I was really feeling sorry for him when Papa San's wife walked over to the pen, reached over me and took the dead one away.

The old Papa San's family was very friendly to us and welcomed us into their house as if by custom. They carried on conversation with us as if they could understand English but couldn't speak it. After listening to his wife as she rambled on and on about whatever, we were offered a spot at the table to dine with the family. I was flattered and accepted. There was, however, no table to dine on. We all squatted in a circle on the floor as the entire menu was placed in the middle of the dirt floor as we assembled around the food items. Mama San handed me a bowl and some very old chopsticks. The sticks were carved from bamboo and seemed so old that they could have been a relic from the Ming Dynasty. I could only imagine how many microbes were crawling on the things so I passed on the sticks and pulled out my trusty plastic fork and spoon.

As I finished the last of the meal, Mama San informed me, in her own way that I had just eaten some of the vasectomy/tubal ligation patient. I felt bad about it but nodded approvingly and stepped outside. Calvin was standing in wait and I suspected he was ready to school me about my activity with the villagers. "You don't know what you're eating." he said.

"I really didn't need to know that time." I replied. Calvin was a control freak bent on imposing his will. He was on his second afraid we might not see the significance. He couldn't have realized how redundant he'd become.

I looked ahead and noticed the spot where I stood and watched the geese had been changed into a place of business. The local hustlers had built a concession stand around the guys which validated what I'd already noticed. The Vietnamese people were natural born capitalists. They knew how to chase the dollar. The saying is that the three main keys to a successful business were location, location and location. There was no need to repeat it to the locals. Maybe it was the reason why the GI was so arrogant. We had the dollars and they wanted them bad. Having that stand built around our chosen spot only made us feel that much more important. The guys were waving MPC around like a bunch of drunks in a bar. Then I noticed that they were drinking beer; larger than usual bottles of strange beer. Boogie Man seemed to be drinking the most of it so I approached him to get a closer look at the label.

"It's what we call Tiger Piss." He said. The label had a picture of a Bengal tiger's head on it. It was probably another French product still under production.

"It's a little watered down, but it'll do in a rush."

"What's he talking about?" I asked Wheelhouse.

"The hustlers always uncap bottles of beer or soda and water the contents down to stretch the profits." The practice wasn't exactly new to any of us. In the old American west, saloonkeepers were famous for it. Later, during prohibition, every speakeasy did it for the same reason. The problem was that in Vietnam, the water quality was almost as bad as Mexico's. I took a chance and found the brew decent but no equal to our own preferred brands. "Heard about Jones?" he asked me.

"No. I did see him get on the slick, though."

"His Dad passed away."

"Sorry to hear about that. I heard them spelling his name out and a moment later he was gone."

"That's the way it's usually done when there's death in the family. The Red Cross takes over and cuts through all of the red tape."

"That fast?"

"Believe it our not Handy, Jones will be home in a little over 36hrs wearing the same fatigues he's wearing now. I hear that they won't even search him going through customs."

Shave's radio was playing a new song by an old familiar voice. It was Brook Benton singing a nice melody called "Rainy Night in Georgia", a real heartbreaker. At that moment I felt as if I were the only one within earshot of the radio who was in love with someone back home. I was definitely the only one moved by the song as it played.

Our strategy while in Tuy Hoa would be for all squads to go on ambush every night. Each squad would also have about 8-10 RF PFs tagging along. The RF PF issue is what stuck in everybody's craw. I saw no reason for the complaining and no resolution to it either. Pacification meant turning the war over to the ARVN and that was what we were supposed to be doing. Getting caught in a firefight with a bunch of tin soldiers on your side was dangerous for sure. I had to believe that they would fight.

When it started to get dark we took our ARVNs out on ambush. They ignored all of the night discipline rules we thought were pretty basic. Things like sight, sound and odor suppression were too obvious to point out. Instead they smoked cigarettes and acted as if they were trying to give away our position. After ambush I complained to Purvis about them but I quickly realized that the rest of the guys were all too familiar with their activities. When I noticed Black laughing at my frustration, I stopped complaining. "Do you see what I was talking about now?" he asked in an effort to drive home his point. I said nothing in reply because the ARVN's actions had planted seeds of doubt and suspicion in my mind about their true allegiance. I figured they couldn't be on our side if they were trying to give away our position. We were faced with an impossible task with the ARVN. Surrendering half of our defensive perimeter to these assholes who appeared to be more like saboteurs than allies seemed suicidal. I couldn't understand the reason for their high degree of non-cooperation. Of course I also didn't know of the ARVN's existence either.

After ambush, we dumped our ARVN's and joined the rest of our company. As the 1st squad returned from their patrol, I noticed that Al, who was with them, was wearing a lot of freshly picked green marijuana for camouflage. As Garson stripped the illegal weed from his steel pot, Al claimed that their ambush spot was in a garden full of it. "I'm telling you man they're cultivating the shit somewhere out there." he continually insisted just as some bad news came across the horn. Another one of the platoons had just encountered a little child with a grenade. The child, acting on instructions, walked up to them pulled the pin on a frag and threw it at them. Fortunately, the kid didn't remove the retainer and the grenade didn't go off. It did, however, demonstrate the kind of enemy activity we could expect. Charlie obviously would stoop to any level to strike a blow. The child's participation made me question our stated reason for being in Vietnam. If the NVA were the intruders the villagers needed to be protected from, someone forgot to tell the villagers. "Now I know what happened at Me Lai." I said to Moose.

"No you don't Handy. That so-called massacre was a matter of eliminating the enemy."

"You mean killing civilians was a part of fighting the war?"

"Absolutely. Who do you think is the enemy anyway?"

"Why don't you tell me."

"Gladly. Children grow up to become VC, so you kill them. Women give birth to children that grow up to become VC, so you kill them. The old men have already fought the war and are trying to hide behind old age so you kill them too. Now that's what I call a pacified village." He laughed.

The trouble with Moose was that I couldn't tell whether he was serious or not. I hoped not because if he wasn't, Calley never should have been placed under arrest. There was something about our being in Vietnam that didn't add up. My continuing learning experience was beginning to shape my opinion on it. I didn't exactly have a library at my disposal and I still wanted to know more than was being explained to me. I was beginning to feel uncomfortable about our role in the war.

Phelam showed up to pretend to be one of the guys again. Chrysler definitely shared the same opinion of Phelam that I did. Chrysler or Chris, as we all called him, was another E-5 from NCO school and seemed to be leaning towards a career in the Army. He was not a head, but he wasn't a hard-ass either. With Chris, you always knew where you stood with him. He provided an effective brand of leadership. Which meant that he led by example. He was not going to pretend to be anyone he was not. Therein was the difference between the two. For an added effect Phelam threw Al into the canal for laughs. Of course he knew that Al was a terrific sport and practically obliged Phelam by allowing himself to be deposited in the water. After the big laugh, he pushed Chris into the drink also. Chris, on the other hand didn't appreciate the joke. Phelam made a quick exit after his second prank. There was no need to hang around any longer than it took for him to make his presence felt. I know he didn't want the lifers to think he had gone over to the other side. Of course Chris was not impressed or amused by anything Phelam did. He was able to see right through his artificial exterior.

Wheelhouse beckoned me from the midst of a group of guys standing around holding a discussion on a news report they heard over the radio.

"Another picture?" I asked.

"No I want your opinion on this bussing issue."

"Bussing?" I said feeling as if I was about to be exposed. The radio report was about bussing and I didn't know anything about it. There was an incident being reported over the radio and I didn't pay much attention to it. All I knew about bussing was that it had something to do with integration. I was sure that he was sampling my opinion on the subject because of the obvious black perspective I could offer. I had to be honest with the guy. "Well, I don't know anything about bussing man. When I was school age, we all attended the nearest all-black school in our area or district." I said feeling embarrassed about my lack of knowledge on such a hot topic.

"What? Are you kidding me man? You mean you never went to school with any white kids?"

"No, for half of my time as a school kid, it was against the law."

"Handy are you trying to tell me that New Orleans had laws like that too?"

"Of course. All of the schools, the neighborhoods, and public facilities were segregated."

"New Orleans?"

"Yes New Orleans. Why is that so hard to believe?"

"It's just that no one would ever associate New Orleans with all of that shit."

"Maybe you wouldn't, but believe me man, that's the way it was back then. There was some token integration in the schools by the time I graduated but I never took part in any of it." I said as he walked away in shock. I then realized that by being honest about my lack of exposure to integration, it covered up my ignorance on bussing. I then went over to the newly created Coke stand and listened to UCLA win another NCAA tournament game and LSU get eliminated from the NIT. I felt tempted to ask Wheelhouse if he ever thought that LSU would recruit the black athlete but didn't because he was from Virginia where integration was obviously in full force. I didn't like the fact that Louisiana was still living in the past.

After the two basketball games and several beers, we went out on ambush again. Although nothing happened, I couldn't help but make comparisons between the two contenders for the hearts and minds of the S. Vietnamese people. Black's assessment of the so-called Ruff Puffs had started to look like an accurate one. They were like little kids tagging along as we went about our mission. Having them around was a joke making Vietnamization an even bigger joke. The ARVN soldier could never measure up to the battle-hardened NVA regular. Anyone who trained at Charang Valley or anywhere else in S. Vietnam could not be expected to fight against a soldier who had run a gauntlet of B-52 strikes down the Ho Chi Minh trail just to get to S. Vietnam. If our plan was to turn the fighting over to the ARVN, we needed a new plan.

We moved our daytime location to another spot. The Coke stand area had turned into a less than desirable location. Staying anywhere else would've been equally bad for us. We attracted such a large crowd of onlookers, curiosity seekers and truant kids that it would become very easy for the enemy to come out, count our heads, take inventory of every weapon we had and plan an attack. Being in a village made us just that vulnerable; which was another reason that pacification was so dangerous. It also added credence to Moose's definition of a "pacified village." If the villagers feared us, they wouldn't be standing around in large numbers watching us. Of course if every village was as pacified as Moose thought they should be, there wouldn't be any villages left standing.

Our new area wasn't as accommodating to the gawking villagers making it an ideal area for us to be working from. The landowner didn't allow trespassers and his spread was huge. He must have commanded a lot of respect for there were no violators to be seen. We were able to slip away into the night on ambush without being detected. Large landowners such as the one who owned that spot stood to lose the most with a communist victory in Vietnam. Almost all of the people we saw on a daily basis were like American sharecroppers. Their only privilege in life was to live on someone else's land and work it for little or nothing. Ho Chi Minh's promise of land distribution had to be more attractive than anything we could offer them. Communist revolutions always strip the "Haves" of all of their holdings to be equally distributed amongst the "Have-nots". To call pacification an uphill struggle was still another understatement. The landowners knew that we couldn't protect them or their land from the enemy. They also realized that Nixon was turning the war over to the paper tiger ARVN and bringing us home. The Saigon government was not strong enough to do any better at defending their village from roaming NVA units when they came along to take a portion of their rice crop. I knew what to expect once Hanoi succeeded in their efforts to win the south. The affluent lifestyle of all landowners was gradually coming to an end. The so-called classless society stood ready to bring them to their knees. Pacification, for all of its good intent, could never work. From where I stood, it possibly never was expected to either.

Every evening we had to take the Ruff Puffs by the hand and walk them through a night of terror in their own country. Our mere presence suggested that there was little that the ARVN was capable of accomplishing without our assistance. Without our presence in Vietnam Charlie, we all felt, would take over in a matter of days. The weather, terrain, and the mosquitoes figured to slow them down more than The ARVN. If the Ruff Puffs were any indication of what the Saigon government had to defend themselves with, the people were in trouble. They had to be the worst soldiers in the history of warfare. I doubted if anyone in D.C. knew about the combat readiness of their so-called army. If they did, I thought, we were truly in a mess.

Our next resupply fell on a Sunday. There was a barber and some chaplains stepping off of the slicks, one for every denomination. I wondered privately if Calvin regarded such gatherings as religious cluster fucks and was certain that Charlie would throw a frag at them without regard to whom they were worshipping. I resisted asking him because he would have probably had some ridiculous answer that I didn't fell like debating.

"We have a barber over there cutting hair Handy. When are you going to get a haircut?" He asked. Jones was right. He was making his rounds trying to get the black guys to get a trim.

"I think I'll pass today if you don't mind."

"Alright, but if you get killed I would just hate to have to send you home to your mother with your hair looking like that." he said with his usual lack of concern for sensitivity. I decided to never get a haircut and for good measure, I also decided to stop combing it. If he thought he didn't like the way it looked, I couldn't wait to see his response after a couple of months without combing it.

Wheelhouse received another box from home. His mother was always sending him some goodies to eat. His rucksack contained all of the brand names found in the supermarket.

"Another Care Package from home?"

"Yeah, want some?"

"What I'd really like is for someone to send me one of those packages that you're always receiving."

"My mom sends me a package of goodies twice a month." He said. If I had to call it as I saw it, those packages seemed to come more like twice a week. He gave me a pack of some Kool-Aid that was pre-sweetened. I didn't even know the product existed. He went on to say that the big Hawaiian "Punch" had been killed charging a bunker. We always figured that someone like Punch would eventually get himself killed. He had a death wish for sure and would have jeopardized our lives with his fanaticism. It was sad, but there was no stopping him. He really wanted to kill somebody and talked endlessly about it. I couldn't figure out the reason for the urge to kill that some of the guys seemed to possess. It was as if an internal demon morphed them into killers. Hopefully mine would stay inside and never surface.

That night we set up ambush alongside of what reminded me of a miniature version of the levee in New Orleans. The area was somewhat compromising but with a little imagination, we used the tall grasses to our advantage and stayed hidden. The location was creative and bordered on being a little more aggressive than we were accustomed to. It should have been a nice attempt at teaching tactics to our allies but they were having none of that. They wouldn't even attempt to pretend they were interested in being on ambush with us. They did a lot of standing up and were again giving away our position all night.

Boogie Man had already started to use the word SHORT. Pretty soon the second squad wouldn't have any of the guys I humped with briefly in the Crow's Foot. Floyd was expected to be the only one left out of the group. They picked up a black guy named Bracey who was from Los Angeles. He was another of the many street-wise black troops that had formed a legion in Vietnam. The inner city seemed to supply the war with most of the black troops. I couldn't understand the demographics behind the statistic but the black guys like Anderson who came from the rural areas were the real minority of the war. Bracey seemed to be very acquainted with Vietnam. He was definitely not a new arrival. He wore too many of the black braided wristlets worn by all of the black troops in country.

Our squad was going through a similar transformation. Most of the faces I had grown accustomed to seeing would soon be gone. It was unfortunate that we couldn't do our time together and most unfair to the guys being left behind. We depended heavily on the guys with a lot of time in country. The way those guys carried themselves was all the inspiration that I needed. They always exuded confidence and there was never enough of that commodity around in the field. I didn't feel, as if I had been around long enough to provide the kind of experience we were expected to lose when any of the guys in our squad left. Witnessing their departure was a gratifying experience just the same. We needed to see them get on the helicopter for the last time to make the trip back home. It had to be like a tonic to see someone make it through the entire twelve-month tour just to demonstrate that it could be done.

As darkness neared, the ARVN's were suddenly nowhere to be found and wouldn't be accompanying us on ambush. Their absence didn't exactly raise any eyebrows either. Ambush would be better without them and was expected to raise our confidence level a few notches. After lounging around the large plantation we had at our disposal, we left under the cover of darkness for ambush. During pacification, everybody patrolled every night. It was an attempt to spread our strength around and disrupt enemy movement. Our C.P. was made up of mostly Ruff Puffs by that time. Garson had nearly two dozen of those paper tigers and their CO with him every night. His RTO Edwards was the only GI with him.

Our ambush site was in a not too populated area of the village. In spite of its isolated location, it still could not be considered a free fire zone. We chose a spot that was near an elevated mound or knoll. The depression gave us a very secure area to defend if only Charlie would accommodate us by attacking from the right direction. As we were deploying our Claymores, we could see another patrol in the distance moving along a trail that straddled a nearby village. As they passed along the trail a figure popped up from behind some hedges and from a relatively close range raked the patrol with automatic gunfire. As the patrol jumped off of the trail and started returning fire, the attacker made a quick escape. Amazingly, no one was hit in spite of the close proximity of the shooters. "Did you see that?" I asked.

"Of course I saw it. It happened right before our eyes." Purvis answered.

"I'm talking about the tracers, man. They were green!" I said still shocked from my first sighting of a live enemy soldier even if it was from a considerable distance.

"Their tracers are green!" I repeated.

"And ours is red so what?" Purvis answered testily. My reaction had really started to wear on him. Having someone like me around would take some getting used to. Only someone as green as I was would come away from a near encounter with the enemy and be mostly impressed with the color of the tracers. "Let's be alert tonight. We know they're out here." said Purvis redundantly. He had to be kidding. After what had just happened, I thought it was pretty obvious. The guys played the Last Guard routine and we retired for the night.

The next sunrise actually stirred me from a deep sleep. I was never awakened for guard duty and we never pulled a stand to. Someone had obviously fallen asleep on guard. I sat up and scanned our ambush site and found Shave at the post sound asleep in a sitting position with his legs crossed and his head slumped forward. I didn't have the heart to be the one to bring the bad news to him. Instead I woke up everyone else up first to let the scene unfold. As I woke each individual up, the bright sun overhead made the same immediate impact on the situation. Then Black crawled over to wake him up. When he opened his eyes, he found the guy who was supposed to be relieved by him, standing over him. He turned and looked around only to find everybody packing and looking at him. He had made the ultimate mistake in the field. The implications were obvious; the vulnerability of our position was absolute. He knew that some GI's, according to legend, had reportedly been executed in the bush by their own for making such a mistake. Remembering how hard they all came down on me behind an allegedly dirty weapon, there was a sharp contrast to how sympathetic they were over Shave's situation. Shave's act was far worse than that little incident back at Beaver. I guess that my being so new and Shave being so short had something to do with it. Considering all that he still had to answer to; like, no response to sit-rep requests, or being pointed out to the lifers as the culprit; made you pity him more than anything else. We were very lucky to wake up at all.

The new day brought on another move to a new location. I had hoped it was not near the area where the kid threw a frag at those guys. The way we attracted kids, it would only add to my paranoia. I loved kids, and was not prepared to blow one away as a safety precaution or because of some preconceived notion. Wheelhouse always entertained groups of kids. He had no fear of what harm they could do. He always had candy or something else to give them. The kids sought him out every morning and flocked around him all day. He looked like the Pied Piper at work. "What are you giving away today?" I asked.

"Pudding. Want some before I run out?"

"I never tasted any before."

"Handy, you mean you never ate pudding?"

"Nope. I never tried the stuff." Pudding never made an entrance into my diet back home. I never thought that I was missing anything but Wheelhouse found it unbelievable. Not ever hearing about Virginia Beach or attending integrated schools, of course, had nothing to do with my choice of desert but I managed to raise his eyebrows again. He gave me a can and it was better than I thought. I even considered asking Barbara to send me a can or two when we got to our new location. Wheelhouse's entourage of little kids followed him to our new location. Maybe he was the Pied Piper of Tuy Hoa because he really enjoyed being with them and he seemed to derive more pleasure out of the war when they were around.

2

We reached our new location where a huge mountain that sat ominously in the middle of a very large populated area of Tuy Hoa. The mountain was about 500 ft. tall and seemed to be out of place in its setting. Situated at the base of the mountain was a considerable portion of the area's population. We approached the area from across a huge rice production field that dwarfed any other I had seen up to that point. The trail that led across the rice field was at least a couple of football fields long. To either side of us, the rice paddies extended all the way to the horizon. It took us almost fifteen minutes to make it to the other side. We were expected to link up with another company of ARVN's that I didn't think would be any better than the last group. One thing was for certain; they couldn't be any worse.

Garson, at first sight of the mountain, put together a patrol to recon the monstrous peak. I was glad that he passed on choosing me to go along with them. The mountain looked every bit like one of the hills that punished us during our stint in the Crow's Foot. The difference was the many dwellings that covered the lower portion of the slope. We took a seat on the ground and waited for the patrol to return. While sitting there, an old Papa San came by with a herd of water buffalo that he easily controlled with a small stick. Suddenly, they seemed startled and very testy at the sight of us sitting along the trail. It was almost as if they could sense something dangerous about us and were reacting to some bad previous experience. As they filed past us they all turned to face us and literally started walking sideways not taking a chance of letting us out of their sights. They were snorting and grunting as if they were ready to stampede us. "Don't move! Don't even flinch!" said Boogie Man as he sat motionless hoping that none of us new guys would make a sudden move. The herd of cattle was seemingly ready to react to any move we made. Maybe there had been some shooting incidents involving some of our troops and they all remembered the threat that we represented. I kept my finger on my trigger not knowing if an M-16 could bring down a water buffalo but I was ready to find out.

After the last animal passed us, we all breathed a sigh of relief. I couldn't help but feel like we had just avoided an ugly incident. Calvin was left behind to keep an eye on us until Garson returned. He liked it; being in charge that is. I wanted to ask him if it was all right to spread out a little to avoid the cluster fuck but my better judgment overwhelmed me.

Directly to our front someone had released a large number of chickens and pigs. It must have been the mating season because there was one rooster going around servicing every hen in sight. Every time he struck seemed like a mugging, with all of the squawking and feathers flying.

I actually considered shooting the damn terrorist to save the hens. The pigs were more co-operative though. There were mountings going on all over the field in front of us. There was also a very small pig with some very adult intentions. He walked up to every adult female and started to go through the motions like all of the older guys. His problem was that he couldn't have reached his target if he had a stepladder. The scene was hilarious and I laughed uncontrollably. Boogie man warned me that my laughing would arouse suspicion about my being under the influence of pot. After he said that, I mustered all that I could to bring it under control. It was the funniest thing that I had ever seen in my life.

We sat for a couple of hours listening to the radio while waiting for the patrol to return. There was a daily re-enlistment pitch on the radio played out in satire. It opened with the voice of an oriental speaking in crude English. It always brought out a few chuckles when we heard it. "Comrade Diem, the time has come for you to consider re-enlistment. As a bonus we will give you one box of bullets and a sack of rice." Then the sound of a rifle chambering a round was heard in the background followed by…"You have ten seconds to decide." Then a very American voice comes in offering anybody the opportunity to get out of the field by signing up for three more years. The promise of a different job away from the fighting was the real incentive or the carrot being waved in front of us. I'm sure that everyone had weighed their options and given it some consideration. I was very amused by the pitch but disappointed by the ploy. Nothing short of the "ten seconds to decide" ultimatum, however, was going to get me to re-up.

Garson's patrol finally returned as "Bridge over Troubled Waters" was being played for the second time which meant that it was about noon. Garson was smiling and that was always a good sign. He held his pow-wow with the squad leaders and then sought to locate the new company of ARVN's. Purvis said that they would be arriving soon and I only hoped that we wouldn't have to conduct a search for them like we did for the previous group.

The company of ARVNs started coming into view from the far end of the rice paddy. They were on line, stretched across the horizon making a sweep of the area. They were wearing the starch fatigues like the last group was. Although they were sweating, Black still lowered his head in disgust. His dislike for the Ruff Puffs ran deep in his veins. He acted as if he hated them more than the enemy. When they finally finished their sweep and assembled near us wiping the sweat from their brow with some very clean white hankies, we weren't impressed. We left them for the rest of the day and would only rejoin them later when for ambush.

Boogie man became ill and had to be taken out of the village and rushed to a hospital. In spite of his many past insensitive remarks, I was concerned about his condition. Bueno said it seemed serious enough to have him taken away immediately. The old second squad was losing its identity. All of the guys were disappearing from the fold.

Working a village at night was unreal. Unlike the mountains or the jungles, there were civilians everywhere. Naturally, it was going to be harder to find as many well-concealed areas to hide in. Our sight discipline was going to be challenged for sure. The area we finally settled in was equally as compromising as anywhere else in the village was. We were definitely going to be an easy target in Tuy Hoa. My fear was just how much longer pacification would last.

When sunrise came, I noticed a pattern had developed. Everybody became depressed in the evening right before ambush and then happy at sunrise. Our spirits would rise and remain high throughout the day and then the night would rob us of our enthusiasm. The last pacification mission was still fresh in the minds of those who were around the year before. Nobody talked much about it and it only increased the fear of the unknown factor to it. There were a lot of booby traps then and that's all they ever mentioned about it. The guys in my squad talked about it even less. Shave, however, always spoke about a night they spent in a place called Phan Thiet when sappers got inside of their perimeter and did some damage.

All of the heads gathered at an abandoned two-story dwelling and started an all day party. Good friends, good dope and good music was about all we could expect out of life. I sat next to Doc John and started to write a few letters home when Al informed me that the Post Office was on strike. I started to panic but figured that if anybody's mail would be delivered, it would be ours. "Handy, is it true that on Mardi Gras day anything goes?"

"No Doc, in fact Parish Prison gets filled every Mardi Gras with people who think so."

"Parish Prison? What's a Parish Prison?"

"It's like county jail in K.C. In Louisiana we have parishes instead of counties."

"When I get out of Vietnam, I'm coming to see the Mardi Gras."

"I'll see you there."

The hookers were out in force everyday. One of them in particular had become somewhat of a favorite because of her persistence rather than her preferred trade. She had already seen better times and was, by then, less attractive than most of her younger counterparts. Out of desperation, she tried to make up for her advancing age and declining beauty with tenacity. Her heavy-handed approach, however, was more a source of comic relief than anything else was. We called her Maggot and she always thought that we were calling her Maggie. The misunderstanding was hilarious. Everybody was short on money but the hookers kept showing up as if we might start printing some for them. Naturally there was nothing that the guys could do for them until April came around.

When the sun went down Garson and his huge entourage of Ruff Puffs accompanied us on ambush. I could have sworn that he had a preference for our squad in spite of our non-conformity. With his temper under control, he was not that bad to be around. Newly commissioned officers like him were big enough of a deterrent to keep me from ever considering a career in the Army though. I couldn't imagine having over twenty years in the Army and having to take orders from someone who hadn't lived as long.

Garson chose a cemetery near the base of the mountain as an ambush site. This was nothing new because we spent a few nights in one at Beaver where that hooker and her 10-year-old pimp worked. I had actually spotted three at Tuy Hoa since we arrived. The graveyard that Garson chose for that night must've been inhabited by some of the "Haves". Each plot was very elaborate. We tried to bed down on top of one made of red granite slabs. The burial spot was in the middle and a fence was constructed around it. The entire plot, including the fence was made of granite. It was very uncomfortable trying to sleep with the gagged edges poking us at every angle. With two dozen Ruff Puffs around, no one was about to sleep. They would've stolen our socks off of our feet if given the opportunity.

The moon was very bright making everything and everybody highly visible. Suddenly Garson thought he saw an intruder through his binoculars. Speaking a little too loud, he claimed that he could see him moving along the periphery of our ambush site. He then got on the horn and while talking to Mercein, he spoke two unmentionable alphabets. [V.C.] It started a panic that quickly spread throughout the entire ARVN contingent. One of the little cowards repeated Garson...BEE CHEE! BEE CHEE!! Before long, the terrified ARVN soldiers were stampeding us. After I was stepped on by two of the retreating bastards, I lost control and started swinging at every one of them that came in my direction. I slugged two of them and they both got up and came again. I grabbed one of them, picked him up and threw him back down the mountain. He also got up and continued to run away. They were all struck with crippling horror. As I stood watching them scramble up the mountain, yelling ... BEE CHEE! I felt outraged at being deserted by the so-called men we were supposed to be fighting alongside. There was no stopping their retreat. I felt tempted to start shooting at them. Garson was laughing his head off at my attempt to force them to stand and fight. It must have been hilarious because there was no one to fight. They were terrified at the mere prospect of facing Charlie. During the briefing the CO delivered before we came to Tuy Hoa, Black insisted they would run from a firefight. What he didn't tell me was that they would also run from their own shadows. It made me re-think my situation. If a half dozen GI's took a dozen Ruff Puffs out on ambush, we would have been asking for trouble. If Charlie came looking for a fight we would have been outnumbered, outflanked and eventually overrun. Pacification was a formula for a disaster waiting to be activated.

The following morning, before we could separate from the rest of the platoon, Garson informed us that we were scheduled to have a mini R&R at a nearby beach. The choppers were already airborne and headed for our location. Before long, we were airborne and on our way. "I wonder if they have any boards? " Wheelhouse asked.

"I hope not, 'cause a guy can get killed doing that shit." I answered as I wondered what it would have been like for my family to find out that I drowned in the S. China Sea surfing while at war.

"Handy, you don't know what you're missing."

"I think that it will be more appropriate for me to just sit and watch the surfers do all of the surfing. Black guys don't surf anyway."

"You know you're full of it. I grew up watching black guys surf everyday. Not many but some."

"Well you won't see this one out there today."

When we arrived at the area we were disappointed to find out that it was no real R&R site. At least not like the one at Qui Nhon. It was just an area designated for us to unwind, I suppose. The place was a poor imitation of an R&R site. The water was too rough for the swimmers to swim in and there were no boards for the great Kahuna Wheelhouse either. It was a bigger disappointment to the rest of the guys than it was to me. I was more than content to sit indoors and watch the film of the Super Bowl that I missed. It was kind of special to watch the game being played in a stadium that I was so familiar with. The game's first touchdown was scored in the South end zone where I once sat and watched the Saints play a preseason game.

It didn't take long for the boredom to set in. I almost wished we were back in the village then. They could never spoil us with R&Rs to places that had so little to offer. Wheelhouse managed to get over not being able surf. It was like some kind of obsession with him. The seas were obviously a lot different at Tuy Hoa than Virginia Beach or at least not to his liking. It seemed crazy for him to give up such a passion to come to Vietnam. Maybe I was just as crazy to not evade the draft. When our time came to return to the village, I had to separate myself from the movie projector and screen. They combined to give me a taste of New Orleans and I loved it. It wasn't the same as being there but was as close as I could expect.

After a measly 2 hours away we were whisked back to the village and deposited into Maggot's waiting arms. Maybe she thought we took a ride to the bank. It was by then time for all civilians to start finding something else to do for the remainder of the evening. It was definitely time for the hookers to return to wherever they came from daily. They couldn't have possibly been one of the villagers. Their presence would've never been tolerated.

Wasting no time, we were moving out to our designated areas almost directly this time. Garson would not accompany us for this patrol. He had far too many Ruff Puffs attached to him for me. Purvis was to take us to a spot not far away from the previous night's fiasco. I was, by then, able to laugh at it and refocus myself on going back out with another group of them.

Before we could fall asleep the quiet night was suddenly disrupted by the sound of another shoot out. Someone was in the shit. I was shaken by all of the machinegun fire and loud explosions. Hopefully, I thought, the sound of machine guns was either Al or Wheelhouse and not Charlie. The chatter on the horn was misleading. It sounded as it they were having fun. As long as they were enjoying themselves, there was no need for us to worry. After all Al could've been squeezing off a few rounds like he did that night in the An Lo's. In the midst of all the shooting, the talk on the radio had turned to near laughter. It couldn't have been a real firefight I thought. Not the kind that people die in anyway. It was unreal to sit and listen to the exchange and not be all too concerned about anybody getting hit.

The shooting and explosions came to a sudden stop. Then the C.O. and Garson conferred over the horn about the engagement. Since Garson was at the location it had to be a firefight and not just a bunch of guys having fun again. I wondered where the old bastard had been hiding since he deposited our asses in the village. I knew for sure that he wasn't with the company. It was obvious that he was making sure he didn't wind up in the body count he guaranteed. He played it safe by staying out of harm's way. Which was not exactly what I called leading by example. It was no leadership at all. Our lives, seemingly, meant even less. To him we were as expendable as a box of bullets. He was right about Tuy Hoa being a hot spot and Charlie was not about to leave just because the Herd had arrived.

After ambush, I couldn't wait to get a blow by blow report from the guys who were in the fight. I wanted a feel about what it's like to get into a firefight. All the training in the world couldn't compare to the real thing. Pop up targets can't shoot back at you. They don't maneuver; they can't flank you; and they don't scare you at all. The attitude of the guys suggested otherwise.

They were full of swagger and acted as if they had just taken part in a play. Everybody was on a high laughing about the firefight, the cowardly ARVN's running out on them and everything else. They were so caught up with their retelling their own personal involvement to each other, that I couldn't get their attention. I was made to feel as if I were on the outside looking in. I had definitely missed out on something that was maybe thrilling. They continued talking but I couldn't get one reply from any of them. I had to wait for them to come down from the tremendous high. They had all walked on the wild side and lived to talk about it. All I could do was listen to them.

We had an unscheduled resupply to replace all the ammo used during the firefight. Although the little battle only lasted for a few minutes, the guys managed to use up quite a few rounds of ammo. Jackson, as did a lot of other guys, got his baptism during the fight. He was not as jubilant as the rest of the guys were but at least he did get his feet wet. He was no longer a rookie. He had become a combat experienced veteran. I on the other hand, had yet to fire my first shot in anger and was beginning to feel like the odd man out.

When the helicopters started to land I could see that there was still some mail coming in. The recent news of the strike by the Post Office really caught me by surprise. I not only didn't know they had a union, I didn't know that any contract was being negotiated. My oldest brother Robert worked for the P.O. He never said anything about it. Of course he never even wrote.

On board were Mercein and the battalion X.O. (Executive Officer) I guess they came out to smell the smoke from the firefight. It was disgusting to have them gloating over putting our lives on the line, or complaining about not coming up with any dead bodies for them to count. The high command believed that Charlie's efficient manner of not leaving any bodies around was an attempt to deny us an accurate count. I never believed it though. We were so hell bent on getting a body count that we, as was policy and standard practice, searched for evidence of bodies being dragged away and factored them into the count. Unfortunately for the keepers of this mentality, our first encounter with the enemy produced no dead bodies and none of those artificial drag trails for them to count either. Personally I couldn't imagine any side leaving their dead behind if it could be avoided. Recon got a few guys fragged trying to recover Sgt. Washington's body in the An Lo's and it wasn't about any body count either.

The battalion XO(executive officer) a Lt. Colonel, walked over to where we were lounging around and as he approached, Purvis called us to attention and whipped out a snappy salute.

"All the way sir." He said in true airborne fashion.

"Airborne." Our high ranking visitor responded as he returned his salute. "The mini R&Rs were instituted so that you could get a break from the action. Did any of you get to see some of the "Round Eyes" stationed on that compound?" Round Eyes, I imagined were American women. This was supposed to be a treat for us to see American women after being around Oriental women who were known to people like the XO as "Slant Eyes."

"Were rotating platoons daily now." He said. I didn't know what he was talking about. All I saw over there was the S. China Sea and the Super Bowl film. "Are there any hookers around here?" Are you getting any pussy?" He asked which surprised most of us.

"Well keep up the good work men, and thank you." He said.

I picked up my mail and just watched the newly crowned warriors reload their empty magazines with some new bullets. There was an air of exclusivity about them that really made me feel uninitiated. Something was happening to me because I started feeling like I wished that I were a part of that club. I wanted to get into a firefight just to feel like I was one of the guys again.

"Is that letter from Barbara?" Doc John asked.

"Yeah, my only letter today."

"Can I read it when you're finished?"

"Okay, let me go over it a couple of times first."

"Can I go over your photo album while you're reading?'

"Doc you're coming up with some weird requests, but if you want to read my mail or look at my photos it's all right with me. I am not going to be the one to say no to the medic."

"Is that your son on Barbara's lap?"

"No it's not my kid."

"There are Boo coo pictures of her and the baby.

"Yes there are."

"Are you sure he isn't your kid?"

"Didn't you already ask me that question?"

"Yeah but he looks just like you Handy."

"He's not my kid Doc."

"Handy, you can admit it to me man. I'm your friend."

"Gimme that album. Here read the letter Doc and tell me what is it that makes you say some of the things you say?"

"I don't know but did I tell you that back home they call me "Babe," after Paul Bunyon's blue ox?"

"Why Paul Bunyan's ox? I mean what is the reason for it?"

"Well in other words they think that I'm as dumb as an ox I suppose." He laughed before coming to Barbara's patented closing to every letter. "Love till Hell Freezes Over."

"Handy, that's going to be a long time." He said with another laugh.

In the distance there was a horde of soldiers and vehicles coming our way. Garson said they were Korean engineers coming to replace the wooden bridge at the near end of the trail we took to get to our new location. The bridge spanned a channel that connected the rice paddies to a reservoir used for irrigation. The stream was at least 10 ft deep and 20 ft across. The job of rebuilding the bridge shouldn't have involved more than a dozen men. There were at least three times as many men getting off of the vehicles. They were all fully armed and appeared ready to do battle. They crossed the bridge, walked past us, moved up the mountain and all the way through the populated area at its base. When they emerged beyond all of the homes, they started shooting their way up the uninhabited part of the mountain. As they continued their assault, I couldn't imagine what they were shooting at. I figured that we couldn't have been so blind so as not to see so many enemy soldiers hiding just beyond the village. The Korean soldiers were really making a big fight out of almost nothing. "Those ROK's are some ass kicking soldiers." said Al.

"Rocks?"

"Republic of Korean soldiers, we call them ROK's.

"I forgot we weren't the only foreign troops over here."

"Oh yeah, man there are Australians, Thais, Turks and some other countries involved here.

He said referring to SEATO (Southeast Asian Treaty Organization), the alliance of non-communist countries in the region that, by decree, had sworn to support and come to the aid of each other whenever under aggression. This allegiance had already created a huge number of US dead in the name of political ideology. It seemed disproportional considering our geographical location in another hemisphere. I remember seeing the acronym in one of my class books when I was a little kid. I just couldn't figure out how we found ourselves in that brotherhood of S.E.Asian countries, or more significantly, who or which S.E. Asian country could we depend on to come to our aid when and if we ever came under aggression. The remoteness of our ever coming under attack by any country or being assisted by any SEATO nation only made our involvement in Vietnam that much harder to for me to accept or understand.

After the Koreans finished their assault, they returned to our area and shared some time with us before they started their work on the bridge. The ROK's treated us like gods. We were not worthy of all of the worship and praise they heaped upon us. I didn't think we were as good as they were but they never seemed to run out of gestures to make toward us. I guess they felt that a great debt of gratitude was owed us for what we did for their country some twenty years earlier. Once they finished exchanging pleasantries with us, they started replacing the old bridge. "You're just going to have to get used to the special treatment because they really like us paratroopers." said Al.

"Yeah the ROK's don't fight the war the way that we do." said Wheelhouse.

"What do you mean?" I asked.

"If they suspect that a village is a V.C. stronghold, they wipe it out."

"No shit. Are you serious?"

"These guys don't play around." He said. I supposed he was right. Considering these ROK's were only engineers, I could only imagine what their combat units were like.

Garson asked Purvis for some names for promotion and he submitted mine along with Diaz's. Speedie was busted down to E-2 when the lifers caught him with the drugs. He didn't expect any true consideration from the lifers though. Jones had been an E-3 for the duration of his tour. I'd heard tales about how minorities had problems making rank in Vietnam. Assuming the stories were true, I decided to approach the matter the way Speedie did. He couldn't care less about rank and rarely spoke of the issue. At least that's the way he appeared to deal with it while continuing to perform his duties.

Wheelhouse took me to a place that was somewhat of a combination grocery store/deli. The place was stocked with lots of can goods. They had a lot of local cuisine to order and eat at the tables. The proprietor was glad to have our business. "I come here everyday," He said as he took out a bag of green marijuana and spread it out on one of the tables. Wheelhouse was not really one of the heads but never passed up an opportunity to be sociable. Being in possession of a bag of green grass was a bit unusual just the same. "With all of the ready rolled dope in this country, why go through all of the trouble?" I asked

"Just something to do. Try the rice bread and the sauce." He said as he ordered some for me.

Black and Speedie walked in and spotted the green marijuana on the table. Speedie inspected it closer and, assuming it was being sold at the establishment, ordered some. "No man, that's for me." Wheelhouse said.

"Why are you smoking that green shit?" Speedie asked ignoring the fact that he had just ordered some when he thought it was available.

"He's not smoking it. He's just drying it out." I said with a mouthful of pink salmon wrapped in rice bread. "You're a weird mother fucker Wheelhouse" Said Speedie as he took a seat at one of the tables and ordered the pink salmon/rice bread combo. The rice bread was actually a pasta product made from rice. It was a tasty meal, especially when dipped in the spicy sauce made from unknown sources. I had been told that eating Vietnamese food was more a risk and definitely an adventure. The locals were also said to eat dogs and cats. I decided to play it safe and avoid any of their suspicious meat dishes. Cultures do vary from continent to continent and in spite of the differences, I couldn't imagine anyone eating a household pet.

Bracey walked in looked around and left seemingly unwilling to fit in at all. He would've clicked with those two ghosters I was with back in December. As I suspected earlier, he had obviously been in country long enough to get tired of the war and was definitely not a new guy. Everything else about him was kept close to the vest. He was as unrevealing to the rest of the guys as he felt he needed to be. Nobody wanted to get killed in Vietnam but many guys in country enlisted for a tour fighting the war and then changed their minds once confronted with the realities of combat. The recent firefight left him rattled. He already knew that Tuy Hoa was no picnic. He wanted out in the worst way and appeared to be looking for a way to get out of his predicament. The Vietnam War was no secret and no one needed to come to Vietnam to realize that people die fighting wars. In time, we hoped, he would realize that we were all on the same boat and equally afraid of dying fighting a war that had already lasted too long.

After we were resupplied, everybody made a quick exit for their favorite daytime spot. We had to get away from the curiosity seekers who had become a major problem. We knew Charlie was somewhere in the crowd watching us. He knew everything he needed to know about us by then. We were definitely at a disadvantage. Our biggest problem was the Ruff Puffs.

Later that day, we bathed near a well that was owned by some lady who didn't seem to object to our presence on her property. Black didn't care what the old woman thought about our being there. We got dressed and moved to another spot to keep the lifers guessing about our exact location. We even charted a course through the village to keep away from the road. We settled at the two-story house we used the day before. It was ideal because from upstairs we could see all avenues of approach. Nobody could sneak up on us there. We could also establish an area that would be off limits to potential thieves. It worked fine because once we set up in our area, only peddlers, pushers or hookers could approach us.

Much later that evening, we started getting ready for our rendezvous with the rest of the platoon. It was time to do what we came to do. It felt eerie because everybody became quiet and serious. We were like a different group of people. The village was emptying rapidly as a mass exodus of civilians flowed to unknown destinations for then night. We remained in position and then headed to our staging area. We arrived early enough to allow Purvis to get our grids for the night. When "Rainy Night in Georgia" started to play we knew it was time to go into our sound discipline routine. I really liked the song no matter how much it made me miss my girlfriend.

When darkness arrived, we all silently moved out under its cover to our ambush site in the rice paddies. We settled in a graveyard located in the middle of it. The flat terrain made it hard to avoid detection and put us into one of the most compromising situations. Complaining was pointless as all sound was forbidden at that moment. Purvis used hand signals and only spoke into the radio.

We arrived under a moonless sky and immediately deployed our Claymores and trip flares. In spite of the darkness, the open terrain made it necessary to literally crawl around our ambush site to avoid giving away our position from a distance. It was not exactly an ideal spot for a late night bowel movement either. Pulling guard was nearly impossible when lying in the prone position. It was like an invitation to fall asleep. Paranoia was the only thing that kept me awake during my shift. We had to watch out for Charlie; because he had made his presence felt. We also had to keep an eye on the Ruff Puffs sector of the perimeter. If Charlie knew exactly which part of the perimeter they occupied, he could have wreaked havoc by attacking from that direction. Vietnamization was a load of manure Nixon had sold to the public and I doubted if anyone back home really knew just how bad it smelled. From where we were sitting that night, the odor exposed it for what it really was. Bullshit.

When the sun came up again it was a relief. My spirits naturally picked up and so did everyone else's. With another day lopped off of our tour we felt that we had something to feel good about. Tuy Hoa was turning into the kind of mission that would make one want to celebrate each sunrise. As we moved to rejoin the rest of the platoon, we noticed that the villagers were returning. That firefight must have alerted them to the dangers of spending the night at home. There were hundreds of them streaming back like rush hour on foot. As I then recalled, the evacuation had been going on for the previous couple of nights. I just hadn't been paying attention to it. They probably spent the night in downtown Tuy Hoa if I could call it that. Garson, while in the middle of one of his mood swings, stopped Al and inspected his machinegun. He declared it dirty and flung it into the rice paddy in his wildest temper tantrum to date. Al went ballistic over the incident. "What the fuck are you doing?" He screamed while standing jaw to jaw with Garson who was equally as loud.

"That mother fucker needs cleaning!"

"You threw it out there, so you'd better go get that mother fucker!" Al replied as they continued to go at it with each other. Calvin tried to intervene but was ignored as the fireworks continued to fly. I took a seat on my rucksack to watch the whole show. Garson was way out of line. I couldn't understand his motive. I always thought that he and Al were close. They seemed to share a friendship that could never turn into something as wild as the scene unfolding before us.I was about to start wagering on who was going to win the fight, when cooler heads started to prevail. Garson even went out into the rice paddy to retrieve the weapon as I detected a little smirk on their faces. Both of them were full of it. Garson walked away. "Let's go." Al said.

"What was that all about?" I asked

"Nothing." he said with a smile.

"Did you guys stage that whole thing?" I asked as he laughed and kept on walking to the grocery store. Wheelhouse was already there with his green marijuana on the table. We all filed in and made ourselves at home. The music was playing and everybody was eating or drinking. As usual we were enjoying the daytime. "What's going on in here?" Garson said as he surprised us with a visit. He looked around the place to see who was in attendance. He spotted the green marijuana on the table and asked about it. "It must be for that guy." Black said as he pointed to the storeowner. Garson knew better. He only wanted to demonstrate how careless we were when we were away from the group. "You guys are half-stepping." he said before leaving almost as suddenly as he dropped in. He was right. Charlie could've sneaked up on us the same way Garson did. After he made his wake-up call, we decided to leave the grocery store and return to our 2-story fortress for the remainder of the day. "What ever happened to Phelam?" I asked.

"I don't know. He hasn't been out here for a while now." Al answered. Phelam's absence became very noticeable after the shooting began. Phelam was always emphasizing his second tour status as if it was both his badge of honor and courage. He should have been in the field exhibiting all of the knowledge and expertise that came with wearing the aforementioned badge. Instead he pulled a disappearing act when we needed people the most. I would've taken

Bear over Phelam any day. Unfortunately Bear was still down with malaria and I didn't know when or if he would ever rejoin us. For the first time in my military life, I understood what real leadership was. From where I stood, it meant having someone to instinctively turn to in those moments of self-doubt; not some asshole pushing you around just because he is in charge.

The ability to lead should have been a prerequisite for the job, but here were too many imposters carrying rank in the Army.

When we arrived at our hangout, there was a crowd of new hookers waiting for us. They were all much younger and more attractive than Maggot. I assumed they were hookers because it only takes one of them to sell grass. They had to be looking for some company. I momentarily suspected that the battalion XO had something to do with their arrival but decided there was no way he would consider it. It would have been more appropriate for him to supply us with some cash first. The girls had a better chance of doing business, I thought, with the non-smokers at the other end of the village. The straight guys didn't spend their money on anything but beer and soda. They had to be in possession of more MPC than we were. To bad the girls came at such an inopportune time. Had they arrived a couple of days later they would have done a ton of business.

In spite of our lack of funds the new hookers continued to feel us out. I didn't know enough of their language to tell them that I was broke. Wheelhouse, on the other hand, was engaged in conversation with at least a couple of them. His Vietnamese was working just fine for that moment as the party continued without their favors. It was amusing the way they continued to wait for some MPC to materialize after being told there was none.

Dowd finally decided to join us at our end of the village. Pretending to be one of the straight guys could have only lasted for so long. He came to the realization that he could enjoy himself and still be an

E-5. Dowd was a slightly built little white guy of about 5'8" and maybe 140 lbs. He was wearing a knife on his boot that wasn't Army issue. He let me inspect it closer. It was stainless steel and quite different from anything else given to us from supply.

"It's for scuba diving. It's used for cutting yourself from the underwater growth that can entangle a diver. My wife bought it for me."

"Wife, you mean you're married?"

"Well you know how it is. She couldn't wait."

"My girl wanted to get married too, but I insisted we wait until all of this shit is history." I said. Barbara would've jumped at the chance to get married before I left for Vietnam, but she had some weird parents who would have stood in the way of anything we wanted to do. Dowd not only had a wife, he also had a kid. War was not exactly something I would recommend for any family man.

Maggot was pissed about all of the new and younger competition around. She was ready to kick someone's butt over the intrusion. I decided to stay out of harms way by writing a few letters to some of the two dozen people that made up my list of correspondents. I even managed to write Gathar another letter to maintain that close link we had formed in training.

We had become nothing more than a couple of pen pals checking up on each other. Writing someone who was also in country, I assumed, was rare. The only thing rare about us was that we had finally been separated. I wished I could have dropped a line extending my condolences to Jones. He had to be coping with a lot at that moment. With the loss of his father and his upcoming return to the war, it was all a young man could deal with I supposed.

I finished writing during AFVN's Country and Western Hour. I had been listening to so much hillbilly music in Tuy Hoa that I had started to appreciate it. There was one song I really liked by a guy named Joe South titled "Walk a Mile in My Shoes." The song really hit home with me and I suppose a lot of other troops in country. The lyrics said it all…"Before you abuse criticize and accuse, walk a mile in my shoes." Every time I heard it, I felt as if he wrote the song about guys like us and had to be singing to honor us.

After we wrapped up another day of leisure, we packed our gear and moved to our rendezvous point with the rest of the platoon. The days seemed very short to us. I supposed it was because of the fun we had whenever we gathered. Along the way we found ourselves in the midst of what had become a daily mass evacuation of civilians. We had to walk at least 100 meters with them and most of them had started to regret our coming to Tuy Hoa. There was a look of scorn on more than one face I noticed. I sensed we hadn't exactly convinced them that we could make an impact on the situation and I couldn't blame them for feeling so.

We hooked up with the rest of the platoon and received the grid co ordinates for ambush. Our spot took us past the grocery store and up the mountain to an open area that I didn't like very much. I felt as if the area was compromising to our safety. I whispered my disapproval to Purvis but was ignored. The scene we made had become all too common. I had become a pain in his ass and he knew how to ignore me when the time was right. He was as irritating to me as I had become to him I supposed. The opium-laced joints I had been smoking all day had me extremely paranoid about our ambush spot.

About an hour after my shift at the post had passed. Another shootout erupted at one of the ambush sites. Someone was in the shit again and judging from the talk over the horn, it seemed like a repeat performance from the previous firefight. Their confidence level was also as high as it was then. Mercein must've been waiting this time because he picked up the horn and weighed in almost immediately. He was more intense than the actual combatants. He was actually trying to coordinate the firefight from wherever he was over the horn. But from where I sat, he was nothing more than another voice cluttering up the airways with unnecessary chatter. No one was paying much attention to him as the two sides seemed to be well engaged. The amount of machinegun fire suggested a firefight dominated by both Wheelhouse and Milles. In training, we were taught that it was always a good situation whenever the M-60 could draw a bead on its target. One of the bursts was extremely long.

The battle lasted about fifteen minutes and then ended suddenly with no reports of casualties. Fifteen minutes is short but even one minute in a firefight was like an eternity. All engagements, I hoped, would be as quick. I also hoped they would all end the same way our first two in Tuy Hoa did; without any loss of life. It had a very euphoric effect on the participants the last time. I fully expected the same spirited response out of them again. The more immediate aftermath, however, had a strange scene unfolding. The C.O. was again dominating the airways with his pompous bluster and, not impressing anybody with it. His tirade did seem odd at the time. The noise he made over the horn was more self-indulging than anything else. It made me feel as If I was in the middle of a weird movie that wasn't ending fast enough. The firefight had ended and he seemed to be just getting warmed up. "Where is the old bastard anyway?" I asked Purvis as the C.O. continued to bitch and moan about nothing in general.

"Tuy Hoa Air Force Base." He replied which should have been the safest place to be for the night. I'm sure that whoever he was talking to was equally unimpressed with him. If he really wanted to make an impact on the situation, he should have walked that mile in our shoes. If the saying about old soldiers never dying was true, it was because there was always a lot of young ones doing the dying for them. Just the same, it was disturbing the way the tough guy came up with the mission for us and then hid out with the Air Force guys. The NVA's commanding officer was out there every night with his men. He had to be in order to keep carrying the fight to us. Maybe the war was always fought without the Captain around. Undoubtedly, getting involved with the actual shooting was not what his job was all about. I just expected more than some voice barking out commands over the radio from a safe distance. He owed us more than that.

Our squad went on alert as soon as the first shot was fired. The last few hours were spent doing an extended stand to. Of course the sorry collection of Ruff Puffs would have never made the move with us if the situation had called for it. As allies went, they were nothing but dead weight. We were truly in a world of shit without any asswipe. At first light we ditched our Ruff Puffs and joined our own to get a report of what happened. There was sure to be another one of those unscheduled resupply days to replenish all expended ammo. It could also mean another visit by those two ranking assholes. I wanted to talk with the guys about the firefight but I didn't want to see Mercein or have his superior ask me if I was getting laid often enough.

The evacuees were returning at the same time. We didn't have to walk far to get to the resupply area which was within hailing distance of our ambush site. The villagers were in a hurry to check for damage to their property. The fireworks were probably visible from where they spent the night. I was sure that it made for more than a few anxious moments sitting watching and hoping for the best. Pacification was not shaping up to be the public relations effort that I had envisioned. It seemed more like an uncoordinated mission by two of the SEATO participants. The Koreans came in and rebuilt that bridge only after storming up the mountain in a saber rattling move and we were only fighting for our lives. In the process, the civilians had become mere observers as we used their village and their homes as a backdrop for combat.

When we came upon the combatants, they were as spirited as the day before. The guys were getting into the shit and laughing about it in the end. This was not what I expected war to be like. I couldn't imagine anyone laughing at the end of an engagement. I had to put the entire thing into perspective. First of all our squad had been extremely lucky. We were pitted against an aggressive foe at Tuy Hoa that could have easily done more damage than they had managed to do so far. Secondly, if they continued to come out to do battle with us, they would eventually cause some casualties. Finally, I needed to ask myself if I was prepared to deal with being shot at for the first time. One thing was certain, at the pace Charlie was setting he would eventually get around to it.

Wheelhouse said he almost burned his barrel off during the last firefight. I did remember a very long burst that was pushing the limit for one trigger pull. In training we were taught to only hold the trigger for no more than a specified amount of rounds for fear of the barrel melting. Wheelhouse probably couldn't afford to take his finger off of the trigger at that moment. "I ordered a spare barrel and a pair of asbestos gloves." He said. It would be just what he will need if he ever let his barrel get too hot again. He would have to change barrels in the middle of the firefight too. "Expecting to do it again?" I asked in jest.

"You never know. Once I centered my fire on their position, I just kept it going. I couldn't help it because they had a machinegun too."

Jackson was not as jubilant as the rest of the guys were. He wasn't too excited the day before either. I had to admit that I was a little bit jealous of my friend but he wasn't about to let his encounters with Charlie go to his head. He was not that kind of guy.

"That fucking Al is a trip man. Go ask him about what happened last night. You will not believe it." He said in exasperation. His reaction was totally different from the rest of the guys. Al and Garson were sharing a good laugh about the firefight.

"Handy! Wait'll I tell you what happened last night." He said still laughing.

"We were situated near a water buffalo pen when the firefight started. All of the shooting made the water buffaloes excited. They started freaking out man. They were threatening to break out of the pen. If they would have made the break, we would have been trampled us for sure. Then Garson grabbed that "Willie Peter" (White Phosphorus grenade) he had been humping forever and fragged them with it. It didn't take them out though. In fact, it only made them more agitated."

"Of course, that shit burns." I said.

"So I stopped shooting at the gooks and turned on the water buffaloes. Man, they must have taken at least 200 rounds before they dropped."

"You mean you killed two water buffaloes?"

"Yeah man, wasn't that wild?"

"Sure it is. What about the owner of the dead water buffaloes?"

"Don't worry; someone will be out here to pay the old fart off this morning. Uncle Sam pays off faster than any insurance company back home. I could have killed a hundred of them and he would have paid off just as quick."

"Where were you guys last night anyway, and where was Charlie?" I asked.

"They were shooting at us from that two story house we were using the last couple of days. We were on the edge of the rice paddy next to the trail. The other position was just up the mountain from us. We had them in a cross fire.

"From our two-story palace? What a coincidence.

The helicopters were bringing in more than ammo, mail and provisions. They also brought out a few new faces. I wondered if they knew what kind of operation they were walking into. It was not the kind I would've wanted to be baptized on. Of course as far as combat was concerned, I was just as green as they were. One of the new guys was assigned to our squad. His name was Dave Nichols. He was a freckled-faced white guy who looked a lot younger than the 21 years he claimed to be. Without the facial stubble, he looked more like he was about 17 tops. I expected him to age another five years before we left Tuy Hoa.

Al informed me that the old Papa San had been paid for the loss of his precious water buffaloes. "He's over there carving steaks right now for half of the villagers." said Al pointing to a long line of villagers waiting for their meat. He was probably charging them for each steak too. Good old Uncle Sam, the man with the deep pockets and the good intentions. Paying off that old man was the closest thing to pacification we had done in Tuy Hoa. Of course if we hadn't killed his cattle, we never would have had a reason to pay him. I wondered what the going rate for two water buffaloes was and assumed he probably picked up a nice profit for his loss. It was probably enough to buy four heads for the two he lost. After the rest of the villagers see what lengths our government will go through to compensate, they'll all be hoping for the same kind of accident to happen to them. Obviously the herd of water buffaloes that was so cautious around us knew exactly what kind of danger we represented.

There were at least two other new guys that came with Nichols or "Nick", as we had started to call him. I hadn't gotten a chance to meet either one of them as the platoon was continually changing over. By June, we were expected to have gone full circle giving us a totally new look. Floyd was the only guy left in Griffey's old squad. He was scheduled to be leaving for R&R the next day. Maybe, I hoped, his disposition would change once he got there. Anderson was rushed to the rear with some kind of sickness. Boogie Man was in a hospital in Japan. Of course, Jones was still home. Ricks took my place on the horn over there and once Floyd goes on R&R the following morning there would be nothing but new faces in the second squad. Up to that point they'd been in every fight we had in Tuy Hoa. It couldn't continue to happen that way. Of course during daylight, we tried not to get preoccupied with the war or the prospects of getting into the next firefight. There was too much fun to be had and the days were much too short. Anyway, as long as our spirit was high, we always could make the best of the madness. Calvin accused us of using drugs to help us get through the war. He said that we couldn't handle it and that we were using pot as a crutch. Personally I thought that it was the music that got me through the day. The pot, it seemed, only helped the music.

Occasionally my mind would drift and I would start wondering what life was like back home. I assumed that my being in Vietnam was putting a damper on everything for my family. I tried not to even think about anything bad happening to me while I was away. Family meant a lot to me. Having all of my close relatives writing and praying for me meant everything. I was envious of all of the guys that still had their fathers alive though. I wished that I had him to write like so many of the rest of the guys. The problem with the war in Vietnam was that nobody really cared about the guys in country except those who knew them personally, and loved them dearly. Once the loved ones returned, all concern ended for the ones left behind. Of course guys like us will always have a place in our hearts for each other. We were just too close to forget the bond. Without that personal connection we had no real value or worth to the consciousness of the American public. To them we were no more than just a bunch of guys caught up in the numbers game. Who could blame them? We weren't exactly trying to save the world. We weren't even saving the Vietnamese from anything that could be remotely mistaken as being a threat to their way of life. We were fighting for our lives and of course each other.

I found Wheelhouse standing with Edwards carrying a smoke grenade in his hand. They were not exactly engaged in conversation and seemed to be waiting for something or someone.

"I'm glad you came along. I need you to take a picture of me bringing in the slick that's delivering my gloves and spare barrel."

"Another picture? How many is this now?" Bringing in a helicopter incorporated the use of a smoke grenade and some hand signals. The smoke gives the pilot an indication of which direction the wind was blowing. Helicopter pilots always preferred landing facing the direction of the wind. After popping the smoke grenade, Wheelhouse's job would first be to hold his arms up as if he were being robbed at gunpoint. Then as the helicopter came up to his location and started to hover, he would extend his arms until they were out away from his body. Then he would tilt them in the direction that the helicopter was listing to give the pilot an idea of how much he needed to adjust. Once the craft's landing gear was close enough to the ground, he would then lower his hands pointing downward until the helicopter's skids were level with the ground. Once the skids were aligned with the landing surface, he would then cross his arms while still pointing them to the ground. The pilot, assuming that his craft was ready to touch down, would then place it gently on the ground completing the process. Or so it always seemed to me. The pilots always came in without that help whenever we were on a terrain as flat and well defined as a rice paddy. The procedure was almost mandatory if we were bringing in slicks on the top of a hill that had been cleared in preparation for these landings. Wheelhouse just wanted to have his picture taken doing just about everything that he could imagine. It was fortunate that the gloves and barrel didn't come in on one of the other slicks. Wheelhouse never would have otherwise come up with the photo opportunity. He chose a spot away from the rest of the group and all I had to do was shoot the pictures for him as he went through the motions.

Edwards popped the smoke grenade and tossed it allowing the wind to leave a signature on its direction. When the helicopter approached him for the landing, Wheelhouse was engulfed by a huge cloud of dust and debris caused by the helicopter down blast. We had forgotten to take into account the dry topsoil of the chosen landing site. It made for one very funny picture of him turning away and covering his eyes and face as the helicopter came in and landed without him giving any signals at all. This was the most memorable picture I had ever taken of him. He also gave the pilot of the helicopter something to laugh at. We retrieved the gloves and barrel and returned to the rest of the platoon.

Nick had by then taken the edge off by smoking his first joint with the guys and showed a willingness to fit in fast. Nobody had to tell him he was the new guy in the squad with everything to learn. He was a team player by heart. His youthful appearance helped make an easy transition from being a total stranger to that of one who could willingly be taken under wing. He was older than most of us but, somehow we just couldn't think of him as being so. To bad he couldn't come in during a quieter period. Things had started to get a little serious in Tuy Hoa. All of the post firefight banter was a misleading indication of just how serious our situation was. By that evening, however, he was fully initiated and had become one of us.

3

As our zero hour neared and all grids had been assigned, I couldn't help but notice that Dowd's squad started out a little early. Wheelhouse was with them and Al was with the first squad. It had to be early because Sly and the Family Stone were singing and that meant the sound discipline routine had not gone into effect. I wished at least one of the machineguns were going out with us. We hardly ever got one of those guys to hump with us since arriving in Tuy Hoa. I missed the days when we were in the boonies. I kind of got accustomed to having one of them with us. Still we had Moose, Ellis and of course Nick to give us that all-important strength in numbers which was very important to me. We waited until it was near dark to move out to our ambush site. It took us across the newly reconstructed bridge and for a great distance along the long trail that crossed the huge rice field. We had been in the area too long. There were no new spots to spend a night in. I hoped the mission would be coming to an end soon because we were beginning to look like an old bad habit. I had developed problems with our being so predictable.

Going out every night was a constant roll of the dice. I felt like praying but I remembered my brother Joe telling me about how prisoners would always pray for their release. It made me feel like one of those hypocrites who only wanted deliverance. I decided to wait until after the war was over for me and then give all of my thanks. A lot of guys had lost their lives in Vietnam and I was sure that most of them prayed for the chance to see home again.

As we walked along the trail, I realized it was the first time we had been that far out from the populated area since we arrived a couple of weeks earlier. Maybe it had been longer since we changed locations. I couldn't recall but if I had counted just the days, it would have seemed like very recent. If I had counted the nights, it would have been more like forever.

Purvis took us for a long trip down the elevated trail which made me feel unnecessarily exposed. Our high visibility made for a very creepy patrol. As we walked, I couldn't help but feel as though Charlie was lurking somewhere out in the area. We were vulnerable to a surprise attack that would have left us a considerable distance from the rest of the platoon. I couldn't see the logic in spreading out at that distance. "Why are we setting up so far away from the rest of the platoon?" I whispered to him totally unaware of where the rest of the ambush sites were.

"Handy, will you please let me handle this."

We finally turned off of the road and moved into our designated area in the middle of the rice paddies. Purvis found a spot that he no doubt felt comfortable with. We quickly deployed our Claymores and settled down for the night. There was no need in fooling myself, Mrs. Handy's favorite son was not about to close his eyes at that ambush site. I expected to be awake for the entire night. The Ruff Puffs were also awake. I was considering facing their direction to make sure they wouldn't steal anything when suddenly a loud explosion went off in the distance that sent a sonic boom echoing throughout the valley. It was louder than thunder and scared me senseless. I crawled over to the post to look for my watch because I figured that our night was at hand and I noticed that it was midnight. "I'm hit." Wheelhouse's voice crackled over the horn under extreme duress.

"Were on our way" I told him while strapping on the radio. Everybody was packing light meaning weapons and ammo only. We waited an extra minute for Nick to get ready. It was his first night in the field and he was about to get into the shit.

The cowardly Ruff Puffs were not expected to join us in making our maneuver to assist the second squad. They were sure that their comrades were by then high tailing it out of harms way. There was too much small arms fire and explosions going on by then to assume that there were any Ruff Puffs around except for the possible dead or wounded. Besides, our contingent of tin soldiers was not going to pass up the opportunity to steal everything that we were about to leave behind. I felt tempted to shoot every one of them on our way out but my ammo was too precious at that moment.

When Nick finally got ready we started to move out. He hit a trip flare and dove to the ground when it lit up the area. He was having trouble coping with his situation and who could blame him. I knelt beside him and gave him some bad news as I helped him to his feet. "Charlie knows were coming this time." I said realizing they had finally succeeded in wounding one of us and they knew we were about to move heaven and hell to try to get our wounded out. Seeing Nick struggle somehow gave me some inner strength and determination; enough to overcome the fact that I was about to also get into my first firefight. Another tremendous explosion then went off in the distance robbing me of all of my newly acquired confidence. "What the fuck is that?" I asked Purvis as we began our maneuver.

"It's a B-40 rocket."

"A B-40 rocket. And what is a B-40 rocket?" I asked as I continued along the trail leading to the second squad's rescue feeling more terrified and further stripped of all of my courage with each explosion.

"It's an anti-tank weapon Charlie uses."

"Anti-tank; we don't have any tanks out here."

"Do you think Charlie cares!" he screamed as we continued to close in our objective. In the distance, it appeared that the second squad was somewhere up the hill behind all of the dwellings. Moose was at point and was walking as if he was on his way to eat or get paid. Shave and Speedie, in spite of being extremely short, showed the same amount of eagerness to engage the enemy. There was no reluctance in either one of them. The distance, however, was starting to work against us. It seemed that we would never cover enough ground fast enough. My initial fear about our being situated so far out was centered on our being rescued. Somehow I never thought about our having to go to anyone else's rescue.

The sound of small arms fire was beginning to take a toll on me as we neared the scene. The occasional explosion of each rocket gave a gruesome picture of an already serious situation. Wheelhouse urged us to hurry and hearing his voice on the radio painted an ugly picture. If his was the only voice to be heard, it meant that both Dowd the squad leader and Ricks the RTO were possibly already dead or severely wounded. I couldn't hear but one machinegun firing so that meant that Young was possibly also wounded or dead. Their situation was only getting worse and we still had some distance to cover. Our rescue attempt was beginning to look like a waste but we continued to press on.

Each rocket that exploded had a disturbing effect on me. I was sure we had covered it in my training back in Tigerland but hearing it for the first time had me shaken. As we started nearing the wooden bridge, I saw our C.P. to my right. Garson was in that group and I didn't know for sure if the first squad was with him or not. Other than about two dozen ARVNs, about all he could count on was his RTO

Edwards. Moose started to run for the last 30 meters and we all followed at his pace. The awkward radio handset started to interfere with my advance. My wobbly legs didn't help either. The loud noise created by the firefight going on beyond the bridge started my heart to beat as hard as it did back at Beaver when Sgt. Washington was killed. As we started to cross the bridge, my radio handset became unhinged. I struggled to continue running while groping and fumbling with it as it dangled and wrapped itself around my right leg.

I finally regained control of the handset as we arrived at the edge of the village located at the base of the mountain. Everybody lined up in the prone position and started to fire in the direction of the village. They had obviously spotted a target while I was both running and fumbling with the handset. I was distracted just long enough to miss locating the enemy and was by then just shooting in the same direction as everyone else. A parachute flare popped overhead and lit up the air but I still could see no target. As I went through my first three magazines, I noticed how fast ammunition was expended in a firefight and realized just how precious our ammo was. After just two minutes had passed I started to make sure that I knew where my target was before firing another shot. The firefight had already lasted longer than the other fights and there was no way to determine how much longer it would be.

Purvis gave the order to flank a fire team to spread out our fire and counter any flanking move on Charlie's behalf. Moose, Shave, Black and Ellis made the move and set up about 40 meters to our left. The move started to pay dividends immediately. Shave was hitting his target as evidenced by the way he kept his eyes glued to his target as he reloaded his rifle. Their new position had placed them in full view of the attackers and put us on the offensive. On our fire team Speedie was laying down the most effective fire. The sightlines caused by the mountain's incline and our prone firing position made it impossible for us to be as accurate as Speedie was with the pronounced arcing trajectory of his grenade launcher. When he hit the tin roof of a schoolhouse with an H-E round, it exploded and showered the occupants with shrapnel. There was an unseen group of attackers using the building as cover to help form the L-shaped configuration that had the second squad isolated and cut off from us. As the flying shrapnel continued to do unseen damage to the flesh, bone and fighting spirits of its occupants, we could hear Vietnamese voices crying out in pain and terror. They were trapped inside of the schoolhouse and were being both terrified by the sound of each round fired from Speedie's tube and punished by its explosion as it shattered the roof with each detonation. They couldn't escape the building because we had each avenue of escape covered. We were bringing a good fight to an enemy that I still hadn't seen but we were not making any headway up the hill to rescue the second squad.

The first squad linked up to our far right for what we all anticipated would be an attempt to make the final push on the second squad's position. Then the C.O. took over the airways again and started to interfere with our communication with each other. He even gave our squad the command to leave our ambush site and get involved with the fight. He was just that far behind on our actual location and didn't realize that we had left our spot at least 20 minutes before he spoke up or woke up. Purvis took over the handset and began talking to him as the parachute flares continued to illuminate the area. They were being delivered by a FSB operating in the area. Being in a village, although unoccupied, kept them from delivering any high explosive rounds. As each flare ignited, the parachute slowed its smoky descent just long enough to keep the area lit up until the next one went off. Each flare rocked side to side as it slowly came down. The pendulum effect caused by the parachute made the shadows below dance eerily in opposite directions. We were taking part in a horror show and time was running out on the second squad. They were cut off and we knew that our assault to rescue them would be their only hope. Unfortunately, it also meant that we could possibly suffer more casualties on the way up the hill.

As Speedie continued to hammer away at the tin roof, we could hear the little bastards crying "I chieu hoi" every time he hit it. There was also a very domineering voice inside seemingly urging them to continue the fight. More like demanding their effort. Then I heard shooting from our rear. I turned to see if we had fallen into a trap and spotted about a half dozen NVA attackers making an assault on our C.P. Three of them were raking the area with AK-47 gunfire. One of them had a shoulder mounted bazooka type weapon, another one was loading it and, the last one was carrying shells for the weapon. All of the terrified Ruff Puffs were running away in a desperate retreat. The attackers were covered with a thin film of mud that glistened in the well lit field as they advanced on CP's position. They no doubt picked up the slime as they crawled through the rice paddies to their destination in order to make their attack. They looked like the ghosts that I used to refer to them as. The scene gave me the creeps.

Garson was already wounded in the arm and lying exposed to more gunfire. His RTO was trying desperately to drag him out of the line of fire as tracer rounds continued to pass over their heads and through their badly scattered ranks. The Vietnamese interpreter was the only one returning fire at the attackers. As Edwards struggled with Garson, the attacker with the shoulder-mounted weapon fired a round at them. The sight of the shell flying through the air leaving a trail of billowing smoke in its wake shocked me. "What the fuck is that thing?" I asked Purvis as I followed its flight over CP's location and watched it explode beyond the retreating Ruff Puffs.

"It's an RPG."

"RPG! What the fuck is an RPG?"

"Listen Handy, I don't have the time to give you the nomenclature of every weapon in Charlie's arsenal. Do you mind!!?" He screamed. He was right. I had to compose myself. We were the only ones within close enough distance to move to Garson's assistance. Their position was crucial and we had to maintain its presence on the battlefield. Allowing the little bastards to over run CP would be the beginning of the end of our battle.

Our other fire team quickly rejoined us and we made a mad dash back across the bridge. As we made our move to help Garson, a rocket, fired from our rear, flew over our heads and passed so close that I could smell the propellant. Our movement had altered the sightline and put us into the crosshairs of the same people we were shooting at moments earlier. The rocket startled Ellis causing him to scamper past me further disrupting our disorganized column as we hurried to CP's rescue. The noise we made crossing the wooden bridge alerted the little bastards to our approach. When we were spotted coming to the aid of Garson, they all fled into the rice paddies to escape us. We didn't have enough time to go after them because we had to get a medivac for Garson and return to the other rescue attempt. We rushed to his position and set up a quick perimeter of our own. There were weapons lying all over the place. Rifles, machineguns, grenade launchers, hand grenades, radios, ammo, they left everything. Their cowardice almost cost Garson, Edwards and the interpreter their lives.

Purvis called for a DUST-OFF for Garson while the rest of the guys administered first aid. In the meantime the battle raged on without us. Garson was extremely grateful for our coming to his aid but right about then we all felt that we were letting the second squad down. I hadn't heard from Wheelhouse in a while and began to fear the worst. There was still a lot of shooting going on over there and a huge cloud of smoke had formed over their location from all of the expended ordinance and flares. It looked like one of those medieval battle mists spun to cloak the attacker. It was frustrating just sitting around waiting for the helicopter to extract Garson. We were needed desperately on the other side of the bridge to continue our assault. Time was precious and was also running out on those guys up there. We needed the medivac to arrive quickly and pick up Garson, so that we would be able to rejoin the first squad and make the assault. Without us, they would have easily been out flanked and cut off like the second squad was.

The chopper finally arrived and Garson, as expected, was able to walk over to it. I didn't think he received any morphine injection either. He had to be in a lot of pain. Calvin, who was with the first squad, was left in charge. We expected to be back as soon as Garson was airborne. Our only hope was whether or not we had waited too long. As Garson walked over to the awaiting helicopter Mercein called for Purvis. I handed him the horn and could hear very clearly every word he spoke. "Listen, I want you to remain at your present location and secure all of the weapons the ARVN's left behind. We don't want those weapons to fall into the hands of the enemy."

"He's got to be crazy." I said. It seemed unlikely for us to sit and watch over the weapons while the second squad got overrun.

"We are going to follow orders." Purvis said setting up an unenviable situation for us. The second squad was counting on us. We were the only hope they had. Being the squad that usually marched to our own drumbeat made sitting just that much harder to accept. Just sitting was not what we had been trained to expect from each other either. Our friends were counting on us and we were being asked to let them down or rather just let them be killed. I started to wish that Bear was still with us but quickly realized it wasn't fair to compare what Purvis was doing to what I thought Bear might do in the same situation. It didn't make it any easier for me to sit and wait for it to end though. I was at an emotional low and felt totally worthless when I realized that someone in the second squad might have heard that last transmission by Mercein. If they did, they knew they were being sacrificed. All they could do was fight to the end and expect to lose their lives when they ran out of ammo. For all we knew, they were possibly already out before Mercein made his decision. Their fate was sealed and all we could do was sit and wait for them to be killed. I felt as if a very large piece of me was dying with the second squad. Wheelhouse was only 19 years old. He hadn't started to live yet. Young was probably the same age as Wheelhouse. Dowd had a family of his own. Floyd was supposed to be going on R&R in the morning. Ricks took my place in that squad. Bracey was one of the most recent additions to the platoon and even more recently added to the second squad. Tragically, one of the new guys who just came out with Nick was up there too. He never lasted 24 hours in the field. I never got to meet him and I didn't even get to know his name.

The helicopter took Garson who had earned both a Purple Heart and a ticket home. In its wake, the Ruff Puffs were slowly returning to the scene of their crime. Their cowardice in the face of the enemy was shameful. Of course in Vietnam, I doubt if there was such a crime and there was definitely no shame. Running seemed more the norm than standing and fighting. A couple of the cowards dragged one of their wounded to me. "I'm not the fucking medic!" I told them, knowing that they couldn't understand me. They started to point to the radio and obviously expected me to call a DUST-OFF for their friend. Unfortunately there were two separate procedures for calling in a helicopter for Vietnamese Nationals and American GI's. I only knew the procedure that we used and didn't even make the call for Garson as Purvis handled it for him.

The ARVN's started to get frantic about their friend's chances of survival. If they would have stood their ground and fought, they could have easily repulsed the handful of attackers. Probably could have wiped them out. They had a four to one numerical advantage but chose, instead, to get up and run. Their friend lying on the ground was an easy target. He got it in the back, and was expected to die because of his choice to expose himself to flying bullets. Obviously the enemy was emboldened by the ARVN's reluctance to fight. They knew that it would only take a few shots fired overhead to set off a panic in their ranks. There were only a half dozen men attacking about twenty giving an unlikely advantage to the attackers.

While lying on the ground, the wounded ARVN started to attract a crowd. Three more of his comrades moved closer and stood around him. As they all stood over their dying friend I wondered if anyone of them knew first aid or if there was a medic amongst them. It was possible that maybe their medic kept running and was by then somewhere near the Cambodian border or the South China Sea. Or maybe the dying ARVN was the medic. His death touched off a scuffle that soon escalated into a fierce battle among the handful of observers over the contents of his pockets. I was surprised to see as much fight in them. I took the radio and moved away from the pack of imitation soldiers disgracing themselves. I felt like crawling into a deep hole and dying and didn't feel as if I deserved to see the sun come up again. I was choking with grief and agony because I was unable to do anything about the second squad's predicament. I couldn't imagine how we could ever get past the humiliation. And I also wondered how much this would weigh on our next firefight. "Look, I can see them from here." Shave said as the sun started to rise. He had spotted the little bastards in the distance moving in on the second squad's position to finish them off. I couldn't bear to look. The hopelessness of it all was too much for me. They must've been scuffling over the contents of their pockets like the Ruff Puffs were doing over their own dead at our location. I felt beyond humiliated at that point. To sit and wait for the enemy to have their way with our dead was like having someone stab me with a dagger in my heart. I was suffocating with the humiliation and had never felt worse.

4

It was sunrise and for the first time in my life it was not a welcome sight. I used to look forward to its arrival but, not that morning. I felt so ashamed that I could hardly face the new day. "Nick, what's today's date?" I asked so that I could remember for the rest of my life the exact date I was humbled so badly. "April 1st." He said making matters worse. It was April Fool's Day. A day we were made to look like fools. Charlie really did his homework. After those two little hit and run episodes, he realized that if he could hit more than one position simultaneously, he could do more damage through all of the confusion. Of course he knew that whatever position he hit would be reduced in number when the Ruff Puffs ran out on us. Once we become badly outnumbered, school is out. By blending in with the crowd and studying us during the day, he also knew how many men it would take to overcome our firepower and wreak havoc on our maneuverability. This time he succeeded in overrunning one of our positions and inflicting a deep psychological wound. There was no doubt that he lost more men than we did. Shave and Speedie probably accounted for more kills between them. One dead GI, however, was far too many dead than I was willing to accept.

Somehow I overlooked a dead NVA soldier lying in front of us about 30 feet away. He was killed making the attack on CP and was left behind when we surprised them by coming to Garson's assistance. The lifers, I assumed, would drool over this. Their precious body count could start at one. We had given them what they had been longing for. The body count, however, came at a high price. By then we should've realized that Charlie was willing to lose the body count game to us. Their strategy was geared to winning the war of will and to outlast our resolve. We were further disadvantaged by Nixon's announcement of redeployment. Although the plan was welcome news to the voting public, it was even more inspirational to the enemy. He would continue to litter the battlefield with dead bodies and drag trails and at the same time claim that he was chasing us out of his country. Nixon's policy was to continue to count the dead bodies; present them as proof of Hanoi's belligerence to the voters and continue to prosecute his brand of warfare. Finally, when all of the troops are home, he would claim an honorable peace in lieu of total victory. The price of pursuing his so-called honorable peace had cost us an entire squad. His reward for it was expected to be a re election in '72. Our misfortune was to be drafted to fight for something as shallow as a President's foreign policy or die in the pursuit of his campaign for re election.

The biggest travesty was that there was nothing that could've been remotely defined as a total victory for us in Vietnam and nothing that we could have possibly demanded as terms of surrender. Five guys had to die in my first firefight before I realized just what a folly we had been involved with in Vietnam.

After going through the humiliation of letting the enemy have his way with our dead, the first squad assembled to make the trip up the hill. I had finally developed the same hate for the enemy that so many others had. I wanted to kill for the first time in my life and there wouldn't be any satisfaction until I'd killed a hundred of them. The enemy had become the gooks that our training cadre had always referred to them as and was desperately in need of killing. I wanted revenge in the worst way. I not only wanted to kill him, I wanted to mutilate his body and send him home to Hanoi in pieces or with my initials carved across his forehead.

Somebody fired a lone shot and quickly alerted everyone in our squad. The shot came from near the second squad's position. Maybe, I thought, we still had a chance to do some damage. Almost all of the Ruff Puffs had returned to retrieve their rifles and we no longer had to stand to watch over them or Lt. Garson because he had been extracted. For one brief moment I thought that I would get a chance to contribute the way I had been trained but it was not to be. The accompanying transmission over the radio told us otherwise. Watson was shot making that last move uphill by one lone shooter who was left behind to put one last dagger in our hearts. He fired one last parting shot at the advancing squad and managed to escape afterward. It was only a flesh wound in the neck but it was, nonetheless, another wound to our pride.

When they finally came upon the ambush site, Calvin started to identify the dead and called them out by name. "Wheelhouse, Welch, Young and Dowd." he said. Welch was obviously the new guy but this was only four. Bracey, Ricks and Floyd had not been accounted for. "We've found Floyd's body lying away from the rest. Ricks and Bracey are here now. Ricks has sustained a wound. So that's five KIA and two WIA." He said ending his transmission with our own body count and none from the other side. And of course all ARVN's managed to escape without a scratch. I hoped the C.O. was happy with his count. He had managed to send five young men to their graves in pursuit of it. I hated him almost as much as I hated the ones that killed those guys. I'll never forget the way he planted us in that one spot to watch weapons and gave up on the second squad. I'll never forgive him for it either. Although I didn't have to go up that hill to look at the dead bodies, standing with a bunch of cowardly imitation soldiers was no consolation. They were still trickling back and, I guess they planned to all be back in another two hours. No need in their taking any chances. They'd give us enough time to finish up first before they all returned. I went to stand near the dead NVA soldier to distance myself from the ARVN's who had contributed to the carnage almost as much as the enemy. As much as I hated the enemy, I did respect his willingness to fight. The dead one lying at my feet died fighting for his cause. The RF PF version of the ARVN would rather die running away.

The area around the dead NVA soldier was littered with pieces of paper with writing on them. Black picked one up and handed it to me after reading it. "Read this shit man." He said.

The crude leaflet had a message to the black GI. It read…

"Black man, why are you fighting this war for the white American government when your people continue to be discriminated against back home? Why are you fighting against the peace loving people of Vietnam who are struggling for the same freedom that is being denied you in America? Throw down you arms and join the war against your true enemy, the white government of America."

I was sure that the message was an overused line preferred by the enemy's propaganda machine. I should have expected as much considering America's history. His war of words fell short of his intended audience though. Of course all of the black revolutionaries back home and over in Vietnam would have agreed with the message but it would have been counterproductive for me to entertain those notions. It was too divisive to even consider at that moment. There was no race problem within our ranks, and I wasn't about to let the enemy conjure up one for me. I didn't like his method of delivering the message while shooting at us anyway. "Are you going to keep it for a souvenir?" He asked me.

"I wouldn't keep it for asswipe." I said as I threw it away.

A deuce and a half pulled up at the base of the mountain. I figured that our dead was about to be bagged, tagged and trucked out. A medivac helicopter arrived at the same time. Over the horn, however, the pilot expressed too much concern about the huge cloud of smoke that was still lingering over the area. He actually thought that the area was still hot. He then ended his transmission and left the area without even attempting to pick up our two wounded men. After hearing all of the stories about daring rescues made by those people, we had to get a wimp for a pilot. Our wounded had to be trucked out with our dead adding salt to our psychological wounds.

The villagers started returning about the same time the truck pulled out. The area was littered with little white parachutes. There were lots of them lying on the ground, in the trees and atop the thatched roofs. The little children were gathering and playing with them everywhere. They had grown accustomed to war and found it entertaining to collect the litter of our battle to play games with. We watched from a distance at our position until we were finally allowed to leave CP and return to our ambush site to retrieve what little the Ruff Puffs left for us. Along the way I started taking an inventory of what I left behind to be stolen by the little bastards. Among the personal items I left was my wallet. I always removed it from my pocket before retiring. There were quite a few pictures of Barbara in it along with thirty dollars. My brother Joe made that wallet for me too. Once we started packing for the firefight, I was focused on weapon, radio and ammo because nothing else mattered at that moment. I was concentrating on the trip and the possibility of not making it in time. The ARVN's were concentrating on their specialty and probably couldn't wait until we made the trip.

We arrived at our ambush site and as we expected, everything was stolen. Our empty rucksacks were strewn about the area as they made a complete haul of our personal items. Our contingent of ARVN's had taken everything but our Claymore mines. I suppose that there was nothing that they could do with an article of war except leave it on the ground as they made their escape. I'd like to think that we learned something that night but it was 1970 and we had been involved in combat for five years. The problem with the ARVN's should have been widely known at that time even if they were RF PF's. It seemed unlikely we were experiencing anything new that night. There were few new lessons to be learned but a lot of new blood to be spilled. At about the same moment those guys were losing their lives on that hill, another 100,000 or so politically naïve men turned 18 in America. Our misfortune was to come of age at the wrong part of the war and peace cycle that had become a part of being an American male.

On our way back to the resupply area, we came upon a commotion involving an old man carrying a pistol. He was being detained and protested his being held. He was lucky he wasn't shot on sight for carrying around a Saturday night special at the wrong time. The last thing he would want to be mistaken for is one of the bad guys by any of us. We were an entire company of short fuses waiting for someone to come along and light one of them. It was commendable of the guys to not let the situation boil over to that point in the face of what had just happened hours earlier.

I ran into the C.O. and told him about the items that were stolen from us during the firefight. He was so caught up in the battle's aftermath that he barely heard a word I said. When he promised me that my Geneva Convention card would be replaced along with my I.D., I was dumbfounded. He was smiling at what we had done in spite of our losses. He was happy about the firefight and more than pleased that we were producing dead bodies. I was angry enough to add him to the body count. Unfortunately I couldn't shoot him and even worse, it appeared as if I would have to deal with him for the rest of my tour. I retreated to the resupply area to refill the magazines I used during the firefight.

When I arrived there, I found an incredible crowd standing around watching us. As I started to help my self to some extra ammo and magazines, I found Doc doing the same thing. He had pledged to hump 20 magazines a Claymore and about six frags.

"But you're the medic. You don't have to even carry a weapon." I told him as I loaded my magazines. He was already carrying about thirty pounds of medical equipment and I doubted if anybody wanted to see him getting involved with the shooting part of the war. "Well Handy I figure that since I've got to be out here I might as well be ready to shoot back until somebody gets hit." He said making me a little bit afraid of what might happen if he got hit. Hopefully after we got out of Tuy Hoa he'd come to his senses and see things differently.

As resupply continued we started receiving more new faces. Naturally it would've been appropriate to replace all that we had lost. We even had to replace Garson this time. It was going to take some imaginative reshuffling of the personnel to compensate for the lack of men caused by the second squad being over run.

After a complete comb over of the battle site, there was a considerable amount of drag trails found near the spot that we fought from. Purvis said they were still being checked out as we were being resupplied. Shave was not surprised at the finding because, as I suspected, the other fire team did hit a lot of people when they flanked to our left. Of course I suppose that bodies are not necessary when calculating the all-important count. All they had to do is factor in the drag trails and use some of that strange math utilized after firefights. "Say Doc, what was it like when you guys got up there?" I asked.

"Everybody's face was shot off. Young must have taken a direct hit from a B-40 rocket. His body was in pieces. We had to round up his parts to put them in the body bag. Ricks was hit in the hand and Floyd was found apart from the rest of the dead lying face down on top of the radio. Bracey says that in the end the three of then tried to get away. As they were being chased down; Floyd was hit and told Ricks and Bracey to make a run for it while he tried to hold them off. In effect he gave his life to allow Ricks and Bracey to escape with theirs. They're assuming that he died lying on top of the radio to keep it concealed from Charlie. As we came upon the ambush site one of them was waiting for us, He shot Watson in the neck. Nothing serious though." He said. Bracey's account sounded thin. His story, however, was the only one available and, that was unfortunate. As for the other four that was killed, I hoped that they were already dead before their position was overrun. I'd hate to think about what it would have been like to be wounded, out of ammo and then to get executed. I remembered back in '65 when the 1st Cav suffered that kind of humiliation at Ia Drang. News accounts told of guys who were caught off guard by an overwhelming force of NVA regulars at the beginning of the battle. The rapidly advancing first wave of NVA troops managed to fight their way past many of the untested troops fresh out of Ft. Benning. Their initial advance left a number of dead and wounded GI's in their wake. As the Cav fell back to re-establish a new line of defense, they were unable to recover their dead and wounded because they were all, by then, lying behind the newly established forward line of the enemy. The dead and wounded were all left where they fell. The rest fought frantically to hold a line and had to spend the night in place. That night, in the darkness, they were tormented by the cries of their comrades lying wounded begging for their lives before being executed by their captors. Their desperate pleas were loud enough to be heard by everybody on the secure side of the line. They were unable to do anything to help them and had to sit in their safe positions and listen to the executions all that night. I had gained a true perspective on that feeling. I understood the frustration of being totally unable to help your own while

105

being counted on to bail them out of their hopeless situation. I doubted if anyone could ever really get over such an experience. I somehow knew that I wouldn't.

Before Garson was placed aboard the medivac, he told Purvis he would submit our names for medals. Fortunately Purvis was smart enough to realize that all we did was sit around and guard weapons while the second squad was having their faces shot off and their pockets rifled. He told him to forget about it. We admittedly did save his life but too many lives were lost in the process. I couldn't accept any citation for what we did either. I would have enough problems dealing with what we didn't do and the fact that we weren't allowed to do anything.

While sitting around licking our psychological wounds, I heard an effeminate voice in the background. The voice seemed to be barking out commands. "Who or what in the hell is that?" I asked Purvis who had just returned from the resupply area.

"It's Garson's replacement. Wait 'till you get a load of this guy."

"I can wait. Believe me, I can wait." He said. With that we took off for the grocery store. I led the way, intentionally avoiding the area where the second squad was killed. I wasn't ready to go near that spot just then. All it represented to me was failure. I didn't even know exactly where they were killed but I knew the general area. I couldn't even bare to look in that direction. When we arrived, we found the old Papa San opening up for business. Not having Wheelhouse to spread his green marijuana out on the table was spooky. In the first few hours after the firefight, I had already turned to look for him once and almost called out his name twice. It would take a while before it sunk in that those guys were all dead but at that moment their spirits were still with us. Doc said he managed to retrieve Wheelhouse's bag of green pot saving him from being branded as a screw-up by the likes of Calvin. He would love to be able to say that those guys were smoking grass and lost their lives because of it.

Jackson came looking for me with a smile on his face. I couldn't believe he had found something to smile about. "There's a new black guy from New Orleans." he said expecting the news to perk me up a little bit I supposed. I was so dispirited that even this ordinarily good news couldn't do the trick. "Have you seen the new platoon leader?" he asked.

"No. I'm avoiding him right now. What happened to that old Papa San they caught holding that gun?" I asked.

"It turns out that the old dude was the village chief." Black answered. He was lucky. Considering that the last chief was assassinated by the NVA, it would have been a real tragedy for his replacement to be killed by one of us. Everything was so hectic at that moment.

Speedie was sitting silently outside of the store. He was down to his last few days and handling being short unlike anything that Jones described. Shave was almost as short and was also as calm and composed as anybody else around him. Doc Bueno was expected to be leaving along with the two of them and he guaranteed that he would not die in Vietnam. I only wished I had the confidence to make a statement like that and hopefully when November came around that everything would be smooth and easy going. No firefights, no pacification or none of the ugly stuff. I probably couldn't handle being short under such circumstances.

Everybody started to open up a bit and retell their role in the firefight. I supposed that it was just too compelling to just keep it all to ourselves. Quite a few of us finally got a chance to shoot at somebody for the first time. Some of the guys were still pumped up. Combat can get your adrenal glands overworked in about ten seconds. A large part of it, however, is nothing but fear. My heart was beating so hard, I was convinced that it was about to explode.

I didn't feel comfortable talking about the firefight as quick as the rest of the guys were. It was fun referring to Ellis as a human jet but it was awkward and it didn't help matters much at all. I left the guys and went to retrieve my mail. The Post Office strike was obviously a quick one because the mail never stopped coming. It couldn't have happened at a worst time for us anyway. We needed to have our mail flowing uninterrupted.

Along the way, I encountered a huge crowd of onlookers just standing around watching us closely. The scene was like a carnival. I couldn't understand the attraction that captivated the civilians. I couldn't make my way through them fast enough. In my haste to escape the crowd I ran into Garson's replacement. I should have stayed at the store.

"Hello soldier. My name is Lt.Jahret. What's your name?" He asked. It was like talking to Jack Benny in jungle fatigues.

"Handy. Aaron Handy."

"Hi Hank" He said which irritated me because I never had a nickname and I didn't want to have him hang one on me. Unfortunately, Al was standing within earshot snickering his head off at my predicament. "Which squad are you in?"

"I'm the RTO for the third squad."

"Well I'm just making my rounds getting acquainted with everyone. You should be wearing a steel pot you know."

"Yes sir. I'll go and get it right away."

Before long I ran into another new guy. He was looking at me as if he had been looking for me. "You must be Handy. Most of the guys have been mistaking me for you."

"C'mon man, you're a lanky black guy with a gold tooth in your mouth. That practically gives every white guy in the platoon the right to call you Handy." I joked. His responding laugh said it all. The guy loved to have a good laugh and soon had me laughing both with him and at him.

"My name is Charles Benn."

"Where you from back in the world Benn?"

"S.Carolina." He said as I offered him a joint. He immediately started to scan the area to see if anybody was looking. He accepted the thing but I could tell that he was no head but it was no big deal. I figured that if he hung around me for a while, I would corrupt him for sure. "The other new guy is from New Orleans you know. His name is Lemar Joichim and he is a lot older than most of us. Check this out man. The guy is 27 years old."

"Are you kidding me man?" I said. At 27 he had to be older than all of us except Calvin and Mercein. He was as old as my brother Joe and I thought that guys his age never had to worry about the draft. I know he (Joe) didn't. "I have to go and find the lieutenant." He said before pausing and breaking into a very infectious laugh. I was again laughing both at him as well as with him and couldn't stop. Maybe having the new platoon leader won't be that bad after all, I thought. If Benn could continue to make me laugh about the new lieutenant without saying a word about him, I knew that I was going to enjoy his company. He was a total riot.

I remembered it was payday and ran back to the resupply area to retrieve my funds. Along the way I ran into the new guy from New Orleans. It had to be him because, like Benn said, he was a lot older than most of us. "Where ya at homes." I said to him.

"Where ya at." He answered recognizing and acknowledging a greeting commonly used in New Orleans.

"Just call me Lee. What part of the city are you from?" He asked me.

"Uptown. I live out by the river on Tchoupitoulas St. What about you?"

"I'm from Ponchartrain Park." He said with a touch of pride. The Park is a section of town where well-to-do black people live. Comparatively speaking he had lived a more privileged life than I.

"What school did you attend?" I asked.

"Carver, and you?"

"Booker T."

"Really, what a coincidence, my cousin, Joanna Hughes, taught there."

"No shit man. She taught me typing during my senior year and was my girlfriend's homeroom teacher for three years. I actually learned to type while sitting in her class and that wasn't easy. She was a good teacher though. So tell me, just how did you manage to get drafted at your age?" I asked curious about his status as a late draftee.

"I was a late draft casualty due to a change in my marital status if you know what I mean. When the breakup was official, Uncle Sam moved in for the kill." he said. It was the same old story. No draft deferment was permanent. The war had lasted so long that it managed to outlive most excuses, alibis, and deferments. All deferments eventually came under scrutiny. No matter if it was school, marital, medical or whatever. Nothing was going to be around forever. The war just outlasted them all. Uncle Sam always had his way with all of us in the end.

After leaving Lee, I retreated to the store. Speedie was playing it safe by sitting outside as he smoked a joint. Garson's little visit was still resonating with us even though he was gone.

"Short! Seven days and a wake up!" He proudly exclaimed knowing no one was shorter.

"I think your math is incorrect." I teased.

"Bull-shit! You just wait. By this time next week, I'll be on my freedom bird flying back to California."

"Are you going back to the America? Take me with you." Maggot shamelessly begged Speedie infuriating him as she continued to make her plea.

"What would I want with a whore like you? Shut the fuck up!" He said and then almost as suddenly as she started begging, she stopped. I realized that as comical as her proposal sounded to us, she was dead serious. S. Vietnam had a lot of desperate people who were looking for a way out of the country. Maggot saw what she actually hoped was an opportunity to get out. She gave it her best shot and came up woefully short. Knowing Maggot, we all assumed she would get over the rejection immediately.

The bloody drag trails found earlier led to an old woman's house. Obviously her place was used as a battle field hospital during the firefight. The place was a bloody mess. There were bandages and gauzes everywhere. The only thing to be determined was whether or not she had any prior knowledge. She was taken away for questioning and of course she denied having anything to do with the whole thing. She claimed that her house was a random selection or designation and that she, along with the rest of the villagers, spent the night in downtown Tuy Hoa. She claimed to be as surprised as anyone else about her home being used while she was away. Although her alibi was strong, her possible collusion remained suspect. I could only wonder how heavy handed would her interrogation be. This was always a big problem for us. Our enemy was feared, tolerated or supported by the people. The same people who we were supposed to be protecting or saving were only paying lip service to our efforts. Pacification was obviously invented to deal with this dilemma.

In an example of how paranoid we had become, the guys in the platoon theorized that an old Papa San who used to come through the village making announcements was actually alerting everyone to an upcoming attack. I only saw him once. I thought that he was sort of like a town crier that I remembered reading about as a little kid. In America's colonial days, the town crier made passes through the settlement ringing a bell and making community related announcements. The old man, I thought, was just a Vietnamese version of this messenger. The third squad had spent so much time away from the rest of the platoon that none of us could pick him out of a line-up if our lives depended on it. All of his daytime appearances, according to the guys, were followed by night attacks. They were, to say the least, on the lookout for him.

As the night started to set in, our anxiety levels started to rise. Everybody was geared up for the worst. The big firefight taught us a lot about our enemy's tenacity. He came expecting to lose men and we feared was willing to come again and again. We also learned about a cruel double standard practiced by our superiors. All of the weapons left behind by the Ruff Puffs and claimed by Charlie were replaced the following morning. On the other hand, the machinegun lost by Wheelhouse would not be replaced until an investigation was conducted on the events surrounding the loss of the weapon. Maybe they thought that we were faking Wheelhouse's death to gain an extra M-60. They were really rubbing our faces in the dirt with their handling of the battle's aftermath. The way Charlie came at us, it wouldn't have been such a bad idea to have 3 or 4 machineguns. Instead we were going out with only one due to our own idiotic procedures. Our morale was low enough yet they were putting us through further humiliation. The Ruff Puffs were packing brand new M-16's, grenade launchers and machineguns. The factory oil was still on them. The sight of them earlier uncrating their new weapons reminded me of that sales line Black claimed was used for selling brand new ARVN rifles.

When Brook Benton chimed in with his Rainy Night in Georgia we knew it was time to go out for the first time after the firefight. As a precaution or maybe a morale booster or confidence builder, we didn't take out any ARVNs with us and we also didn't split up the way we had been doing. There were no scattered squads saturating the area spreading out our influence or diluting our strength either. We went out as a platoon and not very far. I always feared it would cost us dearly by spreading out the way we did. Our problem was that after the damage was done, our strategy was geared around reacting to the enemy's actions and his capabilities.

Our platoon sized perimeter only felt good and reassuring for the first few hours. After that, I felt that we were just a little too reluctant to engage the enemy. We were huddled in the rice paddies near the bridge and we all knew there would be no attack that night. The enemy not only knew we could call out gunships and mortar fire, he had also probably lost too many men the night before. Not having any Ruff Puffs around made us too damned formidable. The enemy knew that and would not be attacking under such conditions. In spite of our superior firepower we still had to take the risks that led to what happened to us the night before. It was the only way we could be effective against our enemy.

Our willingness to adhere to the stupid gentlemanly rules of engagement was our biggest handcuff. Helicopter gunships were not allowed to fire into a village even if it was evacuated so our enemy waged his battles inside of the village. Another tactic we were trained to expect was to be shot at by Charlie from inside a populated area. He knew that we were not allowed to shoot into a village for fear of harming innocent civilians. Any dead civilians resulting from retaliation would have been damaging to our effort. When we called a cease-fire to observe his holiday he pulled an offensive. We recognized Cambodia as a neutral country so he charted his Ho Chi Minh trail through it and set up sanctuaries inside of its borders. We were making the mistake of fighting a war and seemingly enabling the enemy to continue his fight against us.

At midnight everybody was awake and waiting for nothing to happen. I used to laugh at the third squad's Charlie-only-strikes-at-midnight theory but they proved to be accurate. Charlie started that battle at exactly midnight. Call it a flair for the dramatics or anything else. The guys were right about the enemy's tactics. I would never doubt them again but just the same I would still rather be awake. They could have their imaginary security of sleeping or hiding under their poncho liners at midnight. I was having nothing to do with it.

5

We managed to spend a peaceful night in the rice paddies as a platoon. It was quiet enough to give me the creeps. My stomach started to gurgle and made a lot of noise. It was the only sound to be heard during ambush and then I started to belch. I was getting sick and I suspected it was from the Vietnamese food I was eating everyday. Complaining about a bellyache was out of the question at that moment. I didn't want to come across as one of the ghosters looking to get out of Tuy Hoa for obvious reasons. I just couldn't do it. I tried to play it off as just something that would pass with the next bowel movement.

Our lone kill was still over where we left him after the firefight. I wondered what would become of him because the stench from his rotting corpse was going to be unbearable. I would have preferred to let his people come and get the guy so that we wouldn't have to deal with him. Sooner or later that section of the rice paddy would be needed for production and somebody would eventually have to move him out of the way. In the meantime it was business as usual.

Later that day while we sat around being watched by the throng of villagers that came out daily, a helicopter started circling overhead. We'd had so many sorties as of late that our part of Vietnam was beginning to look like an airfield. Then I noticed some more guys were arriving on the slick. At that juncture I figured the more shooters the better. Doc and I took advantage of the distraction and took a walk through the village. We walked for a while and came upon an old woman of about 75 who couldn't speak a word of English. She invited us in just the same and we accepted her offer of hospitality. It was always an interesting experience to enter one of the homes of the Vietnamese. I just couldn't resist. It was the essence of the culture exchange I was seeking. As she walked us through her modest home, she spoke continually about nothing we could understand. We broke out a couple of joints and walked over to her altar and got a light off one of her candles. She took advantage of the opportunity to demonstrate the religion. Doc and I were bombed out on the pot and by then in the mood for a little light-hearted fun. We both followed her lead and imitated her every move. "Well Doc, I guess this makes us practicing Buddhists now."

"So what else do you have for us Mama San?" He asked while failing miserably at holding back the laughter. Almost as if she understood him, she led us to the next room and sat us down on the edge of her bed. She then brought us an old jewelry box with a lot of worthless coins in it. Worthless, I assumed, because they were all from the French Colonial days. She pored over her coins with glee. She was absolutely thrilled to be entertaining a couple of doped up GI's from America. With every coin she showed, she had another story we could not understand. "Doc, we have got to learn some Vietnamese. I can only imagine what she's saying." I said as Doc was by then was laughing at everything. He was actually having a laughing fit and would've probably needed some medical attention had we stayed long enough. We were having fun again and maybe I was starting to climb up from that emotional valley.

Outside of the old woman's house was a commotion. It was the guys making a sweep through the village. Doc and I joined in by slipping out the door and trying to blend in without being noticed. As we left I felt as if there was some good we could do. Maybe after we lost those guys I needed to feel we were fighting for something. I didn't want to ever believe we were wasting lives. The old woman gave me an infusion of worth and necessity. I would have to spend the rest of my life finding a way to define and justify what we had done in Vietnam and to dignify the sacrifices we had made in the process. The survivors of each battle owed it to those who died alongside of us to make sure that they would be remembered for performing in the face of all the negative attitudes surrounding our efforts. It wouldn't be easy but we couldn't just hang our heads in sorrow for what had happened. We also couldn't afford to just be satisfied with surviving each battle.

Pacification, in spite of all of the fun we had during the daytime, was still a very dangerous mission. Yet it still represented the pure essence of what our mission in Vietnam had become. It was the winning of the hearts and minds of the people that the old woman represented. In a small way she had already committed hers to us. She had witnessed a lot of change in the political scenery in her time and she still had some measure of enthusiasm to display for us. I hoped she would be rewarded with an acceptable final solution to the hostilities but the outcome looked bleak for us.

The sweep ended as soon as we joined in. We never got a chance to find out what they were looking for. "Where have you guys been?" Speedie asked as his sector of the line caught up with us.

"We were checking out that house over there." I answered while pointing at the old woman's house as she waved farewell to us. Speedie said that the slick that was circling overhead brought out some more guys and that Burt was one of them. Another was a guy named Katta. There was definitely a concerted effort to augment our numbers in the wake of the firefight.

The landing zone continued to receive slicks. It was almost like resupply day, only unscheduled. Suddenly I heard a very familiar voice making loud idle threats to all who could hear him. It was Kyler. "He's back again." said Purvis.

"I don't care what anybody says. I'm not going back to Uplift. If anybody tries to send me back, I'll shoot him." He said.

He was as serious as a heart attack. Obviously, as they were loading supplies onto the helicopters back at Uplift, he packed a rucksack, grabbed his weapon and jumped onto the first supply chopper heading out and arrived unannounced, undetected and unconcerned about the consequences. Since nobody ordered him back onto the chopper, it was official; he was back. I was glad because he was a real character and a lot of fun to be with. He had a bunch of great tapes and more importantly, he wanted to be in the field. After weighing the pros and cons one had to arrive at the conclusion that we needed more men. Maybe this time the little guy would make it happen. Since Tuy Hoa was not the Crow's Foot and the monsoon season was over we were no longer faced with the arduous task of humping uphill on the muddy trails of the boonies. We were in the low lands, in a village. I felt confident he would make it work the second time around. All we had to do was give him a chance. Somebody wanted that rear job he had just abandoned and we needed men who wanted to be in the field because Tuy Hoa was no picnic. We were getting new men every day but at least Kyler was familiar with what we were doing.

My stomach kept acting up so I told Doc that I might need something for it later on. I still couldn't make it look like I was complaining at that moment. Having Burt and Kyler back made me feel a little better because they made us somewhat whole again. Losing those eight guys took a lot out of the platoon. Needless to say, it also took a lot out of me. I supposed it was unreal to not expect to lose anyone else. It was a war and men do die in wars, it's just that I wasn't equipped to handle it. Anyway I figured it would be good to see the two of them again. Doc would just continue to be himself as he continued to ask me wild questions about New Orleans and the French Quarter. The lewd, tawdry image of Bourbon St. and the French Quarter will always overshadow anything else about the city. New Orleans will always be one big French Quarter to a lot of people who have never been there and, a year long Mardi Gras to many others.

My stomach continued to act up and it became evident I was dealing with something more than just a bellyache. I was hoping that it had passed. The symptoms included a lot of belching accompanied by a funny taste. It was more like boiled eggs. I felt like a kid who ate too many boiled eggs on Easter Sunday. Then the boiled egg taste turned to boiled rotten eggs and the gurgling stomach quickly turned into a case of diarrhea. The belching was nothing that I couldn't handle but the diarrhea was new to me. I never had the experience of passing such a loose stool. I was sure there was some solid food in me but I didn't have one turd to show for it. I barely made it to the bushes where there was no privacy due to the little kids gathered around me to laugh at my predicament. They seemed to know what I was suffering from. While squatting there, I was confronted by an old woman who didn't like my choice of latrine. She berated me as she pointed out toward the rice paddies perhaps suggesting that I use them instead. I had obviously deposited my load onto her property. She continued to complain as I finished and left her standing there in anger.

Speedie's time to DEROS had come and it was time to say our goodbyes to him as he stood waiting for his slick to arrive. He acknowledged all of his well-deserved farewells and somehow knew he would be sorely missed. He had become one of the people who had influenced me the most when I first arrived in the field. Strangely, his DEROS event was not the celebration that I once thought leaving country would be. I expected more from him. I figured that if a guy were lucky enough to do a whole tour in the bush, he would be happier than Speedie was at that moment. Considering what we had been going through, I would have been thrilled to just get the hell out of Tuy Hoa. He was going all the way back to California but wasn't even smiling. When the helicopter came to pick him up, he walked over to the craft, took a seat inside and waived passively as the slick ascended and took him away from us forever. Of course a huge piece of me was on that slick with him. There was something about losing one of the people who had contributed so much to my development in the bush. I felt deflated. "What's happening hardcore?" Kyler asked as he sneaked up from behind.

"Welcome back, dude. I knew they couldn't keep you away for long. What happened to your rear job?" I asked while still watching Speedie's helicopter disappear over the horizon.

"Fuck that job, the lifers were hassling me to death. I couldn't take any more."

"Isn't that the reason you came to Viet Nam in the first place? You volunteered to get away from the lifers remember?" I said as we walked over to the company area for a ceremony honoring Floyd with the D.S.M. The Distinguished Service Medal is one of the highest medals awarded by our country. His name will become a part of an honored legion that probably dates back for two hundred years. By honoring him they will also be honoring all of us at the same time. The award, however, would be a small consolation to his family back home. I wondered how his ex-girlfriend took it when she heard the news. I supposed she felt that she did the right thing because she couldn't face losing him to tragedy. Now that the worst had happened, I supposed dumping Floyd before the worst happened made a difference in the way she received the bad news. I hoped she could live with her decision. "How's the pot in Tuy Hoa? Kyler asked.

"Pretty good. It can't compare to the Bong Son Bombers, but it's some pretty good stuff.

Before the ceremony started we noticed that Bracey was a part of the entourage that stepped off of the slick. We hadn't seen him since the firefight and started wondering if he was avout to rejoin us. When the show began the Colonel was at his eloquent best detailing Floyd's deed. It was as if he was with us during the battle. I supposed those speeches were stored away somewhere in his desk and all he had to do was find the one that fit the occasion. Maybe all he had to do was pull it out and rehearse the lines. In spite of my contempt for the lifers that sent us to Tuy Hoa, I was still impressed with the way he extolled Floyd's bravery. I became choked with pride to be associated with him and felt honored to just be able to say that I knew him. In my eyes, he had become every bit the hero that America worships. I could never forget him or the moment I stood in formation as his name was forever enshrined in our annals. Hopefully the honor will make it possible to gain some closure on the loss of our friend.

In a more puzzling move, they also pinned a Bronze Star with a "V" device for valor on Bracey's chest. I guess since it was their show, they could have written the script any way they wanted to. When the C.O. got a chance to have his say, he spoke about how much the brass was raving about what we were doing there. He was only happy about being in command and totally ignored his nonparticipation. Our losses didn't seem to affect him the way I though it should have. After listening to him hammer out a few more lines, I figured he had an agenda of his own that didn't have much of a place for us except as cannon fodder. He would have wasted every one of us to raise enough of the right eyebrows. He was trying to make Major at our expense with our blood. His blossoming candidacy for a fragging was possibly the reason he spent his time at Tuy Hoa AFB; a safe distance from his potential executioners.

Strangely, at the close of the ceremony, Bracey left with the lifers. I had a feeling that Bracey would not be seeing any more of the field. His experience on that hill had obviously turned into his defining moment of trauma rendering him unable to perform anymore. The brass over at battalion headquarters were obviously in agreement with the premise that Bracey needed some time in the rear to regroup. I suppose they felt he needed to get over his close brush with death. Edwards, comparably, was exposing himself to rocket and rifle fire to save Garson's life and nobody gave him a medal for his actions. What's more, Edwards was still in the village with us. It was a travesty that guys like Kyler was giving a rear job to help out in the field and the lifers were honoring the likes of Bracey. None of the guys actually felt comfortable with Bracey's account of all that happened and the issue was a sore spot with a lot of us. It was too bad that Floyd and the others gave their lives and left him to give us the story. Fate wrote the script and all we could do was accept it as it was.

We also received some mail and Al got a letter from his girlfriend who said she was on vacation in Vegas with a girlfriend of hers. I didn't realize he was still writing her.

"She once sent me a large blow-up picture of herself when we were in the Crow's Foot and I left it tacked to a tree with the inscription; "Here Charlie, eat your heart out." Al never seemed to have any real attachment to the girl and I was sure she agreed that their relationship was platonic.

I congratulated Bracey before he left with his award although it seemed as if he was decorated for merely surviving the battle. Just for getting out alive and nothing else. He left with the medal givers and was nowhere in sight to hear any of the quiet whispers about his award or his continuing absence. Gaining Kyler, or regaining him, was more than a consolation. He started playing his tapes and quickly made an impact on us. He immediately dubbed Jahret as "The Hunter" and was no doubt as irritating to the lifers in the rear as they were to him. He took advantage of the unfortunate situation we were in to just show up to help augment our deflated numbers. He was confident that no one would just send him back and he was right. He was about to get another chance to prove himself and he couldn't have been happier about his change of fortune. Having already failed once at life in the field had only galvanized his attitude toward making it work the second time around.

When the day came to an end, Kyler was assigned to our squad for ambush. Our ambush site for that night was located in the middle of the rice paddies. Our route took us across the entire gamut of different rice paddy terrains. Almost every square, as was common harvest, irrigating and planting practice, differed from the next. There were hardly ever two adjacent squares that were both the same. It was all very confusing. We charted our course through the area atop a dike that separated the wet paddies from the dry ones. Negotiating the dike was a minor balancing act and falling off was no big deal. We only had to make it across the rice field and sneak into the village. Our journey was interrupted by a sudden fall by one of the members at the end of the procession. We turned around and realized that it was Kyler as his ruck had managed to unbalance him enough to lose his footing. He was frustrated yet undaunted as he struggled to his feet and regained his position in line atop the dike. The careless manner in which he brandished his weapon as he tried to get back in line really scared me. We continued on for another few yards and then he fell again. His second fall was into the wet paddy and he went down with a splash. "Shit!" He said loudly.

"Quiet Kyler. You don't want to give away our position." Purvis whispered redundantly as he went to the rear of the line to find Kyler lying in muddy water, cursing his predicament in the dark. He remained with him for a full five minutes before returning to his spot in our procession with a sour disposition and some extra baggage.

"What happened back there?" I asked.

"I've got Kyler's rucksack!" Purvis said dejectedly. Unfortunately for us, Kyler returned to form and reminded us just what it was like to have him trying to do anything else but smoke grass and play music. "He also lost his glasses when he fell and without them he can't see his nose in front of his face so Nick will have to hold his hand and lead him the rest of the way." He said. It would have been tough on him to be sent back to the rear again. He may have been a burden and a pain in the ass for that night but we liked him and that was all that mattered. One thing was certain, if we ever got into a firefight, he could be counted upon to throw some lead downrange. I always felt that his big heart was what would separate him from a lot of lesser men when the moment came to defend our ground. We needed shooters in Tuy Hoa and Kyler, in spite of his poor vision, would not hesitate to squeeze off a few rounds when needed.

We sat at our ambush site until daylight came and then walked straight to the village across the paddies instead of along the dikes. When we made it across the field and into the village, our arrival coincided with that of the villagers returning from town. Their animosity against us was still running high. I felt as if we made a mistake by choosing to walk through the village and maybe Kyler could have used the dike walking practice. Instead we had to run a gauntlet of little kids who were trying to put their hands in our pockets and steal the contents. When we arrived at our rendezvous point, we moved further to escape the crowd of onlookers. The only problem was that everywhere we went, there was a constant reminder of someone who was no longer with us. The absence of the guys who lost their lives in the firefight was wearing heavy on our minds. It was as if someone just ripped the souls out of our bodies. We were like zombies just going through the motions. We were trying our best to overcome more than we had ever faced before in our young lives. Purvis informed us we would be returning to that R&R center again but all I could think about was who would not be returning with us.

Phelam had also returned to the village along with Burt and the rest of the new guys. I hadn't noticed his presence but when he brought his squad back from ambush there was more than one angry face among them. Al was with him and I could tell he wasn't exactly impressed at all. Phelam was walking point, had the radio on his back, carrying both a grenade launcher and an M-16 and smoking a pipe that was no doubt stoked with grass. He really shot himself in the foot when he disappeared in the middle of the real action. His play-acting mattered little after that. The real Phelam had surfaced for all to see and his attempt at pretending to be some kind of brave warrior was not that impressive.

I overheard the new guy Katta talking to Burt about the end of the Beatles. Katta was not exactly a recent arrival in country and was surprised that I hadn't heard about the breakup.

"Everything started happening while I was at Ft. Polk. I wasn't paying any attention at all to the current events. I must have read a newspaper twice during my stay there. I missed hurricane Camille, Helter Skelter and now you say the Beatles have split." I said. Their breakup, admittedly, wasn't as important to me. He was a proud Midwesterner from the big city of Chicago. We then examined pictures of each other's girlfriend and as I admired the photo of his Tina, Purvis interrupted us. "The mass gravesite that Charlie used after the firefight has been located and Calvin has placed you on the detail to dig up the dead bodies we killed." He informed me. Army intelligence, as reliable as it always was in such situations, claimed there were 17 enemy dead buried on the outskirts of the populated area. I was already sick with diarrhea and he wanted me to go dig up some dead bodies. It seemed he would do anything to upset me. "No problem. I'll go in your place." Katta said when he noticed how ticked off I was over the appointment. I was shocked and impressed with the gesture; especially since I had only known him for a matter of minutes. We were definitely off to a great friendship. I quickly yielded my spot to him and he enthusiastically went in my place.

Doc was convinced that my diarrhea was due to a case of amoebic dysentery contracted from drinking untreated water. The water purification tablets were effective in killing the parasites and preventing the sickness but made the water turn brown and taste like chloroform. I rolled the dice and came up with one of the diseases the Brigade Surgeon warned us about during our orientation. Doc ran out of the pills used to treat it and wanted to send me to the rear but couldn't confirm my high temperature. He broke his thermometer during the firefight. Calvin, seizing the opportunity to meddle, played hardball with Doc's diagnosis and prevented me from leaving the field until my fever could be confirmed. Doc was angered by the intrusion but I didn't sulk over the issue. Leaving at that time was like taking the easy way out of a bad situation. If I had to go, it would be over something more serious than the trots.

Al walked up wearing a real angry look on his face. He was furious and I couldn't stay around to find out what it was about. I had to make another run to relieve myself. He was still plenty angry when I returned. Phelps had angered him the night before by lighting a fire to read his map. "Read his map! Who needs a map in this village?" I asked before I realized he was just putting on a show of bravado with his map reading stunt. Al was infuriated by Phelam's attempt to demonstrate how unafraid he was to be on ambush. Of course if he was so unafraid, he would have been with the platoon when it counted. Instead he was hiding out where it was safe and didn't surface until the smoke had cleared. He managed to sidestep all of the danger and then because he thought it was safe, he started a fire to demonstrate his courage. His charade had come to an end as he couldn't fool anybody anymore. I was just glad to see that Al had finally opened his eyes to him.

The grave digging detail came back a couple of hours later with stories of how foul the odor was. I imagined there were probably a zillion flies buzzing around them, too. I still couldn't believe Katta volunteered to go in my place. He said there were lots of body pieces and lots of limbs. Their medic probably did a lot of amputations during the all night battle. While at Ft. Polk we were told that Charlie planned everything well in advance of every attack. The mass grave was also probably dug in anticipation of the heavy losses. It was frightening to think that we had to defeat an enemy willing to make that kind of sacrifice. If he was willing to dig his own grave before the battle, then we would have had to kill them all. Our adversaries had literally been at war continuously since before most of the platoon was born, and they showed no signs of letting up. Their seventeen dead, compared to ours, was the lifer's equation of a victory. Charlie, without a doubt, considered it a victory whenever he could come back to fight again. He was sure to return; we just didn't know how soon. The April 1st battle must have hurt his ability to fight but he was expected to regroup and come back later. "Handy, how long have you been wearing that pimple on your brow? It looks like a sebaceous cyst to me. I think it's going to have to be surgically removed." He said as he continued to examine it.

"Ouch! Be careful with that." I said.

"It hurts because it's infected. It has to be removed and soon." It was obvious that he was only trying to challenge Calvin again over interfering with his duty. He was looking for another showdown and my pimple was going to be where he drew the battle lines. "Are you sure that a little pussy wouldn't cure it man." I joked.

"Yeah I'm sure." Doc was not to be denied this time as he immediately went about preparing for the procedure to be done as soon as possible.

When I heard Stevie Winwood's voice singing "Can't Find My Way Home", I was again reminded why I liked having Kyler with us. It was the music he carried with him and this was a beautiful song with a home theme that had to connect with many of the troops in country. Right in the middle of the song, Calvin informed me that I would be in the 21-gun salute to our fallen. I continued to concentrate on the song since the ceremony was to be taking place soon but not immediately. When the song ended I started to wonder if the salute would one day be performed on my behalf. I was beginning to feel as if I was living out my final days. Tuy Hoa was turning into a huge nightmare that was robbing me of my confidence. I needed to put the firefight behind me and the salute, I feared, would make it that much harder to accomplish. Before Calvin spoke up, I thought that 21 gun salutes were performed at gravesites only. The infantry, it turned out, also performed the salute on the battlefield. For all I knew, we just might have been following an airborne tradition. Paratroopers did seem to do everything different. This ceremony, however, was not a bad idea at all. In fact I liked being considered for it. I only hoped that it wouldn't extend my grief. I still missed those guys tremendously and did not feel whole without them around; especially Wheelhouse. It was still very painful to remember the days when they were still with us and was just beginning to accept their absence.

When the day started to come to an end and our good feeling started to evaporate with the fading sunlight, we were faced with another scary night in Tuy Hoa. At least Shave's radio was not on. Kyler's tapes did more than provide us with music all day. It prevented me from hearing Brook Benton kill me slowly with that song again. A little piece of me was torn away every night in Tuy Hoa. Although Charlie had yet to return, the threat of his doing so was almost as damaging. I was being traumatized by the mere anticipation of his next attack and had become a walking wounded young man. Getting out of Tuy Hoa, I thought, would be all I would need to heal my psychological wounds. The mission's end, however, was nowhere in sight.

We spent another uneventful night in the paddies. Kyler didn't do anything to upset our routine and sort of made our night. There was enough anxiety out there without any drama created by our illustrious reinstated member. My newest concern was centered on Charlie attacking in broad daylight as I didn't want to become too relaxed whenever the sun was up. It just might have been what our enemy wanted us to do making it easy to surprise us. On our way back from ambush, I found myself in the front of our procession. It mattered little since we were in the village and walking along the long trail that lead to the wooden bridge. Jahret, however, saw it differently. In his opinion, I was walking point and he didn't like seeing a radio man walking point. He had a minor fit over the incident but nothing that would cause me to want to frag him. His commission was not enough to make any of us start shaking in our boots with fear either. In Vietnam, one had to earn his respect and the new lieutenant just hadn't made the grade yet.

Burt acquired a hat from one of the little kids who followed us on our way back. When we finally settled down for the day he made a few alterations on it and transformed it into a nice unauthorized boonie hat. It looked like something that Robin Hood would love and something the lifers would love to hate. Burt really did have a touch for artistic creation but got into some trouble with the law. The judge gave him the option of doing some time in the Army or going to jail. So he enlisted." His story was a carbon copy of that of another friend I met at Ft. Benning named Carlton Upton, a teenager from Chicago and a former member of a street gang named the Blackstone Rangers. After jump school, he was sent to Ft. Bragg. I supposed he would eventually be sent to Vietnam also. "What was your offense anyway?"

"I was arrested for possession and since it was a first offense, the judge gave me this option." There were probably at least a thousand Burts in Vietnam at that moment. I was surprised I never heard of the practice before induction because I knew a lot of guys in New Orleans who spent a lot of time in jail. These guys had no problem doing the time. It was like going on a sabbatical or to their second home. They would have laughed at any judge making such an offer. Of course none of those guys were first time offenders either.

The dead body was set afire and drew a huge crowd. My respect for the enemy was sincere and I wished that he could return all of his dead to their families for a decent burial. Then I remembered that our guys had their faces shot off and it made the burning more acceptable. As the body burned, I wrote my brother Anthony a letter because Burt had me worried about him. His recent initiation to pot smoking could put him in the same vulnerable position. He was almost draft age and since he didn't have a record, a judge might offer him the same deal that Burt and Carlton received. Afterwards, we found a well and took a much needed bath and shave. It got pretty hot and muggy during the day in the springtime. The summer, I was warned, would be extremely hot with temperatures exceeding 100 degrees daily.

Katta, to my surprise was a snuff dipper. I had never witnessed the ritual before and was amazed as I watched him filling the space between his lower lip and gum with the substance. I thought that only old men practiced the habit. "Most of my friends back in 'Chicago dips. I've been doing it since high school." he said while standing wrapped in a green towel; his lower lip packed with the black goo.

"You want some?" he offered. "No thanks. I'm sure the cigarettes and the dope will kill me with the same efficiency while leaving my lip and gums intact."

After the bath Al came up with the latest issue of the Brigade's newspaper, "The Firebase 173." The story about our base camp find in the An Lo's was in it. He read it aloud when he found his name in the story. I was surprised that Westy didn't come out to do a story on the April 1st battle. Maybe he didn't want to be too preferential. Considering the way we felt at the time, maybe it wasn't appropriate either. After being in the field and experiencing the pain of losing friends in battle, he would have been affected to the point of losing objectivity. He also knew both Wheelhouse and Floyd. Al read on and came upon a story detailing the exploits of an NCO in our Ranger Company named Patrick Tadina. Tadina, according to legend, was a native Hawaiian who, when dressed like an enemy soldier, could fool anybody who didn't know any better. He took advantage of his likeness and started wearing the enemy's uniforms to fool them. "You mean he wears black pajamas or NVA khaki and carries an AK?" I asked.

"Exactly, he also walks point about 50 meters ahead of his patrol."

"Are you shittin me man?"

"No shit man, he's got so many kills he can't remember or count them." he said which was self-explanatory. Tadina walked up on the enemy, they relaxed when they assumed he was one of them, and then he blew them away. It looked as if by declining the invitation to become a Ranger, I had missed out on meeting a real hero and my idea of the ultimate leader. Of course, there was no guarantee that I would have been in on one of his patrols but meeting him would have made my tour. Still, the story about Tadina was an inspiring one. I was certain that if the war weren't so unpopular, Tadina would have been a national hero. Books would have been written about him and maybe even a movie or two. He was every bit the hero that Sgt. York or Audie Murphy was to their wars. "He seems to be some kind of legend. I'm sure he didn't get this famous on one tour."

"Well, in a way he did. He's been here for years and I'm not sure if he has ever been back to the world yet." He said giving me the feeling that he was pushing his luck with his continuous extension. Hopefully, I thought, he would decide to leave before Charlie punched his card.

Another bowel movement chased me into the rice paddies for another humiliating deposit. Dysentery was something I didn't need to experience. What made matters worse was that I was the only one in the whole platoon suffering with the sickness. I wasn't the only one that drank from that well and I was definitely not the only one who didn't use water purification tablets either. The parasites just picked on me or my canteen I guess. Anyway one more night of suffering and it would be over. There was expected to be either some magic pills or a thermometer come resupply day. Calvin had managed to do his dirt but I could take it. His time would come soon enough. Doc, on the other hand, couldn't wait to see that day come around. He was really angered by Calvin's interference and hadn't shown any signs of getting over it.

When night came around again, we moved down the edge of the rice paddies. The one that lead past the old Mama San's house that Doc and I worshipped Buddha in. Purvis stopped and pointed into the bamboo tree line designating our spot for ambush. It meant that we would be working the trail for the night. I didn't like the spot but didn't complain. Charlie was too smart to come along that trail and our vulnerability was the wide open rear of our perimeter. The selection would only add to my paranoia. I hadn't had more than five total hours sleep since the 1st. I could only hope that my stomach would stay calm for the night. Losing my cookies in my pants was the only other option. Tuy Hoa had become a dread. I couldn't imagine going through eight more months of the same mental torture. The anticipation of the enemy's next move was almost as taxing as facing him in actual combat. My anxiety level was high as Charlie was taking a toll on me without even showing his face. While worrying myself sick over the imaginary rocket and the exposed rear of our perimeter, I noticed Shave was sound asleep.

He only had hours left in the field and was trying sleeping like a baby. I admired the way he handled being short.

Another morning arrived and they just didn't seem the same as they did before we lost those guys. Wheelhouse and I had gotten close those last couple of months and I felt awful about not being able to do anything to help them. The battle's aftermath was proving to be unbearable. It was resupply day and if Doc could cure me I of the trots, it would make him eligible for the Nobel Prize for medicine in my opinion. First we had to fight our way through a throng of returning villagers. Before we made it very far, we noticed a pattern in the rice field adjacent to our ambush site. The plants had been trampled flat and all of the stalks were leaning toward the tree line. It could only mean that an undetermined number of men had slipped into the village undetected by us. We were situated no more than 30 meters away from their path. They obviously knew where we were. "Do you see this shit?" I asked Purvis.

"Yes I do. I'm glad they were just moving." Any assumption of the enemy's demise was a little bit premature. He was alive and still around. Judging by the well pressed rice stalks, he was also still in considerable size and number. One or two men could not have done as much damage to that entire square of the rice paddy. Although our close brush with disaster made us look like novices, we still had to admire the stealth. Charlie never carried as much equipment into combat as we did and never wore much more than a pair of shorts. They were masters of night movement and sound discipline. The rest of the guys, we imagined, would never believe our story when they heard it.

When we arrived at the resupply area Doc had a most unexpected surprise waiting for me. I was expecting my pills and he not only had the pills, he had arranged for my cyst removal to be done at the AFB that morning. Doc had won his little battle over who was boss when it came to the health of the platoon. Judging by the way that Calvin was pouting, I assumed that Doc went over his head. It was probably a done deal before he was even informed of the procedure. I jumped onto the slick and Al was there with his little Instamatic ready to take a picture of me leaving. "Bye Homie. Don't forget to write." he said. The helicopter then slowly lifted from the ground as he waved goodbye with his fist bobbing up and down while taking the picture with the other hand. The flight took me directly to the AFB. I was expecting to spend my first night in a hospital bed and my conscious was clear due to the medic's action. His personal battle with the platoon sergeant was the reason for my being where I was. I didn't have to come up with any life threatening ailment or wound and nothing was faked.

When I stepped off of the helicopter, I startled the ground crew with my appearance and my armature. By flying in, I obviously managed to get around their security and didn't get to check in my weapon. As I walked across the tarmac and past a few Air Force guys standing around in their civilian attire I couldn't help but notice their stare. I supposed they had never seen anyone in full battle dress walking on their blessed air base. I asked him if he would send me back to Uplift to recuperate from surgery and received the anticipated resonse.

I turned and noticed that Shave was handing over the radio to Burt and saying his farewells. I was glad he stayed long enough for me to see him off. We told him to not eat too much of that brown bread when he got back home and not to spend all of his money in one place. Then we sent him back to the world where all of his money awaited him along with all of the things he was planning to do with it. As he left, I witnessed another small piece of me leaving with him. It wasn't fair to have to watch other guys leave ahead of you. Especially when one had as much time still left to do as I did. "Handy, we received a new medic while you were away named Reardon. I'm telling you man, I was being driven by the platoon hypochondriacs." said Doc as Bueno had already gone to the rear and was not expected to return. One medic can not handle the patient load alone. They were coming up with some really mysterious ailments to get out of the field. Most of us however, would rather be together. We just enjoyed the camaraderie too much to want to go in the rear. No matter how depressing or terrifying the nights were we preferred going through them together.

While we were reading our mail, Al sat next to me to read a rare letter from home. He had become one of the many lazy letter writers in our platoon. "Oh no!" he said unconvincingly.

"What happened?" I asked.

"I just got a letter from my buddy and he said that my girlfriend got married to a drummer in Vegas. She just met the guy while on vacation!"

"Bullshit." I said knowing he was just joking.

"I knew she wouldn't wait. I knew it." He said repeatedly while still laughing. Al was full of it and we all knew it. He would always come up with something to make me laugh. No one expected him to commit suicide over his make-believe bad news but he could've overdosed on his own bullshit. We continued to sit after reading the mail and the radio was playing "A Choice of Colors" by the Impressions. It was a song about racial harmony and the irony of the lyrics continued to coincide with our time spent together. In spite of the war, being in Vietnam wasn't as bad as we imagined it would be. Being with the guys I was around made it enjoyable.

As the darkness arrived, I became concerned about our adversaries. Our near encounter with them the previous night had more than alerted me about their presence. I hadn't slept in three nights and for good reason too. Charlie was still around and I could not feel comfortable enough to sleep. I never realized the human body could go as long without sleep. One thing was certain. I was about to extend my sleepless night's streak to four because although my diarrhea had been cured, the pills did nothing for my paranoia.

The entire platoon occupied a large section of rice paddy for the night. Lt. Moore or Moe, as we all called him, had arrived while I was having the cyst removed. Moe was our forward observer. His job was to call in mortar and artillery strikes. His purpose in the field was to act as the eyes of the battery that fires the rounds. Just when I thought it was safe to fall asleep, Moe called a fire mission for no apparent reason. I knew he was good at his job, but artillery rounds are scary. The proverbial "short round" was our main concern. One mix-up in coordinates could have landed one of those shells in our laps. Moe, however, was confident of the rounds' trajectory. He had his eyes fixed through his binoculars on the anticipated impact area. Without a doubt he expected the shells to fall exactly where he wanted them to fall. As the first shell fell on target, Moe had his binoculars in one hand and his radio handset in the other. He gave the order to send more rounds walked in an East to West path. They completed the fire mission with four more rounds. After the explosions, he ended his transmission and his fire mission. Maybe it was a little battlefield saber rattling to give Charlie something to think about as we were positioned a few squares away from the spot where Garson was hit and almost killed. Moe was good at calling in a strike. He looked like a puppet master the way he had that final salvo landing on target. I was glad to have him on our side and couldn't imagine having artillery rounds falling around me.

The sun came up and we were already in place for our planned ceremony to honor our fallen. Since I was scheduled to be in it, I decided to stay sober, out of respect for the five guys that we lost. Jeffrey Morse, one of the new arrivals that came out with Nick, was also going to be in the firing squad if I could call it that. We had a rehearsal before the actual ceremony to go over all of the details. Morse seemed to accept his role as more of an assignment. Of course I could have been mistaken. After all, one of the guys who came out with him was killed that night also. Maybe the two of them jumped together at Benning and he felt obligated to volunteer for the ceremony. Using live ammo only made me wonder where Mercein would stand when the 21-gun salute began. It didn't take much longer because the helicopter carrying the C.O. was coming in at that moment.

There as special formation. The boots naturally represented the ones that we lost. Before the ceremony began, they situated the boots in front of us with an M-16 fixed with a bayonet turned downward and planted into the ground. A steel pot placed atop of the rifle's stock topped off the centerpiece. It was a fitting and proper way to honor the war dead on the battlefield where they fell.

The ceremony began with the CO calling us to attention. He proceeded to make a speech in praise of their valiant efforts. He spoke of the proud airborne tradition that they upheld to the end. He was as eloquent as he was during Floyd's award ceremony. He closed his remarks with, "they made the supreme sacrifice." Those last five words disturbed me a lot. The way I remember, it was his decision to sacrifice those guys. Then he stepped to the rear before the firing of the 21-gun salute. As we were firing, my thoughts were with Wheelhouse's family somewhere in Virginia Beach. Perhaps he was being buried on the same day we were honoring him and the other four guys. It had to be devastating for his parents to be faced with burying their son at such a young age. The situation made me wonder how these families coped with losing someone in such an unpopular war. America was asking too much of its families for a war that mattered so little to them. We were dying in a war our government had literally **already** given up on. Moreover, Nixon's policy of turning the war over to the Vietnamese was a sham. His policy had cost Charlie Co. dearly that day. After the ceremony I felt depressed but at least we did show honor and respect to the five that we lost. To refocus on the mission after all of that pomp wouldn't be easy.

Later that evening our squad was assigned the task of setting up a meaningless checkpoint at the far end of the long road. We were told to detain anyone who didn't have an ID. I didn't even have an ID myself. The Ruff Puffs stole it along with my wallet. Benn was assigned with us to monitor the traffic along the road. He was a real lively soul. The radio started playing "I Want You Back" and he immediately jumped into a little dance. "That's my song." He said as he continued to gyrate to the beat. He was surprised when he discovered I didn't know about the group. I never knew they were a bunch of kids. If they were getting as much airplay back home as they did in Vietnam, they had to be a huge success. I couldn't help but shut down whenever I heard the R&B hits. It wasn't that they didn't sound good anymore. It's just that they made me feel more homesick than I could handle. In spite of all the guys around me, I could find myself feeling lonely at times. The music just made it more unbearable. Especially the oldies which were more damaging than any of the latest top 40 hits. The oldies had all of the associated memories and hearing them made me miss Barbara and being home with her.

Our checkpoint quickly netted three unsuspecting teenage girls for the crime of walking in their own country with no ID. We were ordered to detain them which only brought about more contempt for the lifers. They looked harmless to us. Of course the kid that threw the frag looked harmless too. We were as relieved as the girls were when we finally had to let them go. I hated that duty because they were starting to fear us. In the end, I was more than sure that they were terrified of us. More significantly, they were afraid of what we might have done to them.

When we came back from our checkpoint there was a lot of commotion about the new C.I.B. orders that had just came down and my name was omitted from it again. I brought it up with Purvis but there was little he could do at that time. I was totally frustrated because I had been in the field for almost three months and had definitely been in my first firefight. I wondered what else I had to do. At the rate things were going, I could have gotten wounded and received a Purple Heart before I was awarded my CIB. Nick and Morse earned their badges after their first night in the bush and so did a few other guys. I tried to be cool about it the first time but the second time really had me pissed.

I finally got past the oversight as I realized that there was little I could do about it. The war continued and we again found ourselves out in the rice paddies on ambush. It had become our area of choice since the 1st. Without a doubt we were showing a reluctance to spend our nights inside of the village. Our lesson came at a high price in lives lost and it never had to be that way. We were practically begging for disaster by cutting our strength and diluting it with those ineffective ARVN's. It was only a matter of time before something like that happened. We waited too late for the five guys we lost before playing it safe.

Before turning in for that night, I noticed a lone figure walking in the distance along the ridge extending out from the huge mountain. His silhouette was easily noticeable against the moonlit sky. He was just far away enough from our location to not have to worry about us doing anything to him. We had no sniper weapon to shoot him from that distance. I guess it was because of those days we spent sitting around in full view of the crowd of villagers. It gave Charlie the opportunity to take inventory of our firepower. This guy, I figured, had to know that we couldn't touch him from where we were at that moment. Pacification, it seemed, was not the way to deal with our enemy after all. Maybe the war was made to order for one of those six man teams the Rangers use. Our large contingent was too easy to locate, recon and, whenever necessary, easy to avoid too. Of course there was Moose's definition of a pacified village to consider. Without the hindrance of the civilians, we could have turned the area into a free fire zone and tilted the battlefield to our advantage. But with no village or civilians, Charlie never would have descended on the area and there never would have been a pacification initiative to bring us there.

The following day we were taken back to the compound for our mini R&R and all we could do was sit in the NCO club and just think about the guys we lost and the shameful way we lost them. While we were there sitting at a very large round table, Rachel Coleman, Maleah Johnson and Sandra J. Jones, three Red Cross Girls, walked in and joined us. I understood the reason for having them in country was supposed to be some kind of morale booster but considering the circumstances we were operating under, nothing could've helped. They were three attractive white girls who were having a good time doing their best to cheer up the troops I supposed. Wheelhouse would have probably been impressed with their looks. Their presence had me reminiscing about the day we were skinny dipping in the valley below Fire base Beaver. It seemed as if everything reminded me of the better days we all shared before we came to Tuy Hoa. "How much time do you have in country?" Rachel asked me.

"Four months."

"Four months! You're just a cherry. I've got eight months in country." said Maleah totally unaware of how much I hated being called a cherry.

"Rachel, give him one of those short-timers calendars anyway. He just might make it." said Sandra without realizing how insensitive and inappropriate the remark was to anyone like us who had to face the real part of the war where sometimes some of us didn't make it. "Here you can have Snoopy. When you make it over the hump start coloring in the spaces." she said as she handed me a cartoon of the Peanuts character Snoopy flying in his Sopwith camel chasing after the Red Baron. The cartoon was sectioned in numbered squares to be colored or covered in ink on each succeeding day after the six-month juncture in my tour. The calendar started at the "182 days to go" square so I assumed that the hump she referred to was the midway point in my tour. It seemed like a long time from where I was sitting. Tuy Hoa had turned into a seed of doubt that had grown into huge proportions. I had started to fear I would never live long enough to see the end of the mission. For that moment though, all we could do was sit and listen to Maleah, Rachel and Sandra J do their Red Cross thing in spite of the bad mood we were in. I wondered privately, if they were the "Round Eyes" our XO was referring to earlier. I guess after being here for so long and not seeing any American girls, it would ordinarily be a welcome sight. However, it wasn't an ordinary situation and it wasn't their fault. The girls overlooked the fact that we had to risk getting ourselves killed in the same part of Vietnam they were having so much fun in. It didn't seem fair that less than two clicks away from where we were sitting, we were going to spend another scary night huddled together like frightened kids. Of course they never knew and to them we could only wonder if it mattered at all. I had a feeling that Al was about to say something to the girls that was sure to send them running.

The time finally came for us to leave the bar and not soon enough. If time really flies when you're having fun, then it was truly standing still while in that bar. In fact it stood still for our entire stay because we were all more than ready to say farewell to the so-called R&R site. I decided to pass on the next opportunity to make the trip if the lifers offered. It was a boring charade that we could have all done without. In spite of our overall situation, we were capable of having a better time in the village. We could have sat around feeling sorry for ourselves without the company of the Red Cross Girls.

We arrived in time to hear old Brook Benton chime in with his heartbreaker. The nights were taking me apart and I was still hoping that our stay in Tuy Hoa was nearing its end. Our losses made the stay seem longer than we had been there. I had a feeling that the brass's appetite for dead bodies would not be satisfied with just 17. As long as they didn't have to do the fighting they'd probably let us rot in Tuy Hoa. If there is any truth about old soldiers never dying, it's probably because they always kept themselves at a safe distance.

That night I suppose that someone figured it was time for us to retake the initiative and go back up that mountain where the guys lost their lives. As I should have expected, our squad was being chosen to do the honors. I protested but it was useless. We had to go. Our chosen ambush spot was not far from where the second squad was overrun. There was a huge boulder behind us. It made me paranoid because we were at the mercy of the B-40 rocket. The sight of one flying through the air still had me scared senseless. I still had visions of the one that flew past me while crossing the bridge. The loud sound of one of them exploding was enough to make me shake in my boots.

When the night was over and the sun came up we all felt relieved. There was nothing like a little sunlight to relieve the tension. Of course there was very little sleep during the night due to our predicament in Tuy Hoa. Our enemy was probably laughing his head off at our lack of enthusiasm. We were psychologically defeated and he probably knew it. The only thing that we were looking forward to was the end of our stay in that village and all of its related memories.

When we rejoined the rest of the platoon, I sat and wrote Barbara a letter. I wrote about the firefight about a week earlier as I had already promised to let her in on all that happened. I had second thoughts after sending the letter though. I just had to wait to see how she handled it but somehow I feared that I had made a big mistake. As I wrote, I drank my first bottle of cold Tiger Piss since my bout with dysentery. The Vietnamese people don't chill the bottles of beer. They served it in a glass of ice. The problem was that the water used to make the ice could possibly be the source of the parasites that gave me the disease. Since Doc had the magic pills, I took my chances anyway.

While sitting on display for the throng of villagers and writing the letter, Al approached me with a look of mischief on his face. "Hi Hank, are you writing your girl again?" he asked in his best imitation of Jahret yet. I knew he was going to have fun with the Hank thing. "Al, why don't you write the drummers wife?" I joked.

"I don't know what to say to her."

"I could think of a lot to say."

"Then why don't you write her for me." he said and with that I wrote her a friendly letter that only mentioned the alleged marriage in a congratulatory post-script. It really got a lot of laughs from the rest of the guys when Al read it aloud. Their response was so spontaneous and genuine that I was flattered at having supplied them with such a big laugh. "Say Jackson! Are we carrying enough ammo?" Al yelled.

"Yeah Al, we've got enough."

"Jackson, I've told you a thousand times, it's not "Yeah Al." It's "Yes first gunner", or "No, first gunner." he joked.

"Fuck you Al." said Jackson which triggered more laughter. We were on a roll and as long as we could keep up the humor, being in Tuy Hoa was mostly an enjoyable experience. The chemistry, the camaraderie and the bond was all part of what kept us going. All we would ever need while in the village was each other. I supposed that it must have been the same everywhere else in country during redeployment.

A rumor started spreading about our leaving Tuy Hoa. I didn't want to get my hopes up too high but it was the best news I'd heard since I arrived. I tried not to even think about it. "Say Handy, did you hear about us getting out of this place?" asked Kyler.

"I've heard but seeing is believing."

"Yeah man, tomorrow we'll be smoking Bong Son Bombers."

"Let's wait and see, man." I said trying to end the discussion. Just when I thought I could put the issue out of my mind, Kyler tells me it's tomorrow. It was too much. It was expected to be a long day and an even longer night. Judging by all of the smiling faces, the rumor must have been raging out of control. Getting out of that village must have meant as much to the rest of the guys as it did to me. I doubted if my stay in Vietnam would get any worse than Tuy Hoa and getting out of that village meant everything, so I didn't want to waste any elation over some rumor. I wanted to save it all for the day that we actually left. "Just my luck to come out to the village after all of the action was over." said Walkup, one of the new people who came out after the 1st. His disappointment, though misguided, was genuine. He somehow knew that our leaving the village was no rumor. He also felt as though he had been left behind in the rear during the worst part of our stay in that village. "We missed out on all of the firefights." he said.

"You wouldn't say that if you were here before the big firefight."

"I'm telling you we were in the rear since before the firefight. They could have sent us out sooner." he said making me wonder if he was playing with a full deck. I figured that maybe he had been watching too many war movies or something. As kids we all played war games, cowboys and indians or cops and robbers. It was always a thrill to imagine what it would be like to have a real weapon in our hands and not some cap pistol. I was sure that he would come to his senses when the real bullets started flying and he faced dying in a useless war. "Handy, are you ready?" asked Purvis.

"Right now?"

"Exactly." he said starting a packing frenzy that lasted all of ten seconds. The news of our leaving the village had caught me totally off guard. There was no feeling of jubilation or anything like that but I started to feel as if I had gained the opportunity to see a ripe old age. I was saddened just the same about all that I had lost. There was of course the firefight and its tragic losses, all of the farewells and I suppose a lot of innocence. Tuy Hoa represented a lot of what had been taken away from me. Leaving the village meant leaving it all behind with little hope of regaining any of it. I started to ask myself if I could I live in peace with myself after failing so miserably at what I wanted to do so badly during the firefight.

On the brighter side, I felt that I had survived the worst part of my tour. The war was of course, winding down because of Nixon's policy of redeployment. There would be no more Ia Drangs, Dak To's or Khe Sahns. I also doubted seriously if the enemy would pull any more suicidal offensives like the one during Tet '68. The rest of my tour, I imagined, would pale in comparison to what had happened in Tuy Hoa and that would be fine. Our mission in that village had exposed Vietnamization to me as a charade and it couldn't end soon enough.

When the helicopters arrived to take us back to Uplift, I took one last look at the huge mountain and shivered at the thought of what could have happened. Somehow I knew that it would become a memory that would haunt me for the rest of my life. I imagined that life would go on in Tuy Hoa as it had for centuries. Our stay there was only a moment for those people. The Vietnamese had seen centuries of war and this was only a new year. Certainly there had been other units operating in Tuy Hoa before us and there would undoubtedly be others after we were gone. I just hoped that the next company wouldn't have to leave as much behind as we did. Aside from a higher body count in American lives, they couldn't possibly lose more.

6

When we arrived at Uplift, we all assembled in formation near the company area. The C.O. had bought about ten cases of beer and an equal amount of sodas. There was a barbeque pit burning steaks and ribs. He had a bar set up for all of the juicers, and his record player was playing the songs of Johnny Cash who had to be one of his favorites. There was even a trailer full of ice where one of the NCO's was placing the beer and sodas in it. After a quick speech by the old man, he gave the order to let the party begin. A mad dash ensued for the goodies by all of the guys he hadn't exactly been leading for the past five or six weeks. I guess he thought that it was a reward for his body count but I wasn't impressed at all. The steaks and ribs were nice and the music of course sounded like Johnny Cash. Cash was a C/W superstar for sure but he never really went over big with any of the heads. The juicers, perhaps to impress Mercein, enjoyed his music. It was possible they really believed that Cash had an impressive voice. Naturally, it didn't matter to the half crazed drunks that stood around singing rounds of "Because you're mine, I walk the line." Mercein was in his glory as he joined in with the men who were celebrating the beginning of another stand down as if he was at our side while we were in Tuy Hoa. Of course we did all of the fighting and all he did was hide out at the AFB.

All of the heads, naturally, had to hurry and steal our share of the beverages before the juicers started to get rowdy. "C'mon Al, lets get some of these cans and dash." I said as we started to stuff our pockets. Suddenly Mercein grabbed one of the N.C.O.'s and started wrestling with him. He put him in a hold and threw him into the trailer full of iced beverages. The crowd went wild cheering our ranking hard-ass's behavior. The liquor had barely started flowing and already they were at it. We had to leave immediately because pretty soon, according to legend, we suspected one of the juicers might start shooting.

We left the juicer party and retreated to the bunker line. I started wondering how long it would take for Mercein to come up with another suicide mission. Although Katta came along after the big firefight, he also held the same concern about our wild CO. The old man had already demonstrated a callous attitude toward losing men in battle. He was more dangerous than the enemy was to us. Of course that's what they always said about the war in Vietnam. One enemy was trying to kill us and the other enemy was trying to get us killed. I didn't know what kind of officer Mercein thought he was, but his name had already been jokingly linked to a well deserved fragging. He even planned to lead the Company through a round of PT in the morning. Of course the three of us would find something else to do. At sunrise, the whole company would be expected to be out there with him running all over the place. He probably wouldn't notice our absence. Jahret, of course, was expected to be in that number but we didn't care about him. He looked like he could use a few laps around the LZ anyway.

We partied all night and attracted quite a crowd. Some of the heads from the other platoons were there. We hadn't seen each other since the last stand down. It was nice to see the guys after being separated for the previous six weeks. I was saddened by the absence of all of the guys who were no longer with us. The reunion could have been so much better with them. In time, I expected to have the same kinship with all of the new guys. The experience of life in the bush and its continual bond would offset the adverse effects of the constant personnel turnover. As long as we could count on each other to be there for each other, nothing else would matter.

The bunker was cleared before sunrise leaving the assigned people alone to finish up. The platoon was already huffing and puffing themselves to death to satisfy his majesty Capt. Mercein. Of course we passed on the calisthenics and walked over to the mess hall for breakfast. The Spartan accommodations seemed luxurious compared to what we were used to. Anyone of us could easily get spoiled eating there every day. During breakfast we laughed at the idea of doing PT by order of Mercein or anybody else. After eating we stepped out of the mess hall and ran into the rest of the company running past the mess hall in cadence. "Look at Mercein; the hairy bastard. He's winded." I said.

"And look at Jahret bringing up the rear." said Katta. We stood waiting for them hoping for a confrontation we felt we had earned for non-participation. When Mercein passed by he didn't even look up at us. He just kept walking. By doing so, he denied us the opportunity to vent our anger at him. Jahret, on the other hand, would not pass up the opportunity to berate us. Of course no one cared about his opinion. He did a beeline for us and privately I wondered if he was looking for an excuse to fall further behind while getting a much-needed rest in the process. "I don't know who you guys think you are not showing up like that. If the Captain says PT in the morning that goes for you three guys too. Is that clear?" he said while breathing heavily.

"Yes sir." we replied in unison.

"The next time you pull this stunt, I'm bringing you up on charges." Having said that, he walked away, leaving us snickering at him. In time we expected Jahret to realize that if he kept threatening guys he would get fragged. He was safe with us because we didn't take him serious. Someone else might not hold the same amount of disregard as we held for him. It would only take one person to feel threatened enough by his words to bring about the fatal response. Of course the worst he could've done to the three of us was to send us to Vietnam and we were already there laughing behind his hairy back.

Most of the company later assembled inside of the new barracks constructed to house line companies during stand down. The barracks was crawling with mostly new guys playing loud music. They were lounging around both inside and outside of the quarters. Some of them were writing letters which was a sure sign of a new arrival. Once the guys spend a few months in country, they hardly ever wrote home. I never understood the phenomenon and never wanted to be a part of it. While walking around the new facility, I found a lot of past issues of The Stars and Stripes lying around. One was from back during the Post Office strike. In it was a picture of one of my favorite pro basketball players wearing fatigues and sitting in a New York Post Office sorting mail. Being one of the privileged pro athletes, he never had to worry about the draft and going to Vietnam. Each pro sports team, according to legend, had positions set aside in both the National Guard and the Enlisted Reserves for their players when they were drafted out of college. This arrangement afforded them the opportunity to get paid playing a game and avoiding the other draft at the same time. It was discouraging to find out that he was a draft dodging scab filling in for striking Postal Workers. But since he played for the Knicks, I couldn't let politics stop me from rooting for them.

A middle aged black lifer entered the quarters and started walking around the room. He held the rank of First Sergeant and I had to wonder if he was lost. Then he beckoned us to gather around him. "Say, who is that guy?" I asked one of the new guys.

"He's our new First Sergeant. He was at the party."

"He wasn't at our party." I laughed as I approached him with the rest of the guys. He was a short balding paunchy guy that kept a stinky cigar in his mouth that was sure to keep me at a safe distance as he spoke. "Now, I understand that Charlie co. has just returned from a very trying experience in Tuy Hoa. I know that we lost some men, and losing close friends can sometimes take a lot out of us. When things like that happen, we have to just put it all aside and get on with the mission at hand. Some of us have taken our losses real hard and have chosen to feel sorry for ourselves. Self pity can only make matters worse; so let's try to get back to where we were before Tuy Hoa happened. We still have to function as a unit. That's all that I have to say for now." he concluded as he left me wondering what the speech was all about. Top had a way of saying things that kind of left me confused. It was weird receiving a pep talk from a non-combatant. The higher ranking lifers in the rear always used "we" and "us" as if they had a direct hand in the actual fighting.

Al, Katta and I formed a threesome that had become inseparable. We stepped out of the new barracks laughing at Top's speech and ran into my jump school buddy Byrd. He had re-enlisted to get out of facing a tour in the bush. I redundantly reminded him that somewhere down the line, he would be sent back for another tour. They may have given him a rear job, but his MOS was still infantry. Trusting the Army for an extra three years was too abstract. It was possible that Nixon could have pulled the Herd out of Vietnam before the end of our tour. That would have really made any new re-enlistee look foolish. After deciding to roll the dice with the draft, I wasn't about to change my mind in mid stream. "Guess what? They're sending me to pathfinder school." said Al.

"Pathfinder school? Here in 'Nam? "

"Well pathfinder training anyway. It's a one day deal."

"Will they be assigning you to another company?"

"No. I won't be going anywhere. I'll just be pathfinder qualified, that's all."

"You'll get to wear that patch on your fatigue pocket, right?"

"Of course."

"By the way, what the hell is a pathfinder anyway?"

"Pathfinders always go in first to prepare an area for a landing. Be it helicopter or parachute."

After listening to Byrd talk about that re-enlistment and then Al talk about Pathfinder school, I felt that Byrd had jumped ship. Al, on the other hand, seemed to be embracing everything that Byrd was running away from. I was changing more everyday. Al and guys like him had become my kind of people and Byrd had become a REMF. It wasn't that they weren't as good or brave as we were. It was just that I couldn't identify with them at all.

We decided to take advantage of all of the free time we had and retired to bunker #9 for a day of leisure. Along the way we passed a group of black guys from the first platoon. They were standing around giving each other "Dap". The practice could be mostly described as an exaggerated handshake consisting of a lot of hand slapping, arm waving, chest thumping and finger snapping. The ritual was practiced by all black troops throughout Vietnam. As we passed by, they gave us a black power salute. When they flashed the trademark fist skyward, we returned the salute and continued on our way. "Do you want to be with your brothers?" Katta asked.

"I am with my brothers." I answered trying to understand why Katta asked me that question. He was genuine and sincere but he never had to worry about feeling like he was coming between me and those guys. The guys in the first platoon were only expressing a unity they felt was needed to get them through the war. Their unity shouldn't have been misinterpreted as an expression of separation or racial intolerance. As evidenced by their salute in spite of Al and Katta's presence, it wasn't necessarily an all black thing either. In Vietnam we all needed each other. We were all brothers and nothing could ever change that. I only wished that Wheelhouse and those guys were still with us to share the brotherhood that we all once enjoyed. Their deaths had left a gaping wound in our platoon and I felt that we were still bleeding. To lose those guys and then start separating along lines of color would have been like disgracing ourselves because we had all meant a lot more to each other before we went to Tuy Hoa.

Someone informed us that the first platoon's fearless leader was moving over to recon. He expectedly would've actually been able to better utilize his skills over there. It was more a surprise that he hadn't gone over to our Ranger co. Maybe his superiors wouldn't let him leave the battalion. Those guys in recon were in for a big change in pace. There was a rumor going around that he didn't expect to live to see the end of his tour. Of course a rumor is just a rumor.

We walked over to the mess hall for lunch and came upon three black guys heading in the other direction. One of them seemed to be very ill and was being helped along by the other two. When they got closer, I noticed the sick guy had yellow eyes. I'd never seen anything like it before. He was in dire need of some major medical attention yet they weren't even headed toward the clinic. After passing, we went inside of the mess hall to eat lunch. The place reminded me of a typical restaurant on S. Rampart St. back in New Orleans. It looked like another "greasy spoon" as we called them. Right down to the draped tables. The only difference was the menu. While sitting there, I came up with the idea to write my mom and have her send me some of the foods that couldn't be found in Vietnam.

After lunch, we returned to the bunker for more leisure. War may be hell but we were experiencing as much heaven as Vietnam had to offer. Two guys were lying atop of the next bunker getting a tan. The fun had to stop momentarily because we had to go over to the chapel and pay another tribute for our fallen. This time it would be a religious one. A memorial service was planned for them and although attendance was not mandatory, we went anyway. Most of the guys wanted to pass on it in order to put the episode in the past. I didn't think it would hurt as much as losing them did. It might even start a healing process for some; a process that I really needed to see begin. I still hadn't made any progress in that direction although it had been more than a week since we lost those guys. We still owed it to them to remember and I knew that I wouldn't ever forget.

The Chaplain was another middle-aged man with a lot of rank. He was a major and it seemed that considering his duty; rank seemed irrelevant. He had no command and, I supposed no authority either. Anyway he gave a decent service for the guys. His eulogy was very inspiring. There was speculation that he might even ask one of us to come forward and say a few words. Evidently he planned otherwise because he wrapped it up with a final prayer and ended our stay. When the service ended, I realized that there was little that I could do to feel any different about the ordeal. I could only hope that time would take care of the issue because I still felt like we let those guys down.

There were only about a dozen of us that cared enough to show up for the services and it was par for the course. There was seldom any action over at the Chapel. The Chaplain could only count on giving services in the field because in the rear, no one ever showed up for services. Other than that, he was only needed to force guys to write home whenever their letter writing became too negligent.

A new shake and bake was assigned to our platoon. According to rumor he was a Mormon. I doubted if it were true because I always thought that those guys were pacifists making them eligible for some kind of draft deferment. I wanted to ask Purvis about him but as of late he hadn't been too accessible. He had been acting somewhat withdrawn and distant. It was almost as if he wasn't a part of the platoon anymore. I hoped that it wasn't his girlfriend again because there was so little he could do about whom she went out with while he was away.

Later that day, I found Doc sitting in a four-seater with two other guys. While having his bowel movement he was also experimenting with the first aid tape's surprising ability to disguise the smell of burning marijuana. When either smoking the grass in a strip of the paper tape or applying a strip along side of a ready rolled joint, the smoke produced a sweet aroma. He was in there with two other guys and I couldn't' smell anything but the fragrance that was caused by the burning tape. It had to be the adhesive. We sat laughing at each other for at least a half hour as one unsuspecting lifer after another walked in and out of the outhouse. The little crapper had a cloud of smoke and none of them knew what we were doing. We left because we figured that they would come back looking for us when they started feeling a little light headed. When we stepped out of the little outhouse, we could see some of the guys hitching a ride to Linda & Monique's. There were also a lot of guys coming back from the village. The lifers weren't interfering with our travels at all. If there weren't so many bad experiences to recall, the stand down could have ranked up there with the one we had before we went to Tuy Hoa. Of course that was what made that stand down so special.

I ran into Purvis who seemed to be in a better mood. He was talking about going on leave. It was as if I was talking to a stranger. At that time Purvis only seemed to be withdrawing from us. He had lost all of his enthusiasm and probably just wanted to get back to his girl's side. Purvis never did seem to fit the typical mold of most of the guys in the company. He couldn't have been an underprivileged draftee like so many of the rest of us. Someone once said that as a kid he attended one of those expensive military academies. Maybe he thought that a tour in Vietnam would have topped off his affiliation with the military. He always seemed to put a little more in his pose whenever he was in front of a camera. After his tour turned into more than a photo essay, he seemed to be rethinking his position in Vietnam; a position he could have possibly avoided. That letter from his girl really started the wheels spinning out of kilter. I doubted if one week away could make that much difference in his tour since he had at least four or five months left to do. His job as squad leader was made for a leader willing to set the example and not just exercising the authority. He was no longer exhibiting the example and was definitely backing away from the authority role altogether. I wished him luck and a prompt bon voyage on his upcoming trip to Hawaii.

7

Our stand down ended and we were hustled over to the chopper pad for transport to our next operation. Our destination was not disclosed to any of us. All we knew was that when we disembarked from the slicks we were to move uphill in a hurry. Moving quickly uphill was nothing new to me. Being told to do so, however, was a different story. I imagined the prescribed pace was designed to catch Charlie off guard. I couldn't imagine how an entire company of troops coming in on a bunch of noisy helicopters could sneak up on anyone. It just couldn't be done. If there were any NVA regulars in the area we were on our way to a disaster. Our exact destination was also a mystery. The practice of limiting the number of maps was always puzzling to me. We all went through hours of training learning to read maps but was never issued any. I only wanted to be informed of our whereabouts and to be able to pinpoint our exact location at all times. I remember when we were in the Crow's Foot, there would always be arguments about our exact location between the map holders. All the rest of us could do was sit and watch the privileged few settle the issue between them. Bear used to swear on his last breath that he always knew where we were. He was an extremely confident map reader. Not having him around to lead us uphill once more was discouraging. Nobody ever had to tell that guy to hurry up.

When the choppers landed, my stomach started manufacturing butterflies. As we left our slicks and started struggling our way up the hill, Jahret started barking out commands as if we needed to know what to do next. Redundancy must have been a prerequisite for O.C.S. (Officer Candidate School) cadets. He sounded like one of the training cadre at Ft. Polk as he made a bad moment a little worse with his unnecessary noise. It was a steep mountain and one misstep could have led to a long roll to the bottom of the hill. Jahret could've caused someone to miss that step with his bullshit urging.

We made it to the top and set up a defensive perimeter. It was fortunate to see that the summit was unoccupied by the bad guys. I still couldn't understand the big rush to the top of the hill or the secrecy about what we were supposed to be doing anyway. More importantly, after two stand downs and one long operation in a village, I had to readjust to life in the bush again. At least we didn't have to deal with the monsoon. Climbing up that hill would have been a monster if it were raining.

Al was sent in ahead of us to prepare for the helicopter assault. He loved his new job as our pathfinder. He never mentioned any extra pay either. When he took the job as pathfinder, he surrendered the machinegun to Jackson. Al, along with Katta had also taken up residence in the third squad. Doc John, in the same spirit as Doc Bueno, always had a preference for our squad. He decided much earlier to be like a member of our squad and carried so much extra armature that it was as if he was only a part time medic. He was serious about being a grunt first and a medic only when his services as medic were needed. The squad had gone full circle. We had a completely new group but had somehow maintained the same identity. We were going to carry on the tradition of being the squad that didn't mind doing things our own way and we loved it. The more things changed the more they remained the same. I found it easier than I thought it would be to deal with new faces. I just didn't want to ever be a part of a dull boring group. The guys in the new third squad were fun to be with. I guess it is just the tradition that began before I came over here. That guy Reb started something and he was still influencing us as if he were still around. He would have been surprised to see the residue effect of his stay in Charlie Co.

As we sat around waiting for nothing to happen, a news report came over the radio about an Apollo spacecraft marooned in space. "Did you hear that shit?" I asked."

"Yeah, I'll put a tape on now." Kyler answered showing little or no concern about the astronauts' chances for survival. Surprisingly, the news didn't raise an eyebrow on any of the guys sitting around me. I was almost reluctant to say another word about it. I remembered the way the guys treated Christmas and felt almost as obligated to follow suit with my outward reaction. Maybe they thought that everything would work out and there was no need for concern or alarm. Maybe they were so confident in that good old Yankee know-how that they never worried about the outcome. I hoped so too, but privately I doubted if bringing these three astronauts back would be easy. They were not only in deep space; they were also in deep shit. The guys around me were just so caught up in our own situation that they had lost all compassion and concern for anyone else. I feared for the lives of those three guys marooned in space. I had spent a great part of my adolescence practically worshipping the guys in the silver flight suits. It was a part of that cold war thing. Any trip we made to the moon was like rubbing it in the faces of those communist also-rans. Still, no one cared about what was happening overhead at that very moment.

Jahret planned to send a squad back down the mountain for ambush. Naturally we expected to be that squad so we prepared to go without being told we were chosen. As far as we were concerned, the only thing that had to be decided was how soon we would be allowed to leave. It was getting late and once it started to get dark, it would be impossible to navigate our way down the hill under the extra cover of the trees. We planned to fake our location to avoid fumbling around in pitch darkness. Once out of sight of CP, we would set up for the night and just tell him that we're at the bottom of the hill. "Jahret's coming with us and he's taking a few extra guys along." said Al. It was just what we didn't need to have happen. It sounded like one of those worst case scenarios unfolding. It made me realize that maybe being lost in space couldn't be as bad as I thought. The prospect of spending a night on ambush with Jahret was just that regrettable. I needed to be more concerned with my own situation. Those three crew cuts were making themselves famous. Had we gotten killed during our assault up that hill we would've only been in a body count given at the end of the day's six o'clock news. That body count would have followed the real story for that day, the Apollo astronauts and their date with disaster.

When we descended to mid-level of the mountain, the darkness was worse than I thought it would be. We were slowly inching along the trail due to zero visibility. I couldn't see anything at all. The only sound to be heard was that of an occasional stumble. Even worse, Kyler was with us and he was in his usual form. He could barely see in daylight and having him along was really asking for it. Every time he fell, he let his emotions get the best of him. He was cursing every stumble or missed step and he made more than a few. Jahret was just as loud with his verbal reprimands. It was too dark to tell but, we must have looked like the Keystone Kops. I knew we sounded like them. We were breaking all of the rules of stealth and to avoid getting separated, we had to stay within touching distance. We were virtually holding hands. I didn't know who was walking point, but I hoped he wouldn't fall off of a cliff. Jahret was failing us in ridiculous fashion and exposed himself as being miserably inept as a leader. His performance was only enhancing his candidacy for a well deserved fragging. If he would have done his tour in the earlier years of our involvement, he probably would have been sent back in a body bag a lot quicker than it took me to get as angry or fed up with him.

When we finally made it to the bottom of the mountain, I felt as if somebody was watching over us. I really had my doubts on the way down that trail. It took us over an hour to make what should have been a fifteen-minute hike. As we reached a clearing and started to set up for the night, it started raining hard. Before that cloudburst, I thought that it only rained in Vietnam during the monsoon. It was in fact raining harder than it ever did during the rainy season. "Buddha's really pissing on us now." said Kyler. It was still pretty dark and we still couldn't see each other. All we could use to distinguish each other was voice recognition. We never got a chance to pull out our ponchos. All we could do was sit in the torrential rainfall and get wet like a bunch of assholes. If only Jahret would have stayed up at the top of the mountain we would have set up long before the rain came down. The monsoon had already exposed a lot of us to worse conditions but we would have set up a lot sooner because we never would have come as far downhill as we did either. It was the worst ambush I had ever been on.

The rain finally stopped and we were able to spend the rest of the night in place without further incidence. My anger kept me awake all night. Jahret had to be the worst officer that ever came out of OCS or wherever he came from. I didn't know what the criterion was for a candidate but something was wrong with the screening process. "That was some storm last night wasn't it Handy?" said Doc as he removed his poncho liner to reveal himself. It was so dark when we set up that I didn't know he was next to me. The storm was nowhere near the event that our platoon leader caused by bringing us down in the fist place though. I started wondering how long it would take for him to get one of us killed. His potential for disaster was limitless. It didn't seem fair for us to be the unlucky platoon that had to get stuck with him. There were other companies in the battalion that were equally as undeserving as we were.

We returned to the top of the hill and awaited Jahret's command to move on to our next objective. While sitting around waiting, I privately kept an ear open for news of the ongoing near disaster in space. The rest of the guys were very unconcerned about it, so I kept a low profile on my interest in the event. Before leaving, our squad was chosen to stay behind and spend the night in place alone to catch Charlie following in our wake. The enemy lived off of our garbage. He inspected everything we threw away and expected to occasionally pick up on whatever we accidentally dropped or lost. The area we were covering, however, was too big for one squad to occupy without spreading ourselves thin. Worrying about the astronaut's chances for survival at that point seemed foolish. The rest of the platoon moved along a ridge that connected our location to the next mountain. The distance was expected to be at least 2-3 clicks away. Either we hadn't learned a thing from Tuy Hoa or maybe the lifers just didn't care. Six guys alone separated by that much distance was risky to me. With no other option, we were forced to follow along with Jahret's order to stay behind. At least the area showed no signs of Charlie's presence giving us enough confidence to get through a long night. Our squad was new and about the only thing I missed at that moment was the old "Last Guard" routine. It died before we left Tuy Hoa and the place was just that much less enjoyable without those guys fighting to avoid that particular spot on the guard rotation. I missed the ritual and of course I missed those guys.

The following morning, we left our spot to rejoin the rest of the platoon. We had to take the same route they used which was a violation of a forbidden rule of the jungle; to always avoid being predictable that is. By telegraphing our every move, the enemy would be given the advantage of being able to set up ambush and plant his booby traps along our anticipated route. On this particular day, it was our only option. The enemy had a wide variety of devices designed to maim and dismember. It was hard to concentrate on anything else.

After walking along that trail for at least a half an hour it occurred to me that if we would have come under attack the night before, we would have been on our own. The distance was just too long to expect anybody to negotiate coming to our rescue. We were once again, split up and vulnerable to being outnumbered and cut off. Of course Mercein was again nowhere to be found as we followed a familiar script. We had been placed in a situation similar to the one that had cost us so much in Tuy Hoa. I hoped that everyone else was noticing the pattern.

When the rest of the platoon finally came into view, Purvis radioed ahead to alert them about our approach. We didn't want to spook anyone and get killed by friendly fire and I didn't want to have to shoot one of them to keep from getting killed either. It had already been a harrowing first two days and we needed to settle down and regroup. When we did arrive, it felt great to get the rucksack off of my back after such a long hump. Jahret, however, had other ideas. He had already planned to immediately send us downhill to fill canteens for the entire platoon. I was so angry I felt like punching little holes in every one of them. The trip down was not going to be a piece of cake. The task of bringing all of them back up full of water would be even harder. My anger over being chosen to get the water had become a source of concern for Katta as he tried his best to help me maintain my cool. I felt that Jahret sent us downhill to get back at us for skipping PT. Mercein never said anything to us about it and probably realized how angry we were about Tuy Hoa. His subordinate, however, had appointed himself as the judge who would make us pay for our decision to skip that dumb run around the base camp.

When we made it to the stream at the bottom of the mountain we lit up a joint with. It should have taken us only about thirty minutes to fill up those canteens but we had already decided to have a little fun while we were away. "Hurry up; we've got to move out when you get back." Jahret yelled from atop the mountain. He was practically in full view of us from where we were smoking.

"Is that mother fucker serious or is he just plain crazy?" If he thinks he's going to send us down here on a shit detail after walking three clicks and move out immediately after we struggle back uphill, he's out of his mother fucking mind." I said as I took a seat on a nearby boulder.

"Handy's overcome by the heat." said Katta.

"That's a good one." said Purvis as he picked up the handset and fed Jahret the newly constructed lie about my condition. His quick thinking worked because they bought the story and told us to stay a little longer until I felt better. When we did return to the top, Calvin, of all people, was waiting with a look of concern that appeared so genuine it would have fooled his own mother. "Eat some ham slices; the salt content will help you." He said as I passed by. Katta's smokescreen was working because our planned departure was put on hold until I felt better. This was too much to believe. "Here's some ham slices." Al snickered as he handed me a can of my least favored canned food item.

"But I hate that shit."

"C'mon man, we've got 'em leaning now." He laughed. I ate the slices to keep the guys happy but I didn't like being the subject of their scam. After all, the temperature was nowhere near as hot as it usually gets during the summer in New Orleans. I doubted if it was more than 85 degrees.

When the sham was over, we moved on to another mountain and witnessed another breathtaking view of the countryside. This one was more spectacular than all of the rest. Asia is truly a beautiful continent and sitting atop a mountain looking out at the rolling hills surrounding us was an awesome experience. Sometimes I found it hard to believe I was actually there witnessing it all. I wished Barbara could have been there with me to share the moment but only that moment.

The new buck sergeant I heard about was with us. His name was Keith Mauerman and he was a hulk that stood at about six feet tall and easily tipped the scales at 200 plus. He spoke with a soft voice, one that belied his imposing physique. He was very polite and took everything serious. "Keith, how did the rumor get started about you being a Mormon." I asked.

"It's not a rumor. We are known as Latter Day Saints."

"A Mormon and a Latter Day Saint are both the same?"

"Exactly, I have done some missionary work for my religion that had taken me abroad on occasion. I have also converted and baptized people into the faith." he added, without boasting about how much of the world he had already seen before the war. Everything about the guy suggested that he was a very humble person. "How come you're in Vietnam? Shouldn't there be some kind of deferment for your kind?"

"My kind?"

"Yeah, I mean aren't you some kind of minister?"

"No I only did missionary work. I am not a minister."

"And you're saying that it's OK for Latter Day Saints to fight in wars?"

"We don't take drugs, we don't use alcohol, we don't smoke cigarettes but we are American citizens. Whenever our country calls, we are as obligated as any other religious denomination to comply with the draft." He said. If religion is truly a way of life, then all Latter Day Saints must be like Mauerman. Uncompromisingly committed to spirituality, that is. He was very intelligent and likeable too. Of course what I liked most about him was his intelligence. It was still another argument against the infantry is for the dumb guys theory. I imagined that he would fit in just fine with the rest of the guys in the platoon. He didn't have to be a head either. All he had to be was Mauerman and everything would be alright. If Shave could do an entire tour in the bush as a member of a group like the old third squad then Mauerman should easily do the same with the squad's new collection of free spirits and misfits.

It was still too early to start counting days left in country. Black, on the other hand, was down to his last few and was already in the rear. Hopefully when my days numbered as few, I would only be preoccupied with going home where we all belonged. There was little we could do in Vietnam but fight and die. I might have felt differently a few years earlier but being in Vietnam had taught me otherwise. I had seen enough of the war to question its true objective and direction. Wars should be fought to be won or not fought at all. The Vietnam War had no such objective and it was unfair to those of us who had to participate in it.

Apollo 13 and its crew had somehow managed to limp its way back to a safe landing. I was relieved to hear about their safe return and couldn't imagine how they pulled it off. Of course the guys around me didn't seem to care at all. I wondered if they even heard the news report coming across the radio. As a kid I used to dream about space travel. The only dream that I had in Vietnam was to go home in one piece. Those astronauts had dreams about going to the moon. I'm sure that their safe touchdown became more than a dream come true. Life has a way of rearranging our hopes, dreams and plans. Vietnam was like a demonic roadblock that stood in the way of every young man in America. We could make plans for our future but we had to remove the demon from our path before we could realize any of them. Draft deferments were more attractive than a new car to the average guy back home. One guy that I jumped with at Ft. Bening never reported to Oakland on Thanksgiving. Obviously he let the demon consume him. He probably went to Canada or maybe he just went underground. He would have to live with his decision to desert and make new plans for his future. Who knows, maybe he just decided to make Canada his new home which was too cold and too far away from home for me. All of my plans included Barbara at my side and living together in New Orleans not Canada.

I soon lost all of my curiosity about our exact location. The only thing that mattered was that we were the only troops in the area. It was a good time for Keith and all of the other new guys to get acclimated to life in the bush. Nick had a baptism under fire on his first night. One the other new people that came out with Keith really stuck out like one of those round pegs trying to fit into a square hole. His name was Grove, a curly headed white kid that had to be about 18. He was very much out of place in his new environment and was very lucky to be on a mission where there was no real action going on. It helped me a lot to be in the Crow's foot at the beginning of my tour where there was lots of rain but no shooting. "Handy, did you get any mail from Barbara lately?" asked Doc.

"Of course. Do you want to read it?"

"Yeah, let me see it." I gave him the letter in spite of how odd it seemed to have him reading it. He was the medic so I let him read all of them simply because he wanted to. I still couldn't believe that he didn't have a girlfriend writing him from KC. "Barbara's always talking about how much weight she's putting on. I've gained at least ten pounds since I came in country." he said as he turned a page.

"Yeah Doc. She seems to mention that in almost every letter."

"What about the baby she always mentions? Is it your kid?"

"No Doc. It's not my kid."

"Are you two getting married after the war?"

"One of these days we'll get married. I don't know how soon it's going to be, but we do have plans." I answered. Our plans were real. The demon was the only thing standing in the way of our own little "happily ever after" trailer.

The resupply scheduled for that following morning would have to take place in the middle of our perimeter atop the mountain. We hadn't made any preparations or scouted any other spot. This meant that we didn't have to clear away any trees to create an LZ. Our perimeter was almost ideal for a mountain top landing. When slicks started arriving, the routine of unloading the supplies turned into a rude reawakening. I had forgotten how hard the process was. I usually preferred to run off and pull perimeter guard during the actual resupply.

"Lower your head when you approach the helicopter!" screamed Calvin, trying his best to be heard over the loud noise created by the chopper. I bent over forward and walked over to the slick to retrieve more supplies. After we emptied the helicopter it started to rise straight up.

"Everybody down!" he yelled. Calvin was the reason that I hated the job of lending a hand during the unloading process. He was always trying to orchestrate our every move.

"Let me tell you something Handy, back in '65 when I was with the 101st, I once saw a guy get chopped in half by the rotor blades as a chopper was landing. Never assume that because those blades are 10 feet above ground that it's safe to stand straight up and approach the craft. One slight tilt is all it takes." he said. As much as I hated to admit it, he was right. It didn't take a genius to realize the danger though. Just riding along Highway 1 was hazardous. Of course if I didn't already know that, I'm sure that Calvin was more than ready to give me the number of GI's killed in traffic accidents.

Gathar sent me a letter and spoke about how hard it was for him and other blacks in his platoon to make E-4. We both made rank easily during training but it was going to be different for us in Vietnam. When Garson got hit, my chances of making E-4 took a major setback. It was like starting all over again, proving myself to the new lieutenant. I hoped he was wrong about his situation and that he wasn't just copping out. The black troops in Vietnam were truly being discriminated against, as had always been the case in the military. I could see it all around me every day in my own company. Still, we couldn't afford to let the institutional racism become our reason for falling short of the performance standard. Our detractors needed to point to our failures and shortcomings to justify their biased stance against our efforts. Copping out only played into the hands of those who would deny us at every turn. Getting enraged over the issue only made us vulnerable to disciplinary actions and then susceptible to loss of the little rank that we came over with. In reply, I wrote about my being in the field since December with no CIB. It should've made him feel better to know that although we were separated for the first time in our military careers, we were still together in spirit and suffering.

We moved on after resupply without any knowledge about the operation. They usually knew exactly which NVA regiment was working in the area but had no such disclosure about this mission. I found it odd that Army intelligence always knew who they were but never had a clue about their exact location. I wondered how that arrangement worked out. Either Charlie wrote a letter to our command to misinform them about their location or we just relied on our own contacts without ever questioning their reliability. Whatever the situation was it never really worked out. It always seemed to be hit or miss when it came to locating the elusive NVA.

The next day was all humping and more humping. I couldn't complain because again, it was always better to have missions without any contact with Charlie. My contention that it was good for the new guys to get their feet wet on such a mission. We settled down for the night and started deploying our Claymores. Grove fumbled his trip flare and made it obvious that he was taking our mission about as serious as bivouac during training. When he wrapped the wire around the burned flare and gave it to me asking for another one, I knew that nothing was being impressed upon the guy. "The next time you mess up with the flare; try to remember to say the word "friendly" to alert the others that the flare wasn't tripped by Charlie." I said. He was by far the most interesting case of all the new guys. It was strange the way that Grove and others like him never seemed to grasp the significance of what was going on around them. To be around him was like babysitting an adolescent. While patrolling earlier, he lost contact with the guy in front of him and made a wrong turn leading everyone behind him in the wrong direction. Walking behind him was an adventure. We were rumored to be returning to Uplift shortly and possibly saving Grove's life. Katta was at wit's end and about to resort to choking the kid out of frustration.

Our return to Uplift would not be without note. Our new battalion CO, Col. Clark, was already in place and raising all sorts of hell. He was reported to be cracking down on nearly everything back in the rear. He even wanted the bunker line partying to stop. He had all of the MP's and the officer of the day constantly patrolling the perimeter checking up on every bunker. If he was truly as ornery and intrusive as they said he was, our next stand down was not going to be pleasant. I was not looking forward to meeting the hard-ass. On a more personal level, we had another new guy in the platoon. He was a short blond white guy named Joley who was very eager to meet Charlie. I almost wished that I could have arranged it for him. He was young as Grove and almost as anxious as he was green. Joley was influenced or attracted by that strange seduction of war that one had to experience to understand. He wanted to exchange fire with a real live enemy and I could tell he would not be satisfied until he did. It always seemed to be that the shorter guys were always trying harder to impress. With a chain of command that included the likes of Clark and Mercein, his opportunity would be arriving soon enough.

Considering our diminishing combat role, the chances of being drafted and sent to Vietnam shrunk with the redeployment of each unit. Somehow America was still capable of producing guys like Grove and Joley who would volunteer to go. The draft was the only reason that brought me to Vietnam. It hung over me like an albatross for two and a half years. On the other hand, a number of the guys in Charlie Co. were only 18 and couldn't wait to come over. Maybe they were so bored with life that death or the chance of getting their heads shot off was intriguing. Buckley, another one of the new guys, had a more realistic perspective on the war. He was content to do his time, count his days and get the hell out when his turn came around. He was a 21 year old white guy and had only recently graduated from high school. He must have stayed in high school to avoid the draft. I couldn't imagine any other reason and didn't believe he was as dumb as he claimed to be. Their arrival along with the other new faces in the other platoons was changing the makeup of our company. The 12-month tour may have had an adverse effect on us but we still managed to maintain some cohesiveness.

The mission ended and we returned to Uplift just in time to keep Jahret from driving me insane. Katta, however, did go insane trying to pull Grove's head out of his ass and Col. Clark was awaiting our arrival at Uplift to introduce us to life under his command. He had been rumored by the heads to have transformed Uplift into a concentration camp and had turned bunker guard into some kind of dreaded duty. That might have worked on the previous company but it could never work on us. He could never get Charlie Co to comply with all of his new rules.

When we returned to Uplift we found a new NCOIC named Rudy. Sgt. Rudy tried to overbear but as everyone went through the routine of ignoring the talk he was giving, he tried harder. I actually heard him order all guard duty people to show up for an inspection before reporting to the bunkers. Even more incredible, he expected us to shine our boots. Both Al and Katta were assigned to the same bunker with me and were deep into a serious laughing fit. They were both familiar with Rudy and said that he used to hump with the 1st platoon. Judging from the way they were laughing at him, I assumed he was not to be taken too seriously. "Look, are we going to show up for his inspection or are we going to skip it?" I asked. There was a lot of preparation involved for bunker guard and we needed to act quickly.

"I'm going to the inspection and have a little fun with this clown." said Al.

"Me too." said Katta."

"I'm going over to Linda and Monique's to get a nickel bag before it gets dark. When you guys finish with Rudy, don't forget to pick up a case of beer and a case of sodas too." I said as I took off for the highway to hitch a ride to our favorite opium den. As I stood waiting for a truck to pick me up, I realized that I was standing in the same spot where Wheelhouse and I exchanged those little items we took from that old lady. That was back in February but it seemed like only a couple of days had gone by since it happened. The pain of losing those guys was still lingering inside of me. We were just beginning to get to know each other well before the CO came up with that mission to Tuy Hoa. It was hard to believe they were no longer with us.

I caught a ride on a "Deuce and a half" and took off for the short ride to the village. I got off and started to walk through the village. Pretty soon I came upon an old Mama San using a large stick, actually a small log, to smash some rice placed in a cut out stump. After bashing the rice for a few strokes, she placed the crushed rice on a pan fashioned from dried bamboo leaves. She then tossed the rice into the air a couple of times and, as the rice fell back to the pan, the wind blew away the broken pieces of rice shells. She then walked away with the rice and left the pan lying on the ground. As I passed by her work area I was impressed with the simplicity of the procedure and the practicality of the tools. Before I witnessed the ritual, I never knew that rice came wrapped in those hard shells. This procedure, I imagined, hadn't changed in thousands of years and for the Vietnamese villagers, it probably never will.

I made it to Linda and Monique's place and found the joint crowded with heads.

"What you looking for soul brother?" one of them asked. I never knew Linda from Monique and couldn't make a guess. "A nickel bag baby girl." I answered. She then whipped out a bag as if she knew I was coming. I gave her the money and left immediately. As I walked back to the highway, I found myself running a gauntlet of cold stares, compliments of the neighbors. They obviously didn't care for the constant traffic. I didn't blame them either. I just wanted a bag and was sorry about the inconvenience. Wheelhouse was right. The Vietnamese village people were traditionally hard working people that were only tolerating our stay in their country. I was certain that the black market operators like Linda, Monique and all of the prostitutes were causing a lot of resentment with their contrasting lifestyles. Our presence in Vietnam was corrupting a small segment of people on a grand scale. The pursuit of the almighty American dollar was eroding their otherwise pervasive work ethic. My purchase was only contributing to the problem and made me feel at fault. I left with a new realization of their dilemma.

When I returned to the bunker line, Al and Katta were still laughing and retelling the inspection ordeal. I could only laugh at their stories. "If you two ever show up at another one of my formations with dirty boots, your asses will be grass and I guarantee that I will be the lawn mower." they repeated over and over in their best imitation of Rudy's southern drawl. The ass and lawn mower joke played all night long. Everybody who was somebody was there and nobody was pulling guard. Our main concern was the officer of the day. He was easy to spot as he patrolled the bunker line riding in a jeep. The headlights on the jeep alerted us in advance and that gave us ample time to evacuate the bunker of all unauthorized personnel. Of course, once he made his pass, everybody returned and the party continued. The officer was only going through the motions. He knew that if he became too aggressive it could have threatened his life.

The next morning we had another briefing. Mercein had come up with another mission and Jahret gathered us around to fill us in. "Our next mission is in an area that, according to Army Intelligence, has a large rice cache hidden somewhere in it. We will spread out over the area and conduct patrols in search of this rice." he said which initially didn't sound that bad. It made sense too. We find the rice and deny Charlie his food, which would force him to replenish his supply and also find a new hiding place. Of course I thought that Tuy Hoa sounded like a good idea too. If I'd learned anything from these briefings, it was to ignore my initial feelings about what was being explained to me. On the surface, D-Day probably sounded like a nice mission to some guys who died on Omaha Beach or to the paratroopers who were shot out of the sky when they jumped. We could only find out by searching for the rice, or worse, by finding it.

Jones finally returned from his regretful trip back to the world. Brooklyn must have looked great to him. Those of us who remembered him welcomed him back to the fold. Naturally we all realized that he must've been dealing with a lot of issues upon his return. It had to be hard to lose his squad during his absence. The awkwardness of the moment was very evident as we also readied for our next mission. "What's it like back in the world?" I asked him for lack of anything else to say.

"It's nice, but it's good to see you guys again."

"Did you write Cynthia while you were gone?"

Of course." he said. Jones made me feel like a lesser man. If I had a month back home and had to come to a new squad because of what happened to his, I don't think that I could've handled it. Not the way he did anyway. He was about ten feet tall at that moment and I admired him for it.

8

While on our flight to our next mission, I remembered our fateful day back in the An Lo's when we found that base camp. I hoped the guys would resist letting the lifers in on any subsequent discovery. They made life miserable for us when we shared our findings and it took a while for the rest of the guys to forgive us for disclosing the complex. We learned a lesson that day. One that I hoped we wouldn't soon forget. A heavily guarded rice stash, I feared, would not be given up without a fight. Taking that rice, I figured, would prove to be a costly endeavor. I didn't think that we were ready for any more losses. I knew I wasn't. I was already loaded with guilt and unable to carry anymore. It was also apparent that our finding the rice would only put another undeserving feather in the CO's hat. I didn't know about the new guys but the rest of us shouldn't have been so obliging.

We arrived in our area and immediately took up high ground to set up CP. Our plan was to have patrols patrolling the valley in search of the rice while our squad was stuck with the job of providing CP with security. Keith was assigned to our squad and was expected to take over for Purvis while he was away on leave. One of the squad leaders was a Staff Sgt. who was usually assigned to the mortar crew. I couldn't understand why they had him out in the bush. To also give him a squad was a bigger mistake. It flew in the face of logic to put a guy trained in mortars in charge of a squad. I'm sure he was effective leading a crew from a fixed position to lend fire support wherever needed but in the bush he would be exposed as anything but. "Sarge" as everybody called him was a dark skinned, slightly overweight black guy who followed orders without hesitation. I overheard him responding to Jahret's indecisiveness without quarrel. He took his squad from one location to another and never even sighed in exasperation. With Sarge it was always "Yes sir' or "That's a rog" as he moved his squad around like a chess piece. There was little consolation that we didn't have to go through what he was subjecting his squad to. On the other hand, having Keith in charge as we put in our time with CP gave him a close inspection of Jahret at his worst. It was hoped that he would store some of what he witnessed for future reference. As much as I hated to be on that hill with CP, there was a lot that Keith was learning first hand while we were stuck with them.

The old third squad would have laughed at being told where to patrol. We would have just done our own thing and that was that. It's easy to move a marker on a map from one place to another. Moving a squad around at the order of an idiot, however, was a totally different story. From where we were sitting all we could do was wish those guys luck because if they kept moving around on command, they would pay for it in the end. In all honestly though, I wished that we were out patrolling with them. I would have given anything just to get away from Calvin and Jahret. The free time we spent on the hill meant little to me because we could have made more out of it if we were alone somewhere out in the valley patrolling.

A shootout erupted somewhere out in the valley. Sarge's squad had made contact for sure. I didn't hear any AK-47 return fire, only M16 and a lot of it too. "My point man spotted one Victor Charlie."

Sarge reported over the radio. This meant that we weren't the only damned fools in the valley. Mercein took over the conversation and of course he was asked if they got him. "Negative!" He replied. The news put the old man in a sour mood. He blasted them for their poor marksmanship and ended is transmission. Hopefully Sarge had gained a realization of what a thankless job it was in the bush. His actual job of launching mortars probably looked a lot better from wherever his position was on the valley floor.

The following day found us still on the hill with CP. The other squads were patrolling and we weren't being allowed to do anything but provide the lifers with security. I really wanted to get away from Calvin and Jahret but all we could was sit and listen to their reports over the radio. While lounging around, I decided to make my special hot chocolate drink. 1 canteen of boiling water, 10-15 packs of dairy creamer, one pack of c-rations cocoa and for a special kicker, one pack of instant coffee. It was a staple of mine during the monsoon when I was always wet and cold. I had kind of dropped it from my field menu when the weather turned hot. I took a sip and passed it around. Al drank some and passed it to Katta who in turn passed it to Mauerman after one sip. Mauerman took a sip and started to spit it out. "Yuck! You sneaked one in on me that time Handy." He said.

"But it's just hot chocolate man. What are you talking about?"

"I can taste some coffee in that cocoa. My religion forbids the consumption of caffeine too." he said as he continued to spit and wipe his mouth onto his fatigue jacket while giving me as cold a stare as he could manufacture.

"Well I'm sorry about that man, you only told me about the alcohol and the nicotine. I knew better than to offer you a toke on a joint, but I didn't know about the coffee thing." Unbelievably, they didn't even drink coffee. He continued spitting and wiping making me feel guilty. I imagined he had to get down on his knees and ask or beg forgiveness for his transgression. I had to be more careful with him because I didn't want to offend him or his beliefs.

The following day again found us still on the hill protecting CP. I couldn't believe what they were doing to us. It wasn't that I thought we were missing anything out there. It was just so boring sitting around the radio listening to DJ Chris Noel spin the same records over and over. I never dreamed that we would be sitting in one spot when we knew that Charlie was in the area. I always thought they wanted us to get killed or at least shot at. They were squandering a golden opportunity to get more of us sent home in a body bag.

Suddenly more shooting erupted in the valley again. The firing was intense and heavy. I was certain that someone was shot that time. There was no way, I thought, that anyone could fire an M-16 as much and not get a kill. There just had to be a kill somewhere out there. "My point man spotted another Victor Charlie out there." Sarge said again over the horn. I had a sickening feeling they missed again though. The CO chimed in as expected and just as I suspected they did miss their target again. Mercein was livid. "The next time contact is made, I want some results!" He yelled and ended his transmission. It was probably the same guy they before. The way I figured it, if Charlie was in numbers he would have struck by then. Call it confidence or just cockiness, but I think that if our squad were out there we would have gotten that little bastard the first time around. Anyway, the CO was so pissed that he was probably close to having a coronary. He deserved all of the aggravation and more.

April had finally ended and I was glad to see it pass on. I feared that it would always be an uneasy time for me to relive all of the bad memories of the previous thirty days. It was a scary situation to be in because there was so much time left on my tour that I felt it could happen again. I also hoped the month of May would be all I needed to get out of the funk I had been in over our failure in Tuy Hoa. I continued to feel as if we could have done more for those guys had we been allowed to do so. The guilt had been heavy and my conscience was overloaded. I couldn't have handled anymore losses like that.

It was resupply day and I decided to escape to do some perimeter guard duty. Calvin was overbearing during the previous resupply and I didn't want to see a repeat. I started to find my way out of the area but he followed me to have a private talk. "Handy, I've got a letter from Wheelhouse's mother and she wants to correspond with one of her son's friends. You don't have to if you don't want to but I just thought I'd ask you because you two were close."

"Alright, give me the address and I'll take care of it." I said. I agreed to write the lady out of compassion, but I didn't even know what to say. The poor woman was probably heart broken and distraught. I doubted if there was anything I could do to console her from such a distance. Maybe she would eventually start to feel better when she realized that she had so much to give to the rest of her family. I already knew that she had at least one older daughter and one grandson. Life would go on without her son and it was a tragedy, but life would go on. I decided to write her after I collected my pay.

The paymaster stepped off of the helicopter and everybody was jockeying for position in line and he hadn't decided where to set up shop. They looked like worker bees following the queen around. It was confusing because we were in the bush and there was nowhere to spend any money. They sent out some hot food for us to eat. Sgt. Martin, or Marty as we called him, volunteered to be one of the servers. I thought it was odd because of his rank (E-5) and the authority that came with it. "Why is Marty slinging chow?" I asked Al.

"He used to be a cook in the Marines."

"Marty? You mean to tell me that he used to be a spoon in the Marines. Are you kidding me?"

"No bullshit man, a spoon." he said. Without a doubt, he did look more at home doing the food line than he was on the frontline. Maybe he missed his old job and was just lobbying for consideration. I didn't bother to find out why he left the Marines and joined the Army. Or why didn't he prefer being a cook instead of being in the field. Marty was nearly forty and old enough to know that he had it made in the rear with the gear. His reason would only sound ridiculous to me so I didn't bother asking. It seemed that everywhere I looked there was someone who didn't have to be with me in Vietnam. Marty was only the latest personality.

After eating the food and listening to Katta's critical assessment of the Army lasagna we had just eaten, I constructed the letter for Mrs. Wheelhouse. I started it off by introducing myself and filling her in on my humble background. I told her what a great guy that I along with a lot of other guys thought her son was and that we all missed having him around. I wisely avoided going into any detail about the events that took her son away from us. I didn't want to make her feel any worse than I assumed she already felt. After that there was little else to say so I just closed and let the letter fly. "Handy give me your photo album." said Katta while laughing at Al during another one of their teasing sessions.

"Haven't you seen it enough yet?" I asked as I handed it to him.

"I want to make a comparison."

"A comparison?"

"Yeah, look at this picture of Al's friends." he said as he handed me a picture of a group of white guys posing for an outdoor photograph.

"Collegiate." he said in reference to the style of pants they wore. They were all straight-leg pants and a sharp contrast to the next picture he handed me of his friends all wearing bellbottoms. I imagined that he wanted to show some of those pictures of me and my over-dressed friends. His intention was to drive home his point of fashion with Al. I only carried those pictures to remind me of what life used to be like before the draft. I looked at them every now and then to take my mind off of the war. Katta had found another use for them. The two of them were a riot.

After being paid, fed and resupplied, we settled down and passed the rest of the day with CP. That night I realized how difficult it was just trying to maintain a perimeter of security during our sentry duties. The area was too large and it was ridiculous to believe that because of our patrols in the valley we were safe atop that little mountain. That following morning, I was really leaning towards leaving that spot with CP and had become envious of the freedom the other squads were enjoying. It didn't look as if we were ever going to get a chance to go out on patrol. I was so angry I hoped that the rice would never be found.

While sitting and waiting for contact to be made by any of the patrols, I started to write my brother Joe. I just felt like doing some bragging about my team still being in the playoffs and his team watching it on TV. Writing a letter should have provided me with a distraction from just sitting and waiting for someone else to do something. It didn't work though. Being idle was killing us and we knew it. If those guys would have spotted Charlie again and didn't get him, the old man would surely have that coronary. He really blew a gasket over that second sighting. I was pulling for those guys but they had to do it on their own.

At Uplift, Col. Clark had started showing his true colors. According to word, he had just led Bravo Co. up an NVA infested hill. Obviously he was not the type to sit back and give commands over the horn. Much to Bravo Co.'s dismay, he liked the action. Clark was dangerous. He would definitely get somebody killed. Bravo Co. had found out first hand just how dangerous he could be. On a more familiar note, Lt. Mack was very busy making life miserable for any company that was on stand down. His transition to recon was swift. He had hit the ground running and was making a bigger name for himself than anyone could have imagined. Whenever he took a patrol out, he not only found Charlie, he engaged him no matter how big the contingent was. Both Alpha and Delta Companies were said to have already bailed him out in almost back to back patrols. It was actually safer to be in the bush than it was to be on stand down. Mack, it was feared, was going to redefine a stand down. Whereas it once meant getting lax, laid, drunk or stoned; it would be changed to being on alert. Mack had no qualms about taking on overwhelming odds. He must have been just the kind of lieutenant Col. Clark likes.

A news report, announcing that we had sent some troops into Cambodia, came over the radio. Unlike the near disaster in space, the news of the incursion was naturally a big event to every one of us. Nixon had taken a bold step by sending troops over there. It was a brilliant but long overdue move to drop the kid gloves and stop giving the enemy a safe haven over there. For years Charlie had been allowed to strike and then retreat across the border because we had always recognized Cambodia's neutrality. The nonsense had to end somewhere down the line. Charlie had weapons, ammo, food and hospitals inside of that border and it wasn't much of a secret. Nixon immediately went to the public with a redundant explanation about how the raid would hurt the enemy's ability to fight the war. He added that the move would buy some time in his attempt at accomplishing his Vietnamization policy. Cronkite was by then probably leading the press in the raking over the coals of the president. The reaction was expected to be negative because of Nixon's promise to get the US out of the war. His Cambodian gamble would only be viewed as a widening of the war and that was to be expected. I always thought that Nixon was using the war as a vehicle to get himself re-elected. He was definitely risking his second term by raising the fears of a war weary electorate. Public opinion was sure to crucify him for going into Cambodia. "How about that shit, Keith?" I asked Mauerman as we all gathered around the radio.

"Do you approve of the move?" He asked.

"Hell yeah man. We've been letting Charlie get away with that shit for too long."

"But what about the domino theory?"

"What's that?"

"During the French Indochina war, Eisenhower determined that the fall of any of the Indochina countries to Ho Chi Minh would cause a domino effect on all of the countries in the region. Our country backed the French in its effort to hold onto its former colony and has committed itself to the prevention of this fall of weaker countries into the communist bloc. It is literally the reason we are here today and I think the raid sets up Cambodia as another potential domino."

"That is something to think about. I never heard about that theory before." I said realizing that our commitment in Vietnam seemed to have started a lot sooner than I imagined. I didn't think that our raid into Cambodia was a matter of us bringing the war to another country though. We were only taking away Charlie's convenient safe haven. Keith's presence in our platoon had provided me with a knowledgeable source of information about our involvement in the war. He was at least 25 and a lot more aware of what the war was about. He could have proven to be what I needed to gain a more complete understanding about why we were in Vietnam. Knowing too much about our involvement, of course, had the potential to fuel a lot of the backlash about being there. I still felt like a dummy for not knowing more.

The enemy had usually fought a better fight when allowed to use Cambodia as a staging area. Our method of fighting the war was enabling a tough enemy to continue to fight. It was sheer madness to not go after a crippled wounded army and finish them off just because of the border. We had been bombing the Ho Chi Minh trail in Laos but ignoring the sanctuaries in Cambodia. Raiding Cambodia wasn't expected to get us out of Vietnam immediately but hitting them where it hurt made sense. I was all in favor of making the Russians, the Chinese, the East Germans and whoever else dig a little deeper in their pockets to replace everything we took from them. I hated those damn people for killing my friends and breaking their mothers' hearts. I was never a Nixon fan but I did think that the move was a good one and long overdue. I hoped that Keith was wrong about the dominoes but he seemed too informed to doubt.

Our rice search operation continued without any real participation from us. We were still being kept atop of the mountain providing security for CP while the rest of the platoon continued to search for the rice. The arrangement didn't sit too well with me but there was nothing I could do about it. Our CO probably thought we were a lousy company. He was never around but was always on the horn speaking in rude, gruff, offending tones. He knew he belonged out in the field with us and the fact that he wasn't showed how little he cared about what we thought of him. I supposed he wanted to make the rice mission succeed by imposing his will.

The news started reporting widespread demonstrations across the country in protest of Nixon's move into Cambodia. I imagined that the college students were at it again. I never suspected they were out protesting the inhumanity or the immorality of the Vietnam War. They were only afraid of being drafted and sent over to join us. They were hiding behind their draft deferments and nothing else. They were upset because Nixon had sold them a bill of goods called Vietnamization. They expected the withdrawal to be constant if not swift and without any scary episodes like going into Cambodia. Welcome to the real world.

Jackson received a Care Package on resupply day from his sister. She sent him some sausage and crackers. The sausage had turned green about a week before the package was finally delivered to him.

"You want some?" he offered as he continued to pare away the moldy portion with a bayonet.

"No thanks man. There's hardly any left." I never was the suicidal type anyway. I wondered if his sister knew that the package would take three weeks to arrive from the Homer, LA Post Office. Maybe it was such a favorite of his that he just told her to send it anyway. It made me think seriously about getting my mom to send me something. No perishables though.

The next day when everything started to get quiet in the valley below, I started to wonder just who comprised Sarge's squad and who walked point for him. It couldn't have been Jones. I doubt if he'd miss twice. We were lacking the identity we once had due to the constant changeover. I didn't know which squad was which and hadn't recently heard anyone using any numerical designation. I did know that we were still the third and that much never changed.

More incredible news started coming over the radio. Four student protesters were shot dead by, of all people, National Guardsmen. The Ohio National Guard, who was sent in as a show of force to put down a student uprising at Kent State, actually started to shoot at unarmed students who were protesting the Cambodian raid. It was the most disturbing news dealing with civil unrest since the riots at the 1968 Democratic National Convention in Chicago. This was cold-blooded murder considering that they were just a bunch of harmless unarmed students. We all agreed it was unusual for weekend warriors to be armed with live ammo and couldn't imagine what kind of threat the students posed to a group of armed soldiers. Or just what did they do to make their executioners feel as threatened.

It was a strange reversal of roles and contrasting positions. Before I was drafted I was always shocked at the turn of events surrounding the war. After coming over, however, the news from home seemed even more outrageous. When I thought about the principles involved in the Kent State shooting, I could only see mirror images. College campuses were full of draft deferment seeking students. I had never attended college but I heard there was a waiting list to get into many of them. The ranks of both the National Guard and the Enlisted Reserves were full of these same opportunists. There was definitely a long waiting list to get into any of those units. The wait was said to take years in most instances. Since both groups were going through extreme measures to avoid Viet Nam, it made the shooting just that much more impossible for me to understand.

Grove hit a trip flare and panicked. He squatted in place and repeatedly yelled "FRIENDLY!" out loud. I was impressed that he remembered the procedure for accidental trips. He was following my instructions closely but he was also, getting carried away with the thing. Katta walked over to him full of rage. I thought he was about to choke him for sure but managed to silence him without violence.

"I've got an idea. Let's get a pass when we get back to Uplift." Al suggested. I didn't even know that passes were issued in Vietnam. "Just where are we going to go with a pass?"

"To Phu Cat AFB of course. They have an on site massage parlor." he said as he and Katta nodded their heads in obvious approval suggesting they both knew something about the place that I didn't.

"I'm not into massages man." I said.

"Neither am I."

"I never had one either." Katta laughed.

"Homie, the girls that work in the parlor do very little massaging if you catch my drift." said Al. The Air Force life was full of advantages in comparison to what the Army had to offer us. There was no need in second guessing myself though. I only had 12 months left in the Army and after that, it wouldn't matter at all. I decided to take Al up on that pass to Phu Cat when we returned to Uplift though.

The following day found us still stuck on the top of the mountain with no place to go. The boredom was driving me insane. I almost wished I were out patrolling but not quite. During the last resupply, some of Sarge's squad complained that Walkup was bucking for E-5. They said he had been ordering people around as if he had already been promoted. I guess that was why he was so disappointed at not being sent out to the field earlier when we were in Tuy Hoa. He was in a hurry to make some rank. In his eagerness he was coming across as an asshole to a lot of guys in his squad though. I knew Walkup was a good guy with good intent. I just hoped that he didn't forget who he needed to count on. Or that he needed to count on somebody sometimes. At that moment though, he was irritating a lot of others.

Someone fired a short burst and shortly afterward, Sarge's voice came over the horn. "We just killed one Victor Charlie." They finally got the little bastard and redeemed themselves for all of the misses. Before a minute had passed, Mercein grabbed the horn and took over the transmission. "Listen, I want confirmation on that kill. Get me a picture of the kill and have it sent straight to me." He actually doubted the claim being made by Sarge. This, I thought, would be just the kind of example that should make the right impression on all of the new guys in the company who didn't know the CO. It should have made an impression on Sarge but I doubted it.

I stood around waiting for the guys to come back to congratulate them when I realized that they would not have to take that picture. The job of authenticating the kill would be ours. Jahret handed a camera to Keith and sent us off to do the deed. We quickly got over the irritation of being sent out to get proof of the kill and took advantage of our first chance to escape CP.

We packed light and left immediately. Once we made it to the bottom of the mountain we discovered a tattered, weathered chalk board situated in an area where a number of attendees once sat for some sort of briefing or class. It hadn't been in use for quite a while, but Charlie was definitely there once upon a time. We didn't stay long. We had to move out in a hurry. Fortunately the mountain wasn't too far from where we were. It was nice to go patrolling again even if it was only to take a picture. We continued until we reached the mountain and started our ascent. As we neared the area of the dead NVA soldier, I started to consider mutilating his body. After what happened to the guys at Tuy Hoa, anything revenge I could exact would be acceptable. They shot the faces off of all five of those guys and I wanted to even the score. I was already thinking about lopping the head off of the next dead body that I came across. I had heard stories about dead GI's being found with their severed penises jammed in their mouths and this dead body, I figured would have to suffer some kind of mutilation or humiliation. It was the law of the jungle. Moose once said that carving initials into the chests of the dead and leaving them out in the sun to decompose was a good idea. The skin would peel and reveal the lettering. He was a sick individual but at that time I could relate to what he was feeling.

When we finally came upon the corpse, he was lying on his back with both his mouth and his eye wide open. The flies were infesting him with maggots as we stood waiting for Keith to take the picture. As angry as I was at the time, I could only urinate into his mouth. It bothered me that I could not stoop to the level of our adversaries. The dead body would be sent home with a mouth full of Yankee piss though. As we left the spot where the corpse was, I started regretting not doing something worse to that body. I should have cut his ears off or maybe exploded a grenade in his mouth. Maybe the next time,

I thought, would be different. I was full of revenge but not enough to lose control. We returned to CP and handed the camera over to the lifers so that they could have their proof of death. Mercein's lack of trust in us was the final straw. After those guys took all of that abuse for not hitting their target, he couldn't believe that someone got the kill. He just had to rub it in. It was just one insult after another with that guy.

The next day we ended the mission without any luck finding the rice. Our squad was given the job of going out and finding a rendezvous site for the company to be extracted. I was already looking forward to that pass to the Air Force Base. Although I thought that CP was a fine extraction site, I had no problem with our appointment. It was to be only our second time away from the nest since the mission started. That night was expected to be our first night away too. We left and in no time at all we found a clearing big enough for a platoon sized extraction. Before we could call it in, we had to check out all of the area surrounding it. It was procedure to make sure that there was no sign of Charlie's presence before we started landing slicks in an otherwise unsafe area.

After our recon of the area, we searched for a nice hideaway to spend the night. We entered a bamboo tree line on the edge of the abandoned rice field that would serve as our extraction site. We stepped inside of the tree line and found the area to be perfect. It had ideal cover and adequate space. We dropped our rucks and started to deploy our Claymores and trip flares. Suddenly, while preparing for the night, we heard a distinctive metallic clink coming from our rear. It was definitely an aluminum canteen. My brother Joe had one when he was a Boy Scout. The cap is tethered by a metal chain. The sound we heard was the chain rasping against the canteen. The area was too good to be true and too perfect to be unoccupied. We were not alone. Someone was definitely lurking beyond the bushes to our rear. Al immediately started to move cautiously in the direction of the noise. Katta and I followed him as he disappeared into the tall bushes. We kept close contact behind Al as my heart started to beat as hard as possible and my adrenal glands were pumping full force. My instincts were telling me to retreat but I had already committed to the recon because we had to investigate the sound.

When we entered the immediate area beyond the bushes, we found a stream of water that was at least three feet deep and six feet wide. Inside the stream was a tub or basin fashioned just below the waterline with stones that each weighed about 1 lb. The basin was constructed in a way that allowed the water to continuously flow through it. Overhead was a clothesline that was strung across the stream. Clipped to it were a couple of little green uniforms, undoubtedly NVA, hanging to dry. We had found Charlie's hiding place by accident again. Unlike the base camp we found in the An Lo's, our latest discovery was occupied. Offhand I didn't expect the place to be crawling with the little bastards but it was definitely laundry day for at least one of them.

Al had already crossed the stream and continued the search on the other side. By the time Katta and I climbed out of the stream, Al had discovered a cave dug into the side of the mountain. As he slowly moved toward the entrance, Katta and I took up position atop the protuberance that formed the entrance. Without hesitation, Al boldly walked into the cave. He spent less than ten seconds inside and came out moving fast but very quietly.

"Let's get out of here fast." he said without pausing and started back for the stream. Not needing an immediate explanation, we both followed him. We scampered back across the stream, rejoined the rest of the squad and started to gear up fast. Sensing the urgency, everybody followed our lead. As I scrambled with my gear, I noticed a bamboo pan similar to the one that I saw being used by that old woman the last time I went to Linda and Monique's. Upon closer inspection, I noticed that the ground near my ruck was full of broken rice shells. The rest of the guys never noticed the pan or the rice shells. I tried not to let my discovery delay me as I continued to gear up and prepare for our immediate departure.

Once everybody was ready we started backing our way out, thankful for not having to fight our way out. After we backed through the tree line we made a mad dash in the opposite direction. Not being able to chart our way out of the area, our hastily chosen escape route led us to an area thick with wait-a-minute vines. Grove was with us and chose that moment to get us separated from the rest of the patrol. It was bad timing for sure but under those circumstances we didn't have time to line up in order. Fortunately Nick came back for the rest of us and after reconnecting with the rest of the group we continued our mad scramble. It was already starting to get dark and we had to settle down for the night for fear of running into what we were supposed to be avoiding; the undetermined main body of rice protectors. We called in another grid for extraction and spent the night in place.

"It was supper." Al said the following morning as we prepared to leave.

"Supper?"

"Yeah, we interrupted someone's bowl of hot rice. He left it sitting on a table in that cave. I figured that it was a good time to di-di mau." I agreed with him too. I'd already learned my lesson about reporting something like that to the lifers. They would have only pissed on us in the process of gloating over our find.

We packed up and moved to our rendezvous point. On our way Katta lit up a joint and started passing it back and forth. When I handed it to Doc, I suggested that he not pass it to Grove. He didn't need anything inside of his head that he couldn't handle. An OJ would really scramble his brains. "I can see the rest of the guys now." said Doc pointing to the guys lounging around at the rendezvous point waiting for Jahret and Calvin to arrive from their location. With both of those two away, there was no need to put the joint out so we continued to smoke as we approached them. "Handy, Katta, what are you doing smoking that shit out here?" said Marty as he attempted to self-anoint himself the ranking individual over everybody else and at the same time, failing to impress anyone. We were only concerned about our transports and how long would they take to arrive to extract us.

When we arrived at Uplift, Rudy was waiting for us like a stood up date. He obviously wanted a rematch with Al and Katta because he was demanding that we shine our boots for the next guard formation. Naturally, we ignored him again. He threatened us with the lawnmower line once more and we had another good laugh. Rudy seemingly subjected himself to our brand of ridicule as if he were some kind of masochist. Although we weren't assigned to bunker guard, we put our usual effort into the party planning. The gatherings on the bunker line just seemed to get better each time. The following morning we spent an all day vigil at the newly reconstructed bunker # 11. It was truly a sandbag castle then. The gathering was like a continuation of the party we had during bunker guard. With the sun up though, it was an ideal moment for a few letters. I wrote about 5 or 6 in a row and Jackson asked me to write his sister for him. He had developed a bad case of the I-don't-feel-like-writing-anymore syndrome. I started not to oblige but since we came over together I wrote the letter to his sister. He didn't even bother to rewrite it. He stuffed it into an envelope and sent it to her as written.

Carlos (Speedie) Diaz and Roger (Bear) Hill

Charang Valley

Cliff Wheelhouse

Dave Nichols

Root, Wheelhouse, Edwards and Anderson standing

Kyler and MacMahon

with Gathar

with Milles

9

About three fun filled days into our stand down, Keith handed me an article from the editorial page of BYU's newspaper. An acquaintance of his attended the school. Keith knew how outraged I was about the murder of those students and gave the article to me to keep. The article, written by a student of course, chided Nixon's Cambodian move. It was well written too. The writer was definitely moved by the shooting on the 4th. She wrote that Nixon's explanation for invading the sanctuaries was shallow, and called it a fallacy to widen the war in the name of peace. She was right. It was a militarily strategic raid and nothing else. Nixon should have come clean with the public and admitted it was impossible to bring us back home without making it look like a defeat. Sometimes Nixon seemed to only address his so-called silent majority whenever he explained himself in one of his speeches. The Cambodian explanation was classic Nixon as he took advantage of the opportunity to promote his policy of turning the war over to the Vietnamese. He claimed the move would hurt Charlie's ability to wage war and also buy time to make his plan for Vietnamization work. Actually the raid of the sanctuaries was made because they were there. It also sent a strong message to Hanoi that all future attempts at storing or staging would at least be subjected to being harassed and interdicted by similar incursions. It changed the way that our government had been fighting the war. The absurdity of allowing the NVA to use Cambodia had come to an end. The sanctuaries would no longer be off limits to us.

I was impressed with the article's objectivity and sincerity. Before I read it, I always assumed the student protestors only objected to the war for their own self-serving reasons. I never thought that any of them gave a damn about the ones doing the actual fighting and dying or the poor civilians caught in the middle of the hostilities. Her words changed my opinion about the protesters. It appeared that some of them had genuine feelings about the war and were truly committed to their cause of bringing the conflict to an end. She wasn't only concerned about the war because she had a relative or loved one involved. She believe that it was wrong to have us involved with waging a war thousands of miles from home for reasons that weren't even clear to the ones being sent to do the fighting. However, it had become evident that the students were wasting their time as well as their lives. Nixon would not pull the troops out any faster than he intended to. Hopefully, no one else would get killed in the process of voicing their objections.

The next day we assembled for a meeting to demonstrate the operation of a night vision telescope. The little invention could utilize the limited illumination of the moon and or the stars to produce a picture or image of an area that couldn't be detected at night with the naked eye. It costs a small fortune to produce one but the cost was nothing to Uncle Sam. He could afford anything. It was called the Starlight Scope and its invention was brought about or born of its mother; necessity. Charlie's idea to use the darkness had forced us to utilize our imagination and our considerable resources to come up with a piece of magic. It was a seeing-eye tool that could find its quarry in the dark. To hold the piece of machinery in my hands was like finally realizing that I was living in the age of Buck Rogers. The twenty-first century had arrived thirty years early.

Al and Katta went to Phu Cat on that pass and as I expected, they wouldn't let the three of us go together. They said I could go the following day but that I would have to go with Grove and Nick. Going out there with Nick would be cool and having Grove with us wouldn't be as tough a decision to make as the lifers might have thought. They would do anything to drive a wedge between the guys and the close bond that we shared but they were wasting their time. I only found out a couple of days earlier that passes were issued in Vietnam. I couldn't get that upset about not going to where I once didn't believe we could go legally. Still, it was always more fun to sneak off and venture out on our own. A pass defines your whereabouts and limits your time away too.

Anderson finally returned from the hospital. He had no problem at all with the timing of his illness. He said that it just wasn't his time to die. He had to be feeling some kind of guilt about the whole thing. Anyway he came back ready to resume his role with the platoon. Edwards had already finished his tour and earned his ticket back home to N. Carolina. He put on an inspiring performance at Tuy Hoa that night; which was more than what could be said about the decorated Bracey who had developed the worst case of cold feet in the history of warfare. I didn't know if or when he was expected to rejoin us. During the stand down, he spent his time hanging out with the black guys in the first platoon. He really got along with that group. They all had nicknames like Kool-Aid from Fla., Ice Berg from Chicago and Sugar Bear who was probably drafted from another planet against his will. Sugar Bear was a doe-eyed guy who had a distinct resemblance to the cartoon character on the cereal box. Bracey had formed a close bond with those three and they were almost inseparable. Since that night in Tuy Hoa, Bracey had only been a member of the 2nd platoon by roster. He had been in the rear ghosting for undisclosed reasons and the lifers were not bothering him about returning to the field in spite of the fact that he still had 2 or 3 months left on his tour. When I did seem him we talked about nothing much in general and I showed off a smoking pipe I made while in the An Lo's. I loaned it to him and invited him to our next party not really expecting him to show up. That night everyone was there except Bracey. After going out of my way to make him feel accepted, he continued to maintain that distance from the rest of the platoon. He was spaced just far enough away to make himself feel safe about not ever having to return to the fold. We were on the inside looking out at someone who kept us in his rear view mirror and never looked back. Being on stand down only further exposed the situation.

The following day I took the pass and accompanied Grove and Nick on their first visit to the famous Phu Cat Corner. We hitched the ride and got off the trucks at the corner where the hookers were waiting for them with open arms. I sat and watched for the MPs while the two of them went inside. Nick had a laughing fit over Grove's lack of experience with girls.

"Grove had me laughing. He was asking me for instructions. I told him to take his pants down and stick his dick in her. I was waiting for him to ask me where." he said as he continued laughing. I wanted to ask what happened next but was afraid that it might kill Nick.

Grove was smiling, and didn't seem embarrassed about whatever happened. He had momentarily lost his speech and, maybe more than that. Knowing Grove, I fully realized it just might have been his first time. It was possible that he probably never even held a girl's hand before. Nick was still laughing and I started to worry about him never recovering from his laughing fit. "Soul brother, you want Boom Boom. I love you too much." said a hooker who walked up from behind me. Her proposition sent Nick back into the laughing fit he had just nearly recovered from. We left the corner before someone had to write his mother and tell her that her son laughed himself to death on Phu Cat corner.

When we returned to Uplift, there was word about us pacifying another village. The bitter taste of Tuy Hoa was still fresh in my mouth and the rumor opened up the wounds that had not quite healed. The idea of working with Ruff Puffs once more was demoralizing. They could only be expected to run away again leaving us to do the fighting. I couldn't believe that Nixon actually knew what a horrendous failure Vietnamization really was. Unfortunately, judging from the way everybody was preparing for deployment, we were about to go somewhere. At least there was no promise of a body count awaiting us.

It was scary to think that I had only been in country for five months and was possibly looking at pacification again. With another six months left, there could be more pacification in store for us further down the line. I was getting a lot of bad vibes about working another village so I started planning to go on R&R to get out of country for a while.

Over the radio there was a story playing out about some more campus unrest. This time it was at Jackson State. The news report was followed by that re-enlistment ad that I thought was so funny a couple of months ago. Facing pacification for the second time in five months made me realize the way it worked. First a GI starts having doubts about his predicament or his very survival of the operation he was on and he gives in. It wasn't working on Mrs. Handy's favorite son though. "Man, I'm re-uppin." said Benn after hearing the ad on the radio.

"Did you hear about the shooting at Jackson State?" I asked him.

"Did you hear what I said Handy? I'm re-uppin

"But you haven't seen it get bad yet." I said realizing just how serious he was about bailing out.

"I've heard enough from you guys to know that I need to get away from this."

"In a couple of days you'll feel different. You'll probably be asking yourself, now what was I thinking about? You'll see."

I really hated it when they ran that ad over the radio. Everybody in the field already had a seed of doubt planted in their head. The re-enlistment pitch would only start the seed to grow. To use comedy to make their pitch said even more about how insensitive they were about our position in the middle of a war our country had already given up on. I fully understood his reason for wanting out before getting killed fighting a war that had practically already ended for us. No one could blame him for jumping ship.

We assembled on the chopper pad and after a quick helicopter flight we were deposited onto a small compound situated in the middle of a large populated area. While sitting in a corner of the little compound trying to work up enough courage to light up a Bomber, I remembered the biggest negatives about Tuy Hoa. The worst part was the hopelessness of being there trying to make an impact on the lives of people who hadn't exactly embraced us after five years of fighting for their country. Moreover, half of the platoon would be working in another part of the village. We were cutting our strength in half and diluting it with inept ARVN's.

Kyler was assigned to the other half of the platoon but Ellis had his tapes meaning that Led Zeppelin would be with us at our location. I had come to like the group and its sound. Ellis thought that Kyler was one of the weirdest guys ever and couldn't get over the way he insisted on being a grunt. It was almost as if he had to be in on the action.

That following morning our squad was trucked to our designated location and during the ride we attracted a throng of kids that chased our truck along the way. As I looked closer at one of the little girls, I noticed that she was waving the Starlight Scope at us. We signaled the driver to stop the truck. "Who dropped the scope?" I asked as the little girl was finally able to catch up.

"It came out of the case." said Grove. Keith trusted Grove to hump the scope and he strapped the case to his rucksack upside down. Once the scope was subjected to all of the bouncing around, it easily forced its way out of the case and into the hands of the little girl. Fortunately she was as eager to return it to us. "Give me the scope." said Keith remembering that Grove was suffering from a severe case of head-up-the-ass-itis. Typically, losing the scope meant little to him. It was as if he had only lost a canteen cup. Fortunately Katta wasn't sitting as close to him as I was.

When we arrived at our location, the Ruff Puffs were already waiting for us. Unlike that other group at Tuy Hoa, we didn't have to go looking for them. I was sure that they were equally as incompetent though. Being situated in the middle of the huge village, the rice production field was nowhere in sight. To our left was a herd of water buffalo headed in our direction and probably going to the field for grazing. There were at least a hundred of them being led by one old Papa San who carried a bamboo stick. It was amazing the way he directed the beasts and kept them in an orderly path to the rice paddies that was nowhere in sight. We followed the usual routine of trying not to spook the herd as the old papa san kept them moving along. Occasionally a bull would mount one of the cows for a quick attempt at mating. I supposed that it was the season for the buffaloes or maybe it was the way they always copulated. Papa San showed no concern as long as they did it while moving along.

Suddenly the old Papa San waded into the middle of the moving herd to break up one particular match. He started to beat the heck out of the mounting bull for no apparent reason. He was whacking the beast violently across the back as it cowered in reaction to his attack. According to one of the ARVN's, the old guy had just stopped a bull from mounting his daughter. After protecting the blood line of that pair, the old guy continued along with his herd.

When we chose our spot for the day we immediately started to attract our usual crowd of onlookers. As expected, the villagers would come out again to sit and stare at us all day.

Big Goose was attracting a lot of attention. Some of the villagers had gathered around pointing at him in amazement. "An Ko. An Ko. They said repeatedly.

"What are they talking about Goose?"

"I don't know. I went through the same thing at Tuy Hoa." he said. The villagers were seemingly awed at Goose's presence in their village. It was as if they all knew him from somewhere in their past. The celebrity was, nonetheless, wasted on him. He was an unassuming guy who usually shied away from attention.

Purvis had surprisingly left Vietnam a few months ahead of his DEROS date. There was something about him returning to school and being allowed to return early to accommodate his schedule. The whole thing sounded strange to me but he was history and was on his way back to Memphis to be at his girl's side and protect her from the dating disease. Keith had assumed the duties of squad leader and I surrendered the radio. I took over the M-79 with the intention of humping the weapon until my DEROS. The inquiry into the loss of Wheelhouse's gun was over and Big Goose had become our second machine gunner. Buckley took over the radio and everything would continue to run as before. Doc was with us making the transition smoother than I once thought it would be. I used to dread just thinking about the day when all of the guys in the old third squad would be gone. Once it happened I realized I was over reacting. It never was about the people who comprised the squad; it was about the spirit and the survival of it that made us special. We were still a pretty wild bunch and I couldn't ask for anything more.

Being in a village may have had a lot of advantages but I couldn't get over the Tuy Hoa experience. I couldn't help but wonder if Charlie had a spotter in the crowd of onlookers counting heads and weapons. Our first night in the village was full of trepidation. The Tuy Hoa mission had taught us a little too much as we couldn't get away from our old habits and fears. There was no mass exodus from the village like the one we witnessed over there and we couldn't determine if it was a good sign or not. There was no village crier making a courtesy call and with all of the villagers in place instead of somewhere else, we didn't have the virtual free fire zone to work in. Patrolling a fully populated area posed still another problem. It made us really stand out. There was no stealth and no element of surprise. We would have our work cut out for us every night.

We patrolled until we found an area and spent the night counting the hours until daylight. I loved quiet nights on pacification. After we dumped our Ruff Puffs, we returned to our daytime location where the civilians were waiting for us. We couldn't deal with both the ARVN's and the civilians too. There was a little resentment I detected in them when we made it known that we didn't want them around during the day. Our hands were full just dealing with the throng of villagers standing around us. We couldn't devote any attention to the thieving Ruff Puffs.

The Rascals were on the radio starting the day with "It's a Beautiful Morning." This time it was more than a coincidence. The DJ was definitely using the song as a wake up tune. "I like the Rascals. They ought to play that song every morning." said Al. I liked them too and I remembered all of the airplay they received on the R&B stations back home. While listening to the song, two little girls approached closely inspecting our activity. "So where are you from?" one of them asked me.

"Yes, what part of America do you call home?" said the other one as they immediately became comfortable around the new visitors in their village. They both seemed to be about 7 or 8 years old, spoke perfect English and didn't refer to me as Soul Brother.

"I'm from a place called New Orleans."

"New Orleans. Really?" the first one replied with enthusiasm.

"Why? Have you heard of the place?" I asked.

"Of course we have heard of New Orleans, Mardi Gras, Bourbon Street, the French Quarter and the birthplace of jazz." She said.

"Where in the world did you learn so much about my home and speak English so well? I mean neither one of you are older than 8." I asked in amazement.

"We learned in school of course. Where else can we learn a foreign language?" She answered. I was astonished at what they had accomplished with their comprehension and expression. They spoke better English than a lot of people that I knew.

"My name is Linda and this is my sister Diane."

"Your name is Linda and her name is Diane. You're kidding me right."

"Really. Our names are Linda and Diane. Both Linda and Diane not only handled the English language with ease, they also seemed to handle the village in a way that suggested they were more than just a couple of precocious kids. In the following fifteen minutes they were seen going in and out of almost every house within sight of our little gathering area. The people who occupied the homes seemed to tolerate their intrusiveness with an unusually high degree. They were like two royal brats that no one wanted to offend or would never dare to chastise. It was probably common for Vietnamese girls to adopt names that we were more familiar with. Maybe they did the same during the French occupation. The dope queens (Linda and Monique) of Bong Son obviously used the ploy also.

As I searched through my ruck sack for some food, my photo album came into view.

"May I have a look at your photos?" Linda asked.

"I guess so." I said as I handed it to them. They started going through it and found the many pictures of Barbara.

"Is that you wife?" Diane asked.

"No I'm still single. What about you?"

"Very funny. Are these pictures of the Mardi Gras?" Linda asked when she saw the picture of my two friends Louis and James in a crowd masking as Hobos.

"Yes it is."

"Can we show it to our mother?"

"I guess so." I said without thinking twice before I consented. After they disappeared with it I started to second- guess myself for being so trusting of little strangers. "Handy are you still going to Tokyo for R&R?" Katta asked.

"Yeah, I want to see a World's Fair and I figure this might be my only opportunity."

"I'm going with you."

"Me too." said Al. I had my doubts about whether it would be allowed but agreed to the threesome. It was a great idea and figured to be a memorable trip if they would allow us to go. Having not being allowed to go to Phu Cat on a pass made it unlikely that we would be released to leave country for a whole week.

Linda and Diane brought my photo album back to me after only about a half an hour. All of the pictures seemed to still be there and in turn, had established a little trust. They were likeable little girls in spite of their mock arrogance. They could easily make my stay in the village more enjoyable. Of course they could also turn it into a nightmare. They were cute and adorable but they were still a couple of kids and that was the main issue. Their potential for irritating me was unlimited. The close proximity I had afforded them could prove to be my own undoing. I had to continue to trust them until they showed me that I shouldn't.

A very distraught woman suddenly came running through the village crying her heart out. It was not unlike anything I'd seen before. If I had to make a guess, I'd say it was death in the immediate family. "Al, who do you think she lost?" I asked.

"This ARVN says her husband was just killed in action."

"That's too bad, the poor woman."

"Not bad, big celebration. You see." Said an ARVN who stood nearbyc

"Big celebration? What's he talking about?" I asked.

"The Vietnamese believe that if the body could be returned to its village for burial, it's a good thing. The only real tragedy is when the body is lost and can't be returned. Tonight there will be a big celebration."

"Do you think there'll be lots of goodies to eat?"

"Boo Coo goodies man, boo coo."

"You think we'll be welcome at the party?" I asked

"The whole village will be here. Everybody is welcome and everybody takes part. I've seen this before, man." He was right. The entire village had already turned into a beehive of activity making preparation for the event. Linda and Diane seemed to be in the center of the commotion. The way they were running in and out of the widow's house gave me the impression that they were related. In a way, the ARVN's death seemed to make their day.

The added attraction of attending the party was too tempting to pass up. It was no real problem deciding to make the event. Our mission was pacification and it seemed like the natural thing to do. With no Calvin or Jahret around, we almost had to include it into our itinerary for that night. I was sorry the woman had to lose her husband, but it didn't seem to be appropriate to mourn at that moment. With all of the preparation going on around us it was hard to imagine anyone doing any mourning. In spite of our different cultures, their mood was very infectious. Our anticipation was as high as any of the villagers.

I wrote a few letters to send out on resupply day in the morning. I also wrote Gathar telling him I also hadn't made E-4 and that I didn't think I would ever be promoted. Katta said he hadn't been promoted yet either. Jahret, according to what I heard earlier, appointed Morse as his RTO right after Edwards DEROSed. He was also promoted when he accepted the job. They said that Jahret even back-dated his orders for promotion at least 30 days also. The action made Morse an E-4 a whole month before he knew who Jahret was. It's great when one can make rank fast because we were all equally deserving. However, it would've been more appropriate to give consideration to some of the guys who had been out in the field for months just waiting for nothing to happen.

Katta came up with a brass water pipe he must have been humping in his ruck. He said that a water pipe takes the harsh taste and a lot of the tar out of the smoke. Admittedly, it did come with a lot of novelty attached to it. Everybody wanted a toke on it. We even posed for pictures smoking the thing. It was one hot item for the entire day. The drug didn't have enough effect on my situation though. I was still sitting in the middle of a village and there were also at least 50 people watching us. I kept waiting for the crowd to start thinning out but there was no chance of the people losing any interest in us. It was just like at Tuy Hoa when they came out early and stayed all day. We were their main attraction for our entire stay there and apparently we would be exposed to more of the same in our new location too.

We started packing early so that we could attend the burial fest. I expected to find out just how welcome we were. "Come on, what are you guys waiting for? Lets go." Linda said as I noticed the villagers were all converging on the widow's home. She and Diane had come to bring us to the party. It confirmed what Al was saying about everybody being welcome. The gathering was large and the spirits were high. Their belief in returning their dead to their ancestral home for burial was very evident. Everybody was happy, including the widow. "Here, eat this." said Diane.

"And then you can drink this." said Linda as my two little friends showered me with hospitality. It was similar to attending a wake back home. The only difference was that the widow had yet to receive her husband's body. It was only a few hours earlier that she received the bad news.

"Handy, have you eaten one of these yet?" Doc asked as he showed me a gelatinous fruit dessert wrapped in a leaf. It had a bright red color to it and had left a stain on his entire oral cavity. He looked like a sloppy vampire after feeding. I passed on it and continued eating whatever Linda and Diane brought me until I could eat no more. The crowd was happy and since there was a war going on, I supposed it was a continually practiced ritual affecting all families and villages at one time or another.

We left and continued to do what we came to do. It did give us a chance to experience something else about the Vietnamese culture other than the war, its politics and the drugs.

The following morning, we readied ourselves for resupply day. The rest of the platoon would be arriving to reunite us for the first time since we arrived at Fire Base Orange.

"Handy I want you to pull perimeter guard duty when the helicopters start to land." Said Keith while pointing in the direction of where he wanted me to set up shop. It sounded like a good idea since Jahret and Calvin were coming.

I moved to my post immediately and set up in someone's yard beneath some clothes hanging out to dry. Sitting there reminded me of those NVA uniforms we found on the rice mission. As I reminisced, someone approached me from behind. I turned and found a beautiful young Vietnamese woman. She was smiling and shading her eyes from the sun with her ethnic conical sun hat. "Chow, toi moi nau com neu chi meyon chi an, neu chi chick?" she said in very fluent Vietnamese as if I could understand her..

"I'll bet you tell that to all of the GI's around here." I said jokingly as Linda and Diane suddenly appeared from out of nowhere and started laughing at my reply.

"Chi co hew nyung gi toi hoi?" she said with the same smile on her face.

"No, I'm single. How about you? Do you have a husband? Is he anywhere around right now?" I asked as my two little friends again laughed at my reply. I wondered how much longer they would allow me to make an ass out of myself.

"Lam on vau trong an cung toi." she said and walked back to the house leaving me standing there admiring her beauty.

"You are so silly GI. Do you eat rice?" Linda asked.

"What are you talking about?"

"Do you eat rice, stupid?"

"Don't get carried away with your English. I don't like being called names by little children."

"But do you eat rice?"

"Of course I do. I'm from New Orleans."

"Then let's go inside and eat some rice. She just invited you into her home to dine with her." She said as they began to tug on my fatigue pants.

"Wait until I get my gear." I said as I abandoned my post to accept her invitation.

I walked in expecting to find the meal on the floor the way the family in Tuy Hoa did. Surprisingly, she had a table and chairs. On the table was four bowls of rice. I dragged my ruck inside and sat at the table. Linda and Diane were acting as gracious little hostesses. They seemed familiar with the woman's home. They were assisting her with the preparation of the meal and seemed to know where everything was. It was just like at the widow's house the previous night. The little girls were again being tolerated no matter how obnoxious they acted.

As we sat and ate, the woman continued to make conversation. I felt as if I was in the middle of a very weird movie. Every time I gave a reply, Diane and Linda started laughing again.

"Are you two little girls having fun today?" I asked which only made them laugh harder. I doubted if they would ever finish their meal because they couldn't stop laughing. The woman continued to talk and all I could do was watch her. She seemed to be telling a story or recounting an event she had experienced. She used arm gestures, facial expressions and different vocal tones to get her message across to a listener that didn't understand a word she spoke. Although I wished I had a better understanding of the language, it didn't seem to matter to her.

Our little gathering was interrupted by an ARVN who walked in without knocking. My hostess went silent upon his arrival. He gave her a cold stare as he started to circle the table with an obvious look of disapproval. I fought off the feeling of contempt that I usually had reserved for ARVN's and asked Linda about his identity and the reason for his visit. My usually talkative little friends were also quiet. I couldn't stand it. I exchanged cold stares with the ARVN until he started to prepare himself a bowl of rice. "Who is this guy?" I asked again which only brought about more silence. "Is he her husband? Is this his house?" I asked as they continued the silence. Linda and Diane were actually intimidated by his presence. He didn't scare me at all and I felt like throwing him out on his ass. When I heard the helicopters circling overhead, I walked out of the house and returned to my post. Diane and Linda followed me through the door. Once outside, I asked them again about the intruder and they walked away. I started to wonder about our new location or, more specifically, what kind of village it was. Everything about the place started to worry me including the two little girls that spoke perfect English.

When the rest of the platoon arrived I saw Jackson with some little kid carrying his machinegun for him. He reminded me of Wheelhouse and his weakness for those little brats he entertained daily in Tuy Hoa. When I noticed Jahret and Calvin, I felt fortunate to be on perimeter duty. While standing there watching the guys haul the supplies off of the slicks, the ARVN walked out of the woman's house. I assumed he couldn't stand to see a GI just walk in and enjoy her hospitality as he never said anything to me while in there. He probably used intimidation and the fact that he knew we would not be there very long to get his way with the civilians. The civilians were being caught between believing in our efforts and accepting the AVRN's as a side effect, or going over to Charlie. We were fighting a losing battle.

We completed our resupply without me getting a chance to talk to any of the guys who were over at the other location. The next time I planned not to get sidetracked by another pretty face. At least I received a few letters to read. One of them was from Mrs. Wheelhouse. I hadn't realized that enough time had passed to get a reply from her. I read it immediately. She began her letter with a very cordial greeting for all of us who were still there and said that she was thrilled to hear from me. She mentioned that she had other children besides his nephew's mother. It was reassuring to know that there were enough loved ones around to provide her with support and strength.

Her letter was sprinkled with religious references painting the picture of a woman deeply in touch with her belief in God. There was also a little red personal Bible included in the envelope as a gift offering. She was obviously a very spiritual woman. Her choice of words was eloquent and her handwriting was beautiful. I imagined she was an educated woman. Having an educated woman for a mother seemed abstract to me. My mother never finished school and the difference in the content of their letters was considerable. Her writing was also full of grief-stricken words of despair. She said that she was losing her will to go on. The letter was a little too much for me to bear. My eyes were getting so watery that I could no longer make out the words. I had to put it down to finish at a later time or date. "I hear you got a letter from Wheelhouse's mom. How is she doing?" Al asked.

"Not so good right now. Do you want to read it?" I asked him as I struggled to compose myself.

"Not really. I just thought I'd ask about her." he said in a depressed manner.

"I can't help but feel as if we let those guys down that night. Reading that letter just brought back all of those feelings again." I said.

"Well, anyway, you guys saved our asses that night."

"Saved your asses? You weren't with CP that night. What are you talking about?"

"We were under attack before you guys came storming across that wooden bridge. They were on line making an assault with rockets and AK's. Then you guys came along just in time. I tell ya, it sounded like a hundred boots coming in a hurry."

"Really! I never knew that."

"When those gooks heard you guys coming, they dashed."

"I never saw them. I dropped my handset when we started running. After we got on line everybody seemed to be shooting at somebody but I never saw anyone until CP got hit. It was so frustrating to finally be in a firefight and have so little an impact on the outcome." I said.

"They had B-40's and boo coo gooks coming at us. One rocket passed overhead right between Jackson and me. We were in big trouble before you guys came to the rescue. So don't feel too bad about it." He said with emphasis. I didn't take away any of the futility, I still felt deeply wounded. Reading Mrs. Wheelhouse's letter had re-opened the wound and started the bleeding all over again. Even worse was that I still had to finish reading it. It looked as though I had started something that would only prolong my own healing process. In spite of it all, I planned to continue writing her because I felt as if it was the least I could do.

We returned to our spot in the village to continue our usual routine of smoking pot and listening to music. Katta was practicing his knife throwing, Goose had his usual throng of An Ko stalkers and Diane and Linda just couldn't seem to get enough of me. They were like two constant companions. They sat with me and watched us consume large amounts of marijuana and asked a lot of questions about our smoking habits. They were annoying but at least they didn't steal. They were curious about all of my personal items and looked at my photo album over and over. I never once had to worry about them taking anything from me and they invited me to their theater. I declined and remained in place. They made me feel like a bad guy for refusing but I had enough problems of my own and could not afford to let them overload me with any more guilt. After all, I still had to finish my letter from Mrs. Wheelhouse.

I continued to read the letter as she went on to say that her husband was once stationed at the Algiers Navy Base on the west bank of New Orleans. I used to live about 20 blocks up the street from the base back in the late 50's and wondered if he was stationed there at that same time. Finally and sadly, she stated that the body she buried did not resemble her son. She wanted to know if there was a possibility that her son could've still been alive amongst us and wondered if maybe we made some kind of mistake with the identity. I was almost sorry I finished reading the letter and was at a loss for words to say or write. "Doc, Mrs. Wheelhouse says that her son's body didn't resemble the son she sent over here."

"Well Handy I told you their faces were all shot off. It would be hard reconstructing it from what was left."

"Yeah but she was thinking that..."

"I've already told you what happened. I bagged and tagged them myself. Don't you remember?"

"But what do I tell her?"

"I don't know Handy, you'll think of something."

Mrs. Wheelhouse was really taking her loss hard. Her grief had her so unbalanced that she was reaching for an impossible scenario. I was angrier than ever and wanted revenge in the worst kind of way. I didn't think I would feel any different until I could kill some of the little bastards that took my friend's life and destroyed his mother's heart. I still respected Charlie but I wanted to even the score. His ability to continue to fight no longer impressed me. I wanted to destroy him. I wanted to see his dead body lying at my feet. I felt like lopping the head off of our next kill and couldn't wait for the opportunity.

Reading the letter had me visibly disturbed. Al tried to distract me with conversation about the game of basketball we played on our last stand down but he was wasting his time. I couldn't forget about the letter that fast. In the same spirit, Katta started a conversation about his high school football playing days. Obviously the guys were doing their best to keep me focused on where we were at the moment. They were trying to lift my spirits and I appreciated it but I would have rather had one of them help me to construct a reply for Mrs. Wheelhouse. I was at a loss for words and was beginning to feel as if I had started something that I couldn't finish. I had already committed myself to a correspondence with a very sweet lady and it felt helpless to not be able to console her.

Later, as we went in search of another vulnerable ambush site, the people were waving at us as if we were a bunch of Boy Scouts on a camp out. We went through the motions anyway and I even waved back at them a couple of times. Eventually, we were forced to adopt the practice of using someone's property as an ambush spot. It was very compromising too. We couldn't even use any Claymores because of the villagers. Diane and Linda suddenly showed up and invited me into the nearest home for some rice. They seemed to be everywhere. Their presence was making a mockery of what we were trying to do there. They were begging me to go inside with them and in the process made me feel like a spoilsport for refusing. It was good to see that they had gotten over my not going to the theater with them. After all of those scary nights in the Crow's Foot and Tuy Hoa, I never imagined there would be such contrasting situations. It was dark and we were assigning guard duty to everybody as my two little friends were trying to get me to share a late night snack with them. We were talking in whispers to each other out of habit and the villagers were enjoying a typical evening all around us. We had turned our music off and the villagers were playing theirs loud enough to be heard throughout the entire hamlet. We were supposed to be looking out for movement but none of the people had settled in for the night yet. It was but another scene from that weird movie I found myself in earlier. After Diane and Linda gave up on me they retired for the night and everything returned to normal. Tuy Hoa could have been the same way had it not been for the daily mass exodus. I never realized how accommodating it was to be operating in an evacuated village. Charlie seemingly did us a favor by clearing the place out for us. They managed to create a free fire zone in the middle of what would have otherwise been a populated area. In contrast, the village population wasn't as concentrated as it was at the base of that mountain in Tuy Hoa either. Our new village was a lot more spread out.

The next day I tried to construct that letter for Mrs. Wheelhouse. It was easily the most agonizing letter I had ever written. I planned to stay away from the part about her son's face though. I figured she could do without all of the detail. I didn't want to hurt her anymore than she already was. "Are you writing that girl in the photograph?" Linda asked as they had started the day off at my side. They went on asking more questions about me as I continued to write the letter to Mrs. Wheelhouse. After finishing it, I found it lacking. Mrs. Wheelhouse was too smart to not see that I had danced around the issue. My instincts told me that she would persist. I just hoped that she wouldn't back me into a corner. I could never tell her about what actually happened. I could only hope that someone was on the other end monitoring our correspondence. Maybe they could point out that some things were better off left unsaid; or in our situation, unwritten. "Handy, how come you never comb your hair?" Katta asked.

"Because Calvin wants me to get a haircut. In fact, he practically insists. I told him that the Vietnamese barbers couldn't cut a black man's hair if their lives depended on it but he's always bugging me about it. He eventually said that if I got killed he wouldn't want to send me home to my mother with long hair. He said that if I were dead, I would look better if I had a haircut, even a bad one. Can you believe that shit? My mother wouldn't think that I looked good in a casket even if I did have a haircut. In fact, she wouldn't approve of me coming home dead at all. So not only will I not get a haircut, I won't even comb it. I don't believe that a haircut will look good on me dead. In fact nothing will look good on me dead."

"I agree with you on that." he said while laughing.

Our day again settled into the usual routine of music, drugs and the crowd of villagers staring at us. I tried to put myself in their shoes but it just didn't work. The novelty of having foreign troops around should have worn off during the French colonization. "Handy, let me read your last letter from Barbara." said Doc.

"I haven't read it yet." I had been so occupied with Mrs. Wheelhouse's letter that I'd forgotten about the rest of my mail. Mrs. Wheelhouse had managed to pull on my heartstrings, jerk some tears from me and made me forget to read Barbara's letter.

The ARVN's were always slowly inching their way towards us. They couldn't fool anyone with their approach. We could easily see that they were trying to get their hands on our goods and nobody trusted them enough to let them get too close. I could have been able to relax a little more during the day instead of maintaining a constant vigil just to keep them from stealing our personal items. They might have been awful soldiers but they were master thieves.

That night we again camped near the residence of another villager. I seemed to be the only one with reservations about being in a village again. I wasn't as paranoid as I was after the firefight, but being in another village did bring back some old feelings. I tried to convince myself that our new location could never be as bad as Tuy Hoa was. I wanted to see us regain that swagger that the old third squad once had. When I was a new arrival, I looked up to the ones with time in country. Only they could give me the reassurance that I needed in time of doubt. Whether I liked it or not, the new guys were going to start looking to me for that same reason. I couldn't let them down either. In Vietnam, rank meant little or nothing and time in country meant everything. As I had observed before, we all respected the example, not the rank.

Suddenly Linda and Diane came running out of the house nearest our campsite. Everybody's home must have been open to them. Obviously our new village had to be the safest one in the whole country. If two little girls could go wandering around the village after 9:00 p.m. without fear of consequence, it was time for us to leave. Of course I should have been happy to be in that particular corner of Vietnam wherever it was. I shouldn't have complained at all.

PART THREE

1

At daybreak we returned to our regular spot for another day of leisure and observation. We didn't want to disappoint our audience. They had become so accustomed to our routine that the audience would arrive before us. This ordinarily would necessitate a move to another spot because of the patterns we had set. However since there was no apparent risk involved and because we just felt safe, we remained in the same area. It was almost like being home. In all fairness though, the crowd was a lot nicer than the one in Tuy Hoa. There weren't even any hustlers around. If we needed some pot we had to send a runner and even they had to go far to find some. Linda and Diane, of course, were never too far away. "What do you keep in that bag?" Diane asked.

"They're letters."

"Why don't you mail them?"

"These are letters that I have received. I just can't part with them." I answered as they both looked at each other in mock disbelief. I had to admit that it was unusual to hold on to every letter but I just couldn't help it. I couldn't throw them away. They also made a nice pillow at night.

An old papa san came from out of nowhere talking very loud as he walked through the village. If we were in Tuy Hoa, the old man would have caught a flying bullet as soon as he was sighted. A virtually shooting gallery would have erupted had the village crier made another appearance in April. Fortunately, I thought, it was not Tuy Hoa and the watch for him was off. I had assumed that our paranoia level had subsided and that we had mellowed just enough to allow such every day events to happen without raising an eyebrow of suspicion. Surely our new village was so laid back and peaceful that we could never suspect that this old guy would be Charlie's messenger. We were, I had hoped; too busy basking in the good fortune of being in such a tame village. Suddenly Katta got up and made a bee line for the old man with a mean psychotic look in his eye. I wasn't close enough to prevent him from doing what I knew he was about to do. "You little mother fucker, I know what you're up to. You can't fool me!" He said as he started to choke the old man and shake him violently. The rest of the guys came to the rescue and restrained him. Katta insisted he had just prevented an attempt by Charlie to alert the village of an attack. He demanded to be released. Incredibly the old man was more insulted than terrified. He was glaring at Katta and berating him for his behavior or perhaps his insolence. Our audience, to their credit, was displaying more shock and disbelief than anger or resentment. Katta's temper had gotten the best of him and ruined an otherwise perfect day. If pacification was an attempt to win some hearts and minds, we had just lost a ton of them. I knew Katta had a short fuse and was overdue for another outburst. His chokehold on the old man had put a serious damper on the operation. "Man what are you doing?" Al asked while visibly upset with Katta. I was just glad he didn't shoot the old man. I didn't think that we could overcome a shooting incident. Our new village was not Tuy Hoa and no one was shooting at us.

Diane and Linda were clinging to me like two scared little girls. It was about the most normal action or reaction they had displayed since I met them. "Everything is alright now," I told them.

"Why did he do that?" That old man didn't do anything." Linda said.

"We had a bad incident with an old man doing the same thing in another village. He just overreacted, that's all." I told her. My reply left her as confused as she was scared. It fell short of explaining everything. I wished that the operation could have ended ten minutes earlier and spared us of the ugly incident. The choking scene had soured a pretty decent stay. I was kind of leery at first but it (the mission) had settled into being more enjoyable than any of the previous operations. Everything changed when Katta grabbed that old man's neck though. After that, we were no longer a novelty to the crowd of villagers that sat and stared at us. We had become the ugly Americans and had possibly just worn out our welcome. The complexities of the war and the policy of Vietnamization had placed us in a fishbowl. When we made mistakes like that, it became magnified. Ordinarily the incident would have only been considered a hazard of working around civilians but this, however, was pacification. Essentially, that made the incident a public relations disaster. It wouldn't have been a bad idea to fold our tents and return to Uplift after that. I felt as if our image had been irreparably damaged and our goals for the mission were rendered unachievable. When the day finally came to a merciful end, the choking incident didn't seem to go away with it. We needed to get past the episode in the worst way because the mission continued on in spite of Katta's action. The next day would be resupply day and hopefully a new and different mood would accompany the fresh supplies.

Ambush came and went without incident and without either Diane or Linda. They didn't track me down and although I should have been thankful, I thought they were a little scared of us. I knew I shouldn't have used them as a barometer to gauge the overall attitude of an entire village but I couldn't help it. I was probably overreacting, but I couldn't help that either.

When resupply started, I avoided perimeter duty in order to sidestep any negative reaction from the people. What I really needed was a letter from Barbara to distract me from all that had happened around me. It was more than the "I love you" and the "I miss you" stuff. I needed to hear about all of the little things that were going on in her life. It made me just that much more eager to get back alive. It was as if she was on the other end pulling me home and events like the choking incident were pushing me there.

When the rest of the platoon came, I got a chance to chat with the rest of the guys and find out what it was like at the other location. According to Benn, it was alright but boring. This could only mean that there was too much Calvin and Jahret for their consumption. I could relate to what they were talking about too. At least he wasn't talking about the re enlistment thing again. Pacification had reinvigorated his spirit again. All he needed was a taste of the fun and less of the ugly stuff to make him see that reuppin' wasn't exactly the best thing to do.

As a special favor to our squad, I grabbed our C rations first and then continued to haul all of the rest of the supplies and mail. Mrs. Wheelhouse flattered me with a Care Package and made me feel special. She must have mailed it the same day that she received my letter. I hurried to finish up with the duties of unloading the supplies and sat down to open the package. It had all of the goodies that I had become accustomed to seeing her son receive. There were all of the brand names that were found on the shelves of a supermarket back home; pre-sweetened Kool- Aid, Jello pudding, Oreo cookies, the works. I was speechless. She also had a note with it saying that she hoped that we would enjoy the box of goodies. Privately though, I wondered if it was a good thing for her to do. Sending a Care Package to her son used to be a ritual for her. Preparing this package for us must have been some kind of strain. Just looking at all of the stuff brought back some memories of the last two packages that he shared with me.

When Keith brought over our C rations I remembered that I had already grabbed a box and forgot to tell him about it. Katta suggested we try to sell the box on the black market. His plan was far-fetched but adventuresome. The guys with the rear jobs were the only real dealers. Some of them were making a killing. Those of us who had to do the actual fighting seldom got the opportunity to do any real dealing. The big time dealers were selling cases of the boxes such as the one we had.

After resupply was over and the rest of the platoon had returned to their location, we passed on returning to our usual spot and set a course for our ambush spot for the night. When Keith finally noticed the extra box of "C's," he just shook his head and smiled at our theft. He was an unusually good guy. In spite of his contrasting lifestyle, he managed to co-exist with a squad of drug users and misfits with ease. His tolerance for us was only exceeded by his adherence to his faith. I never dreamed that such a person would fit in with us as well as he did.

While carrying our extra box of "C's", I realized that the weight and the cumbersome load it created would be too much to carry for long. If we didn't sell it soon, it would become a problem just trying to keep it in our possession. The idea was more an attempt at entertaining ourselves than anything else. The black market was just too tempting to not at least try once. It was just like they told us at Charang Valley, the black market was, in some corners, bigger than the war itself. We were happy to just get a chance to give it a try.

2

The following morning, we couldn't find the extra box of C rations. Somebody fell asleep just long enough to allow the ARVN's to steal them. All they needed was a moment to get their hands on anything that wasn't tied down. There was nothing that we could do but take inventory on our personal items and see what else they'd taken. "You little thieving mother fucker!" said Katta as he grabbed one of the ARVNs by the throat and started to shake him worse than he did the old man earlier. He was out of control again and was so angry I was sure he would strangle him to death. The rest of the ARVNs started protesting loudly and cowering at the same time. None of them were about to intervene on behalf of their friend as Katta maintained his stranglehold. Then one of them started to fire his weapon in the air. I immediately grabbed Katta and pulled him aside. "Everybody pack up and let's get away from here. I don't trust these cowards." I said feeling as if one of them would start shooting at us next.

We packed and started to leave the ambush area. I would've ordinarily assumed Katta was the one who fell asleep on guard, but he confused me when he singled out that one particular ARVN for retaliation. His rage and his method of expression had me concerned about our situation in the village. Katta had turned into a bull in a china shop with no control over his emotions. I became afraid of what he was capable of doing or what he might do next. The situation really started to deteriorate when the ARVN's followed us to our regular spot. They were looking for a show down for sure. Our arrogance mixed with their cowardice was about to blow up in our faces and turn into something ugly and possibly deadly. Unfortunately there was nothing I could do to alter the outcome. Two of them approached us as the rest of them started to spread out in the background.

"Chung toi sher tran ank ah day bi yah." said one of them as he pointed at both Katta and the ARVN choking victim. Of course we couldn't understand a word he spoke but his body language seemed to encourage a duel between our Katta and his fellow ARVN. Katta, I figured, would gladly accept any challenge made by any earthly ARVN. I had to start to flank the other ARVNs in the background and quick. I didn't think that anyone of them would open fire on us while their two friends were standing in their line of fire but flanking them seemed natrual.

One of the ARVNs in the background started to follow me as I made my move. His maneuver forced me to watch both him as well as the rest of them. Katta stood toe to toe with the ARVN as the tension mounted. Hoping for cooler heads to prevail was out of the question by that time. They were like two grown men playing that child's game of who would throw the first punch. The posturing, I figured, wouldn't last too long. I tried to put myself into an ideal position before the first blow. The ARVN that trailed me was aware of what I was up to. He followed me until we came to a halt in front of a house that was near the open field where Katta stood face to face with the ARVN.

Without further hesitation, Katta unleashed a vicious smash to the ARVN's jaw and sent him into another state of mind. He crumpled to the ground like a sack of potatoes. Katta had knocked him out cold. The "promoter" of the match knelt over his fighter and tried to revive him. Then one of the

ARVNs sprayed the area with a burst from his M-16. Al and Katta were both hit as the rest of the crowd of ARVNs, GI's and civilians were miraculously untouched by the volley. I immediately turned to the ARVN that followed me and aimed my weapon at him. We both stared each other down as we contemplated shooting each other. I was at a disadvantage because if I shot him with my grenade launcher, the round could have exploded and killed both of us due to our close proximity. "Tooie com myng band anai." He said calmly. He obviously did not want to shoot me. I became angry and frustrated about not being able to retaliate but was not crazy enough to frag someone as close as he was. I also couldn't shoot at the one who fired at the crowd because there were too many of my own standing too close to him. The first few moments after the shots were fired were almost suspended in time. Everyone froze in shock at what had just happened. Once they overcame the initial surprise they rushed to the aid of both Al and Katta who were bleeding profusely. I had to give up on my intention to retaliate and go to their assistance. As I passed through the maze of shameless cowards standing around in regret for what had just happened, I blew my top. I knew I had done the right thing by not shooting back but passing the chance to avenge their shooting was tough. Every moment that passed into history was an agonizing stab at my pride. A cowardly ARVN had just wounded two of my closest buddies and all I could do was stand around and watch them bleed. Doc had already administered the morphine injections and the effect was just beginning to work its magic on them. Their grimace of pain had turned into one of despair as Doc worked feverishly on the two of them. "I couldn't get a clear shot with all of you guys standing around." I said for awkwardly. The humiliation I felt at that moment was beginning to make me feel more wounded than either one of them lying at my feet. I was suffocating with anger. "Handy, it would have only made matters worse. I needed to get to work on their wounds." Doc said. Still, I felt as if I should have done something. Al had a nasty wound to his hip and Katta took a round in his elbow. There was a lot of blood on both of them. Doc continued to work on them as the medivac was called in. I was about to lose two more of my best friends to pacification and I could only imagine how insulted they felt to have been shot by one of the biggest cowards on the planet. It will probably be the most humiliating thing that will ever happen to them. I couldn't accept anymore of the charade. I no longer wanted to fight a war for a country whose soldiers were shooting us. "Fuck this war man. I'm finished with this shit." I said still choking with anger and frustration.

"Don't lose your cool man. We'll be alright." Katta said while trying his best to keep my anger in check after letting his get out of control. Al was silent as Doc worked on his hip that appeared to be shattered. He was visibly upset with Katta more than anything else. Standing over their helpless bleeding bodies was really getting to me. I didn't feel as if I could finish my tour after witnessing the shooting. It was the final insult to have a cowardly thief shoot two of us.

As the medivac landed to take Al and Katta away I felt like getting on the chopper with them. It was hard enough to say goodbye to someone who had finished his tour or someone who was wounded and had to leave but I couldn't imagine accepting an incident like that. I was so angry that when Jahret arrived and tried to restore order and a continuance of the mission I told him that I quit the Army. I was promptly arrested and taken away to wherever CP was. I couldn't exactly say that I was speaking without thinking first either. It was too much to be going against a formidable army such as the NVA and be encumbered with ARVNs at the same time. The job was impossible. Somehow I didn't expect the guy who shot Al and Katta to be punished. He was taken away before I was but somehow I felt I was in more trouble than he was at that time. I didn't think that the Saigon government was anything more than the puppet variety that Hanoi had always insisted it was. It was the puppet masters that I had the problems with. If we were truly pulling the strings over in Vietnam, something should have been done about the farce called pacification. There was too much resentment between the so-called allies to ever believe that it could work. The ARVN hated us and we hated them even more. If pacification had been going on as long as we had been there, then it should have been abandoned long before anyone of us arrived after Nixon took over in '69. The added hazard of being shot by the people we were supposed to be assisting was the last straw. I refused to go on any longer with the ridiculous assertion that we were actually helping the paper tiger ARVN army. They were beyond being helped. I wanted out of the war and the sooner the better.

3

I was dispatched to the rear to be trained as a driver. I assumed it was a sham and that reporting to the First Sergeant was just window dressing. "Go unload your gear at supply and get ready to report to the Sargent Major for your interview." he said.

"I've decided to go for the court martial Top. I don't want the job. Give it to someone else."

"Listen son, I know how you feel right now. You've done a good job in the field. We expect you to do a good job back here now. So go get a haircut, a shave and some clean fatigues. Your interview is scheduled for today."

"Top, when you decide to get the paper work done for my court martial I'll be out there on Bunker # 9 smoking some Bong Son Bombers. Just send the M.P.'s to get me O.K.?" I told him and left for the bunker line. I didn't know how far the charade was going but I had no plans on becoming a driver and definitely was not about to get a haircut.

I spent the next three days and nights on bunker # 9 with three different bunker guard details. They all knew about my status and ignored me every night. After the third night, the armorer came looking for me asking if I had ever reported to the Sergeant Major for the job and proposed that I should at least go through the motions and at least ride around in the jeep with him. He was a nice guy and I didn't like seeing him caught in the middle of the bullshit. Of course it didn't make any sense for me to go through the motions without giving the lifers the impression that I was interested.

We walked over to the motor pool to secure a jeep and while we were inside the quarters for the motor pool guys, I noticed a giant poster of a black left-handed guitarist on the wall. He was dressed in a bizarre outfit with his left hand swung out from the instrument as he bit on his lower lip. "Who's that?" I asked the guy sitting in the chair assuming the huge poster belonged to him.

"Who's that? Are you serious? That's Hendrix. Haven't you ever heard of him?"

"Yeah, I've just never seen him before."

"We're here to get some keys for a jeep." the armorer said.

"Sign here." he told him as he handed him the keys. We took the jeep and drove around the helicopter pad as I attempted to learn to clutch while driving a vehicle across an obstacle course full of mortar craters. Some of those craters would put some of the potholes back home to shame. It was nearly impossible to stay in my seat as we negotiated the no-man's land we used for landing helicopters. I had a better chance of staying atop a Brahma bull at a rodeo. Afterwards, we drove up and down the highway but he complained too much about me picking up guys from the whorehouses and opium dens. The armorer was such a boy scout that he didn't even know where they were. He was a true straight arrow. He had never touched a joint and swore there was no marijuana in his hometown of Tyler, Texas.

After a few more days of driving up and down the highway, the company came in from the field, the charade ended and I was allowed to return to the fold. I was glad to be back with the guys but was not about to let the incident pass without writing Boggs about it. I was still angry about the way they handled me during the days following the shooting. They never had any intentions of bringing charges against me. As I suspected all along, they just wanted to get me out of that village. The armorer was in on the sham also. He knew that the lifers were not serious about letting me become a jeep driver.

Jahret offered me my old job back in the field as if I were auditioning for it. He wasn't very convincing with his artificial gesture. The lifers had practically ignored what had just happened to two of our own. Considering the way the relations were between the arrogant GI's and the cowardly Ruff Puffs, the shooting was probably more common place than I thought.

Later that evening I was placed on an ambush squad and had to leave the base camp for the night. It was near dark, everybody was getting ready to have some fun pulling bunker guard and we had to go out. After being with the boring REMFs for the previous two weeks, it would have been fun to spend a night on the bunker line with the guys again. Instead we were about to leave the perimeter. The designated ambush spot would be somewhere down the highway and the MP's waited for us to start our journey before they closed the highway with the rolls of concertina wire. In our most compromising move to date, we were to walk down the highway until we reached our area. We were then to climb up the mountain to get to our ambush site. It would have been less dangerous if we were in the bush. Our base camp was large enough to always get Charlie's attention. As we marched down the side of the highway, I felt as if Charlie was watching our every move down the wide open and highly visible route. We were sticking out like a bunch of sitting ducks.

We walked along the highway until Uplift was out of sight. Highway 1 snaked through the province and our part of the highway straddled alongside a low range mountain chain. The mountains were patrolled periodically by small teams such as ours and often peppered with H&I (Harassment and Interdiction) artillery and mortar fire to keep it clear of enemy presence. As luck would have it, our number came up to spend the night outside of the village that was nearest Uplift.

After turning off of the highway we climbed up a heavily wooded mountainside and settled down for what would be a very uncomfortable night. The incline was very steep and was expected to provide a difficult night's sleep for any one who was wiling to try. Then just before dark, the sound of a vehicle interrupted our gathering with a disturbing mixture of fear and trepidation. The vehicle was mounted on a track and was either a tank or an APC (armored personnel carrier). The approaching vehicle was undoubtedly one of our own but as we sat there on the mountainside hiding in the bushes, the fear of being mistaken for Charlie consumed us. Our position up the hill was nestled in an overly forested region and we couldn't even see the road below. We could only hope that we were equally as hard to detect by the driver. The closer the sound got, the more concerned we became. Nobody made a move or a sound as we sat like a bunch of scared kids becoming more afraid by the moment.

Suddenly the noise stopped and the air became transfixed with silence and the smell of diesel exhaust. Although we couldn't see it, the vehicle was definitely just below our position. The vehicle was taking too long to move on to wherever they were headed before they became our worst nightmare. My heart started pounding and then the distinct sound of a turret rotating made a sickening turn in what I feared was our direction. It was definitely a tank and I feared that we were about to be killed by friendly fire. Grove was sitting in a crouched position probably ready to start yelling "Friendly" again which might've spooked them into doing what we feared they were about do at that moment. Then the tank opened up a barrage that sent shells crashing into the side of the mountain. The rounds were exploding to our right. The explosions were loud enough to almost crack an eardrum, but no shrapnel. Their target must have been just far enough away from us to keep us out of harm's way. The habit of thinking of all worst case scenarios was at work. I automatically assumed they spotted Charlie near our position. If they did, then he might have tried escaping in our direction bringing us into the tank's line of fire. Keith got on the horn and frantically tried to get someone to get them to cease fire.

When the shooting stopped, we all felt spared. We never found out what or who they were supposed to be firing at but when the tank pulled off, we knew we had just dodged a bullet. Make that several very large ones. Ambush had taken on a new meaning after that firepower display. The following morning we were thankful and relieved to still be alive and left our precarious ambush spot.

We made it back to the highway and started the walk back. Grove found a human skull at the bottom of the mountain and put it in his ruck. Only in a place like Vietnam could a human skull be found just lying on the ground with no other skeletal remains around it. It had probably been gnawed on by some dog or played with by little kids before finding its way to the spot where Grove stumbled upon it. Maybe it was a decapitation job performed by one of us or, who knows, maybe the French or the Vietminh. In combat, mutilations are common. I wasn't the only one who wanted to lop someone's head off. Grove's new toy had to have been there for a long time; long enough for the decomposition process to reduce the body to nothing but skeletal remains. There was no cemetery around so it had to be a war casualty that did not get the burial he deserved. His death and his displaced skull said a lot about the insanity of war and the results of it. It also made me think about Mrs. Wheelhouse's dilemma, or her not wanting to believe the worst had happened to her son. If she knew that Grove could find a skull in the manner he did, she would surely feel that maybe her son could somehow be alive somewhere in Vietnam. We needed to only find him for her. It's amazing the way grief could also contain properties of optimism and hope. Mrs. Wheelhouse needed a dose of heartbreaking reality to shake her from her false hopes of ever recovering her son. She would have had to be shaken by someone else because I didn't have the courage to tell her anything about what actually happened.

Although the stand down was just beginning, it had already lasted a lot longer for me due to all of the extra time I spent waiting for the court martial that never happened. Later that day we were treated to a live stage show put on by a troupe of musicians, singers and dancers made up of a few GI's and mostly Orientals. They were probably making stops throughout the entire brigade. One of the band members, however, bore a strong resemblance to a guy that I jumped with at Ft. Benning. After a few songs I remembered his name. It was Danny Dangerfield; the one who volunteered for a detail while we were at Phu Cat AFB waiting for a truck ride to Charang Valley to begin our jungle training. I positioned myself near the stage and waited for a break in the show to reacquaint myself with him. When the opportunity came, I called him off of the stage and he responded by jumping down to the spot where I was standing. By volunteering for that detail, he managed to get out of doing anything more than punching a cash register or strumming a guitar.

After our talk, he returned to the stage for the finale. The song they sang was unrecognizable to me but when it reached a certain chorus, everybody in the audience sang along and I seemed to be the only guy who never heard the song and didn't know the lyrics. "We gotta get outta this place. If it's the last thing we ever do." they all sang. I turned to Jackson and he just shrugged his shoulders. At least I wasn't the only one who had never heard of it. The rest of the audience treated it like it was some kind of anti Vietnam War anthem. They all sang it with deep conviction and there was even a tear or two spotted among them. "The next time I hear the song I'll be waiting for the chorus to come around." I said to myself. The words did hit home though. We really did need to get out of the place. Tragically for some of us, the place was the last thing that was ever seen because making it out alive was the only thing never done.

The next day we heard news that Col. Clark was killed in action. He was, according to story, killed sitting in the door of a helicopter while hovering over a firefight. He was alleged to have taken one round in the chest while firing his pistol at Charlie below. If the story was true then I don't think he would have wanted to have it happen any other way. The man lived for such action and died from overexposure to it. The validity of the story, as usual, was shrouded in rumor and innuendo. Clark could have possibly died of a sniper's round while looking through a pair of binoculars and the firefight story could have been just a mean spirited jab created by one of his detractors. Our newest problem was dealing with his replacement. He was reportedly on his way to Uplift at that very moment. This Colonel was rumored to be, unfortunately, from the same blood and guts mold as his predecessor. His persona had already preceded him setting us up for a continuation of Clark's iron fisted rule. We were losing one tough guy killed in action and gaining another one as a replacement. Some of the guys at Uplift were really in for a rude awakening if they were anticipating anything less.

The next day, our new Battalion CO arrived and immediately went to work at changing the way things were being done at Uplift. He was succeeding at making life miserable for us while we were on stand down and I supposed we should have all expected as much. He started off with a bang; instituting a bunch of anti-drug use measures that surprised no one. Later that night, he even led a patrol of MP's up duster hill in an attempt to raid the joint. He should've quit the Army and joined the F.B.I. Hoover could have used his brand of enthusiasm.

As the extended stand down continued, we practically lived on the bunker line. On any occasion there was usually at least one sun bather lying out on the top of any bunker catching some rays. One of the guys came up with a tape sent to him from the world that was recorded at a live outdoor concert called Woodstock where, according to him, at least 500,000 were in attendance. His favorite song or performance was by a group named Country Joe Mc Donald and the fish. They sang yet another anti Vietnam War song and he played the thing over and over. He must have played it for at least two hours. The guys just kept cheering him on and he was more than willing to oblige them with another play. The combination of drugs and heat had obviously started to cook their brains. Farris was sure to make a few changes there.

Doc and I had lunch over at the mess hall and I noticed the sick guy with the yellow eyes again. He was even sicker than I first thought and sitting at a table with the same two guys he was with earlier. He wasn't eating much at all. "Doc what is wrong with that guy over there. His eyes are yellow. Look at him man."

"Hepatitis." He said continuing to eat without even looking in his direction.

"I've heard of that before but not much more. Exactly what is hepatitis?"

"It's a liver disease he probably caught from shooting up with a dirty needle."

"Wait a minute Doc. Are you telling me that if you shoot skag into your vein with a dirty needle it will mess up your liver?"

"Exactly."

"That sounds weird. Is he being treated for it or what?"

"He has to come in for treatment on his own. He's reluctant to do so because his heroin use would become a matter of official record."

"Can the disease kill him?"

"Probably will since he has so much time left in country." he said as we finished eating. The level of suffering designated for heroin addicts was as unlimited as their access to the drug. I knew a lot of junkies back in New Orleans but I never heard about hepatitis being a hazard of its use. The guy sitting at the other table was more afraid of being exposed than he was of dying of the disease and almost everybody knew about his predicament. I only hoped Doc was kidding about him being allowed to die of a curable disease by choice.

Word began to spread around that our beloved Recon Company was up to its neck in the shit again. A patrol, probably led by Lt. Mack, had found Charlie. Of course they chose to engage what was no doubt a numerically superior force. This meant that we would probably have to scramble on over to the chopper pad to be inserted into the mess. It was already getting late; which also meant that a number of guys had already left for the whorehouse for the night. Also, some of the other guys hadn't returned from the village yet either. Every one of them would be charged AWOL for missing the headcount that would take place prior to the chopper assault. Lt. Mack's aggressiveness was probably admired by his superiors. They must have really loved the way he went out and got results but I questioned his tactics. Recon's job, by definition, was to find Charlie, not engage him. Sooner or later I knew we would get caught in the rear when it happened. Bravo Company had recently gone through the same ordeal and so did Alpha Co. We just had the misfortune of being in the rear when Mack started some more fireworks. It had reached the point where being on stand down meant being on alert and ready to bail out Recon.

There was no need to wait for the call we all knew was coming. Everybody started packing up and getting ready to head out to the chopper pad. The routine was old. The only new element was the starting point. How badly were they outnumbered? How soon could we get some helicopters? Were they taking any casualties? Had their situation become critical? Could they hold out until we got there? We knew that Charlie was smart enough to try to determine exactly where our slicks would land. If possible, he would have a welcoming party waiting for us at that location. If we chose to avoid landing in that particular area we would have to walk a longer distance making Recon's predicament a little more serious. All of these scenarios were playing in our minds as we continued to gear up. The anxiety was so high I almost threw up. Benn started second guessing himself about not re enlisting while we were on stand down. I couldn't say that I blamed him. He wanted to re up and avoid the situation he found himself in. His hesitation had placed him one helicopter assault away from his worst fear and he was slowly becoming consumed by self doubt.

We made it to the helicopter pad ten minutes after we first got word. But ten minutes in a firefight is like an eternity. The helicopters hadn't arrived and as bad as I didn't want to go, I was hoping for a speedy arrival by our transports. Not arriving in time had become a greater fear than a hot LZ. After that night in Tuy Hoa, I learned that getting there wasn't even half the job. Charlie was not expected to melt away into the woods just because help arrived. We all fully expected to have a fight on our hands when we stepped off of the choppers. My only fear was how big a force Mack had picked a fight with or how big a fight would they put up.

A jeep pulled up with a trailer hitched to it. Inside of the trailer was extra ammo. A bad sign that made me expect the worst. They even twisted Bracey's arm and put him back into the fold for the assault. As absenteeism was still high, they took me out of my squad to fill up the ranks of another one of the squads with a more serious personnel shortage problem.

The Chaplain walked up with an almost empty rucksack and a canteen of water. I guess the only thing he was carrying inside was a Bible. I expected someone to send him back to the chapel because we needed all shooters for the assault. It seemed more natural for him to stay behind and pray for us and we could have done just fine without the extra baggage. His unnecessary arrival at the chopper pad caught a lot of us off guard. There was also, for the first time, a photographer with us. His presence only added more bad vibes to the situation. This one was no GI either. He was one of those free lance guys who worked for a salary.

The arrival of the slicks brought a mixture of fear of the anticipated battle and a strong feeling of anxiousness. The fear of dying was only equal to the fear of not making it in time. I didn't want to find any dead G.I.'s with their faces shot off and no one to exact any measure of revenge from. Whatever was going to happen, I wanted it to happen while we still had daylight. The darkness would put us at an immediate disadvantage. Our initiative would be lost in the cover of the night. Charlie, who ruled the night, would be hoping for a late arrival.

When we started to board the aircraft I was told we would be a part of the lead element. My new squad was made up of so many different faces that I couldn't determine which platoon I was temporarily assigned to. The makeshift squad was tolerable but the mere idea of finding a hot LZ was scary enough to make me wish I was still awaiting that court martial. I also started to regret taking the M-79 because if I were still an RTO, I would've been with my squad. My change of jobs had landed me on one of the first helicopters going in replacing some other grenadier who was spending the night at a cathouse.

The flight was short and agonizing due to all of those worst case scenarios I couldn't erase from my mind. I was totally absorbed by some of the outcomes I had conjured up. Charlie could never come up with anything as bad as the outcomes my mind could manufacture. My heartbeat was, of course, hard enough to crack my eardrums and my adrenal glands were so overloaded that I felt like jumping out of the helicopter. We were doing it again. Tuy Hoa still seemed very recent and already I was on another rescue that was working against the clock. I was hoping to get there soon enough to save them and anticipating the worst when we arrived.

We landed behind the lead slick and started to move out immediately. Chris was at point and seemed to know exactly where we were heading. As we caught up with the point element, the fear of whatever was ahead of us was starting to really set in. My legs were wobbled with fear and interfering with my stride. The sound of small arms fire reminded me of the long walk at Tuy Hoa on April 1st. At least thirty minutes had passed since we first got word of the situation and they were still hanging in. We didn't walk for very long before we came to a halt. The shooting had started to die down and I couldn't tell what Chris was doing up front. He seemed to be throwing a rope with some sort of weight on the end of it. After he took cover and pulled the rope towards him we realized he had found a booby trap, we took cover in anticipation of the explosion. Lee, who was also a part of my new makeshift squad, found an AK-47 lying in the bushes next to him. Unwisely he picked it up to and showed it to me without realizing it could have been booby-trapped. He was lucky to not have his head and arms blown off.

A huge explosion then went off up the trail shaking the ground beneath us. Chris had succeeded in detonating the booby trap and clearing the path of Charlie's unmanned welcoming device. We got up and started to move further up the trail leading up the side of the mountain. Our progress came to another sudden halt. Chris was at it with the rope trick again. We must have been hot on Charlie's tail. The second booby trap was designed to catch us relaxing after finding the first one. Chris was in rare form and probably was anticipating the second booby trap.

The small arms fire had ceased, Charlie had retreated and the urgency of our mission was seemingly over. The Recon patrol, wherever they were, was obviously out of trouble and the mission had neared a successful conclusion. After exploding the second booby trap, Chris pressed on with his pursuit. He then came up to another point along the trail he felt needed further investigation. He signaled for the rest of us to stay back while he investigated the next few meters beyond the second booby trap's intended kill zone. His one man recon took him out of our immediate sight. His demonstration of what it took to be a point man was exemplary. He had been trained well for his job and was going about his duty as if he were on a training exercise. Charlie always marked the trail with an item that could easily be distinguished to mark off his kill zone. An alert point man must pick up on the trail marking before he leads his patrol into it. Failure to do so would cost legs or lives. All too often, both life and limbs were lost by missing them. My position in line made me a potential kill zone victim, I was lucky he was at point.

Chris returned carrying a satchel full of documents. He and the rest of the lifers were poring over them as if they could read Vietnamese. But if the lifers could waste time standing around looking at those papers, everything must have been alright. The rescue mission had really started to take on a sweet smell of success. For all I knew, maybe Recon never was in the kind of jam I thought they were in. "This will be quite a souvenir, huh?" said Lee still showing off his trophy. "You can forget about the lifers letting you keep it man." I said.

"Bullshit, I found it. This sucker is coming home with me." he said believing he would be allowed to take an assault rifle home simply because he found it. In reality, if every GI who found or captured a weapon were allowed to keep it, there would've already been thousands of them on the streets. Lee was in for a letdown that I was sure he would be able to handle. Holding the weapon in his hand was an uplifting experience for him though. He knew just how rare the moment was and was enjoying whatever he could extract from the moment. Capturing a weapon was second only to getting that rare one on one kill. He wouldn't be allowed to take it home with him but, they will never be able to take away the event or the story.

The darkness came before any transports could extract us so we were forced to spend the night in place. It seemed as if we could only count on the Army to give us a ride to the fray but not out of it. We spent a very intense night in the valley amid a lot of suspicious sounds that restarted all of my fears. It felt great to see the sunrise that following morning. We prepared to leave the valley in good spirits. It was gratifying to have arrived in time to save the day for a change. I just wished it could've happened the same way for us at Tuy Hoa. I supposed that I would always be haunted by what happened on that mountain while we sat idly by. Fortunately Charlie was caught this time with no plans to defend himself and just ran. The weapon Lee found, along with all of those documents, were evidence of an unplanned evacuation. Unlike at Tuy Hoa, when Charlie brought the fight to us. He had everything planned in advance.

Our trek through the valley that led to all of those booby traps was slow and deliberate. As each succeeding helicopter dropped off another load of troops, it caused a long line that had no place to go. The guys that got off of the last helicopter would become the lead element on the way out. Chris, feeling in possession of a hot hand, moved to the front of the line to lend his expertise. As effective as he was on the way in, no one should argue with him. He had proven himself and impressed all who witnessed his performance on the way up the mountain.

After we started out way out of the valley, our movement came to an almost immediate halt as I imagined that Chris had spotted something again. Whatever it was could take as long as he felt was necessary. I was in no hurry and felt safe at the end of the line. In a way, coming in first made me deserving of being one of the last going out. It took a lot of pressure out of making those long marches through hot territory and this area was definitely Charlie's turf.

A loud explosion went off followed by a burst of AK-47 gunfire. A booby trap had just been detonated and was definitely manned by at least one shooter. Smitty and Red immediately sped past my position and headed to the front. I instantly followed them because I couldn't bear standing around not knowing what was going on up front. I knew this was going to be ugly.

We ran as fast as we possibly could run in full gear. As we ran along the motionless procession that remained stunned by the explosion, I noticed I still hadn't passed my squad. I hadn't even, in fact, come upon the 2nd platoon's position either. It made me fear the worst. By that time it was obvious that our platoon was leading us out.

Our path straddled along the base of the mountain where Chris found the documents. To our right was a clearing that extended all the way across a valley. As we continued to run past our motionless company, I started to see the familiar faces of our platoon up ahead. I could see everyone but my own squad. The line of men was strung out along a trail that disappeared into a wooded area. The wounded was already being brought out to the clearing just short of it. I could hear screams of pain from one of them as we neared their location. The Chaplain, of all people, was one of the wounded. He was already lying on a poncho bleeding from a wound in his pelvic region dangerously close to his penis. Chris was being carried out next with his pants torn off of him. His scrotum sac had been ripped open and one of his exposed testicles was dangling from his crotch. It was easily the most devastating sight that I had ever seen. In spite of his wounds and his obvious pain, he was screaming insults at the lifers for not listening at his insistence that there was danger just up the trail. Nick was carried out next with his left leg missing. It was his voice that was most prominent as I approached. He was in extreme pain and appeared to be going into shock. He was staring at his leg in disbelief. He could still feel the ghost effect of his toes as he sensed them wriggling around inside of his boot that was at least five feet away from him. He was overwhelmed by the false sensation, the sight of his boot with his foot still in it cut off just above the ankles and the reality of his bleeding stump that was being tended by Doc.

Both of our medics were working frantically on the wounds, starting intravenous fluids, and of course administering the morphine. Nick's cries of pain had dissipated within seconds of his injection. His agony turned into immediate ecstasy and he momentarily forgot his predicament. Keith was carried out next. He had lost both of his legs and was gritting his teeth to maintain his normal demeanor. In keeping with the restraints of his religion, I supposed he declined his injection of morphine as if it were optional. I assumed he had already received an injection just the same. While lying on his back receiving what little first aid that could be administered to such a victim, Keith managed to chuckle at those of us standing over him. "I'm going home now. I'm finished with this war. You poor guys will still have to stay here. I feel sorry for you." He said in mock pity for us as he demonstrated monumental fortitude.

Buckley was assisted out of the wooded area next, the victim of a wound to the shoulder. Doc was walking alongside as he supported him. The photographer was poised right in front of them with his camera at the ready. Ironically, the first time we humped with a photographer, we got ambushed and gave him something to shoot. He seemed totally detached from what we were suffering through as he went about his duty of capturing our moment of tragedy on film for a buck. It seemed insensitive or at least inappropriate for someone to be taking pictures at that time. He obviously would have disagreed.

Benn, who was already out in the clearing when we arrived, was having an emotional breakdown. He was going out of his mind and could not be contained or controlled. "I'm re uppin." he said as he looked at Keith and then Nick. "I'm re uppin. I was standing here and Keith was standing here and Nick was standing there and, and no I'm re uppin, I'm re uppin man. Oh lawd, no! I'm re uppin." he said repeatedly. It was obvious that he was standing between Nick and Keith when the blast went off. The improbability of being able to walk away from the kill zone without a scratch had flipped him out. His emotional display was only adding to the misery of the moment as we all stood around feeling useless and impotent. I was suffering through a lot of personal agony. This was my squad, my family. I felt orphaned by the decimation of our unit. All of those guys were about to go home WIA.

I had been removed from the tragedy in the same timely manner that Jones, Boogie Man and Anderson were back in March. I only assumed there would be some kind of guilt attached to it and I was right. I felt so much guilt that I almost wished I was lying there on the ground with my legs blown off too. I didn't feel lucky at all and couldn't understand how the Chaplain got hit. He looked pitiful lying on that poncho with a number of guys standing around him as he spoke. "As you can see if I step on a twig it will break, just as it would have broken under one of you. The sound of the twig breaking under your foot would be heard no matter who broke it." the Chaplain said. "Doc, what's he talking about?" I asked.

"When Chris found that marking on the trail, he suggested we wait until he investigated the area. Jahret told him we didn't have time. He was in a big hurry to make it to our next destination. They started arguing over the issue and the Chaplain jumped in with this dumb idea about walking point. He said he wanted to lead us through the wooded area that turned out to be a kill zone. Chris was right all along." He said.

"What are you saying? You mean that the Chaplain led those guys into that shit?"

"Not exactly. He wanted to but they placed him about fifth or sixth in line. The Chaplain was the highest ranking individual around so everybody had to at least entertain his idea of walking with the point squad." Chris was real pissed too. It was as if his opinion on what was up the trail took a back seat to the Chaplain's insistence on being near the front. "This is crazy man. Look at this shit." he said while lying on a makeshift stretcher amid a ghastly scene of blood, gauzes, bandages and severed limbs. It was absurd to think that something like that could actually happen but it did. Without realizing his insensitivity, the Chaplain offered his broken twig analogy as a moral to the real life tragedy he had just contributed to. It only certified the theory that one enemy was trying to kill us and the other enemy was seemingly trying their best to get us killed. Only now the Chaplain had proven himself to be an unwitting accomplice to the conspiracy. By then Jahret had become a prime candidate for a fragging that would solve our leadership problem. He would surely get more of us killed and we were being needlessly sacrificed due to his ineffectiveness. Although the likelihood of a fragging ever happening in our company was remote, I began to understand the mentality of the fraggers. It wasn't always an act of murderous revenge or jungle justice; it was sometimes, in a twisted sort of way, an immediate solution to an otherwise hopeless situation. And the Chaplain, who was no doubt exempt from consideration for a fragging, must have also thought he was impervious to injury because of his status as a clergyman. Charlie couldn't have cared less about who he was. As long as he was a GI, he was fair game. If Charlie's mother came down that trail wearing the wrong uniform she would have had her legs blown off too.

The medivac came and took away some more of my friends. Accordingly, three big pieces of me went with them again. At the rate we were losing people, I didn't think I would last to see the end of the summer. My stay in country that was so much fun in the beginning had become one tragedy after another. My squad had been devastated. I was not looking forward to being around when we started the realignment. Keith was a good squad leader. Replacing him wouldn't be easy. I didn't expect Benn to be around much longer either. I assumed he would probably reenlist as soon as we got back to Uplift. This would leave very few of the old faces I'd grown accustomed to being with and I was only somewhere near the middle of my tour.

When the medivac left with the wounded the photographer left with them. He'd take his pictures to be developed and turn them into profit. In the meantime, we would try to adjust to the gruesome images that had been burned into our memories for life. Without, I might add, time to collect ourselves or regain our composure. We still had to reach our destination and move faster because of the delay caused by the booby trap. The device proved itself to be everything we were told it would be. A weapon designed to maim its victim and inflict a deep psychological wound into the spirit of the survivors. It wouldn't be easy to forget what had happened to us and Charlie knew it. What really hurt was that he made such a clean get away after blowing the device. His execution was flawless and made me hate him even more than before.

Jahret was still pushing us to make it to our destination. His haste had already cost us some legs and a lifetime of bad memories yet he was still driving us. He allowed us to take the path that should have been used when Chris told him of his suspicions. Had he insisted on us continuing down that same trail, someone would have surely fragged him. There probably would have been a fight among at least a dozen other willing assassins for the job of eliminating him. I wished I could have been up front with them when the trail marker was found. I would have argued in Chris's favor until the cows came home. I like to believe that a good argument would have placed enough doubt in the minds of everyone else. Of course the Chaplain would have eventually settled the issue with a few well placed twigs. "Say Handy, hold this for me." said Bracey in a low whisper while handing me a very heavy can of M-60 ammo. I was in no mood to just take it from him without a sound reason. I waited a few moments for him to adjust his load or whatever he planned to do. "Oh lawd!" he screamed. I immediately understood his ploy. He was about to fake a heat exhaustion. It was so phony I couldn't stand to even look at the rest of his performance. He was lucky I wasn't in charge of the outfit. I would have ordered him to get up and finish the march or be left behind. Of course, I wasn't in charge; so they went through the motions with him. They loosened his clothes and started pouring their precious water over him. I wouldn't have wasted a drop on him. A minute earlier we were in a hurry to make our destination then we suddenly came up with enough time for Bracey's bullshit. We had to wait in the hot sun for another medivac to pick him up at the risk of exposing someone else to a real heat cramp, exhaustion or stroke. In the meantime we would be stuck with the job of humping the extra load compliments of his big put-on and convince ourselves that we were better off without him. When the medivac came and picked him up we just continued on as if he never came out with us. "Bracey, the platoon hero." someone mumbled from behind mocking the awarding of the Bronze Star Bracey received in Tuy Hoa. I had never sampled opinion on the award but it was obviously questioned by more than just me. Maybe the lifers thought he lost his edge that night and allowed him to ghost away in the rear. Too many of us in the platoon differed with that opinion about Bracey and his special treatment. I was sure that to a man no one ever thought Bracey had the so-called edge. Nor would he ever have anything resembling an edge for duty in the field.

We made it to our new destination; another flyspeck on a map with no defined objective other than fanning out and patrolling the area searching for Charlie. The ambush was still fresh in our minds. The sight of severed limbs and Chris's dangling testicle would be continually replayed in my mind. I could only hope that he wasn't rendered sterile from his wound. That would be almost as tragic as losing a limb. Having one's future taken away like that must be devastating. It really gave me something else to worry about while I was in Vietnam. Having a family was very much a part of what Barbara and I had already planned. I needed to have everything intact when I returned.

After absorbing our losses and due to the personnel shift caused by it, my squad consisted of Benn, Lee, Big Goose, Ellis and myself. Our new squad leader was named Modell. I assumed he was another one of those shake and bake grads from NCO school at Benning. He was new and didn't appear to have earned his stripes in the field. His status was unofficial because everything was still in a state of flux due to the ambush. Modell was dull, boring and impressionable. Unfortunately, those were his good points. He had a long way to go before he could get the same respect as some of the squad leaders who had gone on before him.. At the start, all newcomers had to prove themselves and Modell was just another new guy.

According to my count, I had already reached the halfway point in my tour and gone beyond it without even knowing it. I should have started using my short-timers calendar days earlier. Rachel, Maleah and Sandra J. would be remembered mostly for their attempt at the impossible and their insensitive remarks but I was still thankful for the calendar. I had never even unfolded it. It was significant because I had finally gone "over the hump." Pretty soon I would be in position to start using that magic word, SHORT!

4

Our new location took us over a mountain and onto a valley floor with a landscape that changed drastically every fifty meters or so. In some areas, the valley was as heavily forested as some mountains during the monsoon. And some areas were barely covered with any foliage at all. The valley floor was not conducive for rice production because the area showed no signs of inhabitation and too much of the ground was eroded with deep gullies due to mountain runoff. Charlie, I felt, could hide almost anywhere within. Our last assault and subsequent ambush was obviously still weighing heavily on my mind. Our first night in the valley would be spent on ambush. As evidenced by the terrain, civilians never frequented the valley. It had no signs of it anyway. It was definitely a free fire zone and anything that moved was fair game. No villagers should've been wandering into the area at all. After what had just happened to us, anybody who passed our way would have been shot dead several times over.

We took one of the new guys with us on ambush. There were still quite a few I hadn't gotten to know. It was hard enough to try to face the days ahead without the guys I hoped would be with me. All of the new faces just made it even worse. I was beginning to understand all of the negative feelings about the new arrivals or why they were derided so much. It was just a feeling that consumes you when you watch a lot of guys go home ahead of you. On a personal level, it was a feeling of abandonment and desertion by all of the guys who had left me behind. Even the ones who were killed or wounded had left a void that I couldn't rationalize. Instead of being thankful for having replacements to fill in for the departed members, we treated them like imposters or poor substitutes. It was insane because they were caught up in the same numbers game that we were. Even worse, they held us in the same high regard we had for those guys they replaced.

With new guy in tow, we took off for our ambush site. Modell was calling the shots and choosing the site as well. I was prepared to complain about his selection because I knew Jahret had already given him a grid to use. Jahret likes it when he gets a new buck sergeant to break in. They always followed his orders to a "T". Some of the buck sergeants he inherited would laugh in his face and sometimes did. Modell was definitely a "yes" man though. He took us to the general area of the grid and chose a well-elevated mound to spend the night on. We deployed our claymores and trip flares at the base of the mound and prepared to spend the night.

Directly in front of us about 35 meters away was a heavily wooded area bounded by a culvert about 5 ft deep and 10 feet across. I slept at the edge of the mound directly above the Claymore I set up. In spite of my reservations about the area, I felt relaxed enough to actually try to go to sleep. That night, as I was still not quite asleep, Lee and the new guy started talking in low whispers to each other. I wasn't alarmed enough; however, to turn over and find out what they were talking about. When their talk became a little clearer to me I still wouldn't allow them to disturb my attempt at sleep. Then my head started to clear and I began to pick up on exactly what they were saying. "Let's shoot first, and then blow the Claymores." said Lee very softly.

"No, let's blow the Claymores first." whispered the new guy.

"But if you blow the Claymores first, we might shoot Handy when he wakes up from the explosion." Their conversation had to be a dream I thought. Then I heard the spoon of the frag fly off of the grenade as it passed over my head and with an almost comical redundant whisper..."Frag Out!" They then started firing their weapons. I turned to grab my weapon just before the claymore went off with a loud explosion that really shook me up. Before I could collect myself, the grenade went off causing even more confusion within me. "What the fuck is going on? Are we under attack?" I asked.

"No, there was a gook down there trying to disarm the flare and another one was near the claymore." said Lee.

I looked down the side of the mound, which was barely 20 feet high, to survey the damage. Other than the swath created by the blast of my claymore, all that was left were a couple of Ho Chi Minh sandals on the ground. The sandals were made of tire tread cut into the shape of a shoe sole with inner tube strips. The practical foot ware was worn extensively by the Vietnamese but not good for running at all. Whenever Charlie had to leave in a hurry, he almost always left them in his wake. "Well what happened to them? " I asked while standing at the edge of the mound's summit.

"They're gone now." said Modell as he wrapped himself up and incredibly tried to go back to sleep. I convinced them to recon the area for all of the right reasons. Their fatigue must have gotten the best of them. They all thought it was alright to call it a night because they had scared them away.

I was reluctant to act as if I was in charge of the group but we couldn't just go back to sleep. Our position had been compromised. They knew exactly where we were and we didn't even know how many others were in the area. If all Charlie had to worry about were scare tactics, he would have won the war before I finished high school.

After everyone secured their weapons and got on line, we went to the bottom of the mound. Judging from where I stood, there should have been two dead men lying in front of the spot where my Claymore was deployed. The grass burns indicated that they should have at least lost their legs. It appeared that Lee and the new guy hesitated squeezing that plunger just long enough to let those two get away. Killing is not as easy as we all wanted to believe. It might have been different if we were under fire, but under any other circumstance, it would be difficult. There was a story about the kill that old Sarge's patrol made during our search for the rice cache. The point man allegedly froze up when he came upon the dead guy I urinated on. His hesitation almost got everybody in the patrol shot. Whoever was behind him beat Charlie to the quick and fired in time to save the squad. I only hoped that if I ever got into that kind of situation I would get crazy enough quick enough to put him away. I already had enough anger inside of me to kill a million of them. After losing those guys in that ambush, I was angry enough to kill them all.

When Jahret, Calvin and the rest of the platoon arrived, Modell walked over to them to give his report. I wouldn't have traded places with him for a million dollars. Calvin did a walkover of the area where the Claymore was detonated. "It looks like your Claymore was aimed too low."

"How did you know it was mine?" I asked.

"I just know. Do you know how to deploy a Claymore mine?"

"Yeah. Can you still remember?" I asked with an equal amount of sarcasm.

The next night was another squad's turn to go out on ambush. Old Sarge was still with us and getting close to his DEROS date. He never let Mercein's bitching get to him over those misses they suffered through while looking for that rice but I did. To be sent out to take a picture of the dead body was the final straw in my opinion. Sarge, on the other hand, just took it in stride. Maybe I had been unfair about my assessment of his performance or more significantly, his being placed in charge of a squad at all. He had more than held his own under the circumstances. Of course having Sarge, Modell and Walkup taking out patrols gave me little to look forward to when the time came for us to go out. It would be one "yes" man or another in charge. Jahret and Calvin loved every moment of it. They had finally achieved the kind of network they always wanted. Squad leaders who obeyed their orders and demanded that we stayed in step with the rest of the platoon. I couldn't stand it.

The radio was reporting that Nixon had decided to give the vote to the 18 yr olds. It was a decision that was fair and long overdue. If an 18 yr old was old enough to fight and die in a war, he should at least be old enough to vote for or against the bureaucrat that controls his fate. As for me, they waited until I was on the way to Vietnam to start the lottery then gave the vote to the teenagers after I turned 21. I wouldn't even get an opportunity to vote until I was at least 22. "Handy, when is the Mardi Gras?" Doc asked again.

"The Mardi Gras? Did you hear that news report?"

"Yeah man. So when is it?"

"I've told you it's the day before Ash Wednesday."

"When is that?"

"I don't know. I'm not Catholic." I told him as we both laughed. Having Doc for a close friend had been great for me. I was glad that at least he'd be around for the rest of my tour. Other than Kyler, Mac, Goose, Ellis, Jackson, Red and Anderson, I couldn't think of many others that had a comparable amount of time in country. I was beginning to miss some of those old faces and the turnover had me concerned.

Benn had settled down and was back to being the free spirit he normally was. The ambush really screwed him up for a while. I couldn't imagine how he managed to survive both the explosion and the rifle burst but he did. Unfortunately, I was still having problems dealing with not being there at all. I had hoped that a little more time would be all I needed to get over it. It couldn't happen fast enough and the guilt was mounting. There was a lot happening and it was hard to get past one incident before something happened again. I was afraid to think of what would happen next. At least there were only 165 days left on my tour. "Jackson, did you realize that we had gone over the hump, man?"

"Really, I hadn't been counting the days. By the way, my sister says that you can write all of my letters for me. She likes your writing a lot man and she said that your letter was better than anything I ever wrote."

"Nice try, Jack. I think you'd better write her yourself. My list is long enough." I said as I imagined the first duty for our next Chaplain would be to get Jackson to write home more often.

Resupply day came around again and Mrs. Wheelhouse froze me in my tracks with another heartbreaking letter. She said she was struggling and trying to hold on. She felt as if her world had come to an end. I was really feeling sad for her too. It looked as if she had also backed me into that corner about her son's appearance and was still looking for an answer to why he looked so different in the casket. Feeling convinced the wrong body was sent home for burial, she continued to look for the most unlikely outcome and left me at a loss for words to say or write. Holding on to her belief in God and that her prayers would have brought her son back home alive had failed her. She actually used the word forsaken to describe her feelings about her tragic loss. The letter was distressing and made me feel angry about what was happening to her. I felt hopelessly insignificant and the feeling had a stranglehold on me. I couldn't do anything to help her son that night and there was nothing I could do to console her in her moment of sorrow.

       Spirituality was really taking a beating that day. A little earlier a man of the so-called cloth contributed mightily to a disaster inflicted on some of my close friends. The following resupply day I had to read a letter from a grieving mother; one who felt as if her faith in God had led her to a disappointing realization. It was more than I could stand and really had me rethinking my position on spirituality. I had also become afraid that it would crush Mrs. Wheelhouse if any letter she wrote to me were returned due to my death. She had given me another reason to make it back home alive, as if I needed another one. My getting killed in Vietnam would probably break her heart all over again. I couldn't be a part of any more suffering on her behalf.

Mrs. Wheelhouse also sent me another care package. The guys went through it in a matter of seconds. Some of the new guys had never even known her son but they were impressed by her gesture and excited about getting their hands on some of her goodies. She was a grand lady who managed to make us feel important every time she went through the trouble of making the package and sending it to us.

That evening, Sarge took us out on ambush in place of Modell. We patrolled until we came upon a spot and paused while he read his map and regained his bearings. I saw no reason for it because all we did was walk in a straight line through some rather clear and flat territory. We all just sort of lounged around in place as Sarge started checking out the area and I started to realize that maybe he had already chosen his ambush spot and we were possibly standing in the general vicinity.

Suddenly one of our flanking guards said he spotted someone or something. Sarge was spooked by his sighting and started firing his weapon into the nearest treetops. He had a look of fear and confusion on his face and had us all ducking for cover. I was looking around to see what he could have been firing at and couldn't locate his intended target if there ever was any. Joley never took cover. He wasn't concerned about whatever Sarge was shooting at. He seemed more exasperated over the scene than anything else. "Here we go again." He mumbled angrily as he took a seat on the ground. He was visibly upset at Sarge and his weird behavior. There was little or no concern among the rest of the patrol about who was threatening our position. I may have been right about Sarge's appointment as a squad leader after all. The patrol was made up of guys who were in his squad. Guys like Joley who had been on patrol with him before and was familiar with his behavior. It was his call and I was going to let him sink or swim with his decisions. I just didn't want him near me with his finger on the trigger.

Sarge hesitated for a while before deciding to move into a thicket located behind us. As we all crawled backwards into the bushes and down a slight decline, we were surprised to find a small creek concealed just beyond the foliage. It was about 6 inches deep with lot of long legged insects that walked on the water's surface. I felt like an idiot lying in the water. After our encounter with Charlie a few nights prior, I was hesitant to repeat my takeover performance even if I couldn't understand the strategy of our position in the bushes. Our location was not a good spot to take cover. He had, however, decided to stay put inside the bushes lying in the water for the entire night. Everybody else in the patrol already knew about Sarge's shortcomings. As we spent the night rolling around in that creek, Sarge never gave a second thought about moving to another spot. He was scared senseless and afraid to make his next decision. Our so-called ambush site was a joke and none of us were laughing. Normally a squad leader would have been more afraid of what the guys in the squad thought about his actions but he just remained there in the water poised in anticipation. Taking cover to surprise the enemy would have been a more aggressive tactic but we were just staying hidden.

The following morning when we all had to come out of the bushes, Sarge was still reluctant to make his move. After we all crawled out to begin our return trip, someone spooked him into his treetop shooting routine. As he fired, he started to back into the bushes again and was clearly too afraid to make a step forward. Whatever he was afraid of had to be somewhere at treetop level. I couldn't take anymore of Sarge's self doubt and his wild shooting had me scared. "Fuck this shit man. I'm going back alone. You guys can stay here and keep Sarge occupied if you want to but I'm gonna dash now." I said as I turned away from the dispirited patrol and started walking back mostly in disgust. After I walked for about 50 meters, I looked over my shoulder and noticed the rest of the patrol following me. They actually looked like a group of disciplined soldiers on patrol with their testicles intact. I was proud of them. They had regrouped just in time as we were nearing the platoon's campsite.

When we made it back to CP, Jahret noticed I was walking point with an M-79 and questioned my place in line. I knew he would take it up with the squad leader. His answer had to be interesting. I was sure he wouldn't tell him about how he lost it out there or about how the squad left him because they didn't want to spend the rest of the war waiting for him to get his act together. It had to be embarrassing enough. Joley couldn't let it pass though. He felt extremely disillusioned about the incident. It was about as close to being humiliated as he had obviously been since arriving in the field. "Handy, I'm ashamed of what we did out there last night. We hid last night man. We were hiding from our own shadows because of Sarge. Every time he thinks that Charlie is around, he starts shooting at the trees. He thinks that Charlie hides in the trees to ambush us. He must have shot the fuck out of the treetops when we were searching for the rice.

"Is that what all of that noise was about man?" I asked.

"Yeah, it was him. He did all of that shooting by himself. We were lucky he didn't shoot us in the ass." said Joley who was totally demoralized over the incident. Sarge was suffering from the "Short timers Whores" Jones talked of back in January. The poor guy didn't have a chance. He never was suited or trained for life in the bush and had the added burden of being a squad leader. Rank was never more over-rated and the mission couldn't end fast enough for him or for the men in his squad. At least there was no talk of a fragging going on behind Sarge's back. It was a testament to the squad's confidence that he would eventually get through his ordeal.

On the next night, I had to go back out on ambush again. I couldn't complain because at least we were about to end the mission. While deploying my Claymore I managed to make an ass out of myself by fumbling my trip flare as I attempted to set it. After 6 months in the bush, it finally happened to me. I was so embarrassed that all I could do was sit and watch it burn. Lee was having none of that though. Before five seconds had elapsed he removed his helmet liner from its steel pot, threw it aside and quickly placed the steel pot over the burning flare and sat on it attempting to smother the flame. Actually all he managed to do was cover it up. It continued to burn as smoke seeped from under the steel pot. But it did take all of the illumination and a lot of the embarrassment out of the incident. "I always wanted to do that and see the effect of shutting off the oxygen to the flare." he said while sitting atop his steel pot amidst the smoke that was still escaping from the covered flare. A trip flare is not like a match though. Once it starts burning, it will continue to burn even if submerged in water. Lee sat on his steel pot for a short while but had to get up due to the intense heat caused by the burning flare. Had he sat there any longer, the steel pot would have probably fried his butt and sealed his anus shut. Still, he demonstrated an ability to think and act quick.

When we returned to Uplift, we were ready for our next mission because we didn't want to get caught up in another rescue. Whatever was next on the agenda for us couldn't come soon enough. Getting away from Uplift was, as the locals always said, Number One. I considered going to Linda and Monique's but was afraid of what might happen while I was away. If Recon made contact with Charlie again I'd definitely be charged AWOL. Calvin and Jahret would love it. Besides, Linda and Monique had moved their operation to a new location. I had to find out where they were before I considered going.

Somebody started an ugly rumor about us going on pacification yet again. It seemed as if I had already spent half of my tour working in somebody's village. I needed Boggs' address real soon because I could never begin to feel confident about going home alive if the Brigade kept sending us out on suicide missions. Vietnamization was a hopeless venture and I wondered if any of the other infantry units were repeatedly suffering through the same nightmare. The Herd couldn't be the only unit in Vietnam working in villages as often as we did.

Later that evening, I risked hitching a ride with some of the guys from the third platoon to Linda and Monique's new place. We were lucky enough to catch a ride from one of the ROK truck drivers. The only problem was that there was already a group of rowdy GIs on it making life miserable for every Vietnamese civilian they passed along the way. I remember when I first came to Uplift. I was surprised at some of the anti-Vietnamese behavior. I was told that my attitude toward the civilians would change. They were right but I this crowd was way out of line. One guy was leaning over the side of the truck swinging his rifle at a motorcyclist. Another one was throwing a tear gas grenade at a house. I was glad to get off of the truck before I witnessed a murder.

The new opium den was much larger than the old place. There was a huge patio in the back with a big crowd of customers. Business was booming that day. I also saw a couple of MP's sitting nearby in a jeep. I pointed them out to the guys that I arrived with. "It's OK. They're from English." The MP's form LZ English always used the opium dens nearer to LZ Uplift and our MP's used the dens located around English. It was a neat little arrangement they had worked out as long as they were off duty when they smoked. Judging from the size of the crowd, I'd say that it was a safe day to make a stop at Linda and Monique's.

When we walked in, one of them, either Linda or Monique, walked up and greeted us. I had never been formally introduced to either one of them. She was playing the role of the cordial hostess. She introduced herself as Linda and remembered my last visit to their former den.

"Where's Monique?" I asked.

"She's in the back. Come on, I take you." she said as she led me through her spacious new place. The first room had about ten guys sitting around smoking pot and shooting the breeze as the radio played. The next room was even bigger and had twice as many guys in it. There were two huge vats filled with white powder.

"Coke or Skag. Help yourself." She said. The guys walked over and started to fill the tips of their cigarettes with some skag (heroin). I followed suit but I never was a big fan of the white powder. After I filled the end of a cigarette, I put it in my pocket but was too afraid of the lasting effects of its use. "I just want a pack of Bombers." I told her as she led me to the patio.

"Monique, come and meet our friend." she yelled. Monique was busy inspecting a bunch of syringes with one of the medics. He examined each one and separated the good ones from the bad ones I supposed. Everytime he came across a needle I imagined he thought should not be used, he put it under his boot and broke it in half. The patio was full of guys who were either, cooking up a fix in a spoon, shooting it, throwing up or just nodding out. The grip of addiction was all around us. It was nothing new to me having once lived in a housing project where it was a part of the landscape. I could never understand the attraction to heroin use. It created problems for the users that none of them could handle. Most of the guys on the patio came over to Vietnam full of innocence, but there never should have been enough innocence or naiveté to allow them to be enslaved by the drug. At least I didn't think so.

"This is Handy." Linda said as she formally introduced me to someone that I had known for months.

"Yeah, I know that guy. He's been here before for nickel bags." she said, barely paying attention to us as she collected the "good needles." She never missed a beat.

An old woman wandered in interrupting the gathering screaming loudly at both Linda and Monique. "Tuy mung moo hundan shooie boong bang wan de shuka!" she said trembling with anger. Without hesitation Linda started yelling back at her.

"Com mieu lai toie mung ahn lai dei hong kai kik goo tooie!" she said as she turned around and slapped her butt twice. Her body language said it all. In spite of the new location, the same problem persisted. Having an opium den in the neighborhood naturally brought a lot of resentment from the neighbors. I thought that it was a good time to leave so I grabbed my bombers and left. On the way out, I waived at the two MP's sitting in the jeep. They flashed the peace sign at me and continued their smoke break. That poor old woman was in for a lot of frustration because our MP's would only pay lip service to policing the opium dens. On the other hand, the Vietnamese police were too corrupt to do anything either. American MP's were using the opium dens and their Vietnamese counterparts were receiving a little of the profits from the establishments in return for the harassment free opportunity to do business. The black market had made Linda and Monique rich; as rich as some of the wealthy landowners who, no doubt, resented the new rich duo's status and the nefarious manner in which they had acquired their wealth.

When I returned to Uplift I was relieved to find no rescue mission in process. It was nice to see that Recon was behaving for a change. We all hoped they would continue for just one more night so that we would be able to get out of the place in the morning. I hadn't been back on the base camp very long before Jahret approached me from behind. He offered me the option of staying behind assuming I hated being around the Vietmamese. I refused because anything would be better than staying back in the rear with the rest of the REMF's. Whenever the choppers would take off for our new mission, I expected to be on one of them. Our destination mattered little to me at that moment. I only wanted to be with my platoon. "Say man, are you Handy?" asked a stranger who was wearing new fatigues. Someone had obviously pointed me out to him and he approached me almost immediately. He was a new arrival from Baton Rouge named Clarence Howard. He was a dark black guy who stood about 5' 9" with a stocky build and was definitely a product of the inner city. He wore a crude tattoo on his left forearm that read "Ponson" and had a streetwise demeanor he couldn't hide if he tried his best to. He was concerned about his new surroundings and the people who comprised his platoon. I redundantly reassured him that he only had to listen to the more experienced guys.

"Howard, would you come with me?" Modell said as he walked up and whisked him away.

"I'll rap with you later." I told him as they walked over to supply. Howard, I felt, would do alright in the field. He seemed as capable as any new guy that I'd ever met. His rough edge would serve him well in Vietnam. I figure it would be good to have him around. I was flattered that he sought me out and asked me for my assessment of what Vietnam was like. What I should have done was tell him more about the people who were in charge of our fortunes.

5

We were flown to our new location. A small firebase in the middle of a village located in Phu My District. The name Phu My did not exactly ring a bell and had no history of any battle or massacre that I could remember. I hoped it would remain so until after we were gone. Our being in another village only brought back bad memories. I hated pacification and the foolish notion of turning the fighting over to the ARVN. This time we would be working from a small compound but it changed nothing. Pacification was pacification and all of the headaches, disadvantages and obvious weaknesses were to be expected again. The compound was slightly larger than Firebase Orange but was going to be used as our base of operation. It would keep us from being exposed to the large crowd of onlookers that had plagued us on our previous pacification missions though. Unfortunately there would be a high degree of vulnerability that came with being in a fixed position. Charlie would always know where we were and could plot accordingly. There was no real security involved with being there and most of us knew it. My only concern was how long would we be there.

Our platoon was once again split in half and, unfortunately, Calvin and Jahret were going to be with our half at the compound. It should have been expected because of the garrison and the false security that came with it. There was obviously none at the other location wherever it was. I guess it was too much to expect to be away from the lifers for two consecutive pacification missions. This time, it just had to be our turn to be around them. If we were to spend too much time in Phu My, I felt that it would mean trouble for me. I had a feeling that, given enough time, I would get killed in a village or Calvin and Jahret would eventually get a chance to nail me to a whipping post.

The perimeter of the little compound was ringed with bunkers. Half of the perimeter, of course, would be occupied by the dreadfully inept ARVN's. Their half was easily distinguishable by the thatched roofed bunkers and the ground level design. Our half of the perimeter resembled a number of miniature one-story replicas of LZ Uplift's sandbag castles. More work needed to be done on our bunkers so for the next few days we expected to all be busy bringing our part of the perimeter up to "airborne" standards, I supposed.

Benn and Lee were going to be "hooching" with me so we had to build a larger bunker out of the one assigned to us. Every one of us seemed to prefer the below ground level design. It would call for quite a bit of digging and sandbag filling. I could only hope that both Lee and Benn were willing to dig as much as I was. I had a rather elaborate plan for our bunker.

Among the new faces was another shake and bake from one of the other platoons named Weiss. I didn't know much about him but there was a story that he blew away an old woman in Tuy Hoa with a Claymore. She made the mistake of leaving her home a little too early and startled him. They said he was as skittish as a declawed cat. Old Sarge went home while we were on stand down and Weiss came over to take his place. It was almost like we were being jinxed.

There was another new guy that wasn't exactly new to Vietnam or the Herd. Everybody called him Mad Dog. He was a black guy from the streets of Detroit. Again, it seemed that the inner city was providing the war with most of the black troops. Mad Dog did not appear to be a career soldier. He did a tour with the Herd back in '68 and spoke often about the old days in Nha Trangh and Dalat; two places I hadn't heard about our unit visiting before.

July 1st arrived coinciding with the 150-day mark according to the calendar that Rachel the Red Cross girl gave me. The weather was as hot as I was told it would be. The mid day temperature exceeded 100 degrees daily and we were, at that juncture, digging the hole for our bunker. Lee and Benn had lost their enthusiasm for digging and had started to complain about my design. It was hard to get them to continue to dig after everyone started to complete their bunker but I knew what it would take to house the three of us. Lee started to accuse me of digging my way back to New Orleans but I didn't care. We had barely begun to dig the hole I thought we needed and they had already grown tired of digging and filling sandbags. They wanted to finish the bunker and move in like everyone else.

Every night, half of our contingent was expected to form a patrol and leave the compound for ambush. This meant that aside from the digging and filling, we would have to go out every other night. Modell took out the first patrol and Weiss was to take the other the following night. Pulling ambush in Phu My was expected to be the same as the other two villages, vulnerable and dangerous.

July also marked the end of the Cambodian invasion. Nixon had pulled all of the troops out the day before. I hoped the raid on those sanctuaries would put a hurt on Charlie's ability to wage war just long enough to see us through our mission in Phu My but Charlie had already proven himself to be very resourceful. "Handy, do you remember the cartoon that used to play on TV called King Leonardo? " Howard asked me in his own light hearted way.

"Yeah, I think it's still playing."

"Look at that ARVN over there." he said pointing at an older Vietnamese soldier with an unusually large gut.

"Do you remember the king's no good brother, the one they called Itchy Brother?"

"Yeah I remember Itchy Brother too."

"Do you remember Itchy's podner Biggy Rat?"

"Sure. Why are you asking?"

"Because that mother fucker over there looks just like Biggy Rat!" He laughed. He had just given a nickname to the ARVN that had us all laughing. Howard's sense of humor was infectious. Even the fat Vietnamese soldier was laughing at Howard totally unaware of his being hung with a moniker that could also be regarded as a form of ridicule.

The rest of the ARVN soldiers were equally as unimpressive as the ones we had worked with earlier. They teased us a lot and thought we were all oversexed. They all knew we would be getting paid within a few hours. It wouldn't take long after that for every hooker and hustler within twenty clicks of the compound to converge on our location. I spent those few hours digging as my two intended co-inhabitants-to-be just watched. They had abandoned me because my design was too extensive. I wanted to build the best bunker on the compound and they were willing to settle for less. Working alone was hard because the sun was incredibly hot and made me struggle to make an impact on the huge hole we had started. It had to be at least 6 feet deep and at least 6 feet long and 10 feet across. Gathar and I built a smaller one while at Ft Polk.

For the next two days, I continued digging the hole without the help of my two intended co-inhabitants. I was in no position to drive them any harder than they wanted to work though. "Handy, Lee tells me that you stopped having sex. Is that true?" Howard asked after Lee whispered in his ear.

"Look man, I've had it with these hookers. Paying for sex just aint my bag." I told him.

"Man you can't be serious. You'd better put that shovel down and go get you some pussy." He advised me with a look of concern.

"No thanks. I've had my share of that action."

"You see, I told you he won't do it." Lee added. I was surprised to see that Lee had noticed I wasn't involved with the prostitutes and wondered who else he was keeping tabs on.

Weiss came over to help me dig and fill sand bags. In turn, I decided it would be a good idea to stop digging to deter him from invading my space. He gave me a lot of bad vibes. He had never said a word to me and had probably already been briefed by Jahret and Calvin about who was who in the platoon. Weiss was spending so much time with his nose up the lifers' asses that if either one of them came to a sudden stop he would have immediately been declared MIA. I didn't want him to even feel welcome in my space for one minute.

"I said that's enough digging for now."

"I'm just trying to help you finish." he said.

"The digging's over now. Thanks a lot. We'll finish up here. OK?" I said in an effort to make him feel unappreciated. After he left, I started to put the roof on the bunker. When Lee and Benn noticed that I had finally started the "topping off" ceremonies, they quickly rejoined the project. I told them to stay put in order to keep Weiss at bay because I didn't want him or his kind around. He would only be a problem for me and I could sense his true intentions. They agreed to stay around the bunker and help until we were finish. They worked feverishly at completing the roof. I was sure that when we were finished they would appreciate having the best bunker on the compound. We would be the last to finish but it would prove to be well worth the time and effort.

At one corner of the perimeter was a guard or sentry post set up with an M-60 machinegun. When not on ambush everybody was expected to pull guard at that post at night. During the daylight hours, the spot usually attracts a crowd of music listeners. About all that was being played was the Beatles. Ellis had Abbey Road and the White Album. Howard, on the other hand, was fed up and tired of hearing what was available.

The lack of space on the compound forced all pot smokers outside of the perimeter. I didn't expect it to be long before both Jahret and Calvin picked up on what we were up to. The heads were the only guys who ever left the compound on their own. The only reason most others left the compound was for body functions.

More new faces continued to arrive. One of them came over from Recon whose members seldom if ever left the flock. He made the rare move to join us and seemed to be like one of the guys. His name was Kostrewva. Staff Sgt. Swain was the other new face on the compound. Sgt Swain was another second tour guy of about thirty having served previously with the 1st Cav. He was a black guy who seemed to have chosen to try making a career out of the Army. Howard started calling him Killer Swain whenever he wasn't looking or listening. Swain immediately attained the status of one of those who didn't have to go out on ambush. Weiss wanted to be in on that crowd so bad he could probably taste it.

When it started to get dark, our squad took its turn in the ambush rotation. It was a creepy situation walking off of the compound near dark. I felt extra paranoid and vulnerable passing through the zigzag path that snaked through the barbed wire perimeter. I couldn't understand why the two entrances had to be of a serpentine design. One of the worst case scenarios that I couldn't stop conjuring up in my mind had Charlie shooting and killing a number of us trying to make it through the zigzag opening to the compound. Pacification made me dream up some of the wildest ways to get killed that I never could have imagined otherwise.

Weiss showed reluctance when the moment came to take our squad on ambush. It was as if he hoped Jahret would cancel ambush. I laughed and pretended to be irritated by his stalling tactics. He was being almost afraid of leaving the compound at night. It took him until the last moment to realize that he had to go out. Weiss was probably one of those guys who volunteered for enlistment and in the end, would probably have more fabricated tales of combat to tell than anyone else. Modell was one of those people who didn't seem to take his position in Vietnam serious enough to be scared. Courage, again, had nothing to do with it. He was just that kind of guy. There was very little difference in effectiveness between the two.

After returning from ambush we started to put the finishing touches on the roof of our bunker. Benn and Lee moved in before we could put the last sandbag in place. Their long wait had ended and they were finally able to enjoy the comforts of their new home. There was a feeling of accomplishment that came with finishing the job. Accomplishment was a feeling I had rarely experienced since arriving in country. Our work on the bunker was almost medicinal and, in fact had me standing in admiration of its design and construction. It had sandbags against the wall to keep it from collapsing and sandbags on the floor too. It was spacious enough to accommodate the three of us standing straight up. The roof was strong enough to support a helicopter or withstand any mortar attack. Our bunker was complete.

I dropped in on Mac to check out his place as he was taking it easy going over a picture of a new Chevy. "Super Sport! Looks nice." I said.

"This is what I'm going to buy with the money that I'm saving." We all dreamed of what we planned to do with it. Most guys took their lump sums and spent it on R&R. Barbara and I were saving for our future. Mac's future was red, on a center fold in a magazine with four on the floor. "Good luck." I said as I put the magazine down and noticed a little girl of about 5 yrs old standing outside of the perimeter. "How? Baci Dau? " she seemed to be asking repeatedly.

"She's probably looking for Howard." said Mac. Howard, who shared the bunker with Mac was just awakening from a nop. He emerged from the bunker yawning.

"Her name is Mua. Me and Doc be hanging out at her house every day."

"Where is Doc?"

"Over at C.P. talking to Jahret." he said. I wasn't about to go near that place unless I had too. Our bunker was situated real close to those lifers but I still avoided going over to their place.

Big Goose was attracting his usual crowd of An Ko watchers. The poor guy was not out amongst the villagers but still had to go through the irritation of being gawked at by all of the Ruff Puffs. He just couldn't win. He was a humble guy who didn't care for all of the attention he was receiving. I was intrigued by their attraction to him though. I wanted desperately to understand what it was all about. There was a story behind it that begged to be told or at least revealed.

Biggy Rat grew tired of watching all of our money being spent on beverages sold by the outside hustlers we attracted. He began erecting a coke stand on the compound. We should have expected as much. The hustlers showed up daily with their Cokes and ice and waited patiently for us to come outside of the compound with our precious MPC. They fully expected the gravy train to end upon the completion of Biggy's stand. The little bullies would surely chase away all competition when the time came. The Ruff Puffs had also been using strong-arm tactics on any outsider that exchanged currency with us. They insisted on establishing their own rate. They were insisting on a dollar for dollar rate when their money wasn't worth much more than the paper it was printed on. We were holding out for five for seven. Their persistence forced us to consider using our own paymaster to get the standard rate which was more than what we were trying to establish. The little bastards really believed we would give in and pay their rate.

When Doc finished his talk with Jahret, he approached me with the details. He had talked Jahret into allowing him to set up a Medcap in the village. Medcap, or Medical Assistance Program, is a public relations attempt at impressing the villagers with our goodwill. This meant that he'd be going out to a pre-established spot to treat some of the civilians. This was, in my opinion, what pacification was supposed to be about. It was a method to win some of those "hearts and minds" of the people. He asked me if I would accompany him on his trip into the village. I was surprised he had already agreed to let the two of us go out alone. Doc and I were easily two of the most incorrigible members of the second platoon and was undeserving of that much trust. Our drug use had always been known too. Maybe Doc had also established himself as the medical authority in the platoon and was demonstrating his clout. After that power struggle in Tuy Hoa over my pimple removal, I supposed no one would dare challenge him again.

I grabbed my weapon and joined Doc and the interpreter on the way out of the gate. It felt different walking off of the compound without being under suspicion. Jahret and Calvin may have been aggravating but they were not that dumb. The Medcap may have given us a different reason to leave but they knew we would do as we pleased. When we reached our destination, the villagers were already there in big numbers. It was hard to believe that we were carrying enough pills and potions to cure all that had gathered. As he set up shop at a little table, the people lined up single file for a stretch that covered almost fifty yards. Some of Doc's patients had crutches and some of them were wearing bandages. He had his work cut out for him. I took up a position along a ridge that conveniently stretched nearby. From that high ground I provided Doc and the interpreter with the security. Tuy Hoa never came to anything like what we were doing that day. About all we did over there was fight for our lives. We practically hated those villagers as well as our stay there. We could have also accomplished more had the situation presented itself. Tuy Hoa just turned out to be a combat mission and nothing else mattered more than our survival. As for the last village we were in, our mission there was still a mystery. Maybe Diane and Linda needed a babysitter or maybe not. All we managed to do while there was lose both Al and Katta. Undoubtedly, every Ruff Puff we worked with in the past was still as pitiful and ineffective as they were before we came along. No doubt we'd leave Phu My one day and the local Ruff Puff contingent would be in the same state of un-readiness.

After we put the program in motion, it occurred to me that Doc just might be able to come up with a treatment or a prescription for everybody in line. He was well trained for his job and the villagers had somehow come to expect the level of competence he displayed. It might have been our first Medcap but the people had obviously seen their share of them. He examined babies, changed dressings and dispensed pills with translation from the interpreter. If any VC/NVA soldier was in need of any medical treatment short of a gunshot wound, he would have been in line with the villagers. We never would have been able to distinguish him from the rest and the villagers wouldn't dare betray him. It made sense to allow us to operate without fear of being attacked. I never really needed to be there but I was glad he brought me along anyway. It was real boring on the compound and the opportunity to frolic outside the perimeter was liberating. I even brought a joint to Doc as he attended the sick and lame. I felt uncomfortable having all the fun while he did all of the work. "Here Doc, you've earned this one." I told him as I handed him an already lit joint.

"Thanks, I needed it too." he said while continuing to treat an elderly man's foot. What a country. It mattered little that the medic treating them was doing drugs at the same time. "We ought to do this shit everyday, man." I told him. I'd been asking Barbara to send me a couple of rolls of film but she had yet to respond. I would've loved to have captured a shot of Doc doing his thing with a Bomber hanging on his lips. The opportunity just had to be wasted because neither one of us had a camera.

We wrapped up the Medcap without incident and started back to the compound. I had a lot of fun watching Doc treat all of those people. Phu My, on the whole, seemed rather tame. There was no enemy activity to be found and the natives didn't bother us at all. Even the hustlers lacked the aggressive sales tactics we had grown accustomed to. It didn't change my attitude toward pacification or my fear of it either. I didn't like working in villages around villagers. We were just too dammed vulnerable. "That's Mua's place over there." said Doc as we passed a house not far from the compound.

"Mua's big sister is pregnant. She's gonna let me deliver the baby when her time comes."

"Did they teach you guys how to deliver babies too?"

"Delivering babies isn't as hard as you think it is, Handy. In fact you can assist me when the time comes."

"Yeah, right. Two doped up GI's delivering a baby. You gotta to be kidding me."

"No, I'm serious. If we're still in Phu My when she's due, we'll deliver the baby. O.K.?"

"O.K. Doc. Anything you say."

We returned to the compound drawing stares from Weiss as we passed him by. Weiss, I feared, was eager to impress and seemed to be watching me exclusively. This could only mean that he had been briefed thoroughly about my relationship with the lifers. I expected to be the prime target for anything he could conjure up in that small twisted mind of his. An ass kisser with his kind of intention would try his best to impress.

A slick brought out a new arrival to the fold. With each helicopter landing came a cloud of dust that turned the area into a scene reminiscent of the Dust Bowl. Our bunker was closest to the helicopter pad and we bore the brunt of the dust cloud. The new arrival was carrying a ruck and some rank. He was a Staff Sgt and didn't appear to be a shake and bake. He had too much age on him and in fact was in his thirties. He was on his second tour and no doubt, a career soldier. Some career, every two or three years getting sent back to fight the same endless war.

With resupply coming up the following day, I decided to write a few letters to send back.

"Handy, how come you're always writing a letter or reading one? You must be in love." said Howard as if something was wrong with being in love.

"Everybody writes letters over here. Don't you have a girlfriend back in Baton Rouge?"

"No. I wasn't even in Baton Rouge when I got drafted. I was in L.A. at the time. So, are you in love with that woman?

"Yes."

"Y'all probably get married as soon as you get home."

"We have plans to get married, but not quite that fast." I said. Howard had obviously never met the right girl or maybe he just didn't want to commit. He also showed the same concern for his family as

Jackson did. I had only known Howard for a couple of weeks but he hardly ever wrote home at all. He and Jackson were both two of a kind.

Jackson, surprisingly, had already been promoted to E-4 and never mentioned it to me. He was over at the other location with the other half of the platoon. I hadn't seen any of those guys or the rest of the company since we arrived. We didn't even get together on resupply day like we did on the previous pacification operation. I never heard anything about what they were doing which was usually a good sign.

The following day we received word that our fearless leader, Captain Mercein, had rotated back overseas. His method of departure, all things considered, was true to form. It was inconspicuous, low key and of course a cause for celebration. He left with no farewells, no speeches, thanks or nothing. He never really appreciated having us serving under him. I could only be thankful that I didn't have to suffer through his command for the duration of my tour. Incredibly, Jahret was appointed as his replacement on what had to be an interim basis. It seemed like some kind of cruel joke was being played on us and I hoped his new status wouldn't go to his head. He was probably the lieutenant with more time-in-grade than the rest of the platoon leaders in our company. If a Chaplain could take over the way our last one almost did, anything else was possible in the Army. I hoped that Mercein's replacement would come along soon but then I realized he might be another hard-ass. Remembering how much I was disappointed by Mercein's arrival, I understood there was nothing to look forward to.

6

Doc and Howard took me over to Mua's house and I met her parents along with her pregnant sister, too. They were a real nice family and I had to admit it was kind of weird the way they tolerated our pot smoking. They must have thought that all GI's smoked the stuff. I enjoyed their hospitality to the fullest and always found that good intentions and good people went hand and hand. Mua's family had few possessions other than their overall kindness and nothing else seemed to matter. Their warm reception and humble mannerisms was endearing. It was easy to see why both Doc and Howard kept coming back to visit them. They were literally given total access to the family's home. The practice of making guests feel at home was in full effect and they both loved it. We stayed for about an hour and left with a good feeling.

We returned to the compound where Biggy's Coke stand was doing big business. Mac had named the place "The Rat Hole" and business was booming to say the least. We also had our paymaster bring out some of that worthless Vietnamese money so that we wouldn't get stiffed on the Ruff Puff exchange rate. They were a little upset at first, but they soon realized there was nothing they could do about it. The MPC was such a coveted piece of paper that the hustlers preferred not to receive any Piasters at all. I enjoyed the way they were frustrated at seeing our endless supply of Vietnamese money. We made plans to get paid in their currency as long as were on that compound too.

Barbara's mother wrote me a scathing letter demanding that I stop writing her daughter any more letters about the Vietnam War. Doc read it and thought it was hilarious. He teased me endlessly about it. "Listen boy! You'd better stop writing my daughter about all of that shit going on over there. It's getting her upset." he said in a mock feminine voice. I was paying a price for letting him read all of her letters. Doc and Howard had somewhat replaced Al and Katta as my sidekicks as things were going a little too good to be true. Whenever things were that good, something always happened. I didn't know how long it would take but I felt that calamity was just around the corner. I could almost feel it.

Benn and Lee showed no signs of the fear of the unexpected and were almost always in hibernation. They spent so much time inside of the bunker that I hardly ever saw them outside. They seemed to come out only when they had to and it provided us with continuous security from the thieving little Ruff Puffs. I hated being around them and I didn't like the constant vigil we had to maintain because of their presence.

Jahret planned a sweep through one of the surrounding villages. We all packed light and took off into the sweltering heat. New Orleans has a very hot climate and Vietnam's heat was equally unbearable. Small wonder they called the place hell. The long hot summer was as intolerable as the seemingly endless monsoon. During the daytime we were probably, as Garson once put it so eloquently, "The only damn fools out here." The average GI believed that the locals were not only impervious to the heat and monsoon rain, they were also immune to all of the diseases like dysentery or malaria. The Brigade surgeon told us otherwise during his orientation talk. He said that as humans, they were as susceptible to everything that we were. Their mud huts and loose fitting clothing were the more apparent signs of their adaptation to the heat and rain. And they obviously never drank the water the way that I did In Tuy Hoa. They probably boiled it first to kill the harmful little creatures that caused me so much trouble.

After a long patrol, we made it to the hamlet we were supposed to be searching. We then all got on line and waited for the command to begin a sweep. When we started, our intrusive move through their neighborhood was hardly raising an eyebrow. The right flank of our line consisted of nothing but ARVN soldiers. It should have been a quiet affair but I couldn't tell by the noise coming from their sector. It sounded more like a street fight at their end. There were lots of chickens squawking and pigs squealing. I was too focused on what was ahead of me to be concerned about the ruckus though. We continued our sweep and found nothing we could have regarded as a sign of Charlie's presence. Our so-called allies, on the other hand, found everything they were looking for. They took full advantage of the opportunity to pick up on a few food items. Their arms were full of vegetables, rice, live chickens and pigs which explained the noise they were making. While we were sweeping through the village the little bullies were raiding it. Apparently the ARVN, was as big a threat to the villagers as Charlie was. Howard was amused but more inquisitive about other matters. "Just how long has it been since you had some pussy?" He asked as the novelty of my non-participation hadn't quite worn off yet.

"Uh, it was either March or April. I can't remember."

"March, April! Man its July. Why are you doing this to yourself?" He asked in jest.

Mrs. Wheelhouse wrote me another letter. She also sent a few pictures of her son taken while he was still with us. She started the letter on a more cheerful note but in the end she was pouring her heart out again. I had to put it down for a while. It was too much for me to finish. The pain and suffering she was experiencing was too severe. She had to find a way to cope with life without her son. She just couldn't go on living that way. Sadly, she hadn't turned that corner and her letters kept me from getting past the incident also. Still, I couldn't dare end our correspondence. I wanted to see her reach that point in her life where she could accept what had happened. "Let's go to Mua's house." Doc suggested.

"Yeah, let's go." Said Howard. When we arrived, we found Mua's father at work adding another room to his home. He was erecting the bamboo frame and would construct the walls with mud later. On the third day he would be thatching his roof. I watched another old man in another part of the village doing the same thing. Back in the world he would have needed permits, lumber, carpenters, electricians and a ton of money. In Vietnam, however, all that was needed was the reason to expand and the time to do it. The materials were everywhere to be found and carpentry seemed to be a common trade shared by all of the men. There were some advantages to living in a third-world country that couldn't be ignored.

Doc and Howard, of course, had already made themselves at home inside. I liked being around the real people of Vietnam who maintained the everyday lifestyle of subsistence farming and all of the hard work associated with it. Mua's family was poor and probably living on someone else's land. Their meager possessions did not go unnoticed by us. Doc and Howard suggested we bring all of our excess supplies to them after our next resupply day. I had to agree that it was closely associated with the intentions of pacification; putting our best foot forward, coming to the aid of the people and spreading some of that Yankee goodwill. I knew it would go over better than the sweep we pulled earlier.

Mua's mother was busy cooking the family meal. The rice she cooked, though full of bits of shells and who knows what else looked and smelled delicious. I knew enough about the Vietnamese culture to expect an invitation to dine with them. In spite of all of the stories about how they eat dogs, cats and lizards, I'd take my chances and accept the invitation whenever extended. "Mua's sister is married to an ARVN." Doc informed me.

"Poor girl, I hope it isn't one of those sorry assholes on the compound with us." I said.

"Nah, he's with the regular ARVN Army."

"Say man, is Lt. Jahret funny?" Howard asked. Jahret's effeminate mannerisms always brought up the question about his sexual orientation.

"I doubt it seriously." I answered.

"He's probably a faggot." Doc laughed. It was his brand of leadership that I didn't like. I'd rather have dealt with Garson and all of his temper tantrums any day. Calvin never would have agreed with me but I thought we lost a winner in Garson when we were in Tuy Hoa. His replacement was nothing more than a bad imitation of a leader.

Mua's mother, or Mama San as we called her, prepared three extra bowls of rice without even asking if we were hungry. She was extending a part of their culture that made a lasting impression. Like the family that cooked the vasectomy patient in Tuy Hoa and the pretty girl who fed Diane, Linda and I, Mua's family had continued what had become an enjoyable practice.

We dined sitting in a circle on the floor. The chopsticks Mama San gave us were much cleaner than the ones I had in Tuy Hoa. She grabbed a pot with some kind of sauce and ladled a little bit over everyone's rice. She then opened a server full of meat. I hoped it wasn't Rover. "What do you think it is?" Howard asked.

"I don't care. It's more enjoyable when you just eat it without asking." I replied as I followed Papa San's lead and speared a couple of chunks. She also had prepared some kind of vegetable to round out the menu. The food tasted delicious. They may have been poor but they ate well.

After the meal, Papa San lit up a one of those horrible tasting French cigarettes that were unfortunately still in production in Vietnam. We offered him one of ours. "Now I know what to do with all of those cigarettes that we don't smoke. We can give them to the old guy." I said. We received cigarettes every resupply day and some brands never get used and none of them tasted as bad as the ones Papa San was smoking. Although it was cigarettes, we figured it could still make a nice show of appreciation for all of the hospitality.

After eating we left and on the way back to the compound, we came upon a woman lying in a hammock breast feeding her infant. She spoke to us, but of course we couldn't understand a word she said. She continued on giving obviously complaining about something. I listened patiently but couldn't make much of anything she said. We had somehow offended her and I couldn't understand how considering I just met the woman for the first time.

"She's pissed about us spending so much time at Mua's house and not hers." said Doc who along with Howard must have been acquainted with the angry woman.

"I don't get it. Why is she angry about that?"

"She thinks that Mama San is making money off of us." said Howard.

"Oh, I see." The natives had theorized that GI's were so wealthy that wherever we went, money just fell out of our pockets or maybe we littered the ground with cash so that we would be able to find our way back. Whatever the theory, her attitude created a dilemma.

"Once she notices us bringing our excess supplies to Mua's house the shit will really hit the fan." I said as we continued on.

We returned to the compound and headed straight for the Rat Hole for a round of Tiger Piss. Biggie really had a moneymaker going for him. The guys liked lounging around his coke stand spending their idle time. Someone had placed a sign over it. "Biggie's Rat Hole Est. 1970" it read. Mac and Ellis probably collaborated on the sign. Howard may have given him the nickname but those two made it stick. I left the Rat Hole and retired to the bunker. As usual, Lee and Charles were already inside. They spent a lot of time there in spite of how angry they were about my insistence on building such an elaborate bunker.

Calvin, in a surprising move, found time to try to explain our poor relationship to Howard and some of the other more recent arrivals. He blamed it on the actions of the old third squad that started when Reb was the squad leader and continued when Bear took over. When Howard came to me with Calvin's lame excuse, I countered with the other side of it. When I explained to Howard that Reb was at Dak To, he somehow understood there was nothing Calvin could tell him after surviving the Herd's signature battle. He also understood how the members of the squad would rally around his brand of leadership and emulate his style of soldiering. Bear, he probably theorized, was a Reb protégé cut in the same mold. Reb had left, but his style of doing his own thing had endured. Calvin resented the fact that someone who once challenged his authoritative image earlier in his tour was still around in spirit. I told Howard that Burt and I were the only ones left from the good old days. Keeping up the tradition had fallen into my hands alone and I felt that it was too great a task. Considering there was no one else to help me keep the flame aglow. Calvin's effort try to snuff it out made it nearly impossible. I had somehow come to be the keeper of a flame that was dying a slow death. There were just too many new faces around that never witnessed our rebellion in action. Nixon had turned the war into a final act that everyone wanted to see the end of. Nothing else mattered more than being alive when we all finally get called home. I guess that surviving the war had become what it should have been all along, something greater than any personal squabble that could exist within our ranks.

Two barrels of tar were sent out to be used on our chopper pad. The tar was to be spread out over the landing area's dry topsoil to keep it from being blown all over the place. I was glad I never said anything about it. If the lifers knew I was having problems with it, I don't think they would have acted. When the barrels arrived a passenger came with it. He was a lanky black guy carrying a ruck sack and a rifle meaning that our contingent was still growing. As we ran past him to unload the two 55 gallon drums, he said nothing. He headed to the compound and offered no assistance to the unloading effort. He seemed to have some time in country and displayed an attitude toward his being at our location.

After unloading the tar, Swain decided the best way to disperse the tar would be to lay the barrels on their sides, shoot holes into them and roll them around the LZ. It was ridiculous and messy but after a few hours we managed to spread the tar around the landing area. Afterwards we found a well and cleaned up. Fortunately we didn't have to go out on ambush that night but was later told that the new guy would be assigned to our bunker. Had I known there would be four of us I would have dug a bigger hole. In all fairness though, our bunker was the only one big enough to even consider cramming four guys inside of. He quickly became comfortable in his new surroundings in spite of his objection to being there. His name was Brown and had very little to say. He was from a small town in Louisiana called Baldwin. "How did you wind up in our company?" Benn asked.

"Cuz them mutha fuckahs in Bravo Co. think ahm stupid. Ah don wan fight no fuckin Charlie. Them mutha fuckahs is on dope anyway." he answered. Brown was, no doubt, just a simple country boy who never quiet made the transition after he arrived in country. Maybe, I thought, it wouldn't be so bad having him around and expected him to provide us with a few laughs. I left him to ponder his future with us and collect his thoughts because he had a lot of thinking to do.

I left the bunker and walked down the trench line that connected all of the bunkers. I stopped at the gun placement where all of the music was being enjoyed. It was almost as popular a gathering place as the Rat Hole. At night though, it's a lonely outpost that can be creepy at times. Benn usually got so uptight about being there alone that I often stayed up longer to help him deal with his paranoia.

I started a conversation with Kostrewva and discovered not only that he was from Chicago but was also a good friend of Katta's. They both played on that high school championship football team together. Katta started and Kostrewva backed him up. He said that, after Katta and a lot of other guys graduated ahead of him, the team lost its competitiveness. He said he and Katta were like brothers back on the block. Kostrewva was a former member of Recon and was glad to get out when he did. He was probably inspired to leave by our own Lt. Mack who could scare the grim reaper himself. Kostrewva was of Polish descent and claimed there were more Poles in Chicago than in some cities in Poland.

When resupply day came around I was expecting a letter from Barbara. The first one since she realized that her mother had wrote me. When Calvin gave me the mail for the members of my bunker I noticed that one of the letters addressed to Charles, was from a Vietnamese female named Benn. "Charles, do you have any relatives in Vietnam?" I asked.

"Hell no. What are you talking about?"

"Well there's a letter from some Vietnamese woman named Benn." I said.

"Oh shit! It's that girl I married." he said as he stood up and snatched the letter from my grasp.

"What do you mean married?"

"I met a woman in that village where Al and Katta were shot in and married her so that I could get laid. She told me I could never expect anything to happen between us without matrimony so I married her." My plan didn't work because I was snatched away from her right after the ceremony and replaced you after your arrest." he said.

"That's the wildest shit I ever heard."

Mrs. Wheelhouse sent me another care package, Burt sent me a case of Cokes and of course there were the letters. Barbara had survived the embarrassment and wrote me again.

Barbara also finally sent me Hale Boggs' address. I finally had the opportunity to have my say about the war. Realistically, I didn't expect him to end our involvement in Vietnam single handedly. I just wanted to inform him about the ineffectiveness of our so-called allies and the worthlessness of Vietnamization. I doubted if the generals would ever come clean on the subject. They liked making war and who could blame them.

Brown managed to become more acclimated to his surrounding and was impressed with his new quarters and the case of cokes Burt sent. He drank three of them in succession as if they were his and never even asked where they came from. "Brown, do you realize that you will be expected to go out on ambush occasionally?"

"Bullshit! I aint goin nowhere."

"You're just setting yourself up for a bad discharge, man." I said.

"Ah don need no honorable discharge. Back home all ah need to do is help mah folks plant that crop and turn it over to the owner. He got all the tools, all the seeds and all the land. All we gotta do is make that harvest for him. He gon' let us stay there rent free. What ah need with a honorable goddamn discharge? Ah'll tell you what, if ah had one ah'll wipe my ass wit it." He said with a laugh. Brown, in his own way, was more incorrigible than any of us. I really didn't know what was going to happen to him but he would definitely continue to push the issue.

Katta also sent me a letter saying that he'd already had two operations on his elbow and that there would be more in the future. He had received some incredible surgery to reconstruct his shattered joint. Hopefully, he would one day have full restoration of use in that arm. I'd like to think he would, anyway. At least his spirits were high. As a joke he addressed my letter to Sgt Handy. Surely he realized that I was still a PFC. Charlie Co. hadn't changed that much since he was last with us. I really missed the guy and the good times we shared before the shooting. His absence was still being felt as I was struggling to get past all of the departures without giving up. Just holding his letter in my hand made me angry about what had happened. I felt cursed and was beginning to think twice about getting too close to anybody else who came along. Being a friend of mine was like a kiss of death or at least a ticket home on a medivac. It was good to see that he could still send a letter that didn't contain any bitterness about what had happened. On the other hand, all I had to do was look at one of those imitation soldiers to get angry enough to explode. I hated pacification and all of the bad experiences it provided me with. I'd much rather be in the mountains humping in the middle of the monsoon rather than to be in a village trying to make Nixon's so-called Vietnamization plan work. Without a doubt, if exposed to enough of it, pacification would be the death of me.

Something was brewing over at CP. It was too obvious. Whatever it was would have to wait until the morning. It was almost time for our squad to go out on ambush. I packed early again to appear annoyed by Weiss's delaying tactics. Everybody else followed suit with the get-ready-early routine. As an added act, I gave him a real cold stare to drive home my message. I really enjoyed playing mind games with him. When we did finally go out, it was another shameful exhibition of how to pull ambush. There were two kinds of ambushes. One was when we staked out an area where we were most likely to engage Charlie doing a night maneuver. The other was when we continuously patrolled at night seeking and stalking, which we never ever did. All Weiss did, however, was to find a nice hiding spot to safely spend the night. He must have been suffering from a case of what Jones once called the short-timers-whores. As he noted then, making contact with Charlie was the last thing you would want to do at that stage of you tour. I'd hate to think he was just that afraid of Charlie. Everybody was scared but Weiss took fear to another level. It wouldn't have been a bad idea to let Walkup take out a patrol. He was busting his ass trying to make E-5, putting up with a lot of teasing about how hard he's trying and about all he'd become was the butt of a lot of jokes. Someone was always telling him "Hey Walkup your E-5 orders are on the way down." The teasing went on but never quite bothered Walkup. He just kept pressing on. On the other hand we had Weiss; an uninspiring leader with the stripes.

Later that day, Doc informed me that Sgt Watson had finally returned to Charlie Co. His return was short lived though. Watson was said to have already started walking toward the slick that was to return him to the field when he was turned around. Some orders came down at the last minute sending him back to the world. Watson was rumored to have some very influential parents that pulled some mighty long strings and was the reason he had been gone for so long. Of course all stories are subject to a lot of conjecture due to the amount of rumors that Vietnam was famous for. It mattered less as I had changed my attitude considerably toward the war. I no longer resented the preferential treatment of the affluent and their well connected friends and associates. If the story about Watson was true, then more power to him and anybody who could get out of the war early. If Watson was one of those guys who never had to be in the war I was glad to have known him. Once he was wounded, his parents were probably scared out of their wits. Mrs. Watson came within a few inches of becoming another Mrs. Wheelhouse; another grieving mother struggling to come to grips with the devastation of losing her son to a war being fought for less than acceptable reasons. The war had become a regrettable excursion that we all had to make sense of. We would have to somehow make good on our participation in it and find justification for our losses.

Doc and Howard suggested that we take a load of excess supplies over to Mua's house. I grabbed a few items for that angry woman just in case. The supplies consisted of items like toothpaste and brushes, cigarettes, combs, sewing kits and a lot of other personal items. Everybody uses them so we were sure they would appreciate them. Hopefully it would be just what we needed to keep that angry woman from being infuriated about our visits to Mua's house.

When we passed the angry woman along the way and I gave her my supplies. She went on to say more but of course I couldn't understand a word she said. Doc and Howard were already at home in Mua's house. They were already in the front room smoking as the family pored over the stuff with sincere gratitude and appreciation.

Mua's parents seemed to be a little old to have a five year old kid. Maybe the hard work had aged them beyond their years. Mua's sister appeared to be about nineteen and maybe should have been their last child. Of course there's a big difference between our two distinctly different cultures and maybe having children past forty was the norm in Vietnam.

The aroma in the air could've only meant that it was time for lunch. Mama San was happy about having us over. We were sure to receive an extra helping of whatever she was preparing. "By the way Doc, when is the baby due?" I asked.

"I have no idea."

"Are you serious about delivering the baby?"

"Of course I am. Trust me, when that baby gets ready to come, all we'll have to do is catch it" he said. As he had shown himself to be with just about everything else, Doc was very casual about bringing a kid into the world. I only hoped it wouldn't happen while we were on ambush or on some bullshit sweep. I wanted to see a baby being born. I didn't know how much assistance I could offer; but he asked me and I was more than willing to oblige.

When Mama San served us the meal I found what appeared to be an insect in the gravy. Upon closer inspection, I discovered there were many insects that appeared to be mosquito larvae. I started to pick each one out of the bowl and caught Mama San's attention. "Ahn dang lam gi?" she seemed to be asking.

There's a lot of bugs in my bowl but I'll take care of them." I answered while still picking the little creatures out and wiping them on my shirt.

"Chop chop!" She said. I couldn't tell if she meant hurry up or was informing me that the bugs were a part of the meal.

Doc and Howard never stopped eating. They made me look squeamish without even trying. We learned in our survival training that insects are nutritious but I couldn't have them served to me on a platter. Mama San was doing a better job at pacification than we were. She had easily won our hearts, minds as well as our appetites with her hospitality. We always enjoyed the time spent with her family. The time went by quickly and we had to return to the compound.

At the Rat Hole, where the guys were ordering cokes and piss as if they were back home in a bar, Biggie was in rare form. All he had to do was stand nearby like a waiter anticipating the next round of drinks. "Where's Lee and Benn?" Howard asked.

"They're in that bunker again. The three of them hardly ever come out. Since Burt sent me that case of Cokes, they come out even less now." I said.

"They don't smoke much dope do they?"

"Not much at all. It's ok with me because it means they have fewer reasons to leave the compound. And face it, as long as they're in there, it's hard for those little bastards to sneak in and steal anything from us."

"Man, I bet that if you turned these mother fuckers loose on the streets back in the world, they would all be in jail in a week."

"You think so?"

"Hell yeah! They can't help it. Half of them would be charged with picking pockets." he laughed. Personally I thought they would do very well. They were already natural born capitalists as evidenced by the way they operated their Coke stands. Wherever we congregated they would always come and set up shop and stand around waiting patiently for us to start spending money. The hustlers would not only do well, they would prosper. They had the savvy it took to do business back in the States. All they needed, as Howard said, was to be turned loose on the streets back in the world.

Weiss had requested and received permission to search all of the bunkers for drugs. Lee and Benn immediately started to roll some fake joints and stashed them throughout the bunker. Although they were never under any suspicion of drug use, they couldn't resist having a little fun with the J. Edgar Hoover type who was shaking down the rest of the guys outside of our bunker. I stepped outside and noticed that he wasn't very serious about searching the rest of the quarters either. He took about thirty seconds to go through Mac's place and was working his way down to ours. It was obvious that he only wanted to search my place but I was already expecting his move. I walked back inside, closed my little makeshift door behind me and waited for him to come knocking and knocking he did. "Who is it?" I asked while trying my best to hold back the laughter.

"You already know who it is."

"What do you want?"

"I have orders to search this bunker for drugs."

"We haven't got any." I said trying harder to hold it back the laughter.

"Look, I'm coming in now." he said angrily as he realized that he was wasting his time talking.

"Wait until I put some clothes on." I said in a feminine voice just before he trashed my little bamboo door and stumbled his way inside for the first time since we filled the last sandbag.

"You're gonna pay for that door too." I joked as I exited the bunker. When I returned, Benn and Lee were complaining about Weiss not following their script. His search lost its purpose when I left. "Aw man you messed up our plans." said Benn.

"Yeah homey. I wanted to see the look on that asshole's face when he found the fake dope." Lee laughed.

"He wasn't expecting to find anything. He just wanted to search me. By the way, where did you guys get that rolling paper to make those fake joints?"

"What rolling paper? That's your writing paper." Benn said while laughing.

When resupply day came around again it was All-Star day and Major League baseball was putting on its annual mid-summer classic. Unfortunately I was once again relegated to listening to a major sporting event on the radio. It was one of the things I missed about being home the most. Two new arrivals came out on one of the choppers. One was a tall white guy and the other was a shorter black one. They carried no arms and no rucksack. When they came onto the compound, I noticed that they wore no U.S. Army insignia or any rank either. The white guy wore a baseball cap and the black guy wore a black beret. They carried cameras and did a lot of looking around as if they were inspecting the entire area from the spot they were standing in. I stood just inside of my bunker and became suspicious. They went into the CP bunker and my paranoia really started to work on me. I imagined they were civilian investigators sent out to our location to bring down a couple of us for drug use. After spending a few minutes inside, the two new guys emerged from the bunker and started to draw a crowd around them. I was still too paranoid to approach them. I decided to sit inside of my bunker and just wait for them to leave. If they wanted me, they would have to come and get me out of the bunker. I was not going anywhere near them. Ten minutes later Moe brought the two new guys over to us to show off the work we had put in on our bunker. He had no idea that we hadn't found out exactly who the two new guys were or that I suspected they were C.I.D. They were, instead, a couple of college All American football players winding down a tour visiting the troops in Vietnam. I felt embarrassed but quickly recovered and we all engaged ourselves in a nice conversation inside the bunker about their playing days. The tall white guy was Scott Hunter from Alabama. He was a quarterback that I was quite familiar with being from S.E.C. country. Scott had played for the great Bear Bryant who coached some of the best all white national championship teams in history. I welcomed Scott but couldn't look past how the race issue in America exposed the hypocrisy of our presence in Vietnam and our role in shaping the way we thought the Vietnamese should live. Scott gave me an LSU window sticker for keepsake.

The black guy's name was Bobby Moore who played for Oregon in the PAC 8; a conference which was a lot more progressive than the heel dragging SEC when it came to recruiting athletes of all colors. Bobby was a little more uptight about being in Phu My with us but he was handling it alright. He said he was drafted by the Bears, the team I rooted for when I was a little kid before the Saints came to town. He was a running back and not much bigger than I was. I imagined he possessed exceptional speed to offset his lack of size. Scott didn't have the stature of a Joe Namath and Bobby was no O.J. Simpson but we felt honored to be with them.

After the visit we stepped outside of the bunker and took a few pictures with them. Then as suddenly as they came, they boarded their helicopter and left. It was back to the world for a career playing football for huge sums of money without ever having to worry about the other draft. Scott and Bobby were members of the graduating class of 1970 meaning they finished high school the same year I did. Their athletic prowess and my lack of concern about my future led us down different paths that eventually crossed in Vietnam. I could have possibly been in that graduating class with them but I still would have had to face the draft. Scott and Bobby, I assumed, were both on their way to becoming members of the National Guard or Enlisted Reserves in the state of their respective NFL teams. It didn't matter to me as much as it once did. My attitude had softened against the pro athletes and the charmed life they were allowed to live while America was at war. I was even flattered that they wanted to take some pictures of us. One day when they have grandchildren they would be able to say that they visited the troops and show those pictures of us to them.

Another new arrival came during resupply. He was carrying a rifle but little else. I couldn't say what his status was and whether or not he would become a member of our half of the platoon. Howard received a package from home. He said that he had been waiting for it forever. Maybe, I thought, his mother had sent him some goodies from home. I patiently waited for him to open the package until I realized the baseball game was about to start. I didn't want to wait too long to find out who won the game that had already been played hours earlier.

Soon after the opening ceremonies started, I heard a very familiar voice outside of my bunker singing her heart out like no one else on the planet could. It was Aretha and she sounded better than ever. Actually it was something I had never heard before. Somebody, I thought, had tuned in Hanoi Hanna the DJ who worked for the NVA's propaganda machine. Hanna was one smooth talking bitch who just loved getting inside of your head. In spite of her fame, she practically needed an invitation to get inside of mine. In between the records she played, she offered her own slanted views on the war. Sometimes she told heartbreaking stories about our poor weeping mothers worrying themselves sick about us being in Vietnam fighting the war. Her favorite ploy was to continuously play on our insecurities about the prospects of our wives and girlfriends sleeping with someone else while we're away. Of course she always spoke about the brave NVA freedom fighters kicking American ass on the battlefield. It was her favorite line. Her music was always something off of the list of songs that our radio station never played and Aretha was mysteriously excluded from any airplay. The song playing at the time was, no doubt her newest as I had never heard any of it before. Hanna, on the other hand, would play Aretha all the time along with Hendrix and any anti war song she could come across. Still I couldn't understand why Hanna carried so much notoriety. She was just another voice on the radio to me.

By the time Aretha was into her fourth song. I realized it had to be a cassette being played by one of the guys. Hanna would never give us such a treat. She was always too busy talking trash to allow her listeners to enjoy the music. When Aretha started to sing a song titled Call Me, I was reminded of the reason I never listened to too much R&B in Vietnam. It made me too damn lonely and homesick. I was almost glad to be inside of my bunker alone with my thoughts of Barbara and my dreams of our reunion. "Handy, come here. I want you to listen at this." Howard said as he walked in.

"Listen at what?"

"I just got me a cassette player from home and I've got Aretha's new shit too. I know you're tired of listening to that white boy music."

"What makes you think I can't hear it from here?" I said as we left the bunker and walked down the trench line to the gun post. Howard's music had drawn a crowd of guys who by then were engrossed in the sounds of Aretha She had covered Bobby Blue Bland, Herb Alpert, The Band and the Beatles. I was quite impressed but too deep in love to be listening to it at that moment. Aretha did more damage to me than Hanna could have ever hoped to do. At his insistence, I had to forget about the game and sit with the guys to listen to the new tape.

Our new arrival was not a grunt. His job had something to do with communications. He was probably a signal corps detachment. This meant that he'd automatically assume a spot over at CP with the country club crowd. Their numbers were growing faster than ours. There was Jahret, Calvin, Moe, Morse, Swain and the new guy Jay Hampton or Solo as he preferred to be called. CP had the largest quarters but there was still no room at the inn for Weiss. After all of that ass kissing, he was still knocking at the door. I doubted if he would ever wake up and realize that his job would always be what it always was and would continue to be, a squad leader.

After another unbearable night on ambush with Weiss, we had to go out on another sweep. The Ruff Puffs started a commotion almost as soon as we started our movement. They pretended to spot someone or something up front. They were pointing straight ahead claiming they had identified a lone VC. The only figure ahead had to be at least 300 meters out. At that distance nothing is distinguishable and there was no way that they could make such a claim. Of course that didn't stop them from firing their weapons at their imaginary target and running after it too. No Ruff Puff would be as eager to engage the enemy. It was probably a diversion to keep us from going to our appointed destination which was probably Charlie's place. If it was, then maybe it wouldn't be such a bad idea to let them put on the charade. After all, why should we go all the way to wherever it was and have those same jerks run out on us and leave us to get killed fighting their war.

Weiss took up position behind a rice paddy dike when the Ruff Puffs initiated their charade. He was not taking any chances on their stories being true. He immediately grabbed the horn and called CP. He was hunkered down so low that he resembled one of those Marines at Khe Sahn in '68. I wondered if he could have been calling for reinforcements. We were so close to the compound that all he had to do was yell and Jahret would have heard him. The poor guy, he was traumatized and frozen in his tracks less than 30 meters from the compound. Although the ARVN's managed to take up the entire morning with their show, the only one they convinced was Weiss. Those paper tigers could never pass as the warriors they wanted us to believe they were. They did save us from a long march in the heat though. I hoped they would do the same thing the next time too. We then returned to the compound I could have thanked the little bastards for their theatrics.

Solo, it turned out, was not only a head, he also was a real cool guy. He spent a lot of time with us and left very little doubt about where he stood along that divide that separated us from them. His residency at CP only exposed the hypocrisy of the lifers. They pretended to be on some kind of anti-drug crusade, yet Solo Lived in their midst. The arrangement should have opened Weiss's eyes to reality but his twisted little mind didn't work that way. He was too deep into his role of playing platoon narcotics officer.

I sat to write a letter home and found myself a target of more teasing from Howard. "You writin' that woman again?" He asked as if he was following some script.

"Yeah man. You caught me again."

"Man you're in love. Ya'll gonna get married when you get home. I'll bet y'all get married." He said as I looked over his shoulder and spotted Swain walking in our direction.

"Don't look now but, here comes your boy Swain."

"Killer Swain?" he chuckled keeping his back turned to him as he approached to say that there were no hard feelings between him and us. "Now what was that all about?" Howard asked.

"I think that being over there with that crowd at CP and listening to all of that negative talk and all of that scheming is starting to get to old Swain that's all." I said. Swain was having a difficult time walking the thin line that separated us from them. I was sure he felt it was necessary to get his point across to us.

Later that night after the other patrol left for ambush, the rest of us settled down for a privileged night on the compound. There was nothing to worry about other than a couple of scary hours pulling guard at the gun nest. An extra hour with Benn only extended the paranoia. "The Goose is on the loose." I heard someone say as he ran from bunker to bunker repeating the same message at each stop.

"Handy, the Goose is on the loose." said Ellis.

"What are you talking about?"

"Lenny is drunk." He answered as he continued to pass the word around. I couldn't understand the fuss about Big Goose getting drunk on a night he didn't have to go out on ambush.

"Why do you suppose Ellis is making such a big deal over the Goose?" I asked Doc.

"Goose is an Indian. You know what that means don't you?" he asked as I looked across the compound and spotted Big Goose staggering around ranting and raving incoherently while trashing everything in sight. He had gone berserk. It was dark and we were usually a quiet bunch at night but the Goose was out of control and creating quite a scene.

A sudden burst of gunfire erupted to my right. A lone shooter was standing outside of the perimeter unloading an AK-47 on us from just beyond CP sending everybody scrambling for the cover of the trench line. Nobody was in possession of a weapon to return fire and Big Goose was the only person standing above ground level in harm's way. He was so drunk that he was oblivious to the danger around him. Bullets were flying all over and the green tracers were lighting up the compound. Someone managed to wrestle him to the ground and eventually into the trench line saving him from being shot. The shooting stopped almost as suddenly as it started. The entire incident happened before anyone could get their hands on their weapon. The attacker, taking full advantage of the confusion he had created, vanished into the night. When he ceased fire, it gave us the opportunity to arm ourselves and take a quick assessment of the damage done.

We took up positions inside of the trench line and stared out into our surroundings. Everyone was well aware of how careless we had been up to that point. The Goose chose the worst moment to distract us. He gave Charlie more than enough cover to allow him to walk or crawl up to the wire and open up on us from virtually point blank range. Fortunately for us, he chose to spray the area instead of carefully choosing his targets with single shots. Had he been more selective, we would have been like ducks on a pond. In my paranoid deluded mind, I imagined that the shooter was not alone and that some snipers were waiting somewhere out side of our perimeter. I immediately started to fear the worst for our ambush patrol. They were still somewhere out in the village. The shooting, I feared, might have been some sort of preemptive strike to prevent us from mounting any rescue attempt had Charlie planned to attack those guys. I hoped I was wrong but the experience I gained in Tuy Hoa back in April made me fear the worst. I had visions of us trying to make it through that ziz-zag opening through our perimeter under fire. The worst case scenario was running wild in my mind as we continued to peer out into the darkness for the rest of the night.

After the patrol returned safely, everyone adopted a new attitude towards being on the compound. From that moment on everybody would be in possession of their weapon at all times. Charlie had alerted us to his presence and removed the veil of false security we assumed we had. We were caught half-stepping and got away with it. Fortunately the lesson was learned without our losing any lives. We added vigilance to our relaxed routine of Cokes, piss and music but we stayed loose. "Doc, the Goose has got to lighten up on the juice." I said as the soul queen wailed on in the background.

"He's got to learn to leave the stuff alone altogether Handy. He's an Indian. Haven't you heard about Indians and firewater?"

"I've heard about it but I thought that shit was a myth created in Hollywood."

"There must not be too many Indians in New Orleans."

"Honestly, I had never met any before I came here."

"Well alcohol has always had that effect on his people." Doc continued.

"Are there many Indians in Kansas?"

"Are you kidding? Kansas is Indian country. Why do you think we named our NFL team the Chiefs?"

"Well, do you think he learned a lesson last night?"

"Trust me Handy, he won't remember shit about last night." As I looked at the Goose, I realized just how correct Doc was. In fact, Lenny looked more than a little surprised about the entire ordeal. It was embarrassing learning the truth about the Indians alcohol problem.

Later that day a group of guys were shooting the breeze speculating about the prospects of the Herd being pulled out of Vietnam. They were wasting their time with such talk. I'd been saving an article from our newspaper for a couple of months that read…..

> In the spring of 1969 President Nixon announced redeployment from the Republic of Vietnam would begin, thus reversing the trend of five years. First to go were elements of the 9th Infantry Div., and the third Brigade of the 82nd Abn Div, and the 4th Inf. Div. But the 173rd remains, and as the S.E. Asian reaction force, speculation is that the airborne unit will bear the distinction of being the first in and the last out.

The article, with all of its airborne bravado, typified the attitudes shared by all of the brass. They would love to be the last unit to leave Vietnam. The rest of us would trade the so-called distinction for a ticket on the next flight out. I let those guys continue their conversation without mentioning the article to them. They needed to make up their minds to do the entire 12 months because counting on redeployment would only make matters worse. It was possible that the only early out anyone of us would ever experience would be by medivac or body bag. I placed the article in an envelope and sent it to Barbara to keep her from entertaining the same notion. The thought of her sitting with her fingers crossed hoping for Nixon to pull us out next was disturbing. She deserved a more realistic look at what we were up against.

7

I received a letter from my friend Walter stationed at Clark AFB in the Philippines. Walter and I were classmates and the best of friends throughout high school. He joined the Air Force the year before I was drafted and was officially a career man looking at twenty years of life in uniform. He wanted to know if I'd been on R&R yet; and wondered if I would consider Taipei. He was stationed there in '68 and '69 and said that he always ran back and forth on military hops keeping tabs on his old haunts and connections. I had given up on R&R after Al and Katta were shot. They really had me thinking about how much fun we were going to have at the World's Fair until the shooting incident happened. As it stood, Walter's offer or invitation rather, sounded too good to pass up. He also said that I wouldn't need a hotel, clothes or a woman. He would have everything waiting for me. I sat down to write him a letter informing him of my plans to accept. As I copied his address from the envelope, Doc picked the letter up and started reading it. He came upon a portion of the letter that detailed some difficulties he (Walter) was having with what he referred to as rabbits and assumed he was talking about the white troops stationed with him. I reassured Doc that Walter was not that kind of guy and that he and I hadn't even known enough white people to develop any kind of hatred for them. It was unlikely the Air Force could have changed him much either.

Doc obviously came up in an environment that lacked all of the racial polarization we dealt with in New Orleans. He really couldn't understand why two people of different color couldn't get along and was visibly disturbed by Walter's perceived choice of words.   "Doc, over here we refer to the new guys as cherries and FNG types right?"

"Right."

"Well, maybe rabbits are what the Air Force guys call their new people. I'm telling you Walt is not that kind of guy. I have known him for seven years." He took my word for it and let the issue pass. Doc, in his own way, had never quite given up the innocence he had when he arrived in country six months earlier. At first I thought it was odd that he made himself available for the draft but it seemed possible that, in his own naïve way, he couldn't live with being a deferred student.

In Barbara's last letter she complained about the quality of some pictures I sent her. They were the pictures of the 21 gun salute Jackson gave me. I lost my composure just long enough to write an ugly letter to her and sent it along with the news article. I felt that my requests for some film were being ignored and let her know in my own special way. I regretted writing the letter after sending it off and immediately wished I had it back. I had put my foot in my mouth that time for sure. Our relationship had never reached the depths of that ugly letter.

My frustrations continued to mount as I read some magazines and found one that caught my eye. A LOOK magazine had an article about, of all subjects, the combat readiness of the ARVN soldier. The correspondent who wrote the article was actually humping with an ARVN unit. In his report he detailed all of the things about the ARVN that I had already witnessed in the ranks of their RFPF counterparts.

212

Their reluctance to engage the enemy, the cowardice on the battlefield, the lack of leadership, the corruption and everything I thought no one in Washington knew outside of the Pentagon. If it wasn't enough of a shocker that a magazine with the circulation of LOOK had already written the story, the date was. The issue was from 1967. I was glad that I hadn't written Boggs about it, but I was angered to find out that in spite of the widespread knowledge of the ARVN, Nixon had proposed turning the war over to them. He made a campaign theme out of it and got himself elected. He took office and gave the people the impression he was getting us out of the war through Vietnamization. Instead it seemed he was only using the war as a vehicle to get re elected. America had been sold a bill of goods. Nixon knew the war was complex and that the people had grown too weary to try to understand.

The following night was our turn to go out on ambush. It just had to be our luck to be the squad to go out the night after the shooting. The incident really did a number on our fears and apprehensions. Nobody slept at all and I was sure it was the same on the compound. I was glad to see it end but in a couple of nights we would have to go out again. It took a while for Charlie to make his presence known, but he would no longer be able to surprise us. We would be looking for him after that cameo appearance. It was classic guerilla warfare though; a daring strike and then he vanishes. His ability to hit and run was what made him so formidable. As much as I hated Charlie, he continued to amaze me with his bold tactics. Chairman Mao may have written the book on this type of warfare, but Charlie had elevated its execution level to an art form.

The following morning, during our next resupply, I volunteered to pull perimeter guard and hid in some bushes at the far end of the LZ in an effort to blend in with the background. This was no easy task because we were in a village and there was nothing to really conceal my presence. To make matters worse, a bunch of little kids gathered around me like a pack of cub scouts. They made a mockery of my sentry duty. I was not fooling anybody with that crowd hanging around me. "Go away! Didi Mau! Didi Mau!" I told them in an effort to scatter them without having to wave or point my weapon at them.

Another new arrival stepped off of the second slick. He was in full gear and even from a distance it was obvious he had been in country for a while. Resupply lasted long and but finally came to an end giving me a chance to get away from the flock of kids who were harassing me. They had pushed me to my limit of tolerance for their behavior. They were not only trying to pick my pockets, one of them tried to grab my weapon and make off with it. They were lucky I wasn't one of those guys who would have slapped them around. I could have shot him and gotten away with it but could not have lived with myself.

I received another care package but this one was from Barbara. She even sent me the film that I'd been asking for. She also sent me her high school class ring and told me to bring it home to her in November. All I could do was think about that ugly letter that I wrote her. My timing couldn't have been worse. I was really sorry about that letter at that moment and was really kicking myself for sending it. I hoped that I hadn't over stepped my boundaries with her. I said some pretty bad things in it and she deserved better.

A Vietnamese barber was sent out on one of the helicopters. He managed to cut a few heads while he was on the compound including Benn's. I fully expected to hear from Calvin about it as he had been on my case about not getting a haircut for at least three months. Benn's haircut looked as awful as Jones said it would. I had told him on more than one occasion about the Vietnamese barbers but he ignored me and actually paid for an ugly haircut.

213

The new guy's name was Hugle. He was another head and he managed to fit right in with the rest of the guys. He was a slightly built white guy with thick brown hair and a deep heavy voice. He was as easy going as they came. "Handy, you missed the barber." said Calvin fully realizing that I had no intention of getting a haircut. All he needed was to see one black guy get a haircut and Benn accommodated him.

"I wasn't trying to catch him, Calvin. He's a barber. What on earth would I want with a barbe?"

"I don't think you can get away with that. I could give you an Article 15 you know."

"Who's going to sign it?" I asked. An Article 15 can be regarded as the military's short order brand of justice. The lifers write you up and then present it to you for your signature. The signature is a binding agreement to all of the charges stipulated inside; a signed confession of guilt and an unconditional acceptance of whatever punishment being assessed. The whole deal was a travesty. Agreeing to let Calvin bust me down to an E-2 was unimaginable. It would be like giving him the power of being judge and jury over me. I had already made up my mind to refuse to sign any Article 15 while in the Army and always opt for the court martial for any light offense. It would, in effect, determine how serious the accuser is about the charges.

I left Calvin and joined the guys at the gun placement. Aretha may break my heart but she could never insult my intelligence. "What's he hassling you about?" Hugle asked.

"He has this thing about me getting a haircut. He insists that I would look good with a bad haircut. Can you believe that shit?"

"Is he always like that? I mean, does he go around bothering everybody?"

"I don't know about everybody, but he tries to make my day on a regular basis. He's an asshole." I laughed as we went on listening to Aretha over and over.

The ARVN's suddenly started a commotion outside of the perimeter. About four of them were beating some teenager senseless. Those cowards, I thought, would gang up on an old woman too if she crossed them. The poor kid couldn't have been more than 17 or 18 years old.

"They got one! The ARVNs have captured a prisoner!" someone said.

"A prisoner! You've got to be kidding me!" I said as I grabbed my weapon and left the perimeter to get a closer look. I couldn't believe the Ruff Puffs had actually come up with a prisoner. I imagined he had to be the same one who opened fire on us that night and couldn't wait to get my hands on him. I waded through the crowd of muggers and smashed him in the face with the butt of my weapon. "Take that you cocky son of a bitch!" I said feeling disappointed about not being able to shoot him in the face. Anyway, I wouldn't have wanted to put him out of the misery of suffering through the beating he was taking at that moment. I stomped his head, then sat back and watched as they tossed his near lifeless body onto an awaiting helicopter for what I assumed would be more interrogation.

The helicopter hadn't quite flown out of sight when someone disclosed that he was a draft dodger. The Ruff Puffs were beating up that kid because he didn't want to become a coward like one of them. "Can you believe this shit?" I asked Hugle who was by that time in hysterics laughing at me. I thought we had a VC prisoner and I should have known better. That poor kid was heading for induction into the worst army in history. When he finished his training, he would probably be assigned to one of the fleet-footed ARVN units already bringing shame to his so-called country. At least Charlie didn't get to him first. Those guys would have turned him into a real fighting man. He would have come back to fight against us again and again. "Handy, have you ever heard of Jimi Hendrix?"

"I've heard of him but not that much of his music. I could remember a couple of years ago hearing him singing a song called Hey Joe."

"Really, but he's a soul brother."

"No shit Sherlock. So are a lot of people but I haven't heard all of them sing."

"What about JJ?"

"Now I've heard a lot of Janis Joplin."

"She sounds just like a sister doesn't she?"

"Well she puts a lot of feeling into her delivery if that's what you mean."

"Man, when I get back to the world; I'm going to buy everything they ever recorded." He said.

Mad Dog walked up and silently beckoned for Hugle to come with him. They left the compound together and I rejoined the crowd at the machine gun placement. I let Aretha break my heart while pondering my predicament with Barbara. There was little else to do but start constructing a letter of apology and hope she would accept it. I needed to have her writing me for the duration of my tour. I needed her love and concern to keep me occupied with anything and everything she represented to me.

I stayed awake all night because the recent daring shooting incident had me expecting the worst. There was no way that I could have slept on the compound with my anxiety level so high. I almost barfed from all of the tension and didn't regain my composure until the patrol returned. Charlie had me right where he wanted me; totally obsessed with his whereabouts and his next move. "Handy, when I came in yesterday, I noticed you out there in the bushes with those kids. Are they your runners." Hugle asked.

"Those disgusting kids? Trust them with my money? You gotta be crazy." I said before explaining why I was out there when he came in. We took a walk through the village and smoked a joint together as we got acquainted with each other. "Where are you from back in the world?" I asked "I'm from Virginia man and I have been in trouble since I was first assigned to Alpha Co. The lifers have busted me down to E-1 and there wasn't enough time left in country to make up the lost rank. The MP's have caught me over at Linda and Monique's boo coo times man. They caught me more times than I can remember. Getting picked up by the MP's had become such a routine that I had started referring to then as my personal chauffeurs." He laughed. The lifers, I assumed had offered him the opportunity to finish up his tour with us as the proverbial last chance at redemption. "What are they offering you in return for staying here with us?" I asked.

"They said that they would consider giving me an undesirable discharge; if I can finish my tour here with out getting into anymore trouble."

"Undesirable! That's bullshit man. I'd take the next flight outta here. They're not offering you much. In fact they aren't offering anything. Why are you risking getting your ass killed when there is so little to gain?"

"Because I think I'm going to like it here. You guys are cool." After telling me his story, I started to feel paranoid by walking through the village. We cut our excursion short and returned to the compound. Although it was his choice and his life he was risking, he was ignoring the obvious. He had too much ground to cover and not enough time to make it up. I couldn't understand why he allowed the MPs to repeatedly snatch him from the opium den. Getting caught there once would be one time too many for most others.

As we approached the compound, I could see a little activity going on near my bunker. Some of the guys were constructing something. "What in the world are they doing?" I asked.

"It looks like a shitter to me."

"A shitter! Those dirty bastards, they not only built a field latrine on the compound; they put the damn thing near my bunker." I said. Building one on site, I assumed would eliminate all reasons for leaving the compound. We walked through the zigzag and gave the new shitter a closer inspection. "A one-seater. I'm not surprised." I said as Hugle laughed at my predicament. He wouldn't laugh when the time came to start burning shit. I would have complained to the lifers but it would only make their day. Although I never spent too much time inside of my bunker, I was sure that the latrine's location was chosen by its two chief architects; Calvin and Jahret. They would never see me sitting on that contraption. I'd rather dig a hole somewhere in the village and deal with whatever they plan to do to stop me. The heads would find a way to circumvent its purpose for sure. It was only a matter of whether or not they would ban all movement off of the compound. While contemplating my new predicament, Doc and Howard came to me carrying a load of extra supplies to be delivered to Mua's house. We left under the watchful eyes of suspicion but there was no attempt to stop us from leaving. Their one-seater would not be used if we were allowed to dig our own outside of the perimeter.

When we arrived at Mua's house and unloaded the supplies on our adopted family, we noticed that Papa San was wearing a black Australian type bush hat and carrying a carbine. He was a member of the Peoples Self Defense Corps, a concept designed to arm civilians for the purpose of defending themselves from Charlie whenever we couldn't be around. I disagreed that giving rifles to old men would solve any problem at the village level. The concept would eventually make the situation worse. The potential for more arms falling into the hands of the enemy was scary. At the rate we were going, S. Vietnam would eventually develop the potential to become another armed society worst than ours.

Mama San had insisted on becoming our laundry woman. She wanted to always have a clean set of fatigues from each of us so we gave her an alternate set. We really didn't need the service but she wanted to do it for us. It was hard to say no to someone as kind as she was and in spite of our insistence, she refused to be paid in MPC. I figured it was to keep the Ruff Puff bullies from harassing the family. We took a bath at a nearby well and exchanged our dirty fatigues and left. When we returned to the compound we found the latrine was already in use. Once the thing gained acceptance, there would always be someone taking a crap less than five yards from my place. Suddenly I realized why the thing was built. The CP crowd didn't build it to keep us from leaving the compound. It was constructed for their own convenience. The thought of leaving the compound to take a crap must've been too laborious. With the new one-seater they didn't have to dig a hole or leave the compound and we would have to burn the shit.

Our new NCO's name was Harrington, a ten year man who had been around long enough to remember when they wore a different style uniform and humped some now defunct weapons. He was a grunt's grunt, a dog face that didn't mind getting his fatigues dirty. He loved being an infantryman and was looking at another ten years or more before hanging his boots up. He could never adopt the country club mentality and I figured that maybe it might have led to his possibly being banished from their little club over at CP. Hugle, much to his delight, would also be going out with our squad. "Do you think Harrington would mind if we smoked one on the way back?"

"Trust me won't care what were smoking."

"Handy, have you ever noticed that your first joint in the morning is always the best high of the day?"

"Yeah, I've always noticed that."

"Hell, I can't wait until tomorrow comes." There was something strange about the way Hugle had accepted the worthless deal offered by the lifers. I wondered if anybody ever told him about the shooting that took place the night before he arrived. Considering his reason for accepting the proposition, I also wondered if it would have mattered to him at all.

After ambush was over and we were packing up to return, Hugle was excited to the point of jubilation. All we did was finish ambush. It could have been the sight of the glorious sunrise that always signaled the end of another scary night or maybe the joint he was about to light up. "Handy, have you ever heard of Hendrix?"

"Didn't you ask me that question the other day?"

"Did I? Well, have you?"

"I already told you that I never heard that much of him before I came over here."

"Well what about JJ?"

"You've already asked me about her too."

"Really? She sounds just like a sister, doesn't she?"

"Of course she does," I concurred; wondering if any other answer would have sufficed.

"Man, when I get back to the world, I'm gonna buy everything they ever recorded." he said. Either he was not smoking the same stuff I was smoking, or he didn't realize he was repeating himself.

"Just when are you going home?" I asked.

"In September or October. I've got some bad time to make up so I'm sure you know they're gonna add boo coo days to my tour."

"Man I think maybe you oughtta reconsider and go home now."

"No way man! I like it out here. You guys are cool." he said making me feel guilty for having fun with him while he spent time with us in pursuit of nothing in return. Nothing more, that is, than a good time.

We gathered our gear and left our ambush site. On our way back, we shared that joint and a feeling that a good friendship had begun. Our return seemed longer than it was due to that "morning high" we spoke about. When we made it back to the compound we immediately headed for Mua's house for a few hours of leisure. We walked in and settled down in the new room Papa San had just completed. I stretched out in the hammock and rested while Doc and Howard sat in the doorway leading outside to play some sort of game on the floor with Mua. Whatever they were playing, Mua was beating their pants off. I doubt if they really understood the rules because the two of them were stoned out of their minds. Mua didn't appear to have any little friends her age to play with and seemed content to be at play with a couple of adult men who were both on drugs.

Suddenly Calvin walked up to the door and leaned over both Doc and Howard, who were still sitting in the doorway. They looked at each other and immediately realized that one of them should have or could have spotted him making his approach. "All three of you come with me." he ordered us. We all got up and followed him back to the compound as I tried to get over both Howard and Doc's not noticing Calvin until he was upon us. They were both feeling bad about allowing him to approach us undetected. I reassured them that there was nothing to worry about. If Calvin wanted to do some damage, he would have brought along an officer with him to corroborate his story about whatever he witnessed which was nothing. Jahret was probably too scared and Moe just wasn't that kind of guy. With no other option at his disposal, he undoubtedly made the trip alone to satisfy his ego. He couldn't even expect us to not return to the village; which was fortunate because we loved Mua's family and it would have been the biggest tragedy if we weren't allowed to continue our own brand of pacification.

Calvin was obviously upset at not being able to catch us in the act as he resorted to his own brand of nit picking about everything from my unkempt hair to my uniform or the CIB sewn on the front of it.

"I could write you up for insubordination you know."

"I doubt if you could spell the word." I said challenging him to make an issue of my unauthorized wearing of the badge that they were intentionally keeping from me. Howard had already made me the target of constant teasing, but Calvin was the only one on the compound in need of one of the local hookers.

The following day found us with our usual swagger still intact. Calvin's raid on Mua's house was the worst thing he could have done. Had he just stayed on the compound and waited for us to come back, he wouldn't have to deal with having the issue rubbed in his face. In the end, he just couldn't stay put. He had to come over and play non- commissioned narcotics officer. After his raid, whenever we decided to leave to smoke a joint, we might as well have told Calvin where to find us. We could have also asked when we should expect him to show up.

Hugle found out about my lack of rank and the CIB issue. He immediately sympathized with my predicament and identified with the issue as if it mattered to him. In spite of his insistence, I thought he was making a bad choice staying in Vietnam. I feared that after two or three months with us, he would be sent home and nothing else. Dispatched with nothing more than what he was already in line for.

I walked over to the gun placement and had a nice talk with him about leaving and passing on that deal he made with the lifers. He listened intently and insisted he was having too much fun in Phu My to even consider leaving early. I gave up for that moment but would continue to press on the subject the following day. I hated seeing the lifers get away with what they were doing. He was giving his best effort and they weren't offering him anything in return. I couldn't stand it. To make matters worse, he got himself caught up in the soap opera about my not being promoted. It gave him something to identify with and he didn't need much else. He was truly involved with being a member of our company. "Handy, did you notice that all of the hoes are gone?" Howard asked.

"Of course they're gone. Everybody's just about broke. Why should they hang around?"

"Will they come back on payday?"

"They always do. That's the way the business works."

"When they come back, why won't you get yourself a shot of ass?"

"I'm tired of telling you man. I don't like that wham bam thank you ma'am action." I said realizing that Howard would continue to make an issue about my sex life. In his invented view of life, not having sex with the hookers was unnatural.

Hugle took a seat on the on site field latrine making me feel betrayed. I was hoping the contraption wouldn't catch on. Every time I looked at it, I got irritated. They didn't even care about the lack of privacy. I wouldn't have wanted to be observed by everyone while I was taking a crap. I would have preferred more seclusion. "Handy watch this." Said Mac as he showed me his camera and walked over to Hugle and took a picture of him as he sat on the crapper. He was literally caught with his pants down and provided the entire camp with a good laugh. Maybe the embarrassment of being caught by Mac's Instamatic would stop the guys from using that contraption. I know I wouldn't have wanted to be in his scrapbook as his great-grandchildren looked at the picture fifty years later.

The following day as the ambush patrol returned, I realized that if for no other reason, we were fortunate to be on the compound. The other platoons were scattered out over the village with nothing else to do but put up with the heat all day. They also had to put up with the throng of villagers that were no doubt gathering daily to watch them. Over at the compound, we had the luxury of having our own quarters, which was something that we didn't even have at Uplift. Of course there were the aforementioned disadvantages of being in a fixed position. I had to admit that the advantages outweighed them considerably though.

It was resupply day again and Lee had ordered another case of Cokes for our bunker. Another case could've lasted us until payday but of course I needed to factor in Brown's insatiable Coke habit before making any assumptions.

Sgt Rudy stepped off of the first helicopter and immediately reminded me of the good old days when Al and Katta were still with me. He didn't have his lawnmower with him either. Guys like Rudy were a strange lot. They all felt relieved to be tucked away in the rear out of harm's way. Yet they always find reasons to visit the company in the field. I didn't know what he was missing but he wouldn't find it on our little compound. He was carrying a Claymore bag at his side and headed straight to CP. I took up a position at the gun placement and started to stare at his little gathering with the country club crew. I couldn't figure out the reason for his visit but it couldn't have been to deliver one mine.

After conferring with Calvin and Jahret, Rudy left the compound on foot. When he returned, he took a number of us for a walk outside of the perimeter that led us in the path of a booby trap he had planted minutes earlier. The explosion sent us scrambling for cover. "It's not a booby trap. It was a trip detonated Claymore mine."

"It looked like a booby trap to me." Lee said angrily.

"Sounded like one too." I said. It would have blown our legs right off just like a booby trap would have also. Rudy, in an exercise in semantics, went on to explain how the Brigade had discovered a loophole in the Geneva Convention agreements. According to his explanation, there was a way of detonating the Claymore with a trip wire would have allowed us to use Charlie's tactics without violating the accords. I still couldn't understand the difference and the biggest danger was that any error made while deploying the mine would have cost a life. Everyone had at one time or another fumbled a trip flare. Yet they expected someone to try setting a trip detonated Claymore without making any fatal mistakes. Any mishandling of the contraption could have transformed a human body into about one million flakes and an equal amount of droplets. The potential for disaster was staggering.

That night our squad had the misfortune of being the squad to try the new booby trap first. Modell, strictly on a volunteer basis, was more than eager to test the procedure. "I think you had better bring along an extra canteen cup to retrieve Modell's remains in case he screws up." I told Hugle. We had a good laugh but there was nothing funny about how naïve Modell was. He led us out on ambush and carefully deployed the booby trap. During the early hours of the morning, the booby trap went off killing some dog that wandered down the trail at the wrong time. Forget about writing Boggs, I needed to start thinking about writing the SPCA. The stupidity level had reached new heights and all Modell was disappointed about was not getting himself a kill. He looked pitiful holding the remains of his booby trap, which were only some wires. The dog, no doubt, looked worse. I didn't bother to see how much of him remained after detonation.

When we returned to the compound, we were the target of a lot of dead dog jokes. Modell caught the most because he was the one who wanted to try the thing. Howard came up to me with what I thought would be another joke about the dead dog.

"Handy, listen to me man. This is no joke either." He said with a slight smirk on his face.

"I've heard that if you go too long without some pussy, the cum will start backing up in your system." he said as he placed his hand about crotch level and raised it to his chest.

"And if you still aint fucking by that time, it will back up to here and choke you to death." he said with a laugh as he placed his hands around his throat in mock self-strangulation. I had visions of me listening to Howard and his act until I went home. He was a riot. He passed up a chance to tease us about our dead dog mission to get in another line about my sexual non participation.

In Gathar's most recent letter, he indicated that he just signed an Article 15 for losing his weapon. He had fallen victim to one of those thieves we were warned about during orientation. The cost of the weapon would of course come out of his pocket but the damage was already done. Another weapon had made it to the black market to be bought and used by Charlie to be used against us. Gathar and I came from the same background, living in a housing project; and we knew some pretty desperate people back in New Orleans. Vietnam and its infamous black market, however, was a whole new ballgame. No one could say he had experience anything like the treachery that went on regularly on the streets of Vietnam. The Ruff Puffs were trying to steal from us at Phu My and our own GI's were stealing from us in the rear.

8

Jones had finally DEROSEd and returned to Brooklyn. I also heard they finally promoted him before he left after repeatedly being overlooked for promotion. Jones walked point for his entire tour. Jahret and Calvin were so insensitive to the way they handled some matters that sometimes they didn't seem to care at all. As much as I enjoyed being a part of Charlie Co., I still felt cursed to be serving under those two. They were starting to make an impression on Hugle. He started to notice how much they went out of their way to tick me off and he couldn't understand why. It was typical though. No matter how hard a black worked at his job he would almost always be denied the opportunity to be promoted. In spite of the institutional racism that existed in the Army, there was still an incredible bond in the Herd that existed between the guys in the field. We never let anything interfere with our relationship with each other. "Man, how about that Modell. He finally got himself a kill." Hugle laughed. He was having too much fun. He was still under the effect of his morning high and the dead dog only added to the fun he was having. Then he put me through the Hendrix-Joplin inquiry again. I hesitated long enough to wait for Rod Serling to do his narrative and to reassure myself that I was still in Vietnam. "Just think man, if you go home now you could start that album collection sooner than later."

"No way man! I'm staying right here with you guys." His patented answer had me convinced he would extend his tour another 12 months if he weren't in so much trouble. The dead dog only added to his enjoyment.

The Cokes that Lee ordered were being consumed at an incredible rate; consumed by Brown of course. My guess was that he had been busted down to an E-1 and wasn't receiving any pay at all. He hadn't spent a dime over at Biggie's and as long as we ordered sodas from the rear, we'd never see him go into his pockets for anything but his comb. Brown kept us in stitches without even trying. He was full of that down home humor and his replies were all memorable. There was one thing about him that wasn't funny at all. He was practically illiterate. He said the Army had to teach him to read and write before he started training. Brown was everything most people thought all grunts were. The misconception that a low IQ would automatically qualify one for a stint as an infantryman was bogus. Nothing could be further from the truth. My infantry training class was assisted by a holdover from the previous class. He was a college professor. His being drafted into the Army thoroughly debunked the theory that infantry is for the low I.Q. group. Brown was more like an exception to the norm and nothing else.

Hugle and Mad Dog disappeared again. They had started to develop a pattern of wandering off without notice and the practice was dangerous. I never wanted to come across as being intrusive, but my concern was only about their safety. Mad Dog was on his second tour so he knew all the dangers. He was also knew all of the schemes and was planning to do a little dealing on the black market. He said that a $100 bill could fetch $300 MPC on the market and was considering sending for one from home. Maybe it was the reason he came back for another tour. I couldn't figure out how he was going to send it back though. The Army kept tabs on how much money was being sent back home and forbade possessing excessive currency.

Later that night while I was pulling guard at the machine gun post, it started to rain. After a few minutes, it started to pour. It was only the second time I had seen rain since the monsoon ended. At least this time we weren't on ambush with Jahret.

When the rain became a downpour, I remembered that while we were constructing our bunker, I placed a sandbag in our doorway for flood protection. The trench line, I figured, would collect rain water and start pouring it into our hole. I decided to put another one before the water line breached the one sand bag. The deluge, it seemed, might last a while.

As I walked down the trench line I was hit by a sudden splash of water from my right. It was Hugle inside of his bunker fighting a waist deep flood by bailing out with his steel pot. He was fighting a losing battle. In fact, everyone else was hard at work struggling with their own flooded quarters. I sloshed back down to the machinegun post to pull guard until daylight knowing that our bunker was dry and that I would be the only one available for a while.

The Ruff Puffs were laughing their heads off at their predicament. They knew all along that our below ground design would be under water if such a rainfall did come. They may have been a bunch of sorry soldiers but they knew how to live in the climate.

Daylight found everybody hard at work rebuilding their bunkers. It was a repeat performance of what went on when we first arrived. "Well, now what do you think about all of that digging I had you guys doing?" I asked Benn and Lee as they emerged from the bunker. They could not believe what they saw or that they both slept through it all. I had placed a lot of flood protection in the design. Even if the bunker next to me would have collapsed, it never would have affected our place. We were able to sit and watch the guys the way they watched us during our extended digging and sandbagging period.

Calvin suddenly emerged from CP's rubble with all of his gear. The moment I should have been waiting for had finally arrived. Calvin was finally leaving the fold and not a day too soon. For some reason, I never once assumed he would be going home ahead of me. It seemed that the only guys who left Vietnam were the guys I would miss the most. Calvin had been such a pain in the ass that I had accepted him as some kind of curse. He was like an anathema that could not be removed or a burden that I would just have to bear for the duration of my tour. His comrades over at CP were all gathered around him bidding him a fond farewell. If only Jahret would've followed him on his way out of country, it would have been like a dream come true.

Once Calvin's chopper was airborne I realized that, just like Mercein, he would be replaced and probably by another hard-ass just like him. I supposed that Calvin's replacement would naturally be briefed by Jahret meaning that nothing would change for me. Actually I wouldn't have had it any other way. I was not Army material and that would always be the final analysis. I would continue to be judged by the likes of Jahret and whoever replaced Calvin.

As the day continued, the rest of the guys were busy with reconstructing their bunkers while I sat listening to the music. Then I noticed a familiar sight. Someone was bent over with his pants down being closely examined and tended to by Doc. I hadn't witnessed the scene since the monsoon ended. I couldn't figure out why Doc would be treating someone's asshole in the middle of the dry season because there were no jungle-rot-on-the-buttocks patients to be found in the summer. Upon close inspection, I noticed that Doc's patient was Hugle. He had picked up some pubic lice from the field latrine. "The shitter! Doc, what are you going to do, pick crabs from everyone's ass?"

"No Handy. I've ordered it shut down. They are dismantling it right now." He said pointing to the detail at work near our bunker. This was great news. First Calvin left and then the shitter got the axe. I was on a roll and couldn't go wrong. Maybe Jahret would be leaving next. Maybe someone would frag him for the cause or maybe the war would end first.

The bunker reconstruction ended and the sun came out with a vengeance. The temperature was again over 100 degrees and other than the condensation effect there was no trace of the downpour at all. I guess that Buddha just decided it was time for some wet stuff.

The ARVN's erected a volleyball net on the compound and started a game. Some of the guys wandered over and started looking for a chance to play them. Surely it would be hard for the ARVN to come up with the kind of effort it would take to beat our guys at such an easy game. Even Grove's presence on the court couldn't hinder their efforts. Of course there was no way that I would go out there and play with them in the heat.

When the match started the guys were playing badly. Instead of the lopsided win for Charlie Co., it was a humiliating sweep. They were losing to a bunch of munchkins and nobody seemed to care at all. After watching the uninspiring play of the guys I got ready for ambush early to pretend to be irritated by the volleyball match. The game only delayed our departure from the compound.

That night I finally got a chance to use the Starlight Scope. The thing definitely illuminated an otherwise dark area but its depth-of-field was too distorted. Even worse was the surrealistic image that it produced. It was creepy looking into its viewfinder and seeing green images moving around against an otherwise black backdrop. I'd rather take my chances with my own vision and my paranoid deluded mind when on guard. At least if I thought I saw someone out there I would have known exactly how far away the target was supposed to be.

We returned from ambush and while sitting at the Rat Hole, Doc tried to convince me that the ARVN's were a tough opponent on the volleyball court. I never would have believed that a bunch of little guys had a chance against me.

When resupply day came around again, Burt was on one of the slicks. He was carrying nothing but the third squad's radio that Shave bought back in January. Just seeing the guy brought back memories of the good times we shared when I was new in country. I really missed those good times we had back then. More than anything else, I missed those guys. Bear, Speedie, Shave, Black, Purvis and Burt. Being in Vietnam just wasn't the same without them around. At one time I didn't think that I could have made it without them. I was just that impressionable. The lifers couldn't handle us. We drove them insane with our behavior. "What brings you out here dude?"

"I'm going back to the world man, back to Denver. I came to turn the radio over to you." He said as he handed me the symbol of the old third squad's unity. It was the ceremonial changing of hands that I was expecting since Shave left us in Tuy Hoa. It was the stuff that made us special. The act that we hoped would make a lasting impression on each other. It would for the final four months of my tour anyway. Going it alone was expected to be one tough act though. I may be surrounded by another great bunch of guys but there will never be another group like the one that slowly disappeared from me over the previous eight months.

I accepted the radio and the role of humping it with uncommon pride. After exchanging addresses, I shook hands with Burt and bade him farewell. Another piece of me was going back to the world without me. I hoped to one day go home with the same good feeling that I shared with guys like him. I looked forward to knowing them for the rest of my life. I just hoped that I could survive all of the farewells.

"Say Handy, was that Burt?" asked Hugle.

"Yes it was."

"You mean to tell me that you know Burt?"

"Yes, why?"

"Man that's one heavy dude!" he said.

"He aint heavy, he's my brother." I laughed. I couldn't resist the pun but Hugle, it seemed, was living in another world. I could make silly remarks or crack jokes and he would just go on as if nothing was said. He was just that odd. Nothing ever took him out of his own little world.

"Where did you get to meet Burt?" I asked.

"I met him in the rear. Every time the MP's would lock me up in the Connex, I would go over to Burt's hootch and party." He said as I wondered what it was like to be placed inside of that metal container by those guys. The MP's converted it into a detention cell but wouldn't even stand guard over it. They cut a door and a window in it but they never really locked anyone inside of it. Of course it would have been similar to the conditions that our POW's went through in Japan during WWII, and that was the issue. No one at Uplift had spent more than ten or fifteen minutes inside of the Connex without walking off. Jailbreaks at Uplift were more common than firefights in the field. We were taking part in mad world where police arrested criminals and put them inside of jails with an open door policy and an honor system to match. "Burt used to be a part of our squad." I told him along with a lot of stuff about the good times we had back when all humped together. When I mentioned Tuy Hoa his eyes lit up.

"You guys were there too. I got hit in Tuy Hoa."

"We lost an entire squad one night in that damned village. The damned ARVNs kept running out on us leaving us outnumbered." I said.

"I was out on ambush with a bunch of ARVNs that turned out to be NVA. When they drew their weapons on us we ignored them because we never imagined that they were anything more than a bunch of punk ass ARVN's. I was sitting on the ground with my legs folded when they started popping frags on us where we sat. One went off between my legs." He laughed.

"Man you could've had your dick blown off."

"Everybody tells me the same thing." He said while still laughing. In spite of his having already dodged a huge bullet, he still considered staying with us. He was lucky that homemade frag only wounded him in the leg. He could've suffered a far worse fate than Chris when were ambushed.

A platoon Sergeant stepped off of the next helicopter. He stood at about 5'11" and was less than impressive in stature. He was a spindly white man with thinning hair who reminded me of the Ichabod Crane character in a cartoon adaptation of "Sleepy Hollow". Since he was in full gear, I supposed he was Calvin's replacement. He was wearing a MACV patch on his right shoulder. MACV (Military Assistance Command Vietnam) were the advisors who had been in country since before LBJ started sending combat troops to do the job that advisors could never accomplish fighting alongside the ARVN units. MACV was first deployed to the region during JFK's administration. I remember reading about the war and our questionable presence for the first time while in my reading class. At that stage of our involvement, I supposed that it was hoped and or assumed that advisors and material would be all that would have been needed to keep Ho Chi Minh in check. It will always be debated about whether or not JFK was leaning towards sending in more troops or withdrawing. There was also the conspiracy theory that makes JFK a victim of a ring of policy makers that wanted to go to war in Vietnam.

After resupply, we continued our normal duties. There was still no letter from Barbara but I wasn't ready to cut my wrists or anything like that. I just wished she would've dropped me a line and said something. Even "kiss my ass, you fool." would've been appreciated. I avoided telling Howard about it. I didn't want to hear any of the original lines he was creating.

Sgt. Spurlock, our new platoon Sergeant, was trying his best to make his presence felt. He exchanged pleasantries with everybody and tried to be firm at the same time. Moe brought him over to our bunker to show off the place. I could tell by the way he looked at me that he had been informed on my relationship with the lifers. I could live with having as much known about me. The jury, however, was still out on him. He would have to prove himself to us. He was no longer with MACV. He was with a real infantry unit and not a bunch of baby sitters.

Hugle was angered over my CIB and it raised his level of contempt a notch. I never found out who was informing the guy about all of the bullshit, but they were making it hard for me to get him to consider leaving Vietnam early. He seemed to be more ticked off about the issue than I was. All I wanted him to realize was that going home meant more to me and I hoped that he would've felt the same way. But I was about as close to getting my message across to him as he was to realizing that he had already asked me repeatedly about Jimi and JJ.

With Calvin out of the way, we returned to Mua's house for some more of their hospitality. It was nice to go there once more. It felt good knowing that we could bring so much happiness to them with so little. I knew that I was going to miss them when we left their part of Vietnam.

 Spurlock took us on his first patrol. It was hot and we were not eager to find Charlie. I liked the fact that we had been in that village as long without any fire fights. That one shooting incident we encountered earlier had almost been forgotten. It was almost as if it didn't happen at all. We didn't need to go patrolling to find Charlie. He knew where we were and would definitely come to us often enough to satisfy any eager to impress former MACV NCO.

Almost as soon as the patrol started, we came to a halt to give Spurlock a chance to check his map. Checking a map in a village is sure to make everyone question your navigational skills. I remember when some real heated debates would start up over our exact location. We were in the Crow's Foot then. The place was a virtual no-man's land that would challenge the best map readers. There were ridges, depressions and fingers in that area that couldn't be found on our maps. The surveyors who made the maps took quite a few liberties with its construction. The populated areas were less confusing though.

After Spurlock got his bearings together, we resumed our little patrol. After another 50 meters, someone came upon an old artillery shell that looked as if it had been around forever. The rust had corroded it so much that it had transformed itself into a barely recognizable tube.

"It's an artillery shell." He said redundantly. I couldn't figure out his next move and was hoping that he wasn't considering bringing it back to the compound. Of course all artillery rounds as well as unexploded bombs were used by Charlie to make his homemade frags and his numerous booby traps. They were well trained on how to get to the explosive material inside. Spurlock's intention was questionable. That particular round had been lying on the ground for years and probably had been passed over by the enemy's ordinance specialists. The find posed no threat to our presence in the village and practically begged to be ignored.

After a lengthy conference with the brain trust, it was decided that the best thing to do was to blow it up in place. The idea was not only insane, it was impossible to accomplish with our limited resources. I couldn't even imagine how he intended to detonate the shell. "Is he serious?" Hugle asked.

"I think he is. Let's move away from this asshole and watch from a safe distance." I suggested. We sought the cover of a shady tree and watched in amazement as Spurlock, Swain and Modell took turns throwing frags at the shell while hiding behind a rice paddy dike. I wasn't trained in artillery but I doubted seriously if their method would succeed and fortunately, it didn't. Had it blown up as intended, it would have taken those clowns with it. It did look comical though. Hugle laughed uncontrollably. It was funnier than that little piglet trying to copulate in Tuy Hoa.

After exhausting all of their frags in the near suicidal attempt to blow the round in place, we finished our patrol. Hugle laughed so hard I thought we were going to have to medivac him out of Phu My. He survived though and on our way back we lagged behind to test Spurlock's tolerance for insubordination. About all Spurlock accomplished on his patrol was to demonstrate just how odd he could be.

When we returned to our bunker we each had one of the few remaining Cokes Brown had managed to leave for us. Soon one of us would have to order some more before Brown started to complain about the lack of sodas in our bunker. That night was our turn to go out on ambush again and he was a good distraction. As hard as I tried to not let ambush get to me, it always seemed to take a lot out of my day. I couldn't shake that ominous feeling that something was about to happen on ambush. It was hard to believe that as long as we had been there, nothing had happened to us. The Tuy Hoa experience taught me not to get too comfortable on ambush and that Charlie always came out at night. It was only a matter of time.

Hugle returned from unknown whereabouts and Mad Dog, as usual, was with him. They were noticeable but never to the point where they were causing any suspicion amongst the lifers. I suppose it was to smoke a joint together. Other than leaving and returning, they didn't seem to spend any time together at all. They were close though.

Howard was cleaning his weapon again. He would constantly break down his rifle and oil it with care. His diligence was inspired by a dilemma faced by our troops in the early years of the war. The M-16 rifle had never quite shed the image of being unreliable in combat. The story about how it failed repeatedly just lingered long after the modifications were implemented. I assured him that he no longer had to worry about the problem but he continued oiling the weapon and even had a name for it. "This is my Roscoe. If I take care of it, it will take care of me." I was impressed with the way Howard carried himself. I figured he would do alright in the field and I was right. Whenever the bullets started flying, I knew he would be ready.

After Howard finished cleaning his weapon, we moved over to the machine gun post for the rest of the evening as the volleyball players assembled for another round of competition. The guys seemingly couldn't do without the embarrassment of losing to a bunch of wee people. Meanwhile the radio was playing loud enough to be heard across the entire compound.

"Do you think the brothers would mind playing some more Aretha?" Hugle asked as if listening to Aretha was some kind of exclusive black thing. "Just play it yourself." I said.

"I wish I had a girl back home." He said with a tearful look. Aretha was doing a number on more than just me as she demonstrated her appeal to all listeners.

That night's ambush started off quietly as we all settled down for our usual routine of pulling guard. Our ambush site was situated within a clump of tall grasses that grew around a double coconut tree. It was off the trail that it straddled and had to be considered a very risky spot which would have allowed our intruders to walk very close by. By the time my shift began, the moon had come out and lit up the area around us stripping our ambush site of most of its cover. It would have taken less than that to jumpstart

226

my paranoia. Before five minutes had passed, I started hearing something. It was a rustling sound going on very close to where I was kneeling. There was someone it seemed snaking around in the bushes just in front of me. I was certain that everybody in the perimeter was still in place. But the noise persisted. I must have spent the first half hour trying to convince myself that my mind wasn't playing tricks on me. The noise kept me moving about trying to locate its source. I knew the marijuana had a lot to do with it but it felt so real. I thought for sure that someone was out there. The experience had me considering cutting back on my consumption or stop smoking sooner before going out on ambush. I completed my turn at the post and turned it over to Lee. I stayed awake all that night anticipating something. As we packed for our return to the compound I compared notes on what happened during guard for the rest of the squad. "Did you hear anything last night as you pulled guard?" I asked Lee.

"Yeah I heard something but it was so close that I assumed it couldn't have been Charlie. We would have been killed."

Harrington was the squad leader so on our way back, Hugle and I openly smoked a joint. He also put me through the Jimi and JJ monologue again. It was beginning to look as if he was some kind of mental case. Maybe, I thought, he was experiencing some of that battle fatigue I had heard so much about. If he had already snapped, I was sure he would never listen to my appeal to him to leave early.

When we made it back Sgt Harrington pointed out one of the Vietnamese soldiers on the compound and said that he was our Kit Carson scout. He was a former NVA soldier named Dat who defected to our side back in '68. It was Dat who was making the noise during ambush as I pulled guard. The revelation was reassuring to me. For a minute I thought I was going crazy. I did not want to believe that my paranoia had gotten that much out of hand. I always felt comfortable with being terrified of what might've been out there. It was better than being so relaxed that Charlie would've been able walk up on me with ease. I didn't know what Dat was supposed to be accomplishing by skulking along the perimeter but if I had an itchy trigger finger to match my paranoia, he would've been our former Kit Carson scout that morning. He was obviously exactly where I thought he was. My reluctance to give away our position was the only thing that saved him from being shot. It did prove that I was as sharp as I needed to be while on ambush and good to know the faculties were working at the necessary levels. I planned to acquaint myself with Dat and let him know that no matter how good he was at playing sapper, I almost killed him.

Our beloved leader, Gen. Cunningham had received his second star and was about to go back to the world. According to Jahret, the good General would personally say farewell to every member in the brigade and was already on his way to our location. I quickly made plans to spare myself the privilege of listening to his well-rehearsed speech and take off for perimeter guard when his slick was overhead. He obviously had been a great commanding officer for us all or he wouldn't have been even attempting the farewell tour of the entire brigade. I'll never forget the day he chewed out Purvis at English. He looked every bit the man in charge that day. Purvis was flattered to recieve all of that attention.

When I heard the distant thumping of the helicopter blades whipping through the air, I knew he was on his way. I grabbed my weapon and made a mad dash across the helicopter pad. Hugle, unbeknownst to me, was right behind. We settled in the bushes where I always sat for perimeter guard and of course lit up a joint. When the helicopter landed, the General and his aides disembarked and entered the compound. They were received by the platoon standing in formation at attention. Everybody was fully dressed and looking every bit the close knit, finely tuned fighting men they hadn't exactly been as of late.

Although we had been just the opposite since we'd been there, the General's sendoff was going to be a feel good event.

From our vantage point we noticed that the ceremony was in full swing. General Cunningham was giving his farewell speech and I was beginning to wonder if I shouldn't have been so eager to avoid it. The old guy had done a great job as our leader and all he wanted to do was say thanks. Then just as I started to feel like I owed him a proper farewell, they sent Mac out to our post to give us the chance to do just that. Then we started to regret lighting up that joint. As the General returned to his slick, we made a mad dash back across the landing pad to meet him. The heat, the drugs and the run started to wreak havoc on our faculties as we tried to come to a halt. The blast of the waiting helicopter nearly toppled us as we tried to salute him. The old guy knew what we had been up to but he didn't care. He thanked us for the service we'd rendered during his stay. He told us what an honor it had been to serve as our commander and assured us that Gen. Ochs, his replacement, would be a worthy one. Having said all of that, we shook hands, exchanged salutes before boarding his slick for his next stop. The old guy had a ton of class and he knew how to display it.

9

Doc unexpectedly left our location to spend some time with the other half of the platoon leaving us to fend for ourselves without his services. I only hoped that we hadn't lost Doc Reardon to the aid station at Uplift. There was also, according to word, a new hot area within our battalion's area of operation. They called it the Sui Cai Valley. It was nowhere near Phy My, but I heard that other companies in our battalion had been continually rotating in and out of it for a while. The valley, it seemed, was some kind of infiltration route that Charlie used regularly. Col. Farris was determined to bring all enemy traffic to a halt. They said that the valley was embarrassingly close to Uplift and was more like an insult to the brass. I never thought the day would come when I would feel better off on pacification, but according to Kostrewva, I was. He had already been in the valley and said that it was as hot as it gets over there. The struggle for control of the valley sounded scary because the lifers were expecting to pull out all stops. Charlie was equally determined to continue to use the valley to push as many men and as much material as he needed to. Being in Phu My was beginning to look better every day.

Kostrewva gave me a lot to think about for the rest of the day. I had been wondering how soon we would be leaving Phu My but after listening to those stories about life in that valley, I was wondering how much longer we could stay. Recon practically lived in the Sui Cai at that time and made him glad to be with us. He showed me a leg wound he received from a bullet that passed right through his thigh without breaking the bone. Earning that Purple Heart over there was probably the reason he wanted out. Lt. Mack must have really scared him with his tactics as things were really getting wild in his final days there. The action, he said, bonded them together but that much was to be expected. The camaraderie was just as strong for every one of us who experienced life in the bush and leaving those guys must have been a hard decision for him to make. He at least was still in the third battalion and would be able to see his old friends from time to time. Having taken everything into account, I accepted my situation in Phu My and considered it a lesser of the two evils.

With 124 days left on my tour, I assumed it was proper to consider myself short. Sgt. Harrington was also slated to leave in late November. He had me by about two or three days but I didn't hold it against him. I was more concerned with what was ahead of me though. For that moment it was another sweep. This one, we were told, would be made with the assistance of E troop, our mechanized attachment. The idea of riding instead of walking in the heat was a relief. I hadn't ridden in an APC (Armored Personnel Carrier) since I was at Ft Polk. We were cooped up inside of the vehicle being tossed around like rag dolls. I almost broke my neck. As a trainee, I thought that nothing could hurt us as long as we were inside of its armored plated walls. The dreaded B-40 rocket had since removed that impregnable image.

As soon as Doc left us for the other location, I spotted someone's stomach contents lying on the ground near the mortar pit. I had to admit that the C-rations were barely tolerable but they never made me throw up. It seemed that Doc's absence was felt almost immediately.

I still hadn't received a letter from Barbara but I felt confident that she'd eventually start writing me again. I wrote her another letter while we waited for our armor plated limos. I also planned to write my nephew Robert. He was only six but my brother asked me to write him in order to keep his family abreast of what was going on. The only one in the household who bothered to write back was his wife Pearl. It was a strange writing arrangement for sure but it mattered little to her. Maybe it would have been more appropriate to address my letters to her. Anyway my little nephew would probably like hearing about us riding on a tank. Kids always did have wild attractions to huge vehicles like tanks and fire engines.

After they picked us up and began the sweep, the ride wasn't as bad as I thought it would be. The guys in the lead tank were a pretty confident group. In fact they all were. They were acting like a bunch of cab drivers picking up and delivering their fares. The sweep was as much fun as we hoped it would be. We managed to smash our way through at least twenty rice paddy dikes and of course ruined quite a few crops. Half of our column split off to form a stationary line while the rest of us swung around do the actual sweep. By design, we were supposed to flush out the intended element and force them into the waiting line of vehicles acting as a trap. But other than the damage done by the vehicles, about all we did was anger a lot of villagers and terrify the rest. At least we got a chance to ride atop the APC's instead of inside of them. What impressed me most of all was that all of the guys in E troop were heads. After the sweep we sat around shooting the breeze and getting stoned. Bennett, the guy who drove the lead tank, was a true rebel without a pause. He believed in going as fast as he could push his vehicle. During the sweep all attempts at stopping him or slowing him down were futile. He turned off his helmet communication line and kept on driving. He reminded me of Bear walking point.

I asked them if they ever had any B-40 rocket encounters and if they ever lost anybody to any such attack. Only one of them bothered to answer. He said that a tank was nothing but a pin cushion to a B-40 rocket. Casualties, he added, had been few but all memorable. He said that it wasn't a pretty sight and definitely a nightmare just to have one of them coming at you. Charlie very seldom missed because they couldn't afford to deal with the return fire. So whenever they were under a rocket attack, someone always died. His reply really put the party in a somber mood. It was a dumb question on my behalf. I didn't know what I was thinking about when I asked. When the sweep was over they took us back to the compound and to our surprise, they spent the night at our location and even pulled some ambush duty with us. In spite of my new awareness of the life of a mechanized unit under a B-40 attack, I felt well protected having them around. I really hated to see them go but they had other rice paddies to destroy somewhere else in Phy My District. After weighing the pros and cons, I came to the conclusion that those guys didn't exactly have it better than we did after all. In fact there were very few trade offs. I always thought that grunts had it worse than everybody else in warfare. I also thought that helicopter crews had the best life until I realized how easy it was to shoot down one of their machines.

Later that day, after I had been observing Dat for hours, I realized he had been on the compound for at least a week before Harrington asked me about him. I had initially thought that he was another Ruff Puff. He spoke a little English and was extremely polite. I suppose he felt as if he had to continually prove his allegiance to us. One had to wonder what would become of guys like Dat after Nixon pulled all of the troops out of the war because the S. Vietnamese government couldn't possibly last long after we were gone. By coming over to our side, Dat had possibly committed either treason or sedition. He was another Benedict Arnold as far as Hanoi was concerned and if he had to answer to his superiors, he'd be executed for his actions.

Big Goose was at wit's end with all of the An Ko gawking he'd been subjected to. I read another article in another old Look magazine that might've explained it all. The article dealt with a trip that Jackie Kennedy took to Cambodia. Her itinerary included a stop at an ancient walled city called Ankor Watt. I guess it would be more appropriately considered a ruin since it had been uninhabited since about the fifteenth century and showed considerable neglect. The architecture of the ruin was full of intricate carvings of human figures. There also were lots of statues of Gods and demons. As I had suspected earlier, Goose had the facial features of a number of these mythical figures. I was certain that the Vietnamese were very familiar with the ruin since it was in a neighboring country. I couldn't say for sure but there might have been a connection the people seemed to be making. There was a strong resemblance between the carvings and the Goose. If I was right, the novelty would never wear off as long as they could see him walk among them.

The political climate and landscape of Cambodia had changed considerably during the previous month. There were, according to the news, a number of communist insurgents roaming the countryside creating a lot of instability from within. The Khmer Rouge, as they called themselves, was trying to destabilize the government which appeared to be some kind of monarchy. Eisenhower's domino theory was beginning to materialize. I supposed that all of the pessimists back home who accused Nixon of widening the war were by then all saying "I told you so." I couldn't understand what went wrong after we pulled out our troops but it was beginning to look as if our raid triggered the insurgency or at least exposed it to me. The people in Cambodia seemed to be in for a lot of the same political turmoil the S. Vietnamese people had been going through for years. To make matters worse, they would have to go through it without any help from us. The people back home would overthrow our government if Nixon started to send troops back into that country again. If the countries in the region started falling like dominoes as feared, it would create a serious problem once Thailand were threatened due to our long standing military presence there. The US could possibly have to go through all of the same mess again. It seemed like only a matter of time. The war had already lasted longer than any war in our history and America had grown tired of the endless involvement in the region. As much as Nixon obviously wanted to defeat the little bastards, he had to deliver his campaign promise of '68 to bring the troops home.

Laos, the other country comprising the former French Indochina territory, had an insurgency problem at least as old as the one in Vietnam. The Green Berets had been there since the early sixties battling the Pathet Lao for control of that area. The CIA was even said to be in on the action. From where I was standing, it appeared as if we arrived too late to do anything about the so-called creeping tide of communism. The embarrassment of not knowing much about the war was beginning to consume me. I needed to know more and fast. Unfortunately, everything I learned was disappointing. The little pamphlet we received at Ben Hoa explaining Vietnam's history of being invaded was beginning to look like a product of our own political spin. There was proving to be a lot I could eventually learn about the war from the current events and more than enough to form an opinion.

A patrol was planned for later that day and since we didn't go out the night before, we would have to do the honors. Dat, who had just returned from ambush, was going to accompany us on the patrol. It appeared as if Dat's work was never done. Whether it was ambush or patrol, he was right there. His performance had gone beyond the allegiance demonstration. His efforts were tireless. Everybody realized his expertise would really be needed when we returned to the bush. He had won us over with his commitment.

Later during the patrol, we found ourselves at a far-reaching corner of Phu My with no sign of Charlie. I had already seen quite a bit of the surrounding villages on my own. We came to a halt in front of a Buddhist temple where a number of worshippers were inside. I felt like showing off my knowledge of the religion by joining the ceremony. I intended to repeat what that old woman taught Doc and I back in Tuy Hoa. Inside though, it was a different ritual. There were a group of women stacking and re-stacking some layers of silk-like fabric about the size of throw rugs. Every couple of minutes one of them would walk to the front of the temple and kneel at the altar. There was no incense involved in this version.

The patrol was a waste of time. All we did was walk all the way over to the temple and then headed back. I must have missed something or misunderstood our objective. It seemed as if we were just walking to get some exercise. "Hey guys! Guess what. Hanoi Hannah has just announced that we have been wiped out." Said Sgt. Harrington with his transistor radio held next to his ear. "Wiped out?" I asked.

"Yeah man. She says that Charlie company was just annihilated In Phu My by the brave N. Vietnamese freedom fighters." We all laughed at the important news announcement. Hannah had probably just found out that we were in Phu My. She really went out of her way to give that personal touch. Still, I couldn't understand why she got so much attention. Aside from her mastery of the English Language, about all that was left of her radio show was her play selection.

Suddenly someone opened fire about 100 meters up font. In the distance, a number of civilians came running out of a shelter scattering all over the village. Dat was standing in front of the building with what seemed to be a little boy. He was waiving his rifle, beckoning for us to come to him. We started running to his location while fanning out at the same time. As we arrived we noticed the little boy was actually a man being detained by Dat. Harrington approached him to get a report on the shooting and find out the detainee's status. The rest of us walked into the building, which was some kind of school house. At the front of the classroom lying on the floor was a dead Vietnamese man. Harrington walked in and informed us that the dead guy was giving some sort of class on communism as if it were required listening. Dat sneaked up from behind the schoolhouse and shot the teacher from the back window. Judging from the amount of grey matter splattered on the chalkboard, the cranium fragment on the floor and the huge gaping hole in the dead teacher's skull, it had to be a head shot. The man he was detaining was assumed to be a sentry.

Since there was no way of determining if the civilians were hard core VC supporters or just some terrified villagers who were too afraid to decline the invitation to attend the class, we chose to forget about them. I figured that if there was any reason to hold them, Dat would have done so. He was an exceptional soldier. If he was just a typical NVA soldier, we were truly up against a formidable enemy. Dat sneaked up on that gathering and made the kill before we even realized he had left our patrol. His stealth was amazing. If there was any lingering doubt about the guy's allegiance, he erased it with that one pull of the trigger.

We called a helicopter and had the detainee taken in for interrogation. He was probably recruited on the spot for his lookout duty but of course that much had to be verified through questioning. Dat was able to recognize his role and avoided being detected by him. Had we been without Dat's services, the detainee would have spotted us and alerted the instructor as we made our approach.

We returned to the compound with a feeling of accomplishment. There was also an element of anxiety inside of me. Dat's kill, I feared, just might provoke some kind of response from Charlie and it was our turn to go out on ambush. Our excursion that day planted a foul seed in my mind. The paranoia was already fueling its growth. By the time we made it back to the compound I was consumed.

Back on the compound, everyone else was caught up in the aftermath of Dat's kill. Once again the ritual of retelling the incident had proved to be too strong to ignore. We were excited about his sneaking up on that gathering and scoring the kill. Dat's star was definitely on the rise. In spite of all of the attention and praise, he remained a study in humility and self-deprecation. He had more than made the grade, yet he was seemingly still looking for acceptance and still trying to fit in.

When it was time for ambush, I packed early and went into my routine of pretending to be annoyed by Weiss's stalling tactics. This time he abandoned his practice and just faced the fact that he had to go out. He packed for the event and gave me an angry stare. "Alright, pack your gear and get ready to go!" He yelled. As soon as he raised his voice, I went after him. Mac and Goose grabbed me before I could get close though. Big Goose pointed out that he was bigger than I was but it didn't matter. Although I naturally tend to avoid fisticuffs, I just lost it for a moment. I had never been prone to any sort of violence and yet, I went after Weiss as if it were a common reaction. Dat's kill had me shaken and I suppose had caused me to react. After being restrained, I just forgot about the little episode and decided that I had already gotten away with a lot by just threatening to assault him. In spite of the incident, the lifers allowed us to go out on ambush together anyway. My concern about Charlie exacting some measure of retribution kept me up all night. Weiss's fear of getting shot in his sleep by me kept him up also. I somehow knew that I had seen the last of ambush with Weiss and couldn't have been happier. After we returned he did a bee-line to CP and, I assumed, started pleading a case for some kind of arrangement that would keep the two of us from going out on ambush together. He didn't have to worry about being shot by me.

When resupply day came around again, Barbara finally wrote me another letter. She was hurt, but still in love. The letter had restored order in my world again as I was on the ropes and about to go down for the count. I needed to continue to read her letters for the following four months. I couldn't have continued on without her writing, caring and waiting for me.

Later that day I noticed some more puke on the ground. There were multiple pools everywhere. I just never noticed it because some of the pools were dried hard from long exposure to the hot sun. In fact it couldn't have been the work of just one of us. Somebody was going to puke their guts out.

July had just about come to an end and we were, surprisingly, still in Phu My. The mission had begun to get old as things started getting out of hand. Morale was still about the same but the conduct was deteriorating. At night we had started smoking pot at the machine gun post. It was fun but I couldn't ignore the implications. The lifers knew what we were doing and they didn't even come out of their bunker. It was as if they had started to stay inside after dark because they didn't want to see us smoking it. I never thought I would ever be as concerned about the discipline but I was. I supposed it was the same all over Vietnam. The war had just lasted too long. I had to accept the smoking as part of the landscape. I had painted myself into that amen corner of drug abuse where the OJ was worshipped. There was no room for dissent and no easy way out.

Leading by example was not one of the prerequisites that Spurlock possessed. He was a walking magnet for ridicule. The harder he tried to play the hard-ass role, the more comical he became. He could have taken his act on the road and made a living just being Spurlock on stage. Howard couldn't get enough of him. He often laughed in his face. Things had changed, perhaps, too much. I tried to focus and adopt the same spirit that we used when I was new in country. We had all the confidence in the world then. We simply believed in ourselves and that was all we needed. When Burt dropped off Shave's radio, it wasn't like the ceremonial passing of the torch that I hoped it would be. It only signaled the end of that special time. We had it all back then and it just didn't last long enough for me.

"Handy, payday is coming up soon." said Howard. The thought of getting paid was probably giving him an erection.

"You're right. Just two more days and every hooker within 50 miles of here will be looking for you."

"Don't tell me that you still don't want any pussy!"

"I just don't want to pay for it, that's all."

"Alright, but remember what I told you about that shit backing up in your system and choking you to death. It's true man. Don't let it happen to you." He laughed. He could have at least waited for payday to tease me again.

Al wrote me a letter and thanked me for the pot that I didn't send. I imagined it was hard to go through whatever he was experiencing. He should've still been in traction and unable to get away to take a few tokes anyway. I did notice that the VA Hospital he last wrote me from was located in Pennsylvania and not in upstate N.Y. He was still in good spirits though and that's what encouraged me the most. Remembering the fun we had together before they were shot made being around so many Ruff Puffs again almost unbearable. It was nearly impossible for me to get over the incident. I hated them enough to just start shooting until they were all dead. At least if I killed them, Charlie wouldn't be able to pick up their weapons and use them against us. Hopefully one day I'd be able to get over the shooting the way that both Al and Katta had done.

The Stars and Stripes ran a small story about the Black Panthers announcing their plans to start training troops to fight against us in Vietnam. After listening to Hannah for the last several months, I knew bullshit propaganda when I heard it. Nothing could have been dumber than for them to come over to Vietnam to get killed. North Vietnam, as evidenced by Dat, was putting out some pretty good troops without any outside infusion. I didn't think for one minute that N.Vietnam would even entertain their offer of assistance. Of course I didn't believe the Panthers were seriously offering their help either. The war in Vietnam had only provided them with another propaganda opportunity. There were lots of black troops in Vietnam that identified with their struggle but those of us involved in the actual combat roles were just fighting for our lives. As for me, I just wanted to always think of them as a group of brave black men who stood up for the underprivileged blacks of the inner city; not as American mercenaries who died for N.Vietnam.

Our turn had come around for ambush again. Hugle was looking forward to it with a lot of enthusiasm. All he talked about was going out and coming back with that morning high. "Handy, Jahret just stopped me and you won't believe what he told me." He said changing the mood.

"Tell me anyway."

"He commended me on the job I had been doing and said that if I kept up the good work, I just might get that undesirable discharge."

"What's so unbelievable about that? That was all that they ever offered anyway, right?"

"Yeah but I told him that I didn't believe him because if he was that sincere, he would have promoted you by now. I also told him that if you or anybody else in Charlie Co. had to be in the field as long as you have without a CIB, then I didn't have too much to expect from him."

"Well then just why are you here?"

"Because you guys are cool."

"Cool! Is that all? You're risking your life waiting on a bad conduct discharge because we're cool?"

"Yeah man, yeah." He said with a laugh. I wanted to just give up but I hated seeing the lifers get away with what they were doing. His making a big issue over their treatment of me was not going to make it better. Jahret and Calvin would eventually get theirs one day. Retribution has a way of working itself into every situation. Their day was coming and I knew it.

When the day finally came to an end, we left the compound and settled into a nice cozy spot to spend the night. Ambush had begun to take a little out of me every time we went out. The moonless nights were getting darker and they even seemed longer. It made me realize just why the guys went through that "Last Guard" routine. Being alone at the post at midnight used to be my part of the arrangement. When stand to came around, I looked at my current squad members and remembered that I had become everything to them as those guys were to me.

Mrs. Wheelhouse sent me both a care package and another very painful letter that had me close to tears again. It was near the time that her son was supposed to come home. She said that she was willing to part with him for a year but not for an eternity. She also said that her grief had her going out of her mind. Again she added that she felt forsaken by the tragic turn of events. She wrote of how much she was struggling to hold on and likened her plight to that of someone holding onto a sinking ship. My heart was aching for her and besides that hopeless feeling that consumed me every time I read another one of her letters; I was beginning to feel angry. It angered me that someone who believed in her faith as much as she did had to experience as much disappointment. She felt that her prayers would have been all that was needed to bring her son home alive. Although it had only been four months since her son was killed, I was beginning to feel as if she would never recover from her tragedy. To make matters worse, she was still putting her problem in the hands of her savior to deliver her from the despair she was locked into. This was, of course, same savior that she felt forsaken by. Again, there was nothing I could do for her and it made me feel useless. A painful lesson was being learned from our correspondence. I was learning to never put too much into something as potentially misleading as spirituality. For the rest of my tour in Vietnam, I would only have faith in my own abilities and those of the guys around me to get me out of the war alive. In the end, I would only have the guys, Mrs. Wheelhouse and Barbara to thank for delivering me from it all. There were already tens of thousands of weeping mothers back in the world struggling to cope with losing their sons in the war. I didn't have to imagine what they were going through. Mrs. Wheelhouse had given me a personal insight into their grief. The sad irony of it all was that had her son made it back home alive, she would have thanked God; thanked him for answering her prayers, and for the rest of her life she would have testified to the power of prayer and the glory of God. She was lost in an uncertain cycle that had already failed to produce for her. She, like so many other praying mothers, had never asked God for anything else before. She was confident that she would be rewarded because all she wanted was for her son to live and was probably willing to cut her life short if it meant seeing him return alive. She asked me to forgive her for pouring her heart out but she never had to worry about it. I was willing to deal with whatever she wrote. It was the least I could do from where I was sitting. I was more than willing to accept the pain and the agony that came with our correspondence.

As the supplies continued to come in, a shocking news report came over the radio. In San Rafael California during a trial, a daring attempt at snatching a convict defendant in the middle of his court proceedings had been thwarted by the police in a shootout. The judge, who was taken hostage and used as a shield for safe passage, was killed along with two convicts and a third accomplice who smuggled the guns into the courtroom. It seemed as dangerous back in the world as it was in Vietnam. The defendant was one of the Black Panthers. Their movement was stronger than I thought. The news, as usual, was shocking to me only. The guys around me were only concerned with resupply. "If y'all want some Royal Crown, I got some in the bunker." said Brown. All of the confusion along with the news report had diverted my attention just long enough to miss noticing Brown hauling a case of Royal Crown sodas in the bunker.

"Did I hear correctly?" Lee asked.

"Did he say that he's got some Royal Crown in the bunker?" Benn asked. Realizing what an occasion it was to finally be able to have a soda, compliments of the old guzzler himself, we ran inside to get ourselves a can. We searched the bunker but couldn't find the case of sodas. "Brown is bullshitting us. Ain't no damn sodas in this bunker." Benn complained as Brown returned to the bunker and took a seat.

"Say Brown, where's the RC?" I asked. He got up, grabbed a small cardboard can and handed it to me. "Help yourself." he said. It was Royal Crown hair grease. As the three of us stood there with the hair grease staring at each other, we could feel one of those big laughing fits about to consume us. "OK, let's go finish helping with the resupply." I said as we fought our way out of the door to keep from laughing in Brown's presence. We made it outside just in time to greet another noisy slick that drowned out our laughter. I guess Brown thought we looked a little dry at the top. I hadn't seen that brand in years and didn't know that it was still in production. Brown was a riot and he didn't even know it. I hoped he wouldn't get offended when Charles and Lemar turned him down. As for me, I didn't even comb my hair so he shouldn't have expected me to use any of that greasy kid stuff.

When our turn to go out on ambush came around again, Modell did the honors and led us on patrol. After he chose a spot relatively close to the compound for ambush, we started the guard rotation. After I turned the guard shift over to him, he wrapped himself up in his poncho liner and went to sleep at the post. I shook him and redundantly mentioned the poncho liner puller over his head. "I know. I'm awake." He said from inside his cocoon.

"Modell, wake up man. You're talking in your sleep. You've still got the poncho liner over your head. You can't see shit." I whispered aloud.

"Look Handy, would you please go to sleep and leave me alone!" He said as he turned over in disgust. I assumed that maybe it was just another scene from that weird movie that needed a change in script. I walked over to my gear, exchanged my HE round for a buckshot round and returned to Modell's spot. Then I kicked him in his butt and pointed my weapon at his head. "He always does that on guard." Someone whispered in the background.

"He won't be doing it tonight." I said while standing over him with my M-79 still pointed at his head. Rather than challenging me any further, Modell quickly sat up to pull guard. For the rest of his shift at the post I waited for him to nod off again but nothing happened.

After ambush, I said nothing about the poncho liner episode. I would have handled the matter the same way no matter who was trying to catch a few winks on guard. As far as I was concerned, the incident was history. I couldn't believe, however, that the other guys were aware of his sleeping on guard, or even worse, that they were letting him get away with it. There was a little too much respect for rank if it meant that he could sleep on guard without any fear of consequences. I would have shot him full of holes if he wouldn't have moved fast enough. He never could have made it very long in Vietnam back in '68.

I was still puzzled by the puke on the ground near Mac's bunker. I asked him about the fresh puddle near his door. He said it was Mad Dog and Hugle. They were junkies. His revelation explained it all. Mad Dog had tried to live back in the world shooting that 3% heroin available on the streets and Hugle was in no hurry to test the market. So, one came back for another tour and the other was just trying to stay as long as he could.

Mad Dog, being from the mean streets of Detroit, should have known better. Hugle was from somewhere in Virginia and seemed too smart to even let something like that happen to him. At least, I didn't think he should have. It was obviously the reason the two of them kept disappearing together. I figured it was to get high but not to do heroin. It also explained why Hugle kept getting caught at the opium den. He was probably one of those guys who took full advantage of Linda and Monique's free skag giveaway. He was probably sitting and nodding every time the MP's made their sweep. Once those guys go into one of their drug-induced stupors, they became vulnerable to anything. He had to be as easy a bust as any MP ever had. It also exposed the Army's insensitivity to his condition. He was known to be strung out yet they sent him over to our company as a last chance at redemption. In return, they offer him the remote possibility of getting a bad conduct discharge. He made a dumb decision to start using but his habit was his illness and sending him home in his condition seemed cruel and indifferent. Treating him for his addiction, must have been a little to much to expect from the Army. Instead they ignored his condition and just sent him back to the field for the remainder of his tour. Hugle and Mad Dog were in for a rough life. Once America's involvement in the war ended, there would be no access to the pure grade of heroin available in Vietnam. The life of a junkie was all too familiar to me. I had witnessed the ritual performed by some of my friends in New Orleans. The addiction is a vicious cycle of acquisition and injection that could either put them in a cell, a hospital bed or a coffin.

Payday finally came around again and, as expected, every hooker near and far descended on our area and quickly dried up most of the available funds. Howard couldn't believe that I let the girls get away without sampling their wares. He was beginning to think that something was wrong with me. Nobody in his right mind would go without sex for any extended period unless he was out of cash I suppose. He and the rest of the out of control libidos on the compound had to wait a considerable amount of time before either one of them could do anything. Of course I had money all along and that was the difference or the insanity rather.

Later that day, while sitting atop of my bunker with Morse and Lee, a dog appeared between the wires that formed our perimeter. He was prancing around within the space containing all of the trip flares and Claymore mines. There was nothing we could do but watch him and hope he would be able to get out without hitting a flare. I was sure that no one wanted to go reset any of that stuff. The thought of going into that miniature no man's land was scary.

Suddenly someone fired a shot at the dog. The bullet grazed the animal's back severing his spine and rendering his hind legs paralyzed. He was howling in pain and dragging his motionless legs behind

237

him until he came to a halt and quickly died. "All right now who's going to go get him before he starts rotting out there?" I asked in anger because the dog managed to crawl all the way over to the sector in front of our bunker before he died. Within 24 hours the dog would become our problem and neither one of us shot him.

Before my anger level could get any higher, Biggie Rat approached the wire and climbed over into the area near the dead dog. He carefully avoided all of the wires and Claymores to get to the animal. He picked up the dog by his hind paws and returned to the wire without disturbing any of the trips. After climbing back over the wire he took the dead dog into his bunker. "I guess the ARVN's will be eating dog tonight." Howard laughed.

"Very funny." I said.

"No, seriously. He's the mess Sergeant." Morse said.

"You mean Bigies's actually the cook."

"Yes he is." He said as I realized that it was probably Biggie who shot the dog. Howard wasn't joking at all. The locals actually did eat dogs and, I supposed a tabby every now and then. It was one dish that I wouldn't be sampling.

The day came to an end before I saw the patrol leave the compound. Either darkness crept up on us all and caught them by surprise, or they left through the other exit. When I remembered that Weiss was taking the patrol out I figured that they must have already left. Weiss would never be out after dark patrolling around the village.

The lifers retired to their quarters after dark and the new practice of smoking pot on the compound continued at the gun placement. In spite of my reservations about smoking on the compound, I couldn't resist the opportunity. When the cat's away, the mice do play. "Those guys never left the compound you know." said Kostrewva.

"What guys?"

"Weiss's ambush squad. They're still here faking it."

"Really! Where's that fucking Weiss? I asked. I couldn't resist teasing him when I knew he couldn't say anything. I searched the compound until I found him hiding in one of the bunkers. I blew some marijuana smoke in his face and walked away. I couldn't make too much of an issue of it because I didn't want to offend the guys who was in his squad. I also realized that pulling a fake ambush was nothing new in Charlie Co. I suppose that every one of us had pulled at least one before. I have definitely been in different locations from our reported grid on a number of locations. In fact, our old squad was famous for it.

The following morning as I was working my short-timers calendar I realized that unfolding and refolding the thing would eventually cause it to fall apart at the creases. I put it in an envelope to be sent home to Barbara to finish for me. I wanted to make sure that I had the little souvenir for the rest of my life. As of that moment I had 111 days left in country and it looked good on paper to be closing in on double digits. Once I could see the end of pacification, I would really feel comfortable then.

Weiss's fake ambush went pretty smooth that night. In fact, it went too smooth. It was particularly disturbing the way that nobody saw them return from ambush and no questions were asked. The lifers were unusually accommodating when they chose to be. I didn't think any other squad could have gotten away with it. Of course the other night when Modell was trying to go to sleep on guard, we were extremely close to the compound. It was almost as if we didn't go out at all. We did, however, leave the compound and therein was the difference. Some of those Shake and Bakes were only into wearing the stripes. Leadership qualities had nothing to do with their roles as squad leaders. I'd seen better leaders as a member of the Boy Scouts. Going out on ambush always exposed the pretenders. Weiss was officially exposed as a big phony and he knew it. Modell, as should have been expected, never was considered to even be a pretender. "Who sent the care package man? Was it your mom?" asked Hugle who had became curious about the sender and surprised at the generosity I displayed when it arrived. "It was sent by the mother of one of our former members who was killed at Tuy Hoa. She is, coincidentally, from your home state of Virginia. A place called Virginia Beach. Have you ever heard of it?"

"Hell yeah. I've even been there before. Man, you talk about a small world." he said before he put a familiar look on his face. This time I knew he was about to do the Hendrix/Joplin thing. I answered each question in advance of him asking. He actually looked astonished. He was shocked that I knew every question he was about to ask. When it came to the end where he declared he would buy all of their albums I confronted him. "What about the skag man? I mean face it. If you're still on that shit, about the only thing that you will be interested in buying will be some of that weak shit being sold back in the world. Your love for Jimi and JJ will take a back seat to your habit." I said taking the chance of alienating him. I couldn't pretend not to know about his habit any longer. I had already been fooled for weeks. It was inevitable that I would have found out. Of course as a head there was very little I could say to him along the anti drug use side of the issue. I only wanted to express my concern about his health and his future without sounding judgmental.

With a shrug of his shoulders, he managed to express both surprise and relief. He was surprised about my knowledge of his habit and relieved that he didn't have to continue the charade. I was surprised by his response and, in a strange way, flattered that he tried to conceal his activity from me. I didn't realize he was going through so much to keep up the illusion.

"I think I'll stop when I get back to the world." He said unconvincingly.

"You think it will be that easy?"

"I'll find out." He laughed attempting to downplay the significance of being a heroin addict. If he really thought he could get that monkey off of his back that easily, he was in for a terrible letdown. Of all the junkies back home that I knew, none of them ever just quit. Some of them got arrested for possession or shoplifting but none of them ever quit. As for me, the pot was just fine. I knew the stuff would never control me the way skag would.

The jokes and rumors about Jahret were running wild. Of course, I was so caught up with his poor performance as a platoon leader that I never even bothered to entertain any of the inferences. There was never any testimony about anything, only rumors. My only concern was to make sure that he didn't get me killed first.

Doc was scheduled to return on the next resupply but first we had to do another ambush. Harrington was supposed to lead us out but we were delayed by Lee. He was ill and it was getting late. It was expected to be a problem because nobody wanted to go out on their night off. It would've been like pulling your own teeth and it would also mean that you would have to go out three nights in a row. Lee's illness was about to ruin someone's night because the lifers would not look for volunteers. They would order someone to go in his place.

Jahret designated Mac to take Lee's place and, as expected, Mac was not too thrilled about the selection. He flat out refused to go in his place and he expected to get burned for doing so. I had to admire the way he stood his ground though. He was adamant about it and was ready to accept the punishment for his refusal. This would only make me hate Jahret even more if it was possible. I hoped

Lee would get better soon because I didn't want to go through the same thing two nights later. Assuredly, I'd rather go out feeling sick than to put anyone else through any of that. It just wasn't worth it. Big Goose took Lee's place and we finally left.

When we got back, I sought out Mac to find out what the lifers had planned for him. "It might cost me that car that I was saving for but other than that, I'll be alright." he said. Too bad something had to happen to him because he was a real cool guy. At least Jahret learned that a soldier like Mac, who never made any trouble, would stand up to him whenever he thought he needed to. It felt great to be with Mac and people like him.

When resupply started, I noticed the latest issue of the Stars and Stripes had a story of the daring hostage situation in that California courthouse a few days earlier. There was a picture of the prisoner holding a shotgun taped to the side of the judge's head. The picture was more shocking than the report was back when it happened. It was almost as if it were happening all over again. The revolution phenomenon appeared bigger than I had imagined. I had only been gone for eight months as the new decade had managed to get off on the same tumultuous footing as the preceding one.

Doc returned to the fold and said that the other half of the platoon, as we suspected, wasn't garrisoned on a compound like we were. They were instead making the best of what they had to work with. He said that Kyler was in rare form. Being away from his nemesis "The Hunter" was doing wonders for him. Being in the same village situation we were in earlier had no ill effect on them. They had adapted to the surroundings and were making an impact on the village and the villagers as well. I supposed that I was the only member of the platoon with any reservations about pacification. The others seemed to enjoy being in a village as opposed to humping the boonies. A lot of them hadn't been in country long enough to experience the other side of the coin and never experienced what a nightmare it could become.

Later that day, while strolling through the village looking for a secluded spot for a bowel movement, I found Howard sitting atop a dried up well smoking a joint. At least I hoped it was no longer in use because he had his pants down and was using it for a toilet. He confirmed that it was dry because he never heard any splash. He said he had been using it for a while and that it was his second well. The last one was probably attracting too many flies for him. He offered the use of his new spot but I declined and moved on in search of my own. Howard's ingenuity gave me a good indication of how I probably caught dysentery drinking well water though. The things were wide open to sabotage. Charlie could've even thrown a dead animal into one of them. After my experience with the malady, I stopped drinking from them. Being able to walk around and select a nice secluded spot to relieve myself was a luxury. With the trots, every bowel movement became an adventure.

I found a spot where some large trees were growing in a bowl-like depression in the ground. Upon closer inspection the depression was more like a gulley with the trees on the inner rim. The limbs from the trees were lush with leaves and provided me with perfect cover. Charlie could have never walked up on me from that spot. We could've possibly used the other rim for an ambush site on another date I thought. As I dropped my pants I spotted a couple of women passing nearby. I remembered how low I was on piaster and figured that maybe it would be a good idea to at least find out if they were interested in doing a little money exchange so I interrupted the bowel movement and approached them. With no Ruff Puffs around, it would be perfect if they were willing and also carrying some cash. "Mama San, Mama San, Ladei, Ladei, I said as I emerged from the cover of the trees limbs. The two women kept walking. I walked a little closer and called them again. This time one of them ran and the other one just stood still. I approached the lone woman who was standing looking at me in a most disapproving manner. "What's the matter with her?" I asked hoping that she could speak a little English.

"She scare of GI that all." she said which demonstrated enough understanding of the language for me.

"Well, I don't mean any harm; I just wanted to know if either of you want to exchange some piaster for MPC but I seem to have scared the living daylights out of your friend." I explained.

"She don know that." she said.

"But look at her. She's still running." I said pointing to the terrified woman as she continued to put some distance between us.

"Well, a cuppa year ago, GI, same same you, call mama san to bushes, same same you, and GI did mama san a number ten." She explained meaning that she was lured to the bushes and was raped. I couldn't blame her for running for her life. My coming out of the bushes only created a re-visitation of the attack in her traumatized mind. It didn't help the situation to have my pants almost down when I called them either. I was embarrassed to be in the situation and I should have realized how I must have looked to her. The subject of GI's raping women in Vietnam was a shameful reality of our presence in the war. I felt awful for having reminded her of her humiliation. I wished that there was some way that she could get over it and not have to live in terror. Unfortunately, it would never happen as long as we were still there to remind her of her attack. The other woman wanted to exchange the money but was afraid of what the Ruff Puffs would do if they found out. I thanked her for her time and returned to the compound. The Ruff Puffs were nothing but a bunch of cowardly thugs. They knew we were partially paid in piaster but kept the villagers from making any deals for our remaining MPC. They also knew that we would never agree to their exchange rate, which made their stranglehold on the villagers senseless.

The mysterious Bracey came out on the following resupply day to initiate his out processing. He was on his way back to LA. His ordeal back in April had given him a most peculiar status for the remainder of his tour. I was still angry with him for faking a heat exhaustion and leaving me to carry that can of M-60 ammo. I heard that when the helicopter brought him back to Uplift, he was practically dancing as he stepped off of the helicopter. His miraculous recovery made me wonder how those ghosters could live with themselves. They just didn't have the conscience of most others. They were no more afraid than the rest of us were but couldn't bring themselves to participate when they could easily get out of it. I guess it was a matter of pride. Not in what we were doing in Vietnam, just the way we wanted to be remembered by each other. The guys in the field really cared about what we thought about each other.

After Bracey came out of CP, I stopped him and asked him if he still had my boonie pipe. I loaned it to him months earlier but he claimed he lost it. Even in his conversation he remained as distant from us as he always thought he needed to be. Leaving Vietnam was only a mere formality to him. As for the rest of us, he had already left long ago. In spite of our different opinions, views on life and my disappointment over losing my pipe to him, I gave him some dap and bade him farewell. He then walked to the slick with a look of surprise. He probably never realized I knew how to do the ritual handshake that all black troops in Vietnam practice. Without a doubt, we had parted with, I was sure, similar low opinions of each other too. He probably felt I was not, in his opinion, a real brother. I, on the other hand, felt that he was lacking in even more personal qualities. The usual feeling I experienced whenever another one of us left was missing. There was no little piece of me leaving with Bracey. In fact the only thing that left with him was an honest, accurate, account of exactly what happened on that hill in Tuy Hoa on April 1ˢᵗ. As painful as it would be, I would give my life to know exactly what happened and if it had to happen the way it did. I knew for sure that I would continue to have problems with the story I had been told. I couldn't even say that I hoped that Bracey would find any closure. I was having enough problems on my own.

The following morning there was a possible residue effect lingering after my talk with Bracey. It had me thinking about that firefight the rest of the evening and that night I was awakened from sleep by a nightmare. It was a tormenting re-visitation of the firefight from the perspective of the guys who were on that hill. In the dream I was somehow in the middle of the confrontation but in the weird, complex occurrence that dreams are, I was also a non-participant. I was actually there with those guys but they never saw me. They were exchanging fire, but I wasn't even armed. I knew they were going to lose their lives but I couldn't warn them of their impending doom. The eventual death of the first guy was enough to wake me from my suspended state of torment. It seemed both very real and, at the same time, very weird. It was by far the weirdest experience I'd ever had. My heartbeat was at the same accelerated rate it was that night in April and had me sweating. When I did wake up I was breathing like someone who just ran a mile. The nightmare ended quickly but, like all firefights, it felt like an eternity. Those B-40 rockets were flying everywhere but never exploded denying me of the loud noise that would have awakened me sooner. The air was full of smoke that just lingered and camouflaged the enemy making his job of shooting at those guys easier. The sky was dotted with countless parachute flares that rocked side to side and never quite made it to the ground. The sight of those shadows swaying back and forth again was still very frightening and realistic. Afterward as I sat atop my bunker reliving the dream, I wondered how close I came to losing my mind in my sleep. I feared having the dream again and maybe actually going insane. I hadn't been getting much sleep in Phu My and the nightmare made me feel that it was best. Maybe, I thought, I was better off as a hopeless insomniac who was as afraid of losing his mind as well as his life. Although Bracey's departure was not much of an event to hardly anybody else in the field, just seeing him might have triggered that nightmare.

Bargas was surprisingly awarded a rear job. He was acting as if he'd won a sweepstakes or something. I know he had no idea what it would be like to be in the rear permanently. He had been a boonie rat since he first arrived and a pretty good one too. He did seem relieved to be tapped on the shoulder for the appointment. As long as he was happy about going back to Uplift I was glad to see him go. It's not the same as watching someone leave for home, but we'll miss having the little guy around. He was an inspiration to us all when he was humping a rucksack that was almost as big as he was and probably weighed more. He never once ran out of stamina and his attitude was always positive.

As the time neared for us to go out again, I was hoping for everything to go smoothly. Lee was feeling well and was ready to go. Charles was getting his gear together and so was Brown. Howard was standing with the two of us when we were joined by Mad Dog. He normally didn't go out with us and we were very surprised to see him geared up for the trip on what should have been his night off. His being with us for that night would make him have to go out the following night also and he wasn't complaining. "C'mon, let's go." He said as he walked past us toward the exit.

"Just as soon as we get a squad leader, if you don't mind."

"I'm taking the patrol out tonight."

"But you're no squad leader."

"Jahret wants me to take the squad out tonight." He said completing an odd picture. Every black guy on the compound, minus Swain, was on this patrol. There were no whites at all and to make matters worse, the lifers had turned the reins over to Mad Dog. If they were trying to send a message to us by sending us all out on ambush collectively, it was reading loud and clear.

To avoid looking like a bunch of scared individuals lacking confidence in ourselves we left with a bad taste in our mouths. The incident would not be forgotten. I didn't know whether or not to complain about being on an all black patrol. I started off with literally an all white squad back in the Crow's foot. I doubt if any of those guys were complaining about not having any black guys in their squad before I came over. All I could remember was that they were not complaining about having me aboard and did not ostracize me at all. Our all black patrol, however, was of a different nature. We were all placed together for the purpose of going out on ambush as an all black squad and nothing else. Would it mean that there would be all white squads going out every other night? Would it be in bad taste if I complained about Mad Dog's appointment? Who would I complain to anyway? It seemed useless to complain to the assholes that came up with the idea to send us out together. Whatever I decided to do would have to be done when we returned. It was late and we had to leave the compound.

Our search for that ideal spot for the night took us to an unappealing area. Rather than cause any more problems than we were faced with already, I kept my opinion to myself. Mad Dog, whose appointment never did rate that high with the rest of the patrol, gave the command to deploy the Claymores. Detecting an unwillingness to obey by the others, I almost immediately started unrolling the wire to place my Claymore along the perimeter first. My intention was to hope for some of that "follow the example" stuff to start working its magic. The last thing we needed to happen to us was to fail from lack of co operation. We needed to complete the mission first and then complain later. The rest of the guys quietly deployed the Claymores then instinctively gathered in a circle around the neatly positioned plungers and waited for Mad Dog to assign the rotation of guard shifts, just like we always did. "Everybody go to sleep, I'm pulling guard all night by myself." He said with a smile on his face. His idea of ambush was not going over too big with the rest of the group. Lee sighed in despair, and Charles gave him a look of contempt. "Mad Dog, are you crazy?" Howard asked as he stood. Nobody was moving until Mad Dog changed his mind about the guard rotation. "Howard, you take first guard; Lee you've got the second; Benn third; Brown fourth; Mad Dog you're fifth, and I'll take last guard. We'll all do 90 minute shifts and do a stand to for the remaining time until the sun comes up or whenever we choose to leave." I said.

"What? You just takin' over just like that? Who do you think you are?" Mad Dog asked.

"I'm last guard and you're fifth. That's one hour and a half. Wake me up on time." I said as everybody else retired for the night. He didn't like it but his appointment lost out to the example. It always did work out better that way.

When we returned to the compound and started walking through the zigzag, I noticed that the rest of the guys were waiting for us. Some were livid about the segregated ambush and their anger was very evident when we were reunited. Kostrewva was so angry and apologetic that I thought he was going to hurt someone just to make his feelings known. "I told those mother fuckers they better not try doing anything like that again!" He said angrily. I had never seen the guy that angry before. I noticed that the rest of the guys were pretty upset about the "Soul Patrol" also. The lifers were nowhere in sight. I obviously didn't have to say anything about the issue because the guys had already weighed in with their opinion. I still felt confused about what Jahret was trying to prove, but it was nice to see it backfire in his face. The outcome made me feel very fortunate to be with the kind of guys I had assembled around me. The Herd was without a doubt the premier unit when it came to race relations within the troops.

Nothing could ever divide us along those lines. Jahret was wasting his time playing us against each other. There was too much togetherness in this group to ever let something as ugly as that happen to us. Jahret lost a lot respect by sending out that patrol. I didn't expect to see him try it again.

I started to ask Howard's boy "Killer Swain" why he didn't volunteer to take us out on that all black patrol but it would have been inflammatory. Besides, Swain was already having enough problems walking that line. As much as I resented Jahret for that ambush I wouldn't bother to even go over to him to say anything about it. Nothing other than maybe "kiss my ass."

I was expecting something from Bargas on our first resupply with him in the rear but there was nothing that time. Some guys forget the guys in the field once they accept rear jobs. Bargas would be the exception though. He was expected to remember us occasionally with a case of sodas or two. He would definitely be looking forward to being reunited with the guys on our next return to Uplift too. On an earlier stand down, I remember watching the brothers in the first platoon give a former member of their group a real hard time. They felt he was trying to distance himself from his former mates because of his new duties and were offended by his actions. Bargas would never get too far away from us and he would always be remembered for being the kind of guy he was. Maybe, I hoped, we would get those sodas on the following resupply.

During the resupply, one of the slicks had a passenger inside of it. It was Anderson. He had been with the other half of the platoon. Doc informed me that he was on his way to the hospital again. I never found out what was wrong with him that first time he left us. His new condition was also a mystery to me. That first ailment actually saved his life. Hopefully he'd be returning to the fold before long or maybe he would be going back to the world early. Having done eight months already there was nothing more for him to do but return to the field as one of those short timers cursed with trepidation. He had served long enough to have fulfilled his obligation to America's grand exercise in futility and was scheduled to leave with me which was exactly 106 days and counting. Pretty soon I expected to be in double digits and would be counting down those last few days in country. I could almost smell Mom's chicken gumbo and had already written her asking for a care package from home. "Handy, there won't be any ambush squad going out tonight." said Hugle.

"Great. I didn't feel like going out on ambush anyway."

"Actually there will be a patrol going out tonight but it will be a killer patrol."

"What in the hell is a killer patrol?"

"You know how Recon or the Rangers do with six man teams patrolling at night. We're gonna have six volunteers doing that shit. Aint that wild man."

"Yeah it's wild alright. I like the part about volunteering for the patrol. Because I aint volunteering for shit."

"Well, I kinda like volunteered you for the patrol."

"You kinda like volunteered me to go out with them? Isn't that like the Pope being kinda like Catholic? Man I don't like going out there when it is my turn. I can't believe you did that."

" Aw c'mon man, it will be fun. We'll be wearing camouflage paint on our faces. We'll have the starlight scope; we'll be constantly patrolling and we…"

"Fun my ass. I tell you what. Bring your ass over there to CP and unvolunteer me from that shit pronto. I'm staying on this compound tonight." My demands did little to change his mind as he kept begging me until I gave in. "I promise that I won't volunteer either one of us for any more patrols again." He said unconvincingly after I agreed to go on the patrol. Heroin is more dangerous than I thought.

The stuff must have been eating away all of his brain cells. Of course after agreeing to go with him I must have been in need of some help myself. I just wasn't ready to go through another firefight where my buddies were bleeding to death as we sat and let it happen again. What I really needed to realize was that I could not babysit Hugle and he needed to realize that he shouldn't continue to risk his life unnecessarily.

The killer patrol must have been Harrington's idea because Hugle ran over to him with the news of my committal. I couldn't think of anyone else who would even try to do pull it off. When it's over I planned to sit down and have a real long serious talk with Hugle about his reckless abandon. At times, he seemed totally out of touch with reality and maybe the tendency came with heroin use. I was no authority on the subject and couldn't even make a guess.

We waited for total darkness before we even assembled to leave the compound. Then we sat in a circle smearing the black and green paint on our faces as the reality started to set in. Maybe it was the darkness and the thought of patrolling at night. Maybe it was the sight of some of the other members of the patrol who should have known better than go out on that mission. I could have been a Ranger but I turned down the opportunity to become one because I didn't like the six man concept. Yet I was about to go out in a six man team and aggressively pursue Charlie. I must have been as crazy as Hugle was to have let him talk me into doing it. He had a starlight scope mounted atop of his M-16 and was as happy as a kid with a new toy. He was going to be walking point which would only expose him to more danger. In spite of his drug habit and all of the trouble it had gotten him into, he remained the same thrill seeker that he probably always was.

When Harrington gave us the signal to move out, Hugle started off by slinking his way through the zigzag and quickly ran to the cover of the nearest tree line. Everybody followed his lead one at a time until we had all assembled in the tree line to start out patrol. While patrolling we avoided all open spaces and stayed close to every row of bushes, crawled through some thick garden of an undetermined crop and hugged every tree line we came across. Of course, we were all rookies at it and were following our instincts. Since we all had the same training, there were no unusual expectations of ourselves. Hugle was doing a fine job of walking point. Occasionally, we stopped to scan the area; or rather allowed him to use the scope to see what he could find.

We patrolled for a while stopping occasionally for observation. Whenever we came to a stop, we deployed ourselves in a defensive perimeter while Harrington conferred with Jahret over the horn. During one stop, Hugle spotted a small animal, possibly a rabbit, running away from us. He first aimed at the little critter as if he was about to shoot it and then he continued to lead us further along his randomly selected route. With three hours under our belt and nothing to show for it, I was starting to get bored and sleepy. The killer patrol was about the most insane thing I had done since arriving. I enjoyed going through most of my tour without any encounters with the enemy and only wanted to pass the time counting my precious days.

Suddenly I heard a thump coming from the direction of the compound. The familiar low whistle of an incoming round gave me a bad feeling. A mortar round was drawing a bead on us as we were poised huddled behind the bushes. Then a loud pop went off overhead as a parachute flare opened up and lit up the sky exposing our location. Someone on the compound had illuminated our area with a flare. The mortar placement belonged to the Ruff Puffs and could have only been fired by one of them. The only question was why. Sgt Harrington got on the horn immediately to find out what went wrong. He was speaking in whispers but after that flare went off he might as well have been shouting. Our attempt at stealth had been totally compromised. We were left with no other option but returning to the compound. The killer patrol was over.

The flare was, according to Jahret's story, a mistake. The explanation came with a useless apology and the promise that it wouldn't happen again. They didn't have to worry about it happening to me again. Not on some stupid killer patrol anyway. I had my own suspicions about what actually happened. I felt as if Charlie had radio contact with those little bastards on the compound and probably called in for that flare because they lost visual contact with us. Hell, after that story Hughes told me about what happened to him in Tuy Hoa, any thing was possible. One of those ARVNs might have been Charlie's inside man and maybe it was him that fired that round. I could only hope that we would be leaving Phu My soon. Once my paranoia started working on this new theory, I could have easily gone insane.

As for losing it all, Lee thought that I had already lost it. I had to agree with him too. I had no business going out there. It was a complete departure from who I really was. Lee never would have done anything as foolish as that. He had a lot to live for and wanted very much to see his kids grow up. It seemed unimaginable to be in Vietnam with a family of my own. Of course, I did have a mother and a lot of brothers and sisters who had kids but a wife and kids of my own would have been a different story.

Walkup informed me that I had to go on ambush again, which would make it three nights in a row. The decision to go on that killer patrol was about to haunt me. Hugle, on the other hand, would be staying behind. It seemed that the rotation would continue the way it was in spite of the previous night's deviation.

"Man this is going to be my third consecutive night on ambush." I told Hugle.

"Bummer man." He deadpanned.

"Look, don't even think about this bullshit again."

"Handy, have you ever heard of Hendrix?" He asked me again. His delivery was disarming and took away a lot of the anger I had about going out again. Getting angry at him was a waste of emotions. He probably wouldn't have noticed any change in my demeanor. It had to be the heroin. I couldn't imagine why he kept asking me the same weird battery of questions.

"No but JJ sounds just like a sister to me. What do you think?"

"Yes, she does. Man when I get back to the world, I'm gonna buy everything they ever recorded."

"Lay off the killer patrols and you just might make it." I said before preparing to go out again.

Walkup did the honors for the first time in a while. It didn't bother him to go out on consecutive nights. He was eager to impress the lifers with his zeal. During the killer patrol he really wanted to get some action. He wanted to make a career in the Army and Vietnam was no deterrent to him. Sometimes I wondered if he realized how hazardous our job was. Telling him wouldn't change his attitude about it either. He just wanted to make rank and in the worst way. He was willing to die trying for that third stripe and I was afraid that he just might.

Ambush started off in the usual manner without any of the added drama of a killer patrol. Our squad was soon straddled alongside a trail as we all slept inside of a patch with some small melons growing in some very powdery soil. It was the most unusual configuration we had ever slept in. Our position was concealed from the trail by a row of bushes that was about three feet high. The trail straddled the melon patch and we had the post situated at one end of the trail. Suddenly we heard footsteps running past us as we were lying along the trail behind the bushes. Then there were two successive explosions. Two Claymores had been detonated and sent everyone scrambling for their weapons. "What happened?" I asked Ellis as he was still at the post pulling his shift. "A gook sneaked up from behind me and put his face about this close to me and then ran away before I could get my weapon." he said breathing heavily as he held his hand in front of his nose. Unbelievably, Charlie had sneaked up and eyeballed him momentarily from a distance of about six inches and ran away without getting fired upon. Ellis managed to blow a couple of claymores and scared the hell out of the rest of us but Charlie got away clean and was probably having a bigger laugh than we did over the incident. Ellis was a great sport and would take his teasing in stride. Of course none of us were about to get too carried away with putting him down over the incident. Our adversary was just that competent and daring. He would and usually did anything to frustrate us. It was very funny though. We did manage to continue our ambush and returned to the compound the following morning minus two Claymores.

Later that day while sitting around the rat hole, I was going over the most recent issue of the Stars & Stripes. While reading the paper, a helicopter landed with old Rudy again. I hoped he didn't have any more of those gadgets. I'd have to find a way to report him to the SPCA if he got another dog killed. I heard a rumor that he was going home soon. This story had him down to his last week in country or something like that. He disembarked and headed straight over to CP. As he passed us by, Brown emerged from the bunker wearing all of his gear and carrying his weapon. He headed for the same slick that Rudy had just stepped off of. I didn't remember hearing anything about him going anywhere. He walked past the guys unloading the supplies and managed to get onto the slick before it lifted off. The scene was somewhat reminiscent of his arrival. I had a feeling that Brown had just taken matters into his own hands and decided he'd had enough. "Did you see that shit?" Ben asked.

"Yeah, I'll bet the lifers don't know anything about it either."

"We'll just let them find out on their own." He said. I knew that sooner or later Brown would push the issue. I just wondered how long it would take for the lifers to notice he was gone.

Rudy took off through the other exit with the interpreter, Spurlock and Dat in tow. I felt it was better them than any of us. After his last visit, I wasn't sure if I wanted to be in on anymore of those half baked ideas from Brigade headquarters either.

Resupply ended without any slick returning Brown to the field. He obviously stepped off of the helicopter at Uplift as unnoticed as he was when he got on. Someone like Brown should have never been drafted. He possibly never knew about the draft or heard of the war in Vietnam until they came to get him. Realistically, if a guy can't read, how can they expect him to decipher his draft notice. He probably used it for toiled tissue when it came. They could never get him to fight because he wanted no part of the war and made it known to all. I expected the lifers would court martial him whenever they discovered his most recent transgression.

Suddenly someone opened fire with an AK 47. It was coming from a distance and the initial fear was that Rudy and Spurlock might be in trouble. When the sound of M-16 gunfire became mixed in an exchange, everybody went scrambling for the exits. I was caught wearing a pair of cumbersome Ho Chi Minh sandals I bought from the ARVNs. My movement was slow but the ground was so hot that I couldn't ditch my footwear. When we finally assembled outside of the compound, we started in the direction of the noise that, according to my judgment, was closing in on our location. Suddenly Rudy and Spurlock came into view on our left front. They were running in our direction in a very disorderly retreat as if at least a hundred men were chasing them. Dat and the interpreter were trailing them executing a classic fire and retreat movement. Once they spotted us coming to their aid, the two of them stood their ground and readied to make a stand. My footwear continued to give me problems but I still managed to keep up with the group. The lead element linked up with them as the rest of us fanned out to the right and formed a column. I still hadn't spotted the shooters but the sound of AK-47 gunfire was still crackling in the air. The sweep had begun in the face of some persistent shooting. They seemed to take cover in the village to our front and were in smaller numbers than I first thought. Rudy and Spurlock never stopped running. The fire and retreat movement by Dat and the interpreter was admirably performed. The mad scramble deployed by Rudy and Spurlock was shameful.

As we made a slow careful sweep through the area, the villagers were oblivious to the commotion going on around them. They continued feeding their chickens and tending their livestock as if we weren't there. Then an old woman started scolding me for stepping on her plants. All of this as we continued the sweep; trying to engage an enemy who had already opened fire on us. Their nonchalance seemed strange as they ignored all of the shooting. It was even more unusual for us to press on and not see any of them run for cover. The running, the fear and the shooting had transformed my heartbeat into a chain reaction of miniature explosions, but the villagers didn't even flinch from any of the shots.

Another burst of gunfire went of to my left front. Wherever the little bastards were, they were still shooting at the left end of our column. All of the action was going on over there. Suddenly a burst of M-16 fire opened up to my immediate right. The rounds chewed up the ground directly in front of me. I looked to my right and found Lee looking in my direction.

"What the fuck is going on." I asked, still shaken from the experience of being so close to the impact area of that volley.

"I don't know." he said standing with his still smoking gun. He must have lost control.

Everything started to quiet down. The sweep had come to an end and the shooting had stopped. Either they made a kill over on our left or Charlie got away. It was still a very tense situation as I continued to scan the area in front of me. Walkup came walking down the line in my direction with his weapon on his shoulder like a baseball bat. He said that Mad Dog returned fire and killed an old man in his home lying in his hammock. "I wonder what's going to happen to us now." I said fearing the shooting incident wouldn't go away soon. Although it wasn't like Calley's platoon at Me Lai, it seemed unlikely it would be settled as fast the two water buffaloes Al shot at Tuy Hoa. We were restricted from shooting into a village and we let Charlie sucker us into doing just that. I anticipated an investigation that would take forever because we had to cater to public opinion. Although Mad Dog had just taken away a huge portion of our credibility, no one could charge him for what he'd done though. For in the cold-hearted vernacular of the military, the old man's death would only be considered as collateral damage. Innocent people always die in wars because they often get in the way. Mad Dog may have squeezed the trigger, but I feared the entire platoon would bite the bullet along with him.

We returned to the compound with heavy hearts about the old dead Papa San. Rudy, it turned out, only made the cameo appearance to make one last try at getting him a kill. He had few war stories to tell and he knew it. His status as a REMF had taken him out of harm's way and now that his tour was almost over, he wished he had more encounters with the enemy to talk reminisce; more tall tales to tell his friends about. He used his status as NCOIC and simply arranged to come out to our location and organized his nearly disastrous patrol. It was amazing the way those two assholes managed to nearly get themselves killed in such a short period of time. They must have looked like easy pickings to Charlie. The sight of Rudy and Spurlock running for their lives reminded me of those terrified little ARVNs back at Tuy Hoa. If it weren't for Dat and the interpreter, both of them would have been killed.

The dead Papa San's adult son entered the compound. He had already talked to the lifers before walking over to our bunker where a group of us had gathered. As he approached, I could see the pain etched on his face. He was extremely grief stricken over the loss of his father and spoke softly in the limited English he had mastered. His message was short and simple. He only wanted to profess his father's non-alliance with the VC. It was a very painful moment for us too. What really angered me was that Rudy had returned to Uplift and Mad Dog was inside of his bunker. No one was around to listen to him except Lee, Morse and myself. Being courteous and listening to his redundant reassurance that his father was no VC was about all we could do for him. He was a very humble man of about 30 holding a little toddler in his arms and was in too much pain to imagine. In spite of how much suffering he was experiencing, he felt it was necessary to make his father's loyalty known. At that moment, I only hoped that someday he wouldn't feel as if we were the enemy. That day we failed at pacification and I hoped that all the good we'd done in Phu My someday would be viewed in a favorable way.

That night before we left for ambush again, the lifers to finally noticed Brown's absence. We couldn't help but laugh at the comedy unfolding before us. "Where is Brown?" Jahret asked.

"I don't know sir. He has got to be somewhere around the compound or maybe he took off to dig a latrine outside of the perimeter." I said trying to hold back the laughter. The mission had gotten old. Everything was falling apart, the drugs, the discipline, the accountability everything. We needed to regroup and rededicate ourselves to what we were supposed to be doing. The problem was the initiative would have to come from the top. Jahret was beginning to look more like a part of the problem than the solution, He had lost the respect of most, if not all, of the guys and it was making us all look bad. It not only was bad for the platoon; Jahret was acting CO. That meant that the whole company's efficiency and image would suffer from his brand of leadership. His appointment was beginning to look like a big mistake and his presence in Charlie Co. had become an unending nightmare. He had become what used to be referred to as a candidate for a fragging. He was the kind of leader who was always removed by his men back during the earlier years of the war. I only had to put up with him until November but a lot of the other guys would have to deal with him until sometime in '71.

After several hours had passed, it became apparent that Brown would not be sent back to Phu My. We were curious about what was going to happen to him. His departure from the field was comical but unwise. He had placed himself at the mercy of the lifers and he knew it. Of course he didn't care about the consequences. He was probably planning his exit since he arrived. His execution of the plan was flawless. He only wanted to go home and would never conform, co operate or anything else. He was having nothing to do with fighting the war and it wasn't political. He just didn't want to be a grunt. The strangest thing about his non-compliance was based on his insistence that Charlie was using drugs. He once picked up an empty plastic bag that once contained a pre-packaged rice product made in Vietnam. He pointed to a couple of syllables printed on the bag and offered it as proof that Charlie was on dope. It was odd that someone who could barely read the English being taught in America, would even attempt to translate a foreign language.

Rudy was about to DEROS and his replacement was already at Uplift. The word going around about this one was that he was on his third tour and was reported to have been shot on both of his other two. It sounded like he had a death wish to come back to Vietnam for the third time after being shot twice. Two Purple Hearts would have been enough for the average guy. At least, I thought, it was. Fortunately for him he didn't have to be out in the field going for his third.

The killing of the old man was still heavy on my mind. It's sad to have lived to see a ripe old age and then get killed napping. I hated being a part of the situation that took his life and wished I could've left Vietnam the day before it happened. There was also an air of disregard about the shooting. Mad Dog was showing no remorse at all. Rudy was on his way home and there was no investigation into the shooting. The brief investigation surrounding Wheelhouse's M-60 was apparently deemed more important than an old dead Papa San. Maybe that's the reason the My Lai massacre disclosure took a year before it was so dramatically revealed. What galled me was that the incident happened because Rudy decided to make one more excursion before leaving country.

Charles was talking more and more about getting himself a rear job. He had as good a chance of landing in the rear as a snowball staying frozen on a desert. I would've loved to be out of harm's way during the late stage of my tour but being a REMF just wouldn't work out. I doubted if it would have worked with Charles either. Life at Uplift was anything but uplifting remembering when I first arrived there and was quartered with two ghosters who enjoyed burning shit. There's nothing wrong with dreaming about getting away from the fighting. It was only natural but getting a so-called safer job could become boring, very boring. In the field, boredom was a welcome respite. In the rear, boredom was the norm and might have been the reason for all of the heroin use that went on.

Before we wrapped up our little patrol Howard asked me to accompany him to Phu Cat corner upon our return to Uplift. I couldn't tell if he was looking for a chaperone or a coach. There was only one reason to go to Phu Cat corner and I figured he already knew what to do with a hooker. He still wanted me to go along. When we made it back to the compound, we discovered that one of the ARVNs had ripped us off of some of our extra C-rations and supplies. We all had plenty to give away but it was irritating to find the items missing.

"Have you heard about us leaving tomorrow?" Lee asked.

"Really! Back to Uplift?

"Dig it homey." The sudden news about our returning to Uplift was too good to be true. It was hard to believe the day had come. Phu My hadn't exactly been all that bad but it seemed we had been there forever. The news about our departure immediately erased the bitterness of being burglarized by the little bastards too. By ripping me off they had in fact, lightened my load. I wouldn't need any can goods for a while.

Actually, I expected to miss the place and living in our bunker. We had a lot of fun in spite of being quartered with the lifers and the Ruff Puffs. We didn't get to deliver that baby for Mua's sister but it would have been an experience of a lifetime. It would have been the most significant thing we had done in Phu My.

My worst fears about that big confrontation with Charlie in Phu My never happened. We were on our way out of the place with no casualties. I could've done without the agony of dealing with losing more friends. It would have been nice, I thought, to leave a mission with the whole platoon intact. It hadn't happened often enough for me. I was looking forward to being reunited with the rest of the platoon. Better than that, the whole company would be together for the first time in quite a while. The anticipated party on bunker #9 was sure to be a huge one. With all of the new faces around, there would also be a lot of getting acquainted to do.

"I hear you guys won't be going out tonight. We'll be going out instead." Hugle said.

"Going out tonight? You mean Jahret's going to send out an ambush squad on our last night?" I asked. I thought that it would be dumb to tempt the hands of fate by sending a patrol out at that time.

I confronted Jahret about it and was chewed out. The incident reminded me why I never approached the jerk. His response was too predictable. I was kicking myself for walking into what I should have expected to be another tirade. I deserved to be chewed out in front of everybody. I should've kicked myself in the ass all the way back to my bunker.

That night I wrestled with sleep. There was so much anger inside of me that I never even laid down. I also had a lot of high anticipation about our return to the rear. I had a feeling that this stand down was going to be a memorable one. Maybe as memorable as the one that we had back in February. I couldn't wait for sunrise to come. According to my count, I had exactly 100 days and a wake up left. I was on the verge of breaking into double digits. Everything was going fine for Mrs. Handy's favorite son.

Bravo Co was coming in to relieve us and take on the challenge of coping with the Ruff Puffs. "Biggie Rat" wouldn't have to close down the Rat Hole since he had another group of customers relieving us. Bravo Co. was sure to patronize his establishment about as much as we did. Maybe their medic would even get to deliver the baby for Mua's sister. I hoped so anyway. Bravo Co. deserved a break like Phu My. Col. Clark was once said to have those guys pitted against a large contingent of NVA regulars. He sent them up a hill to attack and when they got bogged down, he had the hill strafed and bombed so much that Charlie almost over ran them evacuating the summit. Clark would have gotten a lot of guys killed had he lived long enough to finish his tour. He probably would have taken a few of us out also.

The early morning calm was interrupted by some gunshots in the distance. It was a brief exchange of AK-47 and M-16 fire. The ambush patrol was in the shit. Everybody started scrambling to move to their assistance. Jahret's decision to send those guys out started turning into a disaster. He couldn't agree to just hunker down for our last night.

Lee said that Hugle was shot and that they were waiting to extract him from the ambush site. "How bad was the wound?" I asked.

"All I know is that he got hit." For a moment I felt there was consolation in that Charlie had succeeded in doing what I couldn't do. I was thinking that his wound could have possibly gotten him on that freedom bird and back to the world. I only hoped it wasn't too serious because he already had a lot to deal with being confined to a hospital bed and dealing with withdrawal symptoms at the same time.

The sun was starting to come up giving me a clear but distant view of the helicopter coming to pick up Hugle. He would be on his way back to Virginia pretty soon. I had already started to miss him and all of the good times we shared in Phu My. I returned to my bunker after standing near the exit waiting for the order to leave for the ambush site. I had been standing there for almost an hour or at least right after I heard the first shot. I felt relieved that I never had to agonize over whether we could reach them in time. The hit and run tactics deployed by Charlie apparently also spared me of being overwhelmed by that agonizing feeling of being sent out on another hopeless rescue attempt.

When the patrol finally emerged from the village and started skirting along the edge of the landing zone, I felt somewhat relieved. I approached Mac to ask him about the severity of Hugle's wound and what kind of condition he was in. The anxiety was killing me and I couldn't wait any longer to hear about exactly what happened.

"They had it all planned, Handy." Mac said.

"What do you mean?"

"Hugle had last guard and must've been the only guy visible. They opened fire on our location and Hugle returned fire in the direction of the shooters. When he opened fire on them, another one of them, who was positioned in the opposite direction, picked him off. The ones to our right were only shooting to get him to give away his position. It was planned that way." he said while slamming his steel pot to the ground in disgust.

"How bad a wound did he receive?" I asked.

"How bad a wound? How bad a wound? What are you talking about man? He's dead!"

"Dead!"

"Yeah man, Hugle is dead!" He said as an eerie silence came between us. I was frozen in shock as Mac turned away, picked up his head gear and retired to his bunker. My worst fears had happened and I felt as if I had failed to make the guy see the danger in his staying with us.

PART FOUR

1

Hugle's unnecessary death fueled an anger inside of me that I felt would not pass until I could avenge his death. The trouble was that the only way I could've accomplished this would have been for me to frag Jahret. Charlie killed Hugle but Jahret got him killed and I couldn't get the incident out of my mind. Getting over the way he was taken advantage of until he died left me disturbed. We shouldn't have had to suffer the humiliation of losing men due to a lack of able, compassionate leadership.

Jahret was nowhere in sight when the patrol returned. His dumb decision to send those guys out had come back to haunt him. I supposed he remembered the scene he made when he berated me for questioning his decision to send out that ambush squad. His callous disregard for the lives of others was exposed for all who heard and or saw him rejecting my suggestion. It would have been so nice if someone would have kicked him out of the helicopter on our way back. He could say whatever he wanted on his way down; as long as he could say it in less than seven seconds.

The shooting took a lot out of what would have been a good day. Other than Mac's reaction to the ambush, I seemed to be the only one who took it hard. I guess I was the only one who made the mistake of getting too close to him. Benn's reaction only seemed to irritate Howard. The death only rekindled the notion that reenlisting was the only way out of the war for him. His second-guessing himself for not putting his name on the dotted line was regarded by Howard as cowardly behavior. On a more personal note, there seemed to be a pattern developing. Whenever I got too close to someone, he either got shot or killed. I remember hearing something about not getting too close for that particular reason. I couldn't understand how we could spend time together under such special conditions and not get close. Maybe it was because the guy who gave me that suggestion did his tour when things were really rough. The years leading up to Tet '68 were the worst years of the war. America was actually trying to win the war and threw everything at Charlie. It was a costly venture back then. The body counts were much higher and contact with Charlie was more frequent. Battalion or even division sized engagements were the norm and Charlie always had more men. It was common back then to see someone get killed more often than we were seeing in '70. The worst thing about being in country during my tour was redeployment. The thought of dying in a war that we weren't trying to win was disturbing to us all. Sadly, I would always regret not being able to talk Hugle into leaving early and stop wasting his time with that worthless proposal. I wished I could have talked him into going back to Virginia and starting his record collection. Jimi and JJ had lost their biggest fan and neither of them ever met him or knew that he even existed.

When Bravo Co finally arrived we knew that our departure was real and was about to happen. It was time to say farewell to Phu My and hopefully to pacification for the last time. I felt lucky to have survived the three we had been through. I remained convinced that there was little we could accomplish in this capacity. As we walked toward the awaiting helicopters we passed Bravo Co. as they disembarked and headed toward the compound. To my surprise, my jump school buddy Byrd was back with the company in the field. He was visibly shook up and ticked off about being there.

"Byrd! What are you doing out here. I mean, didn't you re-up?" I asked as he approached.

"They, they, they, they, f-f-f-fucking over me man. That's what I'm d-d-d-doing out here." He answered. I'd never noticed any stuttering or stammering in his speech before. It must have been triggered by the ordeal of being sent back out into the field after re enlisting to get away from it. He was worried to the point of having to struggle with speech. I almost felt sorry for him but, he should have known better. When we were in jump school together, we all wanted out of the Army after our two year enlistment was over. All we talked about was doing our time and getting out of the military. Byrd changed his mind early in his tour and put his name on the dotted line. He should have been expecting to get screwed in the end. He looked ridiculous standing before me wearing starched fatigues and shiny boots with all of that gear strapped to him. My state of grief was the only thing that kept me from laughing at him. "Well it's not that bad at this location. Try not to go to pieces over it. I've got to go and jump onto one of those choppers now. Take care of yourself and please no half-stepping." I said.

"Look, b-b-before you go; t-t-t-tell me is-is-is they got any gooks out here?" He asked as I fought to hold back the laughter.

"Yeah man. Charlie is definitely out here so be careful. I gotta dash now." I said just before I turned to walk across the chopper pad for the last time. Byrd, I assumed, would just have to find a way to cope with his predicament. I was finished there. We all boarded the slicks and lifted off from Phu My District to Uplift for the first time in almost two months.

It would have been a dream come true to watch someone kick Jahret out of the helicopter but it never happened. Jahret was riding another craft and as expected, he survived the flight. I wanted to feel good about seeing the end of the mission but the loss of Hugle had put a damper on the occasion. It was almost as if I failed to get him to understand that he was taking too big a chance. Within hours, someone in uniform would be knocking on his folks' door to bring the tragic news to his loved ones; a ritual that was being played out daily. It must be agonizing, I thought, to see them drive up to your door. My heart bled for every mother or widow that went through the trauma of having some stranger wearing class A's standing in your doorway bearing the message that didn't need to be spoken.

When we returned to Uplift, we were greeted by Sgt Smith, our new NCOIC. He was trying, of course, to make that good solid first hard-ass impression on us but failed. Our tradition of ignoring what was being said at that moment made his first meeting with us a memorable one. He did manage to maintain his tough guy persona to the end of his little speech that no one heard. We were making our usual plans to go where ever we had planned to go for at least two months. He laid down the law but he was talking to a bunch of lawless misfits who always did as they pleased. That day was no exception.

There were a number of new faces in the company. The first platoon even had a four legged one. They acquired a little mutt for a mascot while in Phu My. The little fellow was probably no older than the two months we were gone. Since the last dog I saw was killed, the first platoon's adoption restored my faith in man's compassion for animals. It might have been alright for them to keep the little mutt while on pacification; but his humping days were expected to come to an end when we returned to the field.

Sgt Smith was giving out orders left and right. He even had a list of bunker guard personnel which was unusual. He didn't even have my name down for guard duty. Sgt Smith was arrogant. He didn't shout, but he could condescend with the best of them. If the story about the two Purple Hearts was true, my guess was that he probably was a fragging victim at least once. He practically begged to be disliked. When he finished his talk, everybody scattered.

"Handy, lets go get a shot of ass." Howard suggested. I was surprised he still had money in his pockets. I thought the hookers in Phu My cleaned him out along with the rest of the guys.

"Don't you want to meet the new guys in the company?" I asked.

"No. I want to get laid."

"There are boo coo guys headed there right now. Why don't you just go along with them?"

"I want you to take me there."

"Maybe later, but not right now." I said. I knew he wouldn't quit until I showed him Phu Cat corner. He would have to wait until I was ready and I wasn't sure if I would ever be again.

I took off for the steak house to get myself a thick charbroiled treat. The Vietnamese fare that I sampled in Phu My was an appealing alternative to the C-rations, but nothing beats one of those steaks. It was everything that America was all about. The excesses of our culture brought halfway around the world to make us homesick. I loved it. I ran into Kyler there. He must have come straight to the steak house the minute the chopper touched ground. He was practically finished eating by the time I joined him at the table. He was glad to see the end of pacification again. He said that he hated it as much as I did. He was counting his days like I was but was not looking forward to returning to Ft. Bragg remembering how he volunteered to go to Vietnam to get out of the 82nd. They never could have driven me to such an extreme. Anyway we were scheduled to leave country together in late November.

Later that evening as we prepared for our bunker guard party, I met a guy from New Orleans named Diamond who attended the same high school that I did. He also recognized some of the old gang from my photo album. When he volunteered to go to the village to buy a nickel bag for the party, I went with him. After boarding a truck, we rode for a few miles before I realized he was counting on me to tell him where to get off. We almost rode that truck to Phu Cat. Once we became aware of our predicament, we signaled for the driver to stop and we jumped off in the middle of nowhere. Before we could hitch a ride in the other direction, a little boy ran us down asking if we were looking to score. We trusted him and he led us to an out of the way opium den that I never knew existed. We scored the bag and returned to Uplift. On the way back, I realized the potential for disaster we had just managed to get around. Diamond treated the incident like nothing happened. We were unarmed and trusting a little kid we didn't know to take us through some territory that was unfamiliar to both of us. We were about as vulnerable as we could have ever imagined being; yet it was no big deal to him. He reminded me of something they taught us at Ft Polk. We were told that anybody who was not afraid of losing his life was a little crazy and too dangerous to be around. Diamond was just that kind of guy.

Diamond was not exactly new in country. It seemed as if he was yet another one of those last chance cases that seemed to always find their way to Charlie Co. He was an ex Ranger who worked the Delta and the "Hook" as he called it. He got into some trouble on the streets of Saigon carrying excessive currency.

"How much?"

"Fifty thousand "P"."

"Fifty thousand in "P". That's a lot of worthless money to be carrying around man."

"Yeah those were the days." he reminisced. As incredible as his story sounded to me, he thought little of it and seemed to relish being in the amount of trouble he was in. Diamond was about as loose as they came. Of course that was the reason he was sent to us. Charlie Company had seemingly become a magnet for his kind. I was glad he was in the first platoon. I was too short to be dealing with a character like him. Being from New Orleans did little for his appeal to me as a friend. He had to be a little cautious or I was sure to avoid him.

We arrived in time to beat the closing of the highway for the night. The party went on all night as usual in spite of Col. Farris's attempt at clamping down on the festivities. Every time they chased us away we just kept returning to resume the party. They were almost as persistent as we were but not quite. It was fun to be reunited with all of the heads of the company. The gathering was a long awaited event.

That morning, Howard reminded me that I was to take him to Phu Cat corner and wouldn't wait any longer. I suggested that we acquire a couple of passes from the First Sergeant's office first. Howard was amused at the way Top handled the awesome duties of being First Sergeant. If he thought that Top was a funny guy, he would probably die laughing at Benn's impersonation of him.

After securing the passes, we set out for my first visit to Phu Cat AFB. I wanted to see if it was as impressive as the one in Tuy Hoa was. Our base camp looked like a shanty town by comparison. Moreover we not only had to be out in the elements exposing ourselves to the danger of being killed by Charlie; we also had to live with the fact that all military personnel in Vietnam received the same amount of hazardous duty pay that we had to earn the hard way. That was the biggest travesty of the war. We should have gotten triple the amount they received.

When we arrived at the Air Force base, their MP's made us check our weapons in at the gate. Col. Farris was thinking about instituting the same measures pretty soon. The act wouldn't go over too big with the rest of the guys. Farris was only concerned about the bad relations between the lifers and the heads. He was, as we always said, braggin for a fraggin. He needed to consider leaving the fraggers alone.

While walking around the base, we ran into Brown. Instead of being locked up at Uplift, he was at the Air Force Base in possession of a pass. Something was wrong with this picture. If Brown could get away with refusing to fight the war and Bracey could get away with faking his way out of it, maybe I should have been excused for the same behavior for being short and scared.

After Howard became irritated with the Air Force base tour, I took him to the infamous Phu Cat corner where the local girls always had the welcome mat rolled out. Only then did he bother to tell me that he didn't have any money. I gave him five dollars for his date, but he wouldn't go in the place without me. I consented and shortly after we settled into our cubicles, one of our cooks came rushing into the place announcing that Charlie Co. was on alert. We had to report back to Uplift immediately. The interruption came before Howard could even get an erection. He had barely undressed. The cathouse, to my surprise, had a no refund policy for such intrusions or dysfunctions no matter how untimely.

We left and hitched a ride hoping for the best and of course expecting the worst.

"It's probably Recon again. That fucking Lt Mack has probably taken on a regiment this time." I said as we sat on the back of the deuce and a half. When I handed my weapon to Howard to retie my bootlaces, he realized that he never picked up his from the Air Force Base. I should have noticed he wasn't in possession of it sooner. Our trip had turned into a disaster. Howard was headed back to Uplift for what was sure to be a firefight and he didn't have his weapon. The lifers, I thought, would crucify him for his oversight. He couldn't get off of the truck and make it back to the AFB and then back to Uplift in time either. It was starting to get late in the evening and the highway would be closing to traffic in less than an hour.

We finally made it back to Uplift in time to report to our Company, which, by that time was well into preparation for extraction. We were to be taken to the site of a downed F-4. The Air Force had their own rescue team and had, by then, picked up both of the pilots. Brown walked up to us as soon as we arrived and handed Howard his weapon. He somehow was able to retrieve Howard's beloved Roscoe, return to Uplift ahead of us and saved him a lot of trouble.

As it got darker, we were still on the chopper pad waiting for our fleet of helicopters to pick us up. I assumed the wreckage was still burning and wondered if we were expected to piss on it to extinguish the flames. I started to get anxious and afraid when word came down that the jet was shot down by a 51 caliber machinegun. Our mission was to go out to the area and search for Charlie and his heavy gun. If his numbers were small, he wouldn't be around when we arrived. On the other hand, if he was in force, our reception wouldn't be pretty. A 51 caliber gun could easily bring down a helicopter.

When the choppers finally picked us up we were whisked to an unknown location. The ride, of course, was filled with all of the usual fear and trepidation that came with rescue missions. The darkness only made it worse. The moonless night sky was so dark that I couldn't see anything other than the horizon outside of the craft. Our pilots must have been flying by the seat of their pants. If Charlie would have opened up on us with that heavy gun, I would have crapped in mine. Hoping for a good landing was too much to expect. In the dark there was nothing of the sorts. We reached a certain spot and hovered over the side of a mountain. Our position along its slope became more precarious when a floodlight, fixed on the underside of the craft, suddenly illuminated the area below us. The door gunner started waving his hands as if he wanted us to jump out of the door. "Are you crazy? We're at least 15 feet up!" I yelled knowing he couldn't hear a word I was saying. He really was telling us to jump. He couldn't get any closer to the ground because of the mountain's slope and the rotor blades were preventing it from getting any closer. The well-lit area below was lush with tall grasses billowing from the down blast of the hovering craft. The movement of the grasses exposed some treacherous boulders that weren't spaced far enough apart. Even worse, the floodlight was creating an inviting target for any potential shooter.

We made the jump and survived the ensuing tumble down the mountainside. Kyler, after tumbling about ten meters, looked up and saw the light from the helicopter he'd just jumped from and fired a shot at it. He thought it was a muzzle flash from an AK-47. Fortunately, his poor vision was just bad enough to not only mistake his target but miss from incredibly close range also. The slick left in a big rush after taking fire from our sight-challenged friend.

We groped through the dark and the tall grasses for our personal items that separated from us during our jump. After which we regrouped, set out and found the downed jet. It wasn't far from our own nearly disastrous landing area. It was just on the other side of a nearby ridge. The crash site had to be about the smoothest crash landing ever. It left a huge grass burn that stretched at least 40 meters before embedding itself into the turf at the bottom of the mountain slope. It wasn't in flames, but if I were a claims adjuster I would have called it a total loss. Those pilots were lucky to bail out of it in time.

After spending the night near the wreckage, we combed the area at sunrise. Charlie obviously made his hit and ran for cover. I wasn't exactly looking for a fight either. It was kind of scary though, knowing that he was somewhere nearby. A 51 caliber could not be humped around like an M-60 due to its heavy weight and cumbersome size. It was usually deployed in a fixed position or mounted on a tank. If it was moved at all, it wasn't moved very far. Fortunately the lifers weren't in a mood to really find it.

I joined Ellis for a prompt photo session and while posing for the picture, some of the guys standing behind us found some spent 51 caliber shell casings lying on the ground in the bushes. It was obviously the spot where the jet was shot down from. The gun was obviously mounted on wheels and the tracks on the ground were situated beside the spent cartridges. The tracks disappeared into a bordering grassy area near the shell casings. Charlie had covered his retreat and there was no way to determine which direction he took after moving atop of the grassy apron. At least the lifers weren't in a mood to investigate any further. We were dealing with a determined adversary who was very cunning and well trained. He would, no doubt, cover his retreat with an assortment of booby traps to alert him to our pursuit. We decided to cut our losses or rather not lose any at all. Other than a few bumps and bruises from that jump, everybody would live to laugh and talk about that one. We geared up and left the wreckage on foot. The Army can come up with helicopters when they need to make an assault but other than that, we could always expect to hump our way around the country. They didn't call us foot soldiers for nothing.

Howard searched himself for some bombers he didn't have and wasn't looking forward to the long trip back without one. He may have dodged a bullet when he left the AFB without his weapon but I wasn't as lucky. Shave's radio was stolen from me while we were in that whorehouse. The radio that represented so much to all of us six months earlier was unceremoniously taken from me along with a carton of cigarettes and some film. I could've kicked myself for losing it so soon after Burt finally handed over to me. Some thieving bastard may have stolen the symbol that represented the special times we shared but I'll always remember them. It shaped and molded me into who I needed to be to get me through the war. I never should have gone into that cathouse with Howard anyway. "Man, I don't know if I can make it all the way to the highway without a joint." He exaggerated.

"No shit, Sherlock." I said as I laughed at his mock desperation. He didn't even know how far it was to the highway.

As we continued to walk and put more distance from the crash site, a village started appearing in the distance straight ahead. The heat was so overwhelming to me that the village started to look like a storybook oasis shimmering in the distance. Thirst usually played a big part in those stories and our situation was quite different. We had plenty of water but no grass to smoke at all. When we reached the village I picked out an older kid and told him to go fetch me a pack of bombers. He was back within five minutes. Afterwards, during a break in our trek to the highway, Howard came and sat next to me still desperate for that joint he claimed he needed. When I reached in my leg pocked and handed him the pack he couldn't believe his eyes. I'd never seen him happier. We smoked as we waited for some trucks that never came. We had to walk all the way back to Uplift. After walking for quite a few clicks, our base camp became that oasis in the distance as soon as it came into view. The Herd needed its own helicopters like those airmobile units. We must've walked at least ten clicks on that highway. Although my feet were killing me from the long march, it was good to get out of that area. I started to feel paranoid about being in the crosshairs of a 51 caliber machine gun totally unaware of its exact location.

"Baby San", a radio operator over at TOC, loved being with Charlie Co. whenever we were on stand down. Nothing could keep him away from the brothers in the first platoon. He was a young black kid from Philadelphia with the facial features, of course, of a 12 year old. He was in trouble for leaving his post at the radio too often just to party with us. He'd already had his share of Article 15's and I supposed that a court martial would be the next action. Baby San, however, cared very little about the consequences. Charlie Co., contrary to his belief, was not that much fun to be with and none of us was about to jeopardize anything just to be with him.

Later that day, we were called to formation near the perimeter wire to watch a demonstration. We were only told that we had to be there. The demonstration turned out to be a little show by Dat. Once we arrived, we were instructed to turn our backs to the perimeter while Dat walked down the highway and nestled in the bushes 50 meters beyond the perimeter. Our perimeter was encircled by rows of concertina wire with tin cans attached to it. The cans made a rattling noise whenever the wire was touched or shaken. Dat was expected to no doubt negotiate all of the barriers and obstacles as he demonstrated his amazing stealth. "All right, everyone turn around and stare out into the open field ahead of you. Dat is going to crawl all the way up to the fence. If anyone spots him, say nothing to the others. He is already crawling towards us as I'm speaking. Try to spot him as soon as you can." said Jahret as he took his position behind us. This, I figured, shouldn't be too hard. I might not have been able to find him that night in Phu My, but in the daylight I figured would be no problem. The guys in the other two platoons were still getting to know Dat but the second platoon was all too familiar with him and his abilities. I just hoped he wouldn't make us look too damned silly out there in broad daylight.

After about five minutes I couldn't find him anywhere in the open area beyond the perimeter. Out of an entire company, only a couple of the guys were able to spot him in those first five minutes. He was putting on quite a show that only a few of us could see at that moment. At least ten minutes had passed before I finally spotted him. In fact everybody was able to see him by that time. He was about thirty meters in front of us as he had already cleared all the rows of wire. He was employing a different method of crawling than we had been taught. Our low crawl was performed on our bellies. Dat was sitting straight up with his back to us reaching out with his left hand and pulling himself in our direction with his right leg aiding his advance and his left leg dragging behind him. The trailing hand could be used to either carry a weapon or some explosives depending on the mission. He had already made it through at least a half-dozen rows of razor sharp barbed wire rolls without causing any of the tin cans to rattle. If we couldn't spot the guy under daylight situations, I figured it must have been impossible to spot him at night. As short as I was then, I also planned to take bunker guard a little more seriously. "This is a demonstration of a sapper attack. Too many of you didn't spot him until it was too late. Our enemy is well trained and highly motivated. We must be on guard at all times." Jahret said redundantly as Dat continued to prove to be a valuable ally to us. There seemed to be little that he wouldn't do either. Comparatively speaking, there was little we could do for him short of bringing him back to the states when the Brigade's turn came to redeploy.

Kostrewva and I left after the demonstration and hitched a ride to Linda and Monique's. While there we were interrupted by a couple of MP's who, after walking through the village undetected, came knocking on the door. This time a Vietnamese National Policeman came along with them. The law in Vietnam forbade our MP's to enter any house on official business without at least one of them present. I thought for a minute that we were going to get busted, but there was nothing but calm on the faces of all the guys inside. They all knew the routine and I didn't have a clue. Everybody retired to the back room, turned off the music and closed the doors. Linda answered the door and spoke only to the National Policeman in Vietnamese, of course. He told Linda that the two MP's claimed she was running an opium den and that the place was crawling with GI's. She acknowledged that she was definitely running one and that the MP's were inconveniencing us. She then offered him what had to be an obligatory bribe if he would get rid of the two MP's and return later for his payoff. The National Policeman agreed to her offer, turned to the two MP's, and told them in English that there were no GI's in the place. He then walked away; leaving the two dumbfounded MP's standing in the door as Linda slammed it in their faces. Vietnam had to be the most corrupt government on the planet. Everybody had a price. It sort of reminded me of Al Capone's Chicago, but even Elliot Ness couldn't do anything with the Vietnamese hustlers.

We returned to Uplift in time for the last formation. Sgt Smith was running it again. He was threatening to bring charges on anyone who got caught on the bunker line if he was not assigned to be there. He was raising the level of contempt for him to dizzying heights. No one cared about his threats because no one took him that serious. If he was really concerned about what went on out there, he could've spent a night at the bunker of his choice. Of course he was too smart to risk getting shot a third time.

When Sgt Smith concluded his oratory, we all made a mad dash for the bunker line. In doing so, I'm sure we made it known that we would not be threatened him or any other REMF. As long as he was in the rear, he could expect to be ignored. Being a third tour guy should have taught him that.

Early that morning during bunker guard and of course in the middle of our party, someone on the base camp fired a burst of M-16 gunfire. It was a commonly heard sound in Vietnam so no one paid much attention to it. We continued the party as if we never heard the noise. It was as if we were only programmed to respond to shots fired from the other direction. We never missed a beat. Someone then popped a Hendrix tape into the cassette player and I automatically thought of Hugle. I remembered the way he would always ask me if I heard of him and was always surprised that I had never listened to any of his music before. After all, Jimi was a soul brother like me. Of course I was still angry about the way he lost his life. It confirmed what I always noticed about how we were fighting two wars. Hugle survived the war but lost the battle against the lifers. He was dead because Jahret refused to give him a chance to live.

Baby San was with us again. I didn't know for sure if he was on duty or what. A couple of the cooks had joined us also. It was unbelievable the way the guys carried on during one of our stand downs. It should've been equally as joyous an occasion for any company to be on a stand down; but for some reason, our being there was always a cause for celebration. The cooks not only let us prepare our own breakfast whenever we wanted to; they also let some members of our company bake marijuana cookies or muffins at night. They just enjoyed having us around.

A stranger suddenly joined the party and helped himself to a beer and a joint. I didn't know him, but as long as he was smoking and drinking, we all figured he had to be cool. The conversation soon turned to the dreaded Sui Cai Valley. While two guys were discussing the valley, one of them pointed to an area about two football fields away and claimed that it was the location of the valley. I was shocked to find out that our base camp was located so close to it. We were practically adjacent to the place. The close proximity was, no doubt, the reason the brass was so serious about the traffic. It's almost as it they were passing right under our noses. I was hoping that I could DEROS before we were sent there. The valley had become notorious for NVA traffic and there were plans to build a fire support base somewhere in the middle of it. If that turned out to be true, we would be rotating in and out of there for sure.

A jeep came into view and sent all of the non-assigned party-goers scrambling. They took the beer and the grass with them also. Uplift had never been like that in the past. I could remember pulling bunker guard all night without ever knowing who the officer of the day was. Col Farris had changed everything. Bunker guard was being done by the book. The officer of the day was making regularly scheduled rounds and they were even using passwords. The prospect of the next visit by our officious intruder was always on our minds. Dat's demonstration had little effect at all on our attitude toward pulling guard. In fact, it had a more adverse effect on us. Most guys realized that if we couldn't spot Dat's maneuver in broad daylight there was no way we could catch one of them during a real attack. Bunker guard was, therefore, regarded as a waste of time. I was too short to be that relaxed though. I only pretended to be less than concerned and managed to keep an eye on the perimeter practically all night.

Being assigned to the bunker, I patiently awaited the jeep's arrival and the drill of asking the password and being scrutinized by the officer of the day. Then I noticed the stranger who had just arrived was still sitting in place still smoking that joint and drinking the same beer. A tough guy who was ready to show his mettle, I thought. There was always someone in the bunch who was crazy enough to try anything. His bravery would be put to the ultimate test because the approaching jeep wasn't the officer of the day. It was the MP's and they were charging up the incline that led to our location and closing in fast. "Better get rid of that joint dude, it's the MP's." I said as he continued to take long drags off of the still burning joint. He was unconcerned, to say the least. "I said the MP's are coming."

"I know." he said calmly. The two MP's stopped the jeep and arrested the guy. While they were handcuffing him he still had the joint in his mouth. He never said a word as they took him away.

The following morning as I exited the mess hall, I ran into Jahret. I tried to sidestep him but he was looking for me. "Hank, I think that it's time for you to be promoted to E-4." He said with his patented artificial smile.

"Well to tell you the truth sir, I'm not impressed at all with the amount of time it took for you to make the decision." I said before I walked away from him. I should have spat in his face. Of course in the Army his actions were too often the norm and black troops always suffered because of it.

After I ran into a couple of other guys who congratulated me on my upcoming promotion, I realized what was going to happen. Jahret was planning to make a ceremony out of the deal at our next formation. I wondered if he would still promote me when I skipped it. His neglect had turned into a little soap opera and he was trying to rewrite the script. He had played the role and then he wanted to change it. If I was wrong, he would have to prove me wrong; but if I was right, he would not get the chance to perform before an audience. There was no way in hell that I'd give him the opportunity to promote me in front of the platoon that no longer had any faith in him. He could always bust me back down to PFC if he objected to my absence.

The stranger that was arrested during the party was rumored to be sought that night for a double murder. The gunfire we heard prior to his arrival was alleged to have been his. According to the story, he walked over to TOC and confronted a lieutenant that had pissed him off about something. He was said to have walked in, found the officer and an NCO engaged in conversation. He told the NCO to leave the room because he only wanted to do the lieutenant. When the NCO refused to be ordered around by an enlisted man, he was shot along with the lieutenant. The shooter then came out to our bunker and lit that joint and opened that can because he figured it would be his last. If the story was true, it explained his willingness to face his captors when they came to get him. It seemed like a waste of one's freedom to execute another GI. Officers and non-commissioned officers had been executed countless times in Vietnam and nothing would ever change along those lines as long as there was enough passion involved. Unfortunately, in Vietnam, there was always plenty of passion.

That night we grabbed some beers and camped out in front of the open air screen to watch a war movie; a WWII flick called "Patton". The movie detailed the exploits of the flamboyant hard-ass general starring George C. Scott in the leading role. Our war would never produce any legendary figures such as Patton, McArthur or Ike. It just wasn't in the cards. I doubted if they would ever make any movies about anything that happened in Vietnam either. The movie going public, I thought, would never want to see any Vietnam War movies. I expected them to only want to forget about Vietnam. It was a shame too.

All of the guys that had been killed deserved to at least be remembered if not immortalized. It wasn't our fault that the war wasn't fought to be won. We didn't have a hand in the decision making, only the fighting and dying. Kyler joined me and asked about my whereabouts during the last formation. He confirmed that I was to be promoted. When he realized how irritated I was about the issue, he dropped it and just watched the movie that lost its appeal when one particular scene turned the audience off. After a tank battle was over; Patton, while standing amidst the dead and wounded surveying the carnage, made a statement that practically trivialized the dead GI's lying around. "God I do love it." he said after which we all went berserk and bombed the screen with every beer can and whatever else we could get our hands on. I didn't know how the movie ended but as far as we were concerned, it ended with those words. They always made movies about the Generals and at the same time made us look more insignificant than we were. I hated the movie as well as the pretense that we were just cannon fodder. It might have been doing alright at the box office but it was a flop at Uplift that night.

Our stand down ended and we were told that before going to our next mission, we were to be taken to an R&R site somewhere on a beach called Lido. It had to be relatively new because we had never heard anything about it. When I heard that we were to be trucked there I imagined that if we could assault the R&R site, we would be flown there by helicopter. I had already earned my Air Medal for making assaults and maybe they didn't want to have to give me another. Baby San was all geared up and ready to go. I couldn't understand where he was going and why he was wearing all of that equipment. Maybe he was planning on sneaking away from TOC to go to the beach with us. The kid was capable of anything. If he was only rebelling, he was in for a rude awakening. I had already heard of situations where guys would get arrested and placed on a plane to be sent back to the world. He could've been sent back to Philadelphia in a heartbeat.

Bravo Co. had already returned from Phu My. Their mission was cut short by a firefight that broke out on the compound with the Ruff Puffs which must have been quite a show. Our government really needed to give up on Vietnamization. The ARVN was more prepared to shoot at us than anything else. If Charlie came along looking for a fight, the ARVN would leave him in a cloud of dust with hopes that he would choke to death in it. Byrd was more than happy to get away from the place. Of course his attitude was expected to change when they went back out to the field again. As for us, it was time to move again. A day at Lido beach awaited us.

2

The truck ride took us down the Highway and then through a mountain range. The course stretched along a narrow twisting road carved into the side of a mountain. The road crumbled along its outer edge as the trucks negotiated its precarious path. I was tempted to jump off of the truck and walk but I managed to stay put. I felt vulnerable to attack the entire time we were going through that man made mountain pass and found it unbelievable that they would bulldoze a path through it. I always thought helicopters were invented to deliver payloads and people over mountains and all other impassable territory.

On the other side of the mountain was, of course the S. China Sea and a beautiful beach. The sand bordering the ocean was a welcome sight. There was a large one story building on the beach to store our gear. Everybody went in and stripped their fatigues off and donned some swimming trunks with our unit insignia sewn on the front. This was definitely Herd territory. I put the trunks on but did not expect to do any swimming. Drowning was, in my opinion, more frightening than any fire fight.

As I stepped outside, I noticed a barbed wire fence at the back edge of the beach that stretched the entire area of the R&R site. On the other side of the fence was a hooch with about a half dozen girls waving at us. I was sure that they were hookers but couldn't understand how they could get away with setting up shop so close to us? Something was definitely wrong with this picture. Howard, I figured, would be able to give me the entire story later. In the meantime, there was a barbeque pit with steaks on it with the usual complement of beer and sodas. I grabbed a can of beer and started to write a letter, only to be interrupted by a group of heads that wanted to go over to the hookers place to get stoned. According to their story, the Colonel knew the hookers were plying their trade over there. They said he didn't care as long as the girls stayed outside of the fence and that we would return whenever his helicopter was on the way. It must have been true because there was a patrol of armed GI's wearing nothing but swimming trunks doing a beeline for their place. I picked up my beer and joined the procession as we walked barefoot across the hot sand.

The girls welcomed us with open arms of course and started providing us with some real hospitality as well as a place to party. Within minutes, the place had transformed into a gathering that rivaled some of the bunker line affairs. Of course all of the heads were there and Baby San seemed to quickly fall in love with one of the hookers. According to his story, his CO grew tired of his antics and had him assigned to our company. The move, though questionable, suited him just fine. Assigning someone to an infantry unit with no real advanced infantry training was a bit risky. There were a lot of things he could get away with not knowing anything about. However, there were some glaring aspects of life in the bush that could expose him like a square peg trying to fit into a round hole. Being on that beach only gave him a false impression of what our life was really like. Maybe I was just comparing his first mission to mine, the Crow's Foot. There really was no comparison. The monsoon, the leeches, the mountains; and, of course, I didn't know any of the guys back then. Baby San practically knew everyone of us already. At least all of the heads knew him. He would never have to experience the FNG treatment. Instead his first mission found him on a beach wearing swimming attire and smoking grass while lying next to some hooker.

The lifers started waving us back to the beach meaning that the Colonel was overhead and it was time for us to make our walk back to appease him. It was bullshit but we couldn't complain. As long as he could see us making the long walk over the burning hot sands, as he had prescribed, it mattered little to him what we did once he took off. Once his slick did leave we all did an about face and returned to the hookers. Not long after we returned, I was summoned back to the building to finally replace my ID. Afterwards, I rejoined the guys and we had an all night party. We were using al sorts of gimmicks for consuming the grass. We blew smoke from the lit end of an ivory pipe through a fatigue shirt sleeve cupped over our nose and mouth. Then we blew some through the barrel of my M-79 in everybody's face. I didn't get us any higher, but the novelty lasted well into the night. The following morning we left by Chinook.

Our flight took us to a dry abandoned rice field. This was another one of those areas that was once populated but later evacuated by the military. It might have been strategic to relocate the people away from certain areas to deny easy access for the enemy but there were some drawbacks. The Vietnamese people had ancestral ties to their villages that spanned millenniums. Moving them around like that had to be devastating to them. I was sure that once we had left Vietnam, Charlie would take over and initiate a complete restoration. Our tactics were inconveniencing the people we were supposed to be fighting for.

Our numbers had shrunk considerably. Charlie Company's overall strength was down to about two full platoons. The first platoon was the only group at full strength. In spite of the small numbers, our arrival sounded like an entire division as we disembarked and started fanning out. It had something to do with hitting the ground running and supposedly catching Charlie napping. Of course it never happened that way. Charlie always knew where we were and was probably somewhere in the distance counting heads.

We started humping through the valley and came to a stop after about two clicks. We dropped gear for a rest and noticed that Barbara's ring was missing. I didn't know how it happened because I had it looped with my dog tags. The tags were intact but no ring. I was sure that I had it when we left the beach and couldn't understand what happened to it. I backtracked but found nothing.

When I made it back, everybody was still in the same spot. Kostrewva met me as soon as I returned and took me to an opium party over at the first platoon's sector. Ice Berg had a tarball as big as a fist. Of course, his two partners in crime, Kool Aid and Sugar Bear were already there. Those three guys were inseparable. Jackson joined in and before we realized it, a half an hour had passed. I couldn't understand the delay but was not about to complain. It turned into a continuation of the fun we were having on the beach. It took my mind off of the lost ring for a while but eventually I would have to deal with losing something that Barbara treasured. I could've kicked myself for not sending it back immediately. Considering life as it was in the bush, I couldn't even hold onto a toothbrush longer than a week.

We finally left the area and moved on for another few clicks across the valley floor. Someone said that we were in an area called the Crescent Ridge of the Hoa An District. which was of little consequence to me. I was just hoping we could get through it soon without any contact with Charlie.

When our procession came to another halt, we were situated at the bottom of a very small mountain. It was covered with a lot of tall elephant grass like the mountain we jumped onto from a hovering helicopter. Walking uphill should not have been any problem. I couldn't understand the reason for the delay. We were stuck in the middle of nowhere and the lead element of our patrol was having some kind of problem conquering a hill that was no more than 30 meters up. We couldn't have gone that soft. "What's the problem up there?" I asked.

"Were waiting on a medivac." Someone answered.

The medivac finally came and hovered overhead as Mad Dog, of all people, was lifted out and taken away. He was walking point swinging a machete on the tall grass when he slipped and fell down the slope injuring his back. Before he was placed into the helicopter, I was informed he had faked the injury to get some ghost time in the rear. There was, admittedly, little that could be done in the field with an addict. Mad Dog could only carry so much skag with him and if he ran out it wouldn't be pleasant. It was smart to allow him to carry out his charade and be done with him.

Later that night, as I tried to remember just which squad if any was out on ambush, someone opened fire from within our perimeter. It was Watson, on the machinegun spraying the area in front of him. He claimed he spotted movement in his sector. "Cease fire!" Jahret screamed. Watson, after firing about 40 or 50 rounds, was insisting that he saw movement. Jahret continued to chew him out for firing without getting permission. It was so dark that I couldn't see anything but the tracer rounds from the M-60 as they streaked downrange. Jahret was still squawking like a mother hen. His loud voice coupled with the total darkness had turned the incident into yet another scene from the weird movie that had visited me repeatedly; a movie that I wanted to see end very soon.

A small brush fire slowly developed down range. The tracer rounds had ignited the dry vegetation that carpeted the valley and added fuel to Jahret's rage. He was going insane. The scene was absolutely wild. The fire was growing rapidly and Jahret was further complicating the situation with another tirade.

I told everyone near me to retrieve their Claymores and start packing. I doubted seriously if the flames were about to die out and if the smoke, wafting in our direction, was any indication of the fire's approach, time was wasting. It was definitely about to get hot soon and I didn't want to be caught standing around listening to our lieutenant raging out of control.

Jahret continued his squawking until he noticed the fire line's creeping growth. Then he gave the redundant order to prepare to move. By that time though, he was the only one who hadn't realized it was time to go. We all should have left him standing in the path of the oncoming flames. He had turned the incident into a ridiculous scene as the smoke was choking us, the flames were gaining on us and he still hadn't shut up. We were lucky the fire wasn't started during a firefight. Charlie would have routed us if we had to depend on Jahret for leadership.

After that incredible night ended I took inventory of all of my close brushes with death and came to the conclusion that combat was only one way to die in Vietnam. Charlie was not the only threat that I had to deal with and it would take a lot of luck to make it to the end. That fire could have been one of the funniest things that ever happened to me but it wasn't. It was scary the way things kept happening to us and I was getting too short to be going through any unnecessary stuff.

When the first platoon left ahead of us, their departure amounted to splitting the entire company in half. The second and third platoons together were barely equal in numbers to the first. Our shrinking numbers had me scared. With only 93 days left, I needed to see more guys around me. It was all a part of that syndrome called getting short. As Jones warned, everything and anything would scare me senseless. Sending half of the company off in a different direction was about as scary as it could get for me.

When we finally moved out, I started thinking ahead to resupply and felt thankful that we weren't in the mountains clearing an LZ. I felt even more fortunate to be in the Crescent Valley and not the Sui Cai. They had started building the two already planned bases in that hot spot. They were going to name one of them after our own Raymond Floyd. The other one was going to be named after Sgt. Washington who was killed when we were at fire base Beaver back in January. The plan was to situate some of those camouflaged listening devices throughout the valley, zero in some mortar and 50 caliber machineguns on their location and open fire whenever they were approached. The brass had come up with a very aggressive plan to interdict the traffic over there. The Crescent Valley, I supposed, shouldn't be as bad. Considering what was going on elsewhere, it seemed to be the lesser of the two evils. In the Crescent, we were looking for Charlie. In the Sui Cai, Charlie was everywhere. In spite of the efforts being made over there, the traffic went on unabated. The struggle for control of the valley was expected to be a continuous one. Kostrewva was right about getting out of Recon. It had become to hot.

We humped for a few more clicks and came to another one of our classic halts again. The first platoon was in the shit without our knowledge. There was a mix-up in radio frequencies and they had to engage without any communication with the rest of the company. They were, however, able to communicate with themselves. Fortunately it was one of those quick engagements where the enemy was content to hit and run for cover. We dodged a bullet that time. Those different frequencies could have been disastrous for the first platoon. They also managed to get through it all without any casualties.

A lot of guys in the first platoon got their first taste of combat in that skirmish making me wonder if Baby San still liked it in the field with us. The day before, I saw him throw his steel pot over a cliff. He was as defiant as he was while working in the rear and showing an unusual disregard for his safety. That firefight probably changed his mind about the necessity of that heavy helmet though. He still had a lot of growing up to do. Once all of those guys he loved to be around would leave for the world, he would feel different about being in the bush. Other than that, he made the adjustment without any noticeable problems. The news about the firefight was depressing to me though. It was just what I didn't want to find in the valley. Charlie was there and he probably initiated that firefight. It was real bad news knowing the NVA was around

Howard took advantage of the lull to clean his beloved Roscoe for the ten thousandth time since I had known the two of them. I liked the guy in spite of the fact that he cost me five dollars with his brief introduction to Phu Cat corner. The only thing that Howard was thinking and talking about as he sat with his weapon in pieces was locking horns with Charlie. He fully realized that his first mission in Phu My was a blessing. In fact, he actually expected to find Charlie in the Crescent. He had a simplistic understanding of the war. In the village, we party. In the bush, we fight. I hoped he was wrong but it looked as if his understanding would prove to be prophetic.

Our small numbers made for an easy headcount. The absence of one particular individual was very noticeable. I hadn't seen Weiss since we left Phu My. He must have been as short as I thought he was. His behavior in Phu My had made me more conscious of my actions in the Valley. I didn't want to appear as if I was as afraid as I really was. I was still wishing that I could handle being short the way that Speedie, Bueno and Shave did. They maintained a demeanor of calm that I could never forget.

When resupply came our nightmare continued. We received a call from the rear inquiring about the first platoon's mascot. It seemed as if the dog had rabies. Once the ownership was determined, the entire first platoon was evacuated to the rear for rabies shots. I couldn't understand why they had to go to Uplift instead of sending someone out to us to administer those shots in the field. We needed those guys desperately and could ill afford to lose that many men to something like that. The timing couldn't have been worse. All I could do was hope for a speedy return to the field for them. I was getting too short to be outnumbered by the other side.

My confidence level took a serious jolt with the combination of the first platoon's firefight and its subsequent departure. I felt as if I was losing it altogether and would only feel better when those guys returned to the field. I figured it shouldn't take any longer than a day to get those shots and convinced myself that they would be back at least by the following resupply day. My fears of being on a mission against a numerically superior force would only torment me for a few days at the longest.

Mrs. Wheelhouse wrote me again. She asked me how much longer I would be in Vietnam. By doing so, she managed to send me on a guilt trip because I had so little time left on my tour. I didn't have the guts to tell her that it was almost over and that I would be reunited with my loved ones soon. My heart ached for the woman and I felt that telling her I only had 92 days left might make her feel worse about losing her son. I knew she wanted me to make it back home alive and she always mentioned she was praying for all of us to make it. She was just that kind of person. I just didn't want to remind her in any way that she had been cheated out of the reunion so many other mothers would get.

After loading up on our fresh supplies, we continued our march through the valley. Getting readjusted to carrying a rucksack on resupply day wouldn't be easy after two months of pacification. We were spoiled rotten. All of that lounging around had ruined us. Being on that compound, having our own quarters, eating at Mama San's and of course, Biggie's Rat Hole had taken a lot out of us. It just didn't seem fair to be subjected to the sudden change in venue. One day we were on a beach with music, drugs and women. The next day it was back to the bush.

Howard, it seemed, had been practically looking forward to life in the bush. He became somewhat enchanted by the stories he heard earlier in his tour. Once the novelty would wear off I expected him to be as disenchanted as the rest of us were. The intrigue and the novelty had already lost its appeal with us. Joley still loved being involved with it; and of course, Kyler was just Kyler. It was strange the way the littlest guys always wanted more of what the bush had to offer.

There was word that Colonel Farris had instituted his much anticipated weapons check-in policy in the rear. His newly instituted plan meant that every time a line company came in the rear for a stand down, all weapons would have to be turned in. Maybe that story about the double murder was true and had convinced him the time had come for a change in the way things were being done at Uplift. The move was sure to be an unpopular one. Being unarmed in Vietnam was like going out in the cold without any clothes on. The fraggers were expected to continue to execute lifers no matter what measures they took. There was too much dissension to expect Farris' program to work.

After humping for a few clicks, Jahret decided to dilute our strength by splitting the remainder of the company in half to continue combing the area. I was sure the practice was standard and should have been anticipated, but the move only raised my paranoia a few more notches. To make matters worse, Jahret and the CP crowd was with us again. For the previous few months, it seemed as if I was always with the half of the platoon that Jahret chose to be with. I couldn't seem to shake him.

As we continued moving along, we came upon a populated area of the valley. It was dark and we hadn't found a spot to spend the night. We continued patrolling through the village until I noticed we had made a series of left turns. Even though it was dark there was no mistaking all of the familiar territory as we passed through for the second trip. This was no déjà vu. We were lost. I said nothing and continued walking. With our numbers so small, I didn't have to worry about the lead element getting into a shoot out with the trailing end of our procession. I'd heard stories about it happening before. By the time we came to another halt, I figured that they'd discovered we were walking in circles. Howard overheard Jahret and Spurlock discussing their navigational error and said they showed more concern about my finding out than anything else. Howard was amused that they were afraid of their big secret getting back to me. I wasn't amused at all. I walked up to the front of the line and told the two of them it was too obvious that they had lost their way. It didn't take a genius to realize we were going nowhere. Getting lost in a village was ridiculous.

We finally made it through the night as well as the village. We resumed our patrol by heading through a low level mountain pass and descended on an area that was definitely familiar to me. This was no déjà vu either. I was pretty sure we had been in the area before. We dropped our rucksacks for a break and I continued to survey the area. I knew I was standing in the same exact spot I once stood before but I couldn't seem to remember when. "I've been here before." I said.

"How long ago?"

I can't remember, but I know that I've been here before and I mean right here." I said pointing to the ground. It felt weird being in the same area and at the same time unable to remember when I was there last. Everything seemed to be the same as it was before. The mountain slope we descended from, the dried up deserted rice field to my right, the gully in front of me, the bushes behind me, everything was familiar. Maybe it was the drugs or should I say the lack of drugs. We managed to consume every bit at the beach and had been without any since we left the place. I couldn't even remember how long it had been.

Once it became obvious that we would be in the spot a little longer than I anticipated, it gave me a chance to try a little harder to remember when we were in that spot last. As I opened my ruck to get a can of applesauce it came to me. We were there back in March. It was the area we were in before we were abruptly brought back to Uplift and briefed about our trip to Tuy Hoa. The mountain slope was the same one that we started to climb when we got the call to turn around. "Howard! I remember now. We were here before we were sent to Tuy Hoa."

"You sure?"

"Am I sure? Go take a look at that coconut tree. I'll bet you'll find bullet holes in that cluster of coconuts." I told him. He walked over and confirmed my story.

"Yeah man, those coconuts are full of holes. Who did it?" he asked.

"Wheelhouse. He thought he could shoot them down from there. He was a wild guy." I said remembering what a free spirit he was.

"Look in those bushes, you'll find an empty applesauce can with a plastic spoon inside of it." I said, feeling relieved that I wasn't losing my mind due to a drug withdrawal symptom.

"Yeah man, here's the can." he said holding the can in the air before discarding it. When we were flown there back in March, I could remember walking across the area to my right. Back then it seemed like a buffer zone between the mountain and the nearest village. I thought I was right about it being so. There was no sign of any civilian traffic on our side of that neutral area. The lack of civilian traffic seemed to confirm my beliefs. We were in the hot zone and I was sure that the other side of the deserted rice field was for habitation. True to form, they decided to split up again. Remaining together until the first platoon returned from Uplift made more sense. Being short, I naturally found more comfort in the strength in numbers theory.

Sgt Smith came out on resupply to augment our dwindling numbers. It seemed as if he was also there to add to the aggravation. I wondered if he felt upset about losing his cushy rear job. His stay, I hoped, wouldn't take longer than it would take the first platoon to get treated for rabies. As was a custom, everybody started calling him Smitty. His sour disposition was a sharp contrast to that of our original Smitty a true free spirit if there ever was one. The old Smitty DEROSed a couple of months earlier and left a void that could never be filled by the likes of Sgt Smith. Smitty was one of those faces that I first encountered back in the Crow's Foot. Sgt. Smith was probably dipped in crow's shit before he was sent over for his third tour. He removed his shirt at every opportunity so that we could all see his surgical scars. It was like a badge of courage that he wore with pride. Unfortunately, no one was impressed at all. His upper torso was so disfigured by his wounds that I couldn't help telling him to cover up. By doing so, I established myself as a smart ass in his eyes which was an even a trade off. He thought I was a smart ass and I thought that he was a big-headed show off. If my body looked like his, there was no way in hell that I would be in Vietnam for the third time pushing my luck. Every time he took off his shirt and exposed his pale, white skin he was practically offering himself as a target to any sniper. I didn't want to get hit by any bullet with his name on it.

His arrival didn't expect to make it any easier for Walkup to be promoted either. He was taking it like a champ though. Nothing ever discouraged Walkup from his pursuit of that elusive third stripe. He took the set back in stride and kept on plugging away at it.

"Handy, get ready for a canteen detail." Said Sgt Smith. He could have gotten someone else to go fill canteens. Ordinarily I wouldn't mind going, but it looked as if he was coming along with us.

To my surprise, our water source was practically right in front of us. We didn't have to walk more than 20 meters. It was right behind a thicket that panned across our view and turned left for at least another hundred meters. The water was at the bottom of a gully that had been carved into the ground by the monsoon runoff. During the dry season, the water level was not expected to be deeper than six inches. During the rainy season it would become a swollen stream with a stiff current that would continually shape the gulley as the water ran through it. We entered the chasm with about twenty canteens and started filling them. From the bottom of the nearly dry channel to the top had to be at least 10 feet deep. "Handy! Go up top and keep an eye out for any intruders." said Sgt Smith.

I climbed up the gully to the top of its rim at ground level and nestled inside of the bushes that straddled its winding path. It was one that stretched from the base of the mountain slope clear across the valley. I was angry with myself for not having a smart ass remark at my immediate disposal for him when he gave me the order to pull guard. Our personalities clashed over everything. I just wished that he would've called on someone else every now and then. It would have been more appropriate to send one of the guys who were carrying an M-16 than it would to send me and my M-79. Of course I wouldn't have had it any other way.

From where I sat, Sgt. Smith looked like a supervisor at an outdoor construction job. He was standing over the workers doing nothing, except watching. Sgt, Smith, without a doubt, only liked being in charge. I'd rather have Walkup leading the detail. At least he would have helped the guys fill the canteens.

There was another much wider gully about 40 meters across from where we were situated. I remember flying over it back in March. A village was another 50 meters or so across from the other side of the larger gully that stretched an equal distance in the same direction as the one we were filling our canteens in.

Suddenly I spotted someone in the distance walking in our direction from my left. He was walking alongside of the other gully and carrying a green sack on his shoulder. It was one of those US mail sacks and it was so full that it almost dwarfed him. There was a lot of waist high bushes on his right so I couldn't determine if he was an enemy soldier. In fact, I could only see the loud green sack moving along the trail. Undoubtedly, he couldn't see me with the sack on his right shoulder. "Hey Sgt. Smith, we've got company. Come and check this guy out." I said sending an alert through the rest of the detail as they frantically scrambled for their weapons and a position on line for a peek. If the intruder was a civilian, he would have to prove it in a hurry. The canteen detail was ready for a kill.

After we were all on line, Sgt Smith eyed the intruder and at the same time, managed to keep his trigger itchy detail at bay. As he made his assessment of the situation, we watched our target as he continued to walk from left to right across our line of fire totally unaware of our presence. Sgt. Smith waited until he was directly in front of us which was still at least 40 meters away. "Dung Lai!" He said loud enough to startle him and send him into a semi squat. As the intruder turned at his waist to pan the area on his blind side, he spotted us all lying on line with our weapons aimed at him and ready to fire. He froze as if it would conceal his position. He was wasting his time. The loud green sack had given him away at least a hundred yards sooner.

"La Dei!" Smitty ordered as the intruder then turned toward the gulley on his left and started to run. As he turned, the AK-47 he was carrying in his left hand came into view. Sgt. Smith gave the command to open fire as if we needed his permission. Everybody opened fire while the intruder scurried for the nearby gully which was only about five or six yards away on the other side of the trail. I launched my first H.E. round and reloaded as I watched the trademark slow arcing trajectory of the round as it flew across the area in front of me. Incredibly the round exploded in the exact spot he had just vacated. Even more incredible, none of the rest of the detail managed to hit him as he started to scamper down the slope of the gully. I adjusted my range for my second shot and fired just before he descended out of view. The second H.E. round disappeared over the horizon of the gully's rim and exploded out of our sight. Not being able to determine the incline of the distant gully, or which direction he ran after getting out of view, I had no way of determining if my second shot was accurate. However, I was sure that if he continued to run straight ahead, I might have hit him.

After the last shot was fired, everybody got up and made a mad dash in the direction of the other gully. "Be careful, he might be waiting for us!" I said remembering that morning in Tuy Hoa when Sgt. Watson was shot. My warning was ignored as they continued running directly to the spot he was last seen running away. I trailed the rest of them as I reloaded my M-79. I ran a path farther to the left of the pack convinced he would be moving away from the spot where he entered the gully. The guys were like wild animals in a feeding frenzy. They were literally engaged in a footrace to get to their quarry first. As they came upon the gully, they found him sprawled on the ground not far away from where he disappeared from view. His sack hadn't rolled far from where he hit the ground. He had a neat puncture wound in his neck. His cause of death was pretty obvious to us all. My second round exploded and sent a piece of shrapnel through his neck. He was killed instantly. "You got him Handy!" someone shouted.

"Nice shooting homey." said Lee.

"I don't know about that. One of you guys probably got him. I only managed to get off two rounds." I said in the most self-effacing manner I could muster in such an awkward situation. As much as I had wanted to avenge the deaths and dismemberments of so many of my now departed friends, I didn't want to accept the credit for finally doing what I had wanted to do for so long. "Bullshit! Look at that wound." said Walkup pointing to the pinhole wound through his neck. He was right. If an M-16 round would have went through his neck there would have been more damage as it exited on the other side. It was just the sight of the dead guy lying at my feet with both his eyes and mouth open and a look of blankness seemingly frozen on his face that had somehow opened my eyes to the brutality of war.

       The dead body was sure to go through some form of humiliation at our hands before his body would be retrieved. The guys were poring over the goods in the mail sack and pocketing them as spoils of war and the privilege to be able to say that, "I got his off of a dead gook back in 'Nam." Now that I had finally taken a life, it all seemed insane. Jahret and the rest of the CP group arrived shortly thereafter and got the report from Sgt. Smith. Jahret then got on the horn and reported the incident to his superiors. Although I didn't want credit for the kill, his report made it a matter of official record. The ultimate dream of every grunt was now turning into an agonizing nightmare for me. Thoughts of retribution jump started my paranoia. The shooting was definitely going to cause me a lot of problems. The first of which was accepting credit for the kill.

I was not accustomed to engagements with Charlie in broad daylight at all. The fact that the dead guy was casually strolling along carrying a loud colored green sack had me more worried. Where was he coming from? Where was he headed? How many of them were in the valley? "Well, you finally got one for Wheelhouse." said Doc.

"I'm not too sure about that, man. There were a lot of shooters with me, you know." I answered.

"Look at all of this stuff." said Joley as he sifted through all of the junk in the mail sack. They looked like a bunch of kids at school recess as they started taking pictures of each other with the dead and basking in the glow of accomplishment.

"We got one of those mother fuckers!" said Lee while pumping his fist in exultation. I liked the "we" part of his statement. I was also glad that Sgt. Smith, Jahret, Spurlock, Moe and Swain were there too. Otherwise those guys might have started cutting ears and fingers off. Ordinarily I wouldn't have cared, but since he did die at my hands, I just wanted to move on and try to forget about the incident.

A lot was learned about our enemy from this kill. His shiny new bullets, his fresh haircut and a lot of the items in his sack told us that the NVA unit operating in the area had been resupplied recently. They were, no doubt, probably being resupplied regularly. It also taught me that their vaunted image of invincibility was but a myth. Our dead friend was half-stepping when he walked up on us. Maybe Dat was just as exceptional as he seemed to be. We never would have caught a soldier of Dat's caliber with his head up his ass like that. Dat would have probably camouflaged that sack and harnessed it on his back. He never would have been carrying it on either shoulder causing a blind side. I'm sure he would have spotted me first. He was just that good.

As if I needed another reason to feel paranoid, Jahret designated our squad to spend the night near the body. The ploy never did work and it was one time I didn't want to be around the dead body that would eventually be retrieved. I just wanted to leave the area with the rest of the group. Our company strength was already down to that of a good sized platoon and half of that platoon was patrolling another part of the valley.

Spending the night near that body gave me the most agonizing sleep of my life. I couldn't get the kill off of my mind and couldn't shake that "my turn is coming" feeling either. The following morning the dead guy naturally was still lying in the same spot we left him in. It was another dumb idea to expect any attempt at snatching the body. Charlie was no doubt watching our every move waiting for us to vacate the area so that he could take away his dead and give him a soldier's burial. Spending the night so close to someone I had just killed was too much for me to bear. I didn't know how much time we had left in the Crescent but the sooner we could have left the valley, the better. That kill was expected to make my remaining days there one tough experience as my worst nightmare had become an ugly reality. The valley seemed to be anything but easy and the daytime sightings and firefights would take some getting used to. It painted an ugly picture of just what kind of valley we were working in.

As we finished packing and started moving out, some shooting erupted in the distance. It was an exchange of M-16 and AK-47 gunfire. The other half of the platoon was in the shit. I expected something like that to happen and it didn't take long. We had barely walked 20 meters away from the dead body and it looked like we would be busy again. Charlie seemed to be everywhere in that valley. Someone announced over the radio that Mac had been hit. Before I could ask about the severity of his wound, bullets started falling all around us. We were standing in the impact area of either the other half of our platoon or their attackers. We made a quick move to link up with CP and took cover. The shooting was continuing and the bullets would have only kept landing there. Our having to take cover didn't bode well for the other half of the platoon. It was hoped that the firefight would be one of those hit and run engagements. The distant sound of the crackling rifle fire, suggested a considerable distance stood between us and their exact location. Moving to their rescue would've taken too long to even consider. Doc Reardon had his work cut out for him. Tending to Mac's wound during a firefight wouldn't be easy.

We moved further out of harm's way while continually monitoring the situation at the other patrol. I began to experience a very sickening feeling when my heart started racing again and my breathing pattern had turned into a series of heaves and deep breaths. About all I could do was sit, wait and hope for the best.

The shooting stopped and Mac was extracted. As short as he was, I figured that I had seen the last of him. Surely he wouldn't be sent back out to us after leaving the hospital. Of course I never found out what type of wound he received and had no idea what to expect. I just hated losing friends to a helicopter and couldn't accept Mac becoming the most recent loss of my tour. Still, I hoped he wouldn't be returned to the field after his recovery. At least he didn't get killed and was expected to be alright. In the meantime, I still had to deal with being in the Crescent with Charlie in large numbers. The place had begun to look like a worse nightmare than Tuy Hoa where the enemy only came out at night.

After evacuating Mac, the rest of the patrol was expected to rejoin us at our new location. The valley was obviously crawling with NVA who could possibly hit them again on the way to our position. We had only been there less than a week and already we had two fire fights and, of course my kill. The numbers were beginning to scare me and it didn't look like we would be leaving the place soon. Apparently we were sent to the valley because of Charlie's presence. Our numerous encounters with the little bastards were no coincidence. Once we had made contact, there was no way we would be getting out of that valley before the brass was satisfied with some kind of body count. The problem was that kind of satisfaction usually came at a price. I had a feeling that Mac would be joined by some of us before very long. We needed to get back up to full strength and fast. "Doc, how much longer are those guys gonna be in the rear taking those shots? They've already been gone longer than I anticipated."

"The process won't be a quick one Handy. I'm afraid that we are going to be in this valley for at least a few more weeks without them."

"A few more weeks! What are you talking about?"

"The administration of rabies shots usually takes around thee weeks. The shots are to be applied to the abdominal region in a ring with a minimum of three days between shots." he said.

"But when I was in basic, they gave us almost ten shots on one day alone. Why do they have to take all of this time? We don't have three weeks to wait for those guys. We need them out here now!" I said without realizing that pressing Doc for an answer was no solution to our predicament. Being short and scared had me so out of touch with reality that I was reaching for explanations that Doc didn't have. Everything was being done according to procedure and the first platoon would have been out there with us if at all possible. The notion that the first platoon was lucky to be in that situation was also untrue. The shots, Doc informed me, would make those guys as sick as a pack of dogs with no pun intended. He assured me that those guys were going through hell but of course so were we.

The spot we ran to for cover turned into a rendezvous point for the other patrol as they were expected to link up with us the following morning. At first, we lounged around in that spot without giving any thought to how vulnerable it was. After a while I started to worry about whether we should remain there waiting for them to come. I didn't like the area but we were with CP so we just had to go against our instincts and stay put. Resupply, I was told, would also take place in the same area.

As it started to get dark it also appeared as if we would be spending the night in the same perimeter that we had spent the previous several hours. The choice was a poor one too. Going to that spot to escape that impact zone was a reaction and almost anywhere would have done in a rush. Choosing an ambush site, we always thought, was a more deliberate process that entailed a lot more selectivity. The area we were in was too large to cover defensively. We just didn't have the numbers to make it work. No matter what configuration we would have applied, there was still a large part of our perimeter exposed. It was equally as compromising as surrendering a portion of the perimeter to a bunch of those ARVNs in Tuy Hoa. The best we could do was deploy ourselves in an "L" shaped configuration and hope that Charlie didn't hit our exposed flank. At least we wouldn't be stampeded by a bunch of cowardly tin soldiers before we got a chance to fire a shot. Having no one covering the area, however, was no consolation. We were trained to take everything into consideration when either choosing a spot to pull ambush or setting up CP for that matter. We instinctively played out all worst case scenarios before making these decisions. Jahret just didn't want to move and that was the reason for our staying in place. In reality, the absolute worst case scenario was having him along with us. The biggest enemy at that moment was our leadership.

I was situated along the short leg of the perimeter along with Sgt Harrington and Lee. We were concealed by a row of bushes that provided us with zero protection from attack. The rest of the guys were stretched along the far end of the long leg of our position which was lined with a few large trees. Comparatively speaking, we were totally exposed at out end. Our makeshift perimeter was also somewhat elevated. The trail that led down the line of defense at the long leg was at least 2-3 feet lower than the level we were situated on. Charlie would've practically had to accommodate us by walking down that trail and sacrificing himself for his cause.

The kill I made was still weighing heavy on my mind. I couldn't get the incident or the look of that guy's face out of my mind. The guys were still excited about it though. It was such a lucky shot that I found it hard to believe I got off two accurate shots at a moving target, no less. It may have been luck in my opinion, but some of the guys thought that maybe I just might be that good a shot. Maybe they just wanted to believe that I was or maybe they needed to, but it was a one-in-a-million shot.

The night silence was suddenly disturbed by the sound of a twig breaking. The sound came from somewhere directly in front of our sector. "Did you hear that? Someone's out there!" said Harrington as he wheeled around for his rifle. Without hesitation the three of us all opened fire and at the same time began receiving return fire. The sound of bullets cracking overhead started my heart racing again. There had to be almost a half dozen A-K's shooting at us. As I fumbled my way through the reloading process I looked to my left rear hoping that someone from the long leg of our perimeter would get up and get on line with three of us. The amount of flying lead, however, was making it extremely hazardous if not impossible. We were, in fact, fortunate that none of us had been hit yet. "I got one of 'em! Did you hear him? Did you?" Harrington asked me.

"Get another one!" I yelled at him. He couldn't hide his excitement and wanted to be sure that he got credit for what he knew would be a KIA straight ahead of us.

Suddenly a small flash went of in front of my face about a foot away. I didn't know for sure if Harrington shot one or not but the rest of them were still putting up a fight. We continued to hug the ground as the bullets passed overhead. I feared it would only be a matter of time before they lowered their aim and started picking us off one at a time. I had to keep firing my M-79 to keep them ducking and blinking their eyes. The sound of the thumper was a bigger weapon than the accuracy. I could only hope for a direct hit to truly be effective due to the prone position of our targets. Most of my shots were just passing overhead and exploding behind them. Some of them never exploded at all. Reloading a grenade launcher during a firefight was challenging. I needed more fire support next to me. The intense AK fire, however, kept everybody else in place leaving us with the task of holding them off on our own.

Lying prone, staring down the barrels of live fire was destroying my concentration. I couldn't reload fast enough and was starting to run low on H.E.'s I was nearly left with only buck shot, tear gas, and parachute flares. We were outnumbered and time was working against us. The way they were firing at us, I was pretty sure they were carrying more than enough ammo. They always did whenever they attacked. Hopefully they weren't planning to rush us after they assumed that we were out of ammo.

Suddenly Grove stood up, quickly walked over to our sector and started to apply some much needed suppressive firepower. He was showering me with some red hot spent cartridges, but I didn't care. I was just glad to have him at my side. He was on one knee practically giving up his entire upper torso in defiance to the rounds flying past us. He did the improbable and the unimaginable deed of coming to our assistance when no one else would dare.

Grove's action seemed to bring their shooting to an end. Everything went silent shortly after he joined in on the fight. It appeared as if the fight was over for the moment. "I'll bet we find one out there when the sun comes up. You'll see, he'll be lying out there straight ahead of me. I don't know how far but you'll see." said Harrington. He was ecstatic over his kill. Nothing would convince him that there wouldn't be a dead body waiting for us to discover when we made our sweep. It was possible that he could have been dragged away. Charlie would do everything he could to keep his dead from falling in the hands of his enemy. I was just hoping that there wouldn't be any live ones out there waiting for us to make that anticipated sweep. It would be one long agonizing stand to, only to be followed by a real scary sweep of the area to our immediate front.

Grove really came through for us that time. It would have taken a lot of courage for anyone else to get up from where he was and come over to our position. Grove just happened to be the only guy in our platoon who couldn't seem to recognize how dangerous it was to do what he did. Anyway, his actions were impressive that night. His head might have been so far up his ass that he couldn't see the danger around him, but he was my hero for the moment.

When the sun came up we got on line to begin our sweep. My adrenal glands were still working overtime. The anticipated sweep was giving me a serious case of nausea. Of course I was only remembering Watson at Tuy Hoa again. I couldn't help but wonder if the little bastards were lying in wait. The field ahead of us had less cover than I could remember. We were staring at a clear field and I feared that we were camped out at or near an opening to a tunnel complex. It would have been our luck to do battle at Charlie's doorstep where he could run back into his hole after expending his ammo. Even worse was the possibility that he had already lined the approach to the complex with booby traps for us and our anticipated sweep? The guerilla warfare thing was doing a number on me once again.

We started our sweep and I immediately spotted a partially exploded chicom grenade. It was made from a C-rations can and was a dud. It had to be the source of that flash that went off near my face during the fight. Fortunately, the can was made to hold food and not the crudely constructed combination of C-4 and the fragments packed around it. The can was partially eviscerated at the bottom with some of its fragments spewed out. Had it not been a dud, it could have blown my head off.

Harrington fired a shot that buckled my knees with fear. He had found his kill and gave him an extra round to make sure he was dead. "What'd I tell ya. Right where I said he would be! Didn't I tell ya! Didn't !" he said unable to hide his glee.

"Yeah man lets finish the sweep." I said as I recovered from being startled by him. The rest of us continued the sweep, as Harrington just stood there for a few extra moments admiring his handy work. I hoped he wouldn't shoot him again. My nerves were already wrecked. We had made numerous contacts with Charlie in the valley and it was taking away my edge. I was losing my mind also. Every step I took during the sweep was full of trepidation. The fear of stepping on a booby trap was killing me. Being short was only complicating my situation. Getting killed in Vietnam should have been tragic enough. I couldn't understand the syndrome we suffered through on the last leg of our tour. It was as if being killed early in our tour wasn't as bad as getting killed as short-timers.

3

After the sweep was over and resupply was underway, I started to breathe a little easier. I grabbed some HE rounds to replace the ones used during the firefight. I was disturbed by the number of rounds that never exploded during that shootout. It could have been due to the low trajectory I was forced to use coupled with the close proximity of the targets that prevented the rounds from exploding. I always felt that shooting straight ahead at a target that was close to the ground lessened the chance of detonation. I hoped so because I didn't want to get into another firefight with non-exploding rounds. I would be better off throwing rocks at them. At least the sound of shooting the thing definitely kept them ducking their heads in anticipation. During a firefight, the sound of the thumper was a necessary ingredient that usually gave us a moment of advantage.

The other patrol finally rejoined us and they all seemed to be in good spirits. Mac was expected to be sent home and recover fully from his wound. He would be missed by all because he had spent so much time with us and he had such an overall good guy appeal. Kyler had his boonie hat shot off of his head during the fire fight. He showed me the bullet hole and talked endlessly about it. It must've been one hell of an experience for him. He was extremely proud of his hat and was probably thinking about what a conversation piece it would be for the rest of his life. He heard about the fire fight we had just completed and of course my kill. He wanted to talk about it, but I told him that I'd rather talk about his bullet hole. Kyler would only make it harder for me to put the incident in the past. He would continue to revel in being involved in what he thought was an adventure.

My mother finally sent me a care package. Among all of the standard goodies were two cans of red beans and some Uncle Ben's converted rice. Red beans and rice is a New Orleans special treat. Lee and I went crazy over it. We were so caught up with the meal that for a minute I forgot I was in that nightmare valley. We started reminiscing about every thing that was unique and common to our local culture and then we got homesick. Jackson was from north Louisiana but was no stranger to kidney beans. Still, he turned down my offer of a sample of the beans and rice. The recent action was having an adverse effect on him and being as short as I was, it was to be expected.

I stocked my ammo vest with some more HE rounds. I also unloaded my tear gas and parachute flare rounds and replaced them with some more firepower. I had a feeling that I was going to need them before long. The word going around was that there was a battalion of NVA regulars operating in the valley. After hearing so much about the Viet Cong, I couldn't believe that I had been there for nine months and had yet to find any. VC was nothing but an acronym. The Viet Cong was no longer a viable entity and had practically disappeared from the battlefield. It was always the NVA. This meant that our company, or what was left of it, would be battling it out with about four or five companies of troops that were as highly trained as we were. It just had to be that way. I felt as if I were cursed. "Handy, you know something? If I keep sending guys to the rear, I won't have enough of them around to protect me." said Doc.

278

"Well stop sending them. You know damned well there's nothing wrong with them." I should have figured it out by then. Our numbers were shrinking even more because Doc was sending guys to the rear for whatever mysterious ailment they could come up with. He was a great guy with a soft touch when it came to using that power he had to determine if a guy needed treatment in the rear. Once the platoon hypochondriacs realized that Doc would fall for any story they brought him, they would've developed the plague. He would probably send one of them to the rear if he claimed to be pregnant.

After resupply, Jahret sent the other half of the platoon out again and kept us back with him once more. It was dangerous out there but I would've preferred to be out on patrol as opposed to being held back with CP. To make matters worse, we were going to spend the night in the same vicinity of the fire fight. It seemed suicidal to be spending so much time in one area of the valley. I could understand his not wanting to go patrolling but staying in one spot was not a sensible alternative. I thought that the most recent firefight would have taught him a lesson, but it seemed as if I was the only one with any reservations or apprehensions about the area. My time spent with the old third squad had instilled a lot of good habits in me that I refused to ignore. Considering our numbers, spending another night in that same spot was a bad idea. The real problem was that no one else felt that way.

That night brought on a moonless sky. I took over the post at around midnight and was greeted by some strange sounds. My paranoia was always running high but the noises were real. There was a distinct rustling sound going on around the periphery of our ambush sight. Dat was still inside of the perimeter so I knew it wasn't him. I struggled for the entire hour and a half trying to convince myself that it was all in my mind. But the noises persisted. I turned the shift over to the next man and tried to forget about the event but In fact, I was still hearing noises. I tried going to sleep but could not get past the unrecognizable sounds. I was literally going to pieces over the noise and couldn't seem to pull myself together.

The noises became more recognizable as the night went on. Pretty soon I heard the sound of a tin can rattling. I then tried to sell myself on the theory that it was probably one of those giant rats trying to get the last morsel out of it. Or was it? "Do you hear that noise?" I whispered to Lee who was doing his shift at the post.

"Yeah man, I hear it Homey." he whispered back to me.

"What do you think? I mean, it is a rat, isn't it?"

"Probably." he answered totally convinced that it was nothing else. I, on the other hand, wanted to be absolutely positive that it was just a rat. Lee's reassurance did little to convince me and I continued to melt down over the matter. It got so bad that every time I heard the noise I felt that there was someone outside of our perimeter harassing me.

"Lee, I'm going to frag whoever or whatever's out there." I said.

"You're gonna to do what?"

"I'm gonna frag whatever the fuck's out there. We might as well be sure." I said as I pulled the pin and whispered …"Frag Out!" The loud explosion managed to wake up everyone but it did little to stop the rattling sound. It was, in fact, rattling louder. The rat theory was definitely out at that time. I was totally convinced that Charlie was out there harassing me and laughing at me because I missed. Without hesitation, I grabbed another grenade, pulled the pin and threw it in the general direction of the rattling sound. "Handy, you threw those frags pretty close, you know." he said after the second explosion. I fully realized how close the grenades were landing, but as long as everyone was lying prone there was little to worry about.

I continued throwing grenades until I had exhausted both his and mine. After I threw Lee's last grenade, his turn at the post expired and he retired to his poncho liner. I then crawled around to see who was willing to part with theirs.

"Who's throwing those grenades?" Jahret asked aloud.

"It's Handy. Give him all of your frags so that he can throw them and then maybe we can all get some sleep." said Lee angrily as he wrapped himself up in his poncho liner and tried to go to sleep. Grove brought me his grenades as well as someone else's and quietly placed them at my side. As he disappeared into the night to his spot, I realized what an ass I had made of myself by throwing hand grenades at a rat. It also became pretty obvious to the rest of the guys that I had possibly gone a little insane. It also said a lot about how much respect for me that the guys had. They had probably come to the conclusion that I was going through a mental crisis of sorts and just accepted it as a part of my newly acquired personality. I admit that I did get a little bit out of hand, but all of my faculties were still intact. Jahret didn't even go into one of his famous tirades over the incident. His unwillingness to interfere with me did not go unnoticed either. He must have thought twice about it.

After stand to, everybody seemed to be giving me a strange look that morning. I felt as if they were looking for some kind of reassurance that my shit was still in order. I wouldn't disappoint them either. Their confidence in me meant everything and I just had to give a better showing than that frag throwing episode. It was another one of those incidents that I hoped I would be able to look back on and laugh. However, it was no laughing matter. I felt like crawling into a very small hole and hiding out for the last three months of my tour. My behavior was about as embarrassing as anything I had ever been through.

After a while it turned out that I was mistaken about those confusing looks the guys were giving me. They were, instead, concerned about the patrol that had incredibly wandered into the middle of Charlie's base camp while patrolling in the dark. We all started packing to move to their assistance. It was happening all over again. Someone was in trouble and I found myself a part of another rescue attempt. The efforts almost never ended the way we wanted to see them end. About all that we ever got out of making such moves was the fear of being ambushed on the way. Of course there was always that hopeless feeling that overwhelmed me every time I realized how much or little we could do in those situations.

We wasted no time moving out. Time, it seemed, was standing still anyway. All of the tension that came with trying to rescue someone who was under fire was absent. All that was left was that gut wrenching hopeless feeling I always had knowing how futile rescue attempts could be. The closer we got to our destination, the worse I felt. Our destination was straight ahead and up the mountains. It seemed unbelievable that those guys actually went as far as they did and in the middle of the night too. According to my headcount, Doc was missing. Of all the worst case scenarios that I could come up with, sending the medic out was the worst. Maybe it was Doc's idea. He must have been anticipating casualties and just volunteered to go along. Of course his "shoot first until someone gets wounded" philosophy was what scared me the most at that moment.

The sound of a lone gunshot sent shivers through me. It was in the distance and came from the direction of the mountain. The RTO said that someone was hit. We still hadn't quite made it to the mountain and the situation had begun to get flaky up there. They were in for a tough fight if we couldn't make it to their rescue in time. There was still a lot of ground to cover and, I was beginning to fear the worst. We weren't' even halfway there yet.

Not knowing how serious the situation was at their location started to destroy my confidence. I felt it was impossible for us to get to where they were fast enough to impact the situation. Our arrival, of course, would be anticipated; which meant a possible ambush or, at least a booby trap might be waiting for us also. Charlie's tactics were well known to us all by that time. It took every bit of courage just to continue the trip. I was personally moving on instinct alone. All of what I considered to be courage had evaporated from me during that last firefight. The wobbly legs, the accelerated heartbeat and the heavy breathing was about to make me collapse. The fear of what awaited us was again equal to the fear of not making it in time. I didn't think that I could live with having to send Doc home in a body bag. It would've been too much for me to loose anybody else to this war. I was convinced that I carried some kind of jinx that would take the life of anyone who got too close to me. The trouble was that I was very close to most of the guys in my platoon.

According to the radio transmissions, the lost patrol was by then making some progress getting out of the NVA base camp. We were not going to have to go up after them after all. The guy who was shot had died. He was a member of the third platoon. I could only imagine what they were going through making an escape while carrying a dead body and all of his gear. The radio reports were all positive though. There was no shooting and they were definitely making headway as our rescue team paused for a reception about one click away from the mountain. We never would have made it in time. The distance and the terrain made it impossible.

When the patrol came into view, they were perched on a ridge awaiting a helicopter for extraction of their dead body. The situation was more stable than I thought. It was reassuring to see them doing the extraction from there. It signified just how safe their position was. We may not have been out of the woods yet, but at least we could all breathe a sight of relief. One dead GI, just the same, was still one too many for me. I was just glad they were able to get out without having to fight their way out. Needless to say it was a relief to know that we didn't have to fight our way up to get to them.

The identity of our newly departed member was unknown to me. It made me feel guilty for breathing that sigh of relief. The fact that I never knew the guy was no real luxury. He was a member of our company. That should have made me feel as angry and or hurt as I would have felt if he were a member of the second platoon. Instead, I was actually looking past his death. He hadn't been dead for two hours and I had already gotten over it. It was as if being short had left me somewhat detached from all concern about the affairs of others. I used to know more of those guys in the third platoon in the beginning of my tour. Things started changing when we went on pacification for the second time back in May. We spent so much time separated that too many of them had become virtual strangers to me. After Phu My, everything changed. The third platoon had become a collection of new faces and very few that I could recognize anymore.

The unreal feeling of being detached was a short lived experience when the sight of those guys placing the dead body on the helicopter brought me back from whatever I had become. The all too familiar stiff, motionless characteristics of rigor mortis were a chilling and riveting picture that gave me the creeps. It was the first dead GI I had viewed. It was an ugly sight even from a distance. Within a matter of hours his body would be prepared for a flight back to the world in an aluminum casket. About the same time his wife or mother would get that dreaded visit from a uniformed messenger telling her of her tragedy. The next of kin of that guy who I killed had probably still not been notified of his demise. I doubt seriously if his body would be returned; at least, not in the immediate future. Our enemy's sacrifices on the battle field were enormous. He was willing to continue to fight until his country was unified under his flag. On the other hand, we were only fighting for our lives. Our only hope was to make it back in one piece and not in an aluminum casket. In the meantime, the enemy's dead would be temporary buried in a plot well hidden form us. I was convinced that somewhere in S. Vietnam or Cambodia was a huge burial plot of dead soldiers from the north. After the war was over they would all be reunited with their ancestral land which was so essential to their culture.

When the extraction was over, the hard luck patrol returned to us. Their close brush with death and or capture was brought on by their disregard for patrolling at night in a hot area. They said it was so dark they were unable to notice they had wandered into that NVA base camp. Of course we did the same thing back in the An Los during the daylight. Fortunately our find was an abandoned base camp. Doc said Charlie allowed them to settle down for the night before they started playing games with their minds. He said they heard catcalls and voices laughing at them all night. It had to be the most intimidating encounter with death they'll ever face. As the sun came up, they started to make their way out of the base camp. There was only one shot fired at them and it was the one that took that guy's life. As I suspected, they were encumbered by having to carry the dead body as they made their way out of Charlie's camp. In a way, it seemed to have afflicted us with a walking wounded. One member of the third platoon had been psychologically scarred by the experience. "What's the story on him Doc?" I asked about the guy kneeling down staring at the medivac as it disappeared over the horizon. He mumbled incoherently to himself and continued gazing into the distance.

"His name is Thaddeus and he's lost it Handy. After the gooks fired that one shot, we had to leave in a hurry. Thaddeus had the job of carrying the body. Every time we rested he would talk to the dead body as if he were only wounded. I think the two of them were close and he's showing signs of having been traumatized by the loss of his friend and carrying his body around. He insists his dead friend will be alright when that helicopter gets him to the 67th evacuation hospital." said Doc as he started to show some signs of dealing with all that had happened since we left the beach. Thaddeus needed help, but for some reason the lifers wouldn't call him a medivac to get him out of the field. It was as if they were trying to ignore what otherwise seemed pretty obvious. Doc was also reluctant because he had already unnecessarily sent so many others in and couldn't afford to send any more unless they were wounded.

The only thing that mattered at that moment was the NVA base camp and their plans to have us assault it. We were outnumbered about 10 to 1 and they expected us to take the fight to them. We were not up to strength, numerically, to make any assault. It would have been suicidal. If we tried to go up the mountain, we would not be coming back down. Charlie would have a field day picking us off as we struggled to make our way uphill.

A helicopter came and picked up Jahret to take him to away to an undisclosed location for unknown reasons. Someone needed to send out a few slicks to pick up the rest of us. It was time to forget about the mission. The particulars involved were starting to disturb me. Charlie was dug in on a hill and we were about to assault it. We were at less than 50% of our strength and going against a battalion. Another Dak To was looming larger as the minutes passed by. I once thought that charging up a hill full of dug in NVA regulars was a thing of the past. I might have been wrong.

Plans were being made to pound the area with some artillery; a move that never seemed to do the job of softening up the target as it was intended to. It didn't work on the Japanese or the Germans during WW11; it had little effect on Charlie at Dak To; and it wasn't expected to have any positive effect in the Crescent valley either. It had to be the kind of situation that the usual deserter went through before he made his first step backwards. When faced with a life or death situation it had to be hard to choose death. About the only reason most of us were probably going along with the assault was because we had nowhere else to go.

After Moe gave the grid co ordinates, the artillery shells started coming in and created a thunderous impact. Charlie was, no doubt, deep underground waiting for the volley to end. The mountain up ahead was possibly honey-combed with an elaborate tunnel complex. I remembered watching the battle at Dak To where Charlie withstood tons of artillery rounds and jet delivered bombs only to keep returning to his post to do battle. I feared we were about to go through something similar to that nightmare.

The shelling stopped and an hour passed while we sat poised in the same position. I doubted if anyone was convinced that it had any kind of effect on our enemy. Charlie was probably cleaning up the damage and was preparing a deadly welcome for our assault. At least there would be a fleet of helicopter gun ships flying shotgun as we made our move on them. Our problem was that someone would have to get shot before we knew exactly where the enemy was. Our primary job during the war was always to draw fire from Charlie so that the gun ships could open fire on their location; of course no one wanted to get shot first. I feared that my moment of retribution was at hand and I was about to get what was coming to me for getting that kill a couple of days earlier.

Before we made our move the area was bombed and strafed by a couple of F-4 Phantom fighter jets. They were trying to build up our confidence level with some well placed bombs and napalm. If they really wanted to use bombing runs to make our jobs easier, they would have done a better job by passing around a few Bong Son Bombers to all of the willing takers. It would have been a lot cheaper.

After the firepower display was over we were quickly joined by a fleet of helicopter gun ships as the assault began. I figured I was in for a very long day or, quite possibly, my last day on the planet. The field ahead of us was full of tall elephant grass with some large waist high boulders scattered throughout. If Charlie opened up on us before we could make it to the mountain, we would at least be able to use those boulders for cover while the gunships did their thing. As we started to move my heart started to beat at that ridiculous rate again.

Our movement was slow and deliberate. Every boulder I passed gave me an exposed feeling until I drew a bead on the next one. We were only half way across the field and already I felt as if I had walked ten miles. Time was standing still as the helicopters hovered to our rear standing ready to unleash their firepower on Charlie. I wished Jahret was there because I felt it would have been his first real chance to get shot at or possibly killed before I get killed. He had been away for hours and his absence was as conspicuous to us as it must have been convenient to him.

Suddenly the gun ships opened fire. We hadn't made it to the mountain and we hadn't been fired upon either. Yet their machine gun and rocket fire was being directed to the open field directly in front of us. Their target was still a mystery to all of us on the ground. There was no one in front of us and their fire was very close.

The gunfire was chewing up the ground and splitting small trees in half. Some of the rockets were hitting the boulders and sending shrapnel flying too close for comfort. Without a doubt, they were shooting at us. We had been mistaken for the enemy and in the ensuing panic; we went scrambling in the direction of the oncoming choppers. We waived frantically hoping to alert them to their target recognition error. As we stumbled along trying desperately to get close enough to the choppers, Ellis was hit by some flying shrapnel and went down. Not being to able watch my step, I tripped and fell just before the pilots finally noticed their mistake. It couldn't have happened a moment too soon. Their line of fire was closing in on our splintered column and there was no way we could have outrun them. We had just avoided a self imposed disaster and immediately started to regroup.

Ellis had a small piece of shrapnel in his back. He was standing up with his shirt off as Doc attended his wound. A medivac was already on its way to get him. He said he was alright but it was obvious that the fragment needed to be surgically removed. Ellis persisted, but it was Doc's call. He was going to be extracted immediately. My anticipated disastrous assault had turned into another kind of disaster. We were already short of people and could ill afford to lose any to friendly fire. Charlie must've been laughing at us.

The medivac took Ellis away and added to the misery of watching our numbers shrink. Our diminishing headcount was also taking a toll on our confidence level. We were in the worst shape of my entire tour. Our company strength was under 40 men and we were locked in a deadly engagement with a battalion of NVA regulars. The mismatch was of little concern to the high ranking hard-asses who thought that our superior firepower was all that we needed to overcome the numerical disadvantage. My last three months in country was off to a scary start. We were going to be in the valley until someone, high up the chain of command, was satisfied with the amount of blood we could shed there. I started having visions of us lying on the ground dead with one of those hard-asses standing over us like George C. Scott in that movie. They'd declare victory; stuff us into body bags and return to their air conditioned strategy room to conjure up another disaster. It was definitely true about old soldiers never dying. About all they ever did was planned our deaths as they continued to write history. They supplied the strategy and we supplied the dead bodies.

There was a change in plans as it was decided to gas the mountain. Unfortunately, the wind was blowing in our faces meaning that we would be in effect gassing ourselves when the nauseous fumes passed over the intended target and eventually over our position. It sounded like a dumb idea but no one ever asked me for my opinion. The brain trust brought in a Chinook helicopter and had it drop a load of C-S canisters over the base camp and of course our own area too. In spite of the amount of diffusion that took place as the gas passed over the field ahead of us, the fumes were still pretty strong. We had already donned our gas masks but we assumed that Charlie did the same also. In training, we were always being gassed during one particular phase of training or another. We were gassed in basic training and AIT, we were even gassed at Charang Valley. I always thought that the enemy would be the ones gassing us in Vietnam though. Instead we were still gassing ourselves.

After the tear gas episode, I began to realize that I hadn't slept since I made the kill. After the previous day's action, no one slept at all. We were in such an intense situation that sleep just could not exist. Moe and Swain were doing their best to keep every one loose, but it wouldn't work. At least the assault never materialized. With 89 days left, I could think of better ways to spend my remaining time than fighting my way up a damned hill. I was curious to know if Jackson was keeping count of our days left in country. However when I asked Doc about his whereabouts, he informed me that he had already sent him in the rear for some off-the-wall ailment.

The assault was scratched but for some reason the lifers wanted to believe that Charlie had vacated the mountain. To prove how safe it was they decided to send us up there to confirm their theory. It was just as I had observed in Phu My, if they really believed that no one was there they would come along. Since they were staying behind, I assumed that the camp could still be occupied. After Baby sitting CP for the previous week, it was finally our turn to go out. It was tempting to complain; but after what the other guys had been through, I couldn't say a word about being chosen to go. We were long overdue. It would've only been fair to send us out.

We started out in a flanking maneuver of sorts. It meant we would be going up far to the left, up the mountain, and then approaching the area from the side instead of head on. Of course if Charlie was still up there, our approach wouldn't matter. He would be looking for us, because he would be looking at us, watching our every move; counting each head and licking his chops at the prospect of being in on such a turkey shoot.

Our pace was a reflection of our collective mood. Our morale was about as low as our numbers were and our confidence in accomplishing our mission was even lower. Our objective was much farther to the right. However, walking straight up to the exact location was too challenging for us at that moment. It was even harder for me because of my short-timer's status. The harder I tried to pull myself together, the worse our situation became. I never imagined things could get worse than Tuy Hoa but they did. I once thought that I couldn't get more dispirited than I was back then, but I was wrong about that also. The Crescent had deflated me more than I was then. Tuy Hoa was supposed to be the biggest hurdle that I would have to overcome. Instead, five months later, I found myself going up a hill to check out an area that had been bombed, strafed, napalmed and gassed yet none of us believed that the area was safe. Tuy Hoa never was as bad.

When our procession reached the base of the mountain, we hesitatingly started our climb. Our avenue of approach took us through the least forested part of the mountain. The only vegetation found in the area was tall grasses and some sparsely spaced bushes. The base camp was about 40 meters to our right. The camp naturally had a lot of trees to provide it with the necessary overhead camouflage. As we reached the level of the base camp, we froze in our tracks. Harrington knew for certain that none of the members of the patrol wanted anything to do with entering the wooded area. As he stood at the front of our patrol, I could sense that he was making an assessment of our willingness to follow him into the ominous camp area. Then Dat walked up to the front of the line and did what he always did.

"I go. You no follow, OK." he said as he slowly walked the remaining few meters and disappeared into the wooded area leaving our shameless contingent behind to await his fate.

"Dat is carrying us man!" Howard said with a hint of embarrassment. He was right. Dat didn't allow us to stand around looking at ourselves very long at all. He'd had enough of the self doubt that we were infected with. He took the initiative and at the same time, made us all look somewhat inferior to him as soldiers. Granted, he was an exceptional soldier; but we had all lost our edge. We couldn't expect Dat to keep bailing us out of tight situations. He was exposing himself to the danger of being captured by the same army that he deserted. We needed Dat desperately. He shouldn't have had to stick his neck out because of our reluctance.

After about ten minutes Dat finally emerged from the wooded area. He said the area was deserted. We all breathed a sigh of relief and returned to the staging area. Charlie had been popping up everywhere in the valley. His absence on that mountain only meant he had relocated somewhere else nearby. He was, no doubt, digging bunkers at his new location as we were having his old camp inspected. His brazen actions suggested he was unfazed by our presence in the valley. He was probably inspired by Hanoi Hanna's constant depiction of America as the latest invader to set foot on Vietnamese soil. When I first came over to Vietnam, our war machine gave us that pamphlet describing N. Vietnam as the aggressor. I supposed Hanoi had always called us the invaders and used Vietnam's history of resistance as an inspirational tool against us just as our writers used that same history to describe Hanoi as invaders. It had begun to appear that maybe Hanoi Hanna was closer to the truth than we were. The mere fact that we were the foreigners and they were native made it painfully obvious that we just might be the invaders no matter how honorable our intentions were. No matter how high in regard we held our democratic beliefs, our counterparts would always point to the fact that we were from another hemisphere and represented a government that they didn't exactly welcome to their soil. To those of us who had to spend time on the ground in the Crescent representing our country, it was frustrating because of our own intentions to pull out of the war. Our numerical disadvantage to that battalion was taking the wind out of our efforts. I felt that somehow our counterparts in the valley knew that we were a bunch of dispirited soldiers. Our resolve had been measured and they stood ready to exploit its low level.

We relocated near the area of my kill for resupply. When I received another letter from Barbara, I realized how important having her correspondence meant to me. For one brief moment I was taken away from all that was going on around me. My entire world consisted of that letter and the memory of the time we shared before the war interrupted us. Nothing else mattered. Of course Doc read it as if it were a requirement. He really got a kick out of Barbara's usual "Love till Hell Freezes Over" closing. He also reminded me that he was going to come to New Orleans one day. I felt rejuvenated by the letter and Doc's standard reminder of his plans to visit me after the war. Doc and Barbara had somehow made me realize that I still had a lot of life ahead of me and that I needed to stay focused on what was immediately ahead of me. The situation may have been bleak but all I had to do was remember that a future awaited me.

In the letter she also added that another two of my friends Sherman and Jessie had been drafted. Another friend, Louis, had already been drafted months earlier. The rest of that old gang of mine had been snatched up by the draft. I hoped none of them had to do any time in Vietnam. Considering our diminishing combat role, I'd say their chances were getting very slim. If I could have held out another year maybe I never would have made it either.

Lee and I finished the rest of the red beans and got past the thrill of having that unique reminder of home. It made us homesick again but we didn't care. I was only sorry that it took mom so long to send the box. After the meal we still had to deal with being in that valley. I wondered if the NVA battalion was occupying the valley back in March when we were taken away so suddenly. It was a real deadly coincidence that we were removed from there and relocated in that hot spot called Tuy Hoa only to return five months later for a worse encounter with Charlie. I was certain that if Mercein knew he stood as good a chance of getting his body count in the valley as he did in Tuy Hoa, I might have been killed months ago. A lot of us would've been dead also. Of course I couldn't be too premature with my thinking. After all we were still in the Crescent and the mission seemed far from over.

Obviously we were a better fighting unit without having to carry those Ruff Puffs around. In that valley Charlie knew we weren't encumbered by the rules of engagement that prevented us from calling in air strikes and artillery or gun ships. With no civilians around, he would either have to fight to death or hit and run. I'd prefer the latter over the former but it's hard to move an entire battalion on short notice. The logistics that came with moving such a large number of men were probably the reason we were not about to leave the valley. I was literally going to pieces thinking about our next encounter.

Thaddeus, it seemed, would never be the same again. When he wasn't babbling incoherently about nothing or everything, he just sat and stared. His situation was starting to anger me. I couldn't believe they were actually ignoring the guy's condition. We couldn't have been so desperate for people that we couldn't afford to let him go to the rear. With all of those guys in the rear faking ailments, the lifers could've done the right thing just that one time and just shown some compassion. His inappropriate and unmanageable behavior would cause a serious problem for whoever had to be alongside him. Hell, even my behavior with that rat and those frags had caused some problems for the guys in my squad. I expected to get better once we left the valley; but Thaddeus, it seemed would never recover from his trauma. His wounds were deep and the effects were going to linger for years to come.

Benn, much to my surprise, had endured the mission better than I had. I was sure it was having some kind of adverse effect on him but he was holding up better than I would have thought. Four months earlier, I figured he would have re upped before we made it to the Crescent. I never dreamed he would have gone through a hot mission without begging to sign those papers. Instead, he had found a way to cope with all that had happened

The helicopters left and with their departure went a good feeling I had come to associate with each resupply day. Every time one came around it represented a milestone of sorts. The most recent one carried the fear of not seeing another one again. We had so many run-ins with Charlie that I was afraid we would get hit during the resupply effort. I never had that fear in Tuy Hoa. Nothing, I thought, would ever happen to us during the daylight. In the Crescent, however, Charlie had abandoned his nocturnal habits and struck at will. The mental strain of adjusting to maintaining a constant vigil was taking a toll on me. I was afraid of letting my guard down during the daytime and couldn't sleep at night. I was also afraid of calling the Crescent the worst mission of my tour for fear of bringing on a bigger monster than all the rest. After all, who knew where we would be going next?

That night was the most sleepless night of all. It was 3:00 AM and again I couldn't relax enough to fall asleep. The rest of the guys had long since succumbed to fatigue and were sleeping like babies. Moe had no problems with sleeping. He was down to his last couple of weeks and showed no signs of the short-timer's dilemma that I was experiencing. I guess he was just a better man than I was. Every little noise in the valley sounded amplified to me. The frogs were croaking, the crickets were creaking and I was sitting there trying to convince myself that it wasn't Charlie somewhere nearby playing tricks with my mind. Life in the bush used to be interesting, challenging and somewhat seductive. Facing my last 86 days turned the ordeal into sheer mental torture. Jones was right about getting short. Nothing scared me more than the prospect of what might happen next. The shorter I got the worse it got. It seemed as if I would lose my mind if I had to stay in that valley much longer. I felt a lot stronger during resupply, but the darkness robbed me of that good feeling I had while reading my mail. It was good while it lasted anyway.

We had gone through at least two weeks without any drugs. Calvin would have been proud of us, I guess. He always thought that we were using the stuff as some kind of crutch and didn't believe we could go through any of the war without it. With his assessment of our abilities proven wrong, I was ready to trade in the next few days in the Crescent for one bomber. Undoubtedly, drugs must have had some kind of effect on our ability to endure. I just never thought of its use as anything but a recreational practice. And I'd always attributed the widespread use to its abundance, availability and, of course, its low price.

Doc informed me that rabies shots are a miserable experience, but I didn't think they were worse than what we were going through in that valley. In spite of it all, I wouldn't have wanted to be in the rear at that time. If our company was in the kind of mess we were in, I had to be in on it too. I didn't think I could stand not being able to lend a hand when my help was so desperately needed. Being unable to do anything but sitting and waiting while someone was in the shit would have destroyed me. I'd gone through the agony often enough to know I would rather die than to experience it again. Unfortunately, being on the scene sometimes wasn't enough. So if those guys could deal with not being able to help out, more power to them. After all, they didn't plan on contracting rabies.

When stand to arrived, it didn't bring on that usual uplifting feeling. Charlie had really screwed me up with his random appearances. The days were almost as scary as the nights. I was afraid to think of how bad or how soon our next encounter would be. There was no use wondering how much longer we would be in the valley. If I had to venture a guess, I'd simply say that we would be there as long as it took. Charlie's persistence would dictate the length of our stay and that was the biggest problem. It was as if we had to spank them for their defiant behavior.

Sgt. Smith and his topless act had become a minor source of irritation. I had never seen an upper torso as disfigured as his; at least not in the Army. The guy really thought his battle wounds were interesting. If anyone would mention anything about them, it practically guaranteed another showing the following day. My lack of enthusiasm and interest in his scars only added to our indifference toward each other.

Doc had a rear job waiting for him at the battalion aid station. He was actually supposed to be with Recon at that moment. I didn't know how he managed to get back with us, but I was not complaining. I liked having him around even if he repeatedly asked me about the Mardi Gras. I really didn't know what it was going to be like without him. Losing him to the rear would be like watching him go back to the world ahead of me. I planned to go see the doctor when we return anyway. Urinating had become a constricted process for me and I suspected that maybe my visit to Phu Cat corner with Howard was the cause. I could have left the field and had it checked but I didn't have the nerve to mention something as insignificant at that moment. It was the easiest way out of a bad situation and taking advantage of it was tantamount to desertion. I couldn't live with myself if I went to the rear and something bad was to happen after I left.

News of Vince Lombardi's death flashed over the radio. The legendary coach passed away after a lengthy battle with lung cancer. Lombardi once said that "Winning isn't everything, it's the only thing." I wonder what he thought about our involvement in Vietnam. I never heard him voice his opinion on the subject; but knowing what a tactician he was, I couldn't help but feel that he was appalled at the endless struggle we were engaged in. I could remember when he was known to call the President, the generals or whoever he had to talk to in order to get his star GI running back available to play on Sundays. I wondered if he ever called Nixon or LBJ to give them his "winning" quotation. I would have loved to spend Sundays at home too.

Both Moe and Swain were begging me for my boonie hat. I didn't know why they wanted a hat with my name and hometown embroidered on it, but they were pressing me for it. I wanted to give it to Moe for a going away present, but I couldn't part with it. He had been carrying around the AK-47 he took off of my kill. It would have made a better conversation piece than my hat if he considered taking it home with him. Officers have certain privileges that might have covered lethal souvenirs like a rifle. I knew that an enlistee couldn't even think about it. "I wish we still had some beans and rice left, homey." said Lemar. Personally, I wished that I were home eating some of my mom's cooking instead of that canned variety. In her last letter, she pointed out that since I only had three months left, it would be a good idea to take me off of the front line and placed in a nice safe area. At first I laughed but I soon realized that she must have been experiencing the same thing I was going through. I left her in November and after ten months, she obviously couldn't bear going through the agonizing finish. Maybe they ought to let mothers run all wars. Our tour of duty wouldn't have been longer than the nine months they carried us. I would have been home a month before she wrote that last letter.

The mid day sun was bearing down on us as we sat exposed to its relentless heat. It wasn't as hot as it was during the summer but under those conditions 80 degrees is unbearable. Charlie was smart enough to take refuge from the heat, but about all we did was suffer like the damned fools Garson referred to us as. The only alternative was to go searching for Charlie, and finding him was too easy in the Crescent. As long as the lifers weren't pushing the issue, I couldn't complain about the heat. I was certain that soon enough, a patrol would be sent out because taking the fight to Charlie was the name of the game. He would sit and wait for us to come after him giving him a tactical advantage over us. About all he had to do was prepare a defense for us, and we all knew it. His unwillingness to attack only fueled the notion that he was respectful of our firepower. This reluctance would only embolden our superiors to plan an aggressive pursuit to push him out of his stronghold, wherever it was at that time. It was a wicked arrangement. The old men did the planning and we followed the plans. It was just a matter of time before they came up with something again. Having Charlie around was all it took to start them dreaming of conquest. We could have gotten annihilated out there but as long as Charlie got bombed, strafed and napalmed to death, it would be considered a victory to the planners. A costly victory is still a victory to the old-timers who don't have to face the carnage.

The conditions in the valley made me feel thankful for not extending my tour. It might have gotten me out of the Army sooner but I had by then realized that I couldn't spend an extra month in Vietnam. I had already lost too many pieces of my former self and couldn't afford to lose any more. Ft. Bragg couldn't have possibly been that bad anyway. I didn't care what Kyler said about the place. I was looking forward to seeing my orders for the place and planning to do another six months of the airborne thing. Like Howard said, it was more important to go home and "Get my momma off of her knees."

I assume that by then, Mac was probably on his way back to Baltimore. I hoped he felt as if he'd seen enough of Vietnam and didn't feel cheated by his sudden departure. He was enjoying his tour and seemed to get a lot out of being in country. Kyler said that Mac received a million dollar wound; the kind that gets you out of combat and out of the Army too. Ellis' wound must have been one of those ten dollar jobs but was said to be in line to receive a Purple Heart for it. I wondered what his views were on being decorated for a wound he received from friendly fire. CIB notwithstanding, I was glad Purvis talked Garson out of considering having us decorated for what we did that night at Tuy Hoa. After that humiliating experience, I would have flat out refused it.

We spent the rest of the day and that night in place. I didn't know how many sleepless nights my body could take, but I was ready to find out. Our stay in the valley had already pushed me to the mental and physical limits of endurance and I didn't have much of an appetite. I only wanted to see the end of the mission. Charlie cooperated by staying out of sight and the lifers hadn't sent us out looking for him for at least the previous couple of days. This trend was about to end. They readied the ill-fated patrol for another trek into the unknown. It should have been well understood by then that we were outnumbered and patrolling stretched our meager numbers to a dangerously low level. All rescue attempts would be both perilous and nearly impossible. I could only hope that they would go just out of sight and play it safe. They'd already lost Mac in one firefight and of course the KIA in that base camp. Surely they wouldn't play with fire again after getting burned twice.

During most lulls, we usually entertained ourselves by playing cards, writing letters or just listening to the music. Instead of the usual activity, we found ourselves staying on alert, waiting for Charlie to strike. At least in Tuy Hoa we had all day to enjoy ourselves. Nothing bad ever happened after sunrise. I thought that all I had to do was survive that village and everything else would be easy. Nothing, however, was more disturbing than dealing with Charlie both day and night. "I wish we had some more red beans and rice with some French bread and a Barq's root beer." said Lee. He was still on that New Orleans high that my mother put him on. He managed to get a lot of mileage out of those two meals. I enjoyed it too but I didn't like being homesick. He was killing me with all of the talk about stuff we couldn't have.

After the patrol left, I started to think about all of the bad luck they had experienced in the valley. They were finding Charlie at every turn. They set a course that took them straight up the mountain we were camped near. If they didn't go too far, it would be the smartest thing they could do. The rest of us just sat tight and waited for nothing to happen. Spurlock and Smitty had assumed command of the company in Jahret's absence. In spite of Moe's commission, he was content with his role as FO. He was not exactly what one would consider a take charge guy anyway. Of course that was what we all liked about the guy. He always went out of his way to be just one of the guys. Pulling rank was not his style. He was a role player and set a good enough example for all of us. He was easily a far better officer than Jahret could ever hope to become.

Somewhere in our loosely defined perimeter, Stevie Wonder could be heard singing "Signed, Sealed, Delivered." It made me wish that I had already been delivered home at that time. In the beginning of my tour, the music would literally carry me through a mission. Some songs used to really pick me up and it was special to hear the DJ Chris Noel occasionally dedicate a number to our Company. Being short had changed everything about being in Vietnam though. The music was nothing more than something that we listened to. There were no magical properties to assist me with my coping abilities. It was foolish to even think that a song would help me through something like what we were going through.

The music was interrupted by the sound of a burst of fire from an M-16. The sound was from a very close range and could've only been one of our own guys shooting at someone.

"A gook was standing right here!" someone shouted. Charlie had boldly walked down the mountain and stood watching us until his presence was detected. He stood within the wooded area of the mountain adjacent to our location. According to the shooter, he was practically standing in our midst. In spite of his close proximity, he managed to get away without being hit. His escape route was the same one taken by our patrol when they left a couple of hours earlier. Charlie had relocated somewhere up the hill and we had been situated just below his new area all day.

Suddenly more shooting erupted further up the hill. Our hard luck patrol was in the shit again. The exchange of small arms fire was intense and was also a lot closer than I first thought. Spurlock was on the horn sizing up the situation. We were about to go through the dreaded routine of going to someone's rescue again. This time it was pretty evident that we would be ambushed before we reached our destination. Charlie's numbers were huge compared to ours. He had the luxury to dispatch a handful of shooters to delay us. We were about to play right into his hand. For sure, there was at least one spotter somewhere up the mountain standing within the wooded area watching us. Our avenue of approach would be reported as soon as we committed. There was little else we could do but assemble to move to their assistance and into the teeth of their well planned ambush.

A fleet of gun ships arrived to provide us with air cover as we made our move. It was probably the same bunch of morons that fired on us the other day. Their presence, thanks to that mishap, was not exactly a reassuring sign. It was only an added element of danger. In spite of all that could go wrong, we still had to make the move.

One of the helicopters landed and dropped off Jahret. He was flying overhead and had gained a better view of what was happening. He was wearing a brand new set of fatigues and walking very casual. Those guys were in the fight of their lives and he showed no sense of urgency. I hadn't heard any reports of casualties but I felt it would only be a matter of time. The AK fire was louder than anything else and I doubted if they could hold out much longer. They were probably surrounded again and this time it looked bad.

Jahret huddled with the rest of the lifers and gave them an appraisal of what was going on at the location of the firefight. His knowledge of the firefight was about as reassuring as those hovering gun ships were. We still had to walk into an anticipated wall of flying lead to find out exactly where they were. Then we would have to survive the gunships return fire while tending to our wounded. At that moment I doubted if I would get out of that valley alive. The worst case scenarios were wreaking havoc with my mind and my ability to move to their assistance.

We all lined up for departure with Sgt. Smith at the point. He was followed by Spurlock and Jahret. It looked like a golden opportunity to shoot Jahret and all I had was HE rounds on my vest. I felt that my life was about to end and I only wished that I could be sure that Jahret would die also. Of course at that point it looked like a suicide mission so the thought of doing him before the shooting started was senseless. The objective of saving those guys at the top of the hill erased the thought of killing anyone else but those who stood in our way.

We started to move around the mountain instead of up. The different approach would make little difference. Their spotter would only notify their ambush team to move to any part of the mountain slope and lie in wait. I was certain that they would be ready to ambush us at the most opportune moment. Jahret and Spurlock, after moving along for only about a few meters, stepped aside to let us pass them by almost as if they were positioning us to get shot first.

"I guess this is where we'll all get killed!" I said as we filed past them. We were moving into another abandoned rice paddy and the area was wide open leaving us fully exposed with nowhere to run for cover. The mountain's apron was only a few meters away from a bordering rice paddy dike and we were slowly approaching it while my heart was literally exploding inside of my chest. The mountainside was not too forested but it had a lot of concealing knee high bushes blanketing its lower face. We could've been staring directly at our executioners without knowing it. They were probably waiting for enough of us to walk into their designated kill zone before opening up on us.

A volley of automatic gunfire zeroed in on the lead element of our column dropping Smitty in the process. Bullets were cracking, thumping and whizzing by us as everybody took cover behind the nearest rice paddy dike. Smitty was still lying wounded and exposed as a full-scale fire fight erupted around him. As he lay sprawled in the middle of the rice paddy, bullets were passing over him in both directions. Doc John immediately ran to his assistance. Doc Reardon joined him and both started to attend Smitty's wound totally oblivious to the flying bullets. They were acting as if they were inside of an operating room. I couldn't believe what was happening before me. I jumped up and ran past the three of them and situated myself at the base of the mountain as if I were covering the medics as they continued to work on Smitty. Joley and Walkup, acting on instinct, had already moved up as the three of us formed our own fire team in support of our medics. "I think I can see them!" said Joley as he started to crawl farther. I grabbed him and managed to keep him on line with us. We were facing nothing but bushes on an incline and somewhere up that hill were an undetermined number of shooters. About all we could do was to lay down the suppressive fire from our position in front of our two exposed medics at work. "Cease fire! Cease fire!" shouted Jahret. He had been trying to get us to stop shooting almost since we started. The unmistakable sound of an AK kept going off repeatedly sending us into another shooting frenzy. As long as we kept hearing it, we never would stop. The gun ships were also scaring the living hell out of me and adding to the chaos with their rocket fire. Their position behind us only made matters worse. Every pass they made raised the hair on my neck. The door gunners all seemed to be able to locate their target which was more than anyone of us on the ground could do. All of which was happening as both medics continued to work feverishly on Smitty in the middle of the firefight.

Nearly half of my shells weren't exploding on impact and reloading duds in the middle of a firefight was frustrating the hell out of me. "Man your shit aint explodin!" Howard yelled as if I hadn't noticed already. Charlie had effectively delayed us with his anticipated ambush. Farther up the hill things were, by that time, getting pretty hot for our hard luck patrol. Unfortunately, we wouldn't be going anywhere until we got Smitty evacuated out of there. Although Alpha Company was on the way to link up with us to make the assault, they weren't coming fast enough. Time was precious and it was definitely running out on those guys up that hill. The helplessness of the situation started to overwhelm me again. The familiarity of it had already started to become second hand. If we had to suffer through letting those guys get killed while waiting for help to arrive I don't think that I could've gone any further with the war. It would have been too much for me.

The medivac finally came and extracted Smitty. Walkup, Joley and I did a fire and retreat movement back to the rice paddy dike where the rest of the guys were on line. As I ran back I noticed that Moe had been firing that captured AK. It was Moe's firing and not Charlie that I heard during the firefight. We actually hadn't been upon fired at since they finished working on Smitty and was obviously the reason Jahret kept yelling at us to cease fire. I was down to about half of the amount of HE's I started off with, and we still hadn't made it up the hill. We hadn't even started. "Doc! What the fuck were you doing out there? I asked.

"I was doing my job."

"But that was Smitty man. He'll just get patched up, sent back to the world only to return next year. He likes this shit. You can't go out there trying to save someone like Smitty." I said.

"Well Handy, I've got to patch him up just like I would if it were you." he said. Of course he was right, but someone like Smitty would just keep coming back to Vietnam until he got killed. He would probably be back in '71. There was a fourth Purple Heart with his name on it already just waiting for him to claim.

As the air war continued overhead, my thoughts centered on what it must've been like up on that hill. There wasn't much shooting going on but we wouldn't dare attempt any maneuver in their direction while the choppers were chewing up the surrounding landscape with machine gun and rocket fire. After Ellis got hit, we all developed a much deserved fear of the term "friendly fire". Their line of fire had to be more accurate this time. It appeared as if the gunships were the only thing that was keeping those guys alive. We were reduced to mere observers as we waited for Alpha Co. to arrive. We were still outnumbered, but at lest we'd have an entire line company to link up with before we make our move. The link-up would make it harder to outflank us with the aid of the gunships. The rules were different out in the field where we didn't have to worry about collateral damage. We were able to bring our full power to bear on them out there.

Although the situation on the hill seemed desperate to me, their confidence level was rising. I didn't know what was keeping those guys from being wiped out but whatever it was, I just hoped they could make it last until we could do something to get them out of their predicament. I was sure that they were practically out of ammo because we were pretty low ourselves. Something needed to happen and quick. The firefight had become a revisitation of Tuy Hoa where Charlie had one element surrounded and cut off from the rest of us. With a little good fortune maybe the outcome would be different the second time around. The constantly recurring situation was taking too much out of me. I couldn't stand the part where we just stood by unable to do anything. I felt like running up that hill alone just to rewrite the script but was too afraid to make a move.

A fleet of helicopters came into view and was closing in on our location fast. They were still quite a distance away, but I assumed they were Alpha Co. Their arrival was not a minute too soon because the situation had to be reaching a critical stage by then. There was no way to determine how much longer they could hold out. It was about to get dark and, in spite of Charlie's departure from the norm, he still ruled the night. We needed to make our move before the sun went down.

A huge fireball was suddenly launched from near the top of the mountain. The orange glowing object streaked across the sky and narrowly missed a helicopter. It was a B-40 rocket and Charlie was trying to shoot the helicopters out of the sky. The slicks carrying Alpha Co started landing at least 200 meters to our right rear. They were all disembarking and taking up positions behind the nearest rice paddy dike. The B-40 salvo gained a measure of respect because Alpha Co. wasn't moving up at all. Alpha Co.'s position hiding behind a dike would be of little help to us. The situation didn't look well for those guys up on that hill. We couldn't possibly make the assault by ourselves and Alpha Co. looked too comfortable back there playing it safe. I really couldn't blame them for what they did. Those rockets could do a lot of damage. I just didn't like sitting stationary and doing nothing to affect the outcome. Even the gunships left to avoid the dreaded B-40. We appeared to be in for an all night stand off because the darkness was creeping up on us rapidly.

As the night descended upon us, it became evident that Charlie wouldn't make an all out assault on those guys. If they did, all hell would have been brought to bear upon that position. I was more than certain that they wouldn't want to take away the only thing that was keeping us from unloading indiscriminately on their position. If they would have over run that position, there wouldn't have been any reason to be cautious or careful of where the ordinance fell. I had heard of similar fire missions being called in by GI's on their own besieged position. Since desperate situations called for extreme measures, plans were made to introduce "Puff" to the skies above the guys on the hill. "Puff," a.k.a. "Puff the Magic Dragon" was an AC-47 workhorse gunship. The plane, an adapted DC-3 commercial airliner, was outfitted with three 7.62mm mini-guns, each firing 6,000 rounds per minute. The plane would circle over head and ring the perimeter of those guys with a protective wall of lead that would make it extremely hazardous for all living objects that got in the way.

Later that night as Puff arrived; we moved our position back about another 50 meters and settled down for the night. My only concern was the remote possibility of having Charlie come running down the hill and over-running our position. Mini-guns were known to create desperate panic and have, on occasion, caused Charlie to make such moves to escape the furious firepower of these rapid firing machines. "Puff" was literally raining bullets down on the area surrounding their perimeter. Any encroachment would've been suicidal. The plane continually circled over head as the NVA battalion tried their best to make what we imagined was a desperate retreat from the area.

We also requested and received a pass by the plane over the base of the mountain. It was extremely dark and we wanted to be sure that they had not assembled near the bottom of the mountain to make a desperate run at us. As the bullets fell over the area it sounded like raindrops hitting the leaves during a rainstorm. It reassured us that no one was hiding in the bushes waiting to launch that ground assault. It was so reassuring that Doc was beginning to relax a little too much. He was nodding out like a junkie. "Doc, Doc! How can you fall asleep at a time like this?" I asked, while shaking him violently.

"Because I'm fucking tired and I'm fucking sleepy!" he said angrily.

"Sleepy! Man Charlie might come down that fucking hill and try to wipe us out. We can't let our guard down now!" I said.

"Well if they come you can wake me up. Now let me get some sleep." he said as he snuggled up against the dike and went to sleep. As I looked around, I noticed that almost everyone had already fallen asleep. For the previous 3-4 days we had practically abandoned the practice for fear of being killed. That moment on that rice paddy was the best opportunity we'd come across to get some sleep during that time period. We knew where Charlie was and he was not about to bother us. We didn't even need to pull guard for a change. However, I still couldn't manage to sleep that night either. My adrenal glands were working too hard to allow it to happen. That B-40 rocket was still fresh on my mind. It had a way of putting fear in the hearts of any who would dare to challenge it. When they fired that first one at those helicopters, it looked as if the side of that mountain just opened up and spat a huge fire ball out of it. I couldn't stop replaying the image in my mind.

4

"Puff" managed to keep a hot perimeter around those guys all night. According to Spurlock, our intelligence reported that there were heavy casualties inflicted on that battalion as it tried to evacuate the area. It must have been hell on Charlie trying to vacate while some plane was raining nearly twenty thousand bullets on him every minute. It really did save our patrol though. After their all night ordeal, they were fortunate enough to see the next day and were expected to return from the top of that hill intact. In spite of how heavy the odds were stacked against them, they managed to survive being surrounded and cut off without suffering any casualties of their own.

Alpha Co. boarded their helicopters and returned to Uplift. They never moved from their spot behind that dike. They just played it safe all night. Again I couldn't complain because everything turned out alright. I wished that all rescue efforts could have ended the same way. Those guys didn't even have to move to an extraction site. They were picked up exactly where they were dropped off. They deserved to return to their much needed stand down. The practice of bailing out another company had become an all too familiar part of being in the rear on a stand down and needed to stop soon.

It was resupply day and everybody would have a chance to replace all of their spent ammunition. It was too bad the brass wouldn't let us leave the valley after all we had been through. They should have listened to their own intelligence reports and called it a victory. Instead I was afraid that they would send us looking for dead bodies and or drag trails on the ground. Their quest for evidence of a body count had to be the most insane pursuit of the war.

The patrol finally began that trip down the mountain and, one by one, started coming into view. They passed through the possible location the shooters used to ambush us and majestically stepped out of the bushes. They then walked the rest of the distance to the base of the mountain and onto the rice paddy square. Their beleaguered appearance was a welcome sight to the rest of us. They were unbowed by their traumatic experience. I was choked with pride just to be there watching them walk with their heads held high. It was an unforgettable moment. In spite of everything that I'd been through in country, I felt proud to be a part of it all. Joe South had to be referring to us when he sang…."Walk a mile in my shoes."

The supply slicks came loaded with that extra ammo along with the mail, food, water and fresh fatigues. Reloading and cleaning our weapons, as expected, was the top priority for that day. Howard, of course, had his beloved Roscoe broken down again and was giving each part a thorough cleaning. He gave a good account of himself during the firefight. For a moment he was displaying the savvy of a more seasoned combat tested veteran. He was as calm as someone on a rifle range as he reloaded magazines under fire. I expected as much from him and he didn't disappoint me at all. Joley, on the other hand, proved the old timers right about being afraid. He was actually about to go crawling uphill into the same bushes that everyone was firing over our heads into. He was as fearless as anyone I had ever met;

a little too fearless for his own good though. His eagerness to engage Charlie could have jeopardized everything.

Among the letters I received was one from Mrs. Wheelhouse along with another care package. Howard became upset at the way the goodies disappeared so fast. He didn't like the way the guys all got to eat the stuff while I did all of the writing. I was surprised that it mattered so much to him. He should have realized that the goodies were to be enjoyed by everybody.

Resupply ended a little suddenly. Before I knew it, all of the helicopters had left before I could send back our trash. I decided to burn all of the trash that our squad created during our C-rations distribution and dug a sump into the ground for all of our discarded boxes. I hated the way we left so much litter everywhere we were resupplied. Harrington informed me that we just might be leaving the valley soon. It was the best news that I had heard since April when the rumor about our leaving Tuy Hoa turned out to be true. It made sense to call it quits after that all night battle. "Puff" had put a savage beating on that battalion. It was time to cut our losses and leave.

The little fire that I started soon grew into a bonfire. Everyone was throwing their trash into the fire as it continued to grow. Jahret spotted the fire and went into another one of his tirades over the inferno. It was foolish to add to the fire but Jahret was going wild again and of course made the situation worse than it had to be. It started to get dark and the fire showed no sign of subsiding. It had become a glaring sight that could've easily been spotted from a distance. Our sight discipline was being compromised which only added fuel to the tantrum that Jahret was having. It had turned into an unusual mission; three firefights and two fires. At least the second fire couldn't spread. After Jahret ran out of words, we packed and left the area. We found a spot nearer the populated area and settled down for the night.

Before retiring, I read Mrs. Wheelhouse's letter. She was still struggling with her loss. I had hoped that by then she would be doing better but her letters were still full of agonizing grief. Her level of despair was deepening. I was convinced that she would never get over the death of her son. Her feelings were only going to get worse as the war continued and constantly reminded her of her sacrifice. Again she mentioned my DEROS date and asked me when I would return. I was torn between wanting to make it home alive to put her fears to rest, and at the same time not making her feel cheated. Being short was also beginning to make me feel guilty. I just couldn't win. One day in the not so distant future, our combat involvement in Vietnam would be coming to an end. Americans back home would no doubt rejoice at the end of the struggle that had torn us apart. The war would continue, but America would be at peace. Nixon would probably extend his so-called Vietnamization bullshit program long enough to be re-elected. N. Vietnam, in our wake, would be expected to sweep across S. Vietnam and through the so-called ARVN army. Vietnam would, no doubt, be reunited under the communist flag and all of us who had fought the war will suffer one last psychological wound as the Saigon Government collapsed. Hopefully the mothers who had lost their sons in Vietnam wouldn't feel as if their sons had died for nothing. This would be the biggest tragedy of the war. We were fighting an un-winnable war that we wouldn't exactly lose. The obvious outcome would hurt our country's pride because we were used to winning our wars and bringing our troops home as conquering heroes. In spite of Nixon's efforts, it would always look like we backed out of this one. Our death toll would continue to climb as we redeployed and in the end, we would blame the anticipated loss on an ineffective, uninspired, but well armed ARVN army.

The following day, we left the Crescent Valley on foot. As usual, the Army could only be counted on to come up with helicopters when we needed to make an assault. I guess they were hoping for us to run into Charlie one last time before we left. Along the way I gave the remainder of the Uncle Ben's rice to an old Mama San who probably never saw rice packaged the way that box was. It would probably be her first serving of rice minus all of the trash that she had grown accustomed to. I hoped she didn't think that Uncle Ben was a relative of mine.

When we finally arrived at the highway, Moe started collecting smoke grenades from some of the guys. After he had at least one grenade of each color, he tied them to a long stick. When the trucks arrived he jumped aboard the lead truck and as we pulled off, he pulled the pins on each grenade. The lead truck was leaving a trail of multi colored smoke billowing in its wake caused by Moe's demonstration of how to go out in style. It was his last day in the field and he was expected to begin his out-processing when he returned to Uplift. The smoke grenade practice was usually preformed from a helicopter but Moe didn't let the mode of transportation prevent him from doing what he had probably been planning for months. It was unfortunate that I didn't have a camera to capture the colorful event. Moe would be missed by everyone in our company. He was a class guy that will always be remembered. Forget about smoke grenades tied to a stick. He had already gone out in style in my book. That last firefight with him blasting away with that AK was unforgettable. I wondered what it would be like when Kyler Jackson and I left. In another 83 days I expected to find out.

Suddenly Uplift came into view. When the trucks rolled through the gate, we were soon joined by the rest of the company. They were, to say the least, glad to see us back again. They were actually thrilled about it. There were hugs, dap, smiles and even a tear or two being shared by everyone. Obviously emotions were running high because of what had transpired in their absence. It was reassuring to know that the guys shared the same feeling about not being able to lend a hand when help was so desperately needed. Without a doubt, that awesome agonizing feeling nearly consumed the entire collection of rabies patients and ghosters. Their welcome was overwhelming. We were a lot closer than most families could ever hope to be. Again I was proud to be a part of this collection of young Americans.

As our new procedure required, we all checked our weapons in with the armorer, a move that didn't sit too well with most of us. It also nearly caused a riot during our last firefight in the Crescent. According to those who were in the rear at the time, they nearly broke into the armory to get the weapons out of desperation. They couldn't stand not being allowed to join in the battle. I didn't know what quelled the near mutiny, but somehow cooler heads prevailed. Being unable to get to our exact location probably had a lot to do with it. It had to be quite a scene. I was right about being in the shit. It's better to be out there getting shot at than sitting around listening at reports about your friends. Just knowing that those guys felt the same way proved that I was with the right kind of people.

After weapons check-in, we all followed our ritual of going to our favorite off-limit spots. I must have been the only one heading to the first aid station. When I told the doctor about my suspicions he went into a tirade about GI's contracting VD. He never even examined me. Instead he went straight to the refrigerator and grabbed some cold penicillin. I was given a very painful shot in the buttocks and sent limping out the door. I was confused by the way the doctor reacted and treated me. I could only hope that I really had the clap, because he had started treating me for it and I had to report for more shots. In his tirade he said that all GI's who caught the clap should have more time added onto their tour. Fortunately he wasn't running the war because somebody would have fragged his ass and quick.

As I limped to the bunker line, I passed Jahret and another Lieutenant engaged in conversation. I overheard him tell the other officer, who wasn't in our company, about how many men he lost on his last mission. He made it sound as if he was trying to one-up him. Maybe weapons check-in wasn't such a bad idea after all. The new weapons initiative could possibly be the only thing that would keep the troops from killing Jahret while at Uplift on stand down. There seemed to be too many guys who were being sent home dead and wounded due to a lack of leadership. I also feared that he would eventually get me killed also. I then realized that maybe that last firefight just might have been the golden opportunity utilized so often in the past to replace ineffective leaders.

I made it to the bunker line and finally got reacquainted with the exhilarating rush of a Bong Son Bomber. For a minute, I forgot about Jahret the doctor and that penicillin shot. Then I sat down and felt the pain again. It started shaping up to be a very forgettable stand down along with some predictably painful sit downs. I had more visits ahead, and I'd already seen too much of the doctor and the aid station.

While on the bunker line, Kostrewva introduced me to Ulion Morris, or Steve as everybody called him. Steve was a black guy from the west bank of New Orleans. He was in Recon and was very close to Kostrewva. Steve said that the Sui Cai was as hot as ever and that they were spending a lot of time there. I knew the time was coming soon when we would be making our much anticipated appearance there. I was already aware that the area was close but not as close as Steve pointed out. The area was in full view from the bunker line. Firebase Washington was practically a football field away from Bunker #11. The two fire bases had been doing a lot of damage, we were told and Charlie had been harassing them regularly. He also said that in spite of their close proximity to Uplift, both fire bases Washington and Floyd were still two lonely, desolate outposts for the few guys inhabiting them. For some reason, the decision had been made to only have about a dozen guys on either base. According to Steve, Charlie sent sappers at them practically every night. My guess was that if things ever got out of hand on either fire base, whoever was on stand down would be sent out to the rescue. Right about then, however, I already had more than my fill of rescue missions. "Handy, is it mandatory to spend your R&R out of country?" Baby San asked me.

"Isn't that what R&R is all about?"

"I was thinking about spending my R&R on Lido beach with…."

"That hooker! You want to spend your R&R with her on that beach?"

"Dig it." he said. Baby San's crush on the whore had obviously gotten out of hand. He should've realized that there was another company of GI's there at all times. His so-called girlfriend was probably laid up with a paying customer as we spoke. Someone needed to tell him that she probably wouldn't put business aside to play house with an infatuated kid. Personally, I had my own R&R problems. Due to my ongoing treatment, I would have to pass on my trip to Taipei. It would have been fun being reunited with Walter but my undiagnosed condition would never permit it to happen in the middle of treatment.

Jackson was very relieved to be reunited with me. He told me how bad he was feeling during that firefight. He actually said that if something would've happened to me, he didn't know how he would have reacted. I had never seen the guy get that serious and didn't know he had a weakness for moments of high drama. This was someone I had served with for the previous twelve months.

That night during bunker guard, firebase Washington came under attack. Actually there were some sappers in the wire trying their best to harass those guys, but they were easily repulsed. Col. Farris and a couple of other hard-asses hopped a slick and flew over to the outpost. I guess they wanted to smell some gun smoke. Anyway we witnessed the entire gun battle. The hill was so close that we were able to easily distinguish the little bastards silhouetted against the muzzle flashes and explosions. I didn't think that

Charlie was serious about attacking those guys though. I thought it was an attempt at intimidating those guys because their presence in the valley was so intimidating to the traffic. It was an equally measured response and nothing more. If Charlie was serious about taking that hill, Uplift would have come under attack simultaneously. Of course you couldn't tell Col. Farris any of that stuff. He had helicopters flying all over the valley looking for the rest of them.

We made our morning formation in time and no one was AWOL. Being AWOL had already cost Jackson a stripe. It seemed that while we were in the Crescent and he was in the rear ghosting, he did a disappearing act. He went to Phu Cat to spend a night at a whorehouse and came back three days later. After being passed over for months for promotion, he had literally given the stripe back to the lifers for some hooker. I thought that I knew the guy better but I guess I didn't. He said it was so good, he couldn't leave her. We agreed to disagree on that one.

Doc had settled into his new job over at the aid station. He told me not to come in during the daytime for my shots. The doctor would only give me another cold injection and the shots were less painful when the penicillin was warmer. He also wanted me to listen to a tape by a group called Crosby, Stills, Nash, and Young titled Déjà Vu. One of the other medics received it from the world and he said that it was the best he'd ever heard. If it really was that good, I figured that maybe I ought to go see him and find out for myself. "Handy, guess what your homeboy did to me?" Kool Aid said to me angrily.

"What happened?"

"He ripped me off of my rations card." he said.

"Bullshit! Lee wouldn't do anything like that." I insisted.

"Not Lee. It was Diamond." he said. Obviously Diamond had yet to realize that he was in Charlie Co as a last chance case and would be shipped out fast for taking that card. Maybe he just didn't care. He was still hooked on that fast action of the Black Market and those rations cards were just too tempting to ignore. He weighed the gain of the betrayal and took advantage of one of the guys he was closest to. His disregard for the bond that normally existed between the guys had left Kool Aid angered as well as dismayed. I was disappointed at what he did too, but Kool Aid had found it necessary to approach me about it. He seemed to be equating our common ties to New Orleans to his loss. "Where is he now?" I asked.

"Nobody knows. He used a story about buying something for his little sister. He claimed he lost his."

"Well be cool and wait. He's got to show up sooner or later." I said.

Later that day Kostrewva and I went over to a new opium den. I never knew anything about its existence, but it was packed with G.I.'s from both LZ English and Uplift. While there, we had to hide in the attic because of a surprise visit from a couple of National Policemen. It must have been a shakedown. The two girls running the place were relatively new and, I assumed, had yet to establish themselves in the trade. After all, Vietnam was the most corrupt country on the planet, and I doubt if there were any Elliot Ness types on the force. Doing business meant paying off the cops. We couldn't go through the routine of climbing up a ladder to hide inside the attic to hide from the police too often.

We made it back in time for formation again and appeased the lifers' demand for that all-important head count. Next to the vaunted body count, the head count ranked a close second. Accountability, however, was far outdistanced by their real motive for the three head counts. I always thought that it was nothing more than a trap set up to penalize any potential AWOL GI.

Thaddeus was still in a daze. Make that in another world. He managed to make it to all formations but was only going through the motions. Some of his close friends approached the lifers about doing something about his condition. His behavior was too obvious to ignore but the lifers were doing a good job of it. He never stood at attention during formation and continually babbled on about nothing in particular. When formation broke, he followed some of the guys back to the highway to hitch a ride to the village. They were literally baby-sitting him.

After our last formation, I paid Doc a visit over at the Aid station. After hours, when the doctors finally retired to their quarters, the Aid Station was transformed into a house party. All of the medics were heads and they all had lots of dope. A surprising number of them were heroin addicts. We sat around smoking and listening to Déjà Vu all night. I liked the tape almost as much as Doc. I immediately recognized their distinguishing harmonizing vocals. They did a song in the summer called Four Dead in Ohio. It was a protest song about those students who were killed at Kent State in May. Of course I heard it on Hanoi Hannah's show because AFVN would never play anything with any anti-war content.

Doc either loved his new job a lot or he was just glad to have me over for the night. I was glad to see him get his much deserved assignment in the rear. As much as I would hate to be in the field without him, I thought he would have a better chance of making it back to the world alive by finishing his time in the rear. After what I witnessed during that last firefight, maybe the rear was the best move for him. Replacing Doc would not be easy as he had contributed a great deal since I first taught him how to clean his M-16. I wished his replacement the best of luck.

During the morning formation, Thaddeus kept talking about some girl he met in the village. He claimed that she was his brother's girlfriend when he was in country before Tet '68. His constant chatter during the formation only exposed the lifers' intentions. They were going to ignore Thaddeus's problem until he came to them seeking help. Of course in his condition he would never make the move. I should've written Boggs about Thaddeus. Sooner or later the race issue was sure to raise its ugly head. Thaddeus was black and that would be all it took for one observer to start pointing it out to the others. In the meantime, Thaddeus would be cared for by the guys in his platoon. They were expected to do whatever was needed to keep him from getting himself killed.

When we broke formation, we made a beeline for bunker #9 and found Baby San arguing with one of his old friends from TOC. They were actually holding a harmless conversation but they addressed each other with a lot of rancor. They were loud and abusive to each other but, in spite of it all, they never came to blows. "Baby San, can I have one of those bombers?" I asked.

"Here take the mother fucker!" He said angrily as he handed it to me.

"Fucking BT's really puts you in a gorilla bag don't they." said Kool Aid.

"BT's?"

"Binoctols, they're on BT's man." Kool Aid informed me. Binoctols were pills that I always thought were downers. I never knew about them causing the user to get angry with the world. I experienced the effect of downers before and never cared much for them. With all of the good pot available in Vietnam, I never considered doing any Binoctols. I was glad that I didn't too.

"Man guess what your homeboy did to me." said Ice Berg.

"Don't tell me he hit you for your rations card too."

"Yeah man, he hit a lot of guys." he said. Diamond was as ruthless as they came. He didn't care at all about what those guys thought of him. He was making suckers out of the entire first platoon. I doubted if he would last much longer than it would take to place him on a plane and sent back to the world. It just might have been his intention all along or maybe the Black Market was so intoxicating that he had problems withdrawing from it. His days seemed numbered in our company. He would not last much longer with Charlie Co. considering all of the problems he was causing.

Kyler informed me that he was planning on taking my R&R to Taipei since I wouldn't be going anywhere soon. There was nothing that I could do about it because of my treatment schedule. With the R&R coming up in less than two weeks, I doubted if I could recover fast enough to make the trip. I figured that I could live without going anywhere until November.

After our last formation, I took in another one of those free first run movies. The screen was still in the same spot that I watched Patton in. The screen was also still wearing all of the battle scars from that pelting that we inflicted upon it. The movie was a much better one than Patton. Rod Steiger starred in "No way to treat a Lady". It was great. Half of us spent the night in the same spot we watched the movie in. Some of the guys were drunk and some of them were on those damned BT's. Of course I left them and joined the heads on the bunker line for another night of evading the Officer of the Day. Col Farris was really serious about putting an end to the bunker line gatherings. He had, no doubt, been informed of the level of non-conformity that he was up against and had stepped up his efforts to change our ways. He was wasting his time, though. Nothing could ever prevent a bunch of heads from doing their thing. After all, what else could he do to us? Send us to Vietnam? Some of the guys didn't want to leave. One of the not so new guys at the party claimed that he had been in Vietnam since '68 and swore that he'd never leave.

During the morning formation, Thaddeus had a glow about him. He spent the night in the village and had been doing so for the previous couple of nights. He also spent the entire day over there too. In fact, he only came back to Uplift for formations and meals. I was concerned about his future and wondered if he would survive the rest of his tour. I felt awful knowing how his family would feel when he returned home. He was nowhere near the same person that he used to be before we went into that valley. I lost a huge part of my former self also. Staying alive was not the only struggle facing me. I was at the mercy of our next traumatic experience. Thaddeus had become another one of those guys that survived that battle on "Hamburger Hill."

Our following formation was to take place at the stage area where I watched the live show that reunited me with Dangerfield; my friend who was serving a tour of duty as a bass guitarist. I kicked myself every time I thought about how he lucked out by volunteering for that detail. He'd never been in the field, hadn't ate c-rations since training, never got his feet wet and definitely hadn't been shot at either.

Our newest arrival from the world was a Puerto Rican from Minnesota named Cruz. He was the kind of guy who was looking for a fight. Charlie, I figured, just had to meet this guy. His biggest problem was that he was also ready to take on everybody else also. He had a huge chip on his shoulder with a matching combative attitude. He claimed that he had never backed down from a fight and had no intention of backing down from Charlie. His favorite line was "If we can't get along, we can get it on." Every time he recited it, he put up his fists as if he was prepared to back up his word. I pointed out to him that everybody in Charlie Co. was his friend and that he needed to accept us as one of his own. He only repeated his line again and with that, I gave up on him. I was convinced that he would eventually get fragged by one of his own. We were already fighting against two enemies and we definitely didn't need another. As ugly as it seemed, his execution would eventually become a necessary action. Contrary to his favorite line, if he can't get along with us, the only thing that he would get on would be a helicopter with his dead ass stuffed inside of a body bag.

Sgt Harrington got into some trouble with the lifers. He had a minor drinking problem that managed to irritate the wrong person. His behavior, in my opinion, was no worse than the rest of those ass hole juicers when they'd had a few too many. At his request, he wanted me to write some kind of letter to his tormentor that would shed some light on his good character and his ability to lead. It all seemed odd for a juicer to come to a head for such a favor. When I imagined myself saving a juicer from being disciplined by another juicer for being juiced, I had to laugh. Harrington had heard about my proclivity for writing letters and thought that I would be a natural choice. I told him how much I wasn't flattered by his assessment, but agreed to do it anyway.

Before writing the letter, I headed over to check on any incoming mail. On the way I ran into Diamond who immediately tried to rip me off of my ration card with a sad song about his grandmother. When I exposed him he only smiled and went seeking his next sucker. It was too bad that Diamond turned out to be one of those uncontrollable guys who didn't care about who he stepped on. His days were definitely numbered and I assumed he was just forcing the issue. He was a real likeable guy and, from what I had heard, one hell of a Ranger before he ran afoul of his superiors in Saigon. He would only be remembered for what he had done in the last few days though. For that he wouldn't be missed at all. I just hoped that all of his victims would forgive me for being the same hometown as he was. I didn't plan it that way. Moose did the same thing before he left us a few months earlier. I would personally prefer to be remembered for what I contributed and that was what confused me about the issue. I couldn't understand how one could share the time and experience of being together in the bush and just piss on the others in the end.

I picked up my mail and joined the crowd on the bunker line. It wasn't easy writing with all of the Binoctol users around me though. It was like trying to write and read letters around the Hatfields and the McCoys. In spite of all of the bad vibes around me, I managed to construct the letter I promised Harrington downplaying the incident and accentuating the more positive aspects of his stay in Charlie Co. I was glad to get it over with. Being around guys on BT's was unreal. I left the combatants convinced that Binoctols would eventually give drugs a bad name.

When we assembled near the stage for the second formation, Jahret came over to me at the last second and ordered me to stand on stage with the others already standing around. I didn't realize what the occasion was, until Col. Farris started reading citations and pinning medals on us. The guy standing next to me did a hell of a lot mote than I did to get his medal. It almost made me feel inadequate to only receive a Bronze Star for meritorious service. After the ceremony was over, I realized that Jahret had seemingly accomplished what he wanted to do, make himself look, that is, like the consummate leader that he had never been. He knew that I wasn't impressed; but of course, it didn't matter to him. It was the other guys in the platoon he targeted with the gesture. Still, I was down to my last three months in country and had yet to receive my CIB. There was nothing he could do about that oversight except admit that he had either blown it or that it was intentional. His audience was well aware of the omission and no ceremony would make up for his mishandling of the matter. I remained convinced that he would eventually get whatever was coming to him in the end.

In spite of all of the unnecessary pomp surrounding the medal, I accepted the congratulations from the guys as we left the area. "That photographer took your picture man." said Kyler.

"Yeah but by the time the photograph is developed, I'll be back in New Orleans." I said. It was not exactly what I would consider a keepsake anyway.

Diamond had succeeded in squandering his last chance. He was placed under arrest and escorted to Camh Rahn Bay and placed aboard the first plane leaving country. The practice of being escorted out of Vietnam was not unique to his particular case. It was a practice reserved for special cases like Diamond. I hoped to join him soon but I wouldn't need an escort to get out of country.

I spent the night over at the aid station with Doc and the rest of the medics. I had my second shot of penicillin and we smoked bombers while listening to Deja Vu all night. I had reached the point that I liked the tape as much as Doc did. One particular song, "Almost Cut My Hair", became a personal favorite of mine. It reminded me of that haircut that I had been refusing to get for months and got a big laugh every time it played.

The party was a blast. It was better than bunker guard. I fell asleep on the floor and staggered out the door to make the morning formation. A lot of the guys barely made it back in time. Thaddeus was officially in love with the girl who claimed she knew his brother intimately. Ordinarily one would assume that the local women would say anything to get next to us but, Thaddeus was no longer in touch with reality. I felt safe and assured that the Army would extend its long arm of prevention and save the guy from himself. He was vulnerable to anything and this woman, I feared, was ready to exploit him. Of course she could be all that would be needed to initiate all of that red tape the Army uses to dissuade us from marrying any of the Vietnamese women. It could have possibly been just what he needed to get the kind of help he deserved.

After formation Charles took off for LZ English. He was going to see a doctor. He never disclosed his ailment but was unwilling to deal with the mad doctor of Uplift. Maybe he was going to see the Wizard of Oz for a second opinion. I couldn't say that I blamed him for feeling that way. Everybody avoided being treated by our doctor because of his stand-offish, indifferent attitude toward us. He seemed to be at odds with everyone who came in for treatment. I hoped that he displayed a different manner when he treated the wounded. Maybe Charles should have taken Thaddeus with him to see the Wizard. He needed to be sent home faster than Dorothy could click her heels twice.

Barbara wrote me and said that the fried chicken franchise she worked for was robbed during her shift. She said a gunman came in and emptied the cash register. She was actually staring down the barrel of a handgun. It made me as worried about her as she was about me. She said that she was alright but her reassurances changed nothing. I had to get out of Vietnam because Barbara was my main source of inspiration. Making it back home alive meant seeing her again. If something tragic would have happened to her, I would have had to stay in Vietnam and not be able to be at her hospital bed or worse, miss her burial. I felt like the song on that Deja Vu tape…Helpless, Helpless, Helpless.

Overall the stand down was turning out to be a pretty nice affair. There were few details and little or no hassling at all. Aside from the formations we had to make, they pretty much left us alone. It wasn't as good as the one we had back in February but definitely not as bad as the time Mercein ran the guys through PT. Without a doubt, the lifers were cutting us some slack for a change. There were plans to send a patrol out on ambush and there was also a counter-plan to fake the ambush. The war effort had gone stale. Nobody gave a care about anything but their own personal DEROS date. It was a bad time to be starting a tour in country. Nixon was pulling units out to keep his approval rating high and Charlie was doing everything he could to make it appear as if he was kicking us out. In the meantime guys like us were just going through the motions. We were just counting days and watching the calendar.

During our next formation, Thaddeus returned from his girlfriend's house too late to make it on time. The lifers ignored it though. When he arrived, he stood still for a few minutes and then left. It was as if he realized he was supposed to be somewhere else. He then returned to the highway and while still in full view of everyone standing in formation on the other side of the fence, hitched a ride back to the village. It was sickening to watch the insensitivity of the lifers. Thaddeus deserved better treatment than that. They should have given him a Purple Heart for what he had gone through. Instead all they gave him was a cold shoulder, a blind eye and a deaf ear. Who knows, maybe he would eventually be disciplined for his odd behavior.

That night during guard duty, I was assigned to the same bunker with Mad Dog and Cruz. I naturally expected the worst. The potential for disaster was just too obvious. A disagreement soon developed over who was going to have first guard. When Cruz gave Maddox his standard "lets get it on" ultimatum, Mad Dog grabbed his M-16 mostly out of fear of having to defend himself against him. At the risk of being shot in the process, I stepped between the two of them and settled the issue by pulling guard all night alone. Neither one of the two combatants ever came to blows or shot each other. I feared for Cruz though. He was not expected to live one week in the bush challenging everybody the way he did. Incredibly, he offered the challenge constantly. He was destined to be fragged after we returned to the field. It was a big mistake to send someone like him to Vietnam. I felt sorry for his parents back in Minnesota. They would have to suffer the loss of their son and never know the truth about the circumstances surrounding his death. He was actually already as good as dead. His attitude would not be tolerated in the bush.

The next day I ran into Charles. He was wearing a brand new very white cast on his arm.

"What happened to you?" I asked.

"I told the brigade surgeon that I hurt my arm and he put a cast on it." He said with a smile.

"Is it broken?" I asked.

"It is now." He laughed. He was in hog heaven knowing he wouldn't have to go to the field for awhile. At least not for a few weeks he wouldn't. I was not disappointed by Charles' new scam. As little as I cared for ghosting, I felt happy about his cast. The brigade surgeon was obviously as cool and easy going as he appeared to be when he gave us that orientation talk during Jungle School. Charles' arm needed a cast about as much as mine did. Maybe the good doctor really was the Wizard of Oz and was a great alternative to seeing our doctor. He provided Charles with exactly what he needed to give him enough time to recharge his batteries.

Later that day, as I left the steakhouse, I noticed a medivac landing with some wounded. They were rushed to one of the sandbagged fortified shelters that were obviously some kind of emergency operating room. As I stood outside I watched as a team of medical personnel prepared the wounded for surgical treatment. There was a lot of frantic action going on inside and the mad doctor was at the center of it all as he barked out orders amidst all of the confusion and cries of pain. When he noticed the audience gathering outside, he yelled at someone and ordered them to close the tarpaulin that acted as a door. The free show was over. I'd been stationed there for months and had no idea that any emergency surgery was performed on our base camp at all. I wondered if our wounded and dead evacuees from the Crescent were sent there also. If they were, maybe that was the reason that everybody was driven to near mutiny. I would've asked but I was reluctant to rekindle any bad feelings about the episode. They were only just beginning to show signs of getting over the incident. Our not so beloved battalion head surgeon gave a good account of himself under duress though.

When another medivac landed with more wounded, I started to fear the worse. I figured that sooner or later someone would give us a call to go out to wherever the action was to lend a hand. There was no getting away from the fighting. It seemed as if we were either in the field or about to be sent to someone's rescue. Before I could get too anxious about our chances of going out again, the helicopters stopped landing. Maybe it was just a booby trap that sent those guys in. If there was a firefight going on out there, I know we would have been at least gearing up in anticipation of an extraction. A fire fight this late in my tour would have been too much for me to handle. I figured that a pair of ruby slippers would have fit just fine on my feet.

The mad doctor may have been in possession of the worst interpersonal skills but he looked very competent in that makeshift operating room. It was pretty obvious that doctors were subject to be drafted also. I couldn't imagine going through all of that schooling and training for a lucrative career in medicine and then volunteering for Vietnam. Being drafted would go a long way to explain the huge chip on his shoulder. However, if he thought he had a rough day at the office, he should have seen our two medics in action with bullets flying by. It would've made him realize how privileged he was.

Kostrewva and I went over to Linda and Monique's for an afternoon of leisure. When we arrived, I saw the heroin addicts sitting outside vomiting and nodding out in reaction to the poison being injected into their veins. One of them was so stoned he couldn't hold his syringe in his hand. For the first time I had to question our reason for frequenting the place. Was it the camaraderie that endeared us or was it the addiction? It was true that I enjoyed being there but the junkies' presence created an ugly backdrop to what went on inside. They looked like miserable victims. I couldn't imagine them enjoying themselves and couldn't help but wonder what would happen if they survived their tours. Just making the return flight would require at least a few injections that I figured would have to be smuggled through customs. Surviving the trip back home would only present them with the problem of finding potent heroin on the streets. Every heroin addict should have been counted in our casualty list. They were as wounded as any Purple Heart recipient. Only their wounds were self inflicted. After we left Linda and Monique's I couldn't stop thinking about those addicts and their plight. They made me feel fortunate to have already witnessed the life of a junkie before I came to Vietnam.

Our stand down was coming to an end soon and the company would be leaving for the field without me. My scheduled treatment for the undiagnosed affliction, real or imagined, would require my staying behind until later. I just accepted it as a gift from the mad doctor. As short as I was becoming, I could've used a little ghost time to help stretch the days out. It was only expected to be a few more days but I was willing to accept every one of them. I was expected to return to the field when I was finished with my shots and stay out of trouble in the meantime.

Good fortune had smiled on the new guy Cruz. It seemed as if he had a brother already in country. The military had a stipulation that no two siblings could be in Vietnam at the same time. As incredible as the story sounded to me, it must have been true. Cruz had already been placed on a fast track back to the world. His brother had, in effect, saved his life by just being there. Hopefully it would keep him stateside until he finished his enlistment. If he came back later, he would still be executed by one of his own. My youngest brother Anthony wasn't even 18 yet and was a safe bet to escape the draft and the war. My family could do without having to relive the experience of worrying about one of us dying in Vietnam.

Our armorer completed his tour and was arrested on his way back home trying to smuggle pot through customs. This was the same guy who wouldn't let me smoke a joint in the jeep during our driving episode. He even told me once that no one smoked pot in his home town of Tyler, Texas. I couldn't imagine why he tried to do it, but the story was not just another rumor that was known to circulate around Uplift. Maybe he wanted to impress some of his friends back home. Maybe after being such a straight arrow for his entire tour, he wanted to walk on the wild side just that once. Whatever was his thinking, he was in a world of trouble and sadly he would not be seeing Texas any time soon.

After our last formation, I headed over to the first aid station for my last shot. I had a good time again but was glad my treatment was over. If I had to go back to their place again, I never would have been able to return to the field. It was too enjoyable. Doc was lucky to be assigned to that job. Being in the rear full time was still a boring experience though. There was just not enough to do and never enough of the right kind of people to be with. Maybe it was the reason that so many of the REMF's were junkies. They just didn't have much of anything else to do at Uplift. My experience in the rear gave me a close insight into just how boring it was. I guess after a few months of the dull life available on our base camp, skag just might've seemed less dangerous than it really was. Later that night while setting up for bunker guard, the new NCOIC walked up to me and asked about my status at the bunker. Before I could answer, Kostrewva walked up and offered the two of us a joint without realizing who he was. When he revealed his identity and his imaginary status to him he not only threatened to charge Kostrewva with possession, he designated me as his witness. I told him to kiss my ass but Kostrewva had already panicked and threw away the pot. "Look what you made him do." I joked.

"Listen, I've already done my time in the bush. I was lucky enough to land this job in the rear and I'm gonna do every thing I can to keep it. I've only got a few months left in country and I refuse to let a couple of potheads like you two get me sent back to the field. I've got a wife and a daughter to get back home to and I stand a better chance of making it home alive if I can hold on to this job." He said as he walked away. He was as serious about busting Kostrewva as he was about extending his tour. After he left we retrieved the pot and pulled guard for the rest of the night. We laughed and joked about the new NCOIC's little speech but, seriously though, we couldn't blame the guy for feeling that way. Vietnam was no place for a dad. Kostrewva was single like me and I didn't know if he even had a girlfriend in Chicago. I always thought that his real love interest was Mary Jane.

The following morning with 75 days left in country, I found myself standing behind the company area watching the company gear up for deployment to the field without me. My normal position within the second platoon made me feel like an outsider that day. I was, instead, a mere observer amidst a very loose formation of excited grunts loading up on supplies, cleaning weapons and, in general, looking forward to what was next. All activity stopped when it was announced that Moe wouldn't be returning to the field with the company. Of course we all knew that his time had come but it gave us a chance to say our last farewells to a great guy who we'd all miss. He made one last plea for my boonie hat but I still couldn't part with the thing. I didn't think he would be bringing that AK back with him either. At least he'd have the memory of shooting it in that last firefight. I knew I wouldn't forget it. I did wish, however, that I could forget the look on the face of its former owner. I still couldn't get that image out of my mind.

Harrington thanked me for that letter. He said that it saved his ass; which was more unbelievable than having him ask me to write it. They couldn't have been serious about doing anything to him. It seemed so unlikely that a letter written by an enlisted man had any bearing on the situation. Normally I wouldn't care about some lifer getting himself in trouble but this guy had been good to us. Every word in that letter was true about him. It made it easy to construct the piece.

The company geared up and gave me the experience of watching them prepare to leave without me. In the process, they provided me with a chance to see the enthusiasm they shared. The same enthusiasm I had lost. It was unnatural and difficult for me to stay behind as they boarded helicopters that didn't have a seat for me. What troubled me the most was the fear that something bad would happen to them while I was at Uplift. My status as a medical detainee would do little to clear my conscience because I wasn't convinced there was anything wrong with me. At least the choppers flew in the opposite direction from that dreaded Sui Cai Valley. Of course our previous mission was in what I thought would be a safe area. Instead it turned into a bigger nightmare than anything I'd been through before. I expected the ensuing few days to pass slowly. In the process, the fear of experiencing that helpless feeling again would surely take away another little piece of me.

I ran into my jump school buddy Byrd. He said that he was going to Hong Kong for R&R late in the month. He was a lot happier those days because he had re established himself in the rear again. I still didn't know what happened earlier when he was reassigned to the field. His world had come to an end when I saw him at Phu My. Being forced to return to the field had shaken him in the worst way. I still felt as if he had made a big mistake by re enlisting to get out of the fighting. Doing another three years in the Army was a bigger nightmare than facing Charlie. Contrary to his beliefs, Uplift was no cocoon that would protect him from harm either. There were booby traps less than 100 yds outside of the perimeter, a major infiltration route nearby and of course the occasional mortar attack that disrupted life in the rudest fashion. Charlie was able to reach out and grab you no matter where you were in his country. Life in the rear was overrated when it came to safety. I couldn't feel safe about being there and would not until I had left Vietnam for good.

The following day, word started circulating that Jimi Hendrix had just died of a drug overdose. He was found alone in a London apartment by the police. He was only 27 at the time of his death. His sad departure sent shock waves of grief reverberating throughout Uplift. I supposed that the news was equally devastating to all of his fans throughout Vietnam. He was almost like some kind of larger than life folk hero with most of the troops in country. His death sparked all sorts of rumors about him. They started one about him being a former paratrooper that did a tour in Nam with the 101st. There was a conflicting story that even said that he was once a member of the Herd. It demonstrated how legend was born. The only thing I knew for sure was that he was dead. His death naturally reminded me of Hugle and his daily inquiry about both Jimi and JJ. That weird ritual he used to put me through was the strangest thing I had ever witnessed in human behavior. Hugle never got the chance to buy all of those albums and Jimi would of course never record again. Tragically, neither one of them had to die.

5

Kyler took what was to be my R&R to Taipei. My medical status forced me to give up my slot on the schedule. It also meant that I would have to stay behind with the REMF's as they continued to suck up to the lifers for fear of being sent back out to the field. The majority of those guys were former grunts. Every clerk, truck driver and miscellaneous flunkie was wearing a CIB. I'd even heard a story about plans to send our company clerk, out to the field just long enough to qualify him for his. I was naturally galled at any intended effort to decorate a clerk with an award that I had already qualified for but hadn't received.

At least I did get to spend more time with Doc. He still asked me about the French Quarter and the Mardi Gras daily. He also constantly reminded me that he planned to come to New Orleans after the war. I spent a lot of time with the medics and that tape by Crosby, Stills, Nash and Young. Barbara, to my dismay, hadn't sent me a letter in a while. Maybe it was because I had become accustomed to having a letter every resupply day and being at Uplift meant having daily mail calls. It was highly unlikely for her to just stop writing me for no reason at all.

The rumor mill was working at full throttle that day. One rumor had the entire brigade moving to Ahn Khe, wherever that was. Another rumor was centered on my hero Patrick Tadina and his demise. According to the story, Charlie had finally caught up to him at long last. I never could have believed that one. The third one was the wildest rumor yet. The story was that the Sui Cai Valley was to be plowed under until there was no vegetation left standing at all. Every tree, every bush and blade of grass was to be removed leaving the entire infiltration route devoid of anything that grew. The theory was, I guess, that a totally denuded valley would be the ultimate deterrent to traffic. We were either very good at coming up with extreme measures or great at creating incredible rumors. Somewhere in our unit had to be a think tank of rumormongers dreaming up the stuff and putting it out. Somehow they never failed to outdo themselves with each succeeding rumor.

Top informed me that Kyler's original R&R was scheduled for the following week and wanted me to consider taking his place since I wouldn't be available for my own. I agreed to consider it but it just wouldn't be the same since I hadn't planned on going to where ever Kyler had originally intended to go. Anyway I wasn't as keyed up about going on R&R after Al and Katta was shot. The World's Fair was very enticing back then. The shooting incident, however, took a lot of wind out of my R&R sails. Walter managed to revive my interest in going but even that fell to the wayside. Everything went wrong at the wrong time, I guess. I should have made plans to go on R&R with Gathar to Australia a month earlier. That would have been fun.

I agreed to take Kyler's spot on the schedule because Doc and Kostrewva were also going the same week to Bangkok. I was destined for Hong Kong and wasn't too excited about it. At least it would take those seven days off of my tour at a time when I felt as if I was running out of gas. The stay at Uplift had robbed me of that feel that I once had for the bush. I had become so short that I couldn't come to grips with returning to the field. Admittedly, I lost my edge in the Crescent but I thought that it would've been temporary. Nothing could have been further from the truth. I was losing it and was just going to Hong Kong to hide out for a week. I'd only have 55 days when I returned and I did want to go out feeling better about my performance in the eyes of those guys around me.

When R&R came up I, The three of us with visions of spending a week outside of Vietnam dancing in our heads, hitched a ride to Charang Valley to pick up our funds. While there we ran into a 17 year old GI being sent home. To my surprise, the military would no longer allow someone to serve in Vietnam at his tender age. I didn't remember when the decision was made but this particular kid was somehow able to lie about his age when he enlisted. Once the oversight was discovered, he was immediately put on that fast track home. He said that he was only 16 when he joined and he did so because he was afraid that the war would be over by the time he turned 18. Foolishly, I not only expected the war to end before I turned 18, I also thought that wars were fought by older men. Still, I wondered how the kid managed to pull it off. They should have court-martialed anyone who signed up an under age recruit. The war may have been an unpopular one but there were more than enough men available among the 18 and over pool of draft-eligible men.

We left Charang under the influence of some BT's to catch a plane headed for Da Nang. It was a C-114, a flying piece of machinery that rattled so much that it earned the nickname "eggbeater." I made a jump from one at Benning. The plane made a stop in, of all places, Tuy Hoa. Just hearing the name of the place shocked me out of my drug induced stupor. When we landed I looked out of the window searched for and immediately found that huge mountain in the distance. I was revisiting, though briefly, the scene of my worst experience in Vietnam. The sight of it made my skin crawl. "Doc! Doc! We're in Tuy Hoa!" I said while trying to wake him from a very deep sleep. "I'm not getting off here! I'm going to fucking Da Nang!" he snapped. Being back in Tuy Hoa didn't affect Doc the same way that it did me. Judging from the way he immediately fell asleep again, I'd say that he never quite understood what I said to him. Still, the haunting memories of the month of April and the tragic event still lingered. Somewhere outside of the perimeter of the Air Force base was a very large piece of me I feared that I would never reclaim.

After picking up a couple of passengers, we left Tuy Hoa and headed for Da Nang. The ride was worse than I expected and the BT's weren't strong enough to give the desired effect of a smooth flight. The vibrations were too powerful and the noise created by the engines was deafening. We arrived and left the plane with the sound of the engines still ringing in our ears. Da Nang was in I Corps; Marine country for the uninitiated. The place was crawling with jarheads, the rough and ready version of America's military might. Everything about the place was different from what I had grown accustomed to. Uplift paled in comparison to this base. The ground was paved, the barracks were permanent dwellings that made those hooches at our base camp look like a shanty town. Finally, their airstrip was more akin to an airport. There were commercial airliners as well as military transports taking off and landing as often as Moisant Airport back home.

We went through our in-processing and were assigned temporary quarters until our flights could be scheduled. The Marines were amused at our obvious contrasts. They were particularly caught up with the patches worn by the "Army guys" as they referred to us. Half of the Marines were juicers and the other half must have been trying to kick the habit. They were all full of that same bravado the airborne lifers were afflicted with. We walked across the highway to the PX for some cigarettes and ran into some of the local hustlers selling joints that tasted awful due to the excessive amounts of rolling paper. I almost died of asphyxiation. "No wonder these Marines are all juicers, there's no decent dope around here." Said Kostrewva. He was right. If all we had to smoke was six sheets of paper wrapped around a smidgen of grass, we probably would have been juicers too. I thought all joints were dipped in opium before being sold in Vietnam. DaNang was an exception and unfortunately, we were out of bombers.

We returned to the base and stood around taking in all the sights and comparing the Navy/Marine helicopters to ours. Their slicks were definitely bigger and flew a lot faster but weren't necessarily better. I was sure that it was just as easy to shoot one of those big boxcars down as it was shooting ours out of the sky. "Say aren't you Aaron Handy?" asked a familiar voice from behind me. I turned around and was very surprised to see an old friend from New Orleans. It was Juan Butler, someone I figured would never get caught up in the war.

"Of course it's me. What in the hell are you doing here?" I asked as I looked down at his dirty boots and realized he was unmistakably a grunt.

"I was drafted last year." He said. I hadn't seen Juan since the ninth grade. He was such a studious kid that I imagined he'd be well on his way to his second degree by then. His presence there, wearing dirty boots, again confirmed my rebuttal to the "infantry is for the dumb guys" theory. He was serving with the Americal Division and was about to go to of all places, Tokyo, for his R&R. We talked for a few minutes before leaving for our R&R destinations. I figured that in a week, I'd talk a little more with him.

After a much delayed take-off and a scary landing at Hong Kong International Airport, I finally set foot in one of its busy concourses. After exchanging my MPC for some greenbacks, I saw an attractive young black woman wearing an airline stewardess uniform. She had a lively step to complement her curvaceous body. For fun, I chased her down and introduced myself to her asking her for her name and writing address.

"My name is Bunny." she said standing before me wearing a name tag that read Annette.

"Well Bunny, I just wanted to let you know that you are the first black woman that I have seen since November '69."

"Let me guess Aaron. You're on R&R right?"

"Dig it"

"And you're stationed in Vietnam right?"

"Yeah. What's the point?"

"Every time I pass through an R&R destination, some brother always feeds me that same line. Sometimes I hear it more than once." She said as she turned and continued on her way. She was unimpressed and was in a hurry to catch her next connecting flight. I was disappointed in her response but quickly got over the way she dismissed me.

My trip to Hong Kong was even more disappointing. It was a seven day nightmare that couldn't end fast enough. The expensive hotel room, a persistent hooker and a near drug overdose convinced me that I never should have left Vietnam. A revolutionary black tried to recruit me to desert and some Australians tried to sell me some land in Florida. I only ate one meal during my last two days there. By the time I left the place, I was near starvation.

Our flight back seemed like a ten minute hop. Da Nang's mess hall was a very welcome sight to most of the returnees. Running out of money while still on R&R was more common than I thought. The place was packed with so many GI's that it looked like a camp full of hungry refugees.

Doc and Kostrewva definitely had a better time than I did. They were talking endlessly about their trip to Bangkok. "Handy, guess what the penalty for possession of drugs is in Bangkok." said Doc.

"I don't know. What is it?"

"Death!" He said as he and Kostrewva started laughing themselves silly. They said it was true but that only made it funnier to them. I'd say they had a wonderful time. Our contrasting experiences had me envious of the two of them. In another 55 days I wouldn't have either one of them around me anymore. Kostrewva was shorter than I was. He was expected to DEROS in a couple of weeks and had a lot of regret about not extending his tour. He was having the time of his young life and didn't want to see it end that soon. I could relate to that but wanted to go home in November if not sooner. I knew I would miss him when he left. I expected him to readjust to Chicago faster than I would adjust to life without him.

I ran into my old friend Juan Butler after he returned from Japan. He was less interested in talking about his R&R than he was about the Jackson Five. We were both from New Orleans and attended the same Jr. High School, but all he talked about was little Michael Jackson. Juan could have probably went on forever about the Jackson 5. He was the kind of guy who, no doubt, had never touched a joint in all the time he had spent in Vietnam. I knew better than to try to get him to smoke with us, so I just sat there on a bench and listened to him talk about his favorite group of singers. I had reached the point where I no longer found it surprising to find someone like him in Vietnam with me. The draft could and would manage to snatch a guy out of college regardless of his GPA. He was living proof that there were no real draft deferments for anyone without connections.

After talking with Juan, I returned to our temporary quarters and overheard one black guy retelling an unfortunate and familiar experience he had in Hong Kong. He was approached one night by a black militant, who talked him into doing exactly what I couldn't be talked me into doing. Not returning to Vietnam. It turned out the guy was no militant. He was just a fast talking con artist trying to steal the guy's clothes. The scheme was to get him to move in with them and then have the girls take his new clothes while they were all out on the town. The apartment was just a temporary shelter until the next victim moved in with them. Once the sham was set in motion, they would lose the victim in a bar and return to the apartment to move everything out to their new location. "I hope I run into that nigger again. I'll kick his fucking ass!" He said angrily. He should have kicked himself in the ass for falling for the bullshit that guy was pushing on that corner. Of course if all he lost were those worthless clothes from the Hong Kong tailors he didn't lose much at all. I would have given him mine if I weren't so much taller than he was. The clothes would only represent and remind me of a lot of money that I wasted because I couldn't handle being short. I wished I had stayed in Vietnam and never considered going to Hong Kong.

6

When we made it back to Phu Cat AFB, we hitched a ride to Uplift and one of Kostrewva's old buddies from Recon was on the truck. They started a conversation about the Sui Cai Valley while Doc asked me for the tenth time about the death penalty in Bangkok. "Twenty Five!!!" said Kostrewva.

"That's right man. Lt. Mack's patrol set up ambush in the valley one night and got 25 kills!" He said. It had to be the most successful ambush ever sprung in the war. Considering how many guys are in a patrol, it was hard to imagine getting that many inside of one kill zone. Three kills was normally considered a lot of men for one ambush. It was impossible to get more than five inside of any kill zone that I had ever set up. Twenty-five was mind boggling. There was no doubt about the validity of his story either. Kostrewva's buddy was beaming with pride as he continued to fill him in on the details. Mack had outdone himself with his most recent exploit. He would be decorated for this one and probably promoted to Captain. His zeal may have bordered on being somewhat maniacal but his effectiveness remained unquestionable. He was a born leader. The likes of which seldom came along.

We arrived at Uplift in the rain and found Charlie Co. on stand down. They also managed to get a kill on their most recent mission. Some of the guys were pissed with Kyler for pumping some unnecessary rounds into the dead body. Of course Kyler cared as little about their opinions of him as ever. He could never change his ways because he would probably relish telling someone back home that he did whatever we thought was excessive.

Howard was in usual form. He went over all of the pictures I took in Hong Kong and wanted to know how good Alice was. I told him she was great to keep from triggering his anticipated response to sexual abstinence. He was impressed with her curves and her unusually long hair. "Did you hear about the big ambush?" He asked.

"Yeah, I heard about it on the way back."

"Jahret has a talk planned for us after the next formation." He said reminding me of one of the reasons I went to Hong Kong. Jahret gave us his talk and I should have expected that it would have been centered on the big ambush. He said that Col. Farris expected all ambushes to be executed with the same imaginative tactics used during the big successful strike. The good Colonel had to be dreaming. Lt Mack, according to the pamphlet handed out before the meeting started, scouted his area first. He spotted an old woman leaving the village carrying two large pots dangling from the ends of a pole straddled across her shoulders as she set a course for the mountains. When she disappeared up a trail leading into a well-concealed area of the mountain, the only logical conclusion was easily assumed. She was obviously going to feed the rice to Charlie. Mack then planned his ambush. They waited for the woman to come down from the mountain with the empty pots and had her picked up for interrogation. Then they moved in on the trail and set up about a dozen claymores in a Daisy chain for simultaneous detonation. The large number of kills started to look more than possible. He positioned two fire teams along the trail along with two well-placed snipers. After the trap was set, they waited for hours before the unsuspecting NVA troops came down the trail triggering the killing spree. In spite of all of the preparation, it still took some initiative on the behalf of his men to subdue the large contingent once the trap was sprung. Some of the stunned NVA soldiers still put up a fight after having their legs blown off. In the confusion, I imagined that some of the 25 kills were victims of their own friendly fire. If there was anything beautiful about killing, the ambush was truly a work of art. And If Farris really thought that any squad could duplicate what Recon did that night, he was crazy. The Colonel had already reportedly spent a night on ambush with one of the squads in Bravo Company. As expected, he came away with an unimpressive assessment of the way a typical ambush was executed. His biggest peeve was sleeping on ambush while only one man pulled guard. He wanted to change that practice to having all men stay up and awake all night. If he thought he could get us to comply with that order, maybe I should have gotten Jones to sell him the bridge that connects his hometown of Brooklyn to the rest of New York.

Then Jahret ended his talk with a warning about drugs. He started off by saying that they were well aware of Linda and Monique's place. His startling revelation brought on a few snickers. Then he informed us that the marijuana cigarettes being sold there were actually treated with opium. "I would hope so." someone muttered in the background. Jahret continued the talk at the risk of being laughed out of country. Everybody was struggling to hold it back.

"So beware of what you're doing when you're in the village. You might get some of that bad candy acid." he concluded in his best Jack Benny impersonation to date. After that line I couldn't hold back.

After the meeting I remembered that I missed payday while away on R&R and my pay was still waiting for me over at the company headquarters. I could have used the money when I was away. Things got so bad for me in Hong Kong that I had to sell my tape player and the Abbey Road tape to one of the hotel workers just to eat. There was no way to get my hands on any funds while there. After being paid, I walked to the steak house with my pay voucher held close to my face. I almost didn't notice a guy who was crying his head off while listening to a Janis Joplin song. "What's the matter man, your girl send you a Dear John?"

"No man, JJ died. Haven't you heard?" He asked as I froze in shock. It was an eerie moment as I immediately recognized what had happened. I struggled momentarily to accept it as mere coincidence that Hugle, Jimi and JJ were dead. But it was creepy to think about how Hugle came into my life and focused so much attention on his two favorite recording artists before they all died in succession. It was almost as if Hugle died and went to that place in the hereafter reserved for dead Vietnam War soldiers and called them over to perform for him. Or maybe somehow both Jimi and JJ found out that their biggest fan had left prompting them to seek him. Hugle's daily ritual of asking me about Jimi and JJ had set up a most bizarre situation for me to recount for the rest of my life.

The news about JJ's death put me into a state of shock that lasted well into the night. The following morning I was greeted with more strange events. The MP's were screening all traffic into the base camp. No one was allowed to leave and there was no immediate explanation for all of the tight security. The rumormongers started a story about a big drug search that never materialized and after about an hour or so, the official word came down. An MPC changeover was taking place. According to the old-timers, the MPC's design was changed annually to wreak havoc with all of the Black Market operations. Once the new MPC was introduced, all old currency automatically became worthless. Only GI's could exchange their old currency for the new design leaving the unauthorized holders with nothing but fancy looking sheets of paper. All of the Black Market dealers would have to start all over accumulating the prized MPC. The changeover had to be taken into account before accumulating too much MPC. It naturally made sense to turn it over to something less subject to change before being left holding the bag. Unfortunately, gold was already being hoarded and turning over MPC for Piaster was a rarity. There was no confidence in the local currency at all. Recent reports of the Piaster being further devalued with the changeover didn't help either. The new rate of exchange made the Vietnamese money worth less than half of what it was before. The actual date of the design change differed every year and had to be the most guarded secret in country. It added a high degree of volatility that should have scared off any smart money dealer. Of course there was no real intelligent speculation going on at the Black Market level. Some of them may have been shrewd but most of them were just desperate, cut throat hustlers. They were expected to accept the losses in stride.

After turning in my recently acquired pay for some of the new money, I picked up my mail and found another letter from Mrs. Wheelhouse. She hadn't made much progress with accepting her loss because her words were still as heartbreaking as they had been for the previous five months. She was struggling to deal with her enormous grief and still wrote letters that painted the picture of a woman overwhelmed with despair. She continued to pray for my survival in spite of feeling forsaken by her spirituality. I was certain that her family was being affected by her extensive grieving process. Their household must have been somewhat dour with the constant reminder she provided. I couldn't wait to get back home to write her a letter. I was convinced that my dying in Vietnam would only make matters worse for her. I wanted to see her get over the pain and suffering she was going through and not to put her through any additional grief. I wished there was something I could have done for her other than reading her sad letters. Each letter she wrote took so much out of me that it made it just that much harder to reply. I could only imagine how much it took out of her each time she sat down to put together each correspondence. Our country owed the Mrs. Wheelhouses of the Vietnam War a debt of gratitude that couldn't be measured and never repaid either.

Over at the bunker line a crowd of heads gathered to celebrate the new monetary exchange rate. The prospect of getting twice as much dope for our money had put them in a very festive mood. "We'll probably get laid twice for five dollars now!" One of them laughed. According to the news report that announced the devaluation of the piaster, Nixon was behind the whole deal. I couldn't understand how or why it was done but it did wonders for all of the heads. It also added fuel to what Hanoi Hanna said about S.Vietnam being a puppet government of the U.S. In one bold stroke, Nixon not only drove the drug prices down, he also robbed the Saigon government of some of its credibility giving the Hanoi propaganda machine more fodder. Our government was really pulling the strings and the Saigon government was dancing to our tune. It was hard to deny it after we tanked the value of the piaster. My understanding of international monetary standards was too limited to make any sense of the move.

The widely spread rumor that our company was to be inserted into the Sui Cai Valley next became a matter of official record. The news gave Lt. Mack's big ambush a new meaning. In essence, it wasn't just a bold ingenious strike; it was also an indication of just how active the traffic was in the valley. I was definitely getting too short to be patrolling there. After what Mack did to Charlie, I was sure he would be looking for revenge. At least I feared he would. Kostrewva didn't have to worry about our next mission though. He was so short that he wouldn't have to be sent out again. He was practically out of the place and on his way home. Too bad he couldn't let me impersonate him and take that flight to Chicago. I would have gladly gone in his place.

The rumor I heard about stripping the entire valley of its vegetation was also true. There was a huge effort underway and from what I heard the place was one big muddy wasteland due to the record rainfall that was wreaking havoc throughout the entire province. According to the news, most of the area was suffering through some of the worst flooding in recent years. The weather had changed dramatically since I left for Hong Kong as the monsoon had obviously started again. As much as I hated the previous rainy season, I should have been happy. After all, it was where I came in and signaled the beginning of the end of my tour.

The week I spent away did nothing to restore my confidence. I was shaken by the mere prospect of going to the Sui Cai with such little time left in country. I didn't know what it was about making it as far and suddenly not being able to function. The so-called Short Timers Whores had a stranglehold on me and I couldn't shake it. My mother was right. They should have found a nice safe spot for her son to spend the remainder of his tour. If only she would have invented one first.

Out of desperation, I cooked up a scheme to fool Top into believing that I had contracted some kind of venereal disease. I took a shower and put some soapy lather under my foreskin to create a superficial rash that would fool anybody. Other than the associated itch and burn, there was nothing wrong that needed any medical cure. Of course I planned to see Doc and not that damned mad doctor. The plan worked like a charm but it would only buy me a couple of days in the rear. Having Doc in the rear was beginning to pay huge dividends. Fooling Top with the soap-under-the-foreskin routine made me feel guilty but I lived through it.

I left my suitcase of Hong Kong clothes and memorabilia over at Doc's quarters for lack of anywhere else to put it. Howard made a daily trip to Doc's hooch just to try on that collection of cheap tailor made suits. He claimed the suits fit him perfectly. I told him I didn't mind at all but maybe he should have given up the drugs. He was almost three inches shorter than I was but insisted the clothes fit. Maybe he just enjoyed wearing civilian attire for a change because no matter how unappealing I tried to make Hong Kong sound, the more interested he became. Maybe it was those pictures of Alice. Anyway, with him leaving for the field, maybe the clothes as well as my stories about Hong Kong would get a rest.

When the company returned to the field, I was left behind in the rear with the gear. I was also left with the ghosters and the REMF's. Kostrewva went to the village to score a nickel bag and almost got caught by our MP's. He didn't say which opium den it was but the proprietor led him and some other guys to an underground bunker to hide in. Privately, I wondered if the owner was VC and if the so-called underground bunker was a tunnel complex. As short as he was it would have been wise for him to lay low but not that guy. He was acting as if there was some kind of cheap thrill he still hadn't experienced and was trying his best to discover what and where it was. He had reached the point in his tour that most of us only dream about. He was through with his obligation, was processing out of the war and would soon be on his way home. He was, as we always said, milking the moment for everything there was. He was already in that comfort zone that I wanted to experience; the part in my tour when I didn't have to worry about going back out to the field anymore.

The weather continued to deteriorate. Remembering how miserable it was out in the field during the monsoon made my upcoming date in the valley even worse. The weather only added to the gloom of not getting any mail from Barbara. It bothered me because our relationship was strong and I hadn't put my foot in my mouth since I was in Phu My. I couldn't understand what was possibly preventing her from writing and I needed to hear form he in the worst way. She had carried me for more than ten months and I didn't think I could have made it the rest of the way without hearing from her again.

It didn't take long for me to start missing the guys after they were deployed to the field. I wanted no part of the valley but I knew I couldn't spend the rest of my tour at Uplift like Mad Dog. He only had to play it cool and spend his time living on the bunker line. I supposed it was what he intended to do on his second tour anyway. He played tapes and listened to the radio all day and of course he easily maintained his habit. I didn't think he would want to ever see Detroit again. After the devaluation, he could get twice as much skag as before and I couldn't imagine what would become of him. His lifestyle would eventually catch up with him though. If he didn't overdose, he'd probably catch hepatitis from shooting with a dirty needle. The war would surely end before he would kick his habit and that would cause the biggest problem for him. Living back in the world with a Vietnam heroin habit had to be worse than coming back for another tour. He was in a world of shit and he didn't even care.

The story about the Herd moving to Ahn Khe was apparently true. I overheard a couple of lifers talking about Uplift and speaking in past tense. They were talking about spending Christmas there making December the last of the Herd's stay in Bong Son. There was no truth to the death of Tadina though. The story, I was glad to find out, was a rumor and nothing more. Hopefully, the guy would decide to leave Vietnam for good. One day, when the war was over, I figure it would be nice to be able to point him out to our spouses and children and say…"That's Patrick Tadina a real hero". He was sure to be the pride of the 173rd for years to come.

I received another letter from Al thanking me for the pot he thought that I sent him. I didn't know who was sending him the stuff but he kept giving me all of the credit. Since he was still in that VA hospital in Pennsylvania, I wondered how he managed to find the time and space to smoke a joint. He was still a riot as evidenced by the promotion to Captain he had anointed me with. I expected the next letter to be addressed to Col. Handy. His early departure came at the absolute worst moment. We were having such a great time in that village. Of course with 52 days left, I still would have been without the two of them for the month of November. Both Al and Katta were going to DEROS around the end of the summer. I really missed those guys and the good times we shared. There was nothing that we wouldn't do to piss the lifers off. It was like a pastime and I never thought I would be able to move on after what happened in that village. It took a lot out of me to see them lying on the ground bleeding. Not being able to retaliate was the ultimate frustration and I still felt like killing a couple of Ruff Puffs for revenge. Any two would have done. The fact that I was not working in another village late in my tour should have been all I was hoping for. The Sui Cai may have been intimidating but at least it wasn't pacification.

A typhoon was brewing in the S. China Sea and it was heading our way. Living with the threat of hurricanes came with the territory back home in New Orleans. All sorts of preparations were usually made every time one entered the Gulf of Mexico. But somehow I didn't think that any special considerations would be made as we started to prepare for resupply. I was sure that resupply would somehow go on as scheduled. It was also a good bet that Top couldn't wait to demonstrate just how inconsequential the weather event was so I went looking for him. My gear was already getting wet on the chopper pad and had been packed for at least three days. I was fed up with Uplift. I was more than ready to return but I didn't let Top know it. "Say Top! What in the world is a typhoon?" I asked while standing with him in the rain.

"It's a tropical storm."

"You mean like a hurricane?"

"Exactly"

"Well I guess all of the companies will be brought back to the rear now right?" I said.

"Bring them back! For what?"

"For the big storm. The wind might blow down a couple of trees on someone out there. Maybe someone might drown. How big is the storm anyway. What's the name of it or do they name their storms in this country?

"No storm's big enough to stop a war. Go pack our rucksack and get ready for the field."

"Top are you gonna send me out there when a typhoon is on the way?"

"You're damned right! Now get your ass on over to supply and get ready for the field. I've had enough of this nonsense!" He said as he chomped on his funky cigar, hitched his trousers and walked away from me. Top was so predictable it was criminal.

I secured my ruck and headed for the chopper pad to be reunited with the rest of the guys. Upon arrival I found the valley to be exactly as I was told it was. An enormous swath had been plowed through what must have been the preferred avenue of travel for Charlie. As much as I hated to admit it, I thought it would work, especially during the monsoon. It might have been Charlie's country but mud is the same no matter who is sloshing around in it. It was very apparent that Charlie would have to find a new route because he could not afford to be caught in the open knee deep in a quagmire. The plowed area was created to funnel the traffic in the path of fire from the bases in the valley.

A command post was set up nestled in the wooded area along the shoulder of the muddy valley floor. As our chopper came in for its landing, a welcoming party greeted me when I stepped off of it. I couldn't understand the reason for it either. I doubted if the guys were that glad to see me again. After all, we were all together only a few days earlier. "Handy! Have you heard about the Hunter?" Asked Kyler with a look of rejoice.

"Did he step on a booby trap? Did one of you guys frag him?"

"Alright, what happened?"

"They came and took him away." He said.

"You're bullshitting me right."

"I'm telling you man, they have relieved him of his duties, stripped him of his command." He said.

"Did you see them relieve him of his duties in the field?"

"No. But I'm telling you that he has been relieved of his command."

I didn't know what happened before my arrival but it didn't take long for the rumors to start circulating. Charlie Co. had to be Rumor Central S. Vietnam. Every time something happened, the rumor mill would put out an unofficial explanation for it. I heard over the radio that Nixon planned to lower the troop ceiling in Vietnam by 40,000. This group, according to him, would be home by Christmas. I assumed that it would be only a matter of time before the guys started floating rumors about the Herd being redeployed back home next. Forget about our impending move to Ahn Khe, the next rumor would probably involve the Herd being redeployed as early as the following ten days.

The platoon had received a number of new faces since I left for R&R. We had a new medic, a new platoon sergeant and a few others. One of the new guys, Larry Gonzalez, had a habit of talking extremely loud. It was almost as if he was unable to speak softly. Larry was a Chicano from Houston. Everybody called him Frito. The changes in our platoon were a welcome sight. No more Jahret or Spurlock. Things were really starting to shape up for us. I couldn't care less about what actually happened to either one of them. An official explanation wasn't necessary. In fact I was just happy that they wouldn't be around for what appeared to be my last mission.

The typhoon threat appeared to be of little concern to the rest of the guys. Our job on that Rome Plow mission, as it was called, was strictly a security fob for the mechanized unit plowing up the valley.

There were several bulldozers at work mowing down trees and occasionally getting stuck in the muddy expanse they were creating. The Sui Cai Valley was less ominous without its foliage. Charlie Co. was about as laid back as we usually were on pacification. I'd been told that the nights were equally as calm. There was literally no enemy activity at all. I hoped that the prevailing attitude about this mission would rub off on me soon. It was hard to match the confidence the others were exuding as they went about doing nothing other than maintaining a presence. In spite of all the mud, their spirits were high. It was like a sloppy picnic. Everybody was in a very good mood and nobody was trying to spoil it either. Not having Jahret or Spurlcok around was doing wonders for morale.

Staff Sergeant Dean, Spurlock's replacement, was like a breath of fresh air. He introduced himself to me and reassured me that my final days in the field would be easy. He said that sending me back alive was his top priority. Harrington, Kyler and Jackson, according to him, had already been told the same thing. It was too bad that it took as long to get a platoon Sgt. Like him. Calvin and Spurlock were two of the most nettlesome hard asses I ever met. To serve under the two of them had been a test of endurance. Dean was a tall white guy with a thick mustache that spoke with the drawl of a Tennessee back woodsman. Everybody liked the guy. He was very protective, they said, and got a lot of respect from the guys because of it. He took us on a patrol and we never covered much ground because he was just that cautious. Of course, there wasn't much left in the valley to patrol anyway.

That night, the typhoon never passed our way. We didn't even get any high winds. It was an eerie night just the same. The event had me in my usual hurricane induced hyper vigilant mode but everyone else was laid back. We were definitely on ambush but the way Howard and Larry kept talking all night, it was more like bivouac at Ft. Polk. We talked all night about the war and its end. Of course the end of the war was what we talked mostly about. Nixon's 40,000 man troop withdrawal had started something that I didn't think was about to end too soon. The prospect of our being in that number was on everyone's mind. I wished it were true because I would have really liked to go home with the unit as a whole. I liked being a member of the Herd and going to Ft Bragg to join the 82nd could never mean as much to me.

After the patrol, Larry treated me to my first jalapeno pepper. Actually I swallowed three of them in succession before I realized they were more potent than any of those red peppers from Louisiana. My mouth and my entire esophagus were on fire and no amount of water could put it out. The education of Aaron Handy went on as I continued to stumble my way through everything about life in America that I managed to put off until I arrived in Vietnam. Those peppers, I imagined, were from Mexico and couldn't be found anywhere in the states.

"Handy do you want another jalapeno pepper?" Larry asked jokingly.

"No thanks. I've already made an ass of myself with those fire balls. You know I still have to pass them and burn my butthole too."

Walkup had finally been promoted to E-5. All of the teasing had ended at last. His orders had finally come down. He was deserving of the promotion after all of the hell he'd been through. I was glad it happened before my DEROS date. He came to Vietnam with the intention of proving his mettle and had succeeded. He was, at times, a better acting NCO than some of the sorry asses that were already wearing the stripes. Some of the guys thought that he brown-nosed his way to E-5 but he could always say that he earned his promotion the hard way and not at some NCO school at Ft. Benning. He would never be called a shake- and-bake.

Kostrewva's DEROS date came and went without my getting a chance to say farewell. They say that he stopped at that new opium den after he cleared battalion and was caught by the MP's. He tried to hide in that underground complex again but the MP's just waited for him this time. After being taken into custody, he was escorted to Cahm Rahn Bay and placed on his plane like so many others had been. He just had to go out in style. I was going to miss him and of course all of the fun we had together.

The rain and the mud was making life miserable for us. I couldn't complain about it though. After all, it was the Sui Cai Valley and we we're the only damned fools out there. The best part was that Charlie would not be using that part of the country for travel while we were there. If the valley was going to be my last mission, I couldn't ask for anything better. I always feared that my last one might be in a hot zone and I truly appreciated being in a lax atmosphere.

It was good to be out in the boonies with the guys and not in some village conducting Nixon's Vietnamization policy. Old tricky Dicky had managed to pull the wool over the eyes of everybody back home. For the first two years of his presidency, he had been using the war as an opportunity to get re elected. Although it appeared as if I would be making it back home alive, a lot of guys hadn't been as fortunate. It disturbed me to think that he had gotten away with making America believe that we could turn the war over to an army that couldn't fight its way out of a paper bag. It was also confusing and frustrating to think that we had managed to get involved in a war that not only couldn't be won, but a war where there was nothing to win. Even if we could have beaten Charlie into submission, there was actually nothing I could imagine that we could have demanded from Hanoi as terms of surrender. Disarmament would have meant occupying Vietnam in the same fashion we had occupied Japan for the previous twenty-five years. We had to use the A bomb on them and using the bomb on the Vietnamese was out of the question because it would only make us look like the bad guys. No matter how we looked at it Vietnam was a big mistake.

I was beginning to feel bad about leaving the guys in Charlie Co. behind. Maybe that was how those guys in the old third squad felt back in Tuy Hoa. There was no real joy in leaving the close knit family we had become, only the pain of separation. In seven months, I'd be finished with my two year military obligation. Regrettably the war would still be going on and some of the guys that comprised Charlie Co. would still be in Vietnam. The situation didn't exactly sit too well with me. I could only imagine what it would be like to readjust to civilian life knowing that some of those guys who were in the Sui Cai with me would still be in country.

Nixon was really working his magic with the war and the public opinion polls. The majority of Americans was still being blinded by his handling of the war and couldn't see through his policy of nightmares and absurdities known as Vietnamization. For the moment though, his most recent troop withdrawal announcement was only enhancing his stature with the electorate.

When I mentioned to Jackson that we only had 44 days left in country, he corrected me and said that he had 47. They added those three days he spent with that hooker onto his tour. It meant that I would have to be going to our reunion at Charang Valley without him. The rest of the jump school class would just have to go home without him. I hoped he felt that she was worth it.

While watching the bulldozers, APC's and tanks scurrying about the valley floor, it occurred to me that those guys had to be E Troop, the same unit we made that sweep with in Phu My. I asked around about that driver Bennet and was told that he was wounded and sent home a couple of months earlier. It was too bad because I liked that guy, he was such a radical. They said that he took some shrapnel in the face during an ugly B-40 attack. Those guys were right about tank warfare. Charlie only attacked them when he had an ample supply of rockets and somebody always gets hit. Fortunately he didn't get killed.

The time was seemingly standing still and the last days were expected to pass slowly. The absence of Charlie was a morale booster that sunk when one of the vehicles hit a mine and provided us with a rare incident. No one was hurt but it did make me wonder how long had the mine been out there in the muck. It would have been a bold move for a sapper to come out and plant the thing in the middle of the night. I could have done fine without the added fear of whether or not there were more mines planted throughout the valley. I was preoccupied with counting days, waiting for my next letter from Barbara and of course my reunion with her in 6 weeks. Charlie or the mere threat of his presence had temporarily disturbed the calm and gave me something to think about.

Benn had recovered miraculously from his mysterious arm ailment. The cast had been removed and he was in good spirits. He didn't wear the thing for the six weeks that I anticipated, but he wasn't complaining. He was in fact, a new person. His ghost time had invigorated his spirits. He seemed to be assuming a role more indicative of someone to seek for guidance. Leadership would be his next step whether he liked it or not. It came naturally to those who had spent as much time as he had in the bush. The new guys were gravitating towards him and he had accepted his role in stride. He had come a long way from being so afraid that he once often considered re enlisting in order to avoid the threat we faced daily. The fear of getting killed was still there but he wore it better. I knew he'd be alright for the rest of his tour.

I met the new platoon leader who walked up on me right after I had just put out a joint. I was sure the guy detected the unmistakable odor upon his approach but he didn't say anything about it. He was an extremely mild mannered guy in his mid twenties. His theme of conversation was the same as Dean's. All he wanted to do was reassure me that my last mission would be as easy and safe as he could make it. Their treatment of me was too much to comprehend. Both of the ranking figures of authority were regular guys. Garson was a great guy but he did have his moments where he showed a weakness for temper tantrums. On the other hand Jahret was abysmally inept and a constant pain in the ass. This guy, I felt, was ideal for taking the platoon through the very crucial future days in Vietnam. His time in Charlie Co. could prove to be the last days in country because I doubted if the Herd would be in Vietnam longer than another year. Our new platoon leader seemed to be capable enough to handle the command of a group of young men wrestling with the anticipated self doubt that was sure to come with being one of the…"last out."

Joley was as daring and head strong as ever. He was, just the same, good to have around due to his willingness to be where he was. As our combat role would continue to diminish, more Joleys would be needed to maintain our presence. He was the kind of guy who would extend his tour to get the most of what was left of our involvement in the war. Guys like him were rare. He had already demonstrated a flair for bravery that could possibly save a life one day or maybe cost him his own. The platoon should benefit from his presence. Overall, his attitude was his biggest asset and should help him deal with whatever came along.

Without a doubt, I was only trying to convince myself that my leaving wouldn't hurt the platoon at all. As my DEROS date neared, I needed to feel that they could get along just fine after I was done there. My obligation had been met and there was no need for me to feel as if I owed anything more but I just couldn't help feeling that I was leaving when I was needed most. It was the most unexpected hurdle ahead of me. I never thought it would be so hard to separate myself from those guys and the life we lived.

When resupply day came there was still no letter from Barbara. It was depressing but the slick did return Smitty for another tour. I should have expected his return because it was impossible to imagine him being anywhere else. I hadn't seen him since June when we hit that booby trap. His old buddy Red was real glad to see him. Red came over with me but had been in so much trouble that I doubted if he would be going home anytime soon. If they added three days onto Jackson's tour for his one infraction, Red had by then another two months added to his. Smitty was of the mold that had given the Herd the distinction of having the highest extension rate of any unit in Vietnam. There was something about the unit that was hard to let go of. Smitty couldn't care less about the fact that our involvement in Vietnam was coming to an end. He just wanted to wear that red white and blue patch on his shoulder a little longer.

When they started passing piss bottles around again, I remembered when I first met Smitty in the Crow's Foot. The more things changed, the more they remained the same. Since I hadn't taken any malaria pills since before I left for Hong Kong, I didn't submit any urine; at least not any of mine. As I turned in the urine I was tempted to jump onto the helicopter the way that Brown did when we were in Phu My. The valley had grown old in the few days that I had spent there. Our permanent position was the only thing to be thankful for. Humping during the monsoon meant incurring all of the little scratches that caused the jungle rot. I needed to go home in the worst way. Mixed emotions aside, New Orleans was calling me and I had to go.

7

When resupply day came around again, Barbara had finally ended her letter writing embargo. As I should have expected, her mother was the culprit for her not writing for so long. Without going into detail she apologized for the incident. I was relieved to finally hear from her and got involved with the rest of the letter. Mrs. Wheelhouse also sent us another package and everybody just waited patiently for me to finish reading Barbara's letter before opening the package. "That woman really got you're nose wide open man. Why don't you put that letter down and open Mrs. Wheelhouse's package so that all of these mother fuckers can eat." Said Howard. He was anticipating the worse from Barbara and predicted that the dreaded "Dear John" letter would be coming before I left country.

"You guys can open the package?" I said triggering a package busting frenzy that really angered Howard. "Look at these mother fuckers; they're taking all of the shit!" He said in anger. My preoccupation with Barbara's letter and my reluctance to intervene only added to his frustration. "Most of those mother fuckers didn't even know Wheelhouse when he was alive!" He said again ignoring the fact that he never knew him either. I paid little attention to them and focused on finishing the letter as Howard stood cursing the entire event.

After resupply we remained in the same spot we had occupied since I arrived. There had been very few patrols and a lot of lounging around. The Sui Cai Valley that I once feared never materialized. The place was about as dangerous as the Crow's Foot. The monsoon, again, was our only enemy. Garson was right. Charlie was too smart to be exposing himself to those elements. We were really a bunch of damned fools for being out there.

"Have you heard about the drops?" Jackson asked.

"Drops?"

"Yeah man. They're dropping up to three weeks off of the tours of the short timers."

"Listen man, I'm having a rough time making it through the last few days left on my tour. I don't need any more rumors to complicate matters."

"I'm just telling you what I heard. Smitty says he heard it before he left Uplift today." Jackson said demonstrating exactly how rumors get started. One tells Smitty, Smitty tells Jackson and before you know it, my mother would be writing me asking about the drops. I had 34 days left and if I was going home any sooner it would be on a plane and not on the wings of a flying rumor. The last thing I needed to do was find myself caught up in that game.

In spite of all the distractions, the only thing that could kill me in the Sui Cai was the boredom. Everybody had their own little spot to occupy and there was no threat to our security. It was the safest corner in Vietnam and I felt lucky to be one of its inhabitants. Our new platoon leader's name was still a mystery to me but he had delivered on his promise of making my last days in the field a breeze. I felt tempted to bring up the CIB issue with him but once my count neared thirty days nothing else counted. I expected to miss Thanksgiving again but make it home for Christmas. Of course after spending a year in Vietnam, holidays had lost its special meaning. The separation from the guys was about the only thing that I was concerned about. Charlie Co. had been my home for almost a year and the guys were closer than family to me. I knew that I wouldn't feel at ease until I knew for sure that everyone of them had made it back to the world where we all belonged.

The Rome Plow operation had taken all of the heat off of both Fire Bases Washington and Floyd. The talk of moving to Ahn Khe meant leaving the security of the valley to the hapless ARVN's. It might have been their country, but they hadn't exactly embraced fighting the war. They were lacking in too many departments to carry on in our absence. With the ARVN soldiers in charge in the valley, it didn't expect to be very long before Charlie started using it again. If fact, he would probably pave a highway through the valley and start driving trucks through the area. As we redeployed it became possible that we could be faced with fighting Charlie back as we departed. Whichever unit does get the distinction of being the "last out" could be faced with the ugliest scene of them all. I had bad vibes about watching the Herd go through that scene on the six o'clock news.

Howard had to eat his words when Barbara's letter arrived. He finally admitted that she and I shared a special relationship and again predicted that we would get married as soon as I returned. He insisted we would get hitched as soon as I stepped off of the plane. "Short! 69 days and a wake up!" shouted one of the guys in the background.

"You call that short. Why in 21 days I'll be doing 69!" Harrington pointed out. He was enjoying his status as being the shortest man in the platoon. It didn't pay to mention how short you were when he was around. Hopefully it would be his last tour over here. I was sure that he would do a lot of boasting when he made it to Ft. Bragg. Guys like him would really get off on being able to say that he'd done more than one tour in Vietnam. It was their badge of courage. It was always who had the most rank and who'd been to Vietnam the most.

Larry, like so many others before him, walked up to me and asked about the drops. The rumor of the drops was raging out of control and it had only been a few hours since we first heard about it. As hard as I tried to ignore what was being said, somehow I just couldn't get around the latest rumor. Every other person in the platoon began each sentence with…."Have you heard?" My curiosity was getting worse than my paranoia ever was. My biggest problem was that I wished it were true about going home early. The entire episode was beginning to consume me and my every thought. The last days were going to be worse than I ever could have anticipated.

We left our little campsite and finally moved over to the compound that contained E Troop's armored vehicles as Kyler said we would. The ground inside of the perimeter was almost as muddy as the chewed up portion of the valley. The guys in E Troop weren't exactly enjoying as good a life as I thought they were. The area we once occupied still had some vegetation left and the trees provided us with some shelter from the rain. The compound had mud everywhere. There was even mud inside of the tents. The grass was definitely greener on the other side. On the compound, unfortunately, there was no grass at all.

After a while, it appeared as if the story about the drops just might have been true. While I was sitting with a group of guys in E Troop and listening to the Four Tops, I overheard one of the guys discussing his upcoming drop of 14 days. He was to be leaving on the 2nd of November. It wasn't one of those "Have you heard?" type of conversations either. He was talking about an official act. The drops, according to him, were Nixon's artificial method of achieving his 40,000 man troop withdrawal. He said that the Christmas deadline was just a big show to impress the folks back home. We imagined there was probably still some kind of fallout from his Cambodian invasion. Nixon, it was assumed, was reaching for a symbolic political gesture that was sure to restore his image as the president who was bringing the troops back home. Anyway, by the time the Four Tops finished singing, I was convinced it was official but I wasn't overjoyed. The feeling was more like being overloaded with guilt; for as I looked around, I saw a lot of new faces. There were guys who were looking at spending most of the next 12 months in Vietnam. There were guys who were going to need someone to go to seeking guidance and everything else that new guys needed during such an awkward transition. I hoped I could convince myself that they would be alright before long. If my tour was going to be shortened by two weeks or more, I could have been leaving the following week also and didn't think I could handle any more guilt than I was already burdened with. Surprisingly, going home or being fortunate enough to realize that you would be going home was a little depressing. I wasn't happy about leaving those guys behind and losing all of the little pieces of my former self could never compare to what I felt I was about to lose.

Feeling a need to be useful to the guys I was about to leave, I approached our RTO and gave him a few pointers on how to keep his contacts clean and dry during the monsoon. I also gave him some advice on how to extend the life of his batteries by turning the radio off when not in use and just about anything else I still remembered from my radio humping days with the old third squad. Jackson followed my lead and started doing the same with the new machine gunners.

That night as total darkness started to approach I felt relaxed and assured that there would be no threat to us in the valley. We gathered at a section of the perimeter's mound of dirt they called a berm. To our rear was an unusual mix of musical sounds from tapes and radios playing loudly in the dark without any regard to the sound discipline we were accustomed to. The guys in E Troop were a loose bunch for sure. I could hear The Who singing "See Me" from one area of the compound and Santana's guitar could be heard wailing along with Rudy Ray Moore's rhyming obscenities from the other end. It was a real weird experience. "Look, a world "J" Shouted one of the guys at the berm with us. Someone had just received a joint in the mail.

"Man what are you supposed to do with that thing?" asked another one of them jokingly.

"I don't know. He couldn't possibly expect me to smoke this little thing." He laughed.

"Those poor bastards back in the world are still paying an arm and a leg for a little bag of grass." Another one of them said. The guys were actually feeling sorry for the heads back home. At the same time they all felt fortunate to be in the land of rice, B-40 rockets and cheap grass. It felt good to hear that from guys who had to stay longer than my DEROS date whenever it was going to be.

That following morning I was wondering why we were on the little compound and not out in the plowed up area. Hopefully it was because we were finished and was about to return to Uplift. My upcoming departure was beginning to make me feel out of place. The news about the drop had made it worse. If we were truly finished with our work in the valley, I wanted to see the end of our presence there. If I was leaving two weeks early, I wanted to see a helicopter or a truck out there to take the four of us to Uplift to start our out processing. "Handy! Handy!" A familiar female voice called from in the distance. I turned and spotted Linda standing about 40 meters outside of the perimeter. I climbed over the berm and walked over to her. She was bold to come out to our location even if it was very close to the village. Of course after the MPC changeover, there was probably an added mixture of desperation compelling her to make the call. Linda was faced with what had to be her annual financial recovery with the added problem of devaluation. "Whatcha got for me baby girl?"

"Two pack of bombers for the price of one." She said as I gave her a twenty and told her to keep the change.

"Thanks man. All of the guys have been nice to me since the new MPC came up."

"I'm being extra nice because I'm feeling extra nice. I think I just might be going home soon."

"You got a drop too?" She asked. Even the opium den queen had heard about the drops. Her disclosure had me laughing all the way back to the compound. Maybe it was possible for my mother to write asking me about the drops after all.

Linda really put me in a good mood. Even the recent news about Muhammad Ali returning to the ring had failed to anger me. I would have been outraged had it happened earlier in the year. Instead, I actually felt good for Ali. He had paid dearly for his induction refusal and now he could get on with his life. Of course there would always be the issue of us lesser known people who would have to continue to serve in the war until it ended for us. His three and a half year exile cannot compare to losing a life or limb but I had to learn to separate the individuals from the issue of the war itself and direct my resentment to the politicians in Washington. It was expected to be easier for me to again root for him and all other celebrated athletes once I returned.

Dean handed me a letter from Burt. He said he and his girl Debbie got married at a Jethro Tull concert and were living in N.Carolina together with their little girl as he finished his time in the Army with the 82nd. I had never heard of Jethro Tull and had to ask around. I found a few guys who knew of the group but no real fans. In his letter he stated that he wished he had some opium tar and I wondered if he was hinting. Anyway, I'd be looking forward to seeing him at Ft. Bragg. "Handy do you think that lady will continue to send those care packages to us after you leave?" One of the new guys asked.

"I really couldn't say." Mrs. Wheelhouse had impressed the new guys with her unusual generosity. Her gesture had far exceeded anyone's expectation. I didn't think it would have been wise to continue the practice it would only further extend the pain of remembering when her son was on the receiving end.

Walkup informed me that we were about to wrap up our stay in the valley. It gave me the opportunity to formally congratulate him on his promotion. I figured he was on his way to a long career in the Army. As far as I was concerned, if nobody wanted to stay in the Army, a draftee's obligation would have been five years. We needed more guys just like Walkup. The Army couldn't have made it as long in Vietnam without the likes of him.

As it started getting dark, the music started getting louder. Being in the field with E Troop was a lot different from what we were accustomed to. Those guys acted as if Charlie didn't exist. Their lifers never intruded and for the most part just stayed out of sight. At one end of the compound, a radio was blaring a new song by the Jackson 5 and at the other end a tape continued playing Rudy Ray More and his obscene exploits of a character named Dolemite. All of which was taking place in total darkness. The kind of darkness that usually had a more ominous association with it but at that moment was just a mysterious backdrop. Hopefully it would be the last episode of that weird movie that had revisited me time and time again for the past year. Everybody had gone insane on the compound. Maybe it was why Linda was able to wander so close to the area. The security was just that lax and who knows, maybe she was expected. The guys had been in the valley since I was in Hong Kong. They all had dope and Linda seemed to be the only logical supplier.

Dat's absence became noticeable to me all of a sudden. He was no longer with our company. I supposed that maybe the battalion was spreading his talents around by moving him from one company to another. Maybe it was noticed that as a unit, our company had developed a dependency on him. Having someone like Dat around could rob you of all initiative. Moving him elsewhere could have proven to be the tonic that we needed. Our company had lost more than its edge with him around. We lost our confidence, our purpose and our identity too. It was like Howard said…"He was carrying us." In spite of being understaffed, we should have been able to put on a better showing than we did in the Crescent. Wherever he was, I hoped he applied what he learned from his stay with us. There was just so much that he should be expected to do. Anything more could and would erode the effectiveness of a unit. Too bad I never got a chance to bid him farewell and thank him for his considerable contribution. He would be missed but we needed to learn to do without him.

The two packs of bombers were expected to be my last score in Vietnam. The year long party was about to end for me. I was going to miss going to Linda and Monique's place. Maybe it was best because life at the local opium den was just too unreal. The addicts, the corrupt police, the frustrated neighbors and all the rest had shown me the reality of just what kind of government S.Vietnam really was. I had ignored the obvious for my entire tour because of the fun that I had. In spite of it all, I wouldn't want to see as much lawlessness back home. I assumed that the end of America's presence in Vietnam would restore the country to what it once was before the French put a stranglehold on the region. Without any foreign influence, the majority of the people would automatically return to being a hard working culture content to live out its existence on subsistence farming and little else. All of the hustlers would have to find something else to do and the country would be better off without their activity. Linda and Monique were as young as I was. They would have more than enough time to find something else to do with their lives after the war ended.

The end of our stay in the valley came suddenly. In a surprise move, they even provided us with trucks for the short ride back to Uplift. Feeling totally convinced it was my last mission, I took one last look around and boarded the truck. I wanted to do the smoke grenade thing but the ride was going to be short and I didn't have enough time to round up the grenades. The news of our immediate departure made me pack so hastily that I forgot my ammo vest on the compound. E Troop would just have to keep it because I would not be going back for it.

When we arrived at Uplift and checked in our weapons, we started a little party. By that time, everyone in the company knew about the drop on our tour. Everybody was happy for us and maybe their congratulatory reaction should have been expected. Instead, it caught me by surprise. Leaving Charlie Co. was going to tear my heart out and I knew it. It wasn't fair to have to leave so much behind. I'd been on both ends of the DEROS event and there was no difference in being left behind and leaving everybody else. It was just a painful exercise that we all had to go through. If it weren't for Barbara, I probably would have extended my tour at least until Doc's DEROS date. Next to the guys that I came over with, Doc had been with me longer than anyone else. He was also my closest friend in the field. Saying goodbye to him was going to be tough.

We started a photograph session that made me realize that I never took enough pictures during my stay. I probably took more pictures of Wheelhouse than anything else. I had lost all of the pictures that I kept with me too. Even my more recent ones that I never intended to keep like the guy that I killed and the pictures of Alice at the Blow Up. I didn't think that Barbara would've appreciated me holding onto any of those. I did send a few to her and they would just have to provide me with the memories of my tour in hell. While posing for pictures, I looked up to my right front and remembered that I also had never made that trip up Duster Hill. I'll always wonder just how much fun those guys had up there.

At the morning formation, Top made a formal announcement of our upcoming DEROS and said that when the Company returned to the field, the four of us (Kyler, Jackson, Harrington and I) would not accompany them. Red had gotten himself into so much trouble that he wouldn't be leaving until sometime after Christmas. Top's announcement officially marked the end of our combat duties and the beginning of our out processing. When formation broke, Top, along with the rest of the guys congratulated us and gave their best wishes on our return to the world. The scene reminded me of Tuy Hoa when Shave, Speedie and Bueno left us. I felt like a mirror image of their dead panned expressions. It made me cling desperately to the last few days that I had left in the Herd. Being a part of it all gave it a special meaning when Top announced it was over for us.

I started my out processing by turning in all of my gear and managed to get away with losing my ammo vest without it being noticed. The new armorer never noticed that I didn't turn one in. I was afraid to ask what they were going to do about it. All of the heads wanted to smoke one last joint and all of the juicers wanted to at least have a beer with me. I couldn't say no to either one of them. In between I posed for many farewell photos and gave dap to every black guy and quite a few of the white guys that knew how to do the handshake. Mad Dog, Sugar Bear and Baby San posed for a Polaroid shot of the three of them and gave it to me as a going away present. They asked me to remember the brothers still over there. I wondered how I could possibly forget any of the guys that had meant so much to me for the entire year. The memories of the times we all shared could never be erased.

That night, in spite of my short-timers status, I was placed in charge of bunker #9 one last time. My last night at Uplift was spent where I had spent numerous memorable days and nights. Before guard started, I was warned in a very threatening manner to keep all unauthorized personnel away. Of course there was no doubt that I would be visited by every known head on the compound for the traditional going away ceremony. The wet dreary weather did little to keep them away either. We smoked an entire nickel bag, drank three bottles of Obisitol and a case of beer. The abundance of alcohol and drugs couldn't lift my spirits. Fortunately the generator was dead again and the entire base camp was in total darkness. It managed to hide my wet eyes from the rest of the partygoers. As we all sat grunting from the influence of the OB, Kyler announced. "I signed up for another tour."

"You did what!?"

"I'm going home for a month and then I'm coming back for a second tour. I signed up before I went on R&R." He said as everyone inside of the bunker was shocked into silence. Even the grunting ceased. His surprise disclosure explained why he was unmoved and not as interested in the drops as the rest of the short timers. Kyler had overdone it with his obsession with proving his mettle. He had a heart the size of which could not be measured and the zeal of a maniac. It was his body's condition that was out of proportion with his drive. He would never be able to hump uphill for more than two hundred feet in full gear and he needed to accept it. All of those we humped with in the Crow's Foot were gone. He had nothing to prove to the people who had arrived since then. They had all gone home ahead of us. He was doing it to prove something to himself. "I hope you know what you're doing." I said.

"I'll be alright Hardcore." He said as we heard a jeep approaching our bunker. It was the Officer of the Day making his rounds. Surprisingly, no one made a move. The jeep drove up and the officer got out and walked up to the bunker. He snatched the poncho from the doorway and was, no doubt, hit in the face with a cloud of marijuana smoke.

"Who's in charge here?" He asked. The only reply he received was the sound of four M-16's chambering four rounds. "I am!" I answered concerned about the mindset of the four people who just might have been thinking about removing the Officer of the Day from the doorway. He hesitated for a moment and then walked away. It was a relief to hear the jeep drive off. There was too much darkness to determine his identity. In fact, I didn't know exactly which four of the bunker party goers chambered the rounds or exactly how many guys were on the bunker at the time he arrived. The total darkness only added to the possibility that one of the guys might have taken advantage of the cover provided by the darkness to pull the trigger. I was glad he was intimidated enough to back down. It was my last night and I didn't need any unnecessary delays.

The following day with a heavy heart and a severe case of reluctance, I said goodbye to all of my friends in Charlie Co. Doc decided to tag along for a while. So we all took off for Charang Valley to pick up our medals and orders, which would also conclude our out processing from the Herd. Along the way, Doc, and I just acted as if we had hitched a ride to the village. Kyler, of course, was only going away for a while. He had no problems with the trip. There was no emotional separation involved with his DEROS. On the other hand, I had to deal with having left behind the greatest bunch of guys that I had ever been around. I was also disturbed about leaving Jackson behind. All of our jump school buddies would be asking about him.

We picked up our luggage and hitched a ride to Charang Valley. When we arrived I was immediately reunited with both Gathar and Larks. Although I fully expected both of them to be there, it was a relief seeing them just the same. So many things could have happened since I last heard from them that I found myself clinging to hope. "Where's Jack?" Larks asked.

"He ran into a delay. He'll be coming along in a few days." I answered feeling reluctant to tell them about Jackson's weakness for Vietnamese hookers. He could fill them in on what happened when we got to Ft. Bragg.

We started our final phase of processing out of the 173rd by receiving all of our medals and ribbons. To my surprise, there were orders for my CIB. "Gathar, I got a CIB!"

"So what's the big deal? Didn't you just finish a tour in the bush?" He asked.

"Yeah but I never received any orders for the damned medal. Check out the date on it. Oct. 12th" I pointed out to them.

"Doc, I got my CIB!" I said as I noticed that Doc was nowhere in sight.

"What happened to the white guy who was with me?" I asked Gathar.

"He's gone. He left while we were standing in line." he said. Doc's quiet departure spared both of us a very painful farewell. Neither one of us wanted to say goodbye so he decided not to. I supposed that one day in the near future, we would get together in New Orleans for a Mardi Gras reunion. It was what the good doctor had been prescribing for almost nine months. I'd be looking forward to it until it happened.

The rest of our old jump school class slowly trickled in throughout the day. Incredibly, there were only a couple of absent faces besides Jackson and none of them were KIA's. We had a big party in the valley that lasted throughout the night. It was like our grand farewell to the Herd. Gathar and Larks spent the entire night praising the works of Isaac Hayes. They were shocked to find out that I hadn't heard his newest release. We were all treated to a free concert by Hayes and the rest of the recording artist from his label while at Ft. Polk. They assumed that I should have been listening to his music like they were.

We all left the valley together and took a scary truck ride to Cam Rahn Bay for the final leg of our one year journey in Vietnam. We posed for a lot of pictures when we first arrived as we basked in the glow of having all made it through the year alive. It felt incredible to be in attendance at the reunion that we all assumed we would put on almost a year earlier. Of course after we realized that we were delaying our own departure and our eventual reunion with our loved ones, we started our final processing. We were issued some khaki uniforms and assigned temporary quarters while we awaited our flight back to the world. Kyler was showing Gathar the boonie hat with the bullet hole in it and it made a noticeable impression on him. He and Larks obviously did not have as many harrowing moments as we did in Charlie Company. Kyler did all of the talking and about all I did was think about all of those guys we left behind. The final separation from them was like a culmination of all of the painful farewells that I had went through over the previous twelve months. I might have lost a lot of me during those farewells but my own departure was even worse. I felt fortunate to have already left the biggest part of me in Barbara's hands while standing at the airport in New Orleans. I had only to finish my time in Vietnam and reclaim that which I left with her.

Cahm Rahn Bay, aside from being totally devoid of Marines, was a sandy version of Da Nang. There were signs of sifting sands everywhere. My entire tour had been spent on or near coastal areas. I had seen the S. China Sea from almost a half dozen spots. This would be my last. We were tempted to leave post and sample the pot in Cahm Rahn Bay but we didn't want to miss our flight and delay our departure for foolish reasons. We figured that we had seen about all of Vietnam that we needed to see and then some.

The bay was also a deep water port for receiving all of those goods that could only be found in a PX or on the black market. In spite of redeployment, the supply line continued and there was always a cargo ship or two in harbor. However it was the giant freedom birds taking off every few hours that had everyone's attention. Our focus, instead, seemed to be on how much time was left on our tour. Our DEROS date was at hand and we all realized just how significant it had been to have spent the previous 12 months as a part of the 173rd. Our year long association with the unit, however, had come to and end. Understandably, there would be little we could do for the rest of our lives that could ever measure up to what had all just experienced but, of course, I hoped that there were still a lot of good years left for us to at least try.

As we waited out our last few hours at the bay, I started to think even more about the guys in Charlie Co and the possibility that I might never see most of them again. The thought of leaving them there and living for the rest of my life without them seemed abstract and almost ruined our little gathering at the bay. Our reunion was a most talked about event a year earlier when we all boldly planned to be there for the very gathering that we were so fortunate to see. Somehow I never expected to meet and get equally attached to another bunch of great guys along the way. After meeting them and sharing the kind of special time we did, it just didn't seem fair to leave those guys at Uplift so abruptly. At least Doc made our separation easier by just leaving without saying goodbye. We had become just that close.

A plane finally landed and the new arriving troops disembarked wearing new jungle fatigues. Their plane would be our transport back home. Our freedom bird had finally arrived. I stood there in our line watching them line up for whatever would be their first leg of processing and started to wonder what would the next twelve months have in store for them. With the war winding down with every troop withdrawal, I could only hope that they could cope with coming over to fight a war that America was extricating itself from. I also found myself hoping for the most unlikely sudden end to the hostilities and an immediate return for all of them. Then my thoughts flew back to November '69 when Gathar and I first landed and took that initial step onto Vietnamese soil. Our first moments in country seemed more ominous because we arrived at night. These guys didn't have to deal with that added element of darkness and our leaving during the daytime only added to the festive mood that we felt coming on as the time neared for us to board our flight.

After the plane was empty, the flight attendant appeared at the door, and beckoned us forward. We quickly ran up the portable stairway to where she stood in the doorway. She started counting each one of us as we boarded the plane. When my turn came to board, the head count stopped right in front of me. It was the cruelest of all jokes as Gathar was the last passenger to get on the plane making me the odd man out. Someone had made a bad count and I was told I had to wait another 12 hours for the next flight out. As I walked back down the stairway, I turned to look and was crushed at the sight of the door being closed behind me. It was frustrating for sure but unlike so often during the previous twelve months, this time there was no well timed song playing in the background on someone's transistor radio to highlight the moment with any incredibly ironic lyrics. Unfortunately there was only me standing in that spot watching those guys leave on a plane that was supposed to have a seat on it for me. I waited for the door to open and one of the flight attendants to call me and say that they made a mistake but no such luck. Then all of my sadness and disappointment turned into anger and somehow it felt appropriate. Vietnam had been every bit as frustrating as missing that all-important flight out and as disappointing as having to wait another 12 hours for it. In fact, I should have expected to be left behind since we weren't making an assault or going to anyone's rescue. Without that necessary objective of someone to attack or the anguish of wondering if we could possibly make it in time to save someone's life, I guess there was no reason for me to expect a flight. Of course being left behind wasn't exactly unfamiliar to me either. Standing in one spot watching an aircraft take off with some of my friends onboard had become one of the most agonizing if not most often repeated events of my stay in Vietnam. It had almost become a signature moment to me. Only this time there were no little pieces of me taking off with the latest passengers. I doubted if there were any left anyway.

THE END

ACKNOWLEDGEMENTS

To my wife Barbara for doggedly insisting that I write the book thirty years earlier. Everything in my life begins with you. This is the book that you asked for.

Many thanks to my son Aaron, my daughter Karen and my grandson Aaron Jasson for giving me three reasons for being a better man.

Thanks to my friend, neighbor, confidant, therapist, editor, steadying influence and proper stranger Kris O'Rourke for just believing in my abilities.

To the guys in Charlie Co. for making my stay in Vietnam as memorable as it was because my memory of what we did seemed almost recent when I started the book.

To the 58,132 names engraved on the black granite panels in Washington D.C. and the Gold Star Mothers who brought them into the world. Your supreme sacrifices made it possible for me to return and honor you and people like you. America still owes you a debt of gratitude that can never be measured. I only hope that I have paid my share in endless grief.

To Janet Salahudin for your lessons in English composition. Your knowledge on the subject was a most valuable aid to my writing.

To Julius Brown who's coaching was very important in building my confidence. Your opinion of my writing was highly valued and deeply appreciated.

To my fellow "18" clerks and all the rest of my ex-coworkers who listened to me for years as I bored them with unending stories of Vietnam. Your tolerance helped me to keep the story alive in my mind long enough for me to finally put it all down on paper.

Special thanks to Iris Montgomery for informing me that the age of the typewriter had passed on into antiquity. The word processor is truly the marvel that you promised it would be.

More special thanks to the personnel at the Work Life Planning Center of the New Orleans Main Post Office whose assistance brought me into the age of the computer. I was very fortunate to be a postal worker and to have the resources of the center at my disposal. Without the aid of Harry Hall, Rosalie Ambrose, Herbert Florrie, Eunice Roots, Linda Payne, Kim Sceau-Goldsby, Toni Brown and the rest of the staff, my task would have been a lot more difficult. Maybe one day management will recognize the true value of the center and make it more accessible in the post Katrina Postal Service.

To Dr. Madeline Uddo, Dr. Joseph Constans, Dr. Cathy Cotton, Dr. Kathleen Coyle, Dr. Michele Hamilton, Herman Woodside and the entire P.T.S.D. staff at the New Orleans V.A. Hospital for getting me where I needed to be to start writing the story. Also a huge welcome home to all of the veterans involved in treatment in the P.T.S.D. program. The support group that you provided me with contributed mightily towards maintaining the constant pursuit of completing the book. Quitting was never an option.

To my brother Robert King, Judy Stoval, Jay Hampton, Janet Harrison, Laurie Cetrone, Raymond Johnson, Edith Johnson, Eugene Major, Annette Hampton, Kaahedrian Williams, Tiffany Hunter, Nancy Webber and all of my computer literate relatives, friends, neighbors and ex-coworkers who helped me make the adjustment to life with a laptop. It wasn't fun being an F.N.G. all over again.

To my friend Chuck Rivett and the class he teaches at St. Martin's Episcopal School on the Vietnam War. It still seems unbelievable but very flattering that every year a bunch of high school seniors could be as interested in learning about our contribution to history. Your insistence on having the book made available to these impressionable teens forced me to self-edit, recognize and delete a lot of the unnecessary expletive language I originally had in the book.

Thanks to the real Danny, Jay, Maleah, Rachel, and Sandra J. for allowing me to use your names to substitute the many that I could not remember and thanks to Annette for the use of your nickname in place of your actual name.

Finally, thanks to my friend and ex-co worker Huck Vo for assisting me with constructing the phonetic Vietnamese used in the story. It sounds more authentic than I thought it would.

MEMORIALS:

Regrettably, there are former members of Charlie Co., other Vietnam Veteran acquaintances and one particular Gold Star Mother who, since the war ended for them, passed on before I completed the book. Most of who left before I even started writing. I wish that all of you could be here to witness my accomplishment; it is a story that we all could have easily identified with.

Emma Wheelhouse
William Gathar Howard
John Degraffenreid
Carlos Diaz
Karl Kyler
Leroy Garrison
Al Milles
Joseph Jones
Gene Talley
Arthur James
Lou Garbers
Alton Minor
Alton P Parker Jr.
Junius Green
David Pagan
Sherman Davis

Willie Gilbert
John Kondas
James Westmoreland
Carter Curtis McKnight
Wes Alford
George Walkup
Henry Singleton
Robert Edwards
Valley Vee
Mike Clausen (CMH)
Irvin Mayfield
David McNeal
Ted Katta
Leonard Mackler
James Moore
Archie Grant